THE MIDDLE ENGLISH
METRICAL PARAPHRASE OF
THE OLD TESTAMENT

MIDDLE ENGLISH TEXTS SERIES

The Middle English Texts Series is designed for classroom use. Its goal is to make available to teachers, scholars, and students texts that occupy an important place in the literary and cultural canon but have not been readily available in student editions. The series does not include those authors, such as Chaucer, Langland, or Malory, whose English works are normally in print in good student editions. The focus is, instead, upon Middle English literature adjacent to those authors that teachers need in compiling the syllabuses they wish to teach. The editions maintain the linguistic integrity of the original work but within the parameters of modern reading conventions. The texts are printed in the modern alphabet and follow the practices of modern capitalization, word formation, and punctuation. Manuscript abbreviations are silently expanded, and *u/v* and *j/i* spellings are regularized according to modern orthography. Yogh (ȝ) is transcribed as *g*, *gh*, *y*, or *s*, according to the sound in Modern English spelling to which it corresponds; thorn (þ) and eth (ð) are transcribed as *th*. Distinction between the second person pronoun and the definite article is made by spelling the one *thee* and the other *the*, and final *-e* that receives full syllabic value is accented (e.g., *charité*). Hard words, difficult phrases, and unusual idioms are glossed either in the right margin or at the foot of the page. Explanatory and textual notes appear at the end of the text, often along with a glossary. The editions include short introductions on the history of the work, its merits and points of topical interest, and brief working bibliographies.

This series is published in association with the University of Rochester.

Medieval Institute Publications is a program of
The Medieval Institute, College of Arts and Sciences

 WESTERN MICHIGAN UNIVERSITY

THE MIDDLE ENGLISH METRICAL PARAPHRASE OF THE OLD TESTAMENT

Edited by
Michael Livingston

TEAMS • Middle English Texts Series

MEDIEVAL INSTITUTE PUBLICATIONS
Western Michigan University
Kalamazoo

Library of Congress Cataloging-in-Publication Data

The Middle English metrical paraphrase of the Old Testament / edited by Michael Livingston.
    p. cm. -- (Middle English texts series)
 Includes bibliographical references.
 ISBN 978-1-58044-150-6 (paperbound : alk. paper)
 1. Bible. O.T.--Paraphrases, English (Middle) 2. English poetry--Middle English, 1100-
1500. 3. Christian poetry, English (Middle) I. Livingston, Michael, 1975-
 PR1837.B6M53 2011
 221.5'201--dc22

                                                                    2011014199

ISBN 978-1-58044-150-6

P 5 4 3 2 1

❧ CONTENTS

❦ ACKNOWLEDGMENTS

I applied to only one Ph.D. program after finishing my first M.A. degree: the English program at the University of Rochester, where I hoped to work with Russell Peck. I got in, fortunately, and on my first visit to the school Russell asked me what I planned to do for a dissertation. I was still finishing my last gasps of an M.A. thesis, so I confessed that I had not given it much thought. Russell reflected for a moment, then suggested I edit the Middle English metrical paraphrase of the Old Testament.

That was some years ago. I took the project on, and an edition of the Octateuch portion of the *Paraphrase* was, in fact, a key component of my dissertation. Between then and now a great many people have contributed to the tasks of completing this work, and I know I will forget more than a few names in composing these thanks.

Surely the most unpayable debt is due Russell, my friend and mentor, without whom this edition — and indeed my career — never gets off the ground. There are no fitting words for his impact on my life. It has been an honor, sir.

As I have noted, I edited the first eight books of the *Paraphrase*, and wrote nearly the whole of the introduction that follows, as part of my Ph.D. dissertation at the University of Rochester. For improvements large and small in those sections, therefore, I owe thanks to the other esteemed members of my dissertation committee: Thomas G. Hahn and Richard Kaeuper, both exceedingly gracious and helpful.

I have numerous reasons to express my gratitude to the impeccable staff of both the Robbins Library and the Middle English Texts Series. Alan Lupack and Rosemary Paprocki were everything one could hope for as a researcher: they were consistently able to act as my missing third hand in gathering materials for the completion of my work. Emily Rebekah Huber and Leah Haught were also essential to finishing this project: over many months they combined to read the whole of my text against the manuscript, finding matters of correction. Daniel Stokes similarly aided with a reading of the introduction, and John H. Chandler, assistant editor of METS, and Martha M. Johnson-Olin supervised final preparations for the press.

In completing this work at The Citadel over the past few years I have been aided by a New Faculty Research Grant from the Citadel Foundation. In addition, I owe personal thanks to Jim Leonard, David Allen, and Libby Walker, all of whom helped expedite my work in one way or another.

As always, I wish to thank the National Endowment for the Humanities for supporting METS, and Patricia Hollahan and the staff at Medieval Institute Publications for taking this volume through its final steps to print.

To family, always first in my thoughts, goes my final thanks. The road has been a long one, and the journey would not have been worth it if I was walking alone.

 INTRODUCTION

The poem's ponderous title befits its scale.

— Morey, *Book and Verse*, p. 146

In a 1996 essay on the characterization of Judith in *The Middle English Metrical Paraphrase of the Old Testament*, Ann Squires notes that the *Paraphrase* "has attracted very little critical attention," especially in comparison with other retellings of the Old Testament like the Old English *Judith*; "indeed," she writes, the *Paraphrase* "is comparatively little known."[1] Given that a complete bibliography of essays to date that take the *Paraphrase* as their primary subject might run to as few as three items, her opinion would seem to border on understatement. If publication is any indication, the *Paraphrase* seems rather worse off than "little known."[2] So the individual who dares to foist upon the world a new edition of this almost universally ignored poem admittedly has some explaining to do. Namely, why has this poem been so neglected? And, if so few ever read it, why is a new edition even needed?

These questions are intimately related, I think, given the two primary reasons that the poem has been ignored. The first reason is its length and subject. Comprised of 1,531 12-verse stanzas, running to a total of 18,372 verses, the *Paraphrase* is unquestionably a mammoth work; James H. Morey, one of the few modern critics to reveal much awareness of the poem, humorously points out that its "ponderous title befits its scale" as "one of the longest and most comprehensive biblical paraphrases."[3] Like the Bible upon which it is based, then, it is unlikely to be a text read cover-to-cover by the fainthearted. Rather, the *Paraphrase* is a text more apt to be regarded as a reference book than as a work of literature: useful, perhaps, for reviewing stories of bulwarks like Samson, David, Job, or Judith. Yet the opinion that this is not a full-fledged work of literature is misinformed. The *Paraphrase* is, in several ways, a remarkable artifact of the Chaucerian period, one that can reveal a great deal about vernacular biblical literature in Middle English, about readership and lay understandings of the Bible, about the relationship between Christians and Jews in late medieval England, about the environment in which the Lollards and other reformers worked, about perceived roles of women in history and in society, and even about the composition of medieval drama.

That such issues have thus far been largely unnoted is surely due to the second problem one faces when approaching the *Paraphrase*: not only is it long, it is unavailable. None of the

---

[1] Squires, "Treatment," p. 187.

[2] I make the distinction of publication because the sales of Russell A. Peck's *Heroic Women from the Old Testament in Middle English Verse* — a volume that includes the stories of Eve, Judith, and Jephthah's daughter from the *Paraphrase* — clearly reveal a considerable readership of some portions of the poem.

[3] Morey, *Book and Verse*, pp. 146 and 69, respectively.

five volumes of the only previous complete edition of the poem, published through the efforts of two editors — Herbert Kalén and Urban Ohlander — over the course of forty years, has found wide circulation. Even more, their edition makes little effort to place the work within the cultural milieu it addresses and lacks substantive explanatory notes that might explore the poet's use of and derivation of ideas from source material.[4] This new edition, therefore, has been set forth in an effort to remedy some of these issues. If nothing else, by bringing fresh attention to the *Paraphrase* within the cultural fields that nurtured it, this edition hopes to invigorate study of what can be viewed as a centerpiece for accessing the burgeoning studies of a rapidly expanding culture.

Still, despite its lack of availability and its massive size, despite even the perceived problems with the Kalén-Ohlander edition, the *Paraphrase*'s inability to garner much critical attention is a strange silence, since academia, like nature, abhors a vacuum. This failure to pick up on the poem at a time when historicist criticism and cultural studies appear to be flourishing becomes all the more curious when one notes that some of the earliest critics to examine the poem came away with distinctly favorable impressions. In 1908, for instance, Wilhelm Heuser regarded it as "an oasis in the desolation of the popular theological literature of the fourteenth century."[5] Though less exuberant than Heuser, John Edwin Wells' original *Manual of the Writings in Middle English*, published before the Kalén-Ohlander edition began to appear, praises the poem for its "well handled" verse, noting especially its "very elaborate alliteration between pairs of lines."[6] And A. C. Cawley, reviewing the second volume of the Kalén-Ohlander edition almost fifty years ago, complained that the poem "deserves to be better known," observing in particular that the poet "excels at straightforward, racy narrative."[7] One would expect that a flurry of essays and studies would have followed, especially after the publication of the fifth and final volume of the Kalén-Ohlander text. Yet this never happened. In fact, although Laurence Muir, the author of the poem's entry in the revised *Manual*, published after the appearance of the full Kalén-Ohlander edition, still regards the poem in a positive light, he is noticeably less effusive with its praise than had been Wells, Cawley, and other early writers: "Impressive mainly for its magnitude, the poem nevertheless narrates the Biblical stories faithfully and straightforwardly, with a certain poetic skill."[8] Strangely, the Kalén-Ohlander edition apparently did little to increase the reputation of the poem. What, one wonders, happened?

Perhaps we need look no further than the first volume of the Kalén-Ohlander edition. True to early editing practices, Kalén wrote a sizable philological introduction for the first

---

[4] Critical reviews of the previous editors' work were nearly universal in pointing out this latter deficiency; see, e.g., that by Liljegren for the first volume of the edition.

[5] "Sein werk steht wie eine oase in der wüste der theologischen massen-literatur des 14. jahrhunderts" (Heuser, "Die alttestamentlichen dichtungen," p. 1). Unless cited otherwise, all translations from Latin, Old English, and, as here, German, are my own; translations from the Bible are from the Douay-Rheims translation as revised in 1749–52 by Richard Challoner.

[6] Wells, *Manual*, p. 398.

[7] Cawley, Review of *A Middle English Metrical Paraphrase*, p. 454. He compares, for instance, the encounter between David and Goliath in the *Paraphrase* with that found in the Vulgate. His opinion is that the *Paraphrase*-poet does remarkable work in rendering both the action and the impact of the sequence.

[8] Laurence Muir, "Translations and Paraphrases," p. 382.

volume of the edition, presenting over 115 pages on matters of phonology, accidence, syntax, and so forth. An excellent comparison of the manuscripts, determining their dialects and relation to each other and to the now-lost original, occupies a further fifty-seven pages. Yet his discussion of the literary aspects of the poem consists of a scant sixteen pages, most of which is concerned with a rough determination of sources. And though he acknowledges that the poem "is a very important piece of work in English literature and compares very favourably with many of its mediæval productions," Kalén is still derogatory in his final regard of the poem:

> A careful study of the poem shows us that it is only very rarely that the author rises above the level of a well-informed, able, conscientious and careful rimer; on the whole, the poem is very tame and colourless, and its monotony bears witness to the great labour the author had in putting the vast material into verse. It is only at the end of the paraphrase, in the *De matre cum VII filijs* and *De Anthioco* that we meet with a more poetical treatment of the subjects and a livelier tone, which sometimes achieves dramatic vividness.[9]

This is not particularly heady praise, and it is certainly not the kind of comment to inspire critical inquiry. Of course, whether the assessment is valid or not depends upon the kinds of questions one seeks to answer in exploring the poem's vast terrain.

And Kalén need not be the final word in such matters. Gustaf Stern, for example, reviewing Kalén's edition in 1925, found the poet far more deft than Kalén gave him credit for, praising the *Paraphrase*-poet as both "well-informed and able."[10] To this we can add the comments of Russell A. Peck, who edited selections from the poem for his thematic collection *Heroic Women from the Old Testament in Middle English Verse*. "The quality of the verse in the poem," Peck writes, "is quite good. The poet has a reasonably good sense of line and often puts together compelling stories. . . . His narrative is pleasantly enhanced with direct speeches that are sometimes vigorous and colloquial, sometimes solemn, aphoristic, or pathetic."[11] I hope to show, through the course of this introduction and the explanatory notes that follow the poem itself, that Peck's regard for the *Paraphrase* — falling somewhere between the dismissive comments of Kalén and the lauds of Heuser — is precisely appropriate to this fascinating poem. To that end, this introduction will briefly lay out the basic bibliographical facts of the *Paraphrase* (its manuscripts, sources, date, provenance); then, after a more extended discussion of biblical canon formation and the poem's possible relationship to Cassiodorus and the Codex Amiatinus, I will concentrate on the place of the poem within the cultural geography of late medieval England, a place that is integral in theory if not in effect. That is, the *Paraphrase* manages to engage primary cultural issues across the broadest possible spectrum, even if its own readership might have been comparatively small. Part of this centrality, of course, is its subject matter.[12] The Bible, in ways

---

[9] *Middle English Metrical Paraphrase*, ed. Kalén, 1:clxxxi.

[10] Stern, Review of *A Middle English Metrical Paraphrase*, p. 286. It is interesting to note that Stern thus chooses only the positive terms from Kalén's own description of the poet, purposefully omitting the negative turn that Kalén had subsequently taken.

[11] Peck, *Heroic Women from the Old Testament*, p. 110.

[12] On knowledge of the Bible and its stories as a key functional component of lay literacy, see Aston, *Lollards and Reformers*, pp. 101–33. That this lay literacy was largely that of a *male* laity is a point made by Blamires, "Limits of Bible Study," and McSheffrey, "Literacy and the Gender Gap." Access points to the Bible were numerous even for the illiterate, deriving chiefly from the liturgy (on which

we are only beginning to understand, might be said to function within late medieval culture just as a glacier of a prior age exacted the geology of the land, moving and shaping the terrain it leaves behind, its defining presence sometimes detected only in the occasional moraines left by its passing.

Lawrence Besserman has recently argued that preoccupation with the Bible so thoroughly saturates the late medieval period that for Chaucer we can (and should) talk productively of a biblical poetic. Using as his starting point Dietrich Bonhoeffer's "faith in the Bible as a sufficient source of divine guidance," Besserman turns to comparison with late medieval England:

> Of course Chaucer and his contemporaries also assumed that the Bible was divinely inspired, an expression of God's will for humankind to follow. And yet, as the various inscriptions of biblical diction, imagery, and narrative in Chaucer's works seem strongly to imply, Chaucer could not possibly have shared Bonhoeffer's strong Protestant faith — it was Wyclif's faith, and would be Luther's, too — in the Bible's ability to convey all that a Christian must know and do for his or her salvation. On the other hand, Chaucer also seems to have been troubled by the opposing view, which held that laymen were not competent to interpret the Bible for themselves — a view espoused as orthodoxy by leading fourteenth-century English and European churchmen.[13]

In the space between those two opposing views, Besserman argues, Chaucer fashioned a biblical poetic, "his creative response to what he and many of his contemporaries had come to regard as the diverse and correspondingly complex poetics of the Bible."[14] More than a glacial force, then, the Bible ultimately functions like a tectonic substratum located just under the more visible but seemingly unconnected features of the surface of the literary landscape in late medieval England.

The anonymous poet behind the *Paraphrase* was among the contemporaries of which Besserman writes, and he composed his massive work at the same time that Chaucer was writing so many of his finest works. No surprise, then, that he is similarly caught between the conflicting impulses of orthodoxy and reform. As he writes in the Prologue to his poem, he is writing for "sympyll men" (line 19) so that they might access the Bible and "our sawlis may be savyd" (line 36) — a position that would seem to be one of relation to Wycliffe and the reformist agenda. Yet the text that he provides is *not* the Bible. It is a translation (and expansion) of the single most authorized paraphrase of the Bible then in currency, that written by the "maystur of storyse" (line 18), Peter Comestor. Thus engaged on both sides of a fundamental and foundational debate, *The Middle English Metrical Paraphrase of the Old Testament*, in a way that few texts can claim, taps into a range of deposits undergirding the cultural geography of late medieval England: the context of vernacular translations of the Bible, the importation of the Bible into romance contexts (and the corresponding morphology of romance into the Bible), the tendencies toward realism in the conceiving of individual and social circumstances, and a generally sympathetic attitude toward the roles of women and Jews that is reflective of a more heterogeneous culture than we might typically expect.

---

see Lamb, "Place of the Bible in the Liturgy," and, in conjunction with discussion of hagiography, Duffy, *Stripping of the Altars*, pp. 155–205).

[13] Besserman, *Chaucer's Biblical Poetics*, p. 7.

[14] Besserman, *Chaucer's Biblical Poetics*, p. 4.

SOURCES AND DATE OF THE POEM

The Middle English Metrical Paraphrase of the Old Testament survives in two manuscripts: Oxford, Bodleian Library, MS Arch. Selden. Supra 52 (fols. 2r–168r), utilized as the base text for both the Kalén-Ohlander edition and this present work, and MS Longleat 257 (fols. 119r–212r) in the private collections of the marquis of Bath. On the basis of dialect, ellipsis (missing material), and matters of content, the two manuscripts clearly represent independent textual lines, neither deriving directly from the now-lost original, probably written in the West Riding of Yorkshire. An analysis of their scribal hands, linguistic features, and physical characteristics reveals that both manuscripts date from the early to mid-fifteenth century. The dialect of the Selden manuscript, which apparently once belonged to the English clergyman Samuel Purchas (1577–1626),[15] is far closer to the original dialect of the poem; the dialect of the Longleat manuscript, which seems to have once belonged to Richard, duke of Gloucester (the future Richard III), is noticeably more Midland in origin. The Longleat manuscript is also incomplete, lacking the first 1,472 lines of the *Paraphrase*, along with additional lines scattered throughout the poem. Since the copyist of this manuscript seems to have been quite careful in his work, we must conclude that his source was likewise missing these lines, placing this text at least one remove from the shared source of both the Longleat and Selden manuscripts.

The poem follows the basic narrative of the Old Testament, though the very nature of a paraphrase indicates that this is not a rote retelling of Scripture. The poet is constructing a work of edification, to be sure, but this edification is built on the use of stories as exempla. Large sections of the Old Testament that are devoted to Mosaic Law, for instance, are excluded from the *Paraphrase*.[16] While Leviticus appears as a running header across several folios of the base manuscript for this edition, the poet has included next to nothing of that book in his paraphrase.[17] In addition to the excision of non-narrative material, the poet also felt free to reorder his materials from his Vulgate source: the very books of the Old Testament, for example, are not in Vulgate order, but in the order given in Cassiodorus' Bible.[18] The *Paraphrase*, then, is at once an abridgment and an expansion of the biblical text, trans-

---

[15] Purchas' name is recorded in the top margin of fol. 2r, in the same hand that summarizes the poem as "The Historie of the Bible in old English verse" on fol. 1v. As his summary implies, Purchas was most likely interested in the poem as an historical, encyclopedic document. Such a viewpoint is not surprising given that Purchas is most famous not for his clerical work but, first, for writing *Purchas His Pilgrimage* (1613), a survey of world religions and peoples that presents itself not as a spiritual journey but as a historical one, and, second, for publishing the four-volume *Hakluytus posthumus*, or *Purchas His Pilgrims* (1625), a compilation of travel literature that included much of the work of Richard Hakluyt.

[16] This is not to say that the poet is uninterested in law per se. Indeed, his work is contained within a greater frame of moral vision that is inextricably bound up with the very definitions of Scripture: though constructed to entertain, there is no doubt the poem is meant to educate, as well. The *Paraphrase* thus functions in much the same way as Gower's *Confessio Amantis* or Chaucer's *Canterbury Tales*: its "tales" serve to reinforce the underlying natural laws it asks the reader to implement in his life, and its ostensible authority is God's.

[17] The headers appear on rectos; "Leviticus" appears on fols. 16r–18r.

[18] For more on Cassiodorus and his possible connections to the *Paraphrase*, see below. For the ordering of the books, see especially note 53.

lated into Middle English and altered, at times, by resort to other sources or to the poet's own invention.

Though the anonymous poet of the *Paraphrase* relied heavily on the Bible as the basis for his work, it was not his sole source for the stories he chose to relate. We know, for instance, that he made extensive use of Peter Comestor's popular *Historia Scholastica* (*HS*) to flesh out the legendary and apocryphal material of the narrative: it is Comestor, the famed *magister historiarum*, who is the "maystur of storyse" that the poet mentions as his primary source in line 18.[19] There is also evidence that the poet used a number of Middle English texts in composing this mammoth work, including the famed *Cursor Mundi*. Arguably more important than these sources, however, was the poet's almost certain — though silent — use of a metrical paraphrase of the Old Testament in Old French. Kalén was the first scholar to make this claim, and it was furthered by Ohlander in his completion of the Kalén-Ohlander edition of the poem. In particular, Kalén and Ohlander were interested in the still-unpublished Old French paraphrase in British Library, MS Egerton 2710. Ohlander produced a more lengthy separate study of the two poems' relationships in 1962, concluding that "the similarity between the two texts . . . is considerable." The Old French and Middle English, he observes, share a "general tone and style," and, even more importantly,

> The same transposition of events as they occur in the Bible sometimes meets us in both texts. There are parallels in many minor details. One important point is the occurrence of Hebrew names that have been taken over by the English poet in their French, often corrupt, form, sometimes based simply on the French poet's need for creating a rime-word.

Ohlander goes on to note, on the other hand, that there are also a number of "dissimilarities" between the two works, such as the fact that "deviations from the Bible are found in one poem that are not found in the other":

> That the English poet has drawn on some French source seems beyond doubt. But that the French text is identical with the one we have been concerned with here, cannot be taken for granted. For we cannot rule out the possibility that our two biblical paraphrases go back to a common source, unknown to us and perhaps lost for ever.[20]

In the course of producing this edition I have made a number of additional comparisons between the *Paraphrase* and the Egerton paraphrase, cited in the notes as *OFP*, yet I cannot improve upon Ohlander's general conclusion. The poems are, at times, close enough to suspect the *Paraphrase*-poet is producing an almost line-by-line rendering of the Old French, yet the number of non-parallels — especially where the Middle English stands alone against all known sources — indicates a greater distance between the two poems. That an Old French source very much like the paraphrase found in the Egerton manuscript has been used by the poet is a near certainty, but beyond this conclusion we cannot now go.

Kalén believed the *York Plays* were an additional source for the *Paraphrase*-poet, having observed that the two works share a number of specific lines and details, an entire stanza at

---

[19] Comestor and the *Historia* are discussed more fully below.

[20] Ohlander, "Old French Parallels," pp. 222–23. For Kalén's original discussion, see his introduction to the poem (1:clxxviii–cxciii). I have included their findings, along with much further evidence along these lines, in the explanatory notes.

one point, and the same rare rhyme scheme throughout: a 12-line stanza rhyming *abab-ababcdcd* that is largely unknown elsewhere in Middle English literature.[21] Kalén then utilized this relationship in order to determine the dating of the *Paraphrase*, using the composition of the *York Plays* in "1340 or 1350" as a terminus a quo. From the poem's linguistic characteristics, Kalén suggested a terminus ad quem of 1440, and he then further honed his linguistic dating down to a final proposal of composition in Yorkshire between 1400 and 1410.[22] But Kalén was more confident than he should have been in both his dating of the *York Plays* and his ability to achieve such a narrow date range on linguistic evidence alone. He was also mistaken on the nature of the relationship between the *Paraphrase* and the *York Plays*. As Richard Beadle has subsequently revealed, Kalén had the relationship backwards. Examining passages common to the *York Plays*, the *Paraphrase*, and the Egerton Old French paraphrase discussed above, Beadle has shown beyond doubt that the *York Plays* borrowed from the *Paraphrase* rather than vice versa.[23] Aside from the two manuscripts of the *Paraphrase* themselves, our only reliable terminus is therefore the single surviving manuscript of the *York Plays*: London, British Library, MS Add. 35290, which itself dates to c. 1430–40. What we now know of the fluid nature of dramatic composition unfortunately does not allow us to predate the relevant passages from the *York Plays* much before this date.[24] Left with only linguistic grounds on which to stand, therefore, we can do little to improve upon the date suggested by Wells in his original *Manual*: the *Paraphrase* was likely written in Yorkshire sometime in the latter half of the fourteenth century, probably around 1380.[25]

THE FORMATION OF THE CANON

> Few cultural paradoxes are so profound, or so unnerving, as the process of religious canonization by which an essentially literary work becomes a sacred text.
> — Bloom and Rosenberg, *Book of J*, p. 35

Segal's Law, one of the many modern add-ons to Murphy's proverbial laws, is particularly applicable to a discussion of the development of the biblical canon: "A man with one watch knows what time it is. A man with two watches is never sure." One faces, in fact, a more perplexing conundrum in the biblical canon; rather than two, today we have at least four primary canons of what Christians call the Old Testament — canons that are similar, to be sure, but by no means identical: Catholic, Protestant, Eastern Orthodox, and Jewish. If a man with two watches is liable to be confused about the time, the person seeking after the authentic form of the Bible is liable to be doubly so. And this is to say nothing of the proliferation of translations of those same sacred texts, each claiming (or, as in Bloom's case, disavowing) their own notions of authority and right.

---

[21] While noting that the form was indeed rare, Stern observed in reviewing Kalén's work that it is not entirely unique to these two cases; it also occurs in MS Harley 2253 (no. 8 in Wright's Percy Society edition). See Saintsbury's *History of English Prosody*, 1:117.

[22] *Middle English Metrical Paraphrase*, ed. Kalén, 1:clviii–clix.

[23] Beadle, "Origins of Abraham's Preamble."

[24] On the development of these plays, see *York Plays*, ed. Beadle.

[25] This location agrees with that found in McIntosh et al., *A Linguistic Atlas of Late Mediaeval English*, which includes Selden. Supra 52 as linguistic profile 30, locating it in the West Riding.

Such a confusing state of affairs is troublesome enough for those who are accustomed to thinking of the Bible as a static text (or for those who desire to think so), but even more difficult to understand is the means by which these various canons have been created. As Bloom observes, the process of canonization is, at its heart, one of altering the mode of a work's place in our discourse: that is, removing it from the realm of the literary to the realm of the sacred. It is the human hand at work in such matters, and the implications of our thereby privileging one discourse over another on the basis of *canon*, that can be simultaneously "profound" and "unnerving." Let us start, however, at the beginning, with a brief overview of the history of the Bible, using the formation of the New Testament as our primary example, since New Testament formation is particularly revealing of the social and political pressures that come to bear on our notions of sacred text. How did confusion ever arise as to what is and is not the Bible?

The first century CE was, in terms of a religious environment, much like the twenty-first. People were relatively free to worship the god of their choosing, in the style of their choosing. From the mystery religions like those of Isis and Mithras to the various sects of Judaism (often termed according to their New Testament labels as Pharisees, Sadducees, Essenes, and Zealots), faith systems were then, as now, placed somewhat in a commercial position, hawking their beliefs as wares in hopes of expanding their hold on the marketplace of ideas. The same was true of that budding Jewish-sect-turned-separate-religion, Christianity. We need look no farther than the New Testament to see that within the first decades after the death of Jesus a number of Christian communities had already sprung up, each with their own individual sacred texts.[26] The Gospel of Mark, for example, was written in Greek no earlier than 70 CE for a Hellenized Jewish audience by an unknown author whose native language was likely Latin and who knew very little about the geography or customs of the Holy Land.[27] This Gospel was later used by the authors of Matthew, Luke, and Acts — with no evidence of the last of these before around 170. John, too, was written later, perhaps around 100, for a community characterized by hints of Gnosticism and Christ-worship (often dubbed the Johannine community).[28] Paul's letters were circulating by 50 and were established fairly quickly as authoritative texts (2 Peter 3:15–16, for example, presupposes knowledge of some of Paul's works), though debate was quick to ensue over which letters were genuinely of his hand and therefore rightly to be privileged. Still other groups had other sacred texts, some of which have managed to survive in whole or in part despite their exclusion from the eventual New Testament canon: works like the Gospel of the Ebionites, the Gospel of Mary, the Gospel of Thomas, or the Gospel of Peter. Indeed, one might regard the very existence of Paul's letters as testament to the wide

---

[26] Though we have no full Gospel manuscripts from before the third century, the various dates presented here are nevertheless those most commonly accepted by scholars.

[27] The tradition that the work was written by Mark, a disciple of Peter who wrote down the remembrances of the apostle, is first recorded by Papias in the second century, though it is important to note that Papias seems to indicate that the "Mark" that he knows is only a collection of sayings, not a narrative like the Gospel as we now have it. Papias, a bishop, does not seem to have seen that text, nor does he affirm the existence of any others.

[28] The dating of the fourth Gospel remains very much uncertain, with scholars falling along a "bell curve" between pre-70 and post-140 dates. John Dominic Crossan has recently suggested that a "first edition" appeared in the first years of the second century, with a second edition appearing between 120 and 150 (*Historical Jesus*, pp. 427–32).

divergence of practice in the early Church, for if unity was the rule there would be no need to write them.[29]

The idea of creating a canon, a stable set of official texts that ought to be shared by all who would call themselves "Christian," was a logical and necessary development as these disparate groups of believers began to connect and interact with each other, exchanging ideas and texts across the spaces that had previously separated them. The very notion of establishing a canon, therefore, is a direct result of the variation that was once available to readers. To control doctrine, it was necessary to control the texts.

In *Against Heresies* (182–88) Irenaeus makes clear that he believes there are only four authentic Gospels: Matthew, Mark, Luke, and John. Likewise, he accepts as "canon" the letters of Paul (minus Philemon and Hebrews). Irenaeus is also one of the earliest writers to mark a clear division between what was increasingly termed the "New" Testament and the "Old." But although Irenaeus' opinions are clear enough, things were obviously more murky at a broader perspective, as the third and fourth centuries saw increasingly vehement arguments about what was to be considered authentic scripture, most keenly seen in the conflicting presentations of Scripture in the works of Origen and Eusebius of Caesarea. Origen accepted as authentic the four Gospels, thirteen Pauline letters, Acts, Apocalypse (Revelation), 1 Peter, and 1 John. Eusebius, however, considered Apocalypse to be spurious, and he added Hebrews to the list of those works "universally accepted" as authentic. Origen, always attracted to the allegorical, also had a high regard for works like the Shepherd of Hermas, the Didache, and the Gospel of the Hebrews, all of which were considered by the more historically-minded Eusebius to be inferior and which the Church would ultimately exclude from the canon. Disputes continued.

In 382 Pope Damasus ordered Jerome, then a young scholar with a penchant for ancient languages and lore, to come to Rome in order to participate in a synod devoting itself to the matter of canon. The result of this small synod was a document outlining the Catholic canon as it now exists (sometimes called the Damasan Canon), though the canon was not officially closed in the Catholic Church until the pronouncement of the Council of Trent in the sixteenth century, at which point the issue had become paramount in dealing with the Protestant Reformation. Politics has always been as vital to the shaping of religion as faith, just as religion, through faith, has always played its role in the shaping of politics. As we will see, this interconnection between religion and politics can be clearly seen in the late fourteenth century through the lens of the *Paraphrase*.

The process of forming an Old Testament canon is, in some regards, more simple than that which occurred with the New for the simple fact that a canon of one sort or another had been extant among the Jews centuries before Christ. Precisely when the Jewish canon was closed has been a subject of some debate, one that has fallen roughly along doctrinal party lines: Roman Catholic and Greek Orthodox writers on the one hand and most remaining scholars on the other. The reason for the discrepancy is the acceptance, in the Catholic and

---

[29] His letters also speak to historical divergence in that they give no indication that he knew of other source texts (such as the Gospels or their hypothetical *ur*-texts like the Q document) or even, upon close reading, of specific details about a human being named Jesus. That is, Paul gives no indication that he has knowledge of Jesus' baptism, His miracles, His beatitudes, His parables, His unique birth, or His fundamentally rabbinical teachings. Perhaps most striking of all, Paul gives no hint that he is aware of Christ's real-world Passion or its theological significance. For a succinct overview of the ramifications of these facts in determining the historicity of Jesus, see Doherty, "Jesus Puzzle."

Orthodox canons, of certain works that are not regarded as authentic in the Jewish Bible — or in the Protestant Bible which bases itself on that of the Jews. These "extra" works, termed the Deuterocanonical Books (by Catholic and Orthodox writers) or the Apocrypha (by most others), constitute seven full books: Tobias, Judith, Wisdom, Ecclesiasticus, Baruch (including the Epistle of Jeremias), and 1 and 2 Maccabees. In addition, there are expansions to books in the universally accepted canon of the Old Testament: an expansion to Esther (10:4–16:24), and a number of alterations to Daniel. These Daniel additions constitute 3:24–91 and chapters 13–14: The Song of the Three Jews and the stories of Susanna and of Bel and the Dragon. The Orthodox canon includes not only this material but also Psalm 151 and the books of 1 Esdras (Catholic Esdras becoming Orthodox 2 Esdras), Prayer of Mannaseh (sometimes called Odes), 3 Maccabees, and, in some traditions, 4 Maccabees.

Whether or not the Jewish canon was itself closed,[30] a clear contributor to these canon differences is the existence of the Septuagint (LXX), a Greek translation of the Jewish Scriptures that includes the Hellenistic material that so characterizes the Apocrypha.[31] This earliest known translation of the Jewish Bible, written in what was the lingua franca of the eastern and southern Mediterranean, is indicative of both the loss of Hebrew among the increasingly Hellenized (Greek-influenced) Jews and the need to maintain unity throughout the diaspora. In any case, the Septuagint was the standard Bible of the early Christian Church: when the New Testament quotes the Old, it quotes the Septuagint in nearly every case.[32] This adoption of the Greek text by the growing Christian community, along with a

---

[30] This possibility has been raised by many Catholic and Orthodox scholars, who supposed that the Jews failed to close off their own canon until the so-called Council of Jamnia in 90 CE, thus giving the first Christian communities some decades to determine on their own the canonicity of the deuterocanonical/apocryphal books. Yet searches of rabbinical evidence reveal no hints that the canon was in such a loose form at such a late date; indeed, such evidence as there is suggests that the Jewish canon had been more or less established perhaps as early as the time of Ezra's return from the Babylonian Exile (458 BCE), which would be in accord with Jewish traditions that follow the first book of Esdras in viewing him as one who "prepared his heart to seek the law of the Lord, and to do and to teach in Israel the commandments and judgment" (1 Esdras 7:10). Ezra thereby becomes the figurehead for the establishment of the Jewish canon, a scribe/poet who consolidates Jewish cultural power by formalizing the word upon which it is based. (For a related discussion of Ezra in the context of poetic theory, see Bloom, *Map of Misreading*, pp. 41–62.) At any rate, most scholars now agree that if the canon was not closed in Ezra's day, it was closed almost certainly no later than the time of the rabbi Hillel (born a generation or two before the Common Era). See, e.g., Lewis, "Jamnia Revisited," or Newman, *Council of Jamnia and the Old Testament Canon*.

[31] The Septuagint, meaning "seventy" and thus often abbreviated LXX, is so named because it was supposedly translated by seventy (or seventy-two) scholars cloistered on the island of Pharos in the Alexandrian harbor at the command of Ptolemy II Philadelphus (285–246 BCE). The basic outline of its construction is given in the *Letter of Aristeas*, which claims to be an eyewitness account of the events but more likely dates to around 150–110 BCE. The story of the Septuagint's translation grew in the telling, so that Philo (in *On Moses* 2.25–44) could report that the translators, working in isolation from one another, came up with identical Greek translations of the Hebrew originals — marking the translation as divinely inspired. This story is itself further embellished by Christian writers such as Irenaeus (*Against Heresies* 3.21.2). For discussion of the later legends, see Jellicoe, *Septuagint and Modern Study*, pp. 44–47; for further overview of the Septuagint itself, see Metzger's discussion in *Bible in Translation*, pp. 13–20.

[32] Metzger, *Bible in Translation*, p. 18.

conservative reaction among Jews to the cultural effects of Hellenization,[33] resulted in the eventual condemnation of the Septuagint by Jewish scholars, "who declared that the day on which the Law was translated into Greek was as unfortunate for the Jews as that on which the Golden Calf was made."[34] This kind of reaction, coming from elite readers responding in self-interest, is seen again and again in the history of Scripture. Indeed, it stands in parallel to the situation in late medieval England as the *Paraphrase* was being written, when a priestly and authoritative caste attempted to outlaw and confiscate vernacular translations of the "original" text: English merely replaces Greek in the equation. At any rate, some Christian communities followed the Jews in attempting to reclaim the Hebrew originals,[35] while most maintained use of the Septuagint, which soon underwent permutations of its own. By the third century CE, the Greek text was so muddled that Origen attempted to restore its sense by collating against the Hebrew, producing a work called the Hexapla.[36]

Thus, despite the best efforts of the Patristic Fathers, or perhaps because of them, the Christian Bible failed from the outset to coalesce into a universally applicable, universally accepted canon or text. And it is here, in the realization that the canon, and thus the text itself, far from being a stable, consistent, and coherent unit, is historically a thing in flux that varies from century to century, sect to sect, and person to person, caught up in politics and in cultural happenstance, that we begin to find important connections to *The Middle English Metrical Paraphrase of the Old Testament*. But before we can move too far into the place of the *Paraphrase* in these matters, we should briefly recall the place of biblical translation in the Middle Ages. In particular, we will need to delve into the works of a "forgotten" Latin translator of the Bible and into the hidden history of one of the most beautiful books in the world, the Codex Amiatinus, which has its own peculiar connections to the *Paraphrase*.

---

[33] The "orthodox" reaction against the process of Hellenization is perhaps nowhere better preserved than in the books of the Maccabees, which detail the victory of Judas Maccabeus and his orthodox followers against foreign elements, culminating in the cleansing/rededication of the Temple in Jerusalem (celebrated at Hanukkah). In a turn of irony, these books are written in Greek, so they are not considered part of the Hebrew canon.

[34] See Metzger, *Bible in Translation*, p. 20.

[35] In contemporary Christianity, this impulse can be seen most clearly in some of the Protestant translations of the Bible, such as the New Revised Standard Version (NRSV), which have attempted to translate not only from the canonized Hebrew text of the Old Testament (the Masoretic text) but also from earlier fragments such as the Dead Sea Scrolls.

[36] The Hexapla presented the Scriptures in six columns: (1) Hebrew, (2) Hebrew transliterated into Greek, (3) Hebrew literally (and painfully) translated into Greek by Aquila (ca. 140 CE), (4) a more readable Greek translation by Symmachus (ca. 180), (5) a "purified" Septuagint translation, and (6) a Greek revision of the Septuagint by Theodotion. While a few fragments of the Hexapla remain, no copy of the whole, which must have been an enormous work in its entirety, exists today. Origen's originals were kept at Caesarea in the library of Pamphilus, but they appear to have been lost to history when Saracens took the town in 638. Origen's version of the Septuagint, however, the fifth column of his text and often called simply the Hexaplaric translation of the Bible, became the basis for many subsequent translations and was eventually recognized as the official Old Testament of the Greek Orthodox community.

CASSIODORUS AND THE CODEX AMIATINUS

Cassiodorus was born around 490 CE, the child of a privileged family in southern Italy, and rose quickly to the stately ranks of the empire, holding the titles of councillor, quaestor, governor, consul, minister, and praetorian prefect as various rulers held sway in Italy. But in 540 he retired from politics and, following the example of Benedict of Nursia who had established Monte Cassino about ten years earlier, set up a monastery on his own estate. It was at this monastery, Vivarium, that Cassiodorus spent the rest of his days devoting himself to religious activities, living to be at least ninety-three years old (at which point, we are told, he was still writing). He wrote or compiled a great many works over the course of his long life, but a few in particular stand out for our purposes here. The first is his *Institutiones divinarum et sæcularium litterarum*, which was written between 543 and 555, in which he attempted to provide the monks of Vivarium with a plan of study that would lead to accurate interpretations of the Bible. As part of this project, he advocated a set of rules for correcting the texts of the Scriptures themselves so that the most accurate copy might be achieved: only from a reliable copy of the Bible might an accurate interpretation of it be made. Foremost among the steps to be taken in checking their texts, as Cassiodorus advises his monks in Book 1 of the *Institutiones*, is to consult those copies of the Bible that he had already collected. Writing for an "in-house" audience of monks who were already familiar with the holdings at Vivarium, Cassiodorus is tantalizingly imprecise in his descriptions of those holdings. Yet the work of modern scholars has filled in such blanks as Cassiodorus left for us, so that there is now a reasonable confidence that his primary source for correcting the Bible was a series of what he considered the four major translations of it: namely, the Greek Septuagint (probably Origen's Hexaplaric text), an Old Latin translation,[37] the Hexaplaric Latin translation,[38] and Jerome's now-standard Latin Vulgate translation.[39] As Marsden points out, this

---

[37] Precisely which Old Latin translation is unknown. Parts of the Bible were being translated from Greek into Latin at least as early as the time of Tertullian (ca. 150–220), and these translations grew organically in bits and pieces under the hands of various and competing translators. By the end of the fourth century, Augustine was able to lament: "the translations of the Scriptures from Hebrew into Greek can be counted, but the Latin translators are out of all number. For in the early days of the faith every man who happened to get his hands upon a Greek manuscript, and who thought he had any knowledge, were it ever so little, of the two languages, ventured upon the work of translation" (*On Christian Doctrine* 2.10 — in Schaff, *Select Library* first series, 2:541). Scholars term these many translations, collectively, the Old Latin Bible (Vetus Latina), though it is important to note that this term does not apply to any single translation of the Bible. Pre-Vulgate full texts of the Bible are known by stemmatic families that are associated with the names of specific representative manuscripts, such as the Codex Vercellensis or Codex Veronensis.

[38] Jerome's first translation of the Bible, based on Origen's Hexaplaric text and begun at the direction of Pope Damasus in 383. For Jerome's own account of the undertaking, see his *Letter to Damasus*, in Schaff, *Select Library* second series, 6:487–88.

[39] Having based his first translations on Origen's Hexaplaric Greek text, Jerome came to feel that a new translation reaching back to the Hebrew originals was required. From 390 to 404 he produced this new translation, which was met with mixed reviews. Augustine, for example, himself a proponent of the Greek and thus no fan of Jerome's work, reports a near riot when a congregation in Oea (modern Tripoli) heard a reading of the book of Jonas in Jerome's brand-new Vulgate translation, one that did not accord with the rendering of the Septuagint. Such was the audience's dismay that the bishop was ultimately forced to change the text of the Latin since "he desired not to be left without a

"complete series of Bibles at Vivarium" accords well with how Cassiodorus tells his scribes to proceed in adjusting their texts.[40] In addition to these matters, Cassiodorus tells us in his *Institutiones* about another Bible of his own compilation: the Codex Grandior, a pandect (i.e., one-volume Bible) with illustrations. He also writes about the Novem Codices, which is, as its name implies, a division of the Bible into nine volumes. What these works might have been has long been considered lost, though they enter into the history of the famed Codex Amiatinus and, in turn, might well enter into the history of *The Middle English Metrical Paraphrase of the Old Testament*.

Now housed in Florence at the Biblioteca Medicea Laurenziana, the Codex Amiatinus measures approximately 505 mm by 340 mm at the covers, 250 mm thick, and weighs roughly seventy-five pounds. It is, by any measure, an enormous book. It is also a strikingly beautiful one, being one of three near-identical pandects made (at what must have been an astounding cost)[41] at the twin monasteries of Wearmouth-Jarrow in the north of England at the beginning of the eighth century. The third and most elaborate of these three pandects, Amiatinus was completed no later than 716 CE, when Abbot Ceolfrith, who had commissioned the works, died in Langres while accompanying the codex to Rome. From Rome the codex passed to the house at Monte Amiato in Italy (from which its name derives); it was at Amiato that the dedicatory inscription on the volume, which named Ceolfrith, was altered, thereby literally erasing its true origins until modern paleographical studies were able to connect it undoubtedly with Wearmouth-Jarrow and Ceolfrith.[42] In time, modern scholars were also able to reconstruct the background of the Codex Amiatinus before its arrival on the Continent, eventually revealing that the pandect's fateful journey to Rome was actually a homecoming of sorts.

The monastery at Wearmouth in Northumbria had been founded a short generation earlier, in 674, by Benedict Biscop, who imported stone masons from France in order to produce a complex for what quickly became a thriving intellectual community. Around five years later, Benedict, Ceolfrith, and an assorted group of other Anglo-Saxon monks — including, quite probably, the future Venerable Bede — traveled to Rome and, while there, bought a number of books to bring back to Northumbria. Among those items purchased, almost certainly, was a copy of Cassiodorus' Codex Grandior, though they did not, apparently, completely understand his hand in the work. After their return to England, the monks of Wearmouth founded a second abbey at nearby Jarrow in 681. Ceolfrith was appointed its

congregation" (Letter 71 in Schaff, *Select Library* first series, 1:327). Nevertheless, Jerome's scholarship (and the papal authority behind it) resulted in his second translation, commonly known as the Vulgate, becoming the standard version of the Scriptures in the West for over a thousand years. Even today, Jerome's Vulgate remains the authorized version of the Bible for the Roman Catholic Church.

[40] Marsden, *Text of the Old Testament*, pp. 137–38, citing *Institutiones* 1.15.11.

[41] In his 1967 Jarrow Lecture on the art of the Codex Amiatinus, Bruce-Mitford famously reported that the parchment sheets used for the three volumes would have required the pelts of approximately 1,545 calves, a daunting statistic, in "Codex Amiatinus," p. 2. More recently, however, Gameson has argued that we should not allow ourselves to be too far swayed by such a large number since, while the undertaking was no doubt remarkable, the actual outlay of resources involved is difficult to determine with any precision: we have little knowledge of contemporary herd sizes, much less how the production of the three pandects would compare to an average scriptorium output during the same period of time ("Cost of the Codex Amiatinus").

[42] The key figure in this discovery was De Rossi, who in 1888 established the English connections (*La Bibbia offerta da Ceolfrido*).

abbot, and he traveled there with Bede and the Rome-bought copy of the Codex Grandior, which was probably placed in the church of St. Paul at Jarrow when it was consecrated in 685. It was sometime in the subsequent decade that the decision to produce the three great pandects was made: one copy would be housed in Jarrow, one in Wearmouth, and one would be a presentation copy to show the Roman Church the skill of a burgeoning community that was, in many respects, at the edge of the world. Their inspiration for creating these enormous one-volume masterpieces was, undoubtedly, the very copy of Cassiodorus' Codex Grandior that they had brought from Rome. And this was only the beginning of Cassiodorus' connection to the work at Wearmouth-Jarrow, for scholars now believe that the text within Amiatinus is likely a surviving example of a revision of the Vulgate text that was authorized by Cassiodorus himself, generally assumed to be that of the Codex Grandior.[43]

The most famous illustration in the Codex Amiatinus is that of a scribe sitting before an open bookcase containing the Old and New Testaments in nine volumes set on five shelves. The scribe is writing in a book, and the implements of his craft are scattered upon the floor around his feet (incidentally making the image one that is useful for understanding medieval manuscript creation) along with another single-volume book.[44] The scribe, we are told via caption, is the prophet Ezra. The theme of the image is clearly not the work of the monks at Wearmouth-Jarrow, as it has much more in common with Mediterranean than Insular art.[45] Scholars have seen in this image, then, evidence that the scribes were copying an existing image from one of Cassiodorus' books. Even more, scholars have come to understand that the hand responsible for the image — Paul Meyvaert argues it is none other than Bede's — was altering his exemplar in the process of composition: the original image was unlabeled but almost assuredly depicted Cassiodorus himself.[46] Yet it is not the identification of the seated figure that is of immediate interest to the study of the *Paraphrase*. Rather, it is the bookcase that is interesting.

Scholarly opinion has long viewed the nine volumes in the bookcase as representing Cassiodorus' division of scripture into nine parts, known as the Novem Codices, since there

---

[43] An opposing view, that the text of the Amiatinus is a Northumbrian-edited composition of texts and thus a parallel to Cassiodorus' work rather than a facsimile of it, was presented by Michelle P. Brown in her 2004 University of London Palaeography Lecture, "Preaching with the Pen."

[44] Reproductions can be found in many places: e.g., Weitzmann, *Late Antique and Early Christian Book Illumination*, plate 48; David Wilson, *Anglo-Saxon Art*, illus. 39; Henderson, *From Durrow to Kells*, illus. 171. A line-art reproduction, useful for its clarity, was made for Garrucci's *Storia della arte cristiana*, table 126, 1.

[45] For a brief discussion, with examples and citations, see Meyvaert, "Bede, Cassiodorus, and the Codex Amiatinus," pp. 870–72.

[46] It has also been speculated that the original could have represented Matthew the Evangelist, an opinion deriving primarily from the fact that in 698 Bishop Eadfrith of Lindisfarne apparently consulted the Codex Grandior at Wearmouth-Jarrow and used the same source utilized for the Ezra image to portray the evangelist in his Lindisfarne Gospels. The argument for Cassiodorus recently put forth by Meyvaert, however, is more convincing ("Date of Bede's *In Ezram*," pp. 1107–26). Ezra, of course, is a fitting figure given his formative role in the Jewish canon (discussed in note 30, above), but one wonders, too, if the Northumbrian monks would have seen a direct parallel between their own work and that of the Jewish scribe/teacher. Of particular note might be 2 Esdras, where Ezra brings the book that he has prepared of the Law of Moses (likely the whole of the Torah) to the people of Israel and reads it to them (2 Esdras 8:5–6).

are no other nine-volume divisions of the Bible that would make sense in this context. More than just representing the Novem Codices, however, the volumes in the bookcase might indicate an even deeper connection between Amiatinus and Cassiodorus' work. Perette Michelli has recently argued that, rather than a random image of a half-remembered collection of books, what's in the cupboard is, in fact, an image of what's in the Codex Amiatinus itself: Cassiodorus' Novem Codices. That is, the portrait could indicate that even the text of the Codex Amiatinus might be copied from the actual text of the Novem Codices rather than, as scholars have previously assumed, the Codex Grandior.[47] And there is some good reason to suspect this, since the Novem Codices as they are pictured in the Ezra image do not directly correspond with the "clues" about the nature of Cassiodorus' text that can be found in his surviving writings such as the *Institutiones*. In other words, an illustrator trying to depict the Novem Codices on the basis of Cassiodorus' other works would not have given us the drawing we now have. If nothing else, the books on the five shelves seem to be neither labeled nor arranged correctly. The labels on their spines, now barely visible, read:

OCT . LIB . LEG	REG . PAR . L . VI
HIST . LIB . VIII	PSAL . LIB . I
SAL . LIB . V	PROP . L . XVI
EVANG . L . IIII	EPIST . AP . XXI
ACT . AP . APOC . IS	

These nine volumes, according to Cassiodorus' outlines in the *Institutiones*, should contain:

1. The Octateuch: Genesis, Exodus, Leviticus, Numbers, Deuteronomy, Joshua, Judges, and Ruth (a total of eight books)
2. The Kings: 1–4 Kings, 1–2 Chronicles (six books)
3. The Histories: Job, Tobias, Esther, Judith, 1–2 Esdras, 1–2 Maccabees (eight books)
4. The Psalms (one book)
5. The books of Solomon: Proverbs, Ecclesiastes, Canticle, Wisdom, Sirach (five books)
6. The Prophets: Isaias, Jeremias, Daniel, Ezekiel, Twelve Minor Prophets (sixteen books)
7. The Gospels: Matthew, Mark, Luke, John (four books)
8. The Epistles of the Apostles (twenty-one books)
9. The Acts of the Apostles and the Apocalypse of John (two books)[48]

The abbreviations for the nine parts of the Bible used in this image are not those that Cassiodorus suggests in his *Institutiones*, nor are these parts in the order that Cassiodorus recom-

---

[47] Michelli, "What's in the Cupboard?" p. 355. Arguing in favor of Grandior as the source, Meyvaert opines that the *Novem Codices* "refers primarily not to physical volumes but to Cassiodorus' own way of conceiving how Holy Scripture was divided" ("Date of Bede's *In Ezram*," p. 1114), though there is no firm evidence to either side of the matter. Meyvaert also does not address Michelli's points about the labeling on the volumes discussed below. Note, for instance, that Meyvaert's excellent reconstruction of the dry-pointing beneath the Ezra image — which reveals that Bede (or another monk) traced the illustration from an extant one presumably in their copy of the Codex Grandior — leaves the interior of the bookcase blank (p. 1118).

[48] I have followed Marsden (*Text of the Old Testament*, p. 134) in both the reading of the labels and the ordering of their interior contents, which would fit with what Cassiodorus presents in the *Institutiones*. Marsden also discusses the labels in detail in "Job in His Place."

mends in that text. In particular, what is here called the Histories ought to be called "Agio-graphorum," be abbreviated "AGI" (rather than "HIST"), and appear after the codex containing the Solomonic material. For Michelli, the only logical conclusion to be drawn from these (and other) discrepancies is remarkable in both its simplicity and its implication: "the books in the cupboard are likely to have been done 'from life', and the *Novem Codices* would therefore appear to have been at Wearmouth-Jarrow."[49] If true, this would mean that Benedict and Ceolfrith bought more of Cassiodorus' works than just the Codex Grandior while in Rome. They might well have bought much of the remains of his library from then-closed Vivarium. What next happens to these works of Cassiodorus is somewhat of a mystery. We know the subsequent history of the Codex Amiatinus after its arrival, sans Ceolfrith, in Rome. We think that Alcuin possibly viewed one of the other pandects around 790, when such a volume was given to Worcester Cathedral by Offa, and we must assume that such valuable items would have been kept safe to the best of the monks' abilities.[50] But beyond this we have silence. Only a few leaves from one of the sister pandects of the Amiatinus have survived.[51] Of Cassiodorus' Novem Codices, no survival beyond the eighth century is certain.

Which brings us, at long last, to *The Middle English Metrical Paraphrase of the Old Testament*. Written in the late fourteenth century, the *Paraphrase* includes seventeen books of the Old Testament: the Octateuch (comprising Genesis, Exodus, Leviticus [largely omitted], Numbers, Deuteronomy, Joshua, Judges, and Ruth), the four books of Kings (1–4 Kings or 1–2 Samuel and 1–2 Kings, into which 1–2 Chronicles have been heavily interpolated), Job, Tobias, Esther, Judith, and part of the second book of the Maccabees. It is not, then, a complete Old Testament. Missing are the Psalms, proverbial material, and, most strikingly, the many books of the prophets.

According to Cassiodorus' descriptions in the *Institutiones*, the books of the *Paraphrase* are the Octateuch, the Kings, and the Hagiography. There is little dissension between canonical traditions on this point. But it is in the ordering of the so-called hagiographic material that we begin to encounter some discrepancies, as the order of these books in the *Paraphrase* is

---

[49] Michelli, "What's in the Cupboard?" p. 354. Meyvaert ("Date of Bede's *In Ezram*," pp. 1114–15) attributes the change to Bede, and attempts to explain it as a correlation of Cassiodorus' divisions with those of Augustine.

[50] As an example of the need for protection, we might briefly recall the history of the Book of Kells, which was probably crafted on the Isle of Iona, perhaps as early as the sixth century but more likely in the late eighth. We know that the book was in existence by 806, when a Viking raid convinced the monks of Iona to move the book to a relatively safer location: Kells Monastery in County Meath, Ireland. In 1007 the book was stolen from Kells by parties unknown (probably raiding Danes), who tore off its bejewelled cover and threw its innards into a ditch. Two months and twenty days later, according to the *Annals of Ulster* (ed. and trans. Hennessy, 1:518–19), these pages were found buried under a pile of sod, which might well have protected the precious folios (though a few pages suffered damage from exposure to water). In 1654, when Cromwell's cavalry was quartered in Kells, the book was sent to Dublin for safekeeping. In 1661, following the dissolution of the Irish monasteries, it was officially given to Dublin's Trinity College, where it remains today. Through these many incidents the codex lost some thirty leaves, its priceless cover, and, in a final trauma, a half-inch of its outer margins (including much art) due to the ignorant trimming of a bookbinder in 1821.

[51] These fragments were being used as wrappers for estate papers when they were discovered, and are now catalogued as British Library, MSS Add. 37777 (the Greenwell Leaf) and 45025 (the Middleton Fragments), and Loan 81 (the Bankes Leaf or Kingston Lacy fragment).

that which Cassiodorus reports as his own preferred order, with the single exception of the "missing" book of Esdras, which would be inserted between Judith and the Maccabees.[52] It is noticeably *not*, however, the order of the material as presented in Jerome's Vulgate, which is so often considered to have been the established authoritative text of the Bible in the relatively stable canon of the medieval church in the West.[53] Even more strange is the connection of the three parts of the Bible — Octateuch, Kings, Hagiography — without any notion of something missing between them. After all, we are missing three parts of the Old Testament, constituting twenty-two books: Psalms (one book), The books of Solomon (five books), and The Prophets (sixteen books). The implication would seem to be that the three parts of the Bible that we do get are paraphrased from a source already set in this order. And this order, as we have seen, is the "wrong" order of Cassiodorus' nine-volume division of Scripture that is otherwise unattested aside from the portrait of Ezra in the Codex Amiatinus.

We are left with remarkable connections in want of firm explanation. One possibility, of course, is that the connection is simple coincidence: the result of an illustrator's lack of care in listing the titles of the Novem Codices in the correct order and a poet's unrelated need, almost seven hundred years later, to place the exciting narrative material of the Bible together into one unbroken strand. Yet one questions such carelessness in the preparation of a presentation copy of a pandect that must have been worth far, far more than its weight in gold, especially if we accept Meyvaert's theory that the executing hand is Bede's. And one wonders, too, about the excision of some quite exciting narrative material, such as that which is found in the book of Daniel, that could have worked well in the *Paraphrase* but whose absence is entirely unnoted by the poet. Against such alternatives, the possibility that the *Paraphrase*-poet had access to actual physical volumes of Cassiodorus' Novem Codices is intriguing. We might even speculate that the poet had at hand only three surviving volumes of the nine-volume work, and the last of those in somewhat fragmented form. Thus we might explain the order of the texts as they are presented, the lack of intervening material between or after them, and the fact that we are given so little of Maccabees, which would have been in the third, fragmented, volume.[54] As we have already seen, the *Paraphrase*-poet was at work in the north of England, where centuries earlier these many strands of Cassiodorus' work had moved in and among the monasteries. It would be a strange set of circumstances that would lead to the otherwise-unnoted survival of parts of the Novem Codices for so many years, but it would be by no means impossible. Beyond this possibility, we dare not move much further, and perhaps

---

[52] Cassiodorus, *Institutiones* 1.6–14.

[53] There is variation among some copies of the Vulgate, but by far the predominant order of the Old Testament books is the Octateuch (Genesis through Ruth), 1–4 Kings, 1–2 Paralipomenon (Chronicles), 1 Esdras, Nehemias (2 Esdras), sometimes 2 Esdras (3 Esdras), Tobias, Judith, Esther, Job, Psalms, Proverbs, Ecclesiastes, Canticle of Canticles, Wisdom, Ecclesiasticus, Isaias, Jeremias, Lamentations, Baruch, Ezechiel, Daniel, the Minor Prophets, and 1–2 Maccabees. For the origins of this order (and its variations), see Light, "French Bibles," especially pp. 159–63. This is the same order as is preserved in Douay-Rheims. Comestor omits certain books in his *Historia*, so that his order is Genesis, Exodus, Leviticus, Numbers, Deuteronomy, Joshua, Judges, 1–4 Kings, Tobias, Ezechiel, Daniel, Judith, Esther, and 1–2 Maccabees.

[54] See the headnotes to the later books of the *Paraphrase* for discussion on some of the literary ramifications of paraphrase ordering as it stands; it may be that these effects are indeed the cause of the "fragmented" quality that is here attributed to sources.

already we have moved too far into speculation. Let us return, then, to the "letter" of the matter, and examine the relationship of the *Paraphrase* to the Master of Stories, Peter Comestor.

STORIES FOR SIMPLE MEN: PETER COMESTOR AND THE *HISTORIA SCHOLASTICA*

This buke is of grett degré,	*stature*
os all wettys that ben wyse,	*as all know*
For of the Bybyll sall yt be	*Bible shall*
the poyntes that ar mad most in price,	*highlights; are made; of importance*
Als maysters of dyvinité	*As masters*
and on, the maystur of storyse,	*and one [especially]*
For sympyll men soyn forto se,	*to understand at once*
settes yt thus in this schort assyse;	*sets it; paraphrase*
And in moyr schort maner	*more brief*
is my mynd forto make yt,	
That men may lyghtly leyre	*easily learn*
to tell and undertake yt.	*recite; understand*
— *Paraphrase*, lines 13–24	

In its second stanza, after an initial prayer that God will look favorably on the poet and will guide him through the mediation of Mary using the full powers of the Trinity, the prologue to *The Middle English Metrical Paraphrase of the Old Testament* declares its basic purpose: to set forth the Bible in a paraphrase that will be more brief than the original text and will present in English the most exciting bits of the narrative in order to provoke "sympyll men" (line 19, likely meaning those unlearned in Latin) into a greater interest in the Scriptures.[55] The poet's primary example in his concept of paraphrasing the Bible stories, and indeed the one on whose text his work is based, is the "maystur of storyse" (line 18), Peter Comestor.

Peter Comestor was born in Troyes around 1100. An able student, he was both dean of its cathedral church and canon of the nearby abbey of St. Loup by 1147. There is evidence that he had studied under John of Tours and that, at some point, he may have heard Peter Abelard. Regardless, his studies in theology advanced to the point that, by 1159, he was living in Paris, studying directly under Peter Lombard. Within ten years his own success at teaching theology won him the chancellorship of the cathedral school of Notre Dame in Paris, a position he held until his death in 1178. It was during his time as chancellor, during the last years of the 1160s, that he wrote and published the work for which he is most known, the *Historia Scholastica*, a work whose impact can hardly be understated. David Luscombe, for his part, notes that Comestor irrevocably "altered the character of Bible studies . . . by widening the range of materials for study so as to include the evidence of the liturgy, of pictures, and of relics. He made a special use of the history, topography, and antiquities of Palestine," including a substantial number of works in Hebrew.[56] Luscombe's term "evidence" is particularly apt, as Comestor was a proponent of the Victorine tradition of literal reading of the Bible, a method of exegesis grounded in the works of the influential Hugh of St. Victor (1096–1141), who had advised his students first to learn and memorize the whole of the Bible's

---

[55] The vernacular quality of the poem is discussed more fully below.

[56] Luscombe, "Peter Comestor," pp. 115–16. Comestor was particularly fond of the Jewish historian Josephus, whom he quotes often in the *Historia*.

literal sense: "First you learn history . . . reviewing from beginning to end what has been done, when it has been done, where it has been done, and by whom it has been done. For these are the four things which are especially to be sought for in history — the person, the business done, the time, and the place."[57] Regarding those who viewed such literal readings as inferior to the allegorical, Hugh had sharp words: "I know that there are certain fellows who want to play the philosopher right away. They say that stories should be left to pseudo apostles. The knowledge of these fellows is like that of an ass. Don't imitate persons of this kind."[58] Luscombe observes that Comestor thus "was in effect fulfilling Hugh's wish for a continuous and comprehensive commentary which took the form of an *historia*."[59] Comestor himself writes in the prologue of the *Historia* that he will keep to only historical matters, "pelagus mysteriorum peritioribus relinquens"[60] ("leaving the sea of mysteries to the more experienced"), an attack, perhaps, on certain commentators who had abandoned all sense of the literal or historical in preference for spiritual or allegorical readings.[61] In fulfilling these Victorine principles, Comestor's work neatly fit into the proverbial gap in the marketplace. The *Historia* thus became an immediate and resounding success. In 1215 the Fourth Lateran Council gave it approval, and it became, along with the glossed Bible and Peter Lombard's *Sentences*, part of the standard theological curriculum of the Middle Ages.[62] Indeed, the *Historia* proved to be, as Morey observes, "the single most important medium through which a popular Bible took shape, from the thirteenth into the fifteenth century, in France, England, and elsewhere."[63] Such was its popularity that it was translated into an astounding number of medieval European vernaculars. Morey lists translations "into Saxon (c. 1248, by order of Heinrich Raspe, landgrave of Thuringia), Dutch (c. 1271, the *Rijmbijbel* by Jacob van Maerlant), Old French (c. 1295, the *Bible historiale* by Guyart Desmoulins), and Portuguese (fourteenth century), and Czech. There are also Castilian, Catalan, and Old Norse translations."[64] The

---

[57] Hugh, *Didascalion*, 6.3. Even Hugh's *summa, De sacramentis*, where we would most expect a defense of allegory, is based on history rather than theology: he there argues that world history is the history of the Church, and thus history is the key to understanding both Creation and the Eschaton, not to mention the here and now between those revelatory end-points.

[58] Hugh, *Didascalion*, 6.3.

[59] Luscombe, "Peter Comestor," p. 119.

[60] Comestor, *HS* Prol. (1054). Citations of Comestor are given by book and chapter and then, in parentheses, by columnation in the Patrologia Latina edited by Migne (PL).

[61] de Lubac, *Medieval Exegesis*, 2:78. By way of example, de Lubac notes the statement of Jerome in his commentary on Mark: "Non historiam denegamus, sed spiritalem intelligentiam praeferimus" ["We don't denigrate the historical, but we prefer the spiritual understanding"] (*In Marcum* 9.1–7, in Morin's *Anecdota maredsolana* 3:2.348).

[62] Morey ("Peter Comestor," pp. 6–7) notes an Oxford University statute from 1253 that "allowed no one to complete theological study 'nisi legerit aliquem librum de canone Biblie vel librum *Sententiarum* vel *Historiarum* vel predicaverit publice universitati'" ["unless he will have studied some book of the canon of the Bible or of the *Sentences* or of the *Historia* or preached the whole publicly"] (from Little and Pelster, *Oxford Theology*, p. 25n2). The verb *legere* here means something much more than "to read": it is the close "study" of a book, which in addition to reading would likely include the production of substantial written commentary (much like a dissertation today).

[63] Morey, "Peter Comestor," p. 6.

[64] Morey, "Peter Comestor," pp. 8–9.

Historia was so popular, in fact, that it began to encroach on the study of the Bible itself. Shortly before 1223, for example, William of Auvergne complained about readers (and presumably writers) who were "satisfied to have heard the preliminaries to Holy Scripture, such as the *Histories* or some other works. The rest they neglect."[65]

Given such obvious and far-ranging popularity, it is striking to find no full translation of Comestor's work in the extant corpus of Middle English. On this note alone, the *Paraphrase* takes on enormous importance in studies of Middle English culture from a historical, literary, and intellectual perspective, for it comprises the most sustained translation — though one that is so loose as to seem at times a paraphrase of Comestor's paraphrase — of the *Historia* into Middle English. As such, it also represents a strong strand of Victorine tradition surviving into the late Middle Ages in northern England, a tradition in which the literal level of the text is privileged over the allegorical.[66]

To see how the *Paraphrase* conforms to Comestor's Victorine principle that the historical or literal level of the text must be thoroughly grasped before the exegete can begin to approach the higher levels of interpretation, let us look at the case of Balaam's prophecy in Numbers 24. Here Balaam, the prophet hired by King Balak to curse the people of Israel who have entered into his lands, has refused to do so. Quite to the contrary, he has repeatedly blessed Israel and cursed Balak for, he says, he can only speak the will of God. For our purpose, let us look at Balaam's final prophecy, in which he prophesies a coming leader for Israel:

> I shall see him, but not now: I shall behold him, but not near. A star shall rise out of Jacob and a sceptre shall spring up from Israel: and shall strike the chiefs of Moab, and shall waste all the children of Seth. And he shall possess Idumea: the inheritance of Seir shall come to their enemies, but Israel shall do manfully. Out of Jacob he shall come that shall rule, and shall destroy the remains of the city. (Numbers 24:17–19)

In his glossing of these verses, the Victorine Peter Cantor (d. 1197) writes: "Note that everything which is said of Christ up to *And when he saw* [verse 20] can be applied to David, except this *he shall waste all the children of Seth*." Peter argues that since Seth's descendants would all have died in the Flood of Genesis, the children of Seth must mean all of mankind: "But David did not waste all mankind, nor the men of all nations, and this at least is true of Christ."[67] The Victorine Stephen Langton (d. 1228) is even more direct in his reading of the verses:

> This is a manifest prophecy of Christ. Hence no literal interpretation other than the prophecy ought to be understood. Thus should we expound the letter: *A star* Christ *shall rise* through incarnation *out of Jacob* the Jewish people . . . *And he shall possess Idumea*; all peoples shall be his, that is Christ's. Literally this was fulfilled under David; that [it might] mystically [signify that] Christ should strike the vices [i.e., *the chiefs of Moab*] and possess their lands, that is the men whom sin has in bondage.[68]

---

[65] William of Auvergne, *Sapiential Books* 1, 2.329, quoted in Smalley, *Study of the Bible*, p. 215.

[66] On the traditional place of the literal within the four senses of scripture, see de Lubac, *Medieval Exegesis*, 2:41–82. For a general historical overview of Hugh of St. Victor and the establishment of the Victorines, see Smalley, *Study of the Bible*, pp. 83–111.

[67] MS Balliol 23, for fol. 42d, trans. Smalley, *Study of the Bible*, p. 233.

[68] Oxford, MS Trinity 65, fol. 241r, trans. Smalley, *Study of the Bible*, p. 233. For further discussion of this passage, and of Langton in general, see Smalley, "Langton and the Four Senses of Scripture."

In other words, the Victorines, so adamant in maintaining and preferring a literal, historical reading of the Scriptures as a necessary foundation for the construction of allegorical or spiritual (and moral and anagogical) readings of the text, here coalesce the literal/ historical and the allegorical/spiritual. The only literal reading possible *is* the allegorical. We find this same argument in place in Comestor, who simply inserts the allegorical reading parenthetically into his quotation of Scripture as if the one flowed necessarily from the other in a technique of interpolated explication that gives equal weight to both: "'Orietur stella ex Jacob et consurget virga,' id est Maria, 'ex Israel . . .'"[69] He goes on, in commenting on the passage, to concur with his Victorine brethren in viewing the allegorical reading — the star is Christ — as the literal in this instance. The particular connection between Balaam's Old Testament prophecy and its perceived fulfillment in the New Testament thus raised the importance of the "star of Jacob": the *Biblia pauperum*, for example, cites Balaam as a pre-figurement of Epiphany (see plate c). The Chester Plays show the importance of the prophecy even more clearly, perhaps, as they include only one play between the Abrahamic covenant and the Nativity: Play 5, the Cappers Play, which constitutes a brief announcement of the Ten Commandments (lines 1–95), followed by a long presentation of the story of Balaam and his prophecy (lines 96–455). While these other literary works clearly reveal the fondness for and importance of the passage, none follows as precisely as the *Paraphrase* the Victorine reasoning; building out of Comestor's *Historia*:

And Balam ther mad prophecyse	
that Crist suld come amang ther kynd.	*peoples*
He sayd a sterne suld ryse	*star*
of Jacob begynnyng,	
And a wand of mekyll price	*scepter of great glory*
of Israel owt suld spryng,	*would spring forth*
Qwylke suld conquere kyng and cuntré	*Which should*
of Moabyse in mony a sted.	*Moabites in all places*
And suns of Seth, also sayd he,	*the children*
suld be hent from handes of dede.	*seized by the hands of death*
The stern to Crist may lykynd be	*star; likened*
to lyght them that lay low os led;	*as low as lead*
The wand, Mary his moyder fre,	*noble mother*
that suld com of the Jew kynred.	*from the Jewish kindred*
Thes wordes was fro God sent. (lines 2503–17)	*were*

The allegorical, then, has become the literal, introducing a surprisingly rare mention of Christ in what is undoubtedly a Christian text. In fact, its seemingly anachronistic incursion into the story of Balaam is one of only eight (previous scholars have counted seven) direct references to "Jesus" or "Christ" in this 18,372-line poem:[70]

---

[69] *HS*, Genesis 33 [1329]. Comestor's interpolation also provides a fine example of how lexicon can itself become a source of allegory: the equation of the scepter with Mary is bolstered by the fact that, in Latin, the terms for "scepter" (*virga*) and "virgin" (*virgo*) are easily (and conventionally) confused.

[70] This is not to say that Christ is not significantly present in other ways throughout the landscape of the poem; in a Trinitarian sense, the many references to "God" (by name, title, or pronoun) within

1. Lines 32–33. The prologue to the poem, in which the poet first reminds the reader that the "figures" he is about to present help us to meditate upon the nature of Christ; he then prays for Christ's guidance as he sets forth into his writing.
2. Lines 2504–13. The poet's explication of the prophecy of Balaam, cited above.
3. Lines 4451–83. In introducing the book of Ruth, the poet notes the genealogical connections between the persons of this book and Christ.
4. Line 4619. At the conclusion of the book of Ruth, the poet again notes the genealogical connections between the persons of this book and Christ.
5. Line 9323. In locating the place at which David built an altar to God, the poet repeats the tradition that Jesus would eventually die upon the same hill.
6. Lines 13081–128. Concluding the story of the siege of Samaria, the poet compares the death of the despairing captain (4 Kings [2 Kings] 7:20) to the suicide of Judas.[71]
7. Lines 13967–68. After reporting that Jonas was in the belly of the whale for three days, the poet notes that Christ was buried three days before He rose from the dead, an association alluded to in both Matthew (16:4) and Luke (11:29–32).
8. Lines 17751–57. In introducing the story of 2 Maccabees 7, the poet observes that while there are martyrs among the Christians, there are martyrs among the Jews, too, even if they did not know Christ.

In not one of these instances is the allegorical reading (we might say the Christological reading) given priority over the literal. And in none of them is much time even given to mention of Christ or the Christian perspective on the text. The paucity of such matters clearly sets the *Paraphrase* within a Victorine tradition of literal readings. Even more, it helps to provide an insight into the intended audience of the poem, a matter that will be discussed more thoroughly below.

IN ENGLISH LEWD MEN TO TEACH: OPENING UP THE WORD

Thus endes the Boke of Judyth,	Book of Judith
als clerkes may knaw by clergy clere.	as clerks may know by good scholarship
God graunt hym hele that hath turned yt	health who has translated it
in Ynglysch lawd men forto lere!	English [for] unlearned; to learn
Insampyll may men here se	Examples
to be trew in trowyng.	loyal in belief
God graunt us so to be	
and to His blyse us bryng!	
— *Paraphrase*, lines 17741–48	

The *Paraphrase* sets forth its purpose, as we have noted, in its opening stanzas, of being written for "sympyll men" (line 19) who need better access to the Scriptures. But it is not until the end of the book of Judith, 17,744 lines into the project, that the poet makes clear what here constitutes a "sympyll" man: the poet asks God for blessings now that he has

---

the poem are co-equal references to Christ. The pressure to read these Christologically is particularly strong in introductory passages focused on God as creator or judge. The point here is, rather, to underscore the relative scarcity of the "naming" of Christ.

[71] This long digression, unnoted as a directly "Christian" moment in the poem by previous scholars, might also refer to Christ by attributing the activity of Creation to God's Word. See explanatory note to lines 13085–86.

translated the text into English so that "lawd" men might learn from it. A "sympyll" man, then, is a "lewd" one — one who does not speak Latin. So at its core the *Paraphrase* is, at least in the mind of its author, an act of translation of the Holy Scriptures. It is with this in mind that the poet asks for favor, and it is on this basis that he places the possibilities of its success, its power, and its authority. The declaration, while innocent enough, is significant. It sets the *Paraphrase* within a long tradition of translation and its associated controversies: centuries of political/religious dialogue between those who wanted to open up the sacred word and those who wished to close it off. The *Paraphrase*-poet is thus placed in the unenviable position of toeing the line of heresy in late medieval England. Even more, as we shall see, the poet's declaration that he is translating the Bible into English for "sympyll men" tells us a great deal about the potential audiences of the *Paraphrase*, another of the cultural cruces upon which this literary artifact is built.

We have already noted that the translation of the Scriptures is no new thing, going back at least twenty-one centuries to the composition of the Greek Septuagint. Yet although it is blessed with antiquity, biblical translation has been, and still remains today,[72] a source of potential conflict and certain uncertainty. Nowhere is the troubling nature of the task of scriptural transmission more clearly stated, I think, than in the words of Rabbi Judah, who taught in the second century CE: "He who translates a biblical verse literally is a liar, but he who elaborates on it is a blasphemer."[73] Judah's conclusion, it would seem, is that the original word is the sole word, and that nothing can come between that Holy Scripture and its audience. Aside from the most basic question of which word is the right word given the tumultuous complexities of textual tradition — a subject we have already broached in canon formation alone, not to mention the scribal inconsistencies between defined copies of a single book or text — Judah's position seems unsatisfactory. Even if we were to confine ourselves to the Old Testament,[74] and even if we were to agree that there is just one version of the original Hebrew of that Testament that is standard and authentic,[75] we are left with the

---

[72] To wit: not long ago I taught a short summer course at a retirement community on the intellectual traditions of the West, and we read portions of the Bible as background material. While I had intended to discuss the content of the select passages, our time was spent instead with my mediating an ongoing conflict among the retirees about the best version of the Bible. Attempts had been made to start a Bible study, apparently, but they had dissolved when half the community desired to use the Revised Version or another "Protestant" version of the Bible, while the other half desired to read the Bible in its "original" — the King James.

[73] Judah, *Tosephta*, Megillah 4.41, p. 228.

[74] The New Testament is particularly tricky since it seems that some of the Gospel material was not originally written in Greek but in now-lost Aramaic versions.

[75] Technically speaking, even the whole of the Old Testament is not in Hebrew: Jeremias 10:11, Daniel 2:4b–7:28, and Ezra 4:8–6:18 and 7:12–26 are in Aramaic. That said, the current standard Hebrew text of the Bible is the Masoretic text, compiled by a group of Jewish scholars called the Masoretes (the "transmitters of tradition") from the seventh to the tenth centuries CE. The oldest complete Masoretic text, and the primary basis for the Jewish and thus Protestant Bibles, is the Codex Leningrad, dating from around 1000 CE. But earlier fragments, such as those found at Wadi Murabba'at (early second century CE) and the Dead Sea Scrolls, have shown the remarkable accuracy of the Masoretic texts. See, for example, Geisler and Nix, comparing the Masoretic text to that of the Dead Sea Great Isaiah scroll (probably second century BCE): "Of the 166 words in Isaiah 53, there are only seventeen letters in question. Ten of these letters are simply a matter of spelling, which does not affect

difficulty of a Scripture in want of translation since so few can read that ancient language. Worse yet, the inevitable relativity inherent in the very act of reading would seem to lead us to the rather untenable conclusion that God wrote a Scripture that can have but one legitimate readership: God Himself, who simultaneously becomes the most literal of readers. Why, then, we might well ask, did He create? How can we be in God's image if true understanding remains beyond our grasp? Is God like the tempestuous gods of Homer, a Creator who enjoys the dramatic contradictions of multiplicity, an entertainment of life that temporarily plays out before His Olympian throne? Is all the world literally but a stage where we devolve into nothing but "sondry folk" who enable God to "despendest tyme"?[76] All of us, as readers, are caught up in the contradictions that afflict the mind of the *Paraphrase*-poet's Job: obliged to read according to his own ingenuity, and inevitably reading wrong, yet being ultimately judged as a reader less by the conclusion of his piteous response than by the integrity (intention) of his honest effort.

The problem is a hard one, and clearly not without import: translation (even in the simple act of reading a text, wherein the words on the page are translated into the mind) is clearly necessary, yet it immediately risks the chance of error and devolution — something that ought to be avoided in what was, and is still by many today, considered to be divinely derived text.[77] Perhaps inevitably, however, the central role of Scripture as a political organizing force has more often than not been the arbiter in determining support for or arguments against its translation. In this context, and pertinent to the later work of the *Paraphrase*-poet, we might observe that almost as soon as Christianity had come to England there were impulses to translate the Scriptures for the newly converted or those about to be so.

Such can be the power of the familiar, of tradition, and of authority, that a translation, too, can be ascribed the status of the original. Thus when Anglo-Saxon scribes and scholars turned to the question of translating Holy Writ, Jerome's Vulgate had, in effect, replaced the various older texts of the Scriptures: their original was the Latin.[78] This, for instance,

---

the sense. Four more letters are minor stylistic changes, such as conjunctions. The three remaining letters comprise the word 'light,' which is added in verse 11, and which does not affect the meaning greatly. Furthermore, this word is supported by the LXX and 1Q Is. Thus, in one chapter of 166 words, there is only one word (three letters) in question after a thousand years of transmission — and this word does not significantly change the meaning of the passage" (*General Introduction to the Bible*, p. 263). Generally speaking, one letter out of a thousand differs between the Masoretic text and the various earlier fragments.

[76] Recall the link between Chaucer's tales of Sir Thopas and Melibee (here quoted from *Canterbury Tales* VII [B²]942 and 931, respectively), in which the pilgrim Chaucer is cut off from his singsong and seemingly pointless Thopas by the Host and urged to tell something "In which ther be som murthe or som doctryne" (935). The question for Chaucer, just as for his reader, is how to access an underlying truth that is presumed to exist. For more on these problems of reader-response, see below.

[77] This issue is by no means confined to the Bible. Note, for example, the 1989 *fatwah* that the Ayatollah Khomeini of Iran pronounced against Salman Rushdie for his suggestion, in *The Satanic Verses*, that the Islamic scriptures, too, are subject to mediation.

[78] Bede reports that in the seventh century Cædmon composed songs rooted in Scripture, though whether these efforts are best considered translations or paraphrases cannot now be known; we encounter similar uncertainty regarding Aldhelm's supposed vernacular uses of Scripture around the year 700 (Remley, *Old English Biblical Verse*, pp. 38–39). The earliest reported literal translation of the Bible into Old English comes from Cuthbert and Ranulf Higden, who both record that Bede himself

was the case with the monk Ælfric, later abbot of Eynsham, who translated parts of the Latin into Old English for his liege, Æthelward, around the year 1000 CE. In the preface to his translation of Genesis, Ælfric writes about his trepidation concerning the task to which he has been ordered:

> Now it seems to me, sire, that this work is very dangerous for me or for any other man to undertake, for I fear that some unlearned man, on reading this book or hearing it read, will believe that he might live today (in the time of the New Law) just as the old fathers lived in ancient times when the Old Law was in place or as men lived under the Law of Moses. I once knew a certain mass priest (he was actually my teacher at one time) who had the book of Genesis and could understand some of the Latin; so this man spoke about the great patriarch Jacob, about how he had four wives: two sisters and their two servants. He spoke complete truth, but he did not know — nor did I then know — how much of a difference there is between the Old Law and the New Law.[79]

Ælfric has personally seen, he explains, how even those who know Latin can misunderstand the text, and he is astute enough to know that only the most learned individuals could comprehend Latin. And if even the most learned can misunderstand the text, Ælfric is right to be worried about the "incorrect" readings (or hearings) that could be committed by an unlearned audience. As a clergyman, Ælfric believes both that the New Law established by Christ in the New Testament abolishes the old Mosaic Law given by the Old Testament and that the Old Testament prefigures the New Testament and the coming of Christ; he worries that the unlearned might not understand this vital distinction and revert to an older — and now sinful — way of living their lives. He also clearly believes in the sanctity of the text that he is preparing to translate: the text that is itself already a translation, Jerome's Vulgate.

Though he realizes that he must fulfill Æthelward's request and complete the translation into Anglo-Saxon, Ælfric is also deeply troubled at the prospect of changing what he feels to be the Word of God. Indeed, it is of no small coincidence that the Anglo-Saxon verb that Ælfric uses for "translate" — *awendan* — means also to "change," "alter," or even "pervert." Thus Ælfric is at great pains to impress upon those who will read his text not only his own fear but also the fear that they, too, should have: knowing that clergy as well as aristocrats will read the text and knowing, too, that copies will surely be made in order to spread knowledge of the Old Testament, Ælfric begs future copyists to preserve his text as closely as possible in order to minimize the chances of misrepresenting what he feels to be an accurate translation of Jerome's text — a rendition that he claims replicates the Latin as closely as possible while preserving good (Old) English sense. In this way, Ælfric hopes that potential

---

translated at least parts of the Latin Gospel of John on his deathbed in 735 (Dove, *First English Bible*, p. 14).

The earliest extensive example of translation into Old English that survives is the ninth-century interlinear gloss found in the Vespasian Psalter. The late ninth century saw Alfred the Great's organized effort to translate major Latin works into the vernacular — including his own translation of the first fifty psalms. A relative flood of material followed in the tenth century, including translations from the Old Testament by Ælfric and interlinear glosses of the Gospels by Aldred.

[79] The Old English text of the preface (from Oxford, Bodliean Library, MS Laud Misc. 509) can be found in numerous places, including Mitchell and Robinson's *Guide to Old English*, pp. 190–95. For the full text of preface and translation, see *Old English Version of the Heptateuch*.

readers (and hearers) of the text will not misunderstand the Word of God, and that the Word of God will remain accurate to the Will of God.[80]

Ælfric's separation between the learned and the unlearned approaches to Scripture can also be seen in his preaching. In his homilies, written between 990 and 994, he was careful to confine his teachings to the literal sense of Scripture, refusing, for example, to discuss the Gospel genealogy on Mary's Nativity Feast because it would certainly involve allegorical interpretations: "This day's gospel is also very difficult for laymen to understand; it is all chiefly occupied with names of holy men, and they require a very long exposition according to the ghostly sense; we therefore leave it unsaid."[81] Smalley points out how much this perspective has changed by the beginning of the thirteenth century, when Orrm, an Augustinian canon in Lincolnshire, wrote a sequence of Gospel homilies generally called the *Orrmulum*.[82] Claiming a desire for his non-Latin reading English countrymen ("læwedd follc" — line 55) to save their souls by understanding the teachings of the Christian faith[83] — the same purpose, of course, as Ælfric's homilies — Orrm "teaches them these doctrines by means of elaborate allegory and number symbolism." Clearly, as Smalley points out, Orrm's "idea of what was suitable for 'simple men' differed profoundly from Aelfric's."[84]

Despite Orrm's high and hopeful opinion of what "simple men" would be able to understand, most medieval writers were more in line with Ælfric's consideration of the unlearned (read: non-Latin speaking) masses. Even many among the clergy were known to have their limitations, especially when it came to allegorical readings of Scripture. Thus the English scholar Alexander Neckham (Nequam), a contemporary of Orrm, observes in a sermon that, if nothing else, parish priests ought "to at least expound the literal sense" of the Bible to their flocks.[85] Neckham's observation calls to mind the Victorines and their demand that students understand the literal reading of the Bible before undertaking other, more complex or subtle readings of the text; indeed, the 1215 papal authorization of Comestor's *Historia* at the Fourth Lateran Council occurred just two years before Neckham's death.

As we have seen, even before the *Paraphrase*-poet took on the formidable task of simultaneously accomplishing both Neckham's and Comestor's goals by turning a literal-sense text into the English vernacular, other writers had been working to provide vernacular avenues for the reading of biblical material in medieval England: Bible translation weaves in and out of the surviving Anglo-Saxon corpus, from direct translations in poetry and prose by men such as Alfred the Great and the aforementioned Ælfric to more *Paraphrase*-like

----

[80] Ælfric was less reticent about translating or paraphrasing other books of the Bible, it seems. All told over his prolific career, he produced Anglo-Saxon versions of all or part of the books of Genesis, Numbers, Joshua, Judges, Kings, Judith, Esther, and the Maccabees, a strikingly similar list to those texts incorporated in the *Paraphrase*.

[81] Ælfric of Eynsham, *Homilies*, ed. and trans. Thorpe, 2:467.

[82] See Hahn ("Early Middle English," p. 85) for discussion not only of Orrm's work but of the need to spell his name (and that of his work) as he would have wished.

[83] See especially the dedication to the *Orrmulum*, lines 1–334.

[84] Smalley, *Study of the Bible*, p. 244.

[85] "Litteratura pollere debetis, ut saltem litteralem sensum gregi vobis subdito exponatis"; quoted by Smalley, *Study of the Bible*, p. 244.

renditions of Bible stories, like the wonderful *Judith* or *Genesis* poems.[86] After the Norman Conquest in 1066, however, there is a long period in which biblical translation into the English vernacular has every appearance of being on hold:[87] the earliest surviving example of such a work in Middle English is the so-called *Genesis and Exodus*, a poem that appears to have been written in the northern area of Norfolk around 1250.[88] This nearly two-hundred-year pause in the tradition of translation might well be due to the facts of the Conquest itself, placing, as it did, a French elite in charge of England and introducing (or corresponding to) a general gap in medieval English literature. But we might observe, too, that *Genesis and Exodus* appears in coincidence with the rising popularity of Comestor's *Historia* and other like narratives that proliferated after the Fourth Lateran Council with its renewed focus on lay spirituality. Indeed, like *Paraphrase*, *Genesis and Exodus* is based in large part on Comestor's work, which had been authorized at that council.

Smaller than *Genesis and Exodus* in scale, but another of the major works in the vernacular Bible tradition, is the Middle English *Jacob and Joseph* (c.1250), a poem that associates itself with the minstrel tradition of stories told to a large and rambunctious gathering.[89] *Jacob and Joseph* narrates Joseph's story (Genesis 37–47) in 538 lines, using a number of extrabiblical legends and details probably culled from French sources. Some of the more fascinating of these additional stories are shared with the massive *Cursor Mundi*, which poem is also worth brief discussion not only as a monument in the chain of English biblical transmission but also as a possible inspiration for the *Paraphrase*.

Cursor Mundi is an enormous work: its several different versions range in length from between 24,000 to 30,000 lines. Written at the end of the thirteenth century, *Cursor Mundi* purports to explain the history and thereby the meaning of the whole of Creation, along the way making use of materials "derived variously from the Bible, the Fathers, the apocrypha, mythology, the *Historia Scholastica*, and French texts such as *La Bible de Herman de Valenciennes*, Robert Grosseteste's *Chateau d'Amour*, and the *Traduction anonyme de la Bible entière*,"

---

[86] While the Bible has a strong and steady influence on a great many other Anglo-Saxon works, whether they are allegorical tales like *The Phoenix* or heroic epics like *Beowulf*, I am regarding such strains as tangential to the line of works presenting themselves as biblical translation.

[87] As in the Anglo-Saxon corpus (see note 85, above), I am here leaving aside those works that do not set themselves forth as biblical translation, though such a distinction does include some fascinating and influential liturgical or devotional works, such as *The Northern Passion* and *The South English Legendary*. On the "peripheral" nature of these works to the translation of the Bible, see Fowler, *Bible in Early English Literature*, p. 127.

[88] I say "so-called" because *Genesis and Exodus* includes, in fact, the whole of the narrative Pentateuch within its rhyming 4,162 lines. The dating of this important representative of early Middle English is imprecise. It survives in only one manuscript, Cambridge, Corpus Christi College, MS 444, which dates to the first quarter of the fourteenth century. Hinckley ("Riddle of *The Ormulum*," p. 193) and Muir ("Translations and Paraphrases," p. 381) both argue for a considerably earlier composition for the poem itself, perhaps even in the twelfth century, while most scholars, including Buehler (*Middle English Genesis and Exodus*, p. 10) opt for a mid-thirteenth century date. For a brief overview of the poem itself, see Morcy, *Book and Verse*, pp. 133–42.

[89] For an overview of the poem, see Morey, *Book and Verse*, pp. 158–59.

just to name a few.[90] It is, as Thompson has called it, an "anecdotal literary-didactic" work.[91] Although a single hand may have made some attempt to smooth out some of its rough edges, *Cursor Mundi* is no doubt ultimately the work of several compilers who have incorporated numerous apparently preexisting poems into long passages of translation from other sources.[92] As a result, the narrative never seems to coalesce into a streamlined, univocal text. Nevertheless, *Cursor Mundi* was widely distributed and widely read; its function as an inspirational text for later writers interested in biblical translation is simply beyond doubt, its influence widely documented. Like *Paraphrase*, it is a work that downplays doctrine in favor of a more Victorine literal level of reading and understanding. As Morey observes, "with no qualms of heterodoxy, such texts become, for practical purposes, vernacular Bibles."[93] That the *Paraphrase*-poet, himself the author of what also amounts to a vernacular Bible, would have known of its existence is almost a surety. He may, indeed, have read (or heard) parts of the earlier text at some point. A number of lines in the *Paraphrase* echo parallel lines found in *Cursor Mundi*, and at times both works concur in their choice of extra-biblical material for inclusion.[94] Such similarities cannot produce a convincing case for direct source study, but they certainly speak to the central place that such texts held within the literary culture of medieval England.[95]

While there are a number of other works of biblical translation that might be utilized to paint the literary background against which the *Paraphrase* was formed, like the psalter of Richard Rolle (c. 1300–1349), some of the poems gathered together with selections from the *Paraphrase* in Peck's *Heroic Women from the Old Testament*, or even the genre-defying mix of art, iconography, and Scripture that is the *Biblia pauperum*,[96] few of them compare in scope to monumental works like *Cursor Mundi* and the *Paraphrase*. One work that must be

---

[90] Morey, *Book and Verse*, p. 101.

[91] Thompson, "*Cursor Mundi*," p. 101.

[92] Morey, *Book and Verse*, p. 100.

[93] Morey, *Book and Verse*, p. 101.

[94] See, for instance, the explanatory notes to lines 273, 781–84, and 1302. We cannot make too much of such similarities, however, as there are just as many differences as there are similarities (see, e.g., the explanatory note to line 4431). Medieval poetry, especially that of the alliterative movement, is notorious for its use of stock phrases, descriptions, and forms. I am disinclined to view *Cursor Mundi* as anything more than a source at a distance: remembered by the *Paraphrase*-poet, perhaps, but not before him as he composed his work.

[95] On the existence of a literary canon of biblical works that stands as an alternative to what we typically consider to be the centrality of Chaucer and romance, see Hanna, "English Biblical Texts." Hanna concludes: "In contrast to the Chaucerian mode, a vernacular bible has, since the tenth century, always been central to English literary production. And the Wycliffite effort proved an enormously successful consolidation of this interest — to the extent that it progressively supplanted, and then thoroughly extinguished, pre-existing indigenous efforts. Rather than an oppositional force, one might find in the Lollard translators and their efforts at propagating Scripture an example of the movement toward (and the recuperation of) a central English literary tradition" (p. 153).

[96] For discussion of the fascinating role of stained glass windows as early Bibles for the poor, including their relationship to the manuscript *Biblia pauperum*, see Caviness, "Biblical Stories in Windows."

discussed here, however, is the hugely successful and controversial translation of the Bible associated with the Oxford reformer John Wycliffe.[97]

WYCLIFFE AND HIS BIBLE

> That wretched and pestilent fellow John Wycliffe, of damnable memory, that son of the old serpent, the very herald and child of antichrist . . . to fill up the measure of his malice, he devised the expedient of a new translation of the scriptures into the mother tongue.
> — Archbishop Arundel, in a letter to Anti-Pope John XXIII, 1412[98]

The desire to bring the Bible to the late medieval English populace, not to mention the idea of translating the text itself, undoubtedly provides some connection between the *Paraphrase* and the Lollard movement associated with John Wycliffe (1330–84), an Oxford theologian, philosopher, preacher, and reformer.[99] The Lollards or Wycliffites, the former term being a hostile epithet and the latter perhaps overemphasizing Wycliffe's position at the head of the movement, preached, among other things, a return to poverty, personal connections to divine will (ultimately leading Wycliffe to condemn the papacy and ecclesiastical order itself), equality of the sexes,[100] and public access to the Word of God, a fundamental principle that caused Wycliffe to support publicly the task of translating the Vulgate into English, beginning in 1378. This task was completed after his death by fellow reformers, and the first Wycliffite Bible appeared in 1388. Wycliffe's movement, and "his" vernacular Bible with it, quickly spread over England and even onto the Continent, where reformers such as John Hus and Martin Luther confessed themselves to be deeply indebted to Wycliffe. Hus, in fact, surrendered his life by doing so: given safe conduct to attend the sessions at the councils of Constance (1414–18), he was found to be guilty of the same heresies as the newly condemned (and very dead) Wycliffe. His safe conduct was revoked, since a promise made to a heretic is no promise at all, and he was burned at the stake on 6 July 1415, his ashes thrown into the Rhine River. The same postmortem fate had been declared for Wycliffe's bodily remains just two months earlier on 4 May 1415:

> This holy synod, therefore, at the instance of the procurator-fiscal and since a decree was issued to the effect that sentence should be heard on this day, declares, defines and decrees that the said John Wyclif was a notorious and obstinate heretic who died in heresy, and it

---

[97] For an overview of the several versions of the Wycliffite Bible, and the controversies about their number, composition, and authorship, see Hudson, *Premature Reformation*, pp. 238–47. I will here treat the translations as a collective impulse associated (to one degree or another) with the name of Wycliffe, referring to a Wycliffite Bible in the same way that one might refer to the Old Latin version of the Bible (on which see note 36, above).

[98] Quoted in Deanesly, *Lollard Bible*, p. 238. Deanesly cites the recipient as Pope John XXII, but this is in error.

[99] One of the finest overviews of Wycliffe is that found in Levy's introduction to his translation of Wycliffe's *On the Truth of Holy Scripture*, pp. 1–40. Another very readable, if somewhat dated, overview of Wycliffe and Lollardy, which specifically addresses their associations with contemporary fourteenth-century literature, can be found in McKisack, *Fourteenth Century*, pp. 499–532.

[100] On women and the Lollard movement, see note 124, below, and the excellent discussion in Hudson, *Premature Reformation*, pp. 99, 186–87.

anathematises him and condemns his memory. It decrees and orders that his body and bones are to be exhumed, if they can be identified among the corpses of the faithful, and to be scattered far from a burial place of the church, in accordance with canonical and lawful sanctions.[101]

Philip Repton, the bishop overseeing Lutterworth, where Wycliffe was buried, failed to act on this decree, but his successor Richard Fleming did not: under his direction, at the urging of Pope Martin V, Wycliffe's earthly remains were disinterred, burned, and thrown into the River Swift in 1428 — more than forty years after his death.

The heretical views of the Wycliffites are generally categorized under five basic rubrics: the nature of the Church, the rights of the papacy, the duty of the priesthood, the doctrine of Transubstantiation, and the use of Scripture. The Church Wycliffe considered to be the body of the Elect, whose head is Christ. In both respects, Wycliffites worked against papal direction: Christ, not the pope, was the head of the Church, and thus Christ alone, not the pope, determined who was within or without the fold of the faith. The Wycliffites repeatedly pointed out that not even a pope knew if he was among the Elect, such knowledge being God's alone. At the beginning of Wycliffe's career he did not consider the papacy as an evil, though he acknowledged from his early years that evil men might be (and had been) pope.[102] But at the end of his career he had come to regard the papal institution itself as evil: at his death he was writing a work entitled *The Anti-Christ*, referring to the papal seat.[103] The root of the papal fall, Wycliffites argued, was Constantine's Donation,[104] a rationale that related strongly to their views on the priesthood: they called for the clergy to denounce all worldly possessions, returning all to the people. All who followed Christ were His clergy, the right to grant forgiveness being God's alone.[105] The Wycliffites were thus merciless in attacking the mendicant orders.[106] And they were similarly forthcoming in their attacks on certain

---

[101] *Decrees of the Ecumenical Councils*, ed. Tanner, 1:415–16.

[102] In *Of Prelates* 11 Wycliffe (or one of his followers) broadens this point to include all clergymen: "a lewid mannus preiere þat schal be sauyd is wiþ-outen mesure betre þan þat prelat þat schal by dampnyd" (*English Works of Wyclif*, ed. Matthew, p. 77). Wycliffe was a prolific writer, but a great many of the writings of his followers were distributed under his name. Of the many volumes of Wycliffite material available in Latin and English I have tried to limit my citations to those English works edited by Matthew for the Early English Texts Society (under the name of Wycliffe alone), as this is likely the most widely available collection of Wycliffite texts.

[103] Compare the Wycliffite *Of Prelates* 22, where it is said that prelates teach that nothing is lawful in the Church "wiþ-outen leue of þe bischop of rome, þou3 he be anticrist ful of symonye & heresie" (*English Works of Wyclif*, ed. Matthew, pp. 89–90).

[104] E.g., *Clergy May Not Hold Property* 5 (*English Works of Wyclif*, ed. Matthew, pp. 376–79). It was supposed that in the fourth century Emperor Constantine the Great had given the lands of the western Roman Empire into the keeping of Pope Sylvester. The supposedly original document detailing this "donation" was proved to be a forgery in the fifteenth century by Lorenzo Valla.

[105] For discussion, see Hudson, *Premature Reformation*, pp. 294–301.

[106] One of the Wycliffites' more witty attacks was the observation that the first letters of the four primary orders — **C**armelite, **A**ugustinian, **I**acobite (Dominican), and **M**inorite (Franciscan) — spell out the name of Caim (Cain), the first murderer. Workman cites numerous instances of the acrostic in Wycliffite works, and he notes that it may have derived from Odo of Sheriton (*John Wyclif*, 2:103). The demeaning acrostic was quite popular, appearing, for example, in *Mum and the Sothsegger* (lines

doctrines of the Church: Transubstantiation, which had been made doctrine at the Fourth Lateran Council in 1215, they declared a wicked lie, their belief being that the Eucharist was a symbol of Christ, not Christ Himself.[107]

As if all this were not enough, the Wycliffites attacked the establishment at its core by declaring that

> it semyþ first þat þe wit of goddis lawe shulde be tauȝt in þat tunge þat is more knowun, for þis wit is goddis word. . . . Þe hooly gast ȝaf to apostlis wit at wit-sunday for to knowe al maner langagis to teche þe puple goddis lawe þerby; & so god wolde þat þe puple were tauȝt goddis lawe in dyuerse tungis.[108]

In reply to the friars' claims that it would be heresy to translate the Holy Bible, the Wycliffites countered by pointing out that their Holy Writ was, itself, a translation. The Church was not amused. Nor was it amused when Wycliffe taught his followers that the only way to be a true Christian was to read and study the Bible.[109] He made few friends among the papacy, too, for declaring that of the four senses of Scripture, only the literal could be counted on for truth: the rest, upon which claims such as papal authority and the doctrine of Transubstantiation relied, at best were dangerous and, at worst, the fancy of the ecclesiastical elite.[110] The Wycliffites' overriding principle that Scripture was the supreme authority — and thus could be the means to judge the Church, its doctrines, and even its personnel — potentially made the Bible, as one critic memorably phrases the matter, "a handbook of revolution as much as *Das Kapital* came to be in a much later age."[111]

While Wycliffe's attacks against the establishment were legion, it was his call for vernacular Bibles that was increasingly singled out for response by the establishment. In a debate in 1401 William Butler stated in his determination that making or possessing *any* ver-

---

500–04) and in the short poem "Preste, Ne Monke, Ne Yit Chanoun" (lines 109–16, in Dean, ed., *Medieval English Political Writings*, p. 50). On a related note, Wycliffites were also fond of calling friaries "Cain's castles"; e.g., *De Officio Pastorali* 9 and 27–28 (*English Works of Wyclif*, ed. Matthew, pp. 420 and 446–50).

[107] E.g., *Of Confession* 13 (*English Works of Wyclif*, ed. Matthew, pp. 344–45).

[108] *De Officio Pastorali* 15 (*English Works of Wyclif*, ed. Matthew, p. 429). While such statements may give Wycliffe and his followers the appearance of being "part of a crusade to take the Word of God to the ordinary people in their own language in the same way that the nineteenth century Bible societies set out to do," Long rightly notes caution against using our own political histories as a lens into this period of history; Wycliffe's desire for translation "was rather the result of a readjustment to authority, the resetting of parameters within which the laity functioned" (*Translating the Bible*, p. 81).

[109] Wycliffe (or a follower) observes that even the priests themselves could benefit from some time off to study the Word in *Why Poor Priests Have No Benefice* 2 (ed. Matthew, pp. 248–51).

[110] E.g., *Of the Leaven of Pharisees* 3 (*English Works of Wyclif*, ed. Matthew, pp. 7–13), *Of Prelates* 21 (p. 89), *How Satan and His Priests* 1–2 (pp. 264–68), and *Of Confession* 12 (pp. 342–43). What Wycliffe and his followers considered the literal was not necessary the historical, as it was with the Victorines, who treated the terms as if they were interchangeable. Rather, the Wycliffites regarded the literal as "that sense of Scripture which the Holy Spirit primarily intends, inasmuch as it promotes the faithful soul's ascent to God" (Wycliffe, *On the Truth of Holy Scripture*, p. 16). On the hermeneutic trajectory of Lollard thought about the preeminence of the literal sense, see Ghosh, *Wycliffite Heresy*, pp. 11–15.

[111] Derek Wilson, *People and the Book*, p. x.

nacular scripture was heresy: "sacred scripture neither in its plain nor in its obscure part[s], nor with the exposition of approved doctors, is to be read by the vulgar people howsoever [they choose]."[112] Even so, the advocacy of biblical translation was not labeled outright heresy until the 1409 promulgation of Archbishop Arundel's censorship laws, which were drafted by synod in Oxford in 1407. The fifth of Arundel's constitutions forbade the reading of Wycliffe's works, a warning given ultimate force in the seventh constitution, entitled "That No One Shall Translate Texts of Holy Scripture into the English Tongue":

> therefore we decree and ordain that no one shall in future translate on his own authority any text of holy scripture into the English tongue or into any other tongue, by way of book, booklet, or treatise. Nor shall any man read this kind of book, booklet, or treatise, now recently composed in the time of the said John Wycliffe, or later, or any that shall be composed in the future, in whole or part, publicly or secretly, under penalty of the greater excommunication, until that translation shall be recognized and approved by the diocesan of the place, or if the matter demand it, by a provincial council. Whosoever disobeys this, let him be punished after the same fashion as an abettor of heresy and error.[113]

As a result of these reactions, it would be over a century before another English translation of the Bible (Coverdale's) was made widely available in England.[114]

Against the background of this tumultuous time, sometime between the beginnings of Wycliffe's career and the exhumation and destruction of his body, *The Middle English Metrical Paraphrase of the Old Testament* was written. One wonders, then, what impact the Wycliffite movement might have had on the composition of the *Paraphrase*. Could it possibly be a

---

[112] Trans. Ghosh (*Wycliffite Heresy*, p. 98); the Latin text reads: "sacra scriptura nec pro parte eius plana, nec pro parte eius obscura, nec cum doctorum approbatorum expositionibus quomodolibet a vulgari populo sit legenda" (from Butler, "Determination against Biblical Translation, 1401," p. 414). For an extensive discussion of this debate, which occurred in Oxford, see Hudson, "Debate on Bible Translation."

[113] Trans. Deanesly, *Lollard Bible*, pp. 295–96.

[114] William Tyndale's translation of the New Testament was first printed in 1525–26, but parts of the Old Testament were left untranslated when he was convicted of heresy and executed by strangulation on 6 October 1536. It is said that his final words were "Lord, open the king of England's eyes." Tragically, it seems that the eyes of the king were already opening. Miles Coverdale's complete Bible translation (partially based on Tyndale's) was printed in 1535 and dedicated to the king and queen of England; Coverdale died a natural death. That said, Tyndale's work has the appearance of opening a floodgate, coinciding as it does with religio-political events in England that would quickly lead to authorized translations of the Bible. Other sixteenth-century translations include the 1537 Bible of "Thomas Matthew" (probably a pseudonym for John Rogers, a friend of Tyndale's); Richard Taverner's Bible (1539); the Great Bible (1539), which was the first "authorized" translation; the two translations by Edmund Becke (1549 and 1551); the Geneva Bible (1560), which was used by Shakespeare; the Bishops' Bible (1568); and the Douay-Rheims Bible (1582–1610), which is utilized for most translations in this volume. It was this wide variety of available English translations that led directly to King James I's 1604 decision to sponsor politically the production of a new translation of the Bible that would act to further social unification. The result was the King James Bible, first published in 1611. For concise descriptions of these various translations, see Metzger, *Bible in Translation*, pp. 56–72. For a fuller account, see Long, *Translating the Bible*, pp. 80–212.

Wycliffite work? And how is it that *any* work of this kind, whether Wycliffite or not, could survive the numerous condemnations of biblical translation?

The latter question is probably the more simply answered. Despite the fact that the Wycliffite Bible was declared heretical, and that just possessing a copy could, at times, warrant the branding of heresy upon one's person regardless of personal beliefs, around 250 copies of the translation survive in whole or in part — more than twice as many as any other Middle English work (the second being *Prick of Conscience*, with 117 surviving copies). Chaucer's famous *Canterbury Tales*, by way of comparison, survives in a "mere" 64 copies. To say, then, that the various condemnations of the Wycliffite work failed to result in its unavailability is an understatement. In fact, careful combing of extant records has shown that many of the orthodox leaders themselves retained copies of Wycliffe's translation.[115] Indeed, it is no stretch to conjecture that so few copies of the *Paraphrase* exist not because of the condemnation of the Wycliffite Bible but because of the *popularity* of that heretical work. That is, the Wycliffite Bible so strongly filled the lay need for vernacular translation that it effectively sealed the market and cut off preexisting traditions of translation.[116] The *Paraphrase* might thus be viewed, dependent upon chronology, either as a premature impulse or a belated addition to what Hudson has provocatively termed the "premature Reformation" of Lollardy. But is the *Paraphrase* a Lollard work?

LOLLARDY AND THE *PARAPHRASE*

> The tradition of biblical paraphrase . . . anticipated and to some degree set the stage for later reformist movements simply because it provided a precedent for the existence of biblical material in English and because it was directed specifically toward a lay audience. The introductions to the paraphrases often express an egalitarian desire to spread the Word among native English who know no other tongue, and who are as much entitled to the saving grace of Scripture as learned clerks.
>
> — Morey, *Book and Verse*, p. 2

We have already seen that the *Paraphrase*, like *Cursor Mundi*, the *Orrmulum*, *Genesis and Exodus*, or a number of other works that fit into this tradition, certainly accords with what Morey calls the "egalitarian desire" to translate Scripture, to render it, as the *Paraphrase*-poet puts it, "in Ynglysch lawd men forto lere" (line 17744). We have also already seen that there is an aspect of such work that is essentially reformist at its core. But the question of whether the lewd audience of such works is necessarily a "lay audience," as Morey suggests, is more difficult to discern, especially in the case of the *Paraphrase*. Who wrote this poem, and for whom did he write it? And can it, when all is said and done, be tied to the Lollards?

The *Paraphrase*-poet, we can be sure, was a man of some learning, well-versed in not only Latin but also Middle English and Old French texts. We can imagine that he was, at the least, a clerk. And, given his desire to translate for lewd men despite whatever warnings might have been current about such activity, we might also consider him a man somewhat on the fringe of orthodoxy. But orthodoxy cannot exist in a vacuum; it is always in need of relative definition for or against one position or another. So if the poet is on the fringe of orthodoxy, it must also be said that he is being compared to orthodoxy in London as it has come down to

---

[115] See Hanna, "English Biblical Texts."

[116] On this point see note 95, above.

us through strong but politically biased voices like Arundel's. What the *Paraphrase*-poet, writing in the West Riding of Yorkshire far away from the primary centers of the Wycliffite debates in London and Oxford, considered orthodoxy, and how he positioned himself relative to that mode of belief, must remain a mystery to us. He certainly gives no indication that he considers himself a potential target for attack on theological or political grounds. He does not spend much time at all constructing a preemptive defense. Quite to the contrary, he goes about his business as if such issues did not exist. And, for him, perhaps they did not.

What that business was, a translation of the literal sense of Scripture, might be thought to have much in common with Wycliffite goals, though it is no more a necessarily Wycliffite work than its many precedents from *Cursor Mundi* to *Genesis and Exodus*. And while it shares with the Wycliffites the desire to present that sense of Scripture to the non-Latin-speaking public, many followers of Wycliffe would no doubt object to the heavy use of Comestor, who habitually moves in and out of the text of the Word itself and has no qualms about altering it in order to make sense of his stories in one way or another. The Wycliffites desired an unmediated Word, a naked text, which a paraphrase most assuredly is not. We might also note that the vocabulary of this translation, as mentioned earlier, includes several terms associated with the ecclesiastical hierarchy. These anachronisms did not need to be added to the biblical account. The fact that the poet chose to add them, however, and chose to do so in a way that did not cast aspersions upon them, is something that might be unlikely in a work influenced by the more radical vein of Lollardy.[117]

More closely akin to the Wycliffites, however, is the treatment of women in the *Paraphrase*. As one can see from the title of Peck's edition that included parts of this poem — *Heroic Women from the Old Testament* — women in the *Paraphrase* are treated quite a bit more favorably than we might expect given the tendency in literature of this period to wax poetic in the misogynist vein. True to Lollard thought, the sexes are placed on relatively equal footing in the text, both having high points and faults, neither naturally superior to the other. Note, for example, the opening description of Judith:

Dame Judyth was a gentyll Jew	*noble*
and woman wyse whore sho suld wende.	*wise wherever she went*
Now wyll we nevyn hyr story new,	*invoke her*
for to sum men yt myght amend	*some*
To see how sho in trewth was trew	*truth was true*
als lang als sho in lyf con lend	*so long as she in life remained*
And lufed the Law als lele Ebrew	*loved; as a loyal Hebrew*
that Moyses tyll hyr kynred kend.	*to her people taught*

       — *Paraphrase*, lines 16957–64

---

[117] The one possible exception to this conclusion is the term "popelard" in line 6650. The word, meaning "hypocrite" or "traitor," derives from the Old French *papelart* or *papelarde*, and typically carries a similar spelling in its Middle English forms. The orthographical appearance here, it might be suggested, reveals some influence of the term *pope* and thus might reveal an antagonistic attitude toward the papacy — though even this would not necessarily speak to a Wycliffite origin for the *Paraphrase*. The "pope" spelling also occurs several times, however, in the Chester Plays (5.296, 5.312, 15.362, 17.157, and 24.589), suggesting that the form might well be a mark of Northern origin rather than a sign of religious or political perspective. See *MED papelard*.

There is much that could be discussed in this passage, not least of which is the favorable presentation of the Jews and of Jewish Law, a standpoint that is taken throughout the poem and is also somewhat surprising given the anti-Semitisms that are so typical of much medieval literature.[118] Aside from this, however, it is striking how Judith is held up as not only a good Jew but also a wise woman — a characteristic that is here made to seem natural to her femininity, not abnormal to it. Joan Ferrante observes that while Judith was often held as an exceptional role model for women,[119] she was typically "divested" of her humanity by exegetes and "made to represent impersonal abstractions like the church."[120] And the *Paraphrase*-poet's refusal to symbolize is all the more interesting in light of the fact that she is held up not just as a role model for women, but for men, too: the poet suggests that men and women both might better themselves by looking to her ("to sum men yt myght amend," line 16960). Squires asserts that the poet has nevertheless labored "to de-fuse the threat" of Judith's "powerful femininity" even to the "expense of the diffusion of the power" of his poem, but if there are efforts to "domesticate" Judith afoot in the *Paraphrase*, one must concede that the poet's heart does not seem to be in it.[121]

Still, one might "excuse" any positive portrayal of Judith as being the result of her centrality to her tale. She is clearly the hero of her story, one with even a heroic Anglo-Saxon cultural forebear, so perhaps we might expect the poet to treat her thus. We would surely not expect, however, a positive spin on the story of Eve, who was almost universally condemned in Christian exegesis both before, during, and after the Middle Ages as the cause of the Fall and thus the origin of the spiritually tainting original sin, however that sin was defined. But if we look at the story of the Fall in the *Paraphrase*, we see that many of the negative connotations associated with Eve, or even the Eva/Ave dichotomies so common to fifteenth-century thought, are missing. As Peck comments, "one is struck by the neutrality" of her character.[122] And while Peck notes that Eve "does play her part in a role that is specifically gendered," the *Paraphrase*-poet refuses to step beyond the strictures of the text in his portrayal of that role. Eve thus becomes a wholly tempered figure, made all the less culpable in the Fall by the wicked machinations of Lucifer, the fallen angel who beguiles *both* Adam and Eve, as the poet makes clear (line 180). And the actual Fall into original sin is attributed to Adam's folly, not Eve's: "Hys boldnes and that balfull bytt / cast hym in care and all hys kyne" (lines 199–200). One might argue that this kinder portrayal of Eve is the result of the *Paraphrase*-poet's deep commitment to literal readings — while Eve is certainly culpable in Genesis, the more negative portrayals of her are largely read into the account — but how then would one deal with the poet's treatment of Rahab? She is unequivocally termed a prostitute in both the Bible (Joshua 2:1) and Comestor (*HS* Jos. 2 [1261]), but here she is described as someone

---

[118] Elsewhere in the poem the poet makes an explicit personal connection between Christianity and Judaism, calling the latter "our law" (line 384) and "our fayth" (line 552). For a terrifying look at one strain of contemporary medieval anti-Semitic literature, see *Siege of Jerusalem*. My edition of that poem includes much discussion of the issue, but see especially pp. 14–17.

[119] On which, see Elizabeth Robertson, *Early English Devotional Prose*, p. 36.

[120] Ferrante, *Woman as Image*, p. 17.

[121] Squires, "Treatment," p. 196.

[122] Peck, *Heroic Women from the Old Testament*, p. 111.

who runs an inn (line 2712).[123] While these relatively positive portrayals of women are not necessarily Wycliffite, they certainly have much in common with the leveling of the gendered playing field that has at times been noted as a hallmark of the Wycliffite movement.[124]

We have in the *Paraphrase* a mammoth undertaking, written at a time when such work could result in the often-fatal brand of heresy. It was on 26 February 1401, after all, that William Sawtrey was burned at the stake for his Wycliffite views, earning him citation as the first confirmed Lollard martyr. And while the *Paraphrase* bears certain affinities with Wycliffe's movement — a desire to bring Latin texts to the "lewd" people of England, a theoretically more equitable regard for women — it seems difficult to call it a Wycliffite text without a great deal of equivocation. The poet uses ecclesiastical terms when he does not need to do so, and one imagines that his heavy reliance on Comestor, at times following it at the expense of Holy Writ, would make those committed to Wycliffite principles very uneasy indeed. We might hope for a doctrinal statement on the part of the poet, a clue that might cut through the gordion knot of the issue of Wycliffite influence, but direct sermonizing is rare in this text. And even when it does occur, as it does at the end of the books of Kings, there are vestiges of both orthodoxy and reform to be found:

Be this ensampyll may we se,	*example*
sen vengance thore so sone was sene,	*since; there; soon; seen*
Us ow to honour ylke degré	*We ought; each rank*
of Holy Kyrke that kept is clene,	*Church; pure*
And noyght to wene ourself that we	*think*
be worthy swylk maters to mene,	*consider*
Bot als thei deme in dew degré	*Except as they judge; manner*
to drese our dedes on days be dene.	*arrange; deeds; straightaway*
God graunt us well to werke	
and so to lyfe and end	
In trowth of Holy Chyrche	
that we to welth may wend! (lines 14077–88)	*bliss; journey*

With orthodoxy, the poet instructs his readers to honor the ecclesiasts. With the reformers, he adds the important addendum "that kept is clene." Both sides of the coin, if the reader wishes to find them, are in play in this poem. And perhaps therein resides much of its power and success. This *sic et non* quality — especially as it relates to Lollardy — might well remind us of Chaucer's Parson, whose Lollard leanings (if he has any) must be sniffed out, as in the epilogue to the Man of Law's Tale:

Owre Hoost upon his stiropes stood anon,
And seyde, "Goode men, herkeneth everych on!

---

[123] On the possibility that the poet has subtly worked implications of her ill-fame into the text, clues that are to be found only if one already knows the biblical account, see the explanatory note to lines 2711–12.

[124] For brief perspectives on the importance of women to the movement, see Cross, "'Great Reasoners in Scripture,'" pp. 359–80, and Aston, *Lollards and Reformers*, pp. 49–70. For an attempted correction of the older view that the Wycliffites were effectively egalitarian, see McSheffrey's *Gender and Heresy*, where she argues that the movement actually disconnected women from those aspects of popular Christianity that were most meaningful to them.

> This was a thrifty tale for the nones!
> Sir Parisshe Prest," quod he, "for Goddes bones,
> Telle us a tale, as was thi forward yore.
> I se wel that ye lerned men in lore
> Can moche good, by Goddes dignitee!"
> 　　The Parson him answerde, "Benedicitee!
> What eyleth the man, so synfully to swere?"
> Oure Hoost answerde, "O Jankin, be ye there?
> I smelle a Lollere in the wynd," quod he.
> "Now! goode men," quod oure Hoste, "herkeneth me;
> Abydeth, for Goddes digne passioun,
> For we schal han a predicacioun;
> This Lollere heer wil prechen us somwhat." (*Canterbury Tales* II[B¹]1163–77)

Harry Bailey's opinion of the Parson was well supported in 1563 by John Foxe, who went even further to consider Chaucer himself "to be a right Wicklevian, or else there never was any."[125] But of course we need not trust either man's opinion, any more than those of later critics who have at various times championed the Parson and his creator as occupying any number of points along the sliding scale between heresy and orthodoxy: Bailey and Foxe (and all their subsequent critics) are readers — with all the power, privilege, and crippling limits that come along with it.

So perhaps what is most important about the inky darkness in which we find ourselves when we try to ascertain the religious or political leanings of the *Paraphrase*-poet or Chaucer (or Gower or Langland) is that the murkiness stands as a testament to the currency of and preoccupation with such issues in late medieval England. Reform, whether termed Wycliffite or not, is yet one more moraine in the cultural landscape in which the *Paraphrase* resides. The poet was no doubt aware of it — how could he not be? — and by composing a literal paraphrase of accepted texts, oxymoronic as that might seem, and refusing thereby to engage in doctrinal debate, the *Paraphrase*-poet deftly avoids much of the difficulty that could have plagued his text and perhaps even threatened his life. By straddling the line between reform and status quo, the poet manages to construct a narrative that spoke to any number of audiences: from reformers seeking access to Comestor's influential work to young clerks not yet well versed in Latin and in need of a crib text to gain an initial understanding of the essential stories of the Old Testament. And if manuscript contexts can tell us anything, we can surmise that he achieved a remarkable success in this regard. In the Selden manuscript the *Paraphrase* is the first item, followed by thirty-four saints' lives from the *Northern Homily Collection* and three tales about holy monks (fols. 172r–239r), with a fifteenth-century love poem (inserted on fols. 168v–169v). Peck concludes that Selden "must have been intended for devotional use, perhaps by a great household or a religious community, or perhaps for private meditational enjoyment and instruction."[126] In the Longleat manuscript, on the other hand, the poem is the final item, preceded by Lydgate's *Siege of*

---

[125] Quoted in Jeffrey, "Chaucer and Wyclif," p. 113. It is possible that Foxe's suspicion was furthered in his mind by the incorrect attribution of works like *Jack Upland* and *Testament of Love* to Chaucer's hand, but the image of Chaucer as a premature Protestant poet continued long after such works were removed from his canon. See Besserman, *Chaucer's Biblical Poetics*, pp. 204–05.

[126] Peck, *Heroic Women from the Old Testament*, p. 109.

Thebes (fols. 1r–48r), the Chaucerian pieces *Arcite and Palamon* (fols. 53r–77r) and *Grisildis* (fols. 77v–89v), and a translation of the romance *Ipomadon* (fols. 90r–105r); as Peck observes: "The compilation . . . is more secular in its orientation than S[elden], and somewhat more aristocratic in its appeal."[127] Which camp the *Paraphrase*-poet imagined he was writing for, if indeed he had one in mind, must elude us, our only final clue being the fact that, within only a few years or decades of the completion of this poem, it was being used as a source for one of the most famous dramatic sequences in medieval England, the magnificent York cycle of plays. But even here we are left with strange leads. For while this cycle is not generally known as a reformative work, and certainly not as one that borders on heresy, in one of his defenses of scriptural translation Wycliffe himself favorably mentions how friars have taught the Paternoster in English, "as men seyen in the pley of York."[128] Like Janus, the *Paraphrase* seems always to be of two faces, a text that is liable to produce what readings are sought within its thousands of verses. It is, in this sense, a quite fitting translation of the Holy Word, which can be so easy to hear but so difficult to understand.

FIGURES FAIR TO TELL: THE ROMANCING OF THE BIBLE

This boke that is the Bybyll cald,	*called the Bible*
and all that owtt of yt is drawn,	
For Holy Wrytt we sall yt hald	*shall; hold*
and honour yt ever os our awn;	*as our own*
All patriarkes and prophettes yt told,	
so ever ther saynges sekerly ar knawn,	*whenever their sayings are known certainly*
And all wer fygurs fayr to fald	*were figures; tell*
how coymmyng of Crist myght be kawn.	*mediated upon*
— *Paraphrase*, lines 25–32	

In his letter to the Romans, Paul writes: "For what things soever were written were written for our learning: that, through patience and the comfort of the scriptures, we might have hope" (15:4; compare 2 Timothy 3:16). Chaucer's Nun's Priest cites this advice at the conclusion of his tale:

But ye that holden this tale a folye,
As of a fox, or of a cok and hen,
Taketh the moralite, goode men.
For Seint Paul seith that al that writen is,
To oure doctrine it is ywrite, ywis;
Taketh the fruyt, and lat the chaf be stille. (*Canterbury Tales* VII[B²]3438–43)

Chaucer again refers to the line in his Retraction, pointing out that while his work may be at the mercy of its readers, his intention was to follow Paul's directive all along: "Al that is

---

[127] Peck, *Heroic Women from the Old Testament*, p. 109.

[128] *De officio pastorali* 15 (Wycliffe, *English Works of Wyclif*, ed. Matthew, p. 429). For discussion about the relation between this early Lord's Prayer Play and the great Corpus Christi Play that we normally associate with York, see *York Plays*, ed. Smith, pp. xxviii–xxix.

writen is writen for oure doctrine" (*Canterbury Tales* X[I]1083).[129] What constitutes that very personal (but very vague) "oure doctrine" is painfully or amusingly unclear, depending on one's point of view about the Retraction. Indeed, it may be its lack of clarity that makes the passage from Paul so popular in the late Middle Ages: Morey cites its use in as varied locations as Caxton's preface to Malory and the *Ovide moralisé*.[130] Looking across the spectrum of medieval citation of the passage, Minnis observes that the "'all' came to mean 'almost anything,' writing of all kinds" as the "discriminating reader" interpreted disparate material to create his own, necessarily personal, "doctrine."[131] For Chaucer, the "all" appears to include nearly the whole of his *oeuvre*; in an exercise in memory at the end of his Retraction he lists nearly the whole of his catalog as needing to be revoked: from the finest fart in the Miller's Tale to Troilus' rise through the spheres at the end of *Troilus and Criseyde*. Only his *Boece* and some clearly pro-Church documents are to be saved. Life is an exercise in reading, Chaucer's Retraction says, and an uncertain one at that. Safer, perhaps, to do away with the chaff of entertainments entirely. They can, after all, be confusing to the "lewd" mind. On the contrary, Chaucer's Nun's Priest, having just told a clearly allegorical tale, trusts the reader in these matters. The difference is one of degree, not kind. Both the Retraction and the Nun's Priest agree that the reading is ultimately up to the reader. For better or worse, the mind determines the moral or the morass.

For the *Paraphrase*-poet, too, the "all" of Paul becomes an exercise in expectation and reader response: just what can the reader be entrusted to understand? And, more importantly, what *must* the reader understand? Clearly, the poet's audience may not understand Latin. But just as clearly, if unsaid, is the poet's opinion that his audience should know what is *in* the Latin. That is, since salvation is to be found in the Scriptures, it is vital that everyone have access to what is found within the Latin text: thus the need for translation. Beyond the Bible, it would seem that the poet would include Comestor as essential writing for the development of proper doctrine. The prologue to the *Paraphrase* places the *Historia* and Scripture on essentially equal footing, and at least one reader of the poem agreed, noting in the margin not only the places where the *Paraphrase* disagrees with Holy Writ, but also where it disagrees with Comestor.[132]

What the poet finds in both the Bible and the *Historia*, and what he expects will be most beneficial to his presumed audience, are "fygurs fayr to fald [tell]" (line 31). Stories, in other words, and exciting ones at that. But of course these are more than just good tales. For although stories can be an end in and of themselves, they are most beneficial as a means to an end. Here again we might recall the introduction to the book of Judith, as the poet there states that by invoking her story anew he hopes "sum men" might amend their ways (lines

---

[129] Chaucer also echoes this sentiment in the link between his own Chaucer-as-pilgrim tales, Thopas and Melibee, where he reports that the *sentence* of the Gospels is one, despite the surface (we might say "literal") differences between their stories (*Canterbury Tales* VII[B²]943–66). One only needs to read correctly in order to discern the underlying, unifying truth. Many critics have read this statement as the defining principle for understanding the *Tales* themselves: so seemingly varied but yet of one *sentence*, one moral substance (see, e.g., D. W. Robertson, *Preface to Chaucer*, pp. 367–69).

[130] Morey, *Book and Verse*, pp. 14–15.

[131] Minnis, *Medieval Theory of Authorship*, p. 205.

[132] These notations are in the Longleat manuscript, not the Selden manuscript utilized as a base text for the present edition. See *Middle English Metrical Paraphrase*, ed. Kalén, 1:viii–ix.

16959–60). Or, alternatively, we might recall the end of her book, where the poet begs God's blessing for he who "hath turned yt / in Ynglysch lawd men forto lere" (lines 17743–44). Like Gower, his contemporary, the *Paraphrase*-poet views his collection of tales, entertaining though they might be, as essentially both an individual and a collective means of instruction. Storytelling is a pedagogical exercise; or, vice versa, teaching is an exercise in telling stories. If the stories fail, so too might the teaching.

But these stories do not fail. The *Paraphrase*-poet is clearly intrigued by the heroic nature of the Old Testament, the unfolding of an epic story, and his selections of Scripture reflect a wider cultural interest in romance narratives, particularly in its concluding episodes of Job, Tobias, Esther, and the tales from Maccabees. Fowler observes how in *Genesis and Exodus* "the influence of romance is clearly evident in apocryphal additions to the life of Moses,"[133] but as romantically involved as that text can be it pales before the more comprehensive *Paraphrase*, where it is not just the life of Moses that garners such treatment but, theoretically, the whole of the sacred Word. The result of this treatment is that "the epic element," as Ohlander puts it mildly, "is everywhere taken care of very conscientiously," and the Old Testament is transformed into something akin to romance — "comparison with chivalric poetry or the 'chansons de geste' is often near at hand," Ohlander goes on to say. The poet thus produces a popularized and at times more sanitized account of Hebraic history, and "the world of the Old Testament is translated into the feudal age."[134] In this vein Brunner has called the *Paraphrase* a "pleasant retelling" that pours the Old Testament "through the alembic of the medieval mind."[135]

Brunner's term "alembic" is, in fact, exceedingly apt. In the poet's hands Scripture becomes a type of still, a textual apparatus that distills his own culture into the document of its foundation, filling it to the point of permeation even at the basic level of vocabulary. Throughout the text we find a lexicon more applicable to the Middle Ages than the biblical age as the poet brings the past action of the Bible into the present thoughts and concerns of his late medieval audience. By making the stories of Scripture more closely related to his contemporary present, the poet surely hopes that his contemporary readers might more willingly listen to the teachings based upon the Holy Word and let it affect their future actions. Thus we find a king's "consaylle" ("council" — line 6216), as well as various dukes, knights, and knaves populating these stories. Similarly, we find the medieval ecclesiastical hierarchy of "byschopes and prestes" (line 7275), as well as "prelettes" (line 7922). We find medieval liturgical phrases such as "*Diligam te, Domine*" (line 9233) or "*Miserere mei Deus*" (line 8225). We find medieval garb, such as Abigail's clothes or Goliath's full steel armor. There is medieval *fin' amors* — Saul's daughter Michel pines for love in the courtly love vein, for example — and the related

---

[133] Fowler, *Bible in Early English Literature*, p. 133.

[134] Ohlander, "Old French Parallels," p. 203. This quality is by no means unique to the *Paraphrase* or even to late medieval literature. The Jewish writer Josephus, for example, carries out the same impulse in constructing his own retellings of Scripture: he is among the first to expand the story of Samson (in *Antiquites of the Jews* 5.8.1–12), adding human motivation and characterization in order to make the story more real, more likely (note particularly his original 5.8.12). In short, he makes Samson a historical man of great sanctity rather than a legendary man of supernatural powers. For more on Samson's literary history, see Krouse, *Milton's Samson and the Christian Tradition*. It may well be this aspect of Josephus that makes him so attractive to Comestor, and Comestor to the *Paraphrase*-poet.

[135] Brunner, Review of *A Middle English Metrical Paraphrase*, p. 477.

excess of emotion that we associate with romantic narratives, such as David's anguished mourning for Jonathan. There are medieval attitudes and behaviors throughout: Shimei spits at David rather than casting stones at him, and David personally forgives him for the act — the biblical story, on the other hand, relates that Shimei just takes part in a general amnesty after David gains the crown. By the same token, Abner tries to bribe Joab's brother Asahel rather than, as the Bible tells it, discuss his issues with him (lines 7445–48). The warfare of the poem, too, is medieval rather than biblical, as "gybcrokes and engyns" ("siege hooks and siege engines" — line 5213) are memorably used in the battle for Jabesh-gilead. "Thus," as Brunner has concluded, "the Biblical story is subtly transformed into a medieval chivalric romance."[136]

Erwin Panofsky terms this process in which authors update earlier models of art or narrative — whether it is to introduce Christian significance to Virgil and Ovid or to invest the past with the setting of the present — the "principle of disjunction."[137] In his study of the ramifications of these disjunctions in the work of Chaucer, A. J. Minnis calls the poems that result "at once anachronistic and historically accurate" (i.e., accurate in presenting the way they think about themselves):

> Their anachronism mainly consists in such things as the late-medieval manners, fashions, ideals of chivalry, and doctrines of *fin' amors* which Chaucer imposed on his pagan materials in an attempt (how conscious we will never know) to up-date the past slightly, to make it more meaningful in contemporary, 'modern' terms.[138]

The *Paraphrase*-poet, working in just the same vein as Chaucer, and presumably for much the same reasons, thus creates the most remarkable kind of document, what we might term romantic Scripture: a holy text that becomes at once ancient history and present reality. In this case, it is a Bible filled with debates of action rather than debates of scholarship and exegesis. While there are correlations with Chaucer and Gower here, there is also divergence. Minnis calls Chaucer "an 'historial' poet," one writing "about events which had long since passed and beliefs which had been rendered obsolete." Chaucer, he says, "did not write exemplary history in the strict late-medieval and Renaissance sense of the term. His concern was with truth-to-life, with verisimilitude, rather than with moral truth."[139] Yet such exemplary history is precisely the *Paraphrase*-poet's goal. He shares with Chaucer the concern for verisimilitude, but it is truth-to-life not for the purpose of showing how ancients "thought and behaved in their historical time and place," but, rather, to make the moral, exemplary lessons of the past all the more real for the present reader. We noted earlier Bloom's observation that "[f]ew cultural paradoxes are so profound, or so unnerving, as the process of religious canonization by which an essentially literary work becomes a sacred text."[140] What we can now see, especially through the lens of a work like the *Paraphrase*, is how medieval literary history essentially inverts this dictum by taking the sacred text and moving it into the literary vernacular with results that are no less profound.

---

[136] Brunner, Review of *A Middle English Metrical Paraphrase*, p. 478.

[137] Panofsky, *Renaissance and Renascences*, pp. 84–85.

[138] Minnis, *Chaucer and Pagan Antiquity*, p. 6.

[139] Minnis, *Chaucer and Pagan Antiquity*, p. 6.

[140] Bloom and Rosenberg, *Book of J*, p. 35.

The idea of utilizing the trappings of secular literature for sacred purpose is nothing new. Fowler notes in his examination of early English biblical literature that the popularity of secular literature could at times cause "an anxiety on the part of the author to persuade his reader or listener to abandon the popular literature of the day and give his full attention to the biblical story, which is good for the soul"; in other words, "clerical authors were feeling the pressure of competition from secular literature."[141] The result at times opens up into what seems to be outright conflict between the sacred and secular in literature. This conflict can be seen at the beginning of *Cursor Mundi*, for example, or in the Middle English translation of Robert of Grentham's thirteenth-century *Miroir*, a Gospel lectionary that describes itself in its introduction as "a litel tretiȝ of diuinite to turn man from romances and gestes, wherein he lesiþ mychel of his tyme þat so setteþ his hert from god, and to give him instead þing þat is profitable boþe to lyf & to soule."[142] And while the *Paraphrase*-poet is not so direct in his rebuttal of "romances and gestes," the content of his poem would seem to indicate that he would be of a mind with the anonymous translator of Grentham's *Miroir*. His concern is with souls and salvation. The romantic aspects of his work are but a means to that end.

The *Paraphrase*-poet is presenting an alternative romance, an epic only scarcely touched with the occasional *lectio* on the morals of the stories that he is presenting. The dramatic nature of his poem's staging, from dialogue to setting, thereby cultivates the seeds of some of the great biblical dramatacists who followed in his wake.[143] Indeed, we know that one of the foremost of their number — the hand (or hands) behind the great *York Plays* — used this very text in the process of composition. The *Paraphrase*-poet's proclamation that he intends to write stories "for sympyll men" (line 19) to understand the Scriptures and be engaged by them — "that men may lightly leyre / to tell and under take yt" (lines 23–24) — thus combines both the profit of sacred literature with the pleasure of the secular. This is Horace's *utile et dulce* ("both useful and pleasing") principle at its clearest, a singular example of the didacticism that characterizes so much medieval literature, an aesthetic of pedagogic efficacy that is inseparably linked to the essential component of true pleasure of the text. In a more doctrinal vein, we might call this the practice by which *ad litteram* makes the Word flesh.

NOTE ON THE TEXT

It has been the policy of the Middle English Texts Series to utilize the spelling of biblical names as they appear in the Douay-Rheims translation of the Bible, since this translation is closest to that of the Vulgate. As this is the version utilized for all translations of Scripture, the policy generally makes good sense. The *Paraphrase*, however, presents obstacles to following this guideline as a hard and fast rule: many biblical names are known almost universally in a form different from that found in the Douay-Rheims or Vulgate. *Noe*, for instance, appears to most eyes as a rather strange spelling for *Noah*. I have decided to

---

[141] Fowler, *Bible in Early English Literature*, p. 133.

[142] Morey, *Book and Verse*, p. 14, citing Goates, *Pepysian Harmony*, xi; compare *Cursor Mundi*, lines 1–28 and 85–88.

[143] This is not to say the *Paraphrase*-poet alone planted those seeds. See Lynette Muir, *Biblical Drama*, for an overview of biblical drama across Europe, much of which predates the great cycles of late medieval England. For more specific looks at the latter, see Woolf, *English Mystery Plays*, and Stevens, *Four Middle English Mystery Cycles*.

err on the side of familiarity in this matter, and thus glosses and references tend to utilize the more common spellings except where the Douay-Rheims is directly quoted.

The presentation of numbers in medieval texts can be a delicate matter for editors. The base manuscript of the poem here edited, for instance, records that Jacob peeled back the bark on the rods where Laban's cattle bred "VI or seven" times (line 966). This is readily understandable enough, but shortly afterward the scribe writes that Jacob made both his wives and their female servants pregnant, "So that he had hymself, . . . Of suns full semly XII" (lines 981 and 983). The meaning here is again relatively clear, though it admittedly looks strange to the modern eye since these two lines are meant to end-rhyme (*hymself* : *XII*). Appearing even stranger are lines such as the statement of the widow of Obadiah about her husband's good deeds in saving those whom Jezabel would have killed: "I C held he hale of hew" (line 12163), in which the first two letters represent "one hundred" rather than the first person pronoun and, as my younger students would imagine it, the verb "see." In the interest of easing the reader's labors here and elsewhere, I have silently replaced such abbreviated roman numerations with spelled-out Middle English words as they appear elsewhere in the base manuscript. Thus, for example, the counting of the tribe of Aser is here "fourty" rather than the scribal "XL" (line 7707). Expanded Latinate forms, such as "mille" (meaning "thousand"), are left as they stand but are usually glossed in the margin.

The scholar wishing a full accounting of the linguistic features of the poem is advised to seek out the first volume of the Kalén-Ohlander edition, which is unlikely to be surpassed in the extent of its discussion. Briefly, though, one might note the following strong features as a guide to reading the poem:[144]

- Midlands -*o*- is usually -*a*- or -*ai*- in Northern dialects, while occasionally Midlands *a*- will be *o*-. Thus *Gast* rather than *Ghost* (line 5); *os our awn* rather than *as our own* (line 28).
- Midlands *sh*- is *s*- in the North. Thus *sall* rather than *shall* (line 27); *suld* rather than *should* (line 87).
- Midlands -*e*- is often -*o*-. Thus *thore* rather than *there* (line 96); *whore* rather than *where* (line 16958).
- Midlands -*e*- in verbal inflections appears as -*y*-. Thus *savyd* rather than *saved* (line 36); *movyd* rather than *moved* (line 48).
- Participial -*ing* is usually -*and* (again, a Northern feature). Thus *lastand* rather than *lasting* (line 82); *schynand* rather than *shining* (line 106).
- The pronoun *she* often appears as *sho* or *scho*.

MANUSCRIPTS

Indexed as item 944 in Boffey and Edwards, *New Index of Middle English Verse*:

- L: Longleat House, MS 257. Fols. 119r–212r. [Private collection of the marquis of Bath.]
- S: Oxford, Bodleian Library, MS Arch. Selden. Supra 52. Fols. 2r–168r. [Base text.]

---

[144] Based on the introduction to Peck's *Heroic Women from the Old Testament*, pp. 116–17.

PROLOGUE

1.

God, Fader in Hevyn of myghtes most,
    that mad this mold and all mankynd,   *made this world*
The Sun that sendes us throwth to tast,   *Son; truth; taste*
    wesdom and welth and wytt at wyn,   *wisdom; intelligence to obtain*

5 The grace of the Holy Gast
    in whom all gudnes behoves to begyn   *goodness must needs begin*
Thrugh mediacy of Mary chast   *mediation; chaste*
    that helpes to safe uus of our syn,   *save us from*
Swylke myght unto me send   *Such*

10   thys boke ryght to aray,   *correctly to compose*
Begynnyng, myddes, and end,   *middle*
    that yt be to Goddes pay.   *liking*

2.

This buke is of grett degré,   *stature*
    os all wettys that ben wyse,   *as all know*

15 For of the Bybyll sall yt be   *Bible shall*
    the poyntes that ar mad most in price,   *highlights; are made; of importance*
Als maysters of dyvinité   *As masters*
    and on, the maystur of storyse,   *and one [especially]*
For sympyll men soyn forto se,   *to understand at once*

20   settes yt thus in this schort assyse;   *sets it; paraphrase*
And in moyr schort maner   *more brief*
    is my mynd forto make yt,
That men may lyghtly leyre   *easily learn*
    to tell and undertake yt.   *recite; understand*

3.

25 This boke that is the Bybyll cald,   *called the Bible*
    and all that owtt of yt is drawn,
For Holy Wrytt we sall yt hald   *shall; hold*
    and honour yt ever os our awn;   *as our own*
All patriarkes and prophettes yt told,

30   so ever ther saynges sekerly ar knawn,   *whenever their sayings are known certainly*
And all wer fygurs fayr to fald   *were figures; tell*
    how coymmyng of Crist myght be kawn.   *mediated upon*

God graunt us Crist to knaw   *Christ to know*
    All our form faders cravyd   *ancestors desired to know*
35 And so to lere Is law   *learn His law*
    that our sawlis may be savyd.   *souls*

[STORY OF CREATION (1:1–2:25)]

4.

In this begynnyng God uus wysch   *guide us*
   well for werke with wyll and toyght.   *thought*
In this boke that cald is Genesis   *book that is called*
40   ther may men see the soth unsoght   *see the truth readily*
How God, that beldes in endlese blyse,   *who dwells*
   all only with Hys Word hath wroght   *created*
Hevyn on heght for Hym and Hys,   *high*
   this erth and all that ever is oght.   *ever has been*
45 This erth was wyde and wast   *wide and empty*
   and no gud on yt grovyd;   *nothing good on it grew*
On the heght the Holi Gast   *On high; Holy Ghost*
   abown the waters movyd.   *above; moved*

5.

Hell He mad marke thrugh Hys myght   *dark (murky)*
50   so that no medcyn mend yt may;   *medicine*
God bad that in the hevyns on hyght
   suld be mad lyght forever and ay,   *forever and always*
And therin mad He angels bryght
   to serve Hymself evermoyr to pay.   *satisfaction*
55 The merknes namyd he to be Nyght,   *darkness*
   and the lyghtnes to be Day.
Of angels on was schefe,   *one was chief*
   and hys name Lucyfer,   *Lucifer*
Unto his Lord most lefe,   *dear*
60   in Ynglysch "Lyght-beyrer."

6.

And for he was so fayr that tyd,   *fair [in] that time*
   angels in hest sone can he hent,   *haste soon; summon*
And sayd he suld be glorefyd
   lyke to Hym that hys lyfe had lent.   *lent (endowed)*
65 Then in this blyse myght he not byd   *remain*
   bott hastely to Hell he wentt,

	For syn in Hevyn is non to hyde,	*Because; not able to be hidden*
	all dyd the same of hys assent.	*all who followed him did the same*
	The tend ordyr of angell	*tenth order of angels*
70	thurgh prid, os kend our clerkes,	*pride; teach*
	Unto fowle fendes fell.	*foul fiends*
	Ther wer the fyrst day werkes.	*These*

7.

	When God that semly syght con see,	*did see*
	Hym toyght yt well withoutyn were.	*thought; doubt*
75	A firmament then bad He be	
	to part the waters in sonder seyre.	*into two parts*
	The watur abown than ordand He	*above*
	to wend abowt with wyndes clere,	*move*
	That other byneth in law degré	*beneath in lower degree (i.e., below the firmament)*
80	To moyst the erth in his manere.	*moisten*
	The firmament namyd He Hevyn,	*Heaven*
	to lend lastand for ay.	*enduring forever*
	Ther ys no moyr to nevyn.	*mention*
	So sessyd the secund day.	*ceased*

8.

85	The waters that wer on erth ordand	
	God hath them geddyrd all in a sted,	*one place*
	And the sted that thei suld in stand	
	ys callyd the Se by ryghwyse rede;	*proper reckoning*
	And the dry erth namyd He the Land,	
90	He bad that yt suld spryng and sprede	*spring [forth] and spread*
	Herbys and treyse with wod and wand	*Herbs; trees; wood; branches*
	and sed to saw when thei wer dede,	*seed to sow; dead*
	So that new suld up spryng	
	there sted forto restoyre	*their place to restore*
95	And flours and frutt forto furth bryng.	*flowers; fruit*
	The thryd endyd thore.	*third [day]*

9.

	God ordand then grett lyghtys two	
	to moyv apon the firmament	*move*
	To parte the days and the nyghtys fro,	*divide*
100	and yer fro yer be sesons sent,	*year from year by seasons designated*
	The moyr befor the day to go	*greater [light]*
	and the lesse to the nyght at attent.	*lesser to attend to the night*
	The Sun and the Moyn namyd He them,	
	by them on erthe the lyght is lent.	
105	Sternys on hevyn He sett	*Stars*
	with bemys schynand for bryght	*beams shining*

By certan mesurs mett.   *certain proper measures*
  Thus was the faurt day dyght.   *fourth day ended*

10.

God bad that in the see suld brede   *breed*
110   dyverse fysches to flett with fyn,   *float (swim) with fins*
And of themselfe thei sall have sede   *offspring*
  allway to wax waters within;   *grow within [the] waters*
And fowls He ordand fayr forto fede   *birds; feed*
  with wynges and wynd ther way to wynd,   *to go their way*
115   By erth and ayer ther lyfes to lede   *air their lives*
  and same won withoutyn fynd.   *together dwell; end*
He blessyd thos werkes fayr
  that thei no myrth suld myse,   *joy should miss*
Bot fyll both watur and ayer.   *air*
120   The fyft day werke was this.   *fifth day's work*

11.

Then bad God ther suld bestes bee
  on dyverse kynd os thei ar kend   *known*
On ylka syd in seyre cuntré,   *every place; diverse (all)*
  and wormes on the wome to wende.   *snakes; belly to go*
125   Then sayd He to Hymself: "Make We
  a man that may bestes mys amend,   *beasts' wrongs repair*
For have power and pausté   *authority*
  on bestes and fowls withoutyn end.
And that man wyll We geyse   *create*
130   aftur Our awn ymage ay   *always*
And like to Our awn liknes."
  So was don the sext day.   *sixth*

12.

God toght the consell was not clere   *thought; scheme; perspicacious*
  a man alon hys lyf to led;   *lead*
135   Som other suld be unto hym nere
  hym forto helpe yf he had nede.
Owt of hys syde Hee sonderd seyre   *sundered apart*
  a crokyd rybe, os clerkes can rede,   *crooked rib*
And therof formyd He hym a fere,   *companion*
140   a female, frutt furth to bred.   *to breed forth children*
He gafe them power playn   *unlimited*
  abuf all erthly thynge,
With all gudes that myght gayn   *all goods*
  tyll thei breke Hys bydyng.   *until they broke His bidding*

13.

145 God gaf man fre wyll to be wyse,   *free will*
   and in certan He sett hys name;
   Then plantyd He Erthly Paradyse,
   and in that place He putt Adam.
   He fyllyd yt full of all delyce   *delights*
150   and made hym suferan of the same,   *sovereign*
   Wyls he wold wone withoutyn vyce,   *While he would live*
   ther forto byd withoutyn blame.   *abide*
   Ther wer all erbys and tresses   *herbs; trees*
   with flours and frutt gud woyn;   *easily obtained*
155 God bad Adam go chese,   *bade; [to] go choose*
   and ette of all bot on.   *eat; one*

14.

   In myddes of Paradyse yt stud   *[the] midst*
   with frut fayr to fede and fyll;   *consume*
   Who of that frutt myght fang ther fude   *take their food*
160   suld clerly knaw both gud and yll.
   Therfor God wernyd hym for hys gud,   *warned*
   and bad hym lett that frutt be styll,
   "Yf thou yt ethe, with wordes wode   *If you eat it, with furious words*
   soyn to be wast owt of thy wyll."   *at once [you will] be deprived of your desire*
165 Of all other that ther wer
   He gaf hym largely lefe;   *free access*
   That bad He hym forbeyr   *That one commanded; forbear*
   for dowt of moyr myschefe.   *fear*

[FALL OF ADAM AND EVE (3:1–14)]

15.

   Bot then the Fend, our fellyst foe,   *Fiend (i.e., Satan); darkest*
170   that fallyn was not fer before,   *fallen; long before*
   For that werkyng he was full wo   *creation; very angry*
   that tho wyghys so worthy were;   *those people*
   Within hymselfe persavyd he soe   *perceived*
   that thei the same sted suld restore   *place should take*
175 That he and hys felows fell fro;
   that mad hym mornyng mekyll more.   *much more angry*
   He toyght yt so suld not be;   *thought*
   therfor in schort qwylle   *a short time*
   He soyght up sotelté   *sought out subtleties*
180   them both forto gyle.   *to deceive*

16.

   He wyst full well withoutyn wene   *knew quite well without doubt*
   how God had demyd in all degré.   *made determination (discerned)*

As a serpent soyn was he sen,   *soon*
   with woman face full fayr and free.   *[a] woman's face*
185   To Eve he sayd, "What may yt meyn
   That ye tent noyght to this tree?"   *attend not*
Scho sayd, "That wold turne us te tene;   *to sorrow*
   God bad that we suld lett yt be."
The Fend sayd, "Foyles the more,   *Fools*
190   by that skyll scornyd ar ye;   *ordinance (ruse) are you scorned*
God wold not that ye wer
   alway so wyse os He.   *forever as wise*

17.
"This frutt may gyf wysdom and wytt;
   als godes so sall ye both begyn."   *gods; become*
195   Scho saw that frutt so fayr and fytt,
   and eth ther of this welth to wyn.   *eats*
Scho bad Adam to ette of yt,   *eat*
   to bytt theron he wold noght blyne.   *bite; tarry*
Hys boldnes and that balfull bytt   *baleful bite*
200   cast hym in care and all hys kyne.   *into sorrow; kind (humanity)*
When thei this frutt had takyd,   *partaken*
   qwerfor thei wer both blamyd,
Thei saw then thei wer nakyd;
   full yll thei wer aschamyd.   *completely*

18.
205   With lefys ther privates can thei hyd,   *leaves*
   and playnly durst thei not apeyre.   *openly*
God callyd on Adam in that tyd,   *at that time*
   and he sayd, "Lord, I hyd me heyre.   *hide myself here*
I hath so doyn, I der not byd."   *dare not pray for anything*
210   God askyd why and in what manere.
"Lord, yf I wer yll ocupyd
   yt was thrugh fandyng of my fere."   *scheming; spouse*
God askyd why that schoe went   *she*
   that forbeyd frutt forto fele.   *taste*
215   Scho sayd, "Lord, the serpent
   gart me do ylka deyle."   *made me to do every bit [of it]*

19.
God told then unto all thre
   what thei suld feyle for ther forfeytt.   *feel (receive)*
To the worme He sayd, "Waryd thou be,   *Cursed*
220   wend on thy wome, ay erth forto eytte;   *go; belly, ever earth to eat*
And, woman, frutt that comys on thee   *fruit (children)*
   sall be broyght furth with paynys grett;
And, Adam, for thou trowd not me,   *trusted*

	wyn thou thy foyd with swynke and swett;	*obtain; food; labor; sweat*
225	So sall all thyn ofspryng	*offspring*
	unto the uttmast ende."	*uttermost end [of time]*
	To manys kynd com this thyng	*man's nature came*
	thrugh falssyng of the Fend.	*deception*

[CAIN AND ABEL (4:1–17)]

20.

	Fro Paradyse thei wer exilyd	
230	withoutyn grace agayn to passe.	*permission to return*
	So went thei both os bestes wyld,	*beasts*
	thei cowd no lovyng. Bot, alase,	*[do] nothing praiseworthy*
	Soyn Eve consavyd and bare a chyld,	
	Cayn, that sythyn so cursyd was	*Cain; then*
235	Because of Abell meke and myld	*Abel meek*
	that he slow with a cheke of an ase;	*jawbone of an ass*
	For the offerand of Abell	*Because the offering*
	was accepte in Goddes syght.	*accepted/acceptable*
	And Caymys went down to Hell	*Cain*
240	and to God gaf noe lyght.	*no light (see note)*

[DESCENDANTS OF ADAM (4:17–5:32)]

21.

	When Adam wyst withoutyn wer	*knew without doubt*
	this wekyd werk, he was full wo;	*wicked*
	He morned ever and mad yll cher	*mourned*
	for meke Abell was murtherd so.	*murdered*
245	Bot aftur that full mony a yer,	
	when he tyll Eve agan can go,	*again can have intercourse*
	Then bare scho suns and doyghters sere,	*she bore many sons and daughters*
	the story says sexty and moe;	
	Then ylke on other toke	*each one another took [as spouse]*
250	and lyfyd be law of kynd,	*nature*
	Als whoso likes to loke	
	may seke and forther fynd.	

22.

	Of Caymys kynd come Tubulcan,	*Cain's kind (family) came Tubal-cain*
	of metall mellyd he amang,	*mettled*
255	And diverse thynges to helpe of man	
	ordand he both schort and lang.	
	Hys brothyr Juball he began	*Jubal; invented*
	musyke, ose mynstralsy and sang.	*song*
	The harpe by hym was ordand then	*created*
260	and other myrth qwer men suld gang.	*wherever men should go*

Of Adam suns the thryd
   hyght Seth, man myld of mode.   *Seth; mood*
He wrott what dedes thei dyd
   that last aftur the flode.

23.

265   Of Seth then com Matussile,   *Methuselah*
   lyfyd he neyn hunderth scxty and neyn yere,   *969 years*
Of hym com Lameth, of hym Noe   *Lamech; Noah*
   that unto God wer gud and dere.
And Noe had suns fully thre,
270   Sem, Cham, Jafeth in fere.   *Shem, Ham, Japheth together*
Then was the werld gone in degree
   thre thowssand yere for neven by nere.   *to figure it closely*
No rayn on erth then fell
   to gayr the gresse up ryse,   *make*
275   Bot faur fludes of a well   *four rivers from*
   that went from Paradyce.

[NOAH AND THE GREAT FLOOD (6:1–9:28)]

24.

Then was no lernyng of no law;
   thei lyfyd in lust evyn at ther lyst.   *pleasure according to their desire*
Ther Creatur thei cowde noyght knaw,   *thought; no one knew their deeds*
280   the wenyd that non ther werkes wyst.
Forto greyfe God thei had non aw,   *grieve; fear*
   therfor all myrthes son thei myst.   *happiness soon they lost*
God spake to Noye and sayd this saw: *Noah; made this declaration*
   "Thou and thy chylder sall be blest;
285   All folke so fowll I fynd
   coruppyd and soyllyd with syn;   *corrupt and soiled*
Me rewthes I made mankynd   *I regret*
   to wond thys werld within.   *dwell*

25.

"And sen I se them so mysegone   *since; misbehaved (mis-gone)*
290   and in hert hath no mynd of me,
I sall dystroy them every ylkon.   *every one*
   Over all this werld sall wax a see   *rise a sea*
So that on lyve sall lefe ryght none   *alive shall live*
   bot thou, thi wyf, thi suns thre,   *sons*
295   And thair thre wyfes, ye aght alon   *eight*
   in land to lyf sall levyd be.   *left*
Bestes and fowles in flygh   *flight*
   non beys for ruth refusyd,   *none should be, for pity, excepted*

	Or all to ded be dyght	
300	for syn ye folke hath usyd.	

26.

	"To make an erke of tymber strang	*ark (boat); strong*
	thou and thi meneye in to abyd,	*your companions to dwell in*
	Thre hunderth cubbettes loke yt be lang,	*300 cubits; long*
	and fyfty cubbeyttes it sall be wyd,	*fifty*
305	And thryty cubbeyttes the heght sall gang;	*thirty; shall go*
	and sett a wyndow in the syde,	*place*
	And cloyse yt well, elles dows thou wrang,	*or else you do wrong*
	to turne the watur in ylka tyde.	*turn [back]; at that time*
	And stages grett plenty	*cages*
310	bus thee make, mony and fayre,	*must you make*
	Wher bestes and fowles may be,	
	of ylka kynd a payre."	*each kind a pair*

27.

	When all was wroygh in hys kynd wyse,	*wrought*
	yt raynnyd, als then was Goddes wyll,	*rained*
315	Faurty days be full asysse	*fourty; count*
	and faurty nyghtys to tell thertyll.	
	The watur over the werld can ryse,	
	fyfty cubbeyttes over the heghest hyll;	
	Yt drownyd the pepyll in all partyse	*people; parts*
320	bot aght that in the arch wer styll.	*except [for the] eight*
	Then monethes yt encressyd,	*months*
	and in Armynie that tyd,	*Armenia*
	When the watur sessyd,	*ceased*
	the arch began to abyd.	*rest*

28.

325	And therby Noe can understand	
	that thei wer sett apon som playn.	*ground*
	A rayven he sent furth to seke the land,	*raven*
	bot that fowlle com not agayn	*bird*
	Then to a dowfe he hath commawnd	*dove*
330	to seke hym sum thyng for certan.	
	An olyve branche full soyn he fand	*olive branch*
	and broyght to schep — then wer thei fayn.	*ship; happy*
	Soyne thei saw then drye	*dry [land]*
	apeyr in dyverse place.	
335	To land thei hast in hye	
	and lovyd God on Hys grace.	*praised*

29.

	The bestes in ther kyndes knew	*by their natures*
	unto what party thei suld repayre	*area they should go*
	To hold them hole of hyd and hew,	*maintain themselves altogether*
340	and fowles flow furth in the ayre.	*air*
	And Noye suns then satt and sew,	*sowed [crops]*
	and soyn thei broyght furth frutt full fayre.	*fruit (offspring)*
	And so the werld then wex all new;	
	thei multiplyd with mony an heyre.	
345	God gafe a sygne to Noye	*sign*
	of the raynbow ryght thore,	*rainbow*
	That He suld never dystroye	
	the werld with watur moyre.	*again*

[NOAH'S CURSE UPON CANAAN (9:18–27)]

30.

	Noye was the fyrst that vynes sett	*vines*
350	wych bare of grapes full grett plenté.	*which bore*
	Of them so sadly can he eytt	*steadily; eat*
	that of the wyn dronkyn was he;	*drunk*
	He fell on slepe down on hys flett.	*in his tent*
	Cham com and scornyd hys prevyty;	*Ham; nakedness*
355	His brethyr duly dyde ther dette	*brothers; duty*
	and hyd hym agayn in god degree.	*covered*
	When Noye his werkyng wyst	*his (Ham's) doings knew*
	he werryd hym forthi;	*cursed him therefore*
	His brethyr both wer blest	*brothers*
360	als ther werke was worthy.	

[TOWER OF BABEL (11:1–9)]

31.

	The pepyll fast then multiplied	
	tho thowssandes moe, or sex, or seven.	*3,000 more, or 6,000, or 7,000*
	Thei fand a feld was lang and wyde,	*found*
	and thor in hand thei ordand evyn	*there by hand; made it level*
365	And began a grett towr in that tyd	*time*
	wych thei sayd suld rech unto Heven.	
	When God saw them sett so in prid,	*pride*
	He kast forto dystroy ther steven.	*determined to destroy their communication*
	Noyne wyst what other wald,	*None knew; meant*
370	bot evyn ose foylles thei foyn.	*fools they acted*
	Wherfor that place is callyd	
	this day Bablion.	*Babel*

[DESCENDANTS OF NOAH (9:28–10:32, 11:10–32)]

32.

Sythyn Noe persavyd by knawyng clere	*Afterwards Noah*
that day was comyn that hym bod dy;	*the time had; he must die*
Then had he lyfyd in landes here	
neyn hunderth wynters and als fyfty.	*nine hundred fifty years*
Yf we suld say hys suns all sere	*assay; separately*
and then depart ther progenité	*list their*
Thatt lesson wer full long to leere.	*learn*
Therfor we lefe them mor lyghtly	*briefly*
And neven bot that nedes,	*mention only what is needed*
and evyn unto understand,	*applies to our understanding*
And that most lely ledes	*faithfully leads*
to lere our law in land.	*teach*

375 (line 3)
380 (at "Therfor we lefe them mor lyghtly")

33.

Of Seme come Phaloge forther than,	*Shem; Peleg*
and of Phaloge come Tharé,	*Terah*
Abraham, Nacor, and Aran;	*Abram, Nahor; Haran*
thare suns wer all thos thre.	*these [latter ones] were sons*
Of Aran com Loth, that lele man,	*Lot; noble*
that honerd God in gud degree.	*who*
Unto this pepyll God began	
to multiplye and make them free.	
Then wer ther systers tway,	*two*
Abram toke Saray,	*Sarai*
And Nacor toke Melkala:	*Milcah*
thei wer ther wyfes worthay.	

385
390
395

34.

Ther was ay wunt to wun	*These were ever accustomed to dwell*
In Urry, whar Caldeis wonnand were.	*Ur; Chaldeans dwelling*
Ther dyed Aran yongest son,	*died Haran [who was the] youngest*
was Loth fader, os we herd here.	*[he] was Lot's father*
And Loth with Abraham furth was fun	*henceforth was [to be] found*
as with hys eme and man most nere.	*uncle; kinsman*
Then Tharé so with yll was bown,	*sickness was taken*
to lyf he myght not langer here.	
He died when he was old	
twa hunderth yer, men wott.	*200 years old, people reckon*
Then is her no ferthermer told	*there no more further*
bot of Abram and Loth.	*except*

400
405

[GOD'S CALL OF ABRAHAM (12:1–7)]

35.

God spake to Abraham for his sped: *advantage*
410   "On this fold may thou not be fune, *In this place; [adequately] supported*
Bot take thy wyfe and with thee lede,
   I sall thee wysch wher thou sall wune *guide; journey*
To have enogh and never nede,
   with Loth also, thi brothyr sune.
415 Thor sall I multiplye thi sed *There; your seed*
   and helpe thee os I hath begune."
To the land of Canan *Canaan*
   so sent he furth thos thre.
God sayd to Abraham then,
420   "This land gyf I to thee."

[ABRAHAM AND LOT (13:1–13)]

36.

Abraham and Loth can same dwell *did dwell together*
   with mekyll myrth full mony a yere; *much happiness*
Thei wex so rych that ther catell *grew; livestock (i.e., property)*
   coverd the cuntré fer and nere.
425 Then mad thei covnand them amell *an agreement amongst themselves*
   that thei suld make ther wonnyng sere, *dwellings separately*
For grett debatt that oft fell
   amang them that ther hyrdmen were. *those who were their herdsmen*
Abraham wonnyd styll at home *dwelled*
430   wher God had byddyn hym come,
And Loth wentt to Sodome, *Sodom*
   a cyté besyd the flume. *river*

[LOT'S CAPTIVITY AND RESCUE (14:1–16)]

37.

Sodome was a grett cety,
   Gommer another nere therby, *Gomorrah*
435 And next them was ther other thre,
   The wych wer fyllyd with syn fouly. *filled; foully*
Thei drede not God in no degré, *feared*
   bot lyfyd in lust and lecheré — *lived; lechery*
And that thei schewyd in syght to see —
440   and agaynst kynd most oncumly. *nature [behaved] most indecently*
Foule is to declare
   how ther werkyns was.
No syb ne spoussyd thai spare, *sibling nor espoused [did] they*
   ne nowther lad ne las. *nor neither; nor lass*

38.

445　Long aftur that this grett warre con spryng
　　　amang kynges of that cuntré.
　　For God sayd thei sall sese for nothyng,
　　　or tho fyve cytes conquerd be.　　　　　　　　　*five cities*
　　Baram was of Sodam kyng,　　　　　　　　　　　*Bera*
450　　and Gomer also governd he.
　　When he herd tell of this tythyng,　　　　　　　*news*
　　　he semyld pepyll full grett plenté,　　　　　　*assembled*
　　Agayns his enmys to go
　　　with schott, scheld, and spere;　　　*missile, shield, and spear*
455　And Loth was on of tho,　　　　　　　　　　*one of those*
　　　a full wys man of were.　　　　　　　*very good man at war*

39.

　　Sone wer thai semyld ylkon　　　　　　　*assembled everyone*
　　　and bett on fast with burnyscht brandes.　*beat; burnished swords*
　　The Sodomites wer soyn sloyn;　　　　　　　*soon slain*
460　　thei myght not flee, thei lefyd ther landes.　*left*
　　And in that batell Loth was tane　　　　　　*taken*
　　　and holdyn in hys enmys handes.　　　　　　*held*
　　Abraham, hys eme, was wyll of wone　*uncle, was distraught*
　　　when he herd tell of thos tythandes.　　　*tidings*
465　He wold not byd ne blyne,　　　　　　　*wait nor tarry*
　　　bott went with power playne,　　　　　　*full*
　　And rescuyd hys cosyn,　　　　　　　　　　*kinsman*
　　　and broyght hym home agayn.

[Abraham blessed by Melchizedek (14:17–24)]

40.

　　Thus savyd he all thies folkes in fere　　*together*
470　　that presond war and putt to pyn.　*were made prisoner*
　　Melchesedeke when he can here　　　　　　*Melchizedek*
　　　how Abraham had savyd hys cosyn,
　　Agayns hym wentt he with gud chere,　　　*To meet him*
　　　and present hym with bred and wyne.
475　He sayd, "I wott withoutyn were　　*know without doubt*
　　　God is thy frend full fast and fyne."
　　He was both prest and kyng,　　　　　　*(Melchizedek)*
　　　and keper of the lay;　　　　　　　　　　*law*
　　He wyst well that this thyng　　　　　*(Lot's rescue)*
480　　was gretly God to pay.　　　　　　　　*satisfy*

[GOD'S COVENANT WITH ABRAHAM (15:1–21)]

41.

The thryd day Abraham was comyn hame
   to se his servandes old and yonge.   *servants*
God come to hym and callyd by name:
   "Abraham, I thanke thee of this thyng.
485   Als I desyrre, thou doys the same;   *Whatever I desire, you do just that*
   therfor thi frutt sall spred and spryng.
Thou sall have welth of wyld and tame
   and myght without more mournyng."
He sayd, "What myrt emong   *happiness among*
490   I have of tame and wyld,
Forto lyfe her thus lang   *here so long*
   And dye withoutyn chyld?"   *die*

42.

God kend hym comforth in that tyd;   *gave him comfort at that time*
   furth of hys hows He can hym lede,   *did lead him*
495   And bad hym see on ylka syde   *every direction*
   over all the land in lengh and brede.
"All sall be thyne and with thee abyd
   and to thyn heyrs ay furth to fede.   *heirs always*
Ose gravell in the se is multyplyd,   *As gravel*
500   so sall I multiplye thi sede.   *seed*
Whoso may tell be tale   *Whoever may number*
   the stern apon hevyn,   *stars in [the] heavens*
Als essely thei sall   *As easily*
   thi sed nowmer and nevyn."   *seed number and name*

[BIRTH OF ISHMAEL (16:1–5)]

43.

505   Abraham was all merveld then   *amazed*
   that ever hys sede suld sogattes yelde   *his seed should yield so much*
Bycause that his wyfe was baran,   *barren*
   and thei wer both in grett eld.   *age*
The wyf wroyght ose a gud woman   *worked as*
510   to geyt a barne to be ther beld;   *child; comfort*
Hyr servant prevely scho wan   *gave*
   tyl Abraham at hys wyll to weld.   *to Abram; to use*
Therfor so yt befell:
   scho beldyd by hym all nyght   *comforted*
515   And consavyd Ysmaell,   *Ishmael*
   that afterward was full wyght.   *strong*

44.

When Agar wyst scho was with chyld,	*Hagar*
hyr hert in pride begane to ryse;	
Hyr maystrys that was meke and myld	*mistress who*
520 in all hyr dedes scho can dyspyse.	
Then Sarai wyst scho was begylyd,	*knew*
bot ever scho wrogh os woman wyse.	*behaved*
Hyr and hyr barn both can scho bylde,	*protect*
and prayd ever God for bettur gyse	*guise*
525 To send them sum ryght ayre	*true heir*
that myght ther welthes weld.	*who; wield*
Bot scho was in dyspayr	
any barn to beyre for eld.	*bear because of age*

[SIGN OF THE COVENANT (17:1–27)]

45.

Aftur, qwen Abraham was old	*Later, when*
530 a hunderth wynters, then wex he tame,	*one hundred years; spiritless*
And in that tyme God to hym told	
wher he wonnyd in his hows at hame,	*dwelt*
"To have a son thou sall be bold,	
and Ysac sall be his name;	*Isaac*
535 He sall have frutt full mony fold."	
Abraham toke tent and trowd that same.	*took heed; believed*
God commaund in that tyd	
that Abraham and all his	
Suld all be circumscisyd,	
540 so to amend ther mys.	*make atonement*

46.

So dyd thei sone and hyght in hy	*promised readily*
the law of God hertly to hold.	
For Abraham it is sayd schortly	*Abram*
that Abraham then he suld be cald,	*Abraham*
545 And hys wyf, that hygh Sarai,	
full Sare suld hyr name be tald.	*Sarah*
Ther kynredyn and ther cumpany	*kinsfolk; households*
wer circumsysed so yong and old.	
For Abraham trowd that thyng,	*Because; believed*
550 ose clerkes declare it can;	
The trowth and the begynnyng	
of our fayth ther begane.	

[A SON PROMISED TO ABRAHAM AND SARAH (18:1–15)]

47.

	Fell aftur long apon a day	*It happened long afterwards*
	Abraham was tyllyd under a tre	*stretched out*
555	In hy seson hym to play	*high (hot); relax*
	bysyd a hyll that heght Mambré.	*Mamre*
	Thre chylder com thor in the way	*Three young men*
	als comly ose ever men myght see.	*as far as*
	And cled in honest wed wer thai,	*simple clothes*
560	all semand on eld to be.	*in flames (see note)*
	For thei wer fayr to syght,	*Because*
	he helsyd them os hende,	*welcomed them as [was] proper*
	And herberd them all nyght,	*harbored*
	and askyd whedder thei wende.	*where they went*

48.

565	Unto hym answerd on of thai	
	and sayd, "We ar Goddes messynger.	
	I am sent unto Sara,	
	scho sall have a son this same yere,	
	And to morn wendes my felows twa	*tomorrow go*
570	to do Goddes bedyng, both in fere;	*together*
	To Sodom and Gomor thei go	
	to synke them down for syns sere."	*destroy; many sins*
	Tokyn of the Trinité	
	to Abraham ther was tone.	*taken*
575	All yf he saw ther thre,	
	all he honerde os one.	

[JUDGMENT PRONOUNCED ON SODOM (18:16–33)]

49.

	Abraham had care then for hys kyne	*kin*
	and for hys frendes that ill suld fare.	
	He prayd God forto abyd and blyn	*wait and refrain*
580	and gud folke fro the yll to spare.	
	God sayd ther was non gud therin	
	bot Loth and tho that with hym ware;	*were*
	And fro that wo well suld thei wyn.	*they escape*
	So was he comforth of his care.	
585	Tway chylder wentt at morn	
	to Sodom the gaynyst gate.	*[by] the quickest way*
	Thei fand Loth them beforne	*before them*
	when thei enterd the gatte.	*gate*

[DEPRAVITY OF SODOM (19:1–11)]

50.

Unto hys hows with them he hyed   *went*

590   and ordand mett for them and mo.   *food*

Hys ennemys com on ylka syd   *every side*

and bad furth tho chylder two.   *summoned forth those two young men*

Hys doyghturs proferd he that tyd,   *he offered at that time*

bot thei sayd nay, thei wold non of tho.

595   Then unto God he cald and cryde

thos byttur folkes to scheld hym fro.   *wicked people; shield*

God mad them blynd to be   *blind*

so that thei toke no tent,   *paid no attention*

Tyll Loth with hys meneye   *Until; household*

600   and tho chylder wer went.   *got away*

[SODOM AND GOMORRAH DESTROYED (19:12–29)]

51.

When Loth was passyd the cyté playn   *had fully escaped*

with hys wyfe and two doghturs dere,

God bad thei suld not go agayn,   *return [there] again*

ne of that fayr forther inquere.   *nor of that affair*

605   Thos cytes sanke ther certan,

and the sownd was herd, a hydwyse bere.   *hideous noise*

The wyf then wyst hyr frendes wer slayn   *knew*

and lokyd agayn with sympyll chere.   *sad mood*

For scho dyd that owtrage   *Because; trespass*

610   that God bad dame do never,

Scho wurthyd to an ymag   *changed; statue*

of salt and sall be evere.   *shall*

[ORIGIN OF MOAB AND AMMON (19:30–38)]

52.

When Loth saw how scho was dyght   *made*

ther styll to stand in a salt stone,

615   To a hyllsyd, that Sogor hyght,   *hillside, that was called Zoar*

hys way full wysly he hath tane.   *taken*

Thor dwellyd thei fere from all men syght,   *There; far*

for cyty neyr them was none.   *near*

The wemen wenyd no werly wyght   *knew no worldly man*

620   wer levyd on lyfe bot them allon.   *remained alive*

Therfor, or ever the fyne   *before the end [of]*

the werld to fulfyll,   *might occur*

Thei gafe ther fadyr wyne

and made hym slepe full styll.

53.

625 The eldyr systur by hym lay,
    the werld to maynten at hyr myght.
He delt with hyr or yt was day, *slept*
    and gatt a son that sythyn Moab hyght. *subsequently Moab was called*
The yonger systur then wold asay *attempt*
630   to fob hyr fader anoder nyght. *trick*
Scho consavyd by ther prevay play *conceived; private*
    a man that semly was to syght. *seemly*
Loth leve we her at home wonnand *dwelling*
    in wastes that wer wyld
635 And tell of Abraham and Sara and
    of Ysaac that was hys chyld.

[BIRTH OF ISAAC (21:1–12)]

54.

Thei wentt wher thei had wonnyd beforne, *dwelled before*
    and in grett lykkyng can thei lend. *pleasure; remain*
Sara was mery evyn and morne, *happy evening and morning*
640   forto be comford well scho kend.
Bott aftur, when hyr sone was borne,
    then was hyr myrth mekyll amend. *mirth much subdued*
For Agar that was wontt hyr to scorn *wont*
    than had no fors hyr to defend. *no strength (privileged position) herself to*
645 Sara, that worthy wyve,
    when Ysac myght oght mell, *anything speak*
Agar owt can scho dryfe *she did drive out*
    with hyr sun Ysmaell. *Ishmael*

[HAGAR AND ISHMAEL (16:6–15, 21:14–20)]

55.

To flee then was scho ferly fayn;
650   with Saray durst scho not be sene. *dared*
In wyldernes scho wonnyd with payn, *lived*
    cared from all comforth clene. *deprived*
An angell gart hyr turn agayn, *did return her*
    and bad that scho suld bowsom bene. *obedient*
655 And Abraham dyd all hys mayn
    and mad acord them two betwene.
Togedder then thei dwell
    in feleschep full fayre;
Grett myrth thei mad them amell *together*
660   for Ysaac theyr ayre. *their heir*

[TESTING OF ABRAHAM (22:1–12)]

56.

Sythyn God Hys servand wold asay   *make trial (assay)*
    yf he to Hym bowsom wold be.   *loyal*
Hee spake to Abraham on a day
    and sayd, "Thi sadnes wyll I se;   *steadfastness; investigate*
665   Take thi sun that thou lufes well ay   *ever*
    and make hym sacrafyce to Mee.   *a sacrifice*
In wyldernes bysyde the way
    a certan hyll schew sall I thee.
An awter theron thou rays   *altar; make (raise)*
670   and offer hym Me untyll."   *unto*
Abraham heyrs how He says
    and grauntt yt with full gud wyll.

57.

Abraham unto hys son beheld,
    a bold man both in bone and lyre.   *bone and flesh*
675   He wenyd that he suld have beyn hys beld   *knew; should; been his comfort*
    when he was old and weke o swyre;   *weak of neck*
Bot unto God he can hym yeld,   *yielded himself*
    ay redy to do Hys desyre.   *ever*
Hys asse he fand furth in the feld
680   And chargeyd hym with wud and fyre.   *loaded*
    [. . .]
      [. . .]
  So went thei furth in fere,   *together*
    qwer God bad thei suld goe.   *where*

58.

685   Ysaac saw in hys fader hand
    a sword and askyd hym what yt ment.
He sayd, "Sun, we sall make offerand   *Son*
    to God; so hath Hymselfe asent."   *summoned*
"Fader," he says, "fyr soyne we fand,
690   bott wher ar bestes that suld be brentt?"   *burned*
He says, "Sun, that God hath ordand,   *arranged*
    for to Hys frendes ay takes He tent."   *always He takes care*
So wentt thei furth ther ways;
     [. . .]
695   [. . .]
    os God wold deme thei dyd.

59.

When Abbraham was werre of the hyll,   *aware*
    qwych God to hym had told before,   *which*

The wud he tok hys sun untyll
700   and bad hym beyre to thei come thore.   *carry [it] until they came there*
Hys fader forwerd to fulfyll   *father's wishes*
         [. . .]
         [. . .]
         was he wyse, os God wold yt were.
705   Apon that hyll on heght,
         os God Hymself had sayd,
      An auter ther on thei dyght   *altar*
         and wud and fyre on layd.

60.
      When the fyre was brynnand bryght,   *burning*
710   than Abraham unto God con see,
      And to hys sun thus sayd he ryght,
         "Sun, I sall make offerand of thee."   *[an] offering*
      Ysaac sayd with semland lyght,
         "Fader, os God wyll, behoveyse yt to be.   *as God wills, so it should be*
715   What hest to Hym that ye hath heght
         leffe yt noght for luf of me."
      Hys sword in hand he hent
         so forto make offerand,
      Bot God His angell sent
720   from Hevyn and held his hand.

[SACRIFICIAL RAM (22:13–19); SARAH'S DEATH AND BURIAL (23:1–20)]

61.
      Hys sun he suld have sacrifysyd,
         bot then he wyst God wold yt noght.   *knew God wanted*
      A wedder he saw hym besyd   *ram*
         that God had sent hym all unsoght.
725   Therof he made offerand that tyd,   *at that time*
         and when thei had ther wrschyp wroyght,
      Hom agayn hely thei hyed
         and thankes God with wyll and toyght.
      Soyne aftur Sara was dede
730   and put unto sepulcure.
      Abraham toke in hyr sted   *place*
         a wyf that heght Sethure.   *Keturah*

[ABRAHAM MARRIES KETURAH (25:1–6); MARRIAGE OF ISAAC AND REBEKAH (24:1–67)]

62.
      Scho was woman wynsom to weld,   *pleasant to possess*
         non heynder haldyn under Hevyn,   *fairer*
735   And wyls scho bode under hys beld,   *while she lived; roof*

scho bayr hym sonys sevyn.   *bore*
Aftur when Ysac wex on eld,   *grew in age*
    a stalworthy man of state and stevyn,   *speech*
Hys fader, for hys sed suld yeld,   *seed should yield [fruit]*
740   a gud wyfe to hym can he nevyn: *call*
Rebecca, a damisell —   *Rebekah*
    hyr fayrer is not fon —   *[one] fairer [than] her; found*
The doyghtur of Batuell;   *Bethuel*
    Nacor is his brothur son.   *Nahor*

63.
745   Full sun he sent his chefe servant   *soon*
    for this mareyg to make yt clere.   *marriage*
He wentt hym furth, and soyn he fand
    the maydyn at a well thor nere.
Hee told hyr fader of this tythand   *news*
750   fro Abraham, his eme full dere,   *uncle*
How his son suld be hyr husband.
    therfor thei wer full fayn in fere;   *happy together*
Wyghtly thei wer acord.   *Quickly they were agreed*
    The servand soyn hyr lede
755   Unto Abraham, hys lord,
    and Ysac with wyne hyr forto wede.   *joy; wed*

[DEATH OF ABRAHAM (25:7–11)]

64.
What worthed qwen thei wedded were   *happened when*
    soyn aftur sall be told uus tyll.
Bot of Abraham now lefe we heyre,
760   and all his story steke we styll.   *conclude*
When he had lyfyd a hunderth yere   *lived*
    and sexty and fyve to fulfyll,   *165 years*
Then dyed hee soyn with seknes sere   *diverse illnesses*
    and went full well with Goddes wyll.
765   Ay whyls he lyfyd in lede,   *Ever while; among his people*
    ever trew was his entent,
And therfor his word and dede
    mun evermoyr be on ment.   *must; in remembrance*

[BIRTH OF ESAU AND JACOB (25:19–26)]

65.
Ysaac lelly led his lyve   *loyally*
770   in the law of God with gud entent.
And Rebecca, his worthy wyfe,
    consavyd two suns so God hir sent.

Betwyx them two began grett stryfe
   within hyr wom, or thei furth went,   *womb, before they came forth*
775   Qwerfor hyr care was kene os knyfe.   *Wherefore; pain; sharp as knife[wounds]*
   Scho askyd of God what yt ment.
He sayd, "Thou sall furth bryng
   two maners of pepyl expresse,
And the more in all thyng   *stronger*
780   sall serve unto the lesse."   *lesser*

66.

And so yt was, os clerkes wott,   *know*
   the lesse was mayster of the more:
For at ther byrth was grett debat   *their; struggle*
   whedder of them suld go furth before.   *which*
785   Bot Esau was mor strang of state,   *strong of body*
   and the fyrst sted he cane restore;   *place*
And Jacob than wentt aftyr latt;   *came last*
   ther moyder was all marryd thore.   *injured then*
Esau, the alder chyld,   *elder*
790   was all over hyllyd with here;   *covered over with hair*
And Jacob was mor myld
   and soft on body and bayre.   *bare (lacking hair)*

[YOUTH OF ESAU AND JACOB (25:27–28); ESAU SELLS HIS BIRTHRIGHT (25:29–34)]

67.

Isaac had both by est and west
   mo catell then men myght nevyn by name.   *more; call*
795   His luf on Esaw he kast   *love; gave*
   and mad hym hyrd of wyld and tame.   *shepherd both*
He sett his hert on hym to rest,
   for he suld be heyr of the same.   *heir; same (his full estate)*
Bot Rebecca lufyd Jacob best,
800   for he wonnyd ay at hame.   *lived always*
Als he satt under hir beld,   *tent*
   hys dyner was well grayd.   *prepared*
His brothyr com from the feld,
   and of sum part he hym prayd.   *asked him for some part [of the meal]*

68.

805   Bot Jacob sayd he suld have none,
   oles then he wold to hym sell   *unless he would*
Hys heritage and thynges ylkon   *each one*
   that aftur hys fader unto hym fell.
Then Esau wyst no bettur wone   *had no better hope*
810   but grauntt this connand them amell.   *covenant between them*
With honger so he was overgone,

     he tent non other tales to tell.   *cared*
     When Ysaac was on eld   *advanced in age*
        a hunderth yere, we fynd,

815   Then wex hee all unweld,   *he grew all feeble*
        and both his eyne wer blynd.   *eyes*

[ISAAC BLESSES JACOB (27:1–29)]

69.

     He callyd Esau, hys elder son,
        and sayd, "I wold thou went in hye   *quickly*
     Unto the wud, os thou was wun,   *wood, as you usually do*

820   and take with thee thyn archerye
     And fand to geytt me veneson,   *work; venison*
        for wyld flesch ette wold I.   *I would eat*
     Then sall thou have my beneson   *blessing*
        and my blessyng befor I dy."

825   "Fader," he sayd, "full fayn."   *at once (full gladly)*
        Therwith he went his way.
     The moyder with all hyr mayn   *power*
        wyll mar hym and scho may.   *stop him (Isaac) if she can*

70.

     For Jacob that was hyr yonger son
830   hath scho soght a sotell gyn: *she has crafted a subtle ruse*
     "Thy brothyr is furth for venyson,
        his fader blessyng forto wyn.
     Go to the feld; ther sall thou fon   *find*
        two fatt kyddes; bryng them or thou blyn,   *fat lambs; before you cease*
835   And in hys wedes thou sall be wonn,   *clothes; dressed*
        and so be blessyd or he com in."   *before he (Esau) comes in*
     "Moder," he sayd, "nay mare   *no more*
        thus to tell in this tyd.   *way*
     My brothyr is hyllyd with hayre,   *covered with hair*
840   and I am soft of hyd.

71.

     "All yf my fader be blynd in bed,   *Even if*
        he wyll feyle that I be noght trew."   *feel*
     "Deyre son," scho sayd, "be not adrede;   *don't be afraid*
        myself therfor sall schape and sew."
845   In kyddes skyns hys handes scho hym cled   *lambskins; clad*
        and mad a broth full gud and new.   *broth [of the lambs]; fresh*
     "Goe fast at thy fader wer fede   *[now] that; fed*
        and say that thou is Esau!"
     He dyde als scho hym bad.
850   unto Ysaac hee wentt.

"Fader, be ye glad;
   heyr is mett that ye of ment."   *here; meat; requested*

72.

"A, sun," he sayd, "well hath thou wroyght;
   thi wysdom now hath thou wun."   *hope*

855 Bot by the voce ay well hym toght   *voice still he thought surely*
   yt was Jacob, his yonger sun.

He gropyd hym fast bot all for noyght,   *gripped; naught*
   be felyn was the falshed fun.   *by trickery; falsehood managed*

He ette of all that he had broght;   *ate*

860   to blese hym then was he begun.

He mad hym over all other
   lord, both lowd and styll.   *in all circumstances*

Thus begylyd he his brothyr,
   bot all was Goddes wyll.

[ESAU'S LOST BLESSING (27:30–45)]

73.

865 Esau veneson hath tone   *taken*
   and broyght his fader for his beld.

"Who is thou?" He askyd on one.   *at once*
   "Ser, Esau, your eldyst chyld."

"A, son," he sayd, "her hath ben on   *here has been one*

870   and brogh me flesch, full fayr and wyld.   *brought me meat*

I hath hym blest, and he is gone."
   Then wyst he well he was begyld.

"Myn heritage he hath
   and power over all oyder.   *others*

875 Now wott I well yt was
   Jacob, thy yonger brothyr."

74.

Esau then with sore syghyng sayd,
   "That ye ar blynd, I by with wo.   *bought*

For now is the secund brayd   *time*

880   that he hath me dyssavyd so.   *deceived*

Fyrst for mett when I hym prayd,   *meat*
   myn heritage he toke me fro,

And now this tym hath me betrayd,
   wyls ye bad me your arand go.   *errand*

885 Well was he namyd for thy
   Jacob, for so he hyght   *promised*

That wyll geytt with gyllery   *trickery*
   that hcc gcyttcs not with ryght.

75.

"Bot fader," he sayd, "I pray yow now
890   yf any blessyng be laft for me."
"Son, I hath gyfyn to hys behofe   *control*
      wytt, wyn, and oyle, all thre.   *wheat, wine, and oils*
And in all maters that may move
      over all my howshald hed is he.   *household*
895   Bot in the dew of Hevyn above
      and in erth sall thi blessyng be."
The fader fulfyllyd his toyght;
      the son was fayn therfor.   *glad*
Thus all this werld was wroght,
900   evyn os God wold yt wer.   *[that] it were*

76.

When Esau wyst this wytterly   *knew this clearly*
      how he hys heritag had lorne,   *lost*
Unto hys brothyr he had envy
      and grett malyce myde day and morn.   *between*
905   Rebecca send Jacob forthy
      into Aran, wher scho was borne,   *Haran*
And als scho wold, hee wentt in hye.   *haste*
      bot seyre ferlys he fand beforne. *many wonders he found*
Als he lay on a land,
910   sclepand abowtt mydnyght,
A stegh he saw up stand   *ladder*
      from erthe to Hevyn on hyght.

[JACOB'S DREAM AT BETHEL (JACOB'S LADDER) (28:10–22)]

77.

That stegh began evuynly at his crown; *ladder; the top of his head*
      unto his syght yt semyd so
915   Als angels wentt evyn up and down
      full mony tym both to and fro.
God told to hym in that seson
      how that he suld wede wyfes two,   *wed two wives*
And how his generacion   *children*
920   over all the werld suld grathly go.   *subsequently*
Hee sayd, "For Abraham sake
      that was thi fader free,
Whedder thou slepe or wake,
      thy beld ay sall I be."   *comfort always shall*

78.

925   Than Jacob of ther maters mels   *these matters speaks*
      and says he saw God in gud astate.

And in his tale this furth he tels
   and says, "By this werke well I watt   *know*
That in this sted is nothyng els   *place is nothing less*

930   bot Goddes awn howse and Hevyn gate   *than*
And dredfull to them that heyr dwels,
   bot yf thei flee fro all debate."   *strife*
A stone lay at his hede;   *beneath his head*
   that rayssyd hee up on end,

935   In a tokynyng yt levyd   *As an indication; left*
   how God hys myrth thore mend.

[JACOB'S SUCCESS IN HARAN (29:1–30:24)]

79.
So went he furth, and sone he fand
   Laban and his two doghturs dere.
For Rachell was then his connand[1]

940   forto be servand sevyn yere.
And at the end, to understand,
   when Rachell suld have neghyd nere,   *come to him [as wife]*
Then was Lya by hym ligand: *Leah*
   no wounder yf he schawyd no chere.   *showed no happiness*

945   Jacob was full evyll payd,   *ill paid [for his seven years of service]*
   for he had noygh his awne.   *nothing to call his own*
Bot Laban to hym sayd,
   this custom thor was knawne: *there was established*

80.
The elder systur to sett before   *to wed*

950   in wrschype that to wemen fell.
A new forward the festyd thore: *agreement*
   oyder sevyn yere that he suld dwell   *another*
To be most maystur of ther store,
   and then he suld resave Rachell.   *receive*

955   And forto make hym myght more,   *further incentive*
   this connand mad thei amell: *contract they made between them*
To have yf ther fell any   *[For Jacob] to have*
   bestes of colours sere. *livestock of diverse colors (i.e., not unicolor)*
Swylke mad Jacob mony.   *much wealth*

960   How, that ye sall heyre.   *hear*

---

[1] *To [wed] Rachel was then his (Jacob's) agreement*

[JACOB PROSPERS AT LABAN'S EXPENSE (30:25–43)]

81.

When bellyng tym of bestes begane,	*breeding*
os men by course of kynd may nevyn,	*mention*
Unto the wud he wendes then	*wood he goes*
and gat hym wandes mony and evyn.	*gathered to himself rods*
965 The barke warly away he wan	*carefully he peeled*
in sonder places, sex or seven,	
And sett them wher the bestes rane.	*passed*
And so thrugh grace of God of Heven,	
On the wandes ose thei lokyd	*as they looked*
970 and toke to them reward,	*took regard to them*
Som bar blake and som brokyd,	*Some bore black; variegated*
sum skellyd and sum garde.	*speckled; spotted*

[JACOB FLEES WITH FAMILY AND FLOCKS (31:1–21)]

82.

By the faurt yere were fully gone,	*By [the time] the fourth year was*
Jacob had catell grett plenté.	
975 He toke his wyfes and welth gud on,	*in abundance*
and karyd unto his awn cuntré.	*carried [them]*
Hys wyfes had servandes, ayther on,	*either one*
that servyd them in seyre degree.	*various*
Jacob fro spoushed sparyd none,	*wedlock*
980 bot made them all berand to be,	*pregnant*
So that he had hymself,	
to rekyn old and yonge,	
Of suns full semly twelfe;	*twelve fine sons*
of them grett sede myght spryng.	

[JACOB'S CHILDREN (29:31–30:24; 35:23–26)]

83.

985 Sex of the suns com of Lya:	*Six*
Judas, Semeon, and Levi,	*Judah, Simeon*
Ighachar, Zabulon, Ruben. All tha	*Issachar, Zebulun, Reuben; those*
war born of hyr body	
With a doghtur that heght Dyna.	*Dinah*
990 Then this two servandes had in hy	*servants*
Dan, Neptalyn, Gad, Asser, no ma;	*Naphtali; Asher*
so wer thei ten to tell schortly.	*ten [sons]*
When Rachell can begyn,	
then bayr scho, that worthy wyfe,	
995 Joseph and Bynjamyn;	*Benjamin*
with hym scho lyfyd hyr lyfe.	*(i.e., she died in childbirth)*

[JACOB WRESTLES WITH THE ANGEL (32:22–32); RETURN TO BETHEL (35:1–15)]

84.

Jacob was noyed on a nyght   *troubled*
   in his way os he wentt:
Hee wrestyld with an angell bryght
1000   that his on schank was all to schent.   *one hip was utterly broken*
That angell com from Hevyn on heght
   and told unto hym Goddes entent.
Israell was his name be ryght,
   and Jacob suld no moyr be ment.   *called*
1005 Wherfor thus forther fell:
   all his lyneyg lese and moyre   *his people all together (most and least)*
Wer namyd chylder of Israel
   in werld heyr whyls thei woyre.   *while they were in this world*

[JUDAH AND TAMAR (38:1–30)]

85.

Now in this processe or we passe,   *narrative before we pass [on]*
1010 is gud the dedes forto dyscrye   *describe*
Of the eldyst brothyr that hyght Judas;   *who was named Judah*
   for on hym jones the genology.   *hinges the genealogy [of Jesus]*
His brothyr rewll he refusyd has   *dominion (rule)*
   and karyd into Chanaan,   *journeyed into Canaan*
1015 And in that land wed he was
   with mekyll welth, os was worthy.
His wyf was fayr and free
   and bayre of hyr body   *bore*
Thre suns semly to see;
1020 ther names heyr say sall I.

86.

The fyrst hyght Her, os I herd tell,   *Er*
   and Onam was the name of an other.   *Onan*
Thei wer both fayr of flesch and fell.   *skin; complexion*
   and Sela men callyd the tother.   *Shelah*
1025 Full mekyll myrth was them amell,   *among*
   for thei had mobles mony afore.   *movable goods*
And forthermer so yt befell
   that wedd was the eldyst brothyr.
He was eldyst and heyre.   *heir*
1030 Ther weddyd thei were,   *(i.e., in Canaan)*
He and a woman full fayr;
   hyr name was Thamar.   *Tamar*

87.

Moyr semly woman myght none see,   *A more beautiful*
  yf thei suld sech on yche syde.   *seek on each side (i.e., everywhere)*

1035   Bot he was evyll in his degree;   *(Er) was wicked*
  therfor he myght no langer abyd.   *live*

For wekydly then wastyd hee
  the sed that suld be multiplyd.   *seed (i.e., the semen)*

Therfor God ordand hym to be

1040   funden ded in that same tyde.

For he rewllyd hym not ryght,
  als course of kynd wyll tell: *the course of nature will guide*

The Fend on the fyrst nyght
  had forse hym forto fell.   *to die*

88.

1045   Then of this dole had Judas dred   *sorrow*
  And sayd unto his secund sun,   *second son (i.e., Onan)*

"Go thou, rayse up thi brother sed!"   *children*
  ose men then in this werld was wun.   *in this world were accustomed [at that time]*

Bot hee unethly dyd his dett   *scarcely (not properly); duty (had sex)*

1050   evyn os his brothyr had begun;

Wherfor he servyd the same mede: *(the Fiend); reward*
  or yt was day, ded was he fun.   *before; dead was he found*

Then Judas was full wrath
  when this tene was betyde,   *sadness had occurred*

1055   And toght yt was grett wath   *thought; danger*
  to wed hyr with the thryde.

89.

And he was yong to tell that tyd;   *he (i.e., Shelah) was young*
  therfor he hath consell tone: *he (i.e., Judah) has given advice*

He send hyr home — yt is nott to hyd —

1060   to hyr fader, that scho was fro gone,

And bad that scho suld thor abyd
  in wedohede with welth gud one.   *in abundance*

And Judas wyfe in thos days dyed;
  then was he wedow levyd alone.

1065   Servandes semly to se
  had his katell forto kepe,

For he had grett plenté
  of asses, nawtt, and schepe.   *oxen*

90.

When Thamar herd thies tyghynges tell

1070   that Judas wyf was ded hym fra,

With hym then wer scho lever to dwell   *would she rather live*
  then with hys yongest sun Sela.

	Of this mater mevyd scho amell	*decision she acted immediately*
	and watyd hyr tyme forto ta.	*bided; take*
1075	And forthermer yt so befell	
	that with his servand suld he ga	
	In clowes to clype his schepe,	*an enclosure to shear his sheep*
	als custom was then thore.	
	Than Thamar tuke gud kepe	
1080	and ordand fast therfor.	*arranged things securely*

91.

	Hyr wedow wedes scho layd away,	*widow's weeds*
	and hir face to schyn os glasse,	*and [made] her face shine as glass*
	And cled hyr in full rych aray;	*clad; clothing*
	for so scho trows to jape Judas.	*thus she intends to trick*
1085	Scho sett hyr on a somer day	
	in the way wher he suld passe.	
	When he hyr say, soyn can he say,	*saw, immediately*
	"Fayr woman, all my hert thou hasse."	
	His servandes gart he go	
1090	befor furth on ther way,	
	And allon levyd bot them two	*alone left*
	to make them myrth and play.	

92.

	Then his entent he hyr told untyll;	
	that yt was Thamar trowd he noyght.	*believed (knew) he not*
1095	"Woman, and thou wyll wyrke my wyll,	*if you do what I want*
	then sall I send thee sone unsoght	
	A fayr kyd lame to kepe or kyll."	*baby lamb*
	The woman answerd ose scho toght,	
	"Syr, I wyll have, as yt is skyll,	
1100	a wede to byd tyll yt be broght."	*a pledge to await*
	He sayd, "That sall thou have."	
	He toke the be all of his herme	*bracelet off his arm*
	And also his walkyng stafe;	
	he kast both in hir berme.	*bosom*

93.

1105	Then was scho bown what he wold byd,	*willing*
	for scho kepyd to have helpe therby.	*intended*
	And in that tyme so yt betyd:	
	tway chylder bred in hyr body.	*two children (i.e., twins)*
	Then Judas went and deuly dyd	*properly (dutifully)*
1110	hys schepe clyppyng withoutyn cry.	*shearing*
	And scho wentt home and helyd and hyd,	*kept quiet and hid*
	and all this processe prevely.	
	Judas a kyd then sent,	

	as he had heght certayn.	*promised*
1115	Bot the woman was went,	*gone*
	and the kyd broyght agayn.	*brought [back to Judah]*

94.

	Then Judas was grettly agayst	*taken aback*
	and wroth, for his wedd was away.	*pledge*
	[. . .]	
1120	[. . .]	
	When thre monethyse wer playnly past,	
	then Thamar feld full fell afray:	
	Hyr wome so wex that folke full fast	
	demyd of dede ylke day.	*judged her worthy of death then*
1125	Sum sayd that scho was gylty	
	to God agayns ther law,	
	And sum sayd scho wer worthy	
	therfor to hange and draw.	

95.

	When Judas herd how all this wentt,	
1130	he was full wroth, we may warrand.	*warrant*
	He bad scho suld be aftur sentt,	
	for all the dome hang in hys hand.	*judgment*
	[. . .]	
	[. . .]	
1135	To tell the sothe or take jugment	
	aftur the law of the land.	
	Than Thamar was furth broyght,	
	as the law was then usyd,	
	Bot so wysly scho wroght	
1140	that scho was well excusyd.	

96.

	Judas then spake with word bold	
	and sayd, "The suth sall non man spare.	*truth*
	Thamar, the trewth bus heyr be told.	*must here*
	who is defawt of all this fare?"	*guilty*
1145	Then schewde scho furth his bee of gold,	*bracelet*
	and hys stafe had scho redy ther.	
	[. . .]	
	[. . .]	
	Then Judas knew all dele,	
1150	and thus he sayd in hye,	*aloud*
	"By this werke now wott I well	*I know well*
	that scho is wyser then I,	

97.

"And hyr ow forto beyr no blame."   *she ought to bear*
    So was scho savyd from scath and scorne.   *harm*
1155   And with wrschyp scho wund at hame   *dwelt*
    tyll tym hyr chylder suld be borne.
The meydwyf wyst and sayd the same
    that scho suld have twa men at morn.
The fyrst scho gafe Phares to name   *Perez*
1160   bycause that come furth beforne;
The secund son furth yede
    so like unto his brother
At the mydwyfe fest a thred   *That; fastened [on his hand]*
    to knaw on fro the tother.

98.

1165   When the secund past from his place,
    thei namyd hym Yaram, that thor werre.   *Zerah, who there were*
The moyder, quen hyr was over past,   *when her [childbirth] was finished*
    was ferly fayn that thei well farre.   *very happy*
Then Holy Wrytt schews how yt was
1170   in genology of this charre,   *business*
And says thus, "Judas gendyrd has
    Phares and Yamar of Thamar.
Then gatt ther Phares Esrom."   *Hezron*
    Thes processe leve we playne,   *These narratives*
1175   And tell how Jacob come
    to his cuntré agayn.

[DEATH OF ISAAC (35:27–29)]

99.

When Jacob com to his cuntré,
    of hys moyder dede herd he tell.   *death*
Ysac, his fader, myght no see;
1180   for febylnes son seke he fell.   *soon he fell sick [and died]*
Ten of his suns then ordand hee   *his (i.e., Jacob's); then he (Jacob) ordered*
    to kepe his catell tham omell,   *among*
And Joseph and Bynjamyn to be   *Benjamin*
    ay styll at hom with hym to dwell.   *ever remaining*
1185   An auter ther thei rayse   *altar*
    to make sacrafyce,
And honerd God all ways
    with wrschyp on ther wyse.

[JOSEPH'S DREAMS OF GREATNESS (37:1–11)]

100.

	Then Joseph dremyd with Goddes wyll	
1190	and says his brethyr how he beheld,	
	How thei and he under a hyll	
	geyddyrd scheffes fayr in the feld.	*gathered sheaves*
	He sayd that hys schefe stod up styll,	
	and elevyn unto his can held.	*eleven; did bow*
1195	His brethyr toke gud entent ther tyll	*brothers paid close attention*
	and toght that he wold wrschep weld.[1]	
	He sayd, "Sone and the mone	*Sun; moon*
	and other sternys elevyn	*stars*
	War bown both morn and noyne	*Were bound; afternoon*
1200	to honour me full evyn."	

101.

	The elevyn had full grett hethyng	*eleven [brothers]; contempt*
	and sayd to hym, "Be lyve, lett se:	*Quickly, let [us] see*
	What wold thou deme of this dremyng?	*make of these dreams*
	Hoppes thou to guferne grett degree?	*Do you hope to govern [in]*
1205	Or that thou sall over us be kyng,	
	and we all suggettes unto thee?"	*subjects*
	Than hatreyd in ther hertes thei hyng	*hung*
	and toght that bargan suld not be.	*thought that that outcome should*
	Jacob in hert can hyd	*did hide in heart*
1210	ther stevyns and held them styll.	*their opinions and kept them quietly*
	And what so suld betyde,	*whatever should happen*
	he prayd God to wyrke His wyll.	

[JOSEPH IS SOLD BY HIS BROTHERS (37:12–36)]

102.

	Bott well he trowd in his entent	*he (i.e., Joseph) believed*
	that dreme suld men of myghtes more.	*should mean more powerful things*
1215	Hys brethyr of grett malys ment	
	and sayd that suld hym son ryght sore.	*aggrieve*
	Sythyn on a day was Joseph sent	*Then*
	to se hys brethyr and als ther store.	*also their goods*
	Thai saw and sayd he suld be schentt	*killed*
1220	for talys that he had told before.	*the stories (i.e., his dreams)*
	Bot his brothir Ruben	*Reuben*
	held hym owt of ther handes	*kept him from their hands*

---

[1] *and thought that he wished to hold power [over them]*

And sold hym to strang men,   *foreign*
   and forto led into fer landcs.   *far*

103.
1225 Then all tho ten hath tane to red   *those ten [remaining sons] have decided*
   to feyn a falshed for that fude,   *invent a lie; child*
To say he was etyn in a sted   *eaten in a place*
   with wyld bestes, os thei understud.
And this to maynten with holhed   *convincingly*
1230 thei wett his coyte with kyddes blud.   *coat with the blood of a goat*
When Jacob herd his sun was ded,
   no wounder was thof he wer wude.   *thereby; mad*
Of hym and all that hepe   *group*
   now lett we leve in hand,
1235 And tell furth how Joseph
   was ledd furth into Egype land.   *Egypt's*

[JOSEPH AND POTIPHAR'S WIFE (39:1–23)]

104.
Puthefar he can hym lede   *Potiphar; did; lead*
   to Pharo, that ther was kyng.   *Pharaoh*
That stewerd wyf for his fayrhed   *handsomeness*
1240 can waytte Joseph in bowr to bryng.   *did contrive*
And for he wold not do in dede,   *Because; have intercourse [with her]*
   in downgyn depe scho dyd hym thryng.   *dungeon; caused him [to be] thrown*
And to hyr lord scho spake gud sped   *right away*
   that he suld hast hym for hyng.   *[to] hang*
1245 Bot when he presond was,   *imprisoned*
   two felows ther he fand
That wer for ther trespasse
   haldyn full herd in band.   *hard in bondage*

[JOSEPH INTERPRETS THE DREAMS OF TWO PRISONERS (40:1–23)]

105.
The kyng was with ther werkes wrath;   *their behavior angry*
1250 butler and baker ther namys call.
Apon a nyght thei dremyd bath   *they both dreamed*
   and told yt furth to grett and small.
And Joseph rede ther dremys full rath   *interpreted their dreams quickly*
   and sayd what son suld aftur fall: *soon*
1255 The butler forto scape all scathe,   *escape all harm*
   and the baker to by for all.   *pay for everything (i.e., to be executed)*
So was the butler ryght
   resavyd the kyng beforne;   *brought; before*

| | The bakster, als he heght, | *as he (Joseph) predicted* |
| 1260 | was hangyd at morne. | |

[Joseph interprets Pharaoh's dream (41:1–36)]

106.

	Sythyn dremyd the kyng another nyght	
	that mad hym mervell in his mode.	*what made him wonder in his mind*
	Hym toght he saw a selcoth syght:	*It seemed to him; marvelous*
	sevyn bestes com fatt from the folde,	*beasts; fattened from the pen*
1265	And aftur them saw he ryght	
	sevyn bestes leyne for fawt of fude.	*lack of food*
	Bot the leyn ware moyr of myght	*strength*
	and stroyd the fatt evyn os thei stud.	*killed*
	His dreme he told the clerkes	
1270	to constru by clergy,	*by means of [their] wisdom*
	Bott non cowd wytt what werkes	*know*
	that syght suld sygnyfye.	

107.

	The butler spake then for his sped,	*benefit*
	"Lord, in your preson lyges in bend	*lies in bonds*
1275	A lele man of the Ebrew lede;	*loyal; Hebrew blood*
	of this mater can he make end."	*give a solution*
	Then was Joseph tan forto rede	*taken to give*
	this consell, ose the butler kend.	
	He bad the kyng tent and take hede	*listen*
1280	how God suld in sevyn wyntur send	
	Of catell, corne plenté,	
	all men to weld at wyll;	*use*
	And other sevyn, sayd hee,	*following seven years*
	men suld for hungur spyll.	*die*

[Joseph's rise to power (41:37–57)]

108.

1285	And when the kyng can understand	*did understand*
	that swylke defawt suld aftur fall,	*such famine*
	He mad hym stewerd of his land,	
	all men to come at his call.	
	Then in fyrst sevyn yere he ordand	
1290	and geydderd corne of gret and small,	*gathered*
	Wher with the folke ther fud he fand	*Therewith to; there food he provided*
	whyls hungur was in werld over all.	*while; (everywhere else)*
	Hys kyn in Canaan	*[Joseph's] kinsmen*
	for hungur was nere lorne.	*were nearly lost (dead)*

1295   His fader herd tell then
              that in Egyp was corne.   *grain*

[JOSEPH'S BROTHERS GO TO EGYPT (42:1–25)]

109.
        Ten of hys suns sent he ther then
              for corn yf thei therby myght wyn.   *grain; buy*
        To wen thei were full mere men,   *go; merry*
1300   non levyd at home bot Byngemyn.   *none remained; Benjamin*
        When Joseph saw his brethyr ten,   *brothers*
              he knew all ware comyn of a kyne.   *one family*
        Bot none of them cowd hym kene,   *recognize*
              for hegh a state that he was in.
1305   He askyd them when thai come.
              Ruben and noe nother,   *no other*
        He sayd, "Ser, we have at home
              our fader and our yongest brothyr.

110.
        "That we were twelfe cownt we cane,
1310   bot on was dede, down in a dale,   *one; killed*
        With wyld bestes in Chanaan;
              for hym our fader hath mekyll bale."   *has much sadness*
        When Joseph herd, he wyst well than
              how that his fader in hele was hale.   *was still alive*
1315   In werld was not a myryer man;   *merrier*
              "Bott ferther," he toght, "asay I sall."   *I shall test [them]*
        He toght to geddyr them, bryng   *thought to gather*
              Benjamyn hym beforne,
        For thai twa was most yong   *those two (Joseph and Benjamin)*
1320   and both of Rachell borne.

111.
        He sayd, "For soth, I sall you spyll   *execute*
              bot yf ye be to my bedyng bayn.   *obedient*
        Fyrst your sekkes sall I do fyll   *sacks*
              of corne to make your fader fayn.   *happy*
1325   Bryngys than Benjamyn me untyll;   *Then bring; unto me*
              that yong boy wyll I se certayn.
        And Symeon, he sall heyr byd styll   *Simeon; here await*
              in preson tyll ye come agayn."
        Thus sayd he to asay   *test*
1330   yf ther luf war fyne   *genuine*
        Unto ther fader all way,
              and to that barne Benjamyn.   *child*

[JOSEPH'S BROTHERS RETURN TO CANAAN (42:26–38)]

112.

	Thei wentt furth, os he can them warn;	
	ther was no consell forto crave.	*help to beg*
1335	Thai told ther fader how thai had farn,	*fared*
	and Symeon laft, them all to sayve;	
	And them bad bryng the yongest barne,	*child*
	his helpe or hele yf thei wold have.	
	The fader toght loth hym to tharn,	*to lose*
1340	for rowth he remyd als he wold rave.[1]	
	Ther sylver, that thei noyght wyst,	*did not know about*
	was in ther sekkes certayn,	*sacks*
	That made hym have moyr trest	*trust*
	to send them save agayn.	

[JOSEPH'S BROTHERS COME AGAIN, BRINGING BENJAMIN (43:1–34)]

113.

1345	Agayn thei wentt full fayr in fere	*together*
	hertly to hold os thei had heght.	*promised*
	Then Jacob satt with sympyll chere,	
	full drery both day and nyght.	
	Tyll Egypt son thei neghyd nere,	
1350	and to Joseph thei went full wyght.	*speedily*
	Of Benjamyn his brothyr dere	
	had he grett hast to have a syght.	*great eagerness*
	Bot that he was ther brothyr	
	wold not he lett be herd,	*be known*
1355	Bot askyd ever on and other	
	how ther fader ferd.	

[JOSEPH DETAINS BENJAMIN; JUDAH PLEADS FOR HIS RELEASE (44:1–34)]

114.

	Ther sekes he dyd to fyll that tyd	*sacks*
	and bad them wend ther way with wyn	*go their way with joy*
	With Symeon, that was besyd.	*beside [them]*
1360	Bot hastely ther blys can blyn.	*bliss did cease*
	A cupe of gold gart he then hyd	*he caused to be hid*
	within the seke of Benjamyn	
	So with that gawd to garre hym byd,	*trick to cause him to stay*
	for he toght thei twa suld not twyn.	*be separated*
1365	In ther way as thei wentt	

---

[1] *for sadness he frothed (at the mouth) as if he would go mad*

and trowd of nokyns trayne,   *suspected no trickery*
Sun armyd men war scntt   *Soon [after them]*
and broyght then Benjamyn agayn.

115.

To Joseph fell thei down be dene,   *forthwith*
1370   and he lett os he lufyd them noyght.   *pretended that he loved*
Unto them carpyd he wordes kene   *he uttered sharp words*
and sayd, "Fals thefes, what was your toght?
Yow forto beld bown have I bene,   *comfort I have been prepared*
and wekydly heyr have ye wroght,   *wickedly here*
1375   And of yourselfe yt sall be sene."   *shall be repaid*
Als he dyd ther sekkes be soght,   *caused their sacks to be searched*
His cowpe was fun with schame   *found*
in the yongest brothir seke.
Joseph sayd he that same   *same [one]*
1380   suld hyng hegh by the neke.   *hang high*

116.

Judas sayd, "Mercy, lord, lett be;   *let [it] be*
lett us not lose that lytyll knave.   *child*
Our fader toke hym unto me;   *placed him in my keeping*
I hyght hym sothly hym forto sayve,   *made him an honest vow to protect him*
1385   And sertes bott yf he sound hym see,   *certainly unless he sees him safe*
full sune sall he be grathyd in grave.   *soon; laid in [his]*
Lett hym go home, and dwell wyll we
in hold, wherso ye wyll us have."   *captivity*
When Joseph wyst ther wyll   *knew*
1390   and saw them wepe so soyre,   *so sorely*
"Brethyr," he sayd, "be styll
and mowne ye yow no more."   *moan*

[JOSEPH REVEALS HIMSELF TO HIS BROTHERS (45:1–24)]

117.

This tokyn to them he told,   *evidence; he gave*
"When my fader to feld me sent,   *field*
1395   I am the same man ye sold
for twenty pennys of payment."   *pence*
Then all ther hertes began to cald;   *to [grow] cold*
full well thei hopyd to have ben schent.   *they expected; been killed*
Bot Joseph sayd then, "Brethyr, be bold;
1400   I forgyf yow with gud entent."
Thei kyssyd and for joy grett
myrth was them amange.
And thus this meneye mett   *company reunited*
that mekyll spech of sprange.   *much talking arose*

[JACOB BRINGS HIS FAMILY TO EGYPT (46:1–12), DIES, AND IS BURIED (49:29–50:14)]

118.

1405	Then Joseph sent his brethir ten	
	to foche his fader, wher thei hym fand,	*fetch; left*
	And all ther kyn that thei cowd ken	*know*
	gart he bryng into Egyp land.	*he caused [them to be] brought*
	And in on yle that hyght Jessen,	*region; Goshen*
1410	thor was ther wunyng well ordand.	*dwelling*
	His dreme was fayr fulfyllyd then,	
	for all thei heldyd to his hand.	*bowed*
	When Jacob das war weryd	*days were done*
	unto a hunderth faurty and sevyn,	*147 [years]*
1415	He dyed and was enterd	*interred*
	in Chanan, wher he had bene.	*Canaan*

[JOSEPH'S LAST DAYS AND DEATH (50:22–26)]

119.

	Then had Joseph welth in weld	*in hand*
	of gold and sylver and gud store.	
	His brethyr gudly can hym be held	*well were under his protection*
1420	with men and wyfes that with them were.	
	And aftur when he was of eld	*of age*
	a hunderth yer ten and no more,	*one hundred ten years*
	His saule to God then can he yeld,	*soul; did he yield*
	als all his helders had don before.	*as; elders*
1425	His brethyr ylkon	*brothers all*
	within schort tym war dede;	*[a] short time were dead*
	Bott folke war full gud one	*very much in abundance*
	that com of ther kynred.	*family*

120.

	And tho that aftur them can dwell,	*those who after*
1430	thei multyplyd ay mo and moe,	*ever more and more*
	And wer namyd chylder of Israel,	*children*
	for Jacob name was schonged so.	*Jacob's name was changed*
	Thei mad grett mornyng them amell,	*mourning among themselves*
	for Joseph was so fer them fro,	*Joseph's greatness was so far from them*
1435	For afturwerd, os men may tell,	
	ther welth was turn to wer and wo.	*war and woe*
	This buke then ende we thus,	
	that is namyd Genesis.	
	To begyn Exodus	
1440	God with His wyll us wysch.	*guide*

# Book of Exodus

EXODUS INCEPIT.   *Here unfolds Exodus*

[ISRAEL'S BONDAGE IN EGYPT (1:1–14)]

121.

When Joseph and hys brethyr ylkon   *each one*
  wer ded, then com ther a new kyng.   *came there (in Egypt)*
Of Joseph wyst he ryght none,   *knew he nothing at all*
  ne noyght wold knaw of his comyng.
1445 Bot he levyd, and thai myght all one,   *believed, if they should continue*
  ther kynred suld overcome all thyng.   *their kindred (the Israelites)*
Therfor he hath the consell tone   *counsel taken*
  in gret thraldom them forto bryng.
He gart them beyre and draw   *caused; bear*
1450 and do both dyke and delve,   *make both ditch and digging*
So forto hald them law   *hold them in servitude (low)*
  and lose ther lyneg twelfe.   *lineage*

122.

Now wer thei sett in sorow sere;   *many sorrows*
  thei fand never of defawt beforne.   *experienced never such loss*
1455 And so thei fayr faur hunderth yere   *endured*
  with grett myschefe mydday and morne.
Bot unto God ay war thei dere,   *always were they dear*
  all that of that blud was borne: *bloodline*
Hee multiplyed in all maner
1460 themselfe, ther catell and ther corne.
The kyng was kend by clerkes   *told*
  a chyld of them suld spryng
To wast hym and his werkes   *destroy*
  and unto bale hym bryng.   *woe*

[SLAUGHTER OF INNOCENTS AND THE BIRTH OF MOSES (1:15–2:3)]

123.

1465 To lett this harme then ordand hee   *prevent this harm; ordered*
  all man kynd in ther byrth to qwell   *male children at; kill*

	That of the Israel borne suld be,	*Israelites*
	bot all woman kynd to dwell.	*let live*
	A man wonnyd in that same cyté,	*dwelled*
1470	heght Amryn and his wyfe, Jacabell.	*named Amram; Jochebed*
	Scho bare a sun semly to see,	*She bore a handsome son*
	by qwom seyr farlys aftur fell.	*whom many wonders*
	Thre monethes thei hym hyd,	*Three months*
	and lengur thei durst not abyd	*dare not wait*
1475	Bott in a case hym dyd	*container (i.e., an ark) placed him*
	and layd hym by the seesyd.	*seaside (i.e., riverside)*

[INFANCY OF MOSES (2:5–9)]

124.

	The kyng had then a doyghtur dere,	
	Tremouth scho heght, os I herd say.	*named Thermuthis*
	With hyr maydyns fayr in fere	*together*
1480	in that place wentt scho to play.	
	Thei saw the case in watur clere	
	in poynt to falle and flett away.	*about to slip (decline) and float*
	At hyr byddyng thei broyght yt nere;	
	a full fayr chyld therin fand thei.	
1485	For hyr sun scho yt chese	*chose him for her son*
	and was full mery in mode	*mood*
	And gart name yt Moyses	*did; Moses*
	als funleng of the flud.	*foundling of the flood (river)*

125.

	The lady trowd full well that tyd	*knew quite well at that time*
1490	that yt was on of Ebreus lede,	*one of the Hebrews' people*
	And at thei sent yt so to hyd	*And that they had sent it thus to hide [it]*
	and durst no nother do for dred.	*could do nothing else for dread*
	Scho sent to lades on ylka syd	*two ladies on each side*
	the chyld to norysch and furth fede.	
1495	Bot the barn wold not with them abyd,	
	ne towch ther papes for nokyns nede.	*breasts for any reason*
	Then had the lady kare;	
	that syght full sore hyr rewys.	*grieves*
	Scho bad them seke yt ay whare	*seek out everywhere*
1500	a noryse of Ebreus.	*nurse*

126.

	This chyldes systur, a damsell,	*(Miriam)*
	then with that lady was dwelland.	
	Scho herd how all this ferly befell,	*wonder*
	and socur sone therfor scho fand.	*relief soon*
1505	Scho mad hyr moder Jacabell	

	that chyld to warysch and warrand.	*save and protect*
	The lady dyd hym with hyr dwell	
	and payd hyr hyre in hyr hand.	*her hire (payment)*
	The chyld with all his mayn	*strength*
1510	fell to the pappe full nere.	*breast at once*
	Then was that lady fayn;	*that lady (his mother) joyful*
	so wer all foure in fere.	*all four [family members] together*

127.

	For he to sowke so had begun,	*suck*
	The lady bad no bettur yele.	*reward*
1515	The chyld was fayn when he had fown	*glad; found*
	the moder pappe fully to fele.	*feel*
	The systur wyst how thei had wonn	*knew; won*
	hyr brothyr lyfe, that lykyd hyr well.	*her brother's; pleased*
	Bot the moder was most fayn of hyr sun,	
1520	that scho went had ben drownd ylk dele.	*she thought; drowned entirely*
	Scho fosterd hym full fayre	
	tyll he cowd styr and stand.	*until he could walk*
	To court then can scho care,	
	als the lady had hyr cummand.	*as; her commanded*

[MOSES GIVEN TO THE PHARAOH'S DAUGHTER (2:10)]

128.

1525	For all ther consell well scho knew;	
	unto the lady scho hym toke.	
	And Tremowth toke hym for hyr trew	*true [child]*
	and for hyr sun hym never forsuke.	
	He was so fayr of hyd and hew:	*skin and complexion*
1530	all men had lyst on hym to loke.	*desired*
	Befor his tyme was never Jew	
	so fayr to syght, so says the boke.	
	And yf men myght hym see,	
	that were sory oft sythe,	*chronically depressed*
1535	Trugh blyse of his bewty	*Through delight in*
	thei suld be glade and blythe.	*happy*

[THE INFANT MOSES IN PHARAOH'S COURT]

129.

	So yt befell apon a day:	
	the kyng and the lordes that with hym wore	*(i.e., Pharaoh); were*
	Sat in the palys them to play,	*palace to enjoy themselves*
1540	and cunnand clerkes was with them thore.	*cunning*
	A damsell in rych aray	
	broght the chyld them furth before.	

And of that fayr full fayn war thei,   *fair child very glad*
    for all men lufyd hym, lese and more.
1545   The kyng can on hym loke
    and was ryght glad forthi.   *therefore*
In hand sone he hym toke
    and kyssyd hym curtasly.   *courteously*

130.

Betwyx hys schankes he sett hym ryght   *legs*
1550   and lappyd hym to hym for grett lufe.   *gathered him to himself*
And for he was so worthy a wyght,   *a young man*
    hys pertenes he toght forto prove.   *cleverness he thought*
His crown of gold, full fayr and bryght,
    that barne hed sett he above.   *he set above that child's head*
1555   And sone was schewyd in ther syght
    a wonder case forto controve: *event; contrive*
That chyld full lyghtly lete,   *very frivolously acted*
    the crown kast he downe,
And fylyd yt with his fete   *defiled; feet*
1560   forto breke yt full bowne.   *eagerly*

131.

So qwen thies clerkes this syght can see,   *when these [gathered] wise men*
    unto the kyng thei said full sone,
"Syr, wott thou not we wernyd thee   *don't you know we warned*
    with on Ebrew to be undowne?   *a Hebrew [you would] be undone*
1565   Se this sygne: that same is hee!   *See this sign*
    Therfor be wyse with wordes fone.   *few*
Hys bane belyv bot yf thou be,   *Unless you quickly become his killer*
    thynke thor to abyd ne bettur bone.   *no better reward*
The case sen thou knavs,   *circumstances since you know*
1570   rewle thee by ryghwyse rede."   *rule yourself; proper advice*
The kyng sees by ther sawys   *sayings*
    that barne behovys to be ded.   *child ought*

132.

Then a wys man of ther law   *their*
    sayd the chyld suld not be schent: *killed*
1575   "This dede that he hath done this day,   *deed*
    yt ys not doyn be yll entent;
That sall be seyn sone on asay."   *seen at once through trial*
    Hott colys he gart bryn in present   *coals; bring in*
And proferd the chyld with forto play.   *offered [them to]*
1580   And in his mowth he soyn them hentt.   *soon placed them*
He kyd well he was yong,   *showed; young*
    and no man wold hym marre;   *would [therefore] hurt him*

The coylys brynt so his tong
   that he spake ever the warre.   *worse*

133.

1585 This mater sone was movyd and ment   *told and known*
   in chamber emang this madyns all.
Tremuth toke therto full gud tent,   *very careful attention*
   and fast scho hyed into the hall.   *rushed*
The chyld in ermys sone hath scho hent   *[her] arms*
1590 for no defawt to hym suld fall.   *guilt*
Loe, how sone God hath socur sent;   *See, how quickly; succor*
   that He wyll save, be savyd thei sall.   *whom He would save, they shall be saved*
To chamber scho hym bare;   *bore*
   then was he owt of drede.   *danger*
1595 All that the clerkes sayd ayre   *before*
   was aftur done in dede.   *deed*

[MOSES MURDERS AN EGYPTIAN AND FLEES EGYPT (2:11–15)]

134.

Scho was full fayn to be his belde,   *comfort*
   and in hyr boure scho cane hym hyde,   *bower she did hide him*
Tyll he was waxin well of eld.   *had grown well in age*
1600 Was none so semly in no syde;   *seemly; place*
All folke had hele that hym beheld,   *comfort*
   so was he fayr of hew and hyde.   *skin and complexion*
And sythyn when he myght wepyns weld,   *then; weapons wield*
   he mustyrd manhed mony a tyde.   *showed courage many times*
1605 And on a day yt betyd   *happened*
   he hard and was nerhand   *heard; nearby*
How on of Egypt chyd   *one of Egypt (an Egyptian) quarreled*
   with a chyld of his land.   *man; (i.e., a Hebrew)*

135.

Then Moyses meud hym them omell   *moved himself among them*
1610 both for his kyn and his cuntré.
The man of Egypt can he qwell   *did he kill*
   and hyde hym that none suld see.
Full soyne the kyng therof herd tell   *[Yet] very quickly*
   and demed that Moyses ded suld be.   *should be killed*
1615 And ther he durst no langer dwell,   *there [in Egypt] he (Moses) dared*
   bot fast to Madian hastyd hee,   *Midian*
A cyté sett before
   under Oreb hyll to be.   *Horeb*
Getro was byschope thore   *Jethro*
1620 and goverynd grett degré.

[MOSES IN MIDIAN (2:16–22)]

136.

	Hys doyghtyrs keped his fee in feld,	*possessions*
	os custom was than cumonly.	*as was then common custom*
	The wemen myght no watur weld	*women; get [for their flock]*
	for hyrdmen that ware moyr myghty.	*[because of] herders; more strong*
1625	Then Moyses stud and them beheld	*stood up and saw them*
	and helpyd the wemen with maystry.	*gallantry*
	Thei told ther fader under teld,	*in a tent*
	and he bad bryng hym home in hye.	*haste*
	Sythyn Getro gafe hym to	*Then*
1630	hys doghtur, heght Cephoram.	*Zipporah*
	Scho bare hym chylder two:	*bore him two children*
	Eliazar and Gersam.	*Eliezer; Gershom*

[MOSES AT THE BURNING BUSH (3:1–4:31)]

137.

	With hym laft Moyses, for his lay,	*[Jethro] left Moses alone, due to his loyalty*
	to be hys hyrd, yt is not to hyd,	*shepherd*
1635	Als his doghturs wer wontt all way,	*were previously accustomed to do*
	for wrschyp was yt cald that tyde.	*it was considered an honor at that time*
	With his schepe wentt he on a day	
	under the monte of Synay syde.	*side of Mt. Sinai*
	Ther fand he farlys hym to flay;	*marvels; terrify*
1640	abayst he was ther forto abyde.	*dismayed*
	A buske he saw up stand	*bush*
	with floures and leves grene,	*flowers*
	And that buske was byrnand,	*burning*
	bot sulpyng was none sene.	*consumption*

138.

1645	Of mervyll myght no man hym blame;	*astonishment*
	swylk ferlis ner before hym fell.	*such wonders*
	God carpyd to hym and cald by name	*spoke; called [him] by name*
	within a buske wher He can dwell.	*bush*
	"Moyses, I am God the same	
1650	of Abraham, Ysac, and Israel;	
	For the chylder that suffers schame,	*children who suffer shame (i.e., the Israelites)*
	all myn entent I sall thee tell.	
	I wyll mustyr My myght	
	and owt of bale them bryng,	*bondage*
1655	Als I before hath heyght	*promised*
	to them and there ofspryng.	

139.
"My messynger I wyll make thee
    to Pharo of Egypt kyng:
To byd hym lett My folke go free   *command him [to]*
1660   owt of his land at ther lykyng,
To make ther sacrafyce to Me
    In wyldernese of werldly thyng.   *worldly goods*
Thy brothyr Aron sall with thee be   *Aaron*
    and beyr wytnese to old and yyng   *bear witness*
1665   How thou spekkes with Me here.   *spoke*
    And yf thei trow thee noght,   *believe*
Sygnes, sore and sere,   *Signs, painful and abundant*
    sall I send soyne unsoght."   *at once, whether desired or not*

140.
Then sayd Moyses, "Lord, understand
1670   this; I wold sum other wentt.   *would [prefer that] some*
Thei lufe me noyght in Egypt land;
    unto my talys thei wyll not tent." *words they will not listen*
He bad hym then cast down his wand, *He (God) told him (Moses); staff*
    and sone yt semyd os a serpent.   *as [if it was] a serpent*
1675   And mesyll-lyke yt made his hand   *leper-like*
    to apeyre in the kynges present.
"Yf thei aske thee of whom
    thou had their segnes and whore,   *where*
Say, 'I am that am';
1680   that is My name evermoyre."

141.
Moyses says, "It sall be done
    in this case, ose Thou hath commawnd."
He toke his leve at Getron   *from Jethro*
    and held the way to Egypt land.
1685   Als God hym heyght, his brothir Aron   *promised*
    evyn in the way befor hym he fand.
Of his fader and his kyn ylkon   *all of his kin*
    he told to hym full gud tythand,   *tidings*
And how all his enmys
1690   wer dede and done away.
And he told on what wyse
    God sent hym for say.

[AUDIENCE WITH PHARAOH (5:1–23)]

142.
His fader and all hys frendes wer fayn   *glad*
    of his cummyng to that cuntré.

1695   He sayd he suld them bryng from payn
            unto a place of grett plenté.
        And to fulfyll the purpase playn
            to Pharo went Aron and hee,
        And schewyd to hym the segnes certayn   *signs*
1700   wylke God bad thei suld lett hym see.   *which*
        "For the schylder of Israel,"   *children of Israel*
            thei say, "God sentt us hase."
        Bot for oght thei cowd tell,   *aught*
            he sayd thei suld not pase.   *leave*

[MOSES' MIRACULOUS ROD (7:10–13)]

143.

1705   Moyses then cast down his wand,
            and soyne it semyd os a serpent.   *at once*
        He toke the tayle up in his hand,
            and ase a wand agayn yt went.
        As mesyll furth his fyngurs stand,   *As a leper's*
1710   and hole agayn sone he them hentt.   *whole; made*
        The kyng sayd he hade clerkes connand   *cunning wise men [who]*
            cowd do the same by experiment.   *through their own knowledge*
        He sett ther segnes at noyght,   *[the worth of] their signs as nothing*
            and sayd ther folke therfore
1715   Suld be in bondom broyght   *bondage*
            wele wers then ever thei were.   *much worse*

[THE TEN PLAGUES (7:14–12:32)]

144.

        God sent unto them venjance ten   *ten vengeances (plagues)*
            so forto make theym turne theire moode.   *change their minds*
        All the waters of Egypt then
1720   in feld and towne were turnd into blude   *blood*
        So that it myght noght helpe to men,
            ne unto bestes, ne fowles fode.   *beasts, nor bird's food*
        Bot swylke fawt fell not in Jessen,   *such troubles did not occur in Goshen*
            wher thei wonyd that to God wer gud.   *lived who; loyal*
1725   The secund soyne can fall   *the second [plague] soon*
            to greve them als God wyld: *as God desired*
        Both feld, hows, and hall
            with taydes and froskes wer fyllyd.   *toads and frogs*

145.

        All was venomd with the vermyne   *Everyone was poisoned; vermin*
1730   that suld oght reche ther releve.   *bring about*
        Bot Pharo therfor wold not fyne,   *cease*

	bot Goddes folke more then can he greve.	
	Then the thryd God send them syne:	*the third [plague]; quickly*
	grett myse that made them mor myschefe.	*many midges*
1735	Thei stroyd and corumpyd both corn and wyne.	*destroyed and corrupted*
	No man myght for ther malice meve.	*move*
	Nothyng myght byd ther byte	*endure their bites*
	yf thei safe aftur suld be.	*and manage to be whole afterwards*
	Bot Pharo wold not yett	
1740	therfor lett this folke go free.	

146.

	He sayd he suld them bynd in band;	*bind them in bondage*
	God send the faurt venjance forthye:	*the fourth vengeance (plague) therefore*
	Grett fleand loppes over all the land	*flying fleas*
	batte men and bestes full bytturly.	*[that] bit*
1745	Wherso thei fell on fott or hand,	
	full hedos herm had thei in hye.	*hideous harms; immediately*
	Bott Goddes folke non swylke fawtes fand;	
	thei wonnyd in well, as was worthy.	*dwelled in safety*
	Kyng Pharo was frowerd	*malevolent*
1750	and ever of wekyd wyll.	
	His hert was mad so herd:	
	Goddes folke ay haldes he styll.	*ever he holds [captive]*

147.

	Therfor the fyft come aftur fast,	*the fifth [plague]*
	that well wers then any other was.	
1755	Moran was over ther catell kast,	*Murrain*
	on schepe, swyn, oxe, and asse	
	So that in lyfe ther myght none last.	*(i.e., they would all die)*
	the kyng therof most herme has,	*harm*
	Bot when this perell was overpast,	*peril was finished*
1760	he wold not lett the pepyll pase.	*pass [from the land]*
	Therfor the sext was sene:	*the sixth [plague] was seen*
	when Moyses movyd his wand,	
	A powder yll and unclene	*dust*
	was cast over all the land.	

148.

1765	That powder blew over all bylyve;	*at once*
	wherso yt blew, sone wex a blayne.	*grew a boil*
	Yt mad like messels man and wyfe	*leprosy*
	that ware not to Goddes bedyng bayn.	*bidding obedient*
	Both nyght and day swylke dust can dryve.	
1770	Than was the sevynt of frost and rayn	*the seventh [plague]*
	With halestons that dyd them stryve;	*hailstones*
	wherso thei bett, thei brast ther brayn.	*burst their brains*

Swylk thonour and lefynyng · *thunder and lightning*
in all that land was wroght
1775 That herbes and all maner of thyng · *plants*
was waist and broght to noght. · *laid waste; nothing*

149.

The aght was yll wormes fleand; · *The eighth [plague] was ill worms flying (locusts)*
thei coverd over all that cuntré.
Agayns the storme myght no thyng stand: · *storm [of locusts]*
1780 thei left no fruttes, ne levys on tre. · *fruits, nor leaves on the trees*
The neynt then fell neyr at hand: · *The ninth [plague]*
so marke that none myght other see; · *such darkness*
No lyght was levyd in all that land,
and that enduryd by days thre.
1785 The tent was sodan ded · *The tenth [plague]; sudden death*
of all folke, fo and frend.
Then toke the kyng to red · *advice*
to lett the pepyll wend. · *people [of Israel] go*

[THE EXODUS BEGINS (12:33–13:22)]

150.

The kyng gafe leve unto Moysen
1790 and Aron to wend os thei wold.
On mold wer non more meri men · *On earth*
fro tym thei herd ther talys bee told. · *these sentences pronounced*
Thei hyghed them fast unto Jessen, · *hastened*
wher the Jewes wonnyd both ying and old, · *dwelt*
1795 And sett them certan tyme and when
to wend, and bad thei suld be bold
To borow and with them beyre · *obtain; bear*
all guds that thei myght gette.
And so ordand thei here · *provided*
1800 full smartly small and grette.

151.

Sexti and ten in yowth and eld · *(i.e., seventy)*
wer told when thei enturd that land. · *numbered; entered*
Now wer thei that myght wepyn weld · *wield weapons*
to reckynd thre hunderth thowssand,
1805 Owttakyn wemen and hyrdes in feld · *Not counting; shepherds*
and chylder that in na stoure myght stand. · *struggle*
Thei prayd all God to be ther beld, · *security*
and furth thei went, as was ordand. · *ordained*
On days at ther desyre · *During the day*
1810 with all fudes wer thei fede;

On nyghtys with flawme of fyre   *flame (pillar)*
  in lyghtnes ware thei lede.

[CROSSING THE RED SEA (14:1–31)]

152.

When Pharo wyst that thei wendyd ware,   *knew that they had gone*
  Moyses and Aron and ilka Jew,   *every Jew*
1815   He commawndyd all men, both lesse and mare,
  aftur that pepyll forto persew
With chares and mules and mekyll store.   *chariots; many supplies*
  to the Greke Se he gart remew.   *Greek Sea (Mediterranean) he moved away*
Full well he hopyd to have them thore,
1820   for kyndly course no ferre he knew.   *no further natural road*
He sayd, "Forsoth, we sall
  bynd them full soyre in bandes."   *securely (cruelly)*
Bot God that goverans all,
  He savys ay his servandes.   *always*

153.

1825   When thei herd, yt is not to hyd,
  the kyng was command on swylke a wyse,   *[that] the Pharaoh was coming*
Thei saw the see on that on syde   *sea on that one side*
  and on that other all ther enmys,
For ferd full fast then can thei chyde   *fear; complain*
1830   and sayd, "Oure lyvys not lang lyse;   *remain*
Bettur had us ben forto byde   *wait*
  and have bene savyd in the kyng servyce."   *to have been kept; Pharaoh's service*
Thei wend Moyses had wyst   *believed; known*
  and tylyd them furth with trayne.   *drawn; duplicity*
1835   Hee sayd, "Be ye of gud trest;   *cheer*
  God sall us save certayn."

154.

To God he bad them crye and call,
  and to the see wyghtly he wentt.   *quickly*
Hys wand he lete in the watur fall
1840   and prayd to God with gud entent.
The watur stud upe ose a walle: *like*
  swylke grace God to them thor sentt.   *there*
Thurghtowt the see so wentt thei all
  that nowdyr chyld ne wyf wer schent.   *hurt*
1845   Pharo con aftur fownd   *did pursue*
  and trowd well them to have tane.   *thought; taken*
He and his meneye wer drownyd;   *retainers*
  on lyfe ther lafte not one.   *alive*

[SONG OF MOSES (15:1–19)]

155.

When Moyses and all hys meneye
1850   stud on land and lokyd agayn
And saw how thei ware past the see,
        and all ther enmys sleghly slayn,   *cunningly slain*
To call on God then commawnd hee,
        and this songe sayd he certayn:
1855   "*Cantemus Domino Gloriose*,   *Let us sing to glorious God*
        love we God and His power playne,
That savys us on this wyse   *in this way*
        owt of all wo to wende,
And hath stroyd our enmys
1860   that soght us forto schend."   *destroy*

[BITTER WATER MADE SWEET (15:22–25)]

156.

Moyses thus and hys folke in fere
        mad joy to God, both moyre and lesse.
So wentt thei furth and neghed nere   *came near*
        A forest that was fayr to gese.   *look upon*
1865   Thore fand thei wellys fayr and clere,   *wells*
        with watur semand fayr and fresche.   *that seemed*
Bot to asay on sydes sere,   *to the taste in all ways*
        yt was all blend with bytturnese.   *mixed*
That gart them be grochand   *This caused them to begin grumbling*
1870   and murmerand in ther mode.   *murmuring in their spirits*
Then Moyses with hys wand
        thrugh Goddes grace made yt gude.

[BREAD FROM HEAVEN (16:1–36)]

157.

Thus lovyd thei God of all His grace   *praised*
        that for them wroght swylke werkes grett.
1875   Thei sojourned thore a certayn space
        tyll thei were rest and well refette.   *refitted*
Sythyn past thei unto another place,
        a forest of Syne, was fere to gette.   *Sin, [which] was far to cross*
And thore theim fell a febyll case: *befell*
1880   defawtt of fude, both drynke and mette.   *[a] lack of food*
Bot God herd Moyses stevyn,   *speech*
        and Aron helpe he wold.
He send them foyde fro Hevyn,   *food*
        flour that "manna" was cald.

158.

1885	Thore fell before them foulys sere,	*many birds*
	aftur ther lyst and lykyng was.	*pleasure; delight*
	And so thei were fede faurty yere,	
	ay qwyls thei wonnyd in wyldernese;	*all the while they lived*
	Ther cloghyng was ever in lyke clere,	*clothing*
1890	and ever ther fude was fayr and fresche.	
	So wer the folke fede fayre in fere;	*altogether*
	ther bestes lyved with grouand gresse.	*their beasts lived on growing grasses*
	Then past thei furth fro Syn,	
	a forest fayr and wyde,	
1895	To the forest of Raphadyn,	*Rephidim*
	and thore thei buskyd to abyde.	*prepared to sojourn*

[WATER FROM THE ROCK (17:1–7 AND NUMBERS 20:1–13)]

159.

	Watur befor them fand thei non	
	in ryver, ne in dyke to stande.	*canal*
	Therfor thei mournyd and mad grett mone.	*moan*
1900	To Moyses ware thei all grochand.	*grumbling*
	God spake to Moyses and Aron	
	and bad that he suld with his wand	*he (Moses) should*
	Before the folke stryke on the ston,	
	and watur suld he have at hande.	
1905	Moyses sayd, "Men, take tent	*pay attention*
	to me, both most and lest."	
	He stroke, and watur went	*struck [the rock]*
	owt both to man and beste.	

160.

	For Moyses sayd, "To me take hede,"	*Because*
1910	and mad no mynd of Goddes myght,	
	God spake unto hym ther gud sped	*there at once*
	and reckynd to hym this reson ryght:	
	"For that thou demyd not of this dede	*Because of the fact that*
	that yt be Me was done and dyght,	*through Me; accomplished*
1915	My folke, I say, thou sall not lede	
	into the land that I them heght."	
	Then word of them sprang	*news of them (Israel)*
	in cytys on ylka syde.	*cities on each side (i.e., in the area)*
	Thai say, "Yf thei last lang,	
1920	our remys thei sall overryde."	*realms they shall override*

[AMALEK ATTACKS ISRAEL AND IS DEFEATED BY JOSHUA (17:8–16)]

161.

	Faure kynges hath horssus and harnes hent,	*Four; have horses; harnesses taken*
	Amalec and other thre.	*Amalek*
	Thei say, "This Ebrews sall be schentt,	*destroyed*
	bot yf thei sped them fast to flee."	*unless*
1925	Bot Moyses sone hys men hath sentt	
	and made ther cheftan Josue.	*Joshua*
	He prayd at home with gud entent	
	so that the vyctory hade hee.	
	Whyls Moyses held hys hende	*While; hand*
1930	up unto Hevyn on hyghte,	
	Ther myght non enmys lend	
	agaynys hys folke to fyght.	

162.

	Josue overcom all thos enmyse,	*enemies*
	and full grett welth he wan therby	
1935	Of catell and of cloghes of price,	*clothes*
	and home agayn fast can thei hye.	*come*
	Moyses gart make grett sacrafyce,	*prepared [to]*
	for God had gyfyn them the victory,	*given*
	And ordand pristys and princis wyse	*caused*
1940	forto kepe furth ther cumpany.	*maintain*
	Getro of Madian,	*Jethro of Midian*
	that Moyses founded fro,	*had departed from*
	He soght unto hym then	
	with wyf and chylder also.	*[Moses'] wife and children*

[THE THEOPHANY AT MT. SINAI (19:1–31:18)]

163.

1945	Aftur that tyme thei toke the ways	
	wher the montt of Synay was nere,	*mount of Sinai*
	Wher Moyses for the pepyll prays,	
	and God unto hym thor can apeyre.	*there can appear*
	He fastyd full faurty days,	*forty days*
1950	the Law of God for he wold lere.	*learn*
	Then Commawndmentes, os clerkes says,	*Ten Commandments*
	war to hym takyn in tables sere.	*on several tablets*
	Bot whyls he thor can dwell	*there (on the mountain)*
	to lere Goddes laws lely,	*loyally*
1955	Hys folke full fowll fell	*so foul fell [away]*
	and made them mawmentry.	*idolatry*

[THE GOLDEN CALF (32:1–35)]

164.

A calf of gold thei gart up stand   *made to stand up*
    and honerd yt with all ther mayne.   *honored; power*
"This broyght us owt of Egyp land
1960   and sall us save," thei say certayn.
Then God unto Moyses commawnd:
    "Wend down unto thi pepyll agayn,
For thei have synnyd and tone on hand   *taken*
    a werke that wyll wurth to payn."   *turn to pain*
1965 Moyses then from God past
    and hyed hym to that halfe.   *hurried; place*
He fand his folke full fast   *discovered his people*
    kneland befor that calfe.   *kneeling*

165.

That mawmentry that thei of ment   *intended*
1970   was hedows thyng to hym at here.   *hideous; for him to hear*
He brake ther calfe and sone yt brent   *broke; burnt*
    and kest the powder in watur clere.   *cast*
Thei dranke therof ever os thei went,
    for other watur was non so nere.
1975 On thos that to that syn assent
    the venjance of God cane apere,   *did appear*
For he wald have them spylt   *destroyed*
    aftur ther awne desyre.   *as a result of their own desires*
The berdes of them wer gylt   *beards; were gilt*
1980   like unto the gold wyre.   *golden wire*

166.

When Moyses and his brother Aron   *Aaron*
    saw sygne of God in that sted,   *God's sign in that appearance*
Other wyttenese nede them none   *witnesses*
    bot at ther here was waxin rede.   *that their hair; grown red*
1985 Of them that was with tresone tone   *taken*
    and bold to breke that Moyses bede,   *what Moses bid*
Ware twenty-thre milia sloyne;   *Were 23,000 slain*
    then wer the remland wyll of rede.   *remnant helpless (at a loss for a plan)*
To fete thei can them fald,   *[their] feet; bend*
1990   and Moyses gatte them grace,   *granted*
And then to them he told
    how God spake in that space.

[THE COVENANT, THE ARK, AND THE TABERNACLE (33:1–40:33)]

167.

An Arke, he sayd, thei suld do make,
 therin to hold that holy store:

1995 The tables that God can to hym take,   *tablets; made him to take*
 with manna and with mekyll more: *much more*
All ther sacrafyce for Goddes sake
 and all that offerd suld be thore.   *should be there*
And therwith suld none wune ne wake   *no one dwell or watch*

2000 bot folke that were ordand ther for.   *ordained for that*
This Arke thei made in hye   *haste*
 of gold and prescius stone.
The lynege of Levy   *lineage of Levi*
 to tent therto was tone.   *to attend to that was chosen*

168.

2005 Aron was ordand byschop to be
 forto resave the sacrafyce,   *receive*
And prestes and dekyns in ther degree   *deacons*
 at serve to hym in sere servyce.   *various services*
And ryght so the duke Josue

2010 was chosyn os a prince and most in price,   *worth*
Wherso thei come in ylke cuntré
 to sett the batels in asyce.   *reckoning*
A Tabernakyll thei toke
 to kepe Godes Arke ay clene.   *always safe*

2015 So endes the secund boke,
 that of Moyses wyll mene.   *will be dealt with*

 # BOOK OF NUMBERS

NUMERI.

[DEPARTURE FROM SINAI (10:11–13) AND THE FIRST CENSUS OF ISRAEL (1:1–54)]

169.

	When Moyses thus had ordand all,	*ordained*
	full cunnandly os he well can,	*very cunningly as well he can*
	Unto Goddes servyce what suld fall,	*what should relate to God's service*
2020	and what to werres that wyrschyp wan,	*what [should relate] to wars; win honor*
	Then remevyd thei both grett and small	*they went off*
	to a forest that heght Faran.	*was called Paran*
	Ther Tabernakyll ther can thei stall;	*Their; build (install)*
	with the Arke of God thus thei begane.	*began*
2025	God bad Moyses, Hys Jew,	
	suld fayre on the feld	*go into the field*
	And nowmer his men all new,	*count*
	all that myght weppyns weld.	

170.

	Then Moyses dyd os God commaund:	
2030	he toke all that past twenty yere	*those past twenty years [in age]*
	Sex hunderth and thre milia	*603,000*
	acowntyd of knyghtes in armys clere,	*[were] accounted as knights in good arms*
	And fyghand folke on fote he fand	*fighting footmen he found*
	sex hunderth and fyve milia in fere,	*605,000 together*
2035	Withoutyn clerkes that were ordand	*Without the priests*
	to serve God on sydes sere.	*in other ways*
	And thei wer told be tale,	*those [who were not counted]*
	of the lynage of Levy,	
	To thryty milia hale.	*30,000 altogether*
2040	That was a fayr cumpany.	

[AARON AND MIRIAM DISPUTE MOSES' AUTHORITY (12:1–16)]

171.

	Sone aftur then begane debate:	
	Aron and his systur Mary	*Miriam*

Moyses, ther brother, can thei hate   *[To]; their; did they become hostile*
  and had to hym full grett envy.
2045 Thei say it falys not for his astate,   *it is not proper to his estate*
  and als that he was not worthy
To goverand them and gyd all gatte   *guide [them] in every way*
  or forto make over them maystry.   *exercise; mastery*
Thei sayd he was to bold   *too*
2050 at bryng them from ther blyse   *bliss [in Egypt]*
To suffer hungur and cald,
  and all ther myrth to mysse.   *lose*

172.

For this defawt gret venjance fell,   *trespass*
  os God Hymself vowched save to send:
2055 Mary all sone was fowl mesell,   *[made] foully leprous*
  and that endured aght days to ende.   *eight*
When Aron saw this and herd tell,
  hys awn defawt well he kend;   *knew*
To Moyses fette fast down he fell   *feet*
2060 and prayd to God his myse to amend.   *wrongs*
Then Moyses for hym prayd
  And for his systur also.
Lepur that on hyr was layde   *The leprosy*
  full tytt was tane hyr fro.   *taken from her*

[SPIES SENT INTO CANAAN (13:1–24)]

173.

2065 Then made thei myrth everylka man   *each and every*
  and toke ther tentes in that tyde   *took [down] their; place*
And flytted furth fro Faran   *journeyed; Paran*
  unto a forest fast besyde.
And fude enogh ther fand thei than;   *food*
2070 thei beld them thor a whyle to abyde.   *dwelled; there*
Ther myght thei se to Canan,   *Canaan*
  qwylke God had heyght them not to hyde.   *which; promised; (i.e., to reveal)*
Bot thei fand fandyng   *had hardships*
  or tyme that thei come thore.   *before the time; came there [to Canaan]*
2075 Then Moyses mad gedderyng   *made a gathering*
  of all folke hym before.

174.

And sayd, "Sers, ye sall understand
  how God hath sent yow solace sere,   *great solace*
That led yow owt of Egypt land
2080 fro Pharo and his folke in fere   *together*
And broyght yow soundly over the sand,   *safely*

	when all drowned that your enmys were.	*enemies*
	And for your hele He hath ordand,	*comfort*
	and for your fode, this fawrté yere.	*these forty years*
2085	And thynk als on this thyng:	*also*
	how your elders and ye	
	Hath groned and made gruchyng	
	both unto God and me.	

175.

	"Therfor all myse forto amend	*misdeeds*
2090	honers Hym ever with all your myght	*honor*
	And kepe His law ose I hath kend	
	in word and dede both day and nyght.	
	And certan men I rede we send	*advise*
	to serche the land that He hath heyght,	*promised [to us]*
2095	And se how the folke may them dyffend	*defend themselves*
	and aftur ther rede rewle us ryght."[1]	
	Josue toke he then,	*Joshua*
	and Calafe, to wende ydder.	*Caleb, to go there*
	The folke toke other ten	
2100	and send furth all togeydder.	

[THE SPIES RETURN FROM CANAAN AND REPORT (13:25–14:10)]

176.

	In Canan ther cowrse thei cast	
	and soyght the land in lengh and brede.	*reconnoitered*
	By fawrty days war fully past,	
	had thei notyd all that was nede.	*necessary*
2105	The ten com fyrst, that went furth last,	
	and to Moyses thei spake gud spede.	*productively*
	The folke then floked abowt them fast	
	All forto herkyn and take hede;	
	And frayned how thei had faryn	*asked; fared*
2110	owt in the uncuth land,	*unknown*
	And yf thei suld yt tharne,	*lose*
	or have yt in ther hand.	

177.

	The ten then can ther tales tell,	
	that stound them gretly in ther stevyn.	*stunned; their assembly*
2115	Thei sayd ther was not into dwell	
	a bettur land under Hevyn,	
	For thor was wyn and watur of well,	*there was wine*

---

[1] *and after their (the spies') counsel we will decide rightly*

whett and oyle all ordand evyn,   *grain*
Bot at the folke ware ferse and fell,   *But that; fierce and cruel*
2120   and nowmer of them myght no man nevyn.   *the numbering; know*
"Thei ar wytty of were   *clever at war*
    and well of armys kend;   *accomplished in arms*
Hors, scheld, and spere   *shield*
    have thei redy at hend.   *hand*

178.
2125   "Thei ar so grett on grone to gang: *large on the ground to walk*
    we seme bot barns to ther bodes.   *seem mere children to their bodies*
And ther cetes ar sett so strong   *their cities*
    thei cownt no cumyng of enmys.   *fear no onset of enemies*
Yt is no tyme to tary lang
2130   to loke wher no releve lyse."   *relief lies*
Then wax thor murmur them amang,   *grew there*
    as rebels thei began to ryse.
And to Moyses thei sayd,
    "How durst thou do this thyng,   *dared you*
2135   Thus traturly betrayde
    us all and our ofspryng?

179.
"We myght have lyved in Egypt land
    and governd us in gud degré.
Now hath thou stald us heyr to stand   *placed*
2140   to dye in payn and poverté."
To kyll hym have thei made connande.   *made a pact*
    So come Calafe and Josue.
Thei toke unto them new tythand   *tidings*
    and bade abayst thei suld not be: *said [that] fearful*
2145   "Yf ye in trewth be ryght   *righteous*
    and to God call and crave,
The land that He hath heyght,   *promised*
    that hette we yow to have.   *assure*

180.
"For all the ways os we can wend,
2150   we fand fell folke full of envy
And grett. Bot God is not ther frend,
    for thei lyfe all in mawmentry.   *idolatry*
Ther cetys sone we sall do schend   *cities soon; ruin*
    and stroye ther borows by and by.   *destroy their towns*
2155   For thei ar folke full of the Fende,   *Fiend (the Devil)*
    and in God sall we fast afy.   *soon trust*
Sen that He fayled us never   *Since; failed*
    in stowre when we war stede,   *battle; were troubled*

He wyll be with us ever."
2160   Then war the rebels rade.   *were; afraid*

[GOD CONDEMNS ISRAEL TO WANDER FORTY YEARS IN THE WILDERNESS (14:10–45)]

181.

To Moyses fette thei fell in hye   *feet; in haste*
   and mad grett sorow in Goddes syght.   *made*
Then Moyses prayd God Allmyghty
   forto have pety of ther plyght.   *pity on their plight*
2165 God answerd to hym opynly
   and sayd, "For that thou trawd not ryght,   *believed not rightly*
Ther sall none of that cumpany
   cume in the land, qwylk I have heyght.   *which; promised*
Thoo ten that told tythand   *Those; tidings*
2170   my folke so to greve,   *grieve (affright)*
Thei sall lend in this land   *remain*
   with mornyng and myscheve.   *mourning and mischief*

182.

"And all that trowde unto ther tale   *believed*
   to tene Moyses, my servant dere,   *harm*
2175 Here sall thei abyd and be in bale: *sadness*
   all that ar past over thryty yere.   *thirty years [of age]*
Ther chylder and ther heyrys all,   *Their; heirs*
   sall fyll that land both ferr and nere.   *far and near*
Josue and Calafe thei tway sall   *they shall together*
2180   be soverans in all sydes sere;
For thei went wysly thore
   and told yow trew thythand;
Thei and ther heyrys ever more   *heirs*
   sall be lordes of that land."

183.

2185 Then all tho rebels them repent
   and prayd to God for bettur bone.   *boon*
Bot to ther tales toke He no tent;   *no heed*
   als He had demed, so most yt be done.   *must*
And neverthelesse lyght he them lent
2190   abowt mydnyght withowtyn moyne,   *moon*
And fresche watur wherso thei went,
   and fode, yf that thei wer fele or fone,   *many or few*
Evyn at ther awn likyng
   aftur ther tonges wold tast,
2195 And keped ay ther cloghyng   *ever their clothing*
   withowtyn wem or wast.   *stain or waste*

[REBELLION OF KORAH, DATHAN, AND ABIRAM (16:1–50)]

184.

For this debate began to be
    grett murmur all thos men amang.
A crewell man that heyght Core   *cruel; was called Korah*
2200   agayn Moyses moved mekyll wrang.   *against; did much wrong*
Full rych he was of gold and fee;   *tribute*
    therfor he toyght hymself more strang   *thought; strong*
And mekyll more worthy then hee   *than he (i.e., Moses)*
    to govarn folke and for them gang.   *govern; go before them*
2205   He gatte of hys assent   *got*
    Datan and Abyron,   *Dathan and Abiram*
And told them his entent,
    and gart them fondly fon.   *made; foolishly behave*

185.

Tway hunderth rebels gart he ryse   *Two hundred; did he raise up*
2210   and fyfty at ther stevyn to stand.   *place*
To the Tabernakyll, as wreches unwyse,
    went thei furth to make offerand.
Thei senssed thor and dyd servyce,   *spread incense there*
    as byschoppes had before ordand,
2215   And sayd Aron was not of price   *worth*
    swylk werkkes to take on hand,   *such works*
Bot Core suld be then
    ther hed, os hym well aw,   *their head [priest]*
And Abyron and Datan
2220   byschoppes to led ther law.   *lead their*

186.

God was not of that purpasse payd;   *pleased*
    therfor yt turned them unto tene.   *it turned into misery for them*
Moyses and Aron to them sayd,
    "Sers, ye wot well withowtyn wene   *know; doubt*
2225   Thrugh grace of God we two war grayd   *were groomed*
    to be in state as we have bene.   *in the estate; been*
Yf any other be bettur arayd,   *prepared*
    to morn then sall the soth be sene."   *shall truth be seen*
To come then have thei hyght   *promised*
2230   on the morn, both lest and mast.   *both small and great*
Bot God ordand that nyght
    that all that werke was wast.   *that work (of Korah) was wrong*

187.

God send His venjance sone certan   *soon*
    wher Datan and Abyron can dwell.

2235	The erth opynd, yt is not to layn,	*earth opened up; [be] denied*
	And sodanly thei sanke to Hell	
	And all that of ther fayr ware fayn,	*their behavior were glad*
	wyf and chyld, down with them fell.	
	The erthe sone was closed agayn;	
2240	ther was no tokyn of to tell.	*sign of [them]*
	Bot Core come on the morne	
	with fele folke on fotte,	*many; foot*
	As connand was beforne,	*cunning [as he]*
	agayns Moyses to mote.	*argue*

188.

2245	Moyses spake then unto Core	
	and to two hunderth and fyfty,	*to [Korah's]*
	"Go se, both my brother Aron and ye,	
	and gyfe sense unto God Allmighty,	*incense*
	And by sume seyn then sall we se	*sign*
2250	qwylke man of all this cumpany	*which*
	Ys best worthy byschop to be!"	
	To this asent thei sayd in hy.	*haste*
	Unto the Tabernakyll	
	full tytt thei toke the way.	*very quickly*
2255	God send full sone merakyll	*miracle*
	thos fals folke to afflay.	*terrify*

189.

	As Core to the auter went	*altar*
	forto gyfe sense as sufferan syre,	*to give incense as a sovereign leader*
	A sodan fyre from Hevyn was sent	*sudden*
2260	and brent them up both bone and lyre.	*burned; flesh*
	Two hunderth and fyfty war schent	*destroyed*
	with other that dyd ther desyre.	
	Yet ware thei mo that malyce ment	*more whom malice brought*
	agayns Moyses with grett yre.	
2265	To be soveran, thei sayd,	
	he had over grett gylt,	*surpassing fault*
	For he had thor betrayd	
	ther folke and fowle spylt.	*shamefully destroyed [them]*

190.

	Her for full hyddos herme thei have:	*Here; hideous harm*
2270	thonour and lefnyng down dyscend	*thunder; lightning*
	And stroyd them up, both knyght and knave.	
	Then Moyses, all mys to amend,	*[their] misdeeds*
	Gart kepe the sensurs, whoso wold crave,	*Made the censers be lit, [by] whomever; pray*
	in the Arke of God to be kene	*shown*
2275	How God wyll ever His servant save	

and fro ther face ay them dyffend.   *from their foes ever defend them*
And thus this story twyns   *ends*
     that is cald Numeri,   *Numbers*
And a new boke begynnys
2280   that is named Dewtronomij.

DEUTRONOMII.

[AARON'S BUDDING ROD (NUMBERS 17:1–12)]

191.
Thoo folke, fulfylled with felony,
　　that God fed faurty yer before,
To Moyses had thei ever envy
　　and unto Aron mekyll more. *even more*
2285　Thei sayd all he was unworthy
　　to be ther sufferan byschop thore. *their sovereign bishop at that time*
Then Moyses had ordand in hye
　　to wytt of God qwylke worthy ware. *learn from God who was worthy*
"Lordyns," he sayd, "take tent *Gentlemen; take heed*
2290　to stynt this stryvyng strang. *cease*
Fro God sall grace be sentt *shall*
　　who dos well, and who wrang.

192.
"To morne I byd ther be ordand, *Tomorrow*
　　of all the kynrendys of alevyn *eleven tribes (kinfolk)*
2295　A man to take ther cawse on hand
　　In all that nedfull is to nevyn, *necessary to invoke*
And ylkon of them bryng a wand *each one*
　　Into the Arke of God of Hevyn.
Aron, my brother, his sall stand *his [wand] shall*
2300　als for the twelft; then ar thei evyn. *as; twelfth [tribe] (i.e., Levi)*
Ylk man, that thei not myse, *deceive*
　　sall wrytt his kynraden name, *tribe's*
And Aron sall wrytt on hys
　　'Levy' and lay that same." *lay [it there] in the same way*

193.
2305　So on the morn thei mett on ond, *all together*
　　the elevyn princese mekyll of price. *eleven princes of much worth*
And ylkon wrott within his wand. *wrote [his tribe's name] upon*
　　And Aron wand for Levy lese. *Aaron's rod for Levi stands*

109

	Then unto Moyses war thei tane	*taken*
2310	as formost wytte and most wyse.	*since [he was] of the most wit*
	In the Arke of God he layd ylkon	
	And closed yt at ther awn devyse.	
	Thei prade with hert and hend,	*prayed*
	ylkon in ther degree,	
2315	That God sume seyn suld send	*sign should send*
	who suld ther byschope be.	

194.

	Full sone on the morne thei com clene	
	that specialté to spyre and spye.	*favor to spy out and see*
	The alevyn princes all be dene	*forthwith*
2320	fand all ther wandes ded and drye.	*dead and dried up*
	Bot Aron wand bayr leves grene	*Aaron's; bore green leaves*
	and flowrs fayr to syght semly.	*flowers*
	Therby thei wyst withowtyn wene	*without doubt*
	God lufed the lyneg of Levy.	*lineage (tribe)*
2325	That wand was done to tent	*afterward placed*
	in the Arke of the Tabernakyll,	
	For yt suld be on ment	*henceforth remembered*
	how God dyd ther merakyll.	

[THE INCIDENT AT MERIBAH (NUMBERS 20:1–13)]

195.

	Then sessed ther stryve, yf yt ware late,	*ceased their anger, though*
2330	Agayns Aron, that ay was clene.	*who always was pure*
	And he stud styll in his astate,	*still remained in his estate*
	byschop, os he had eyr bene.	*been before*
	To Cades then thei toke the gatte,	*Kadesh; path*
	a soyle that was full seldom sene.	
2335	And ther began a new debate	
	for watur wantyng, os I wene.	*as I understand*
	Then Moyses, os God wold,	*desired*
	owt of the roche full ryfe	*out of the rock abundantly*
	Broyght watur, qwylke was cald	*which; called*
2340	allway the Watur of Stryfe.	*(i.e., Meribah)*

[DEATHS OF MIRIAM AND AARON (NUMBERS 20:1, 23–29)]

196.

	Becawse of stryvyng in that stede	*place*
	agayns Moyses with yll entent,	
	Thor Moyses systur Mary was dede;	*There Moses' sister Miriam died*
	for hyr mekyll mone was ment.	*much moaning was made*
2345	And Aron sone wex wyll of rede	*soon grew helpless*

for eld and seknes that was sentt. *age*
He dyed with mony bowsom bede; *died; humble prayers*
    we hope his sawle to welth is went. *soul to reward (i.e., Heaven)*
His soyne Eleaser *son Eleazar*
2350   to byschope then chase thei. *chose*
And how thei forthermer fare, *further fared*
    yett sume dele sall we say. *some more will*

[BATTLE OF HORMAH (NUMBERS 21:1–3)]

197.

Herrott, the kyng of Cananews, *Arad; Canaanites*
    when he herd tell the new tythand *tiding*
2355   How Moyses come with mony Jewes
and wold with strengh dystroy his land,
With them wold he take no trewse, *truce*
    bot sone his ost he had ordand. *soon his host; gathered up*
And Moyses furth his men remeuys *moves*
2360   tyll thei thoo folke on feldes fand. *those; fields found*
Sone ware thei in prese, *the press [of battle]*
    and full smertly can smytte. *hard they strike [each other]*
The overhand had Moyses, *upper hand*
    and the kyng was dyscumfete. *defeated*

[THE ISRAELITES COMPLAIN AND ARE PUNISHED WITH SERPENTS (NUMBERS 21:4–9)]

198.

2365   Thor gatte thei gudes full grett plenté, *There they got goods*
and for that welth thei wold not fyne, *cease [the battle]*
Bot furthe thei sewed more forto se, *forth they pursued*
    and that suyng thei rowed syne. *pursuing they regretted afterwards*
For thei come in a wast cuntré, *desolate country*
2370   wher thei fand nother bred ne wyne. *found neither bread nor wine*
Therfor begane debate to be
    that Moyses wold thai war putt to pyne. *[saying] that; wished; pain*
Bot he sone them releved *relieved*
    and mend ther myschawnce.
2375   Then was God with them grevede,
    and sone He sent venjance.

199.

Wyld wormes wex them amang, *serpents came up*
    full mekyll of fors and fell os fyre, *great of strength and cruel as fire*
Qwylke sume with toth, and sume with tang, *Which some; tooth; tongue*
2380   bott and brent them bone and lyre. *bit and burned; flesh*
To Moyses fast then can thei gang *quickly; they go*
    for socur os to ther soveran syre. *succor as; high lord*

	And all yf thei had wryed hym wrang,	*accused*
	his wyll was to do ther desyre.	
2385	He prayd God them to amend	
	and forgyf ther trespasse.	
	And thor God hath hym kend	*there; ordered*
	to cast a worme of brasse	*serpent of brass*

200.

	And als a seyn hym forto rayse.	*as a sign to raise it*
2390	And thus then told He in His tayle:	
	"Als sone os thei yt sees," He says,	
	"of all hurtes thei sall be hole."	*whole*
	And so was done by dyverse days,	
	wherso thei went be down or dale.	*wherever; by hill or dale*
2395	To Arnon Fluyd thei toke the ways,	*Arnon River*
	that lyged then low in a vayle.	*lay low in a valley at that time*
	A sutherun syre Seon	*sovereign sire [named] Sihon*
	was kyng of Amaryce;	*the Amorites*
	Abowt that flud Arnon	*river*
2400	was he man mekyll in price.	*a man of much worth*

[KING SIHON DEFEATED (NUMBERS 21:21–32)]

201.

	And for Moyses hys men wold save	
	and hald them sownd by se and sand,	*safe in all ways*
	He send to Seon leve to crave	*to ask for permission*
	to lede his folke thrughowt his land.	*lead his people (i.e., the Israelites)*
2405	Bot Seon sayd he suld not have,	
	bot sone thei suld be bon in band.	*bound in irons*
	Seon was strekyn with his awn stave;	*stricken with his own sword*
	Moyses dystroyed all that wold stand.	
	Ther wan thei welth gud on,	*won; in abundance*
2410	more then men myght of tell.	
	In a cyté cald Esmon,	*Heshbon*
	thor drest thei them to dwell.	*they prepared*

[DEFEAT OF KING OG (NUMBERS 21:33–35)]

202.

	Whyls thei sojornde in that cyté,	
	a land was nere that heyght Basan,	*Bashan*
2415	And Og was kyng of that cuntré.	
	Of Ebrews herd he tythand then.	*news*
	He ordand hym ther bayn to be,	*determined himself to be their destruction*
	bot God that all gud consell can	*knows*
	Ordand that overcomyn was he,	

2420	and Ebrews all that wrschepe wan.	*honor won*
	Thus logyd thei in sere landes	*lived; several*
	and conquerd sere kyngdome	
	And held them in ther handes,	
	or thei come to the flome.	*before they came; river [Jordan]*

[KING BALAK, BALAAM, AND BALAAM'S ASS (NUMBERS 22:1–24:25)]

203.

2425	Yett wonned on, ose ther way lyse,	*dwelled one, as their direction took them*
	heyght Balake, a kyng full cruell,	*called Balak*
	And he was mayster of Moabyse,	*the Moabites*
	a folke that was full fers and fell.	*cruel*
	How Ebrew over all then wan the price,	*won the glory*
2430	be dyverse tythynges herd he tell.	*by diverse tidings*
	And for thei ware of were so wyse,	*because; war*
	he drede hym more with them to mell.	*feared; to meddle*
	He cald to hys consell	*council*
	to se what ware to do,	*[it] were [best]*
2435	To take trewse or batell.	*truce or battle*
	And thus thei told hym to:	

204.

	"The Ebrews ar men full myghty	
	and mony mo than we may bryng.	*many more [in number]*
	To fyght with them ware grett foly;	*folly*
2440	ther God is with them in all thyng.	
	Bot Balam, the prophett, wones herby,	*Balaam; lives close by*
	that God wyll graunt all his askyng.	
	Make hym go curse that cumpany	
	and wary them both old and yong.	*trouble*
2445	Then sall ther god withdraw	*their*
	his helpe, wher in thei treyste.	*in whom they trust [so much]*
	So sall thei lyg full low	*lie very low (be brought low)*
	and lyfe evyn as us lyst."	*it pleases us*

205.

	The kyng in hast, ys no at hyde,	*there is nothing to hide*
2450	hath send his servant, os thei ordand,	*as they instructed*
	And Balam wold no langer byd,	*delay*
	he com furth as the kyng cummand.	
	His ase stud styll when he suld ryde,	*ass stood still*
	and Balame bett hym with a wand.	*beat; stick*
2455	The best spake and told in that tyde	*beast spoke; place*
	how that he saw an angell stand	
	The way hym forto lett.	*prevent*
	Then was the prophett flayde;	*terrified*

Hamward his hede he sett,   *his (the ass's) head*
2460   bot sone the angell sayd,

206.
"Hald furth thi gatt, os thou began,   *gait, as you*
     unto the kyng of Amoryse.
When thou comys to Flom Jordan   *the River Jordan*
     and sees wher the chylder of Israel lyys,   *children; lie*
2465   God bydes thee that thou them not ban   *curse*
     bot blesse them all on the beste wyse.   *from this wise beast*
And He sall be with thee thor then   *there at that time*
     and save thee from all yll enmyse."   *wicked enemies*
Then past the prophett playn,   *went; openly*
2470   evyn os the angell hym lede.   *led him*
The kyng was then full fayn,   *very glad*
     for he wened well have spede.   *had high hopes to have success*

207.
All his entent he told hym tyll: *his (Balaam's) intent he (Balak) told to him*
     that he suld wary the Jews allway.   *how he should fear; always*
2475   He sayd, "Ser, have us unto an hyll   *(Balaam); take*
     wher we may se all ther aray."   *their numbers*
Then was he fayn that to fulfyll.   *he (Balak) happy to fulfill that [request]*
     Unto the heghtest hyll hasted thei.   *highest*
And ther the prophet stod full styll,
2480   and thus to them cane he say,
"Ye chylder of Israel,
     that myrth full lang hath myst,   *happiness so long have missed*
Tythynges to yow I tell: *Tidings*
     God byddes that ye be blest

208.
2485   "With all gudnese, ase he begane
     To Abraham your fader free,
To Ysac and to Jacob then,
     of whos kynradyn all comyn ar ye.   *lineage you are all come*
Ye sall conquer all Chanan
2490   and have yt in your pawsté."   *power*
Then was the kyng a carefull man,   *sorrowful*
     when that he herd yt so suld be.
Full sore he was aschamed,
     for he that fyght had soyght.
2495   And Balaam fast he blamed,
     for that he band them noyght.   *cursed*

209.

He prayd to wary them on all wyse *curse them in all ways*
  so that he myght them bett and bynd. *beat and bind [in irons]*
Agayns hys boyde he blyst them thryse, *command he (Balaam) blessed*
2500   and als he sayd, so suld thei fynd. *experience*
Then Balac, kyng of Moabyse,
  went away as wroth os wynd. *angry as wind*
And Balam ther mad prophecyse
  that Crist suld come amang ther kynd. *peoples*
2505 He sayd a sterne suld ryse *star*
  of Jacob begynnyng,
And a wand of mekyll price *scepter of great glory*
  of Israel owt suld spryng, *would spring forth*

210.

Qwylke suld conquere kyng and cuntré *Which should*
2510   of Moabyse in mony a sted. *Moabites in all places*
And suns of Seth, also sayd he, *the children*
  suld be hent from handes of dede. *seized by the hands of death*
The stern to Crist may lykynd be *star; likened*
  to lyght them that lay low os led; *as low as lead*
2515 The wand, Mary his moyder fre, *noble mother*
  that suld com of the Jew kynred. *from the Jewish kindred*
Thes wordes was fro God sent. *were*
  Kyng Balake cursed that qwylle, *time*
Bot Balaam, or ever he went, *before he left*
2520   he wroyght a weked wyle. *wicked stratagem*

[APOSTASY AT PEOR DUE TO BALAAM (NUMBERS 25:1–18, 31:16)]

211.

He saw the kyng was not well payd, *very pleased*
  therfor sum comforth wold he kene. *make known*
"Ser, I sall thee lere," he sayd, *teach*
  "to stroye Moyses and all his men. *[how] to destroy*
2525 Gayr damsels be gayly gratt *Cause damsels that are finely attired*
  to seke in cytes, neyn or ten. *to be sought out in the cities, nine*
And when thei ar ryghtly arayde, *rightly gathered*
  unto the Ebrews send them then. *Hebrews*
Grett myrth ther sall thei make
2530   to yong men evyn and morne *evening and morning*
And gayr them God forsake. *cause them to forsake God*
  So sall thei sone be lorne." *soon be lost*

212.

The kyng hath sent, os he can say, *as*
  for fayrest wemen that men fand. *for the fairest women that men could find*

2535	He did theym cloth in rych array	*clothe in rich garments*
	and thus to theym he command,	
	"Loke wysly that ye wend your way	*you make your way*
	to our enmyse of uncowth land,	*enemies of foreign*
	And fowndes to gayr them leyf ther lay.	*hasten to cause them to leave their faith*
2540	Lett Belfagor be ther warrand."	*Baal-peor be their protector*
	Tho wemen werly soyght	*carefully*
	this falshed to fulfyll.	
	The Ebrews groched noyght	*complained not*
	forto werke all ther wyll.	

213.

2545	Thei leved the law that Moyses lent	*abandoned*
	and unto mawmentré mad ther mene.	*idolatry cast their lots*
	And for thei so to syn assent,	*because they thus to sin assented*
	God was greved unto them ylkon.	
	To Moyses told He His entent	
2550	and bad tyte venjance suld be tone.	*quick vengeance should be taken*
	With wo so twenty milia went,	*20,000 died*
	and wemen war full wyll of wone.	*and women[, too,] were fully without hope*
	Fynnes, a full fell man,	*Phinehas; dangerous*
	Eleazar son was hee,	
2555	Sloght ther maysters than;	*Slaughtered their [the idolaters'] teachers*
	the remnand fast can flee.	*remnant*

214.

	And forthi that this Fyneys	*because*
	dystroyed them that ware Goddes enmyse,	*enemies*
	Forto be byschop God hym chese	*chose*
2560	aftur his fader for His servys.	*service*
	And for His sake He grawnt peyse	*peace (life)*
	unto all Ebrews that ware wyse,	*were wise*
	And sayd He suld ther kynd encresse	*their lineage increase*
	unto grett reverence forto ryse.	
2565	With Moyses then was none	
	that he lede over the se,	
	Bot thei ware ded ylkon	
	bot Calaphe and Josue.	*Caleb and Joshua*

[CENSUS OF THE NEW GENERATION (NUMBERS 26:1–65)]

215.

	Then commawnd God unto Moysen,	
2570	for he suld fayn his foes to fere,	*should be glad to make his enemies afraid*
	That he suld reckyn the remnand then	*count the remnant*
	of all tho that myght armys bere.	*bear arms*
	He fand thre hunderth thowssand men	

that myghty were to wend in were
2575   Withowtyn prestes and clerkes to ken,   *to count*
        qwylke twenty-thre milia ware.   *which were 23,000 [in number]*
        God bad Moyses be wyse
        and that his host ware grayde   *were prepared*
        To stroye the Moabyse,   *destroy the Moabites*
2580   that had them thor betrayd.   *there*

[HOLY WAR AGAINST MIDIAN (NUMBERS 31:1–54)]

216.

        Moyses withowtyn more abayd,   *more waiting*
        twelfe milia toke he them amang;   *12,000 [men]*
        Ther leder Fyneys he made   *Phinehas*
        them forto gyd wher thei suld gang.   *guide; should go*
2585   To Moabyse full ryght thei rode   *the Moabites*
        and stroyde them all with strokes strang.   *slaughtered*
        Fyve hethyn kynges with cuntreys brayd   *heathen; countries broad*
        in few days to ded thei dang.   *they beat to death*
        Balam thei have not leved,   *left [alive]*
2590   that fyrst conseld the kyng: *counseled*
        Fynyes stroke of his hed   *struck off*
        for his fals consellyng.

217.

        All batels thus thei broyght to end;   *battles*
        then past thei home with mekyll pride.   *went; much*
2595   No tong in Erth myght tell the tend   *tongue on Earth; tenth [part]*
        Of welth that thei have in that tyde.   *time*
        Ryght to the flome all folke was frend;   *river [Jordan]; were [now] friendly*
        to do them dere durst non abyd.   *none dared to cause them hurt*
        Two of ther lyneg ther wold lend,   *lineage (i.e., twelve tribes); remain*
2600   bycawse the land was large and wyd;
        That was Gad and Ruben.
        The kynrendes toke to rede   *These kindreds; advice*
        And asked leve of Moysen   *permission*
        to dwell styll in that stede.   *place*

[GAD AND REUBEN DESIRE TO STAY IN JAZER (NUMBERS 32:1–42)]

218.

2605   Thus prayde thei throly, all and sume,   *earnestly*
        bot Moyses made this connand then   *pact*
        That thei suld passe over the flome   *river*
        and helpe to conquere Canan.   *Canaan*
        And when thei Gerico had wun   *Jericho*
2610   into ther boundom, best and man,   *their possession, beast*

Unto that cuntré suld thei come	*they should*
and be ther styll, os thei begane.	*be there again, as*
Ten cytes made Moyses	*cities*
in tyme thei sojournd thore,	*in [the] time they sojourned there*
2615 To them that cuntré chese	*For those who; chose*
to have and hald ever moyre.	

[MOSES' DEPARTING WORDS TO THE PEOPLE (DEUTERONOMY 31–34)]

219.

Then Moyses both with hert and hand	
loved his God of grett powere,	
For he wyst that he suld from them wend.	*knew; go*
2620 He told the folke his consell clere.	
He sayd, "Sers, I sall sun make end,	*soon make an end [of life]*
for Canan come I not nere.	*near*
Kepes commawnmentes, os I have kend,	*Keep the commandments, as; taught*
and other law loke ye non lere.	*not learn*
2625 Elyazar sall byschop be	*Eleazar*
to stand in Aron stede,	*Aaron's place*
And ye sall hald Josue	*consider Joshua*
your duke when I am dede.	

220.

"That on may mekyll you avayle	*That one (Eleazar); avail*
2630 that God yow here gyf mynd and myght;	
That other sall wend in batell	*That other (Joshua) shall go*
and fell your foys with fors in fyght.	*foes; force*
Therfor in fayth loke ye not fayle,	*in your faithfulness*
bot ever in trowth be trew and ryght.	
2635 Then nawder enmyse, ne yll consell	*neither enemies, nor wicked counsel*
sall do yow dere be day or nyght.	*wound by*
Have mynd how God hath wroght	
for yow and your ofspryng.	
Loke ye forgeyt Hym noyght,	
2640 bot thanke Hym over all thyng.	

221.

"Sone sall ye passe Flom Jordan	*the River Jordan*
to the land that yow levest wore.	*you were promised*
And when ye come to Canan	
and hath all that God heyght yow thore,	*promised to you there*
2645 Loke ye dystroy all mawmentes then	*idols*
of fendes that ye fynd yow before,	*fiends*
And part the land as ye well can	*divide*
aftur your lynage, lesse and more.	*lineage*
Whoso hath most meneye,	*the most numbers*

2650	born all of a blode,	*a [single] bloodline*
	Them nedes the most cuntré	*They require*
	to fynd ther bestes fode."	*find food for their beasts*

222.

	As Moyses thus his consell kend	*counsel told*
	to can the law and kepe yt well,	*know*
2655	A whyt clowde down fro Hevyn dyscend	*descended*
	and coverd hym over ylka dele.	*entirely*
	He was away when thei lest wend,	*least knew*
	bot wheder ward wyst thei not well.	*to where they knew not*
	Ne more thei herd of his end,	
2660	ne his grave cowd no man fynd ne fele.	*nor; could; nor feel*
	Thei soyght and sayd "Alas!"	
	with mornyng them amang,	*mourning*
	Os yt no wonder was,	*As it was not surprising*
	for he had led them lang.	*for a long time*

223.

2665	Moyses mad end in this maner.	
	Full mekyll mone was for hym ment.	*A very great moaning*
	To God his dedes war ever dere,	*deeds were always dear*
	for trew in trowth was his entent.	
	Full leve he was Goddes law to lere,	*glad; know*
2670	os long os he on lyfe was lent.	*as long as he was living*
	Wherfor we wott withowtyn were	*know without doubt*
	his sawle unto Hevyn is hent.	*gone*
	This boke thus end wyll we	
	that made is of Moysen,	
2675	And tell furth of Josue.	
	God grawnt us myrth. Amen.	*joy*

 # BOOK OF JOSHUA

JOSUE.

[JOSHUA SENDS SPIES TO JERICHO; RAHAB AIDS THEM (2:1–24)]

224.

	Moyr of the storé may men se	*More; story*
	what was done aftur Moyses dede.	*died*
	A nobyll duke, heyght Josue,	*called Joshua*
2680	was ordand to stand in his sted;	*ordained; place*
	Elyazar, byschope was he	*Eleazar*
	the pepyll forto rewle and rede.	*rule and guide*
	Then neght thei nere that cuntré	*When they came close to*
	God them heyght of His Godhede,	*promised*
2685	So that yt myght be sene,	*seen*
	the land of Canan:	*Canaan*
	Noyght bot the flome betwen.	*river [Jordan]*
	And thus thei ordand than.	*gathered then*

225.

	Becawse the cyté of Gerico	*Jericho*
2690	was next the flome and fast therby,	*strong*
	Josue had ordand two	
	most cunnand of that cumpany	*most cunning [men]*
	Unto that cyté forto go	
	and bad that thei suld spyre and spye	*look and spy out*
2695	The wardes and the wals also	*watchmen; walls*
	and all that passage prevely,	*way secretly*
	How thei myght tytyst take	*quickest*
	that cyty be on asent.	*by one assent*
	This message forto make	*mission to undertake*
2700	two wyght men furth ther went.	*two fellows went forth there*

226.

	To Jerico thei toke the way,	
	a cety semly unto syght.	*beautiful to look upon*
	Thei spyrd full ryght all ther aray,	*spied; their array*
	both ways beneth and wals on heyght.	*the ways beneath [the city]*

2705	So dyd thei dewly all that day	*duly*
	to tyme that neght nere the nyght;	*until; the night came near*
	Ther thar loygyng in a place toke thei	*lodging*
	with a woman that Raab hyght.	*Rahab was called*
	Scho had fayr rent in hand,	*a substantial legacy*
2710	laft of hyr elders beforn;	*before*
	Bot scho was commyn kend	*commonly known*
	as hostler evyn and morn.	*innkeeper evening*

227.

	Whyls thei the cyté thus aspyd,	*spied out*
	all yf thei ware wytty and wyse,	*although they were careful*
2715	To the wardyns thei wer ascryde	*watchmen; reported*
	that Raab herberd swylk to spyse.	*harbored such two spies*
	The bayles went in the evyn tyde	*bailiffs*
	to foche them furth befor the justyce.	*fetch; judge*
	Bot prevely scho can them hyde	*secretly*
2720	and hold from handes of ther enmyse.	*enemies*
	Scho lett them lang or day	*let them down long before daybreak*
	over the wals of that cyté	
	And teched them the redy way	*taught; best way*
	from all enmyse to flee.	

228.

2725	Bot fyrst scho festend this connand	*she pledged this agreement [between them]*
	or ever scho wan them over the wall:	*before she got them over*
	"When ye sall entur into this land	
	and govern this cyté, grett and small,	
	Me and myn, loke ye warrand	*be sure*
2730	that no defawt unto us fall."	*disadvantage*
	Herto thei both held up ther hand	*To this; their hands*
	and sayd, "This cunnand kepe we sall.	*agreement*
	Thou and thi meneye both	*your household*
	sall well be sayved," thei say.	
2735	Thei went withowtyn wothe	*danger*
	over the flome the evyn way.	*river the quickest way*

229.

	Unto Josue thei reckynd ryght	*reported*
	of Jerico all poyntes playn,	
	And wher thei suld muster ther myght	
2740	to wyn yt well withowtyn payn;	*without loss*
	And how thei had to Raab heygh	*agreed*
	so that scho suld be saved certayn,	
	Bycawse scho sayved them in the nyght,	
	when bayles suld them have slayn.	*officers*
2745	Thei loved God with gud wyll	

	that tho yong men so yemed,	*those young men so guided*
	And hetes yt to fulfyll	*assures*
	and do evyn os thei demed.	*just as they had said*

[JOSHUA LEADS ISRAEL ACROSS THE JORDAN (3:1–17)]

230.

	Josue bad the pepyll pray	
2750	and honer God with mayn and mode,	*might and spirit*
	And ordan that on the thryd day	*ordered*
	suld thei passe furth over the flud.	*river*
	The suns of Levy, befor went thai	*(i.e., the Levites), in front*
	berand the Arke of God full gud.	*bearing*
2755	Thei fand ther wath and redy way,	*there a ford*
	wher never folke befortym yode.	*had before gone*
	Wemen and chylder yyng	*young children*
	then next them fowled fast.	*followed closely*
	The flud sessyd of fluyng	*river ceased flowing*
2760	whyls all the pepyll past.	*while; passed*

[MONUMENT COMMEMORATING THE CROSSING; PASSOVER CELEBRATED (4:1–24, 5:10)]

231.

	When thei war past, both best and man,	
	the stremys wex agayn full strang.	*grew; strong*
	Thei loyge them in Canan,	*lodged*
	that land that thei had coyvet lang.	*coveted long*
2765	Elyazar has ordand then	*Eleazar*
	that certan men sone suld gang	*go*
	For twelf stones to the Flome Jordan	
	and make an auter them amang.	*altar*
	Thei purveyd sone a place	*provided soon*
2770	wher God honerd suld be.	
	Ther held thei fest of Pasce	*Pasch (Passover)*
	with grett solempnité.	

[JERICHO BESIEGED (6:1–20)]

232.

	And when the solempne day was done	
	And all the folke refreyshed were,	
2775	Josue semled hys host full sone	*assembled*
	of lysty men, both lesse and mayre;	*strong men*
	Pristes and dekyns gart he gone	*Priests and deacons he ordered*
	and beyr Goddes Arke up them beforne.	*bear*
	To Jerico thei went ylkon	*each one*
2780	and hastely, when thei come thore,	*there*

A day jornay abowt   *[And everything for] a day's journey*
   be strengh thei have dystroyde.   *by*
Then thei within had dowtt   *those within [the city]*
   full sone forto be noyde.   *killed*

233.

2785   Then Josue bad the clargy gang   *go*
   with all the lynage of Levy
And beyr the Arke up them amang
   abowt the town to ylk party,   *each side*
And at thei suld syng solemp song   *that they; solemn songs*
2790   and make all maner of mynstralsy.
And yf the wals war never so strang,
   so suld God send them the vyctory.
"Bot o thyng I yow of warne: *one*
   when ye entur within,
2795   Sparse no manys wyfe ne barne   *man's wife nor child*
   bot Raab and hyr kyn.   *Rahab; family*

234.

"For scho our messyngers con sayve   *did save*
   when we them sent over the flude."   *river*
And also he commawnd knyt and knave   *knight*
2800   and comyns that with hym yode   *common [soldiers]; went*
That thei suld nawder hyde ne have   *neither hide nor keep*
   to themselfe sylver ne other gud,   *goods*
Bot stryke them down with sword and stave
   and stroy all that befor them stud.
2805   Gold to that Tabernakyll
   he bad that thei suld beyre,   *carry*
To God that dyd that merakyll
   to them in all ther were.   *their wars*

235.

That thei suld kepe this commawnment
2810   he charegd the ost, both old and yong,   *army*
And sayd forsothe thei suld be schent   *destroyed*
   that to themself toke any thyng.
Abowt the cety then thei went   *Around*
   full solemply and sanges can syng.
2815   And on the sevynt day hath God sent
   entré ewyn at ther awn lykyng.   *entry even as they had desired*
Wher the Arke of God can dwell,
   the folke abydyn styll.   *remained silent*
The wals fayled and down fell,
2820   and thei enturd at wyll.

[Jericho destroyed; Achan breaks God's commandment (6:21–7:1)]

236.

	So when thei had this cyté wun,	
	thei slow and brent both best and man.	*killed and burned*
	Bot Raab, os thei had begun,	
	and hyr kyn thei keped as thei cane.	*as they were able*
2825	On Achor, that was Caryn son,	*One [man named] Achan; Carmi's*
	A full rych mantyll fand he then;	*cloak he found*
	He hyd yt when he had yt fun;	*found*
	that boldnes aftur myght he ban.	*regret*
	He brake Goddes commawnment,	
2830	that Josue forbede.	
	Therfor fele folke war schent,	*many people were killed*
	and he had dulfull dede.	*a piteous death*

[Defeat at Ai (7:2–26)]

237.

	Bot how that care began to com,	
	the story furth reherses ryght.	
2835	Thor stud afferrom, ner the flome,	*stood afar, near the river*
	A rych cyté that Adan hyght.	*Ai was called*
	Josue semled all and sum	*assembled*
	his knyghtes that ware wyse and wyght,	*capable*
	And thryty thowssand on a thrum	*30,000 together*
2840	sent he with tho folke to fyght.	
	Bot thei that ware within	*who were*
	so boldly batell bede,	*carried out*
	The Ebrews, moyre and myn,	*altogether*
	war sum slayn, and sum fled.	

238.

2845	When Josue herd this folke to flayd,	*heard that these men were dispersed*
	no mervell yf he war yll meved.	*surprise; ill at ease*
	"Sum of ourself has synd," he sayd.	*sinned*
	"Wherfor our God is to us greved."	
	Lottes amang them sone thei layd	*Lots; soon*
2850	so forto se the soth, thei beleved.	*thus to reveal the truth*
	Thei fand how Achor them betrayd,	
	and how the mantyll had them myscheved.	*had worked against them*
	To ded sone was he staned,	*death soon; stoned*
	as his werke was worthy.	
2855	And Josue fast wold fownd	*attempt*
	forto venge this velany.	

[VICTORY AT AI (8:1–29)]

239.

To Adan he ys wentt agayn
   with thryty milia and well moe.   *30,000; more*
And when he come nere on a playn,
2860   he parted hys pepell evyn in two: *evenly*
The on half to a mowntan   *one*
   prevely bad he them go.   *he ordered them to go quietly*
To tyme the saw his syng certan,   *At the time they saw his sign*
   the cety suld thei entur so.   *city*
2865 Thei past furth prevely   *secretly*
   In buschement so forto be.   *ambush*
He and hys company
   asawted that cety.   *assaulted*

240.

Within thei ware full sterne and stowte,   *strong and stout*
2870 for them had falyn so fayr befor.   *they (the Hebrews) had fallen so quickly*
Thei opynd the gattes and wentt owt,
   all men of armes, lesse and more.
Then Josue feyned to fle for dowt   *pretended to flee out of doubt*
   to thei fare fro the cyté wore;   *until they were far from*
2875 Then to the mowntane he made a schowt
   and set his syng to them thore.   *sign; there*
To the cety then thei wentt
   and fand full evyn entre.   *found very easy entry*
Full fast thei schott and brentt   *Very quickly; shot and burned*
2880 that folke myght farre see.   *see [it] from afar*

241.

When Josue agayn can loke
   unto the cyté styfe of stone,   *made*
He saw thor fyre and full grett smoke   *there fire*
   and sparkes fleand full gud one.   *flying in great numbers*
2885 To his men then he undertoke
   that that cyté to them was tone.   *taken*
He bad them wett wele ylka noke   *to check each nook thoroughly*
   that ther enmys scaped none.   *so that none of their enemies escaped*
All that behynd oght dwelt   *ought to remain*
2890 be lyve ware dongyn down;   *quickly were struck down*
That wentt before ware feld   *felled*
   with them that toke the town.

242.

Ther ware the panyms put to payn;   *pagans*
   thei had no bodes them to beld.   *assurances to comfort them*

2895	And the Ebrews ware farly fayn	*greatly gladdened*
	to se ther enmys feld in feld.	*fallen in the field*
	Thrughowt the cyté past thei playn	
	and spared none in yowth ne eld.	*spared neither young nor old*
	Thei gatt ther gold that myght them gayn	*profit*
2900	and other welth at wyll to weld.	*wield*
	So went thei, old and yong,	
	to ther awn cumpany	*in their own tribes*
	And mad full grett offeryng	
	to God, os was worthy.	*as was right*

[GIBEONITES TRICK JOSHUA INTO PEACE (9:1–27)]

243.

2905	When thei had wonn this grett renown,	
	grett word of them began to ryse,	*rumor; arise*
	How Jacob suns wold dyng al down	*soon would take down all*
	and in were how thei wan the prise.	*war; won the rewards*
	So was a cuntré heyght Gabown,	*called Gibeon*
2910	and the pepyll heygh Gabonyse.	*Gibeonites*
	Thei sembled in that same seson	*at that same time*
	and toke ther cownsell on this wyse:	*held their discussions*
	To putt them furth in presse	*en masse*
	ther land forto dyffend,	*defend*
2915	Or elles persew for peyse,	*else pursue peace*
	and thus ther consell kend.	*decision was made known*

244.

	Thei toke twelfe of that same ceté,	*twelve men from*
	qwylke that thei for most cunnand knew,	*whom; knew to be most cunning*
	And sent them unto Josue	
2920	for sympyll peyse forto persew.	
	Thei sayd, "We cum fro far cuntré	
	with ye, ser, forto take peyse and trew.	*you, sir; truce*
	By our cloghys that may thou se.	*cloths; see*
	When we went furth, then ware thei new.	*journeyed forth; were they*
2925	Or we wyn hom agayn	*Before we reach home*
	wyl be full mony a day."	
	Thei toke trewse by this trayn,	*truce by this trickery*
	and fast thei went ther way.	

245.

	When Josue thus ther peyse had sworn,	
2930	he trowed them folke of full far land.	*believed*
	Bot hym was told sone on the morn	*he was soon told*
	that thei ware neghbours nere at hand	
	Of Canan — this toyght hym scorne —	*thought*

	not thre days jornay thens dwelland.	*three days' journey away they lived*
2935	Bot for sewrty was fest beforn,	*because the pact was made before*
	he sayd the peyse suld stably stand.	
	So that thei suld not fall	*fail*
	that land whyls thei wonned in,	*dwelled*
	To bere wode and fuell	*bear wood*
2940	ther sacurfyce to begyne.	*there*

[JOSHUA STILLS THE SUN AND DEFEATS FIVE KINGS (10:1–27)]

246.

	Kyng of Jerusalem herd tell	
	of bayle that in that land began:	*misery*
	How that the chylder of Israel	
	ware comyn fare over Flom Jordan,	*far over the River Jordan*
2945	And how thei hade wun them omell	*won; among*
	fyrst Jerico and sythyn Adan	*Jericho and then Ai*
	And Gabonyse with them to dwell.	*Gibeonites*
	That mad hym a full mornand man.	*very mournful man*
	Hee sayd hys men to ryse	*told*
2950	and prestly to persew	*promptly*
	To stroy the Gabonyse,	*destroy*
	for thei had takyn trew.	*truce*

247.

	For faur kynges sone had he send,	*soon*
	qwylk well he wyst wold with hym last.	*who; knew would*
2955	To Gabonyse wyghtly thei wend	*strongly they went*
	them and ther cytes down to cast.	*their*
	Bot Josue wold them dyffend,	
	for thei in fayth war festynd fast.	*compact were well allied*
	With his meneye them to amend	*help*
2960	to paynyms planly ys he past.	*against the pagans has he moved*
	He tokyd them in that tyme	*defeated*
	so that ther fled bot fone,	*there fled but few*
	Fro on howr aftur prime	*one hour after prime*
	to fowr howrs aftur none.	*four hours after noon*

248.

2965	Hym toyght the day went hastely;	*thought; [too] swiftly*
	therfor he prayd God for His grace.	
	And God of Hys gud curtasay	
	lenghed that day two days space:	*lengthened; [to] two days in length*
	He made the sone to stand forthi	*sun; therefore*
2970	and passe not furth his kyndly pase	*natural pace*
	Tyll Josue had the vyctory	*Until*
	and overcomyng of all hys foyse.	*foes*

	Sqwylke grace os God dyd thore	*Such grace as God*
	Agayns the cowrse of kynd	*Against the course of nature*
2975	Was never seyne before,	*seen*
	als fere os men may mynd.	*as far as men can remember*

249.

	The paynyms os in parke war pynd,	*pagans as if in an enclosure were pinned*
	to byd them batell was not to byd.	*make; happen*
	The fyve kynges held them behynd,	
2980	and in a hole thei have them hyde.	*cave; hid themselves*
	Bot Josue furth can them fynd.	
	That he was kyng thore well he kyd.	*there; made known*
	Thar handes to ther bakkes gart he bynd,	*backs he had bound*
	and on this wyse with them he dyd:	*in this way*
2985	He gart them lyg on lang	*at length*
	apon the grownd thor grayd	*arrayed*
	And Ebrews on them gang,	*walked*
	and thus to them he sayd:	

250.

	"Als ye fare with kynges fyve	
2990	that fulse them heyr under your fette,	*prostrate themselves here; feet*
	So sall ye be lordes in your lyve	
	of paynyms kynges, her I yow hett,	*here I promise you*
	And have maystry of man and wyfe	
	that wyll no to yow make them mett.	*complaint*
2995	Ther sall none stand with yow to stryfe,	
	whyls ye your God with gud wyll grett."	
	Then gart he hang thos kynges,	*ordered those kings hung*
	als other had bene before,	
	And sythyn of other thynges	*then*
3000	sone made he maystry more.	

[SOUTHERN CANAAN CONQUERED (10:28–43)]

251.

	Sex cytes wan thei that same day	*Six cities they won*
	and on the morn als other mo.	*as many more*
	To Galgala then toke thei way	*Gilgal*
	unto ther frendes that thei wentt fro.	*allies; left behind*
3005	Of all this fayre full fayn ware thei	*these happenings very glad*
	and thanked God wherso thei go.	
	Then made thei myrth and mekyll play;	*much play*
	thei wyst of non to werke them wo.	*knew*
	Bot sone aftur thei war	*they were*
3010	noyd of new maner:	*troubled with a new problem*

Kyng Jabyn of Dasore   *Jabin of Hazor*
   geydderd full grett power   *gathered*

[NORTHERN CANAAN CONQUERED (11:1–12:24)]

252.
Of kynges and dukes and mony a knyght,
   that wysly cowd the wepyns weld;   *knew how; wield*
3015 Thre hunderth chareottes hath he dyght   *chariots*
   of vetell and tentes with to teld,   *victuals and tents to pitch*
Fowr hunderth thowssand folke to fyght
   Full well at hors with spere and scheld.
To see that was a semly syght   *wondrous sight*
3020 when that thei fared furth on the feld.   *went out*
When Ebrews con them se,
   thei ware adred sum dele,   *were frightened somewhat*
Bot God sayd unto Josue
   he suld overcom them well.

253.
3025 Duke Josue and Fynyes   *Phinehas*
   wold take no tyme to tary lang;   *wait long*
Thei putt them furth full fast in presse   *en masse*
   agayns ther enmys forto gang.   *against; to go*
Ther was no poynttyng unto peyse   *signaling of peace*
3030 bot ylk man his fere to fang.   *adversary to catch*
The Ebrews con ever incresse,   *grew strong*
   bot paynyms toyght the stoure full strang: *the pagans thought the battle*
Thei had no strengh to stand
   agayns Goddes folke to stryfe.
3035 Of faur hunderth thowssand   *400,000 [men]*
   ther leved bot few on lyfe.   *remained only a few alive*

254.
Ther chareys was fest on fyr ylkon   *Every one of their chariots was set on fire*
   with vessell and with mony a tent.
Thei spoled and spylt and spared non,
3040 tyll all was wast and schamly schent.   *shamefully destroyed*
Bot tresour to them have thei tone;   *taken*
   Cytes and burghes have thei brent.   *Cities and towns; burned*
When thei had wonn so welth gud wone,   *in abundance*
   to Galgala agayn thei went.   *Gilgal*
3045 Then was none leved in land,   *no one left*
   kyng ne prince with pryde,   *nor*
That them durst more gayn stand,   *That any more dared stand against them*
   ne in batell them abyd.

255.

    Ne forto fle war leved bot fone;   *Nor were any left to flee but a few*

3050   thei conquerd all thos cuntreys clene.   *whole*

    Thyrty kynges to ded was done   *death*

      withowtyn dukes and knyghtes kene.   *keen*

    Bott all this werke was not wroght sone;   *done quickly*

      thei toke full mony tym betwene.   *a great amount of time*

3055   Then forto noye them fand thei none,   *to trouble*

      bot all on myrth thei wold mene.   *in joy*

    Thei made grett sacurfyce

      unto God Allmighty,

    Wyt wrschepe on this wyse,   *Did worship in this way*

3060   als yt was well worthy.

[Division of the land (13:1–19:51)]

256.

    Duke Josue then folke arayse   *gathered*

      on Sylo. That was a solempne syght.   *at Shiloh*

    And all thus to them he says,

      "Hevys up your hertes to God on hyght

3065   And wrschep Hym with wyll all ways

      that now hath fulfylled that He heyght   *what He promised*

    In Abraham and in Ysac days:

      that thei suld have this remes be ryght   *these realms by right*

    To them and ther ofspryng

3070   and weld yt with honowrs.

    For now is all that hetyng   *are all those promises*

      fulfylled in us and ours.

257.

    "The grownd therof in them begane   *foundation [of this promise]*

      and past furth to ther progenyté.

3075   Yow menys how Moyses commawnd then   *remember*

      to us and to all our cumpany,

    'Qwen ye have conqwerde Canan   *When*

      and hath yt at your awn maystry,   *under your own control*

    Depart yt als wele os ye cane   *Divide*

3080   to the twelf kynradyns communly.'   *twelve tribes*

    Thus was his bydyng last,

      and so part yt we sall.

    Sythyn sall we lottes cast

      qwylke part to qwylke sall fall."   *which; which [tribe]*

258.

3085   Ten of the wysest furth can fayre

      and mett the land in lengh and bred.   *measured*

When thei had done that charge and charre,   *chore*
   agayn then hastely can thei sped.   *back again*
Then Josue and Elezaar
3090   to ylke a kynradyn toke gud hede   *each of the tribes*
And gafe ylkon aftur thei wayre   *each one according to whether they were*
   mony or few ther on to fede.   *feed [themselves]*
So wentt thei all and sum
   aftur ther cowrsc was cast.
3095   And thei beyond the flome   *river [of Jordan]*
   unto ther partes past.   *to their lands went*

[JOSHUA'S FAREWELL AND DEATH (23:1–24:33)]

259.
Qwen twenty yeres war full spend
   fro tyme thei past Flome Jordayn,   *the River Jordan*
Then Josue full clere kend   *very clearly knew*
3100   that he most passe by kynd of man.   *pass by the natural course of man*
Aftur the Ebrews hath he sent,
   and to them thus sayd he than,
"Syrs, I may no langer lend   *remain*
   to governe yow, ose I began.
3105   My tyme neghys nere   *grows near*
   that me behovys fownd yow fro.   *I must leave you*
My consell sall ye heyre   *counsel shall you hear*
   and takes gud tent therto.   *pay careful attention to*

260.
"Honowrs God ever, old and yyng,
3110   and kyndly kepes Hys commawndment.   *naturally keep*
And coveyttes now non other kyng,
   bot trows in Hym with trew entent.   *trust; proper will*
Whyls ye do so, all erthly thyng
   that nedfull is is to yow sent.   *that you need*
3115   And what tyme ye breke this bydyng,   *command*
   full sodanly ye sall be schent.   *destroyed*
Hath mynd, both more and lesse,   *Keep in mind*
   what dedes He for yow dyde   *deeds*
And of seyre grett kyndnese   *the many*
3120   He to your kyndradyn kyde.   *to your tribes showed*

261.
"He lede them fayr fro Fayran   *far from Pharaoh*
   and mad ther way thrugh waters clere
And drowned ther enmys ylkon
   that none with noye myght neghe them nere,   *harassment*
3125   And sythyn in wyldernes gud wone   *then during their long sojourn*

sent them of foyde full faurty yere.   *food for*
This land to ther lynag alon   *people alone*
    He heyght, and now ye have yt here.
Therfor forgeyttes Hym noyght
3130   bot nevyn Hym in your nede.   *invoke*
Whyls ye of Hym hath toyght,   *While you have Him in mind*
    allway ye sall well spede.   *always*

262.
"I warn yow all so and all Ebrews
    that ar of Jacob kynradyn knawn   *Jacob's kindred*
3135 That ye comyn not with Cananews,   *commune*
    nor with non nacion bot your awn.   *nation*
For yf ye mell yow with swylke schrews,   *mix yourself with such cursed people*
    in donger sone sall ye be drawn.
And whyls ye use all honest thews,   *while you; habits*
3140   full savely sall your sede be sawn."   *seed be sewn*
Thus lerned he lest and most   *taught he one and all*
    to eschew all yll thyng.   *bad things*
And then he gafe his gost   *gave over his soul*
    to Goddes awn goveryng.

263.
3145 Thus qwen this nobyll duke was ded,   *when*
    the folke made doyle withowtyn drede.   *grief certainly*
And whyls thei wroyght aftur his rede,   *performed after his advice*
    thei had lordschep of ylke led.   *each nation*
Elezaar, ther sufferan hed,   *Eleazar, their sovereign chief-priest*
3150   the same way sone aftur yode.   *soon afterward went*
And hys sun Fynyes in his sted   *Phinehas; place*
    was ordand furth thos folke to led.
This boke ys of Josue
    sen tyme thei past the flome.   *since; passed the river*
3155 And other new say sall we;   *narrate*
    that is called Judicum.   *Judges*

JUDICUM.

[CONQUEST OF CANAAN COMPLETED (1:1–36)]

264.

When Josue, that gentyll knyght,   *Joshua*
    was hent to Hevyn, ose men may here,   *as men can hear*
The Ebrews, men of grett myght,   *strength*
3160   then leved in myrth full mony a yere.   *joy*
And forto wyn that was ther ryght   *to win that [land] was their right*
    sadly thei soyght on sydes sere,   *many sides*
And Fynys for them to fyght   *Phinehas*
    ferd with the folke both farre and nere.   *fared; far and near*
3165 The cyté of Salem
    in the sort of Bynjamyn,   *holdings*
Sythen cald Jerusalem,   *Then*
    that went thei forto wyn.

265.

The cyté was both lang and wyde,
3170   warded and walled full well for were.   *guarded; for war*
Thei segede yt on ylka syde   *besieged; each side*
    with men of ermys and other geyre.   *arms; gear*
The Cananews war bold to byde;   *endure*
    thei dowtede non to do them dere.   *feared none; harm*
3175 Bot at the last layd was ther pride;   *laid [low]*
    thei fand full fell folke them to fere.   *found a very strong people; frighten*
Had thei lufed God lely,   *loyally*
    no man myght them have noyde.   *destroyed*
Thei lyved in mawmentry,   *idolatry*
3180   that dyde them be dystroyde.   *caused*

266.

The Ebrews enturd as thei toyght,   *desired*
    and all ther enmys fast thei feld.   *felled*
Thei spoled and spylt and spared noyght   *nothing*
    bot tresour that thei toke unteld.   *untold*

3185	And when thei hade ther werkes wroyght,	*deeds*
	at home no langer thei them held,	*remained*
	Bot in Ebron fast have soyght	*Hebron*
	unto mowntans wher gyantes dweld.	*giants lived*
	When Fynyes them fand,	*found*
3190	he stroyde them in a thrawe	*destroyed; brief time*
	And delyverd all ther land	*their*
	to clerkes that keped the law.	*who maintained*

267.

	Thei conqwerd marches, lesse and more,	*borderlands*
	and welth enogh so can thei wyne.	*wealth; did they win*
3195	Bot Salem, os I sayd before,	
	fell in the sort of Byngemyn,	*holdings of Benjamin*
	And therfor thus was ordand thore	
	that thei and thers suld dwell therin.	
	That cyté sone can thei restore	
3200	in grett comforth to all ther kyn.	*family*
	Thei partyde them amang	*shared among themselves*
	thresour by chaunse to chesse,	*treasures chosen by lot (chance)*
	And so all can thei gang	*go*
	unto ther awn cetyse.	*their own cities*

268.

3205	Thus ware the Ebrews ylkon	*every one*
	logyde in the land of Canan.	*established*
	Thei had no lord bot God allon	*alone*
	forto do sewtt ne servyce than.	*homage nor service then*
	Ne forto noye them fand thei none,	*harm*
3210	The commawnmentes kepe whyls thei cane.	*[were] kept; can*
	Bot hastely thei hath mysgone,	*soon; misbehaved*
	and Bynjamyns folke fyrst begane.	*began [the trouble]*
	Both Moyses and Josue	
	bad that thei suld them kepe	*keep themselves [away]*
3215	Fro folke of that cuntré	*(i.e., Canaanites)*
	and paynems feleschepe.	*pagan fellowship (i.e., contact with Gentiles)*

269.

	The lordes of Bynjamyn lynage	*lineage*
	to breke this bedyng hath begune,	*command*
	When thei sufferd for certan stage	*a certain time*
3220	the hethyn men amang them wun,	*to live*
	And towns lett thei for tripage,	*subjected; tribute*
	wherin Philystyyns was fun.	*were found*
	And paynyms, both man and page,	*pagans; boy*
	to be ther servandes hath thei bun.	*taken*
3225	And evyn os thei began,	

all other soyne assent, · *other [Israelites] soon assented*
That unethes on man · *So that scarcely one*
  toke kepe to the commawndment.

270.

In hertes thei war so sterne and stowt, · *hearts; stout (i.e., hard-hearted)*
3230   for weltes of gud and grett maystri, · *wealth of goods; mastery [of lands]*
The law them lyst not leve ne lawt, · *pleased; believe; revere*
  bot lyved in lust and lechery.
By cawse thei had no werre withowt, · *wars without*
  amang them wex full grett envy, · *grew; contention*
3235 And the Bynjamyns was most abowt · *Benjaminites were most likely*
  to groche and greve God Allmighty. · *vex and anger*
That was schewed in schort tyd · *revealed in a short time*
  at the cyté of Gabaon, · *Gibeah*
Next Salen nere besyde, · *Jerusalem*
3240   how fowle ther thei fon. · *acted*

[THE INCIDENT AT GIBEAH; WAR AGAINST BENJAMIN (19:10–20:23)]

271.

Ther yt befell apon a day
  prowd Benjamyns with ther meneye · *company*
Wentt in a place them forto play
  befor the gattes of that ceté. · *(i.e., Gibeah)*
3245 An Ebrew com ther in the way · *An Israelite*
  with his wyfe, full fayre and fre.
Amang themself then can thei say,
  "Yond woman this nyght weld wyll we." · *possess*
Ther curstnes so the kyd, · *wickedness so they showed*
3250   qwat for scath and qwat for scorne, · *whether; harm; contempt*
For dedes thei to hyr dyde, · *deeds*
  scho was fun dede at morn. · *found dead*

272.

Hyr husband then had mekyll care; · *much sadness*
  no wonder was thof he were wo. · *that because of this he was woeful*
3255 The body he toke and with hym bare · *bore*
  to his cuntré, wher he com froo.
He sent to cetys lesse and more
  to Gabaon be lyfe at goo · *at once to go*
Thor forto venge that fellows fare. · *There to avenge that man's reception*
3260   And hastely thei hafe done so.
Bott thei that wroght this woghe · *woe*
  within ware sterne and stowt; · *inside [the city] were strong*
Ten thowsand sone thei sloghe · *soon they slew*
  of them that ware withowt. · *were outside [Gibeah]*

[THE DEFEAT OF BENJAMIN (20:24–46)]

273.

3265	Then ware the Ebrews put to payn,	
	for that asawt full sore them rews.	*they rue*
	For Fynyes then was not fayn	*pleased*
	of the feyghyng, for all ware Jews.	*fighting*
	His host he sembled sone agayn,	*assembled*
3270	and to the rebels he remews.	*and against; moves*
	Twenty milia sone ware slayn,	*20,000*
	for with them wold he take no trews.	*truce*
	Both wyf, chyld, and page	*boy*
	thei byrttynd sone and brent.	*immediately cut to pieces and burned*
3275	So was all that lynage	
	for ther syn schamly schent.	

[BENJAMIN REPOPULATED (20:47–21:24)]

274.

	Bycawse thei toke the trew manys wyfe,	
	that progenyté was put to pyn	
	Bot sex hunderth that fled on lyve.	*Except for 600 who fled alive*
3280	Ther lyved no mo of all that lyne,	
	Qwylke aftur, qwen thei toyght to thryve,	*Which; when; thought*
	with other Ebrews acordyd syne.	*[were] accorded then*
	And stylly so withowtyn stryfe	*quietly thus; battle*
	thei saved the sort of Benjamyne.	*people of Benjamin*
3285	All ther possessions playn	
	to them thei con restore	
	And so ordand agayn	
	twelfe, os thei ware before.	*twelve [tribes], as*

275.

	In Gabaon thei con them sese	*seize*
3290	with other cytes large and lang.	
	Then leved the Ebrews all at ese;	*lived; ease*
	wold non with greve agayn them gange.	*grievance against; go*
	Als lang os thei wold God plese,	
	was non in ward to wyrke them wrang.	*in [their] rule; wrong*
3295	And when thei melled other ways,	*But; did otherwise*
	sone mengyd myschef them amang.	*soon mischief mingled*
	When they left Moyses Law	*Moses' Law*
	and to maumentres theym mende,	*idolatry; turned*
	So Cananews couth knaw	*Canaanites came to know*
3300	that God was not ther frend.	

276.

	Then Fynyes dede aftur tytt	*Phinehas soon afterward died*
	that them to maynten ever hym melled.	*to assist them ever busied himself*
	Thei folowd all ther flesch delytt,	*their fleshly delights*
	and God His helpyng from them held.	*withheld*
3305	Then Cananews withowt respett	*respite*
	dang them down qwerso thei dweld:	*wheresoever*
	Thus scaped thei not undyscumfeytt;	*escaped; punishment*
	Fylysteyns in feldes them felled.	*Philistines; fields*
	Thus aboyde thei sorows sere,	*endured; many*
3310	and no wrschepe thei wan.	*honor; won*
	This lastyd twenty yere,	
	and thus fell aftur then.	

[THE JUDGES OTHNIEL, EHUD, AND SHAMGAR (3:9–31)]

277.

	A semly man, that Cenys hyght,	*seemly; was called Kenaz*
	of Judas generacion,	*Judah's tribe*
3315	He proferd hym for them to fyght	
	and unto batell mad hym bown.	*battle; ready*
	Phylysteyns he putt to the flyght	
	and feld ther foys in feld and town.	*felled their foes in field*
	Sythyn faurty yere he rewled them ryght	*Then; ruled*
3320	and dyed sone aftur that seson.	
	Then sone the folke can fon	*began to behave wrongly*
	and wroyght as wryches unwyse.	*wretches unwise*
	So come the kyng Eglon	*came [against them]; Eglon*
	with full mony Moabyse.	*Moabites*

278.

3325	He conquerde cuntres to and fro	
	and greved them with full grett owtrag:	*injury*
	Sum to byrn and sum to slo	*slay*
	and sum thei sett in sere servage.	*servitude*
	He toke the cyté of Jerico	
3330	and putt the pepyll to pay trypage.	*made; tribute*
	Hyt was his ded, for he dyed so;	*death*
	his lordschep last bot a lytill stage.	*little while*
	An Ebrew, that hyght Howade,	*Ehud*
	that well cowd plese and playn,	
3335	Made Kyng Eglon oft glade	*often happy*
	with fals talyes that he cowd feyne.	*false stories; feign*

279.

	Fell on a day the kyng and he	*It happened*
	ware in a chamber them alone.	*were*

3340	He slogh the kyng in prevyté	*slew; privacy*
	and laft hym ded, styll ose a stone.	
	And he wentt in the same ceté	
	and warned the Ebrews ylkon	*all*
	And bade thei suld son arayd be;	*should immediately be prepared*
	ther enmys suld als tytt be tone.	*quickly be taken*
3345	When Moabyse wyst ther kyng	*knew their*
	was so dede, sone thei remeved	*removed [themselves]*
	And fled both old and yyng,	
	and Ebrews fast persewed.	

280.

	In that persewyng hade thei payn:	
3350	ther wold no cety them socour.	*succor*
	Ten milia of them was slayn,	*10,000*
	so ware thei stound in that stoure.	*staggered in that battle*
	The Ebrews can then ordand	*did*
	Howade to be ther governowre.	*Ehud*
3355	To aghtene yeres was past playn,	*Until eighteen years were fully past*
	full surely saved he ther honour.	
	Then regned Senagar,	*Shamgar*
	that sex hunderth ons sloght	*once killed*
	Of panyms, that prowd ware,	*pagans; were*
3360	with a soke of a ploght.	*plowshare (coulter of a plow)*

[DEBORAH AND BARAK (4:1–5:31)]

281.

	Sythyn Ebrews assent to syn	*Then; assented to sin*
	and cowd not kepe ther laws clene,	*their laws*
	Then com on them Kyng Jabyn	*Jabin*
	with Cananews that ware full kene.	*keen*
3365	He wold no sesse to slo and byrn,	*cease to slay and burn*
	bot sone aftur hade he tene.	*pain*
	Two Ebrews, comyn of gentyll kyn,	*noble line*
	in batell to hym them betwene.	*took*
	Barrett and Debora	*Barak and Deborah*
3370	thus ware thei named thore,	
	And well goverand thei two	*those two*
	full faurty yere and more.	

[MIDIANITE OPPRESSION (6:1–6)]

282.

	When faurty yeres was fully past,	
	for thei to God ware ever grochand,	*complaining*
3375	In grett dyscumforth war thei cast	*discomfort*

for hungar that fell in that land.	*famine that occurred*
And sevyn wynters, so lang yt last,	
to sympyll folke no fode thei fand.	*food; found*
Then unto God thei cryed full fast	
3380 and prayd his help with hert and hand.	
For als thei fayled mett,	*even as they lacked food*
yett had thei mo enmys	*more enemies*
That dyde them grevance grett:	*distress*
Madyans and Malachys.	*the Midianites and Amalekites*

[CALL OF GIDEON (6:7–12)]

283.

3385 When thei to God ther kayrs knew,	*sorrows confessed*
how thei agayns Hys wyll were went,	*against; had gone*
On Gedion, a gentyll Jew	*One [man named] Gideon*
of ther awn lynage, hath He lent.	*their own people, God gave to them*
And for He in His trowth was trew,	*because; promise was true*
3390 God hath His angell to hym sent,	
Like unto a man in hyd and hew,	*flesh and appearance*
and told hym how His maker ment	*intended*
Forto aray hym ryght,	*arm*
both hert, hed, and hend.	*hand*
3395 And then wend furth to fyght,	*[he] went*
Goddes folke forto dyffend.	

284.

Gedeon was that same morne	*morning*
purveyd in a prevé stede	*private place*
To clepe his schepe and thresch his corne	*shear; thresh*
3400 so forto ordand cloghes and brede.	*make clothes and bread*
The angell that com hym beforne	
and broyght bodword os God hym bede,	*message; ordered*
He wened full well yt had ben scorne.	*fully imagined that it was a joke*
Therfor he was full wyll of rede	*counsel*
3405 And toyght he suld asay	*test*
by some experiment	
Whedder yt ware trew or nay	*true or not*
that God His servant had hym sent.	

[SIGN OF THE FLEECE (6:36–40)]

285.

A flesse he sprede befor his fette	*fleece; feet*
3410 on the erthe and all nyght lett yt ly.	*lie [there on the ground]*
He sayd, "Yf this flese be wett	
tomorn at morn and the moldes dry,	*tomorrow; earth is dry*

	Then wyll I trow and hertly hette	*believe and heartily be assured*
	this message is of God Allmighty."	
3415	On the morn full drye was all the strett,	*place*
	and the flese wett. That was ferly.	*wondrous*
	Then the contrary	*opposite*
	he ordand at evyn latte:	*bade late that evening*
	At the morne the flese was dry	
3420	and all the ways full waytte.	*wet*

[GIDEON'S ARMY CHOSEN (7:1–8)]

286.

	Gedion then trowed with trew entent	*believed*
	that thies tokyns was trew and ryght.	*signs were true*
	He told the folke Goddes commawndment	
	how he suld them dyffend in fyght.	
3425	He samed sone by on assent	*gathered soon by one*
	neyn milia to beyre armys bryght.	*9,000 [men] to bear arms*
	And God hym wysched, or ever he went,	*guided him, before*
	forto asay them in His syght.	*test*
	He sayd, "Wende to the flome	*Go; river*
3430	with all thi folke in fere	*together*
	And make them all and sum	
	to drynke of that water clere.	

287.

	"All thoo that on ther fette up standes	*those who on their feet stand up*
	and fenys not for scheld ne spere	*let go*
3435	Bot takes the watur up with ther handes	*their*
	to drynke, tho sall do enmys dere.	*do the enemy harm*
	And tho that lyges low on the sandes	*those who kneel*
	to drynke os a mule or a mere	*mare*
	Ledde them no ferther to other landes;	*Lead*
3440	thei ar not worth to wend in were."	*worthy to go in war*
	When thei com to the flude,	*river*
	ylk on heldyd down his hede.	*each one bent down*
	Of tho that evyn up stude	*still*
	ware bot thre hunderth leved.	*remaining*

[GIDEON ROUTS THE MIDIANITES (7:9–8:27)]

288.

3445	When Gedion saw that yt was so,	
	his hert began to hover and hone:	*waver and hesitate*
	He wyst panyms wer mony moe,	*pagans were many more [in number]*
	for of his folke wer left bot fone.	*only few*
	Bot God bad he suld boldly go	*ordered*

3450	and mell with them both morn and none.	*intermix with them (the enemy)*
	"For sone," he sayd, "thou sall them slo."	*slay*
	And als he demed, so was yt done.	*decreed*
	Oreb and Zebe, thei two	*Oreb and Zeeb*
	the hethyn folke con lede,	
3455	Zebee and Salmana,	*Zebah and Zalmunna*
	tho faur dyed at that dede.	*died at that battle*

[DEATH OF GIDEON; RISE AND FALL OF ABIMALECH (8:28–9:57)]

289.

	All ware thei dede and dyscumfeyt,	*dead and discomfited*
	the hethyn folke fully in fere.	*heathen; all together*
	Bot all this was not done so tytt;	*quickly*
3460	that batell was full strang to stere.	*very difficult to manage*
	Gedion to rewle them had respeyt	*rule; respite*
	in rest and pese full faurty yere.	*peace for forty years*
	He leved lyfand withowtyn lyte	*left alive without flaw*
	sexty fayr suns of wemen sere.	*sixty fair sons from many mothers*
3465	The eldyst, Abymalech,	*Abimalech*
	putt his brethyr to pyn;	*brothers to pain*
	He wrogh a wofull cheke,	*slaughter*
	that slogh fyfty and neyne.	*slew*

290.

	When he had so his brethyr sloyn,	*brothers slain*
3470	of Sychym was he soveran syre.	*Shechem; sovereign sire*
	Bot God hath vengiance on hym tane	*taken*
	that sone he past fro that empyre:	*at once he disappeared*
	Hys harnys was strekyn owt with a stone;	*brain was struck out*
	he served to have no bettur hyre.	*end*
3475	Then ware the Ebrews left alon;	*alone*
	ylkon mygh do ther awn desyre.	
	Of God thei had non aw	*no awe (reverence)*
	for gold and grett maystry.	
	Therfor thei left His law	
3480	and lyved in mawmentry.	*idolatry*

[OPPRESSION BY THE AMMONITES (10:6–18)]

291.

	Thei mad them goddes of gold and brasse	*themselves gods*
	and sayd tho same ther seyle had sent.	*those; their happiness*
	Then God full gretly greved was	
	that thei so wrang agayns Hym went.	
3485	Enmys He putt on thcm to passe	
	that them slow and ther cetes brynt	*killed them; cities burned*

	To tym thei kneled and cryd "alas"	*Until [such] time [as]*
	and turned to God with gud entent.	
	When thei ther trespasse knew,	*trespasses confessed*
3490	God send them sone socour:	
	On Gepte, a gentyll Jew,	*One Jephthah*
	to be ther governowre.	

[JEPHTHAH (11:1–28)]

292.

	Gepte was a knyght in armys clere;	*bright*
	fro bayle, he sayd, he suld them bryng.	*confinement*
3495	A fayre lady he hade to fere,	*to spouse*
	and both thei lyvyd to Goddes lovyng.	
	He had a doyghtur that was hym dere	*[to] him dear*
	and no mo chyldder, old ne yyng.	*no more children, old nor young*
	To hyr befell, os men may heyre,	*her; hear*
3500	full gret myschefe, a mervel thyng.	*strange*
	He send to cetys and town,	*cities*
	to all that myght armys beyre	*bear*
	And bad thei suld be bown	*bade; ready*
	to wend with hym in were.	*go; war*

[JEPHTHAH'S VOW (11:29–33)]

293.

3505	Then unto God hertly he hett	*heartily; promised*
	and mad a vowe with all his mayne:	*strength*
	That yf he myght the maystry geytt,	*victory get*
	als sone os he com home agayn,	*as soon as*
	The fyrst qwyke catell that he mett	*living creature*
3510	of his for Goddes sake suld be slayn,	*God's sake should*
	In sacrafyce so forto sett.	*thus to set*
	Thus sayd he suld be done certayn.	
	To batell then thei went	
	withowtyn more respyte.	
3515	Ther enmys sone was schent,	*enemies soon were destroyed*
	both slayn and dyscumfeytt.	*defeated*

[JEPHTHAH'S DAUGHTER (11:34–12:7)]

294.

	Then past thei home with mekyll pride	*journeyed; much*
	becawse thei wan the vyctory.	*won*
	His doyghghtur herd, is not to hyde,	*heard, it cannot be hidden*
3520	hyr fader suld come home in hy.	*haste*
	Be lyfe scho went, and wold not byd,	*Quickly; wait*

agayns hym with gud mynstralsy. *toward; singing*
When he hyr saw, "Alas!" he crycd,
"My doyghghtur dere, now sall thou dy!" *shall you die*
3525 To his hors fette he fell — *horse's feet*
in sadyll he myght not sytte. *saddle*
No tong in erth may tell *tongue*
what kare his hert had hytt. *grief; struck*

295.
So when he myght hymselfe stere, *control*
3530 he toyght in hert how he had heyght: *promised*
To slo the fyrst that suld apeyre *slay*
and sacrafyce yt in Goddes syght.
"Alas," he sayd, "my doyghghtur dere,
for my doyng thi dede is dyght." *death is assured (predestined)*
3535 Scho prayd hyr fader to mend his chere *amend his mood*
and mad hym myrth all that scho myght. *made*
The more that scho mad glee
to comforth hym with all,
The more sore hert had he, *heart*
3540 for he wyst how yt suld fall. *knew; befall*

296.
"A, doyghtur," he sayd, "I made a vowe
to God when I to batell wentt:
Yf I of panyms myght have prow, *over the pagans; victory*
what so com fyrst in my present, *presence*
3545 That suld be slone — that same ys thou. *slain*
Alas for my sake now bees thou schent." *you will be killed*
"Fader," scho sayd, "I beseke yow
be trew and tornes not your entent. *true; turn*
For bettur is that I dye,
3550 that may no thyng avayle, *avail*
Then so fayr cumpany *Than*
os ye broyght from batelle.

297.
"Sen ye heyght sacrafyce to make *Since you promised*
to God that goverans gud and yll, *who governs*
3555 Leues it not, fader, for my sake *Abandon*
bot all your forward fast fulfyll. *promise precisely fulfill*
Bot graunteys me grace two wekes to wake, *grant; two weeks to mourn*
to speke with lades lowd and styll, *ladies publicly and privately*
And of maydyns leve to take,
3560 and then do with me what ye wyll."
He gafe hyre leve to gang *gave her permission to go*
with grefe and gretyng sore. *weeping sorrow*

| | All that scho come amang | *Everyone* |
| | ay menyd hyr more and more. | *always grieved for her* |

298.

3565 So went scho furth to mony a frend,
          that for hyre syghyng sayd, "Alas!"
      All weped for wo os scho can wend,   *woe as she did come [among them]*
          when thei wyst how that it was.   *knew*
      And when the tyme drogh nere the end   *drew near*
3570   that hyr fader assygned has,
      Scho went agayn with wordes hend   *courteous*
          and proferd hyr with payn to pas.   *get on*
      Therfor hyr fader noyght leved;   *delayed not*
          his sword in hand he hent   *took*
3575 And swythly swopped of hyr hede   *quickly struck off her head*
          and bad scho suld be brent.   *ordered [that] she should be burned*

299.

      Grett sorow yt was this syght to se;
          all weped that wyst of hyr wo.   *wept*
      Bot most sorow in hert had he
3580   that heddyd hyr and had no mo.   *beheaded her; more [children]*
      Swylke folys suld men be fayn to flee   *Such follies; eager to avoid*
          and be avysed or thei vow so.   *considerate before*
      Foyle vow is bettur to broken be   *[A] foolish vow*
          then man or woman sakles slo.   *than; guiltless slain*
3585 Sex yere governd Gepte Ebrews   *Six years*
          and saved them from all angers yll
      Both of Phylysteyns and Cananews,
          and then he dyed os was Goddes wyll.

[JUDGES IBZAN, ELON, AND ABDON (12:8–15)]

300.

      Next aftur Gepte regned Abessan,   *reigned Ibzan*
3590   os clerkes knawn that con theron.   *acknowledge who know about it*
      Grett wrschep in his tym he wan,   *honor; won*
          and aftur hym regned Achyron   *Elon*
      Ten yere; and aght yere aftur than   *eight years afterward*
          gufernd a gud man, hyght Abdon.   *called Abdon*
3595 And sythyn thei hade no mayster man: *then they (the Israelites)*
          that mad them fowly to fone.   *made; foully to live*
      Thei forsoke Goddes servyce
          and to mawmentes tham ment.   *idols; returned*
      Therfor with sere enmys   *many enemies*
3600   sone ware thei schamed and schent.   *shamed and killed*

[BIRTH OF SAMSON (13:1–24)]

301.

To God thei fast con call and crye
    and dyd grett penance for ther plyght.
And He ordand then helpe in hye.   *ordained; haste*
    An nobyll man, that Many hyght,   *Manoah was called*
3605   Was haldyn chcfe of chewalry   *considered supreme in chivalry*
    and had to wyfe a worthy wyght.   *person*
Bot chylder bare scho non hym by;   *children bore she*
    therfor scho drowped day and nyght.   *drooped (moped)*
Grett mornyng made that myld   *mourning; gentle [woman]*
3610   and prayd in town and feld   *field (i.e., everywhere)*
That God suld send sum chyld
    that myght ther welthes weld.   *their happiness secure*

302.

So ose scho prayd with hert and hend, *heart and hand (i.e., with all her being)*
    hyrselfe alone in her selere,   *private room*
3615   An angell saw scho by hyr lend   *her standing*
    in forme of man with face full clere.   *bright*
"Woman," he sayd, "thi mornyng mend;   *amend*
    God takes entent to thi prayer.   *heed*
A sone He sall to thee send,
3620   that sall governe tho folke in fere.   *those peoples together*
Of myght sall none be more   *strength*
    on mold amang mankynd.   *earth*
I warne thee thus before,
    as thou sall forther fynd.

303.

3625   "The Ebrews that in bayle ar brast   *captivity are bound*
    sall he dyffend with forse in fyght.   *force*
Cutt not hys hare of for no hast,   *his hair off for any reason*
    for therin sall be most his myght.
Ne lycour loke he non tast   *Nor liquor allow; taste*
3630   to make hym dronkyn day or nyght,   *drunk*
For therwith may his wyttes be wast   *wits be wasted*
    to werke wrang, all yf he be wyght."   *brave*
When he had told this tale,
    no ferther of hym scho fand.   *found*
3635   Scho toyght hyr hert was hale   *thought; glad (whole)*
    for joy of this tythand.   *message*

304.

Unto hyr lord sone can scho tell   *her lord (husband)*
    of all this case, os scho can kayre:

	How scho was werned with Goddes angell	
3640	to beyr a chyld to be ther ayre,	*bear; their heir*
	And how he suld be ferse and fell	*fierce and fell*
	and his forse in his fax suld fayre.	*strength; hair*
	The gud man sayd, "No more thou mell;	*speak*
	of swylke dedes I am in dyspayre."	*events*
3645	He trowde yt bot a trayn,	*believed; trick*
	and to hymself he sayd,	
	"Sum foyle to make hyr fayn	*fool; glad*
	hath broyght hyr in this brayde."	*deception*

305.

	Than all thof scho before was glade	*Then although*
3650	throgh bodword of the angell bryght,	*good news*
	Sone was scho sore and sume dele rade	*Now; she annoyed; a bit angry*
	bycause hyr lord sett yt so lyght.	
	Scho prayd to God with semland sade	*a grave face*
	to send sume tokyn to his syght.	*some sign*
3655	So that he myght have, als scho hade,	
	gud hertyng from Hevyn on hyght.	*good hearing*
	Hymselfe made sacrafyce	*[Manoah] himself*
	and prayd God of His grace	
	Forto wytt on what wyse	*know in what way*
3660	this process com in place.	

306.

	Sone aftur this then fell yt so,	*it befell*
	as thei prayd both with stabyll stevyn,	*voices*
	God send His angell to them two,	
	and that same note he can them nevyn.	*news; mention*
3665	Manne then toke tent therto	*Manoah; took heed*
	and loved the Lord of Lyght and Levyn.	*Lightning*
	For when the angell ferd them fro,	*went from them*
	thei saw how he was hent to Hevyn.	*taken*
	The wyfe sone wex with chyld	*grew*
3670	and bare withowtyn blame	*bore without blemish*
	A barne to be ther byld.	*child; their comfort*
	Sampson thei cald his name.	*Samson*

[SAMSON'S YOUTH (13:25)]

307.

	Phylysteyns had then maystry,	
	And Ebrews was withowtyn beld.	*comfort*
3675	This chyld was tent full tenderly;	*attended [to]*
	all wold his hele that hym beheld.	*desired his safety*
	To batell bede he his body,	*he took his*

as sone ose hee myght wepyns weld.   *soon as; weapons wield*
On mold was no man so myghty;   *earth*
3680   The Phylystyens his felnes feld,   *fierceness felt*
Ay whyls he leved Goddes law   *All the while*
   and keped His commawndment.
All men of hym had aw,   *awe*
   in werld wherever he wentt.

308.
3685   His moder herd the angell say
   how that hys hore suld not be schorne.   *hair; shorn*
Therfor scho dyde yt wex allway;   *allowed it to grow*
   so wex his myght mydday and morne.   *thus grew his strength*
Phylesteyns oft can he flay   *terrify*
3690   that was full fers and fell beforne,   *fierce*
Tyll ay at the last he lufed ther lay   *Until; loved their law*
   and went with them that wold hym scorne
To ther cyté that heyght   *their city that was called*
   Tanna, with thourys clene.   *Timnah*
3695   Thor saw he sone a syght,   *There*
   that sythyn turned hym to tene.   *later; sadness*

[SAMSON AND A PHILISTINE WOMAN (14:1–4)]

309.
Evyn os he enturd that ceté,   *as; city*
   a semly madyn sone he mett,   *beautiful maiden soon*
Of fygur fayre and face full free;
3700   with full grett gladschepe scho hym grett.   *gladness she greeted him*
Hym toyght her semly on to se;   *He thought; look*
   hys hert at all on hyr was sett,
And to hyr kynradyn carped he   *kindred he announced*
   that hyr to wed wold he not lett.   *hesitate*
3705   Then was the Phylesteyns fayn   *glad*
   to gare hym luf ther lay,   *cause; [to] love their ways*
For thei trowde by sum trayn   *intended by some guile*
   sum tyme hym to betray.

310.
He playd hym thor lang os hym lyst   *there [as] long as he desired*
3710   with mekyll myrth betwen them twa.   *much mirth; two*
His kynrede of this werke noyght wyst,   *family; knew not*
   for that cety was farre them fro.
His moyder morned, fro scho hym myst.   *mourned; missed*
   Then toke he his leve in Tanna   *Timnah*
3715   And turned agayn unto his trest,   *trusty ones*
   his frendes that sojornde in Sarra.   *Zorah*

He told them tales to the end
  of his dedes day and nyght,   *deeds*
And of that maydyn hende,   *fair maiden*
3720   how he hys hert hade heyght.   *heart had promised*

311.
His moyder mornyd, and mony moe   *many more [did so, too]*
  qwen thei herd tell of this tythyng.   *news*
Bot no of them durst say hym so   *dared*
  to wreth hym, all yf he was kyng.   *anger*
3725   His fader sayd betwen them two,
  "Sun, yt is no semly thyng   *seemly*
With Philysteyns us forto go;
  thei hatte us Ebrews, old and yynge.   *hate; Hebrews*
And Moyses in his law
3730   amonyst, als us menys,   *admonished, as we recall*
That we suld ever us withdraw
  fro fals Phylysteyns.

312.
"Us ow to lufe God Allmighty,   *We ought to love*
  as our forme faders dyd beforne.   *founding fathers did before*
3735   Phylesteyns makes them mawmentry   *for themselves idols*
  and honers them both evyn and morn.   *honor*
Therfor, dere sone, sett not therby.
  We have thee sayved sen thou was borne;   *preserved since*
Sayve now thiselfe fro socerry,   *sorcery (corruption)*
3740   els may thou lyghtly be forlorne."   *forsaken*
His moyder weped allway   *wept*
  and sayd he suld be schent.   *destroyed*
Bot all that thei cowde say
  myght not turne his entent.   *alter*

313.
3745   And when thei saw yt myght not spede   *help*
  more forto lerne hym lowd ne styll,   *teach him publicly or privately*
Sum dele for luf, sum dele for drede,   *Somewhat for love, somewhat for fear*
  thei grawntt hym to have his wyll.
Sone afturward all same thei yode   *all together they went*
3750   this foly forward to fulfyll,   *silly promise*
And with fayr wordes tho folke to fede,   *those folk (the Philistines) to feed*
  throw spech yf thei myght yt spyll.   *through speeches to see if they might undo it*
So soyght thei fro Sarra   *Zorah*
  by wuddes and wastes wyld   *woods and wild wastes*
3755   And toke the way to Tanna   *Timnah*
  with Sampson, ther semly chyld.   *fair*

[SAMSON KILLS A LION (14:5–9)]

314.
Then of sum torfurs men may tell,   *troubles*
  qwylke in that tyme to hym betyde.   *which*
For os thei wentt, swylke ferles fell,   *such marvels happened*
3760   his herdenes may not be hyde.   *[that] his hardiness; hid*
Behynd his frendes os he con dwcll,
  under a wud syde what so he dyde,   *wooded area whatever he was doing*
A lyon come hym forto qwell,   *lion; kill*
  for he saw none with hym abyde.   *he (the lion); waiting*
3765   And the lyon ther he slogh   *he (Samson) killed*
  evyn his twa handes betwen   *only his two hands*
And tyll a dyke hym drogh,   *into a ditch he dragged it*
  for he suld not be sene.   *seen*

315.
When he had doyn this doyghty dede,   *brave deed*
3770   that non wyst of bot only hee,   *knew*
Aftur his frendes full fast he yede,   *went*
  os thei raked to that rych ceté.   *progressed*
Thor fand thei folke full fayre to fede,   *There found; feed*
  of Phylysteyns full grett plenté.
3775   Bot that thei hethyn lyve can lede,   *Except; led [a] heathen's life*
  more plesand pepyll myght non be.   *pleasing*
To Manne and his fere   *Manoah; company*
  full grett myrth can thei make
And gaf them drewres dere   *dowries dear*
3780   for Sampson, ther sun, sake.   *their son's sake*

316.
To loke his lufe he wold nott lett   *look [on]; cease*
  for nothyng that myght betyde.
Befor hyr frendes furth was scho sett
  with mynstralcy and mekyll pryde.   *songs and much pride*
3785   Qwen Manne and that meneye mett   *When; company met*
  and cause of ther comyng dyscryde,   *was made known*
A certan seson sone was sett,   *certain date soon*
  and sewrty layd for ayder syde   *securities laid; either*
That Sampson suld hyre wede   *would her wed*
3790   be swylke a certayn day.   *such*
His frendes was sore adrede,   *afraid*
  bot thei durst not say nay.   *dared*

317.
When all was sett so in certayn,   *certainty*
  thei sojournd thor bot schort seson.   *remained there only a short time*

3795	Full fast thei hyed them home agayn	*hastened*
	to Sarra, a cety of renown.	
	Sampson was of this fayre full fayn;	*pleased*
	to batell fast he made hym bown.	*ready*
	He kyd that he was mekyll of mayn;	*knew; great of strength*
3800	Phylesteyns oft fast dang he down.	*struck*
	Thai that ware all abufe	*all above [the ground]*
	and leved ay so to last,	*believed ever thus to endure*
	He putt them to reprove	*reproof*
	in all place wher he past.	*places; passed*

318.

3805	All Ebrews folke he can dyffend	
	and made fre that before was thrall.	*free; enslaved*
	And when the tym come nere the ende	*came near*
	that was ordand amang them all,	
	Hys kynradyn holl that he kend	*family whole; honored*
3810	bade he to be at his brydall.	*wedding*
	And os thei ydderward can wend,	*as they thitherward*
	a farly fare yett can fall:	*wondrous thing*
	That place persayved he	*perceived*
	wher he the lyon slogh,	*slew*
3815	And the bayns forto se	*bones*
	to the dyke he hym drogh.	*ditch he drew himself*

319.

	Evyn to that corse hys cowrse he kest,	*corpse his course he followed*
	and sone he fand the bones dry.	*soon he found*
	Bees in the mowth had mad ther nest;	*made*
3820	a honycame he fand in hy.	*honeycomb he found*
	He brake yt owt, so toyght hym best,	*broke*
	and menyd to make some bourd therby.	*intended; jest*
	Then raked he furth withowtyn rest	
	tyll he come to his cumpany.	
3825	With the fayrest hony he fede	*fed*
	his fader and moyder also,	
	And sythyn he brake and beyd	*then he broke and gave*
	to other frendes moo.	*more [of it]*

[SAMSON'S MARRIAGE (14:10–11)]

320.

	And sum dele held he styll in store	
3830	forto part with his paramowre,	*beloved*
	For of all wemen that then wore	*were [living]*
	of fayrnes myght scho beyre the floure.	*bear the flower (be the best)*
	And hastely when thei come thore,	

thei ware resayved with grett honowur.
3835   And to fulfyll forward before,   *covenant*
        assygned thei certan day and howre.
    Sampson wede that free   *wedded that lovely damsel*
        with both ther frendes assent,   *their friends' assent*
    With all solempnité,
3840   and myrth that myght be ment.

321.

    Thor was solace of servyce sere;   *diverse courses*
        thei had sene non swylke bot the same.   *seen nothing like it until this*
    Both beyrys and bullys and baran dere,   *bears; bulls; fallow deer*
        ther wanted none wyld ne tame.   *there none lacked wild or domesticated meat*
3845   Of turnamentes ther men myght lere;   *tournaments where*
        who wold not hurle, hald hym at hame.   *joust, kept himself*
    Bot to Sampson durst non apeyre: *none dared challenge*
        all dowt his hand that herd his name,   *feared*
    Becawse he was so strang.
3850   The Phylysteyns forthi   *therefore*
    Ordand them amang
        of tresty men thrytty,   *thirty trustworthy men*

322.

    Qwylke thei well wyst was wyse and wyght   *knew were wise and capable*
        and stalworthest in stede and stall,   *in every way*
3855   Forto be nere hym day and nyght
        for ferd of fare that myght befall.   *fear of events that might happen*
    And when Sampson persayved that syght
        and all ther gawdes, grett and small,   *tricks*
    A reson he devysyd and dyght
3860   forto asay ther wyttes withall.   *test their wits*
    Of the lyon that he slogh   *slew*
        and of the came with hony   *comb with honey*
    He made game gud enoght   *good enough*
        forto abays them by.   *abash*

[SAMSON'S RIDDLE (14:12–18)]

323.

3865   "Sers," he sayd, "I sall yow tell
        a taylle that sall our bowrdyng be,   *entertainment*
    And yf ye thrytty yow amell   *among*
        what it suld sygnyfye can see,
    Thrytty cloghes of sylke to sell   *garments of silk*
3870   sall I gyfe yow in gud degré,   *shall I give*
    And yf ye fayle how yt befell,   *fail*
        so mony sall ye gyf to me.

Avyse yow in your mode;   *Consider; mind*
   the question this es: *is this*
3875   Owt of the herd come fode,   *strong [thing] came food*
   and of the swalowand swettenes."   *swallowing [thing came] sweetness*

324.

To them this reson he arayd
   and bad thei suld that case dyscrye.   *expound*
Of the purpas thei ware not payd,   *task; glad*
3880   bot his wyll durst thei not denye.   *dared*
Of sevyn days respeyt thei hym prayd,   *For; respite*
   to be avysed therfor fully.   *take counsel*
"I grawntt your askyng, sers," he sayd,
   and with tho wordes thei went in hy.   *those; haste*
3885   Thei dyde ther besenes   *their busyness*
   this ylke lesson to lere.   *same answer to learn*
Bot what the menyng was
   cowd thei not all cum nere.

325.

When thei had soyght faur days or fyve
3890   by consell of ther clergy clene   *counselors; their simple clergy*
And oft reherssed this lesson ryve,   *often; frequently*
   thei cowde not say what yt suld mene.   *mean*
Then ware thei stede to strutt and stryve.   *disposed; strive [in anger]*
   So sayd on that had mekyll sene: *one; much seen (experienced)*
3895   "We wytt yt never bot yf his wyfe   *unless*
   may geytt yt told them two betwen.
Sen scho ys of our kyn,   *Since*
   assay hyr sone we sall.   *ask her soon*
So may we wrschep wyn."   *honor*
3900   To this assentt thei all.

326.

Two wysest of them to hyre wentt   *her*
   and sayd, "Syster, thiselfe to sayve,
Wytt of thi maystur what it ment,   *Learn*
   the mater that he wold us crave.   *subject; from us seek*
3905   For and thou tell us his entent,   *if you*
   grett helpyng of us sall thou have.
And yf thou suffer us to be schent,   *destroyed*
   thee ware os gud be grathed in grave: *are as good [as to] be laid*
Sore vengance sall we take
3910   on thee and all thin."
Scho sayd, "Sers, for yowr sake
   I sall assay hym syne."   *then*

327.

Sone afturward, when scho myght wyn
   alon with hyr lorde to dele, *alone*
3915 Scho kyssed hym kyndly cheke and chyn *on cheek and chin*
   and lett ose hyr luf was full lele. *pretended that her love; loyal*
"A, ser," scho sayd, "ye sall have syne, *have committed transgression*
   your hert fro me yf ye oght hele. *anything conceal*
I wyll forsake both kyth and kyn *cuntry and family*
3920 and wend with yow in wo and wele; *go; woe and weal*
My hert ware comforth clene. *pure*
   Wole ye kyndly me kene *explain*
What that mater may meyne *tale might mean [that]*
   ye told to the thryty mene?" *men*

328.

3925 "Gud leve," he sayd, "lett be thi fayre *Good love; your concern*
   to tyme that thei have done ther dede. *until the time; their deed*
That mater wyll I not declare
   forto be nevynd for nokyns nede." *mentioned for any kind of need*
Then sone scho sobed and syghyd sare *sobbed and sighed sorely*
3930 and feyned hyr febyll by falshede. *feigned herself enfeebled through*
Scho rent hyr cloghes and ruged hyr hare, *tore her clothes; messed up her hair*
   os scho wold dye withowtyn drede. *doubt*
When Sampson con hyre see
   so mowrne and make swylke chere, *thus mourning; such moods*
3935 He said, "Lemman, lett be; *Lover*
   the lesson sall thou lere." *learn*

329.

He lered hyr fyrst of this lyon, *told her*
   how that he slogh hym with his hand, *slew*
And aftur when that thei come to town
3940 by the same way os he can wend, *as he can go*
How he in a dyke ther down *ditch*
   fand the bones clene that he kend, *found; knew*
And how bees then had made them bown *themselves a home*
   in the lyon mowth to loge and lend. *lodge*
3945 "The mowth," he sayd, "that ette, *ate*
   and the bownes war hard and drye, *bones were*
And the hony was swett; *sweet*
   this case thei suld dyscrye. *describe*

330.

"Bot wyfe," he sayd, "this that is wroyght
3950 lett no man wytt be way ne strette." *know in any way*
"A, ser," scho sayd, "that wold I not,
   for all this werld heyre I yow hette." *here I promise you*

Bot in all hast that ever scho myght
 scho made hyre with tho men to mette.   *those men to meet*
3955 A blyth bodword to them scho broyght   *glad tidings*
 of all this fare fro hed to fette.   *from beginning to end*
Scho sayd, "This is certayn
 and soth, so sall ye say."   *true*
Then ware thei ferly fayn   *wondrously pleased*
3960 and bold to byde that day.

331.
Be this was sex days comyn and gone;
 the sevynt day was ther seson sett.   *appointment*
To Sampson wentt thei ylkon   *each one*
 and sayd, "We come to do our dett.   *debt*
3965 What ys more hard then is the bone
 amang all fude that furth is fett,   *taken*
And swettur thyng then hony is none
 in mowth, when yt is melled and mett."   *mixed*
When Sampson herd them say
3970 so evyn unto his merke,   *close to his mark*
He wyst full well allway   *knew*
 his wyfe had wroyght that werke.

332.
And then persaved he properly
 qwy scho so stretly can hym enquere   *why she so earnestly*
3975 The question forto com by,
 hyr lynage for scho wold yt lere.   *tell*
Then carped he to that cumpany   *called*
 and told before tho folke in fere,   *those gathered folk*
"I knaw all your confyderacy,
3980 And I answer in this manere:
What may bettur begyle   *beguile*
 A lele man, lowd or styll,   *good; aloud or silently*
Then weked woman wyle,   *a wicked woman's wile*
 wher yt is turned unto yll."

[SAMSON DESTROYS ASHKELON (14:19)]

333.
3985 He wyst well how thrytty wore   *thirty [men] were*
 ordand, for gape men hym to geme.   *ordered, as bold; guard*
Forthi, all if his myght was more,
 that tyme wold he not be breme.   *fierce*
Ther falshed schewed he them before   *falsehood*
3990 that the woman wysched them well to deme. *had guided; to make answer*
Than langer hym lyst not sojorne thore: *he desired to remain there no longer*

	he wyst thei ware fayn hym to fleme.	*anxious to drive him away*
	He toke his men ylkon,	
	all that myght armes beyre,	*bear*
3995	And went to Askalone,	*Ashkelon*
	A cety walled fore were.	*for war*

334.

	The cety fell, so has he fun,	*found*
	to Ebrews, his helders of old,	*elders*
	And then in bondeyg ware thei bown.	*bondage were they (the Jews) taken*
4000	Swylke tales to Sampson sone thei told:	*Such*
	Phylysteyns had the gaudes begun;	*tricks*
	sone ware thei feld os fee in fold.	*felled as cattle*
	That cety sone so he wun	*won*
	Ebrews to weld yt, as thei wold.	*rule*
4005	Then fayrd he furth them fro,	*he went away from them*
	And so his way he wendes	*goes*
	To sojorne in Sarra	
	with his fader and his frendes.	

335.

	Ther wuned he with them mony a weke,	*stayed; many weeks*
4010	for of his fayre thei war full fayn.	*deeds; glad*
	Of Sersyns syde none he forsoke;	*He refused to fight against pagans (Saracens)*
	who wold hym ware, sone ware thei slayn,	*anger, soon were*
	Tyll at the last talent hym toke	*desire*
	to Tanna forto turne agayn	*Timnah*
4015	Hys wyfe, that he lufyd, forto loke,	*loved*
	for whor he lufed he cowd not layn.	*where; deny*
	All yf scho fawted before,	*defaulted*
	yett wold he frayst hyr ferr.	*try her further*
	And so when he come thore,	*there*
4020	he fand hyr werkand werre.	*found her behaving even worse*

[SAMSON DEFEATS THE PHILISTINES (14:20–15:17)]

336.

	Sampson was forgeyttyn than,	*forgotten then*
	os unkouth man that is unknawn,	
	And scho wede with another man,	*she (his wife) wed to*
	that used hyr evynly os his awn.	*just as his own*
4025	Then Sampson bytturly can bane	*curse*
	and sayd scho suld be hanged and drawn.	
	And bettur consell none he cane	*knew*
	bot stroye the sede that thei have sawn.	*destroyed the crops; sown*
	He was so mased and moved,	*amazed*
4030	full mony he dang to dede,	*beat to death*

And cautels he controvyd   *wiles he contrived*
  to harme all ther kynred.

337.
In that same tym men suld begyn
  ther cornes into ther howse to kest.   *grain; cast*
4035   He sembyld be a sutell gyn   *subtle contrivance*
  thre hunderth fers foxys from est and west,   *fierce foxes*
And fyrebrandes that well wold byrne   *firebrands (torches); burn*
  full fast unto ther taylis he fest;   *tails he fastened*
That made them rasydly forto ryne   *swiftly to run*
4040   to all was brent; so toyght hym best.   *until; burnt*
Cornes and wynes he dystroyd
  that suld susteyn ther lyve.   *life*
Of swylke maner he noyed   *troubled*
  Phylysteyns for his wyfe.

338.
4045   Yf he was wroth, none myght hym wytt;   *angry; blame*
  he went and wund wher he was born.   *dwelled*
Phylysteyns had full grett dyspytt,
  for he had so dystroyd ther corne.   *their crops*
Thei sayd thei suld yt qwykly qwytt,   *quickly avenge*
4050   and therto have thei othes sworne.   *oaths*
Full grett ost geydderd thei full tyte
  and sayd all Ebrews suld be lorne   *destroyed*
On lese then thei wold send   *Unless*
  Sampson them untyll,   *unto them*
4055   Bonden both his hende,   *Bound; hands*
  to werke with hym ther wyll.

339.
When that this soynd to them was send,   *message*
  the Ebrews made full mekyll mone.   *moan*
Thei had no fors them to dyffend;   *army; defend*
4060   therfor thei ware full wyll of wone.   *were utterly lacking hope*
No consell in that case thei kend,   *solution; they knew*
  bot to Sampson thei wentt ylkon
And told hym all ther tale to end,
  and helpe bot hym how thei had none.   *except for*
4065   He bad thei suld hym bynd   *ordered; bind*
  be lyve, no langer sese,   *quickly; wait*
Both hys handes hym behynd
  so forto make them pese.   *peace*

340.

Then ware thei bold when he them bade:

4070   thei band his hend with cordes new. *bound his hands*

Unto the lordes thei have hym lede,

    and in that tyme thei toke a trew. *truce*

When he with his enmyse was stede, *enemies was placed*

    thei wer full bown his bale to brew. *eager to make trouble for him*

4075 Bot of them was he not adred; *afraid*

    he toyght thei suld that ryot rew. *trouble rue*

So were Ebrews certayn

    that pese suld stably stand,

And Phylysteyns was fayn, *were glad*

4080   for thei had hym in hand.

341.

Hys frendes wer yett full wyll of rede, *were at a loss for a plan*

    for thei wyst not what wold betyde. *knew not what would come about*

His enmys bed no bettur bede *made; command*

    then umsett hym on ylka syde. *surrounded*

4085 He herd them deme he suld be dede, *deem; dead*

    and when thei war most in ther pride,

He stert up sternly in that stede. *stood up strongly*

    to breke his bandes he wold not byd, *break his bonds; wait*

Sone ware thei sonder ylkon: *Soon; sundered altogether*

4090   thei myght dere hym no dele, *could harm him in no way*

Bot wepyns had he ryght none *Even though weapons*

    and thei war armed well.

342.

Non armowrs ne no helpe he hath, *No armor*

    bot well he treste in Goddes grace. *trusted*

4095 And als God wold, ryght so yt was:

    sone had he comforth in that case. *soon*

He fand a cheke bone of an asse *jawbone of an ass*

    full sodanly in that same place.

Therwith of panyms gart he passe *pagans did he take*

4100   a thowssand lyves in lytyll space;

All that hym batell bede

    ware skomfett sone and slayn. *discomfited soon*

Thei ware full fayn that flede, *glad that fled*

    and he leved alon. *left [them] alone*

[SAMSON AND THE SPRING AT LEHI (ENHAKKORE) (15:18–19)]

343.

4105 He musterd that he was myghty *showed*

    amang them that ware maysters mast. *most dominant*

Then thanked he God full inwardly
    that hym hade helped so in hast.   *quickly*
For feghyng was his flesch so drye   *fighting his throat was*
4110   that bown he was to gyfe the gast.   *ready; give up the ghost (i.e., die)*
And watur myght he non come by;
    in byttur bale so was he brast.   *misery; bound*
Then prayd he God in hy,   *[to] God in haste*
    als He at His awn lyst   *pleasure*
4115 Had send hym vyctorye,
    vochsave to sleke his threyst.   *slake*

344.
God was ay bown his bale to bete   *ever ready his misery*
    and unto beld hym forto bryng.   *comfort*
The asse bown lay at his fette,   *[jaw]bone; feet*
4120 wherwith he can his enmys dyng.   *strike*
Therof com watur cold and sweytt,
    os yt ware of a well spryng.   *sprung*
That slekyd hys threyst and slaked his hette.   *request*
    He thankyd God ever of all thyng:
4125 Fyrst for the lyon
    He gafe hym grace to slo   *slay*
And sythyn in this seson   *then at this time*
    hath sayved his lyfe also.

345.
Then wex he wygh, os he was are,   *he grew strong, as; before*
4130 by wonder werke that ther was wroyght.   *[the] wondrous work*
Unto his frendes fast can he fare,
    that for hym had full mekyll toyght.   *much concern*
All that for hym before had kare,   *sadness*
    he made them myrth all that he moyght,   *might*
4135 And all tho that ther enmys ware,   *enemies were*
    under ther bondowm hath he broyght.   *their power*
Whyls he wund in Sarraa,   *While he dwelled in Zorah*
    all folke he fand his frend,   *found*
Bot sythyn to Gasa   *then to Gaza*
4140 toke hym talent to wend.   *desire to go*

[SAMSON AT GAZA (16:1–3)]

346.
This Gasa was a grett cety;
    to fals Phylesteyns yt fell.
Of panyms wonned ther grett plenté   *pagans (Gentiles) dwelled*
    that made grett maysterys them amell.   *warriors; among*
4145 Ydder wentt Sampson oft to see   *There*

                a damsell that ther can dwell.
        None durst hym warne wher he wold be   *dared warn him [off from]; wanted to be*
            for talys that thei of hym herd tell.   *tales*
        He fand defawtes before   *failures*
4150   Phylysteyns forto treyst;   *trust*
        Bot sythyn he mett with more   *afterwards*
            that made hym more abayst.   *abashed*

        347.
        Hys lufe he wold not hele ne hyde,   *conceal*
            for no man sayng sett he by.   *man's words*
4155   And so betyd yt on a tyde   *happened*
            to Gasa past he prevely.   *he went secretly*
        Bot sone Phylesteyns hym aspyd,   *soon; espied*
            how he come with no cumpany,
        And how he buskyd hym forto abyd   *was accustomed; stay*
4160   and all nyght with his leman ly.   *lover lie*
        By ther consell thei kest   *determined*
            how that he suld be tone   *taken*
        And raysed owt of his rest
            and so sodanly slone.   *slain*

        348.
4165   Thei wyll not fayle whatso befall;
            therfor ther gattes speyre thei fast,   *their gates they bolted shut*
        And sett gud wache apon the wall   *good watch*
            with wepyns that full well wold last.
        Thei say no sylver sayve hym sall;   *silver (i.e., ransom)*
4170   his pompe and pryd suld sone be past.
        Bot Sampson hath persayved all,   *perceived*
            how thei his ded devysed and cast.   *death devised and planned*
        When he hopyd no man herd,
            at mydnyght furth he meved   *moved*
4175   And fand the gattes all sperred;   *found; barred*
            that gart hym be yll grevede.   *grieved*

        349.
        Then wyst he well he was in wath;   *knew; danger*
            to God he prayd with stevyn full styll   *small still voice*
        Att helpe hym forto scape fro scath   *That he should; escape from harm*
4180   sen all hys wele was in His wyll.   *welfare*
        Thor schewed he sone that he was wrath: *There; angry*
            both gattes and postes he puld hym tyll,
        And on hys bake he bayre them bath   *bore; both*
            to Tabor, that was a heygh hyll.   *Tabor; high*
4185   Phylysteyns that hym hattes   *hate*
            than fand a fowle affray   *scare*

When thei saw ther gattes
both brokyn and borne away.

350.

Full mekyll mone thei made that morne,   *great moan*
4190   and carfull was that cumpany;   *full of sadness*
That he ascaped them toyght yt scorne,   *seemed shameful to them*
for wo thei wyst wold fall therby.   *troubles they knew; as a result*
Wher he was sum dele frend beforne,   *in some ways a friend before*
then was he foo and full enmy;   *foe; enemy*
4195   Wher he them fand, none was forborne   *spared*
that in Phylysteyns wold affy.   *ally [themselves]*
Them forto schame and schend   *kill*
with hand hade he none aw,   *no fear*
And Ebrews he mayntend
4200   and govarnd in Goddes law.

[SAMSON AND DELILAH (16:4–22)]

351.

With wemen wold he wun and wend;   *women he would dwell and hang out*
he ne royght whedder yt ware well or wrang.   *did not care*
All yf Phylysteyns ware noyght his frend,   *Even if*
of them the fayrest wold he fang.   *catch*
4205   In Soreth can a lady lend   *Sorek did dwell*
that lemans lyfe had leved full lang.   *a harlot's life*
Hys hert all hale to hare he mend;   *altogether to her he gave over*
full mekyll myrth was them amang.   *much pleasure*
For scho wold hym begyle,   *beguile*
4210   with fayre chere scho hym fede.   *fed*
Bot he wyst of no wyle   *knew; deception*
and was nothyng adrede.

352.

Scho was full fayre of hyd and hew,   *beautiful skin and complexion*
bot of hyr luf scho was full lyght.   *love; fickle*
4215   Of hyr condicions noyght he knew;   *plans*
Dalyda that damsell heyght.   *Delilah; was called*
Phylysteyns was ever untrew:
when thei of Sampson saw this syght,
Full prevely thei can persew   *secretly*
4220   to marre his maystry yf thei myght.
Thei wyst that woman cowde   *knew*
dyssayve hym by sum gyn.   *deceive; contrivance*
Therfor thei melled with mouyth   *spoke*
to gayre that bourd be gyne.   *capture that man by trickery*

353.

4225   Thei sayd thus: "Dalida, doyghtur dere,
              Phylysteyns in thi fayth affy.   *trust*
       Sampson, thi felow and thi fere,   *companion*
              thou wott he is our werst enmy.   *know*
       Wold thou qwayntly of hym enquere   *cunningly*
4230   wher in his wyghtnes most may ly   *strength*
       And warne us, for we sall be nere.
              Grett wrschep may thou wyn therby.   *honor*
       So may thou stynt all stryve,   *stop all strife*
              and gyftes we sall thee gyfe
4235   To lede a ladys lyve,   *lead a lady's life*
              os lang os thou may lyfe."   *as long as you may live*

354.

       "Syrs," scho sayd, "I sall asay   *try*
              and fand sum of his fors to fell."   *find; strength to quench*
       Sone aftur os he by hyr lay,
4240   full grett myrth made scho them amell.   *between*
       Scho sayd, "Gud paramowre, I thee pray   *lover*
              A lytyll tale me forto tell,
       Sen thou so mekyll of myghtis may,   *Since; great*
              wherin thi strengh is dyght to dwell.   *made*
4245   So may I fully fele   *feel*
              how thi luf to me lys."   *lies*
       He dowted hyr sum dele   *somewhat*
              and answerd on this wyse: *in this way*

355.

       "Yf I ware bown, both hend and fette,   *were bound; hand and foot*
4250   with cordes that wald ryght well last,
       So myght ylk man to be me mette,   *any; my match*
              for then ware all my power past."
       That scho hym lufed full well, scho lett,   *pretended*
              tyll he on slepe was faln full fast.   *until; fallen*
4255   Scho band hym full herd, I yow hette,   *bound; assure*
              and then a grett cry up scho cast,
       For thei that can aspy
              suld wyn hym in ther weld.   *overtake their power*
       He stert up stalworthyly;   *started*
4260   of hyr fayre noyght he feled.   *her workings (the bindings); felt*

356.

       He wyst nothyng how scho had wroght
              for he persaved no perell yett.   *peril yet*
       And that hyr warke was wast, hyr toyght;   *so her work was wasted, she thought*
              therfor scho frest another fytt.   *attempted; wicked stratagem*

4265	Scho sayd, "Ser, and thou luf me oght,	*aught*
	thou wold not se me soroand sytt	*sit in sorrow*
	And namly for a thyng of noyght,	*nothing (i.e., not worth a trifle)*
	qwylke by thi word that I wold wytt:	*which; know*
	Wherin thy strengh is hyde.	
4270	I kepe noyght elles to crave.	*have nothing else*
	Sythyn als thiself wold byde,	*Since you expect to stay*
	I wyll se yt to save."	*I expect to see it or else*

357.

	He sayd, "Dame, whoso wold me bynd	
	with twanges schorn owt of a hyde,	*straps cut*
4275	Both my handes fast me behynd,	
	then hastely war past my pryd."	*would my pride be passed away*
	When he on slepe ware wardly blynd,	*asleep was blind to the world*
	to bynd hym wold scho not abyd.	*wait*
	And for Phylesteyns suld hym fynd	
4280	or he was lawse, on lowd scho cryde.	*before; loose*
	He waked, os he noght wyst;	*nothing knew*
	the bandes in sonder brayde.	*broke asunder*
	For scho hyr purpase myst;	
	scho was nothyng well payd.	*not a little angered*

358.

4285	Bot furth yett, for scho wold not fayle,	
	scho sayd, "Sen I no ferther found,	*Since I've nothing better learned*
	Yll may me lyke my long travele	*My long labor suits me ill*
	to be beswyked." With that scho swound.	*hoodwinked; swooned*
	He sayd, "Whoso wold take a nale	
4290	and fest yt fast into the grownd,	*stick*
	Yf enmys wold me then asayle,	
	I suld have no strengh in that stownd."	*place*
	Scho broyght both nale and band	*bonds*
	and fest yt when he sleped	*fastened*
4295	And drof yt with hyr hand	
	down into the erth full depe.	

359.

	Scho wakyn hym then with a cry,	*woke*
	for his enmyse suld here in hast.	*should be here quickly*
	And when he start up stallworthyly,	*stoutly*
4300	then wyst scho that hyr werke was wast.	*undertaking*
	Full mekyll moyne scho made for thi	*lament; therefore*
	and sayd, "In bayle ever I am brayst,	*sadness*
	Sen I se grayth incheson why	*Since; clear cause*
	thei lufe not me that I luf mast."	*love most*
4305	Scho sayd in yre and angere,	

"Sen I werke so in vayne,
I sall lufe them no langer
   that lyst not luf agayne." *will not love in return*

360.
Sone has scho chosyn another chare: *mood*
4310   scho weped and wrang both hed and hand. *wept and wrung*
I deme hyr a dewle os I dare; *deem her a devil*
   scho mad hyr als scho myght not stand. *made as [if] she*
Now nedes Sampson forto beware,
   les he be wrethed with his awn wand. *lest; grieved; own rod*
4315 Bot for he saw hyr sogaytes fare, *regarded her as exceedingly fair*
   he wex a foyle, and that he fand. *grew a fool, and that he revealed*
He sayd, "Leman, be styll, *Lover*
   no lenger lyst me layn. *does it please me to lie*
Thou sall wytt all thi wyll; *know all you want*
4320   I say thee in certayn.

361.
"My myght is haly in my hare *wholly; hair*
   so that yf yt were cutt of clene, *off cleanly (shaved bare)*
Then suld I be of myght no mare *strength no more*
   then other men before hath bene.
4325 Bot leman, loke thou layn this lare; *conceal this information*
   tell yt never bot us two betwene!"
"A, luf," scho sayd, "well lever me ware *love; I would prefer*
   forto be kylled with cayres kene. *terrible woe*
Derly I sall yt dyght *take care of it*
4330   both by nyght and day
Forto maynten thi myght
   in all that ever I may."

362.
So sall Sampson be putt to pyn, *pain*
   that maysteres mad full mony a myle. *who had made masteries for a long time*
4335 A woman with hyr weked ingyne *guile*
   has lorne that led — alas that whyle! *betrayed that man*
Of hyr falshed scho wold not fyn; *stop*
   full freke scho was hym forto fyle. *eager; defile*
Scho dyd hym drynke of dyverse wyn *wines*
4340   with grett gladnes hym to begyle.
So yll wemen wyll glose *deceive*
   them that thei wold have schent, *destroyed*
For men sall not suppose *suspect*
   in them none yll entent.

363.

4345	Hyre solace was to hys unsele,
	becawse scho kest hym to betray.
	When he of wyn was dronkyn wele,
	then was hys wytt all wast away.
	He fell on slepe and myght not fele
4350	what folke to hym wold do or say.
	Hys hare scho cutt of ylka dele,
	wherin his strengh and lykyng lay.
	This was a delfull dede
	of all that ever was told,
4355	For trest of mekyll mede
	made hyr to be so bold.

Glosses: *comforting; misfortune* / *intended* / *wasted* / *feel* / *hair she cut off every bit* / *pleasure* / *woeful deed* / *trust of much reward*

364.

	When this was done, scho mad a schowtt,
	for enmys suld here, that was hyd.
	He wakynd and went withowtyn dowt
4360	forto have done, os he are dyde.
	Bot fals Phylysteyns flokked abowt;
	to bynd hym sore non thurt them byd.
	And sone both his eyn putt thei owt,
	because no kyndnes suld be kyd.
4365	To Gaza thei gart hym ga
	both blynd and bun in bandes.
	And the dewle Dalyda
	was made lady of landes.

Glosses: *shout* / *enemies to hear, who were hidden* / *awoke; without fear* / *he did before* / *gathered* / *needed* / *soon; eyes* / *shown* / *made him go* / *bound in bonds* / *devil Delilah*

365.

	He that myght fell all folke beforn,
4370	now is he fast with feturs fest.
	Phylysteyns fast can hym scorne,
	for he had bene a grevus geyst.
	At qwernes thei gart hym grynd ther corn,
	and fylth oft in his face thei kest,
4375	And grett byrdyns that suld be borne
	to gayr hym beyre so toyght them best;
	Tho fellows folke ware fayn
	to se hym fowle fare.
	Ebrews ware put to payn;
4380	his kynradyn had gret kare.

Glosses: *destroy all people before* / *fetters strong* / *grievous guest* / *mills; made* / *threw* / *burdens* / *make him bear* / *Those; happy* / *fare badly* / *kindred; trouble*

366.

	In byttur bayle thus can he byde,
	ay bon to beyre what thei wold byde.
	All way with hym thei flott and chyde,
	bot in the meyn tyd thus betyde:

Glosses: *sorrow* / *always made to bear* / *shout* / *meanwhile thus occurred*

4385   His hare was waxin sum dele syde,   *growing*
        wherin his strengh was holy hyd.   *wholly concealed*
    Therfor to venge hym he aspyd
        on dedes that Dalyda hym dyd.
    Thrugh hir gyltry was he   *deceit*
4390   full yll turment and tened.   *tormented and aggrieved*
    And venged wold he be,
        yf he hymself suld schend.   *[even] if; die*

[SAMSON'S VENGEANCE AND DEATH (16:23–31)]

367.
    Ylke yere thei used to make a fest,   *Each year; feast*
        qwylk may not fayle, bot yf thei fon,   *which*
4395   And sacrafyce full mony a best   *beast*
        unto ther god that heyght Dagon.   *their god who was called Dagon*
    And now thei mad yt more honest,   *splendid*
        for thei had maystry of Sampson.
    Ydder thei semled, most and lest,   *There they assembled*
4400   and broyght hym to be wonderd on.
    As a best that was blynd   *beast*
        he balturd furth them by;   *hobbled along*
    Both before and behynd
        thei bunsched hym bytterly.   *struck*

368.
4405   In a palays thei hath purvayd   *palace*
        ther mangery with mekyll pride.   *their banquet; great*
    Full ryally it was arayd   *royally*
        with wyndows and with wardes wyd.   *courtyards*
    Bot all on heyght the halles was grayd   *were prepared*
4410   and selers beneth in to abyd,   *cellars*
    And on a pyller war thei brayd   *pillar were they supported*
        that bare up all on ylka syde.   *every side*
    Sampson befor had seen
        the purpase of that place;
4415   He toyght at turne to tene   *thought in turn to harm*
        ther sang and ther solace.   *their song*

369.
    He prayd a boy that lufed hym best   *asked*
        unto the pyler hym forto lede   *lead*
    That he ther by his bake myght rest,   *back*
4420   for of swylk helpe had he grett nede.
    Dame Dalyda on deese was drest   *dais; seated*
        with mony a wyght in worthy wede.   *man; clothes*
    The pyler gart he bow and brest   *burst*

	that all the halle in sonder yede.	*into pieces went*
4425	Yt bare down man and barne	*It bore (fell) down*
	and slew them all at ons	
	Bot the boy, that he can warne	*Except*
	to wend owt of the wons.	*building*

370.

	Ten milia Phylysteyns and mo	*10,000*
4430	gart he be lorne in lytyll whyle,	*caused he to be killed*
	All for he wold that woman slo	*because; slay*
	that with hyr gaudes can hym begyll.	*tricks; beguile*
	Sampson hymselfe was ded also;	*dead*
	he mogh not passe from that perell,	*may; peril*
4435	So wakynd weyre and mekyll wo	*Thus arose strife and much woe*
	all throw a wekyd woman wyle.	*through a wicked woman's wiles*
	The Ebrews all and sum	
	governd he twenty yere.	
	Thus endes Judicum,	*Judges*
4440	bot more yett men may lere.	*learn*

BOOK OF RUTH

RUTH.

[RUTH AND THE LINE OF KINGS (4:17, MATTHEW 1:3–6)]

371.

	God that weldes both wyld and tame	*controls*
	in all our spekyng be our spede	*language; help*
	Forto begyn withowtyn blame	
	this boke and make yt for our mede.	*reward*
4445	A woman, that heygh Ruth be name,	*who was called Ruth by*
	now forto nevyn of yt is nede.	*note; necessary*
	And this boke is named of the same,	
	the Boke of Rewth so we yt rede.	*Ruth; read*
	Scho was playn pupplyst	*widely known*
4450	of kynred fayr and gud.	*[to come] from family fair and good*
	Of hyr kynred com Cryst	*came Christ*
	and of the Jewes gentyll blud.	*noble bloodlines*

[NAOMI'S FAMILY (1:1–18)]

372.

	Aftur Sampson dede, that was dughty,	*Sampson's death, who was brave*
	of whom we told in tym beforn,	
4455	Of Ebrews reygned on Ely	*ruled one [man named] Eli*
	that mayntend them both evyn and morn.	
	And in Bedlem, a burgh ther by,	*Bethlehem*
	on Emalec was bred and born.	*Elimelech*
	He had a wyfe, heyght Neomy,	*called Naomi*
4460	and in ther tyme fell defawt of corn.	*occurred a lack of grain (i.e., famine)*
	Semly suns had thei two:	*Beautiful sons*
	the on was named Chelon,	*Chilion*
	And that other of thoo,	*those [two]*
	he was named Maalon.	*Mahlon*

373.

4465	Hungur was in that reme so ryfe,	*realm so widespread*
	all Ebrews mad full yll chere.	

	Emalec toke chylder and wyfe,	*[his] children*
	and went ther way thei fawre in fere,	*those four together*
	To paynyms land to lenght ther lyfe,	*heathen lands to lengthen their lives*
4470	wher corn enogh was and not dere.	*not scarce (expensive)*
	And thor thei wund withowtyn stryfe	*there they dwelled*
	with Moabyse more then tene yere.	*the Moabites; ten years*
	A wyfe thor wed Chelon,	
	Orafayn, a woman wyse.	*Orpah*
4475	Ruth mared with Maalon,	*Ruth married*
	a paynyn of grett price.	*pagan (Ruth) of great virtue (honor, gentility)*

374.

	Of Ebrews born both ware the men,	*Hebrew descent were both*
	of Jacob kynd and Jews cald;	*Jacob's kind and called Jews*
	Phylysteyns ware tho fayre wemen,	*Philistines (i.e., pagans) were those fair*
4480	and paynyns law holy thei held.	*pagan laws they considered holy*
	On this wyse ware thei wede then	*way were they married*
	agayns ther law, bot so God wold,	*against their; willed*
	For Crist suld com, os clerkes ken,	*understand*
	of both the braunches I are told.	*earlier*
4485	Emalec and his suns	*sons*
	in that land left ther lyves,	*left their lives (i.e., died)*
	And sythyn all same thor wonnes,	*then all together there lived*
	the mother and two suns wyfes.	*sons' wives*

375.

	Bot then the mother Neomy	
4490	langed into hyr land agayn:	*longed to return into her land*
	Hyr lyked not paynyms cumpany,	*She; pagan*
	for of hyre fare ware thei not fayn.	*behavior; pleased*
	Hyr suns wyfes was full wylly	*willing*
	to wend with hyr, this is certayn.	*to go*
4495	Scho tuke Ruth furth to be hyr by,	*beside her*
	and in that land scho leved Orfayn.	*left Orpah*
	Of on enogh hyr toyght	*one; thought*
	to led the landes throgh.	*lead*
	So Ruth with hyr scho broyght	
4500	evyn unto Bethlem burgh.	

[NAOMI RETURNS TO JUDAH WITH RUTH (1:19–22)]

376.

	Ydder thei wan withowtyn stryfe.	*There; trouble*
	Hyr frendes befor full fayr scho fand,	*[from] before*
	And sone thei asked hyr resons ryfe	*many questions*
	both of hyr suns and hir husband.	
4505	Scho told how thei had leved ther lyf,	*left their lives*

and how thei past in paynyms land,   *passed away in pagan lands*
And how Ruth was hyr on sun wyfe   *one son's wife*
    and wold werke evyn os thei ordand.   *directed*
She wold leve paynyms law   *leave pagan belief*
4510   and lere with all hir mayne   *learn; power*
The God of Jews to knaw.
    Therfor thei ware of hyr fayn.   *glad*

[RUTH MEETS BOAZ IN THE FIELDS (2:1–18)]

377.
Ruth was ryght fayr of hew and hyd,   *face and skin*
    and scho lyved lely os a Jew.   *loyally*
4515   Togeydder so furth can thei byde;   *afterwards; abide*
    all folke hyr lufed fro thei hyr knew.
So yt betyd in hervest tyde,   *happened at harvest time*
    when men suld schere that thei ar sew,   *reap; have sown*
Ruth sayd scho wold wend ther besyd   *go*
4520   and glene them corn as for hyr dew.   *gather; as her proper work*
"Doyghghtur," sayd Neomy,   *Daughter*
    "go furth in my blessyng;
Thy dyner dyght sall I   *prepare*
    agayns thi homecomyng."

378.
4525   So went scho furth on the morne
    to glene and byrdyns forto beyre.   *gather and burdens to bear*
A Boze, that was in Bethlem born,   *[man named] Boaz*
    a dughty man in dedes of were,   *brave; deeds of war*
He geydderd his folke hym beforne   *gathered*
4530   into the feld his corne to schere   *crop to harvest*
And fand this woman gedderyng corn   *found*
    in doles wher scho myght do no dere.   *dales; do no harm*
He asked of them ylkon
    whethyn was that woman fayre.   *who*
4535   The sayd, "The wyf of Maalon;
    to Emalec next hayre.   *heir*

379.
"Scho sojourns in this same cety
    with Neomy, thy nevow grett."   *niece*
Unto that semly then sayd he,   *lovely [woman]*
4540   "Wend with my men to drynke and ette   *Go; eat*
And werke with them in stede of me;   *on my land*
    all sal be thin that thou may gette."   *yours; gather*
Scho thanked hym with wordes fre
    that so vowchsave hyr to rehete.   *comfort*

4545	All day with them scho wroyght;	*worked*
	that dede dyd hyr no dere,	*deed; harm*
	For at evyn hom scho broyght	*evening home*
	als mekyll os scho myght beyre.	*much as she could bear*

[NAOMI PLOTS RUTH'S MARRIAGE (2:19–3:5)]

380.

	Scho told hyr dame how scho had done,	*lady*
4550	for that scho lengyd so lang a stage,	
	And how Boze bed hyr swylk a bone	*gave her such a boon*
	and werke and take hyr werke to wage	
	That Neomy toyght hyr allon	*thought to herself*
	Amang them forto make maryage.	*Between; marriage*
4555	Scho wyst of Boze: wyf had he none,	*knew about*
	and he was lord of hegh lynage.	*good family*
	Scho sayd, "My doyghtur dere,	
	unto my tale take tent!	*advice take heed*
	Tomorn loke thou be nere	*Tomorrow; close*
4560	ay in his awn present.	*always; own presence*

381.

	"And when thou hath bene all the day	*after*
	with hym and his folke in felles,	*in the fields*
	Wayt at evyn well, yf thou may	*Await that evening, that*
	lige in the loge that he in dwelles;	*sleep in the lodge*
4565	And when thou sekes, yf he ogh say,	*search [there], if he says anything*
	say that thou sekes hym and noyght elles,	*seek; nothing else*
	Thee forto wys the redy way	*You to guide in the best way*
	to sum maryag that he of mellys.	*some marriage; might arrange*
	Loke thou be homly hyd	*humbly hidden (i.e., chaste)*
4570	to mette with hym at morne."	*meet*
	Evyn os scho demed, scho dyd.	*directed*
	Boze fand hyr hym beforne.	

[BOAZ AGREES, NEGOTIATES WITH ANOTHER MAN (3:6–4:12)]

382.

	When Boze hyr herd, he hade pety	
	how scho hyre mane unto hym ment.	*complaint; told*
4575	He sayd, "Here wuns in this cety	*dwells*
	a yong man with ryve elders rent.	*much older claims*
	Hym sall I make to mary thee,	*marry*
	or elles the same sall I assent;	*else to the same [contract] I will agree*
	The herytage then weld sall we."	*protect*
4580	Thus told he hyr all hys entent.	
	Scho was full fayn forthi,	*glad therefore*

and als sone as scho mogh,   *might*
Scho told to Neomy
   on what wyse scho had wroyght.   *way she had worked*

383.

4585   Then Neomy was farly fayn: *wondrously glad*
   on grownd was no thyng that hyr greved.   *earth; upset*
For well scho wyst hyrselfe certayn   *knew*
   that Ruth full sone suld be releved.   *settled (given comforts in a marriage)*
Sone Boze gart summond ilke cyteseyn   *each citizen*
4590   and sayd them how this mater meved.   *thing had gone*
And to the yong man told he playn   *clearly*
   how that the woman was myschewed,   *had come to grief*
And that he suld assent
   to be husband and hede,   *head*
4595   Or els refuse the rent   *property*
   that com of hyr kynred.   *came from her family*

384.

The yong man answerd curtasly   *courteously*
   and sayd thus in thar aller syght,   *all of their sight*
"I luf another to lyg me by;   *desire another to lie beside me*
4600   hyr wyll I hold, os I have heyght."   *promised*
Then answerd Boze, "Ruth wed wyll I
   and have hir rent os yt is ryght."   *property*
To this acordes this cumpany,   *agrees*
   so wedded he that worthy wyght.   *woman*
4605   The rent he con restore
   unto hym and hys wyfe.
Os elders dyd before,   *As previous generations*
   he used yt in ther lyfe.   *enjoyed it (the rent) in their lives*

[RUTH MARRIES BOAZ (4:13–22)]

385.

In the spowsall ware thei copyld clene;   *marriage; chastely married*
4610   os God wold, so was done in dede.   *God willed; deed*
He was Ebrew and scho panym,   *pagan*
   bot by Goddes law ther lyfe thei lede.   *lives they led*
A sone thei hade sone them betwen,   *son they had soon*
   qwylke Obeth heyght, who wyll take hed. *which Obed was named, whoever*
4615   And of hym withowtyn wene   *doubt*
   Jesse was rutt; of hym we rede   *Jesse was begot; read*
How sythyn com Davyd Kyng,   *later*
   that was chefe Juge of Jewys.   *who was foremost Judge*
Thus Jesus Crist wold spryng
4620   of paynyms and Ebrews.   *pagans and Jews*

386.

	And on what wyse He sprang and spred	*way He (Jesus)*
	mone aftur com in carpyng clene:	*must afterward; simple speech*
	Then ware no ledes that lyf led	*people*
	bot only Ebrew and paynym.	*Jews and pagans*
4625	The Boke of Ruth thus have we rede	*read*
	of faders that before have bene.	*forefathers*
	In lytyll spech we have yt sped,	*brief; related*
	that mony mater may be mene.	*many matters; considered*
	And next now aftur this	
4630	begyns the Boke of Kynges.	
	He bryng us to His blyse,	*[May] He; bliss*
	that Lord ys of all thynges.	

FIRST BOOK OF KINGS (1 SAMUEL)

[ELKANAH AND HIS FAMILY (1:1–8)]

387.

	God that goverans all thynges	*who*
	and myght fully made more and lese,	*[whose] power; (i.e., everything)*
4635	In whom our helpe all holy hynges,	*completely hangs*
	He graunt us grace of His gudnese	*[may] He grant; goodness*
	Forto begyne the Boke of Kynges	
	and further yt furth in fayr processe,	*set it forth in fair terms*
	Als Holy Chyrch heyre says and synges,	*here; sings*
4640	and as the Bybyll proves expresse	*proves best*
	How prophetes fyrst begane	
	Goddes banere furth to beyre,	*banner; bear*
	How kynges wrschepe wane	*honor won*
	be dyverse dedes of were.	*diverse deeds of war*

388.

4645	Ther wuned a man in Ramatha,	*dwelled; Ramathaim*
	a gentyll cety of the Jury,	*noble; Jewry*
	And his name was cald Elcana;	*Elkanah*
	amang all other most myghty.	*[thought] most strong*
	He had two wyfes. On heyght Anna;	*One was called Hannah*
4650	scho was barand of hyr body.	*barren*
	Hys secund wyfe heyght Fenenna,	*Peninnah*
	bot scho had barns hyr husband by.	*children*
	The costome then was thore,	*custom; at that time*
	that sythyn hath bene untoyght:	*which since has been out of use (unthought)*
4655	No wemen wrschept wore	*women were honored*
	bot thoo that frutt furth broyght.	*those who children (fruit) brought forth*

389.

	Helcana, that was full wyse,	*Elkanah; very wise*
	lufed Anna well, for scho was fayre.	*loved; beautiful*
	Bot all way was scho lesse in prese,	*[in] all [other] ways; honor*
4660	bycawse scho broyght hym furth non ayre.	*no heir*

Thei used then ylke yere ons or twyse   *each year once or twice*
   unto the Tempyll all folke to care
And ther forto make sacrafyce
   to God, that goverans erth and ayre.   *air*
4665   And fell that Helcana
   with wyfes and chylder wentt
Thar sacrafyce to make
   to God with gud entent.   *proper intentions*

390.
Thei broyght with them both bred and wyne,   *bread and wine*
4670   aftur ther folke ware fele or fone.   *many or few*
And thor thei sett them down at dyne   *there; eat*
   when thei ther sacrafyce had done.   *their*
He parted then Anna to pyne,   *distributed; pain*
   for unto hyr he gaf bot one,   *gave only*
4675   And to Fenenna fele and fyne,   *many and fine [offerings]*
   for scho had chylder and that other none.
When scho saw Fenenna
   for hyre chylder well fayre,
Scho weped and was full wo,   *wept; very sad*
4680   for scho no barns bare.   *sons bore*

[HANNAH MOURNS AT THE TEMPLE (1:9–19)]

391.
Scho rose and went withoutyn rest
   to the Tempyll wher the Arke of God stud.   *stood*
And thor scho fell in prayers prest   *eager prayers*
   and prayd to God, that gyfes all gud,
4685   Hys grace in hyre forto fest   *provide*
   and send a sun to mend hyr mode.   *sadness*
So carefull cowntenance furth scho cast   *Such a lamenting look*
   that Ely wened scho had bene wode.   *Eli believed; made mad*
And unto hyr sayd he,
4690   "Dame, thou takes no kepe   *are not watchful*
All yf thou dronkyn be.   *If you are drunk*
   Greve not God. Go slepe!"   *Aggrieve; Take rest*

392.
"A mercy, ser," scho sayd. "Do way!
   My sorow sall thou understand.
4695   To God is that I cry and pray   *[it] is*
   to have a sun with my husband.
And sertes, ser, yf I so may,   *certainly*
   to God here sall he be servand."
When Hely herd hyr so say,   *heard her say this*

4700   he prayd for hyr with hert and hand.
        Then sone toke Helcana
            his chylder and wyfes two
        And went into Ramatha,
            that town that thei come fro.

[SAMUEL'S BIRTH AND CHILDHOOD (1:20–2:11)]

393.

4705   Sone aftur this so yt befell:
            Anna consaved, os God vowchesayve,   *conceived; granted*
        And bare a sun heyght Samuell,   *bore; named*
            as scho full oft cane aftur crave.   *because she did ask [for him] so often*
        Grett myrth was made then them amell   *among*
4710   for comforth of that lytyll knave.   *gladness in; boy*
        In the Tempyll was he dyght to dwell,   *made*
            ose sone os he hymself can save.   *as soon as he could take care of himself*
        Hys moyder made offerand
            of hym, os scho had heyght,   *promised*
4715   Forto be Goddes servand
            dewly both day and nyght.   *dutifully*

394.

        In Goddes servyce so con he lend,   *would he live*
            a full fayre chyld of hyd and hew.   *in all ways*
        And by twelfe yeres was past tyll end,   *by [the time] twelve years were ended*
4720   he cowth enogh of nurtur new: *he was mature enough*
        The gast of God in hym dyscend,   *spirit; descended*
            wherby he cowth tell talys trew.   *make true prophecies*
        How thynges suld both begyn and end,
            be prophecy full well he knew.
4725   So aftur yeres twelfe
            Ely, the prophett wyse,
        Held Samuel nex hisself   *Considered; nearest to himself*
            in all sufferand servyce.   *sovereignty of service*

[ELI'S WICKED SONS (2:12–17, 22–36)]

395.

        Two suns with his wyfe had Ely,
4730   for samyn wuned, both scho and hee: *[they] lived together, she and he*
        On Fynyes, that other Ofny,   *One [named] Phinehas; Hophni*
            two semly chylder forto se.   *fair children in appearance*
        Bot both thei lyved in lechery
            and dred not God in no degré.   *feared*
4735   Ther fader them faverd, and forthi   *Their father favored them; therefore*
            to fowll endyng thei fell all thre.   *foul*

	The sacrafyce thei stall	*stole*
	to fynd ther barns brede;	
	Therfor themself had bayle	*woe*
4740	and other of ther kynred.	*others of their family*

[ON THE NEED FOR PRIESTS TO BE WORTHY]

396.

	Forthi ys goyde thei tent to skyll	*Therefore [it] is well [that] they take every care*
	that haluyd thyng has forto geme,	*who hallowed things must protect (observe)*
	Be ther defawt that nothyng spyll;	*So that by their failures nothing is soiled*
	ne in beyryng be not to breme,	*neither in bearing to be too rough*
4745	Ne take nothyng themself untyll	*Nor to take anything unto themselves*
	that unto Goddes servyce suld seme;	*should be suited*
	And be ever ware with werkes yll	*always be cautious to avoid ill works*
	for dowt of Hym that all sall deme.	*fear; judge*
	And chastys ther chylder well	*chastise their*
4750	allway when thei do omysse	*amiss*
	That thei no fawtes fele,	*faults suffer*
	as Ely feled for hys.	*suffered*

[GOD SPEAKS TO SAMUEL (3:1–21)]

397.

	Now wyll we rede and reherse ryght	*read and recount properly*
	how God to Samuell can apeyre.	*did appear*
4755	As he lay slepand on a nyght	*sleeping one night*
	in the Tempyll, hys mayster nere,	*nearby*
	He herd a voyce call hym on heyght,	*aloud*
	"Samuell, Samuell!" sithes Ser.	*many times*
	He rayse hym up and wentt full wyght	*woke; at once*
4760	unto his mayster with myre chere	*merry*
	And sayd, "Ser, wyll ye oght,	*whatever you desire*
	I com yow forto kepe;	*fulfill*
	Ye cald me als me toyght."	*so I thought*
	He sayd, "Nay, sun, go slepe!"	

398.

4765	He wentt and layd hym down agayn	
	and hastely on slepe he fell.	*quickly asleep*
	And sone he herd the same stevyn certayn	*at once; voice*
	cald on hym and sayd, "Samuell!"	
	He royse and wentt with pase full playn,	*pace*
4770	and to his maystur so can he tell.	
	Then Ely wyst and was full fayn	*knew; very glad*
	that God apered thore them amell,	*there among them*
	"Go slepe, my son so dere,	

	and yf on speke thee tyll,	*one speaks to you*
4775	Say thus: 'Lord, I am here;	
	tell me what is Thi wyll.'"	

399.

	He sleped in his howse at hame,	
	and sone when he to bed was broyght,	
	A voyce come and cald hym by name;	
4780	and he sayd, "Lord, Thi servaunt unsoyght	
	Wyll werke Thi wyll of wyld and tame."	*(i.e., anywhere)*
	Then answerd God, as Hym gud toyght:	*thought*
	"All Jacob suns sall suffer schame	*(i.e., All Israel)*
	for wekyd dedes that thei have wroyght.	
4785	Ely that thou wyt wunes	*live with*
	sall sone dye sodanly,	*soon die*
	For he suffers hys suns	*allows*
	use theft and lechery."	*[to] partake [in]*

400.

	Thus sayd God unto Samuel	
4790	of fell defawtes that folke suld fele.	*terrible calamities; people should experience*
	Unto his maystur con he tell	*did*
	how God had demed ylka dele.	*judged each thing*
	And when Ely had herd his spell,	*news*
	that God was greved then wyst he wele,	*knew*
4795	And in prayers full fast he fell	
	to save hys suns fro the unsele.	*ruin*
	Bot no poyntt myght be feld:	*detail might be altered*
	that Samuel sayd suld sew.	*occur*
	From thenfurth folke hym held	*thenceforth*
4800	for prophett, trest and trew.	*trusted*

[WAR WITH THE PHILISTINES (4:1–2)]

401.

	Sone aftur fell that Phylysteyns	*[it] happened*
	mad grett semblyng on ylka syde	*assembling on every side [of them]*
	Of pepyll that were all paynyms,	*pagans (i.e., non-Jews)*
	for both tho names thei bare that tyde.	*held at that time*
4805	On Jacob suns, that heyght Ebrews,	*[were] called Hebrews*
	come thei to were with mekyll pride	*[make] war; much*
	And says thei sall, whatso yt mevys,	*whoever it upsets*
	be bet or bun all that wyll abyd.	*beaten or bound; would abide*
	Cetyes and towns thei breynt	*burnt*
4810	over all in Ebrews land.	
	Both cornys and wyns thei schent	*grains and wines they spoiled*
	and stroyd all that suld stand.	*destroyed*

402.

Sone Ebrews herd and saw this syght
    that forto byde thei had no beld;   *remain; courage*
4815   Trowghowt ther reme thei raysed ryght   *realm*
    all wyght men that myght wepyns weld   *strong*
Agayns Phylysteyns forto fyght.
    Thei sped them fast with spere and scheld.
Bot smertly ware thei putt to flygh,   *quickly; flight*
4820   and fals Phylysteyns had the feld.   *battlefield (i.e., victory)*
That day was dede and takyn
    ten thowssand, says the Boke.   *Bible*
So God had them forsakyn,
    for thei His law forsoke.

[THE LOSS OF THE ARK; DEATH OF ELI AND HIS SONS (4:3–18)]

403.

4825   The Ebrews toyght both scath and scorne   *injurious and scornworthy*
    that thei suld fro Phylysteyns flee.
Thei sembled folk fast on the morne   *gathered men*
    and sayd thei suld ther solace see.
The Arke of God furth have thei borne;
4830   therwith thei wene to wyne degré.   *hope to win well*
Bot for thei had ther laws lorne,   *forsaken*
    God wold no werke ne with them be.
Of Ebrews sone was slayne   *at once were*
    moe then thrytty thowssand;   *more*
4835   The Arke of God was tone   *taken*
    and led to hethyn land.   *heathen lands*

404.

Thus Ebrews that was putt in prese   *were put into difficulty*
    war all umcast with cares cold.   *surrounded*
Felesteyns ther can full fast encresse,
4840   for thei had Godes Arke in wold.   *possession*
Bot both Ofny and Fynyes,
    Ely suns that I ayre of told,   *I told of before*
Thor leved ther lyves, withowtyn lesse.   *left their lyves, no lie*
    And ther fader, for he was old,
4845   When he herd tythynges tell   *[this] news told*
    that his two suns was slayn,
Down fro his sege he fell   *seat*
    bakward and brast his brayn.   *burst*

[THE ARK AMONG THE PHILISTINES: DAGON BROKEN, A PLAGUE OF MICE (5:1–12)]

405.

Thus Ely and his suns was sloyn,

4850   and Ebrews all was schent for syn.

The Arke of God from them was gone

   with fellows folk Fylystyen.

Thei sett yt be ther god Dagon,

   for thei to hym wold wrschepe wyne.   *make obeisance*

4855 Bot vengance sone on them was tone: *soon; taken*

   he fell and brake both bone and skyne.

And more harme sone at hand

   fell over all that cetye:

Grett myse groyved owt of sand,   *mice appeared*

4860   an ugly syght to se.

406.

Thei ette tho folke, both flesch and blod;   *ate those*

   thei had no fors them to dyffend.

Ther bowels royted wher thei stod;   *rotted*

   ther was no medcyn them to mend:

4865 Mony thowssand for woo were wod.   *woe went mad*

   This vengiance God apon them send,

For the Arke of God, that was so gud,

   was haldyn then in hethyn hend.   *held; heathen hands*

Thei toke consell that tyde   *council at that time*

4870   and send yt fro Assoton   *Ashdod*

To a cyté ther besyde,

   that named was Askalon.   *Ekron*

[THE DECISION TO RETURN THE ARK (6:1–11)]

407.

Bot als sone ose thei toke entent

   to mayntein yt thor them amell,   *there among them*

4875 All the same harme sone had hent: *occurred*

   thei royted and ranked flesch and fell.

To fyve cetys so was yt sent,

   and in ylka place os yt can dwell,   *each*

Sone all the folke ware schamly schent,   *terribly diseased*

4880   so grett nowmer that non myght tell.   *no one might count them all*

Then thei toyght and sayd,   *thought [about it]*

   when thei sufferd so sore,

That God was noyght well payd   *not well pleased*

   his Arke was holdyn thore,   *held there*

408.

4885	For yt gart all that grevance groyve
	of sorows that ware to them soyght.
	And yett thei toyght that poynt to prove
	whedder yt was therfor or noyght.
	A sotell case thei can controve:
4890	A ryall chare sone have thei wroyght
	And coverd yt clenely above;
	the Arke of God thorein thei broyght.
	Fyfe myse then gart thei make
	and fyfe rynges of gold fyne
4895	For the fyfe cytes sake,
	wher folke ware putt to pyne.

Because it caused all the terrible calamities
placed upon them
possibility
that way or not
subtle
royal carrier soon

therein
Five mice then caused they to be made

torment

409.

	Two oxin that myght yt well weld
	sone have thei schosyn that chare to draw
	And led them fere furth into the feld,
4900	the wyll of God for thei wold knaw.
	Thei lete them be withowtyn beld:
	none forto lede them, heygh ne law.
	Thei stode of ferrom and beheld,
	and thus then sayd thei in ther saw:
4905	"Yf the bestes bryng yt nere,
	then wyll God with us lend;
	And yf the flytt yt ferre,
	He ys not fully our frend."

manage
chosen
far out; field
guidance
to lead them, high or low (i.e., anyone)
stood aside
in their way
near
dwell
they (the cows) take it far away

[RETURN OF THE ARK (6:12–7:2)]

410.

	Thoo oxin went with pace full playn
4910	and led the Arke to Ebrews land.
	Phylysteyns, for thei past fro payn,
	was glad that yt was ferre from hand.
	Bot Bethsamys was ferly fayn
	when thei the Arke in ther feld fand.
4915	Procession went thei thore agayn
	and gafe to yt full grett offerand:
	The oxin and the chare thei bryntt
	before the Tabernakyll.
	To the jewells toke thei tent
4920	in mynd of this merakyll.

steady

were relieved of their pains
were; far
[the people of] Beth-shemesh were joyous
field found

large offerings
burnt

they made note

411.

	Then wrschept yt was worthyly
	bot for that thei unworthy were.

except for [the fact] that

Moyses ordand in all the Jewry
    that non suld negh Goddes Arke so nere *approach*
4925 Bot only the lynage of Levy, *lineage*
    pristes or dekyns knawn for clere. *priests or deacons known to be pure*
Thies folke was not so, and forthi *therefore*
    ther boldnes sone thei boyght full dere: *rewarded them quite poorly*
Vengiance com sone unsoyght
4930   apon sexty thowssand.
Sythyn Levy barn yt broyght *Then children of Levi*
    and sett yt where yt suld stand.

412.

Amynadab, a nobyll Jew, *Abinadab*
    when that he saw thies folke mysfayre, *these people fared ill*
4935 He ordand offycers all new,
    swylke os he wyst worthy ware, *such as he knew were worthy*
Of the most cunnand that he knew;
    and his awn sun Eleazare *Eleazar*
Ordand he byschop forto be trew
4940   and tech the folke for all swylke chare. *such matters*
Then lyfed Ebrews at es *ease*
    and forsoke synfull dede. *abandoned sinful ways*
Ay whyls thei wold God plese, *Always when they*
    of nothyng had thei nede.

[SAMUEL JUDGES ISRAEL; WICKEDNESS OF HIS SONS (7:15–8:3)]

413.

4945 Samuel was sufferan cald *considered [their] judge*
    and leyrer of ther laws full lang. *teacher; for a long time*
Two suns he had, wyght men and bold, *brave*
    that melled them of the law amang. *meddled*
Bot ther jugementes oft sythys thei sold *ofttimes*
4950   and turned the ryght oft unto the wrang.
And ther fader, for he was old,
    myght noyght them mare of myse to gang. *stop them from doing misdeeds*
Fro pure men held thei fode
    and fold them monyfold, *animals*
4955 And rych men for ther gud
    myght werke whatever thei wold. *meddled*

[THE CALL FOR A MONARCHY (8:4–22)]

414.

All gude men had full grett dedyne *indignation*
    that ryght suld be so mysarayd. *displaced*
And comyn pepyll can them pleyn *complain*

4960   to Samuell, and thus thei sayd:
         "Syr, thee semys sone to passe hene,   *seem soon to die*
           for eld thi face is all afrayd.   *age; weathered*
         To forther us thou suld not feyne,   *further [lead] us; avoid*
           our governance of mysse is grayd.   *is all out of place*
4965   Therfor, ser, of this thyng
           we pray thee evere ylkon: *always as one*
         Ordand over us a kyng   *Ordain*
           to gyd us when thou art gone.   *guide*

415.
         "Ever ylka nacion bot we   *Every other*
4970   hath kynges chosyn at ther awn chose.   *own choice*
         And, ser, thi suns, soth we see,   *truly*
           thei wyll not leve our laws to losse.   *cease to destroy our laws*
         Therfor a kyng in this cuntré
           grawnt us to have withowtyn glose."   *deceit*
4975   He wyst full well God wold not be   *(i.e., Samuel)*
           plessed nor payd of this purpasse,   *pleased or satisfied with*
         For prophettes, pristes, and clerkes
           governd allway before,
         And God ordand ther werkes.   *governed their works*
4980   Forthi thus sayd he thore:

416.
         "Syrs, ye wott what God hath wroght   *know*
           for yow and all your ofspryng: *children*
         Your elders owt of bondeyg He broyght   *bondage*
           fro Pharo, that cursed kyng.   *Pharaoh*
4985   He send them fode enogh of noyght   *food enough from nothing*
           in wyldernes — that was a wonder thyng!
         And to yourselfe He sendes unsoyght
           to lyfe heyre at your awn lykyng: *own recognizance*
         He sayves yow lyth and lym.   *joint and limb (i.e., in whole)*
4990   Therfor now forto have
         Oyder thyng then Hym,   *Another*
           I consell noyght ye crave.   *counsel you not to ask for*

417.
         "I sall yow say encheson why,   *tell the reason*
           and ose I say, so fynd ye sall.   *as*
4995   Ye have now non bot God Allmighty,
           that wele may govern both grete and small.
         Fro a kyng have of you maistry,   *But if; mastery*
           now are ye fre, then ware ye thrale.   *you would be in thralldom*
         Your corne, your catell, ox and kye,   *grain; livestock, oxen; cows*
5000   bus redy come unto his call.   *must be ready to come*

As hym thynke yt wyll seme,   *it would be best*
    so bus yow ryde and gang   *you must ride and go*
And do os he wyll deme,   *however he desires*
    wheder yt be ryght or wrang."

418.

5005   Thus preched he them by processe playn
    qwat care suld come in all swylke case.   *what ills should come; such cases*
Bot all his wordes was in vayn: *were in vain*
    thei answerd spytfully in that space,
"Ser, we wyll have a kyng certayn,
5010   as the pepyll hath in other place,   *have in other places*
To mayntein us with myght and mayn   *strength and stoutness*
    Agayns Phylysteyns, our face."   *foes*
He heyght them forto have   *promised*
    a kyng in tyme comyng.   *the times to come*
5015   Thei keped noyght els to crave;   *would be satisfied with nothing else*
    then hom went old and yyng.

[SAUL ENCOUNTERS SAMUEL (9:1–27)]

419.

In Masphat sojournd Samuel   · *Mizpah*
    and mad gret mornyng for ther mysse.   *mourning; sins*
And in that same cyté can dwell
5020   A nobyll man, was named Cys.   *Kish*
He had a sun, Saul to tell,   *son*
    a cumly chyld to clype and kyse.   *comely; embrace and kiss*
And in that same tym so befell
    that asses was with-rachyd of hys.   *his donkeys had gone astray*
5025   He bad with wordes meke   *asked; meek*
    Saul, his sun certayn,
Wend furth his bestes to seke   *To go forth to seek his beasts*
    and bryng them home agayn.

420.

Saul was both meke and myld
5030   to fyll his fader commawndment.
He toke with hym another chyld
    for feleschepe, and furth thei went.   *for company*
Thei soyght be ways and wastes wyld
    the assys that thei to seke ware sent.   *donkeys; seek*
5035   Thei fand none that cowde be ther byld   *comfort*
    to tell in what land thei ware lent.   *they had gone*
Saul sayd, "We wyll gang   *go*
    unto my fader agayn;

Hym thynke we dwell full lang,   *too long*
5040   and our gatt ys in vayne."   *journey is in vain*

421.

Hys servand sayd, "Nay, ser, lett us byde   *No; await*
    sum bettur bodword home to bryng.   *better news*
Samuel wunes heyr besyde,   *dwells here*
    a wyse prophett that wott all thyng.   *knows*
5045   He sall us tell in full schort tyde   *in a very quick way*
    of our bestes sum trew tythyng.   *true tidings*
Sen we have wasted ways wyde,   *Since*
    our help now in his hand may hyng."   *hang*
Saul full sone assent;   *quickly agreed*
5050   this way he wold not lett.
To the cyté thei wentt,
    and Samuel sone thei mett.

422.

Thei prayd hym wysch them, yf he myght,   *inform*
    to ther assys that went ware wrang.   *about where their donkeys went*
5055   He sayd, "Suns, dwels with me all nyght;   *stay*
    then sall ye wytt, or ye gang."   *know, before you go*
He saw Saul semly to syght   *seemly*
    and of fayr stature to be strang,   *strong*
And werned he was from Hevyn on heyght   *notified he (Samuel) was; on high*
5060   that he suld be kyng Ebrews amang.   *he (Saul) should*
Folke dyde servyce that day,   *People performed services*
    full grett ose custom kend,   *as custom called*
And to God can thei pray
    sum gud kyng them to send.

423.

5065   And when that wrschepe was all done   *worship*
    and tyme was for the folke to twen,   *depart*
The prophett at the howre of noyne   *hour of nine (i.e., noon)*
    toke thoo two chylder to his yne,   *those; house*
And wheder folke ware felle or fone,   *whether [or not]; many or few*
5070   he dyde Saule the deyse begyne   *made Saul sit at the head of the table*
And made hym to be served sone,   *at once*
    als he ware comyn of kynges kyne.   *as if he were come from royalty*
Ebrews had all ferly   *were all curious*
    why that this werke was wroyght.
5075   Samuel wold not say why;
    he wyst that thei wyst noyght.   *knew that they knew not*

424.

That he suld be kyng well he kend;   *knew*
   therfor he rewled in swylke aray.   *conducted [himself] in such*
In his awn loge that nyght thei lend.   *own house; spent*
5080   And on the morn when yt was day,
With them he ordand hym to wende   *go*
   and toke Saul besyd the way   *beside [him along] the way*
And sayd, "Thus God hath me send
   all his entent to thee at say.
5085   To I have told my toyght,   *Until I have revealed my thought*
   byd thi felow furth goo,
For what God wyll be wroyght
   sall non wytt bot we two."   *no one know*

425.

He dyde hys servant hym withdraw,
5090   and then he sayd, "Saul, take hede!   *heed*
God hath so ordand that thee aw   *instructed; ought*
   His folke in land to lere and lede.   *teach and lead*
And for ther kyng thei sall thee knaw   *their*
   and sewt and servyce to thee bede.   *suit; present*
5095   Ay whyls thou lufes God and His law,   *As long as you love*
   He wyll be nere in all thi nede.
And yf thou wyll ga wrang   *go wrong*
   and werke agayns His wyll,
Thi lordschep lastes not lang.
5100   Therfor take tent thertyll!"   *take heed to this*

[SAUL ANOINTED BY SAMUEL (10:1–16)]

426.

He toke oyle, os God had hym kend,   *announced*
   that blessed was of God before,
And anoynt hym both hed and hend   *head and hand*
   and cald hym "kyng" and kyssed hym thore.   *named*
5105   And sythyn to God he hym be kend   *made him known*
   and told hym wher his assys wore   *donkeys*
And the ryght way how he suld wend,   *go*
   and yett that tym he told hym more.
"Full semly chylder III,
5110   sun," he sayd, "sall thou mette.   *meet*
Thre loyvys sall thei gyf thee   *loaves [of bread]*
   with wordes wyse and swete.

427.

"And forthermer then thee avyse: *furthermore for your consideration*
   in Gabatha thor sall be seyne   *seen*

5115	Prophettes that ar provyd in price	*honor*
	and cunnand clerkes in clergy clene.	
	Thou sall speke with them profecyes	*prophecies*
	and tell what maters may be mene.	*what portents may mean*
	Thei sall wounder on ther wyse	*wonder in their way*
5120	and say thus, 'Wher hath Saul bene?'	
	Sun, yf thou se in certayn	
	this fulfyll in all thyng,	
	Trow then withowtyn trayn	*Know; doubt*
	that God wyll have thee kyng.	

428.

5125	"Grete well thi fader as faythfull frend,	*Greet*
	thi moyder and other meneye mo.	*your other companions*
	And when the terme is comyn to end,	*time*
	that we have tane betwyx us two,	*taken*
	To Masphat sall we same wend."	*together go*
5130	So ylkon cayred wher thei come fro.	*each one traveled*
	The maters that the prophet mened,	*mentioned*
	evyn in ther fayre thei fand them so.	*journey; found*
	Saul sone told full evyn	
	his fader of all his fare,	
5135	Bot nothyng wold he nevyn	*mention*
	of kyndom forto declare.	*kingdom*

[SAUL CROWNED KING (10:17–27)]

429.

	When the seson come that thei had sett,	*season came*
	to Masphat geydderd full gret wone.	*gathered a great many people*
	Ther Samuel and Saul mete	
5140	with myghty Ebrews mony one,	
	For in that place he had them hett	*promised*
	to have a kyng whore thei had none.	*where [before]*
	And lottes thei layd withoutyn lett	*lots; hindrance*
	of what kynred kyng suld be tone.	*from which family the king should be taken*
5145	For so assent thei all,	
	and sone when thei begyne,	
	The lott con lyght and fall	*did alight*
	on the lyne of Benjamyn.	*lineage*

430.

	Then sone thei layd ther lottes agayn	
5150	to wit which man shuld amend theire mys,	*know; their distress*
	And soone it light, is noght at layne,	*it is no lie*
	apon Saul, the sun of Cys.	
	Then Samuel sayd, "Sers, certayn	

	be cowrse of kynd your kyng he ys."	*by course of nature*
5155	The Ebrews answerd and ware fayn.	*glad*
	Kyng myght he be with mekyll blyse.	*much happiness*
	He was cumly to ken,	*fair to see*
	of breyd and heyghnes als	*breadth and height*
	Abowe all other men	*Above*
5160	both be the hede and the hals.	*by the head; neck*

431.

	Thei rayssed hym up into a stall	*seat (throne)*
	on heyght that all men myght hym see.	
	Thei kneled on knesse and kyng hym call,	*knees*
	as costom was in that cuntré.	
5165	Then Samuel sayd unto them all,	
	"Sers, all your yernyng now have ye.	*yearning*
	What fayre to yow ferther fall,	*Whatever should further befall you*
	sett no defawt to God ne me.	*guilt [for it] upon God nor*
	Sen ye have God forsakyn,	*Since*
5170	and His doyng ylka dele,	
	And to a kyng yow takyn,	*you are given over*
	loke that ye luf hym wele.	*love him well*

432.

	"And kepe the lawes that Moyses kend,	*Moses made known*
	leese that ye yeld yourself to spyll."	*lest you yield; death*
5175	Then lyst them thore no langer lend,	*desired; there; to remain*
	bot ylk man went at ther awn wyll.	*each*
	Wyse Ebrews with ther kyng con wend	*go*
	redy hys bedyng to fulfyll.	*ready to fulfill his bidding*
	Sum other foyles can yt dyffend	*fools did oppose it*
5180	and sayd thei assent not thertyll.	
	Bot sythyn when thei saw	*then*
	his gudly governance,	
	Then to hym can thei draw	
	for dowt of aftur chaunce.	

[NAHASH THE AMMONITE BESIEGES JABESH-GILEAD (11:1–4)]

433.

5185	Saul was ordand on this wyse	
	kyng of the Ebrews, all and sum.	
	He sett his reme in gud assyce	*realm in good assize*
	and wroyght by Samuel wysdum.	
	Sythyn Naas, kyng of Amanys,	*Nahash; Ammonites*
5190	that wund full ferre beyond the flome,	*dwelled very far; river*
	Ordand hym redely forto ryse	*Prepared himself quickly to rise up*
	with cuntreys that to hym wold come.	

Ebrews he con dystroy,   *did*
  ever als he myght them geyte,   *all of them that he might get a hold of*
5195 And none myght to hym noye,   *harm*
  so was hys power grete.

434.

He byrns ther towns and ther cetyes
  and stroys ther catell, corn, and wyne.   *destroys*
The febyll folke that hym not flees
5200 to fell also he wyll not fyne.   *kill; cease*
All that he sees sone sall chese
  on of tho twa to take or tyne: *give or lose*
Auder the ryght eye forto lese,   *Either; lose*
  or suffer ded with dewlfull pyne.   *death with terrible pain*
5205 Thus mekyll folke was slayn,   *many people were slain*
  that wold them fend with fyght,   *would defend themselves*
And mony was put to payn   *many were*
  thrugh losyng of ther syght.

435.

So wendes he furth and never fynys,   *goes; finishes*
5210 bot ever his cumpany encrese   *armies increased*
Unto he come to Galadyns   *Gibeonites*
  in a cyté, that heyt Jabese.   *Jabesh-gilead*
Ther settes he gybcrokes and engyns;   *siege hooks and engines*
  of that sawt he wyll not sese   *assault; cease*
5215 Tyll all within be put to pyns.   *Until; to pains*
  and at the last ther cheftans chese   *their leaders chose*
At yeld them to Naas,   *To yield everything to Nahash*
  ther cyté so to have
And weld all that thor was,   *rule; there was*
5220 ther lyfes alone to save.   *lives*

436.

When Naas herd ther resons ryfe,   *many reasons*
  he sayd thei suld chese on of two:
"He that wyll yeld hym sall have lyfe,   *yield himself*
  bot hys ryght eye sall he forgo;
5225 And all tho that wyll stand with stryfe
  we sall not sese, or we them slo."   *until we slay them*
Then weped sore both man and wyfe.   *terribly*
  Thei cowd not wele the werse of tho,   *determine the worse of those [choices]*
Bot of pece thei hym prayd   *peace*
5230 to sevyn days ware past,   *until*
"For sertes, ser," thei sayd,
  "no langer may we last."

437.

The kyng kest hym noyght to remove   *decided not to move away*
   bot styll to abyd in that same stede.   *place*
5235   And comforth to them non he knew
   bot the sevynt day to suffer dede.   *seventh; death*
Therfor that tyme hee grawntt trew,
   and thei sent furth full fast on hede   *forth with headlong speed*
To Saul that was kyng of new
5240   and told how thei ware wyll of rede.   *devoid of options*
"Our carfull end we kene   *sorrowful end we perceive*
   bot thou us sone releve.
Sen we ar made thi men,   *Since we are*
   helpe to mend our myschefe!"

[SAUL DEFEATS NAHASH (11:5–15)]

438.

5245   When Saul herd tell this trayn,   *news*
   amang his men he made grett mone   *moan*
And sayd he wold dyffend tham fayn;   *gladly*
   so sayd his Ebrews ylk one.
He bad the messyngers wend agayn   *to return*
5250   and hald the trew that thei had tone.   *hold the truce; taken*
For socour sall thei have certayn
   or thre days next be comyn and gone.   *before; were come and gone*
Thei wentt, as he them bad,
   full tyte unto Jabes.   *very quickly*
5255   Then Gabonyse was glad   *the Gibeonites were*
   when thei happyn to have pese.

439.

The kyng Saule in his mynd hath ment
   how he myght semyll his pepyll sone.   *assemble his people quickly*
Ane ox he dyd bryng in present   *One*
5260   and bad he suld to ded be done.   *he should be slaughtered*
Thareof to sere cetys he sent   *numerous*
   and sayd, whedder thei had fele or fone,   *many or few*
Thar bestes suld have the same jugment   *Their livestock*
   bot yf thei hastyd withoutyn hoyne   *unless; without hesitation*
5265   To wend with hym in ware   *war*
   ther enmys owt to dryfe.   *to drive out their enemies*
All that myght armys beyr
   was bown to go be lyfe.   *bound*

440.

The kyng gart nowmer them and tell,   *managed to count*
5270   them that suld come in company.

Thei fand of folke of Israel   *found*
    sex hunderth thowsand men myghty,
And of Juda als fell ther fell,   *as many as there appeared*
    the nowmers ar not forto dyscrye.   *to be determined*
5275 Unto them all sayd Samuel:
    "Wendes furth, ye sall have the vyctory.   *Go*
Forto dyffend your ryght   *To defend*
    that enmys hath outrayd   *violated*
God wyll enforc your fyght.
5280   Therfor be noyght afrayd!"

441.

Kyng Saull with his host is wun   *journeyed*
    to Jabes, wher the Phylysteyns dwell.
The fellows folke sone hath he fone,   *wicked people soon he has found*
    that sorely sojornd in ther sell.   *small dwellings*
5285 In a mornyng befor the sun
    with all host on them he fell
And bett them down os bestes bun.   *as bound beasts*
    Thor was no more tale to tell.
Or thei myght wepyns weld   *Before*
5290   to were themself fro wo,   *guard; woe*
Ware thei feld in the feld   *killed on the battlefield*
    that none myght flytt therfro.

442.

Naas, that wold no rawnson take   *ransom*
    bot eyne of all that he myght hent,   *except the eyes; seize*
5295 Now myght no man his sorow slake   *relieve*
    tyll eyne and eyrs and all ware schent.   *ears; cut off*
The Ebrews now may myrthys make,
    that late befor of mornyng ment,   *mourning voiced*
And fals Phylysteyns for ther sake
5300   owt of this werld with wo ar went.
Kyng Saul slogh that day   *slew*
    a hunderth with his handes,
And wan wrschepe for ay   *won worship forever*
    to hym and all his landes.

443.

5305 This was fyrst chaunce of chevalry   *feat*
    that Kyng Saul fell in this case.
Grett boldnes hath his folke therby   *courage had*
    and grett ferdnes to all his face.   *fierceness took over his face*
Folke that before was not frendly,
5310   now ware thei fayn at fall to grace.   *glad to fall*
And he had myght then and maystry

on all Ebrews in ylka place.
  Thei gat, both grett and small,
    that myght full gretly gayn,
5315 And home thei went with all;
    than ware the folke unslayn.

444.
  Thei thanked Samuel of this thyng,
    for by his wytt thei wroyght allway.
  And lowd thei kest up a cryyng,   *a cry*
5320   and to the kyng thus can thei pray:
  "Yf any Ebrews, old or yyng,   *young*
    that ow to lyfe be Moyses Lay,   *by; Law*
  And wyll not knaw thee for ther kyng,"
    that "thei be done to ded this day,   *executed*
5325 All for thei suld be flayd
    that fyrst was turned hym fro."
  Bot he answerd and sayd,
    "God wold not we dyd so.

445.
  "Sen God hath gyfyn us vyctory   *Since*
5330   and our enmys on kares cast,   *in sorrows thrown*
  He wyll that we forgyf gladly   *desires*
    all tho that to us have trespast.   *have done trespass*
  All that wyll mekly aske mercy
    sall have our frendschep full and fast."
5335 The pepyll prayssed hym fast forthi   *praised*
    and sayd his lordschep lang suld last.
  So was all folk his frend,
    and none groched hym agayn,   *complained against him*
  For hys wordes fayr and hend
5340   all ware to his bod bayn.   *commands obedient*

446.
  Samuel says, "Sers, yow avyse   *witness*
    qwat lordschepe God hath yow sent:
  Loves Hym with all your sacrafyce
    of all His grace with gud entent!"   *good intentions*
5345 So dyd thei ylkon on ther wyse,
    and unto Saul sone thei went
  And raysed hym kyng. Then was yt thryse
    with the fyrst tyme that he toke untment.   *took ointment (was anointed)*
  So was he kyng hymselfe,
5350   lordschep to have and hald
  Over all the kynredes twelve   *kindreds*
    that Jacob suns was cald.

[ON ISRAEL AND THE NAMES OF THE JEWS]

447.
Now for ther names so oft tyms news,
  to what entent now wyll I tell:
5355 Of Abraham ware thei cald Ebrews;
  with forme faders so yt befell.
And of Juda thei ware cald Jews
  and with sum chylder of Israel.
Of Canan ware thei cald Cananews.
5360 So in sere cuntres os thei dwell,   *Thus in various countries where*
Be sere names ware thei kend,   *were they known*
  als clerkes well declare,
And God can with them lend   *did with them remain*
  ay whyls thei luf His lare.   *as long as they loved His doctrine*

[SAMUEL SPEAKS TO THE PEOPLE (12:1–25)]

448.
5365 Then Samuel sayd, "Sers, I yow pray
  that ye wyll tell heyr to your kyng   *here*
Yf I dyd ever by nyght or day
  trespase to yow, old or yyng,
Or toke your catell, corn, or hay,
5370 ox or asse or other thyng."
Thei sayd, "Ser, forsoth, nay!
  Ye greved us never in governyng."
"Then have ye now mystakyn
  and served to suffer pyne,   *deserved; pain*
5375 Sen ye hath both forsakyn   *Since*
  Goddes governance and myne.

449.
"And yf God with yow greved be,   *is aggrieved*
  for ye have groched Hym agayn,   *complained against Him*
Pray we Hym, both I and ye,
5380 that He send us sum seyn certayn   *sign*
Of His grevance in this degré."
  And soyn He sent a proyfe full playn: *proof plainly seen*
Swylke wedder that wonder was to se   *Such weather*
  of thonour, levynyng, hayle, and rayne *thunder, lightning, hail, and rain*
5385 And frost, full fell and kene,   *foul and sharp*
  that before was full clere.   *where before [the weather]*
Swylke wedders was never seyne   *weather patterns were never seen*
  in that tyme of the yere.

450.

For then thei had ther harvest grayd *prepared*
5390   to geydder home, both wyn and corne. *to gather*
Then wyst thei well God was not payd, *pleased*
    and that thei had on myse them born. *they themselves had done amiss*
Unto the prophett fast thei prayd:
    "Have mercy, els we be lorne." *destroyed*
5395   "I sall pray for yow, sers," he sayd,
    "bot haves mynd mydday and morn
What grace God hath yow sent,
    als all your kynredes knaw.
Kepes well His commawndment
5400   and lelly lufes Hys law. *dutifully love*

451.

"For what tyme ye breke His bedyng, *bidding*
    your blyse mun with bale be blend; *bliss might with sadness be mixed*
And bees curtase unto your kyng *be courteous*
    with all your myght his myrth to mend;
5405   And honers hym over all erthly thyng,
    and wendes, ylk man, wher he wyll wend."
And thus thei parted, old and yyng,
    wher thei ware levest forto lend. *they were most desirous to go*
Kyng Saul had a sun,
5410   that named was Jonata, *Jonathan*
Qwylk aftur furth was fun *afterwards was found [to be]*
    gentyll with mony ma. *noble; more [qualities]*

[The Philistines invade Israel (13:1–7, 19–22)]

452.

In this meyntyme the kyng herd tell *meantime*
    of new tythandes that was nere at hand: *tidings; near*
5415   Phylysteyns that ware fers and fell *fierce and cruel*
    war enturd into Ebrews land.
In Gabatha thore con thei dwell *Geba*
    and stroyd all that thei before them fand
And hasted to have them omell *among them*
5420   all that to armys war ordand. *were assigned*
And smithes smertly thei slogh *blacksmiths quickly*
    and of iren ylk thyng,
Both fro wayn and ployght, *wagon and plow*
    and gart yt to them bryng. *caused it all to be brought to them*

453.

5425   The Ebrews then yll angerd er: *very angered were*
    away was born that them suld beld. *taken what they should use*

Thei had no wepyns them with to were,   *to make war*
    all myght thei never so well them weld.   *wield*
Phylysteyns myght thei do no dere,   *harm*
5430   all yf thei fele say in the feld.   *field*
Kyng Saul wold fayn them to fere;   *desire to make them afraid*
    he hastyd hym fast with spere and scheld.
He toke thre thowsand men:
    to hymself tha twa   *[of] those [he took the] two*
5435   That he cowd kenest kene,
    and on to Jonata.

454.
And fast thei went furth on ther way
    with other folke foloand in fere.   *following in company*
Sone when Phylysteyns herd say
5440   that Kyng Saul suld com so nere,
Thei governd them in grett aray   *gathered themselves*
    and sembled folke on sydes sere   *many sides*
That sexty thowsand sone had thei
    of knyghtes kene in armys clere   *gleaming armor*
5445   And thrytty thowsand els,   *besides*
    that well myght wepyns beyre,
And mo that no man tels   *more; can count*
    on futte full wyght in were.   *foot full strong in war*

455.
Yt was full semly syght to see
5450   of charyottes and of chyvalry.   *chivalrous [knights]*
Had thei lufed God in gud degré,
    then ware yt daynty to dyscrye.   *then it would be a pleasure to describe*
When Kyng Saul come in cuntré
    in space, wher he myght them aspy,
5455   Dred sum dele in his hert had hee   *Dread somewhat*
    becawse of so grett cumpany,
And for dedes thei had done
    to dyverse man and wyfe;
And his folke ware bot fone   *ill-prepared*
5460   with swylke a strengh forto stryfe.   *strive*

456.
Bot his kenes full well he kyd   *fierceness; proved*
    with all hys myght them forto mare.   *injure*
And when his folke herd how thei dyd,
    then howped thei well forto have ware.   *hoped; war*
5465   Sum fled, and sum in hoyles them hyd;   *holes*
    for ferd then wold thei found no fare.   *fear; get no farther*
Ther ware bot few with hym abyd   *remaining*

	or that wold negh the pepyll nere.	*approach*
	When he saw thei ware gone,	
5470	his teyne myght no man tell.	*grief*
	He wyst no bettur wone	
	bot sent unto Samuel.	

[SAUL MAKES THE OFFERING WITHOUT SAMUEL (13:8–12)]

457.

	Hys moyn be messege can he ma	*entreaty by message he did make*
	that he was ferd and faylyd myght,	*fearful and failed in strength*
5475	How he and his sun Jonata	
	ware ordand with ther foys to fyght,	*foes*
	And how his folke ware fled hym fra	
	when thei of enmys had a syght;	
	And prayd hym come to Gabatha,	
5480	for thore thei suld abyd hym ryght.	*await*
	When Samuel herd certayn	
	how stratly he was sted,	*how he was placed in such circumstances*
	He send sone word agayn	
	and bad, "Be noyght adred!	*afraid*

458.

5485	"For within sevyn days aftur this,"	
	says hymself, "I sall be thore,	
	And tyll that tyme, be gud avyce,	
	that he gett bestes abowt ay whore,	*beasts from whatever places are around*
	So that we may make sacrafyce	
5490	unto our God tho folke before."	
	The kyng hath ordand on all wyse,	*ordered all these things*
	als he send word and sum dele more.	*somewhat more*
	Bycawse the prophett dwellyd	*[But] because; delayed*
	over the terme that was sett,	*past the time*
5495	The kyng more furth hym melled	*interfered*
	then he suld do be dett.	*duty*

459.

	When the tym come that was ordand,	*agreed*
	and no man come hys sytte to slake,	*because; troubles to relieve*
	And hys men wold not with hym stand	
5500	(for wo unwynly con thei wake),	*joyless did they live*
	Foleherdenes he toke on hand	*Foolhardiness*
	hymselfe thore sacrafyce to make.	
	Then the prophett come and foyles fand;	*fools found*
	he was full ferd for dred of wrake,	*very fearful for dread of [God's] wrath*
5505	For he had messege sent	
	with wordes on this wyse,	

    Or he com in present   *Before; person*
       to make no sacrafyce.

[SAMUEL TAKES THE KINGSHIP AWAY FROM SAUL'S FAMILY (13:13–15)]

460.

    Therfor he sentt hym sone his wage   *immediately his reward*
5510   and sayd, "Had thou not done this dede,   *deed*
    Thi suns suld have born heritage;   *been endowed with*
       now sall no frutt be of thi sede
    Bycawse thou hath done this owtrage,
       that suld not passe bot be presthed.   *occur except through the priesthood*
5515   God hath ordand a lytyll page   *page (youth)*
       aftur thi days this land to lede."   *lead*
    Thus told he his entent
       to the kyng and Jonata,
    And wroth his way he went   *angered*
5520   agayne to Ramatha.

[SAUL FIGHTS ON; JONATHAN'S NIGHT RAID (13:15–16, 23–14:23)]

461.

    Then was the kyng in mekyll dred,   *much dread*
       for hertyng of helpe he ne has.   *the encouragement (heartening); does not have*
    He toke apon hym hegh manhed,   *much courage*
       and furth full playnly con he pase.
5525   And thre hunderth then with hym yode   *went*
       of thre thowsand that with hym was.
    That was full lytyll folke to lede
       to hym and hys sun Jonatas.
    Jonatas persayved that thei
5530   myght not eschew that chaunce
    To wyn wrschepe away   *honor*
       bot be Goddes governance.

462.

    The panyms was so grett plenté;   *pagans were so very plenteous*
       on a hegh hyll loged thei lay.   *they lay in their tents*
5535   To stroy ther strengh fast stud he
       and mare ther myght yf he may.   *mar their strength*
    He toke on of his awn meneye,   *one of this own company*
       qwylke he treyst wold not hym betray,   *whom he trusted*
    And sayd, "Felow, com furth with me!"
5540   So prevely thei went ther way   *secretly*
    That none wyst bot thei two;   *knew [of their going]*
       and evyn abowt mydnyght

To that hyll con thei go,   *did*
    and thus then sayd he ryght: *straightway*

463.

5545   "What I do loke thou do the same,   *Whatever; see that you do the same*
    and this sall be our segne certayn: *sign of assurance*
Yf any of them nevyn me be name,   *call*
    then sall we have our purpase playn.   *have our way with them*
And yf thei boldly wyll us blame
5550   and none answer gyf us agayn,
Then is gud that we hast us hame,   *haste ourselves home*
    or els our traveyll turnes in vayne."
Thor was no way to wend
    bot a strayt sty of stone.   *vertical path*
5555   Clamerand on knese and hende   *Clambering on knees and hands*
    by that gatt ar thei gone.

464.

With mekyll payn so can thei pase
    and come into that evyn entré.
On of them wyst well who yt wase,   *knew*
5560   and to his felow thus sayd he,
"Yonder ys comyn the Jew Jonatas
    with mony mo of his meneye."   *more [men] of his company*
Thei loked on them, thei cryd alas;
    soyne ware thei feld that myght not flee.   *soon those were killed who*
5565   Thei ware kylled all uncled;   *unclad*
    none myght helpe other harmes.
Down fro that hyll thei fled
    and brake both leges and armes.   *broke*

[SAUL FOLLOWS UP THE ATTACK; JONATHAN EATS FORBIDDEN FOOD (14:16–35)]

465.

Kyng Saul sadly spyrd and spyed   *sought and looked for*
5570   ther cowntenance forto kene,   *(i.e., to find Jonathan and his armor-bearer)*
And when he herd how hegh thei cryed,
    unto the hyll he hasted then.
Hys folke full fast to hym relyed   *rallied*
    that before dared os dere in den,   *were as brave as deer in their dens*
5575   So that he had be undertyde   *undrentide (morning)*
    mo then ten thowsand feghyng men.   *more; fighting*
He saw Phylysteyns fled
    and full radly remowed,   *readily driven away*
His folke he fast arayd
5580   and then prestely persewed.   *eagerly*

466.

Fayn wold he venge the velany   *Gladly would he revenge*
   that thei had stroyd both wyn and whett.
On payn of cursyng dyde he crye
   that non that day suld tent to mette,   *stop to eat food*
5585 And whoso dyd, he sayd, suld dy,   *be executed*
   and therto swere he othes full grett,   *he swore oaths*
So that thei myght have the vyctory
   or evyn, and then suld all men ete.   *before evening; eat*
Bot hys sun Jonatas
5590 with his felow furth went;
He wyst not, thore he was,   *did not know, where*
   of the kynges commawndment.

467.

Agayns his strake myght no man stand,   *Against his attacks*
   he feld Phylysteyns, grett plenté.   *killed*
5595 So be a forest syd he fand   *by; side*
   honycamys in a holoo tree.   *honeycombs; hollow*
Sone hent he owt on with his hand,   *At once he took it out*
   to hold his hert therof ete he.   *support his strength he ate of it*
He dyd not ose the kyng commawnd,
5600 so greved he God in that degré.   *grieved; by that means*
By the sune was went west,   *By [the time] the sun*
   thei had wun wrschepes grett.   *victories*
Then bad the kyng them rest   *ordered*
   and boldly drynke and ete.

[JONATHAN'S GUILT DISCOVERED (14:36–46)]

468.

5605 Full sewrly that nyght sojournd thei,   *securely*
   for of enmys had thei no dred.   *enemies; fear*
And on the morn, when yt was day,
   the kyng his folke wold ferther lede.   *further lead*
Unto a prophett can he pray,   *did*
5610 Achyas heyght he, os we rede,   *Ahijah he was called, as we read*
That he to God suld sumwhat say
   and wytt yf that thei suld well spede.   *well proceed*
He prayd, os the kyng hym bade,
   and fraynd how thei suld fare,   *inquired*
5615 Bot non answer he had.
   then was the kyng in care.   *nervous*

469.

Then trowd he sum had done trespase.   *he believed somewhat*
   Therfor he fraynd his folke full fast,   *questioned*

And forto wytt how that yt was,
5620   lotes he cummand them to cast.   *lots*
Sone the lott fell on Jonatas.
     Then was the kyng gretly agast
And sayd, "My sun, forfeytt thou has;   *you have forfeited yourself*
     thi lyf may now no langer last."
5625 Then all tho folke in fere,   *together*
     when thei the wordes herd,
Mornyd and made yll chere,
     and Jonatas answerd.

470.

He sayd, "Sers, ye sall understand
5630   I forfeyt noyght, that is my treyst.   *belief*
I herd not how the kyng commawnd,
     ne of his wyll nothyng I wyst.   *knew*
An honycombe forsoth I fand   *I truly found*
     and ete therof to slake my threyst.   *ease my thirst [for sustenance]*
5635 Yf I therfor be law of land   *by the law of the land*
     sall lose my lyf, do os yow lyst!"   *desire*
Thei sayd all schortly, "Nay,
     that was never Goddes wyll.
Or thou suld dy this day,   *If*
5640   fele folke suld fare full yll."   *many people*

471.

Unto ther kyng all are thei gone
     and sayd, "For thi sun we wyll us mell,   *plead*
Sen he hath sayved us ever ylkon   *Since he has always saved us all*
     fro the Phylysteyns fals and fell.
5645 So sewr a soverand have we none   *stalwart a leader*
     sayve thiself, the soth to tell.   *truth*
Therfor we say, and he be slayn,   *if*
     we wyll no lenger with thee dwell."
The kyng herd and toke hede   *took heed*
5650   how hertly thei hym crayved.   *passionately; begged*
For luf and als for dred
     he sayd he suld be saved.

472.

Then ware thei glad, no wonder was;
     full mekyll mon for hym was ment.   *very great moans; were made*
5655 Thei prayd the prophet Achias
     that he and thei be hole assent   *by one assent*
Suld pray God forgyfe that trespase,
     and so He grawnted with gud entent.
Then the kyng and Jonatas

5660	with mekyll gold agayn ar wentt	*much*
	Unto ther places playne,	
	wher thei before had bene.	
	Sexty thowsand ware slayn	
	of fals Phylystyene.	

[SAUL AS KING; HIS FAMILY (14:47–52)]

473.

5665	When thei had thus Phylysteyns feld	*killed*
	and had over hand of all ther foys,	*had the upper hand on all their foes*
	The kyng of Ebrews with hym held	
	of the most hertyng that he has.	*encouragement*
	Then was no man agayn hym meld	*remaining*
5670	bot playn pece in ylka place:	*simple peace in every part of the land*
	Thei sett and sew and boyght and sold	
	and lyfed in lykyng full long space.	
	He lede them be ther law	
	and governd them be Goddes bydyng.	
5675	All Ebrews, als thei ow,	*ought [to do]*
	honerd hym as ther kyng.	

474.

	Kyng Saul had suns thre	
	all dedes to do at hys devyce.	
	Jonatas the fyrst was he,	
5680	that in all place wan grett price;	*won great renown*
	The secund, semly forto se,	
	heyght Jesus and the thryd Melcheys.	*Ishyo; Malchishua*
	All ware thei fayr of face full free	
	and ther warkes full wayre and wyse.	*works [were] very prudent*
5685	And he had doyghturs two,	
	at home wonnand with wyn.	*dwelling with joy*
	The ryght names was of thoo	*those*
	Mycoll and Merobyn.	*Michal and Merab*

[WAR AGAINST THE AMALEKITES (15:1–8)]

475.

	Thus in delyce os he can dwell,	*happiness*
5690	all folke attendand hym untyll	
	God sentt His prophett Samuel	
	at warn hym forto werke His wyll.	
	On Goddes behalf he con hym tell	
	how that ther elders war angerd yll	
5695	with Malachys, a folke full fell,	*the Amalekites; cruel*
	that spetuusly ther sped con spyll.	*spitefully their fortunes*

When thei past fyrst the flome,   *river*
  that folke, full of the feynd,   *devil*
Letted them forto come   *Prevented them from going*
5700   be ways wher thei sull wende.   *desired to go*

476.

Therfor he bad Saul suld passe
  and putt tho paynyms all to pyn,   *those pagans; pain*
Wyfe and chyld, all that thore was,
  cytes, castels, corn, and wyn,
5705   And leve on lyve nawder ox ne asse,   *alive neither*
  cow ne calf, schepe ne swyne:
"Tyll all be lorne that lyf has,   *Until; dead*
  for nokyns fayntnes loke thou fyne.   *no kind of weakness; cease*
Take no parte of ther pelfe   *their property*
5710   to part thi pepyll omang!
Ne sayve noyght to thiselfe;
  wast all els dose thou wrang!"   *[put to] waste everything or you do wrong*

477.

Kyng Saule to his saws assent,   *advice assents*
  and therto hertly hath he heyght
5715   Forto fulfyll Goddes commawndment
  of Malachys with all his myght.
Hee sembled folke, and furth thei wentt   *assembled men*
  with sexty thowsand at a syght.
Thei stroyd cytes and burghys brentt;   *towns burned*
5720   Phylysteyns fast thei feld with fyght.   *quickly they killed*
Fro thei come in cuntree
  that Malachys wund in,   *dwelled*
Thei feld both folke and fee   *livestock*
  and wasted all that wold bryn.   *burn*

478.

5725   Agag was kyng of Malachys
  and led the lordschepe of that land.
Soyne when he wyst on what kyn wyse   *knew in what kind of way*
  Kyng Saul styrd with strang hand,   *stirred [against him]*
Hee redyd all his reme to ryse   *prepared all his realm*
5730   ther enmys styfly to gayn stand.   *stand against*
Of knyghtes kene and princes of price   *brave; worth*
  full fell Phylysteyns furth he fand.
Ther way thei wold not lett
  bot putt them furth in prese.   *battle*
5735   When thei and Ebrews mett,
  thor was no poynt of pese.   *no bit of peace*

479.

To se yt was a semly syght,
  whoso hegh stud and beheld,
Of penons and of baners bryght   *pennons*
5740   with schaftes and mony a schynyng scheld.
Kyng Saul kyd that he was wyght;   *showed; strong*
  his Ebrews boldly can he beld.   *protect*
Phylysteyns so the feld with fyght   *field*
  that sum for ferd forsoke the feld.   *fear*
5745 Men myght see stedes stray   *horses*
  that thore allon was leued,   *there were left alone*
And ther lordes how thei lay
  in ways withowtyn heuyd.   *without heads*

480.

Phylysteyns myght no langer last;
5750   all went to bale that wold abyd.   *into custody who would remain*
With Ebrews ware thei all umcast;   *surrounded*
  the fand no socur in no syde.   *they found no relief*
When thei ware all with payns past   *with pain killed*
  that in the feld was fun that tyde,   *were found at that time*
5755 Ebrews then fowled furth full fast   *went forth*
  to stroy ther landes, lang and wyde.
Thei leved nothyng on lyfe   *found nothing alive*
  that ne to ded war dyghtt: *they did not cause to be dead*
Both man, chyld, and wyfe,
5760   bestes and fowls of flyght.

[AGAG AND SOME RICHES ARE SPARED; SAMUEL'S CONDEMNATION (15:9–26)]

481.

When thei had wasted on this wyse
  ryche and pure, both old and yyng,
Saul was sett on covetyce,
  and sone forgatt he Goddes bedyng.
5765 For Agag was a prince of price;   *much worth*
  he heyght hym help, that hethyn kyng,
And fayrest bestes for sacrafyce
  he bad men suld furth with them bryng.
His folke saw he forfeytt,   *surrendered*
5770   and lett so lyghtly therby.
Thei toke what thei myght gett
  to beyre with them boldly.

482.

So went thei home and wold not dwell;   *remain*
  of ther werkyng well them toygt. *they thought they had done well*

5775	And sone the prophett Samuel	
	come furth to wytt how thei had wroyght.	
	And when he herd the bestes bell	*beasts bellow*
	and saw Kyng Agag with them broyght,	
	He made grett manace them omell	*among*
5780	and sayd that dede suld dere be boyght	
	For thei toke no reward	
	to werke agayns Goddes wyll,	
	That bad none suld be spayrd,	
	nother gud ne yll.	

483.

5785	Full sore he syght for ther sake	*sorrowfully he sighed*
	and sayd thus to Saul, the kyng:	
	"How durst thou werke this werke for wrake:	*vengeance*
	other man or best from theyn to bryng?"	*thence*
	He sayd, "Ser, sacrafyce to make	
5790	and gyfe them unto Goddes lovyng."	
	Then Samuel sayd, "God wyll not take	
	offerand of yll-gottyn thyng.	
	Bot tho that lely lyfes	*who live loyally*
	and kepes Hys cummawndment,	
5795	What gyft so thei to Hym gyfes,	
	therto wyll He take tent.	*take heed*

484.

	"How suld He take offerand to gre?	*favor*
	All thyng Hymself sayd suld be lorne.	*destroyed*
	Both man and best He bad suld be	
5800	fordown, wher thou them fand beforne.	*undone*
	Heyr is the kyng of that cuntré,	
	and best I here yow hath for borne.	*beasts I hear*
	I warne thee: God is wrath with thee,	
	for thou hath wayt Hym with this scorne.	*inflicted*
5805	Thy werke thus wyll He yeld:	
	thi lordschep sall not last,	
	And other thi welth sall weld	*others; wield*
	that in fayth wyll be fast."	

485.

	When Kyng Saul herd Samuel	
5810	so spytfully speke in that space,	
	Unto his fette oft sythys he fell	*knees many times*
	and prayd of God to geyte hym grace	*grant*
	And to amend yt them omell,	*among*
	als he wold consell in that case.	
5815	Bot for his wordes he wold not dwell;	*despite his (Saul's) words he (Samuel)*

	he saw no plessance in that place.	*pleasure*
	Sone fro that pepyll he past	*At once; he [started] to pass*
	ryght way to Ramatha,	*Ramah*
	Bot the kyng folowd fast;	*followed close behind*
5820	in hert he was full wa.	*woe*

[SAUL RIPS SAMUEL'S CLOAK; SAMUEL KILLS AGAG (15:26–34)]

486.

	Full well he wyst he suld be schentt;	*destroyed*
	that made hym hertly forto hast.	*quickly to haste*
	The prophett by the mantyll he hentt	*cloak he grabbed*
	so that yt rayve and worthed to wast.	*ripped; lost its value*
5825	Then sayd the prophett, "Ser, take tent!	*take heed*
	This sall thou trow and trewly trayst:	*believe and truly trust*
	Ryght os thou has the mantyll rentt,	*Just as; garment ripped*
	so sall thi reme fro thee be rast."	*realm; be taken away*
	Then had the kyng grett care,	*sadness*
5830	and oft he askyd mercy:	
	"And thou thus fro me fare,	*If; depart*
	my folke wyll have ferly,	*terrifying [experiences]*

487.

	"And traw that I have done sum trayn	*know; treachery*
	and with sum grett thyng greved thee.	
5835	And therfor, gud ser, turn agayn	
	with glad sembland that thei may see	*countenance*
	And schew to me sum seyn certayn	*certain signs*
	of lastand luf and of lewté."	*lasting; loyalty*
	He grawnted, and then the kyng was fayn	*glad*
5840	sen that myght no bettur be.	
	The prophett come and plessed	*came and made an offering*
	and alowd ylka dede.	*acknowledged each deed*
	Then the kyng was well esed,	*relieved*
	bot in hert had he drede.	*fear*

488.

5845	When thei herd tell of this tythyng,	*heard word; news*
	the pepyll was payd well enogh.	*were satisfied*
	The prophett bad thei suld furth bryng	
	Agag that ever on dregh hym drogh.	*who had withdrawn himself*
	When he was broyght at hys bydyng,	*command*
5850	he sayd, "Thou hath wroght mekyll wogh.	*wrought much woe*
	That sall thou fynd befor our kyng."	*discover*
	Ther with his awn hende he hym slogh.	*own hands*
	Then ryght to Ramatha	
	the prophett wentt in hy.	*haste*

5855   The kyng to Galgala   *Galgal*
           went with his cumpany.

[SAMUEL ANOINTS DAVID AS KING (15:35–16:14)]

489.
     Samuel of soroyng myght not sesse,   *sorrowing; cease*
           for Kyng Saul so wrang had wentt,
     Bycause when God to kyng hym chese   *chose*
5860   then he anoynt hym with an oyntment.   *anointed*
     He prayd to God forto relesch   *release*
           that grett grevance with gud entent,
     Bot he had answer to hald hym pece;   *hold his peace*
           all that was sayd behoved be sentt.   *was said was necessary to be said*
5865   Thei ware fast frendes before
           and of on consell kend;   *known to be of one counsel*
     His mornyng was the more   *mourning*
           when he myght not amend.

490.
     God sayd he suld swylk lufyng lett,   *such emotions cease*
5870   for new gam us bus begyne.   *a new business was needed to start*
     "Take thou thi boyst with the oyle benett   *your box; blessed oil*
           and wend to Bedlem or thou blyne.   *go to Bethlehem before you stop (right away)*
     Thore sall thou fynd, fayr on his flett,   *in his home*
           a Jew, Jesse, of Jacob kyn.
5875   Gayre hys suns befor the sette,   *Gather his sons*
           for on of them sall wrschep wyn.   *one; honor win*
     Enoynt hym to be kyng,   *Anoint*
           Saul stede to restore,   *Saul's place*
     And have the same blessyng
5880   that Saul had before."

491.
     He wentt and wold no langer stand   *remain*
           or he the wyll of God hath wroyght.
     Jesse, that gentyll Jew, he fand   *noble; found*
           in Bethlem cyté sone unsoyght.   *at once*
5885   Fyrst he made them make offerand   *offering*
           and honer God, so hym gud toyght.
     Sythyn he told hym new tythand   *Then; news*
           and bad hys suns suld furth be broyght.   *asked [that] his sons*
     Sex suns ware sett on raw   *in a row*
5890   be lyve at his bedyng.   *quickly; bidding*
     Then prayd he God to schaw   *show*
           qwylke of them suld be kyng.   *which*

492.

All ware thei semly unto syght;	*impressive by sight*
full wyght men ware the eldyst two.	*very strong*

5895
He asked whedder of them suld be dyght.	*which; chosen*
God answerd and sayd, "Non of tho."	*those*
Then unto Jesse wentt he full ryght	
and asked yf he had any mo.	*more [children]*
"Ya, ser, a yong, that David heyght	*young [one]*

5900
is in the feld full fere us fro	*field very far from us*
Our catell forto geyte."	*gather*
Then Samuel with gud chere	
Sayd, "Sertes, I sall nott ete,	*For certain; not eat*
or that hyrdman be here."	*before; herdsman*

493.

5905
David sone was aftur sentt,	*immediately*
and fro he wyst, he wold not byde.	*once he (David) knew; tarry*
He saw the prophett in present	*presence*
and heylsyd hym hendly, noyght to hyde.	*welcomed him properly, hiding nothing*
The prophett hym in armys hentt	

5910
and told hym all what suld betyde.	*happen*
Unto ther dyner then thei wentt:	*their*
he sett the chyld hymself besyde,	
On that other syde Jesse	
and sythyn his breyther all,	*then his brothers*

5915
Ylk on in ther degree,	*Each one; their*
aftur ther eld suld fall.	*age*

494.

Hee honerd hym on deyse that day.	*on the dais*
his fader merveld what yt mentt.	
Sythyn to a prevay place went thei,	*private*

5920
and thore he told all his ententt.	
"My sun," he sayd, "I sall thee say,	
fro God of Hevyn thus am I sentt	
To warn thee of His wyll allway:	*notify*
grett lordschep sal be thee lentt."	*lent*

5925
He wyst withowtyn fayle	*without doubt*
God assent to that same	*same [thing]*
And bad hym kepe consell	
and anoynt hym be name.	

495.

When he hym so anoynt hath	

5930
with holy oyle both hed and hende,	*hand*
The gud gast, that in Saul was,	*good spirit*
in David soyne con descende,	*at once did*

And into that place soyne con passe   *in its*
  An evyll sprett of curssed kynd   *evil spirit*
5935 That dyd Saul oft say, "Alas!"   *made*
  when hys blyse was with bale blend.   *torment blended*
Oft sythys hys solace sessed   *ended*
  with syte and sorow sere.   *anguish; sorrows great*
And David ever encressed
5940 in wytt, als we sall here.   *knowledge; hear*

[SAMUEL'S ADVICE TO DAVID ON GOOD GOVERNANCE]

496.
Samuel sayd, "Sun, whyle thou is yyng,   *young*
  lok that thou gyfe thee to gud thewes,   *yourself [over] to good manners*
For God hath sayd thou sall be kyng
  and keper of all Hys gud Ebrews.   *loyal*
5945 And therfor, sun, lufe lele lyfyng   *son, appreciate loyal*
  and flee fro feleschep of schrews,
And honere God over all thyng,
  that swylke gud grace unto thee schews.   *is revealed*
For whyls thou lufes Hys lare   *lore (wisdom)*
5950 and kepes Hys cummawndment
All whyle sall thou well fare
  and never be schamed ne schent."   *destroyed*

497.
When this was sayd, then Samuel
  wentt to lend wher hym levyst wore.   *reside where he was living*
5955 And David styll at home con dwell   *did*
  in feld with his fader store.   *field; father's herds*
And in that meyntym he con hym mell   *meantime; practice*
  of mynstralcy ay more and more   *minstrelsy ever*
Tyll he cowd herpe, os we here tell,   *harp*
5960 als well as ever was kend before.   *known*
Now David leve we here   *leave*
  with hys herpe and hys slyng   *harp; sling*
And tell how sorows sere   *many*
  come to Saul the kyng.

[SAUL PLAGUED BY AN EVIL SPIRIT (16:15–16)]

498.
5965 The sprett, that I spake of are,   *spirit; earlier*
  that loged was with hym to lende,   *lived; dwell*
Assayd hym oft with sorows sare   *assailed; dreadful sorrows*
  and wroyght hym wo when he lest wened.   *least desired it*
He sentt for feysyke full wyd whare,   *physicians from all over*

5970	and clerkes that in swylke craftes was kend.	*such; were knowledgeable*
	Amang them all thei cowd no mare,	*could do nothing to stop [his ills]*
	bot mynstralsy, thei sayd, myght mend.	*music; alleviate [it]*
	The harpe when he myght here,	*hear*
	the sprett that was within	*spirit*
5975	Suld have no grett powere	
	to dere hym for that dyne.	*hurt; because of the music*

[DAVID WINS A POSITION AT SAUL'S COURT (16:17–23)]

499.

	Then for ther tythyng in that tyde	*their duty at that time*
	he bad men gang to gette that glee.	*ordered the men gathered*
	And so sayd on, that satt besyd,	*one [man]*
5980	"In Bethlem, ser, wuns on Jesse;	*lives one*
	Lett on go loke, no langer abyd,	*Let one [of us] go search him; [to] await*
	for a yyng sun at home has hee,	*young*
	That herpes well, ys not at hyde,	*harps*
	and at your bydyng wyll he bee."	
5985	Messyngers sone was sentt	
	to Jesse for hys sun.	
	So yyng David is went	
	with the kyng in cowrt to wun.	*dwell*

500.

	And soyne when Saul saw that chyld,	*soon*
5990	he made grett solace for hys sake,	
	Bycawse he saw hym meke and myld	
	and mynstralcy that he cowd make.	
	For when the fend was woyd and wyld	*fiend was mad*
	and with sere turmentes wold hym take,	*many torments*
5995	Then was the harpe his boyt and byld,	*relief and comfort*
	and song myght sone his sorow slake.	*quickly slake his sorrows*
	Therfor was David dere	
	and in wrschep all way.	*honor at all times*
	None was the kyng so nere,	*kept so close to the king*
6000	nother by nyght ne day.	

501.

	Thus with the kyng wonnand he was,	*living*
	full well belufed withowtyn wene.	*without doubt*
	Of prowes in all poyntes con he passe	*prowess in all things did he surpass*
	over all that on his eld hath beyne.	*who were of his age*
6005	Bot the kynges sun, heygh Jonatas,	*called Jonathan*
	he lufed hym best of all be deyne.	*straightway*
	Hys hert all holly to hym he has,	*heart completely*
	and that was oft sythis aftur seyne.	*often times seen afterward*

	None wyst he was anoynt	*knew he was anointed*
6010	bot the prophett and hee	
	Tyll yt come to the poynt	
	that God sayd yt suld bee.	

[ANOTHER PHILISTINE ATTACK (17:1–3; 12–15)]

502.

	Soyne messyngers musters them omell,	*Soon; mustered among them*
	of harms hard thei hard at hand:	*heard close by*
6015	How that Phylysteyns, fers and fell,	*fierce and cruel*
	dystroyd all that thei before fand,	*found*
	And how thei dyght them forto dwell	*promised; remain*
	tyll thei had wasted all Ebrews land.	
	Kyng Saul herd this tythyng tell,	
6020	hys ost full sone he had ordand.	*army (host) very quickly*
	The chyld David he sentt	
	to soyjourne forsoth in lye.	*in safety*
	To Bethlem is he went	
	and keped his faders fye.	*herds (property)*

503.

6025	Kyng Saul wold not rest to ryde,	*wait to ride [forth]*
	ne sesse to he of them had syght	*nor cease [riding] until*
	Under a banke, wher thei abyde,	*Beneath a hillside; waited*
	with baners spred of brad full bryght;	*abroad*
	Kyng Saul on the other syde,	
6030	the hyll betwen, was on a grett heght.	*one of great height*
	So nother towched other that tyd.	*neither engaged; at that place*
	Phylysteyns ware the mo of myght.	*stronger force*
	Kyng Saul wyst full well	*knew*
	God was not fully his frend.	
6035	Therfor he drede sum dele	*feared somewhat*
	agayns enmys to wend.	*to go fight*

[GOLIATH TAUNTS ISRAEL (17:4–11; 16)]

504.

	Phylysteyns ware the feller then	*mightier*
	for a grett freke that thei furth fand.	*giant man; sent forth*
	On Golyas ylk day began	*The one [named] Goliath each*
6040	upon that hegh hyll forto stand.	
	He bad Ebrews send furth a man	
	to fyght with hym, hand for hand,	
	And wheder of them so maystry wan	*which; thus mastery won*
	suld have the lordschep of that land.	
6045	He was both grettur and grym	*larger and [more] grim*

then any man myght suppose.

Ther durst non dele with hym   *dared no one to fight*

    for dred that land to lose.   *fear*

505.

Hys armour was passand to prays,   *remarkable to valuate*

6050   and fyve hunderth on his hed he has.   *500 [measures of metal]*

Hys heyberke held of hevy pas   *hauberk; heavy weight*

    sex hunderth to wey with brase.   *600 [measures] to weigh with brass*

In hys ax hede that he suld rayse   *the head of his axe*

    well sexty hunderth weght ther was;   *6,000 [measures of] weight*

6055 And all of stele, the story says,

    and brygh glyterand as any glas.

He was a gremly geyst   *a grim guest (fellow)*

    in feld to fynd before.   *field*

Allway this cowrse he kest   *behavior he did*

6060 full faurty days and more.   *at least*

[DAVID COMES TO THE FIELD (17:17–30)]

506.

In that seson was David sent

    to the sege at see his breyther hende.   *battlefield; brothers [who were] fair*

He asked of men what he be ment   *he (Goliath) intended*

    that on the hyll alon can lend.   *who*

6065 And when thei told hym ther entent,   *understanding*

    and how none durst fyght with that fend,   *fiend*

He sayd, "All grace fro God is lent;   *given*

    unto yond warlaw wyll I wend."   *against that infidel I will fight*

Hys breyther can hym blame,   *brothers did*

6070 and fro care hym to kepe   *from injury*

Thei bad he suld hast hame   *go homeward in haste*

    and fede ther fader schepe.   *feed their father's sheep*

[DAVID WILL FIGHT GOLIATH (17:31–37)]

507.

The kyng herd tell of this tythand,   *news*

    he gart foche David hym before.   *caused David to be brought before him*

6075 "Sone," he sayd, "to leve this land   *Young man; leave*

    and lose thi lyf full lothe me ware.   *very reluctant*

Thou hath no strengh with hym to stand."

    And thus the chyld answerd hym thore:

"My helpe ys holy in Goddes hand,   *completely in God's hands*

6080 I wot His myght is mekyll more.   *know; much more [than Goliath's]*

All yf yond man be strang,   *Even if that man is strong*

    he lyvys not lafully.   *lawfully*

In Goddes name I sall gang *go*
and fell hym sone forthi." *at once therefore*

[DAVID'S ARMAMENTS (17:38–40)]

508.
6085 When Kyng Saul saw for certayn
that hc wold found that fend to fere, *attempt to defeat that fiend*
He armyd hym at all peyssys playn *armed him with all the requisite pieces*
and ordand hym scheld and spere.
Bot the chyld had no myght ne mayn *strength*
6090 swylke weght on his body to bere. *carry*
He sayd, "Takes all this geyre agayn; *Take off; gear*
I am not wunt swylke wed to were. *do not want to wear such armor*
My slyng is nemyll enogh *nimble*
and best dyffence for me.
6095 Wyld bestes therwith I slogh,
that flayd my fader fee." *flayed my father's cattle*

[DAVID AND GOLIATH EXCHANGE WORDS (17:41–47)]

509.
He toke his slyng and furth can found
that mawment yf he myght to marre. *idolater; kill*
He geydderd stones apon the ground, *gathered*
6100 swylk that for his craft accordand were. *were appropriate*
Golias steyted in that stound *came out at that time*
and cald hym fole when he was fere. *called him a fool; far away*
"Boy, hopys thou I be a hound?" *do you hope*
David sayd, "Sertes, I hold thee werre." *I consider you worse*
6105 Golyas says, "Go hom,
thou barn, and leve thi berre! *child; abandon your boast*
Tho folke that thou fro come
sall by this dede full dere." *deed [pay] full dearly*

[DAVID KILLS GOLIATH (17:48–51)]

510.
David fast toke furth his slyng
6110 and a ston that therfor was fytte. *fitting*
Abowt his hed he can yt bryng,
to tyme he saw wher yt suld sytt. *until*
He wated the warlaw with a wryng *struck the idolater; throw*
and made hym wode owt of hys wytt: *mad*
6115 For armour or for other thyng, *Despite; any other*
into the harns he has hym hytt. *brains*
For all the lakes he lerd *boasts he pronounced*

	the lyve thor he leved.	*this life there he left*
	David with his awn sword	*his (Goliath's) own*
6120	swythly swapped of hys hed.	*quickly lopped off*

[PHILISTINES ROUTED (17:51–54)]

511.

	Phylysteyns herd this note new;	*heard of this matter at once*
	yf thei had noy ys not to hyde.	*anxiety [it]*
	Full rasydly thei can remew	*swiftly; retreat*
	and reydyd them to ryn and ryde.	
6125	Kyng Saul prestly can persew	*pressingly did pursue [them]*
	and foled fast to fell ther pryde.	*followed*
	That day was joy to mony Jew	
	to here the hethyn how thei cryde:	*heathens*
	Thryty milia war slayn	*30,000 were slain*
6130	of folke that myght not flee.	
	Thei turned then home agayn	
	into ther awn cuntré.	*own*

[SAUL GROWS JEALOUS OF DAVID (18:1–9, 13–16)]

512.

	With Kyng Saul was David dere,	
	for he had done this doyghtynes.	*act of martial bravery*
6135	And all the folke, both ferre and nere,	*(i.e., everywhere)*
	gaf hym the price of that prowesse.	
	So ose thei com by cyteys sere,	*through many cities*
	all welcomd them, os worthy es,	*as is proper*
	With mynstralsy and mere chere	*merry cheer*
6140	of wyfes and maydyns, more and lesse.	
	Tho wyfes sang how Saul slogh	*Those; killed*
	a thowssand with his hand;	
	The madyns sang and loghe,	*laughed*
	"David slogh ten thowssand."	

513.

6145	When Saul herd, he was sory.	
	Wyfes sayd he sloght a thowsan playn,	
	And maydyns made ther melody	
	that David had ten thowsand slayn.	
	Of this began full grett envy	
6150	and lasted lang, ys not to layn.	*it is not to be hidden*
	For in hys hert he thynkes holy	
	how Samuel prophett sayd certayn	
	He suld his lordschepe lose,	
	for he brake Goddes bydyng.	*defied God's instruction*

6155   This sang made hym suppose   *song*
           that David suld be kyng.

514.
           Bot he wold mare hym, yf he myght,   *would harm*
           that he suld never that fare fulfyll.
           He saw, for this werke he had wroyght,   *(i.e., the killing of Goliath)*
6160   that all men lufed hym lowd and styll.   *publicly and privately*
           Sere sutelteys oft sythys he soyght   *Many tricks he often times sought*
           how he myght sped hym forto spyll.   *quickly kill him (i.e., David)*
           Bot to hymself he wold say noyght;
           ne David toke no tent thertyll.   *nor did David take any heed thereto*
6165   He provyd passand his eld   *proved himself surpassing of his age*
           of gud maners and myght.
           For he cowde wepyns weld,
           to were was non so wyght.   *to make war; capable*

515.
           Kyng Saul fayged hym with fayrhede   *flattered; speciousness*
6170   and wayted ever to werke hym wo.
           He wyst well for hys doyghty dede   *knew; brave deeds*
           that Phylysteyns ware hys foo.   *foe*
           He ordand hym his ost to lede
           all way when thei to were suld goo.   *war would go*
6175   That was nother for lufe ne dred,   *neither for honor nor fear*
           bot that Phylysteyns suld hym slo.   *slay*
           Bot God was ever hys gyde
           his werke forto warrand.
           Wher he suld gang or ryde,   *walk*
6180   gud hape was in his hand.   *good fortune*

516.
           Then went David with scheld and spere
           and styfly stud in mony a stowre.   *stalwartly stood in many an engagement*
           Phylysteyns was he fayn to fere,   *glad to frighten*
           in ylka feld he bare the flour.   *on each battlefield; bore the flower (achieved victory)*
6185   All welthys that he wan with were   *goods; won with battle*
           he sent to Saul for socour.
           And that he dyd David to dere
           God turned yt to his grett honour.
           The kyng ay waytand was   *ever waiting*
6190   how he myght werke hym wo,
           Bot the kynges sun, Jonatas,   *Jonathan*
           fendyd hym ay therfro.   *always defended him from that*

[MICHAL'S LOVE FOR DAVID; THE BRIDE-PRICE AND THEIR MARRIAGE (18:20–29)]

517.

	As brether ware thei fast in fere	*Like brothers; dedicated in company*
	ather to beld os other bad.	*either to do as the other needed*
6195	All folke them lufed, both fere and nere,	*far and near*
	in ylka sted wher thei ware sted.	*each place*
	And Mycoll, the kynges doyghtur dere,	*Michal*
	David hyr hert all holy hade.	*her heart completely had*
	When he was moved to make yll chere,	
6200	no myrth on mold myght make hyr glad.	*on earth; happy*
	And when the pepyll hym plessed,	*pleased*
	and scho hys conforth kend,	*knew of his comfort*
	Yf other had hyr dysplessyd,	
	that medcyn moght amend.	*medicine might amend it*

518.

6205	In luf thus lang was scho led,	
	scho had no lykyng of hire lyfe.	
	When he in any stoure was sted,	*battle was engaged*
	then was hyr mynd in mekyll stryfe.	*much anxiety*
	Scho swere that no wyght suld hyr wede,	*swore; man; wed her*
6210	bot scho myght ever be his wyfe.	
	Scho had no beld at bowre ne bed;	*comfort in bower or bed*
	hyr care was kene as any knyfe.	*sorrow was as sharp*
	Scho changed hyde and hew,	*color and complexion*
	hyr fayrnes fast can fale.	
6215	At the last the kyng yt knew	
	and asked of his consaylle	*council*

519.

	If them toyght yt ware well to do	*thought it was the right thing to do*
	to gyf his doyghhtur to David.	
	And thei gafe consell all therto:	
6220	"Non is so kumly in this kyth.	*fitting in this country*
	A semly copyll is of them two,	*beautiful couple would be made*
	for both ar large of lym and lyth."	*prodigious in limb and joint*
	The kyng assented it shuld be so,	
	bot this forward he fest therwyth:	*contract he made*
6225	Heydes of Phylesteyns	*Skins (hides)*
	two hunderth suld he bryng.	*he (i.e., David) bring*
	With this ylk wyle he wenys	*same stratagem he believes*
	David suld make endyng.	*be killed*

520.

	Full well he trawd by this yll trayn	*thought; wicked guile*
6230	David to lose in lytyll stound,	*in no time at all*

	And or he had two hunderth slayn	*before*
	forto have mony a wekyd wound.	*many terrible wounds*
	Bot David of that fayr was fayn;	*business was glad*
	he gatt felows with hym to found,	*got; go*
6235	For Mycoll luf hym lyst not layn.	*Michal's love he did not deny*
	Philysteyns fast he fell to the ground.	
	Two hunderth hedes certan	
	ware nevynd to hym be name,	*called; by name*
	Bot when he come agayn,	
6240	fyfe hunderth broyght he hame.	*home*

521.

	Then was he praysed with man and page	
	with sere solace that to hym soyght.	
	Thei sayd he was well worthy his wage	
	for this ylke warke that he had wroyght,	*very work*
6245	That so had sterd hym in that stage.	*Who thus had conducted himself*
	Fyve hunderth hedes with hym he broyght.	
	The kyng then made the mayreg,	*marriage*
	bot evyll ay was in hys toyght:	*evil ever; thought*
	Sere cawtels oft he cast	*many cunning tricks*
6250	David to schame and schend.	*destruction*
	All turned to the best,	
	for God was ever his frend.	

[DAVID'S CONTINUED SUCCESS (18:30, 19:8)]

522.

	Soyne aftur this so yt fell:	*happened*
	Phylysteyns, full of envy,	
6255	Dyght them and wold no langer dwell	*Readied themselves; wait*
	to be venged of ther velany.	
	When Kyng Saul herd tythyng tell	*news told*
	that enmys com in opynly,	*[their] enemies came against [them]*
	He demyd David with them to mell,	*instructed; deal*
6260	and als he heyght, he dyde in hye.	*ordered; in haste*
	Felows that wold not fayle	
	ar gladly with hym gone.	
	Thai vencusyd the batele	*won (vanquished)*
	and gat gud full grett wone.	*got goods*

[SAUL AND THE EVIL SPIRIT; HIS ATTEMPT ON DAVID'S LIFE (19:9–10)]

523.

6265	Then with all folk was David dred	*fearfully acclaimed*
	and hownerd for his dughty dede.	*martial deeds*
	When Saul herd he had well sped,	

	then in his hert he had more drede.	*doubt*
	Down he fell seke in his bede,	*sick*
6270	for ferd David that land suld lede.	*fear; would lead*
	Hys yll sprett soyn hym spred;	*wicked spirit quickly struck him down*
	no speciall spech myght hym spede.	*comfort*
	David was aftur sent	
	by hym to harpe and syng	
6275	And all to evyll entent:	*intention*
	in bale hym forto bryng.	*grief*

524.

	David hym dyght to do his dett:	*prepared himself; duty*
	the kyng fro wo yf he myght were.	*might protect [him]*
	As he with harpe to syng was sett	
6280	the fend fers so forto fere,	*fierce fiend (wicked spirit) thus to drive away*
	The kyng hath cast his lake to lett:	*tried to stop his (David's) playing*
	withowtyn spech he spens a spere.	*grasps a spear*
	To David evyn he toke his mett	*aim*
	thrugh the body hym to bere.	*bear [the point]*
6285	Then Mycol kest a cry,	*cried out*
	and David turned hym soyne.	*turned around immediately*
	Fast home he can hym hye.	*hasten*
	God wold noyghth yt were doyne.	*did not want it done*

[SAUL AGAIN ATTEMPTS DAVID'S LIFE; MICHAL HELPS HIM ESCAPE (19:11–17)]

525.

	The kyng was then all wode for wo;	*crazed*
6290	that he so scaped, hym toyght scorne.	*thus escaped*
	He bad wyght men be lyve suld go	*ordered strong men at once*
	and lyg in wayt untyll morn,	
	And that he suld not scape them fro,	
	for forfetur myght fall therforn.	*forfeiture [of their lives]; (i.e., if that happened)*
6295	He suld not lett for frend ne foo	*pass*
	no langer tyll his lyf ware lorn.	*taken away*
	When Mycol hath this herd	
	how hyr fader can say,	
	Full ferdly furth scho ferd	*Very frightened; went*
6300	to marre yt, yf scho may.	*mar it (Saul's plan)*

526.

	"David," scho sayd, "my husband hende,	*fair*
	my fader hath full hertly hyght	*sincerely sworn*
	He sall not fyne for fo ne frend	*cease*
	to morn or he hath marde thi myght.	*mourn before; marred*
6305	Thi way wyghthly behoves thee wende	*quickly*
	and leve me here a wylsom wyght.	*helpless person*

For bettur is thou lyfe and lende   *remain*
    then that we both to dede be dyght."   *death*
He assented certayn
6310   syghand with sympyll chere.   *sighing; mood*
Yf thei parteyd with payn,
    no question is to inquere.   *ask [why]*

527.
Swylke wemen were worthy to wed   *Such women*
    to helpe ther husbandes in a nede.
6315   For hyr ded was scho not adred,   *death*
    bot yit scho dyd another dede:
Scho layd a dry stoke in his bed   *log*
    and covert yt with worthy wede.   *clothes*
When knyghtes come hym to have dede,   *killed*
6320   scho sayd, "Sers, sen he fro cowrt yede,   *since he left the court*
He toke so hertly care   *sincere ills*
    his lyf days ar nere done."   *[that] his life's days*
Thei wened well yt so ware;   *knew; were*
    agayn thei went full sone.   *they returned [to court] at once*

528.
6325 And evyn os thei in syght com see,
    unto the kyng so con thei say.   *did*
He bad be lyve, "Bryng hym to me;   *quickly*
    he sall dee with dole this day!"   *die with grief*
Thei saw yt myght no bettur be;
6330   unto his hows agayn go thei.
In his bed thei fand a mekyll tree   *found a big tree*
    hyld, and he was went away.   *covered over*
When the kyng saw he was hale,   *healthy*
    hys hert had sorow enogh.
6335   [. . .]
      [. . .]

[DAVID ESCAPES TO RAMAH AND SAMUEL (19:17–18)]

529.
He sware his doyghtur suld be schent;   *destroyed*
    full he leved to lose his land.   *believed*
To Ramatha is David went,   *Ramah; gone*
6340   wher Samuel is sojorand.   *residing*
He told to hym all his entent,
    how that the kyng so fellows fand,   *such fellowship found*
Bot that he so the lyfe was lent.   *remained alive*
    Both loved thei God with hert and hand.   *praised*
6345 He sayd, "Sun, for this thyng

in hert have thou no toyght.	*care*
God will that thou be kyng	*desires; you [should] be*
when all his whylys ar wroyght."	*his (Saul's) wiles*

[SAUL'S FAILURES TO GET DAVID; HE AND JONATHAN MEET (19:19–23)]

530.

	Aftur this ware long to tell	
6350	how ever the kyng hys kindes kyd.	*made known his nature*
	For messeg made he mony amell;	*between [them]*
	to be his bayne ay can he byd.	*bane always did he work*
	When Jonatas herd how that yt fell,	
	grett hevenes in hert he hyde.	*heaviness*
6355	For dowt of dede that con hym quell	*fear of death*
	he wold bot wytt how David dyde.	*would nevertheless know*
	Ryght unto Ramatha	
	he went the gaynest gatte.	*[by] the straightest road*
	The trew lufe betwen them two	*true love*
6360	myght no bale gare abate.	*for no sadness could be weakened*

531.

	When David herd say for certayn	
	that Jonatas wold com hym tyll,	
	Ful gladly went he hym agayn	*he went to meet him*
	and thanked hym oft of all gud wyll.	
6365	Of his frenschepe he was full fayn,	*glad*
	for he lufed lely lowd and styll.	*loyally publicly and privately (i.e., in all arenas)*
	He told hym all the procese playn	
	how the kyng aspyd hym to spyll.	*worked to kill him*
	To fotte can David fall	*To foot (i.e., kneeling) did*
6370	for his God wyll all way.	*God's will in all ways*
	Jonatas says he sall	
	helpe all that he may:	

532.

	"To the kyng, my fader, wyll I fare	
	and faynd his frenschepe forto geyte.	*attempt; to get [for you]*
6375	For thee to speke I sall not spare,	
	all thof he wold me bynd or bete.	*even if; beat*
	At erst that I her answer	*As soon as I hear*
	of lastand luf or like to thrett,	*unfailing worship*
	That thou may kepe thiself fro care,	
6380	thou sall be wernd, or ever I ette."	*warned, before ever I eat [anything]*
	David says, "For mercy,	
	thou mendes all my myschefe."	*mends all my sadness*
	Thei kyssed full curtasly,	
	and so thei toke ther leve.	*their leave [from one another]*

[JONATHAN SOUNDS OUT SAUL (20:24–34)]

533.

6385   Jonatas went with sympyll chere,
      unto the cowrt he come in hye.   *haste*
   When grett fest was of folke in fere,   *in company*
      unto his fader he sayd sothly: *truthfully*
   "Ser, David that is to yow so dere
6390   and in his dedes ys ay doghty,   *deeds is always brave*
   How ys yt so he is not here?
      He myght menske all this mangery.   *honor everyone at this feast*
   He is your sun by law
      and my brother also.
6395   Be oght that ever I knaw,   *anything*
      he trespast never yow to.   *against you*

534.

   "He is ay redy in your ryght   *always ready*
      agayn your rebels forto ryse;
   Phylysteyns hath he feld with fyght   *slain*
6400   and owtrayd all our enmyse.   *overcome*
   In cowrt is non so cumly knyght,   *no one so fair a*
      ne non so wyse, yf he us avyse."   *thinks of us*
   The kyng then loked on hym full lyght   *at once*
      and sayd, "Lossell fowle, thou lyse.   *Scoundrel foul, you lie*
6405   That sall ye both abye,   *atone for*
      als sone os I hym see.   *as soon as*
   Thou maynteyns with maystry   *honors*
      the most enmy to me."   *the greatest enemy*

535.

   Jonatas answerd with word hende:
6410   "Ser, yt hath not so bene sene;
   Ye have fun your faythfull frend;   *wronged*
      to your bedyng bown hath he bene."
   Then wex the kyng full of the Fend;   *grew; Devil*
      he wared fast with word kene.   *cursed; sharp words*
6415   Hys sun he schope forto schend,   *son he attempted to destroy*
      yf wyght men had not gone betwene.   *strong*
   Jonatas wyst well enogh   *knew*
      then how the game wold go.
   Of dregh he hym withdrogh   *Aside he withdrew himself*
6420   and fled his fader fro.

[JONATHAN SPEAKS WITH DAVID (20:35–42)]

536.

To David wyghtly is he went,	*quickly*
wher he was in grett stody sted,	*anxiety remaining*
And sayd how he suld have bene schent	*killed*
befor his fader, had he not fled,	
6425 And how no mercy myght be ment,	
ne specialty may none be sped.	*expected*
"Ther is no other tale to tent	*listen [to]*
bot wend or wage thi hede in wed."	*depart or place your head at stake*
To his fette then David fell	*feet*
6430 and thanked hym of all thyng.	
Luf that was them omell	*among*
made payn at ther partyng.	

537.

David sayd, "Ser, sen yt is so,	*since*
for soverayn God thus he be soght!	
6435 All yf thi fader wyll be my foo,	
be thou my frend and fayle me noyght!"	
Jonatas sayd, "For well or wo,	*good or bad*
what warke in ward with me be wroyght,	
The cunnand made betwyx us two,	*promise*
6440 that sall I hald with hert and toyght."	*heart and mind*
Thei durst no langer dwell,	*dared; remain*
for folke ware not ther frend.	
Thei kyssed and morned omell,	*together*
and so ther way thei wend.	*took*

[DAVID MEETS WITH AHIMELECH (21:1–9)]

538.

6445 Jonatas went with sympyll chere	
agayn unto that same cety,	
And David soyght with sorow sere	*many worries*
untyll a town, was named Nobbé.	*Nob*
Thor wuned a byschope of grett power,	*dwelled*
6450 Abymalec at home hegh he.	*Ahimelech; called*
He welcumd David os his dere	*friend*
and asked hym aftur his meneye.	*company*
He sayd, "Ser, I am sent	
in messege fro the kyng.	
6455 My meneye furth ar wentt	
for other nedfull thyng.	

539.

"Myn armour gart thei me forgete.   *they caused me [to] forget*
   Yf thou have any, helpe me!" he says.
"And als yf thou have oght at ette: *also; anything to eat*
6460   for sene I ette ar gone thre days.   *since I ate have passed*
And ser, I have meystur of mette,   *need of food*
   for I have to wend wylsom ways."   *to follow a winding road*
The byschope says, "I have of whette   *grain*
   blessyd bred that is to prays.   *sacred bread*
6465 Bot armour none I bere,
   ne wapyns with to fyght   *nor weapons*
Bot a gud sword of were;   *except a worthy; war*
   that sall be thin be ryght."

540.

He cald hym kyndly, as he can,   *refreshed*
6470   with mette and drynke and myrthis more.   *joys*
Golias sword he gaf hym then   *Goliath's*
   qwylke hymselfe wan in feld before.   *which*
In this meyn tyme com in a man,   *meantime came*
   Odeth, that keped the kynges store.   *Doeg; king's herds*
6475 He wyst not how debate began,
   ne of the kyng how wroth thei ware;
Bot that he thore can see,
   and talken them betwen,
In hert well haldes hee,   *remembers*
6480   for so was aftur sene.

[DAVID AS OUTLAW LEADER (21:10–22:5)]

541.

Then David furth his frendes soght;
   he fand bot few in to affy.   *found; trust*
In certayn sojorne wold he noyght: *safety he could not travel*
   that folke by spech myght hym aspy.
6485 Full mony wonder werke he wroyght,   *wondrous works*
   als he com in sere cumpany.   *various*
And how all was to endyng broyght,   *completion*
   the Bybyll bers wyttenese therby.   *bears witness*
Yt ware long tyme to tell
6490   how he hys cowrse kest   *took his course*
And what ferlys be fell   *wonders*
   or he was broyght to rest.   *before*

542.

Bot poyntes that falys to our procese,
   sum of this werke we wyll begyne:

6495	How that he wund in wyldernese,	*dwelled*
	in a forest that heygh Sephyn.	*called Ziph*
	Thore come men to hym, more and lesse,	
	of cosyns and of other kyn.	*family members*
	And thos that owtlayd or exyld ys,	*those who were outlawed or exiled*
6500	thos went to hym, all that myght wyne.	*manage [to do so]*
	Thei bede hym forto be	*promised*
	his men in all manere.	
	So in schort tyme had he	
	fawre hunderth folke in fere.	*four hundred men together*

[Philistines attack Keilah; David saves the city (23:1–13)]

543.

6505	Now in this meyn tyme herd thei tell	
	with folke that ferd thore to and fray	*went to and from there (Ziph)*
	How the Phylysteyns, fers and fell,	*fierce and cruel*
	inseged a cyté that heght Ceilay,	*besieged; that [was] called Keilah*
	And how thei made maystrays omell	*tyrannies among [them]*
6510	and sayd that thei suld bryn and slay	*burn*
	Ebrews that in that ceté dwell	
	and all ther thresour to them ta.	*take*
	Thei brynt and wold not blyn	*set fire; cease*
	abowt both lengh and brede.	
6515	Then thei that ware within	
	lyfed in grett dole and drede.	*woe and fear*

544.

	Qwen David wyst thei suld be slayn	
	he wrscheped God with wyll and toyght.	*honored; thought*
	Then unto God fast can he frayn	*inquire*
6520	whedder he suld helpe them and he moght.	*if he can*
	And sone he had answer agayn	*at once*
	and sayd, "Go furth and drede thee noyght!"	
	To geydder his folke he was full fayn,	*gather; joyful*
	and unto Cyala sene thei soyght.	*Keilah then they journeyed*
6525	Thor was no tale of trewse;	*talk of truce*
	Phylysteyns fast thei feld.	*speedily they killed*
	And thei resaved the Ebrews	*welcomed (relieved)*
	that in that cyté dwelled.	

545.

	The soverance of that same cyté	*governors*
6530	honerd David with hert and hende	
	And bed at his bedyng to be	*promised; bidding*
	and at his wyll to wun and wende.	*to do all things*
	In that cyté then sojornde he,	

	and in grett lykyng thor thei lend	*pleasure there they remained*
6535	So that hymself and his meneye	*company*
	with mette and drynke ware mekyll amend.	*food; much strengthened*
	Thore gatt thei gold gud wone,	*in good amount*
	armurs and other wedys.	*clothes*
	Sum that before had none	
6540	hose now all that them nedes.	*had now; needed*

546.

	Word of this werke full wyd can spryng	
	with lernd and lewd in all that land.	*among the learned and the unlearned*
	And sone was told to Saull the kyng	*soon [it]*
	how David was so sojornand.	*sojourning*
6545	He was full fayn of that tythyng,	*pleased; news*
	for ther he hopyd to have hym at hand	
	And into a bale hym forto bryng,	*sadness*
	for his strengh myght no man stand.	
	He sayd, "Sone sall we see	*At once*
6550	hys bost proved full prest,	*boast; very quickly*
	When he haldes that ceté	*holds [himself within]*
	and levys the fayre forest."	*leaves*

547.

	He purpassed hym full prevely	*privately*
	David to schame and to schend	*kill*
6555	And ordand with clene cumpany	*ordered with a whole company*
	to Ceila sodanly to wend.	*go*
	He sent sere men to spyre and spye	*various; inquire*
	how David tytest myght be tened.	*most quickly might be harmed*
	Bot he had hertyng hastely	*he (David) had advice*
6560	fro God, that ever was his frend.	
	God werned hym fast to flee	
	with his men, old and yyng,	
	And in the forest to be	
	for the kynges comyng,	

548.

6565	For yf the kyng that ceté crafe	*desired*
	or any sawt to yt sett,	*before any assault was set to it*
	The cyteners themself to sayve	*citizenry*
	sall sone delyver yt ose dew dett.	*as due debt (i.e., a sign of loyalty)*
	Then suld David no helpyng have	
6570	bot be tane os a fysch in a nett.	*caught as*
	And sone went both knyght and knave	
	to forest, where none wold them lett,	
	And when the kyng yt knew,	
	that thei ware past fro playn,	*had passed from the area [of the city]*

6575   No ferther wold he persew
             bot tytt turned hom agayn.   *quickly*

[DAVID AND JONATHAN MEET IN ZIPH (23:14–18)]

549.
         Thei toke to a wod that heyght Gedyn,   *En-gedi*
             bot thore thei sojornd bot lytyll whyle;
         Then to a forest that heyght Cephyn;   *Ziph*
6580   thore hoped he non suld hym begyle.
         Thor Jonatas fro all his kyn
             to see David soyght mony a myle.
         He was wel glad his wrschepe to wyn,   *love to achieve*
             all yf his fader wold fayn hym fyle.   *even if; be glad to dishonor him*
6585   Yt was myrth, when thei mett,
             to wytt how all yt was.
         Thei kyssed and for joy grett,
             and sone sayd Jonatas:

550.
         "David," he says, "drede thee no dele,   *fear you in no way*
6590   all yf the kyng threpe again thee,   *even if; inveighs against you*
         For aftur wo all sall be well:
             thou sall governd in grett degree.
         I am thin freynd; that sall thou fele: *trust*
             ther sall not fawt be fun in me.   *never fault be found*
6595   To sayve thiself seke thi sele;   *seek your safety*
             yt is the fayrest forto flee.
         Thou sal be kyng be kynd   *natural process*
             and full grett lordschepe lede.
         Make me then in mynd   *Hold*
6600   and thynke on ayre don dede.   *our accomplished deeds*

551.
         "Yt is wysdom, os wysmen says,
             at suffer welth forto wyn.
         And in no poynt he is to prays   *in no way; praise*
             that cannot byde his bale to blyn.   *wait for his sadness to cease*
6605   All yf the kyng thee wayte all ways,   *ambushes you*
             he sall not dere for all his dyn.   *harm [you]; noise [about it]*
         Thou sall endure aftur his days
             and stand in state that he standes in."
         Thus bad he hym to beld   *take courage*
6610   and sayd he suld be kyng.
         David curtasly kneled
             and thanked hym of all thyng.

552.

Then parted thei, yf yt ware payn,   *even though it were painful*
    for full trew luf was them betwen.

6615   And Jonatas went home agayn
    so that non wyst whore he had bene.   *knew where*

And David held his peyse full playn   *peace*
    in wodes, for he suld noyght be sene.

And ever he has in uncertayn

6620   whore he myght dwell withowtyn tene.   *trouble*

He durst not dwell for dyn   *dared*
    in town, ne in cyté.

In the forest of Cephyn
    ay toyght hym best to be.   *he always thought it was best to be*

[DOEG'S BETRAYAL OF AHIMELECH (22:9–19)]

553.

6625   All in desert so con thei dwell;
    of ryall ryches noyght thei reke.   *royal; heeded*

Thei dranke no wyn bot of the well,   *wine except from*
    ne beyre bot of the reynnand beke.   *beer except; running brook*

In this meyn tym is so to tell

6630   how the kyng in yre was ever freke,   *anger; eager*

And of falshed that then befell
    thrugh Odeth to Abymaleke.   *Doeg against Ahimelech*

The kyng for David spyred   *inquired*
    forto bryng hym in bale.   *into grief*

6635   Odeth his mayster herd,
    stert up, and told this tale.   *stirred himself*

554.

"Syr kyng," he sayd, "I mervell me   *am amazed*
    that thou for David hath any drede.

I saw hym in thin awn ceté,

6640   wher thi frendes fayre con hym fede.   *feed*

Abymalec, byschope of Nobbé,   *Nob*
    full mekyll beld con to hym bede.   *much comfort; provide*

Golias sword to hym toke he   *Goliath's*
    and kyssed hym kyndly when he yede.   *left*

6645   I wened noyght ye ware wroth,   *knew*
    and sertes, ser, had I wyst,   *certainly; known*

I suld have bun them both   *captured*
    and led them to your lyst.   *to [deal with at] your pleasure*

555.

And, ser, to prove this that I say,

6650   sendes for that popelard prevely."   *traitor at once*

The kyng therin made no delay;   *at that*
    full herdy men he sentt in hy.   *strong; haste*
The byschop broyght thei the same day
    with his kynred in cumpany.   *family*
6655   The kyng hym asked in rude aray   *a rude manner*
    why he mayntened his most enmy.   *maintained his greatest enemy*
Abymalec hym excused
    be wytty wordes all ways.   *clever*
Hys resons ware refused,
6660   bot softly thus he says:

556.

"Syr kyng, thou may full wynly wake   *happily live*
    whyll luf lastes betwyx yow two.
Me toyght full well sett for thi sake   *thought; to set forth*
    all the eys that I myght to hym do.   *food*
6665   He sayd he suld thi messege make,
    And for he suld more sewrly go,   *securely*
Golias sword I cowd hym take,
    qwylke hymself wan in feld in wo.
He standes in mony a stowre   *battle*
6670   and ys ever bown to wende   *bound [by oath] to venture*
Forto sayve thin honowre.
    Therfor, ser, he is thi frend."

557.

Then was the kyng wode, I warrand,   *enraged, I'll wager*
    when he of all this werkyng wyst.
6675   Hys kenyst knyghtes then he cummand   *fiercest*
    to kyll hym that hys enmys kyst.   *kissed*
Bot non on hym wold lay ther hand
    because he was Goddes byschop blyst   *blessed*
Owtakyn Odeth, that fawtt fyrst fand;   *Except Doeg, who the fault first discovered*
6680   to werke wo that was hys lyst.   *desire*
Hys sword full swyth he droghe   *quickly he drew*
    with other of his assent.
The byschope thor he sloygh   *slew*
    with all his clene covent.   *pure company*

558.

6685   He wold noyght stynt so forto stryfe
    with all that come that close within,
So that thei slogh fowr score and fyve   *killed eighty-five*
    of the byschop clerkes, or ever thei blyn.   *before ever they ceased*
Then bad he them wend be lyve   *ordered; go quickly*
6690   the burgh of Nobbe forto bryn,   *burn*
And that thei suld stroye chyld and wyve   *destroy*

        to the otterest end of all his kyn.   *uttermost; family*
        Thei wasted all that thore wore   *killed; were there*
            that non away was wun,   *dwelled*
6695   Owtake Abyathar,   *Except Abiathar*
            Abymalec eldyst sun.   *eldest son*

[ABIATHAR ESCAPES SAUL'S WRATH, GOES TO DAVID (22:20–23)]

559.

        Yt schope so that he was not schent;   *happened; destroyed*
            God ordand hym to flee before.   *ordered*
        To David wyghyly is he went   *quickly; gone*
6700   and sayd to hym with syghyng sore
        How all was tan with turnament,   *taken*
            his fader and his clerkes, faur score,   *eighty*
        And how Noabbe with bale was brent   *dread was burned*
            and non on lyfe left, lesse ne more.   *alive*
6705   David says oft, "Alas,
            that folke for me ar dede!"   *dead*
        Abyathar then byschop was
            furth in his fader stede.   *father's place*

[DAVID ELUDES SAUL (23:19–29)]

560.

        Kyng Saul ever by consell cast
6710   how that he myght best do David dere.   *harm*
        And full oft sythyes he fowled fast   *very many times*
            with all his fors hym forto fere.
        Bot David ever fro perels past,   *perils*
            als was Goddes wyll hym forto were.
6715   And so befell yt at the last
            that David myght have done hym dere.
        And how that tym be tyd,
            we wyll take time to tell,
        Both of dedes that thei dyd
6720   and what wordes wore them omell.   *among*

561.

        The kyng full raythely can ryd   *quickly*
            David to wast for werldes wele.
        And David durst not well abyd;   *dared*
            so ware the kynges folke ferly fele.
6725   Under a hyll he con hym hyde
            in a depe hole to hald his hele   *cave to maintain his health*
        So that the kyng suld passe be syd,
            and nother suld with other dele.   *engage*

	Bot or thei past that pase,	*passed that pass*
6730	evyn bot them two betwen	
	Befell a ferly case,	*wondrous occurrence*
	os then the soth was sene.	

[DAVID DOES NOT KILL SAUL IN EN-GEDI (24:1–22)]

562.

	The kyng sone of the hole had a syght	*soon; cave*
	that yt was merke and owt of mynd.	*dark*
6735	Down of his palfray con he lyght	*from his palfrey did he alight*
	to eyse his womb be way of kynd.	*relieve his bladder; nature*
	And als he in his ded was dyght,	*deed was engaged*
	David folke soyn con hym fynd.	*David's men thereupon did*
	Thei sayd, "Ser, go ryve throwgh hym ryght;	*slice him through at once*
6740	oft hath he thee persewed and pynd."	*pursued and pained*
	David says, "God forbede!	
	He is a kyng enoynt."	*anointed*
	Bot or ever thei yede,	*before they left*
	he playd a perlus poyntt.	*perilous feat*

563.

6745	Full prevely his space he spyde;	*secretly*
	of the kynges cloyght a peyse he kytt.	*cloak a piece he cut*
	The kyng then reded hym to ryde,	*prepared himself*
	and als he was bown furth to flytt	*ready to fly forth*
	David curtasly thus cryed:	
6750	"Ser kyng, to wend thus ys no wytt.	
	I myght have made thee here to byde.	*suffer*
	Behald thi mantyll and yt ys slytt!	*cloak*
	When I this fro thee reved	*robbed*
	away, and thou not wyst,	*knew*
6755	I myght have hade thi hede	*head*
	als lyghtly, yf me lyst.	*easily*

564.

	"And therfor, ser, persew me noyght;	
	I am not glad thee forto greve,	*aggrieve*
	Bot bown in all that ever I moght	*bound*
6760	thee and thi reme forto releve."	*realm; protect*
	The kyng then herd and hym be toyght	
	how he was thore in grett myscheve,	*trouble*
	And how wysly thore David wroyght;	
	no more in malyce wold he meve.	
6765	He trowd be this tokenyng	*believed*
	within hymselfe alsone	

That David suld be kyng
   when he had his dedes done.

565.

He saw David was well arayd   *prepared*
6770   with feyghyng folke full fayre in fere   *fighting; together*
And toyght, yf he to batell brayde,   *rushed*
   whoso suld wyn wrschepe wore in were. *win honor (victory) was in doubt*
Therfor all sothly thus he sayd,
   "David, this ded thou hath done here   *deed*
6775   And thi grett meknese made me payde;   *glad*
   I grawntt thee peyse be my powere.   *peace*
Sen thou so sufferand ys,
   thi lordschep lang wyll last.
I grawnnt thee forgyfnes
6780   of all poyntes that ar past,

566.

"So that thou faythfully sall fulfyll
   the forward fest betwyx us two,   *contract made*
And that thou do gode and non yll
   to my folke when I found them fro."
6785   David sayd, "Ser, with gud wyll,
   als thou wyll say, so wyll I do."
The kyng then cald hys folk hym tyll;
   to Galgala agayn can thei go.
And David wentt then hyne   *quickly*
6790   with his men ever ychon   *all together*
To the forest of Cephyn;   *Ziph*
   he wyst no bettur wone.   *knew no better hope*

[Samuel dies; Nabal's wealth (25:1–4)]

567.

In this meyn tyme that I of tell
   dyverse farles con befall.   *happenings that did occur*
6795   The nobyll prophett Samuell
   then dyed, as erthly men bus all.   *must*
Then David men meved them omell,   *grumbled among themselves*
   for fude in forest fand thei small.   *food; scant*
And thore besyde Cephyn con dwell
6800   a full ryche man, his name Noball.   *Nabal*
He had ryches by raw   *plentiful*
   of rent and ryalté,
Bot he lyfed not by the law
   of Moyses and Josue.   *Joshua*

568.

6805	No man cowd rekyn hys ryches ryfe;	*count; plenteous*
	he was ryall in his aray.	
	Bot ever he was with sturt and stryfe	*contention*
	that no man myght hym do his pay.	*satisfaction*
	A gud woman hade he to wyfe,	
6810	and hyr name was cald Abygay.	*Abigail*
	Scho wrschept God in all hyr lyfe	*honored*
	and at hyr myght mayntened His lay.	*law*
	Scho was full trest and trew	*trustworthy*
	and lufed with more and lesse	
6815	And fayr of hyd and hew,	*skin and complexion*
	als the Boke beyrs wytnese.	*bears witness*

569.

	His catell was in sesyn sett	*(Nabal's); season*
	als over all in that cuntré.	*as [they were]*
	David oft with hyrdes mett	*herders*
6820	and mayntend them als his meneye.	*company*
	Wyld wulfes and lyons oft he lett	*obstructed*
	to do dysese to Naball fee.	*Nabal's herds*
	All yf his fod was ferre to fett,	*Unless; far to fetch*
	nothyng unto rewll take wold hee.	*nothing would he take unlawfully*
6825	So ose the yere con slype,	*year did pass*
	the seson fell therfor	
	That men ther schepe suld clype,	*sheep should clip*
	and this was costom thore.	

570.

	And so be tyde yt in that tyd	*it happened; place*
6830	that Naball hath his fest ordand.	*feast*
	In all the cuntré was yt cryd,	*publicized*
	os costom was in that land;	
	[. . .]	
	[. . .]	
6835	Fast under that ylke forest syde,	*same*
	swylke solace suld be so nere hand.	*such*
	He made wyght men to wende	*strong*
	at muster ther myschefe	*trouble*
	And pray Naball to send	
6840	sum fude for ther releve.	*relief*

[NABAL DENIES FOOD FOR DAVID'S MEN (25:5–11)]

571.

	Then of the wyghest furth ar wentt	
	to Naball, whore play was plenté.	*merriment*

When thei had told all ther entent,
    dyspytusly answerd then hee: *spitefully*
6845   "Who is he that thus yow hath sent?"
    Thei sayd, "David, the sun of Jesse."
He sayd thei suld be schamed and schent   *killed*
    as felons that ar fayn to flee: *caused*
"He is the kynges enmy
6850   and hath full wekydly wroyght.
All hys fors I dyfye;   *force*
    here sall he have ryght noyght."

[DAVID SWEARS VENGEANCE (25:12–13)]

572.

The messyngers agayn thei goo
    and told David evere ylk a dele.   *every point of it*
6855   When he yt wyst, he was full wo   *knew*
    and sayd yt suld be venged well.
Hee sware grett othes that he suld slo   *oaths; slay*
    Naball for all his hertly sele.   *great wealth*
And aftur hym all other mo
6860   that to hym fell suld angers fele:
Both man and wyfe and chyld,
    he sayd thei suld be lorn.   *destroyed*
And bestes, tame and wyld,   *beasts*
    no thyng suld be forborn,   *spared*

[ABIGAIL'S WISDOM (25:14–23)]

573.

6865   That thei ne suld passe by sword or knyfe
    in what syd so that thei myght be sene.   *whatever place they might be found*
Sone aftur raked ther resons ryfe   *went their many reasons*
    amang the hyrdmen all be dene.   *forthwith*
Thei went and told to Naball wyfe,
6870   that wytty was withowtyn wene,   *clever was without doubt*
How that hyr lord suld lose his lyfe,
    for he had carped wordes kene   *said bold words*
And myssayd David men   *abused*
    that folke ware fayn to plese.   *were desirous to please*
6875   Fro scho his cawse cowd kene,   *determine*
    hyr hert was not at esse.   *ease*

574.

Scho menys to mend yt, yf scho may,
    that thei suld not be putt to pyne.   *pain (death)*
In gud garmentes scho made hyr gay   *herself fair*

6880	with pelure and with pyrre fyne.	*fur and precious stones*
	And grett presentes scho con purvay	
	of bred, flesch, and nobyll wyne	*meat*
	And wentt to mete hym on the way	*meet him (David)*
	towerd the forest of Cephyn.	
6885	So leved scho forto lett	*intended she to alleviate*
	the harmes he can them hette.	*against them promised*
	And sone when scho hym mett,	
	scho fell down to his fette.	*feet*

[ABIGAIL'S PLEA TO DAVID (25:24–35)]

575.

	"A, gentyll knyght of Jesse kynd,	*Jesse's family*
6890	that sal be kyng be reson ryght,	
	Gayre not the pure pepyll be pyned	*Cause; [to] be pained*
	in dyverse place for a man plyght.	*one man's sin*
	My lord is maysed and owt of mynd;	*bewildered*
	anentes hymself hath he no myght.	*concerning*
6895	God forbed that the folke suld fynd	
	thi felnes with a foyle to fyght!	*boldness; fool*
	I wyst not thi men wore	*knew*
	to aske us oght of our gude.	*goods*
	Sertes, ser, had I bene thore,	*Certainly; been there*
6900	thei suld have faled no fud.	*lacked no food*

576.

	"And therfor, ser knight, no ferrer kare	*sorrow no more*
	bot take of me this pure present."	
	Then David saw scho was full fayre;	*beautiful*
	grett favour in hyr face he fand.	*found*
6905	He sayd, "Dame, be not in dyspayre.	
	I graunt thee, he to thi husband.	*haste*
	Non of thi pepyll sall we payre."	*hurt*
	Scho thanked hym with hert and hand.	
	Thei toke mett and drynke;	*food*
6910	therof the folke ware fayn.	*glad*
	He thankes hyr, als hym thynke,	*as he thought*
	and so he turnys agayn.	*returns*

[ABIGAIL TELLS NABAL, WHO DIES (25:36–38)]

577.

	Abygay told hyr husband hale	*whole*
	what sorows he suld full sone have sene	*very quickly have known*
6915	And sufferd dede in his awn sale,	*death; own hall*
	had not hyr witt and werkyng bene.	

And when he herd hyr tell this tale,
   unto his hert he toke slyke teyne,   *heart; such grief*
Within ten days he dyed with bale.   *sorrow*
6920   Few of his meneye can hym meyne.   *company; mourn*
To David sone was sayd
   that Naball endyd so.   *ended (died)*
Then was he ryght well payd   *glad*
   that he helped not thcrto.

[DAVID MARRIES ABIGAIL (25:39–44)]

578.

6925   When Naball thus with wo was went
   and dede withoutyn darte or knyfe,   *dead*
For Abygay hath David sent
   and weded hyr unto his wyfe.   *wedded*
This woman thus turned evyll entent   *subverted*
6930   and helped to stynt full mekyll stryfe.   *much*
And therfor God slyke grace hath sent   *such*
   in lykyng forto lede hyr lyfe.
Another he wan also   *Another [wife] he (David) gained*
   thrugh dughty dedes he dyde.   *bold deeds*
6935   Thore had he wyfys two,   *In these he had*
   and Micoll was the thryd.   *Michal*

[SAUL AGAIN PURSUES DAVID (26:1–5)]

579.

Then folke of Cephyn had grett envy,   *Ziph*
   for David sojornd thor so lang.   *lived there*
To Saull sent thei prevely
6940   and bad that he suld make hym strang,   *strong [in presence]*
For David that was his enmy
   suld not be mayntened them amang.
Thei hete he sall have hym in hy,   *promised; haste*
   for with hym gudly wyll thei gang.
6945   When Saul herd this tale
   folke ware not David frendes,
His ost he ordand hale,   *ordered altogether*
   and wyghtly ydder he wendes.   *thither he went*

580.

When David herd muster omell   *heard it said among [the people that]*
6950   Kyng Saul in that reme can ryde,   *realm*
He sent his folke by fyrth and fell   *through forest and field*
   whore he wold buske to abyd.   *prepare*
And sone con thei to hym tythynges tell

	he sojornde by a cyté syde,	
6955	And that thei dyght them thore to dwell	*were making themselves there*
	and telled ther tentes apon that tyde.	*pitched their; place*
	David hymself hath soyght	
	tyll he of them had syght,	
	For in his hert he toyght	*thought*
6960	to be nere them that nyght.	

[DAVID SPARES SAUL'S LIFE (26:6–25)]

581.

	Two felows that he trew had fun	*had found loyal*
	chesed he furth for sych a chare:	*chose; job*
	On Abysay, his systur sun,	*One [named] Abishai*
	and a bold man Abyathar.	*Ahimelech*
6965	Thoo three ther gatte so hath begun,	*Those; their way*
	and any wyght of them was warre	*and no man; aware*
	That to the kynges tent ar thei wun,	*gone*
	wher he lay and the duke Abnare.	*Abner*
	All folke war fast on slepe	*secure in sleep*
6970	aftur the mydnyght tyde.	
	Thor was no cowrs to kepe;	*There; man to watch*
	thei ware sure on ylka syd.	*secure on every side*

582.

	David that ever was myld of mode	
	sees how sadly thei slepand are.	*soundly*
6975	All yf thei aspyde to spyll his blud,	
	unto them wold he do no dere.	
	Bot a grett coupe of gold full gud	*cup*
	and als the kynges chefe chasyng spere	*also; hunting spear*
	Thei toke, and evyn agayn thei yode,	
6980	and over a burn thei con them bere.	*hill; bear*
	And on that other syd,	
	whore thei no harme myght take,	
	David full kenly cryd,	
	"Wake, Ser Abnere, wake!	

583.

6985	"Ye werke os ye ware chylder yeng,	*work as [if] you were young children*
	that kepes a kyng and slepis so sade	*guard; sleep so sound*
	Qwyls men beyre away his thyng."	*While*
	The duke of hym the heryng hade	
	And answerd hym os in hethyng,	*contempt*
6990	"Why cryes thou so, unknawn lade,	*lad*
	And makes swylke noyse thus nere the kyng?"	*such*
	Then Saul wakynd and was rad.	*afraid*

He trowed sum ware untrew *believed; unfaithful*
   of tho that wuned hym wyth, *dwelled*
6995 For the voyce well he knew
   that yt was of David.

584.
And to wytt how yt was begun,
   he cryde to hym and cald be name:
"Is thou not David, Jesse sun?"
7000   "Yis sertes," he sayd, "I am the same. *certainly*
This ylke nyght myght thou me have fun *same; found*
   in thi tent, wher thou haldes thi hame. *maintain your home*
Yow both I myght have bett and bun *beat and struck*
   and went my way withowtyn blame.
7005 I toke thi coupe of gold
   and bare thi spere thee fro *bore*
And myght well, yf I wold,
   have tane thiself also. *taken*

585.
"Therfor, ser, it were fayr to sesse *cease*
7010   of swylk dedes os thou uses at do, *deeds*
And suffer me to passe in pese *peace*
   that tryspase noyght thee unto.
Thou lefes the lessons that ar lese *believe; false*
   and waytys ever to werke me wo.
7015 Now have I mett thee twyse at mese; *twice in good range [for killing]*
   thou wot thiself that yt is so." *know*
The kyng sayd, "Wele I knaw,
   and here the soth I se. *truth*
Thou dose all that thou aw *do; ought*
7020   in meknes unto me.

586.
"And also I se well for certayn
   thou sal be kyng; this is no nay. *there is no denying it*
Therfor I graunt thee pardon playn
   never forto dere thee aftur this day." *harm*
7025 Then David of his fare was fayn, *glad*
   bott ferrer he fled for more affray. *farther; fear*
The cowpe and the spere he sent agayn. *returned*
   Ylkon at wyll then went ther way. *Each one willingly*
The kyng abatyd his breth
7030   and toyght his werke not wyse;
And David went to Geth, *Gath*
   unto the kyng Achyse. *Achish*

[ACHISH OF THE PHILISTINES GIVES DAVID LAND (27:1–11)]

587.

The kyng Achyse that I of meyne

    was wyght enoght and wyse of were,   *strong; war*

7035   Bott he was full a Phylysteyn

    and his men in the same manere.

He hard well how David had bene   *heard*

    before abowt to do them dere.   *harm*

Bot now he wott withoutyn wene   *without doubt*

7040   Kyng Saul and he enmys ere.   *he (David) were enemies*

All yf he ware Ebrew,   *Even; Jew*

    sen thei his enmys wore,   *since they (David and Achish) were his (Saul's) enemies*

He trowde he suld be trew   *believed; faithful*

    to Phylysteyns therfore.

588.

7045   He gaf hym landes a lytill fra

    to loge hym and his pepyll in,   *lodge*

A grett ceté, Cissylla,   *Ziklag*

    to hym and to hayrys of his kene.   *heirs of his family*

Ydder went he and his wyfes two,   *Thither*

7050   and ther thei wuned with mekyll wyn,   *dwelled with much joy*

Sex hunderth men withoutyn wo

    owt of the forest of Cephyn.   *Ziph*

Semly thore sojournde thei: *Gladly*

    David and his Ebrews.

7055   He honerd God allway

    and fayged the Cananews: *beguiled the Canaanites (i.e., pagans)*

589.

To brew them bale bown wold he be.   *He would always be ready to cause them sadness*

    Over mownt he went to Malachis,   *mountains; Amalekites*

And thore he stroyd up that cuntré.

7060   And sythyn he wentt unto Serrys.   *then; [the city of] Shur*

Ther gatte thei gold full grett plenté,   *won*

    pellour and pyrry of grett pryse.   *furs and stones of great worth*

And grett presandes oft sythyes sent he   *tributes often times*

    unto the kyng of Geth, Achys.   *Gath, Achish*

7065   Achys noyght understud

    what Phylesteyns can fele: *did suffer*

David sayd he gatt that gud   *won those goods*

    of Ebrews ylka dele.   *entirely from Jews*

[PHILISTINES ATTACK ISRAEL (27:12–28:4)]

590.

	Then was Kyng Achis ferly fayn	*very glad*
7070	that he and Ebrews enmys ware.	*were enemies*
	He trowd he wold never turne agayn	
	so frenly als he was before.	*as friendly [to the Jews] as*
	He sembyld men with all his mayn	*strength*
	of all his landes, both lesse and more,	
7075	And sayd the Ebrews suld be slayn,	
	and on lyfe suld he leve no store.	*alive; livestock*
	He prayd David als frend	
	that he and his meneye	*company*
	With hym in were wold wend,	*war would go*
7080	and gladly grawnthed he.	*he (David) granted [him that]*

591.

	Then was full grett myrth them omell;	*mirth among them*
	thei styrd and wold no langer stand,	*stirred; be still*
	Bot furth thei fare over fyrth and fell	*went over forest and field*
	and fullyd all that thei before fand.	*killed; before [them] found*
7085	When Kyng Saul herd tythynges tell	*heard the news told*
	that Phylysteyns enturd his land,	
	He sayd thei suld not soundly dwell.	
	A full grett ost sone he ordand.	*army at once*
	And with them all went he	
7090	with mekyll prese and pryde	*much fight*
	To the mount of Gylboy,	*Mount Gilboa*
	and thore he busked hym to byd.	*prepared himself to wait*

[SAUL CONSULTS THE WITCH AT ENDOR (28:5–25)]

592.

	He myght se on that hyll on heyght	*high*
	in the low land what lyfe thei led:	*gathering they made*
7095	Towns of fyre byrnand full bryght	*on fire burning*
	and all over was with enmys spred.	
	He saw them mony and mekyll of myght.	*their numbers and great strength*
	Sum dele in hert he was adred	*Some bit; afeared*
	And prayd to God to schew sum syght	
7100	how that he suld in that stowre be sted,	*battle be placed*
	Whedder his folke suld be flayd	*Whether*
	or ellys ther enmys slayn.	
	Bot howsoever he prayd,	
	he had no tokyn agayn.	*sign in return*

593.

7105 His prophettes also for hym prays;   knew; was not pleased by
    of helpe unto hym herd thei noyght.
Then wyst he well that God not pays   knew; was not pleased by
    sum werkyng that he has wroght.
He bad his men go dyverse ways   ordered
7110   that sum wyche sone to hym ware soyght,   witch at once
That by hyr craft cowd ded men rays   raise dead men
    that sum body be lyve ware broyght
To tell how he suld chefe,   should end [the fight]
    awder lyfe or ellys be sloyne.   either live
7115 One sayd, "Lord, with your lefe,   by your leave
    in Endor dwels swylke one.   En-dor lives such a person

594.

"Scho con by craft of socery   witchcraft
    tell all that ever in erthe sal be."
The kyng went to hyr prevely   secretly
7120   and bed hyr gold, full grett plenté,   offered
To rayse hym up sum ded body,
    to say whedder he suld fyght or fle.
Scho asked in whom he wold affy.   trust
    "In Samuel, forsoth," says hee.
7125 Sone thrugh hyr soceris   At once; witchcrafts
    and thrugh the Fendes rede   Devil's counsel
Samuel scho gart up ryse,   caused to rise up
    that lang whyle had bene dede.   dead

595.

Als Samuel stud them beforne,
7130   the kyng sayd, "Tell us, or we twyn, before we part
Whedder syd sal be up born   Which side shall be raised up
    in this batell that we begyne,
And who sall have ther lyvys lorn!"   taken away
    Then answerd he with dedly dyne: deadly noise (speech)
7135 "Thou and thi suns sall wun to morn   expect to mourn
    in the same wyse that I wun in."   dwell
Then was he hent in hy   taken away in haste
    away, thei wyst not whore.   knew not where
Kyng Saul then was sory.
7140   Hym rewed that he come thore.   He rued

[DAVID IN THE PHILISTINE ARMY (29:1–11)]

596.

He teldyd hym within his tent   secluded himself
    on Gylboy batell forto abyde.

Now leve we hym wher he is lent
    and tell how David con be tyde.   *did fare*

7145 Kyng Aches boldly borows brent   *burned towns*
    and stroyd cytes on ylka syde.   *every side*
David ay wyghtly with hym went;   *always quickly*
    non was so well arayd that tyde.
The Phylysteyns ware not payd   *pleased*

7150   that he suld with them wun.   *dwell*
Ylke on tyll other sayd,   *Each one to the*
    "Ys noyght this Gesse sun?   *Jesse's son*

597.
"With Kyng Saul he ys at hame
    and of his howshold hath bene lang."

7155 Sum other says, "This is the same
    that maydyns made of in ther sang."   *their song*
"Syr kyng," thei say, "we ar to blame,
    and he with us to batell gang.   *if; goes*
His awn kyng wyll he kepe from schame   *own; save*

7160   and turn to mell hym us amang.   *speak [to] him about us*
The more that he us shendes,   *humiliates*
    the more thanke sall he have.
So sall thei bee full frendes.
    Therfor se us to save!"

598.
7165 Kyng Aches saw his folke afrayd;
    of David fare thei ware not fayn.   *David's accompaniment; glad*
Therfor thus to hym he sayd,
    "I thanke thee, ser, with all my mayn   *strength*
That thou thus prestly is purved,   *are so eagerly prepared*

7170   bot now I pray thee turn agayn
And see my reme be ryght arayd.   *realm be properly governed*
    I grawnnt thee heyre my power playn."   *make you heir [to]*
Then David home can fare,
    all ware yt not his wyll.

7175 Bot lang or he com thore,   *long before; there*
    new tythynges com hym tyll.

[AMALEKITES ATTACK ZIKLAG (30:1–10)]

599.
Amalachys we ment of ayre,   *The Amalekites we spoke of earlier*
    that David angerd oft before,
Thei wyst full well how that thei ware   *were*

7180   went to were, both lesse and mare.   *gone to war*
Therfor full fersly con thei fayre   *fiercely did they come*

	to Cesilla, whore his wyfes ware.	*Ziklag, where his (David's)*
	Thor forto spoyle wold thei not spare;	
	thei brent and stroyde up all ther store.	*burned; their goods*
7185	Thei toke his wyfes two	
	and home with them thei lede.	
	And of his meneye moo	*company more*
	wore thor full stratly sted.	*were there placed in straits*

600.

	David was never ayre so wo;	*before*
7190	no wounder yf he wex nere wode	*grew near to insanity*
	When that he wyst his wyfes two	
	war led away with all ther gud.	*their goods*
	Hys meneye made mornyng also,	*company; mourning*
	becawse ther wyfes with them yode.	
7195	Thei sayd thei suld never hamwerd go	
	or thei had schamly sched ther blode.	*before*
	David prayd God to send	
	sum comforth in that case.	
	He had wernyng to wend	*advice [from God] to go*
7200	and well overcom his fayse.	*foes*

[DAVID ATTACKS THE AMALEKITES (30:11–31)]

601.

	To fell them down full fast thei thrett,	*threatened*
	and furth thei cayred to that cuntré.	*traveled*
	On of tho Malachys thei mett	*those Amalekites*
	that for mete myght no ferreur flee.	*hunger might no further*
7205	To have his hele David hym hett	*health; promised*
	to tell hym how the best myght bee.	
	He sayd, "Ser, I sall thee sett	
	whor thou the Malachys may see."	
	Hee wysched them redy way	*guided*
7210	tyll thei had knawyng clere	
	Whore all ther enmys lay,	*Where all their enemies*
	makand full mery chere.	*making*

602.

	Thei made then myrth with all ther mayn	*strength*
	and trowed that no man myght them marre.	*believed; harm*
7215	Then David and his folke was fayn	*were glad*
	and toyght that thei suld fownd no ferre.	*go no farther*
	Thei pressed to them in that playn	
	and so with skelppis thei con them scarre	*blows they did*
	That sodanly thore ware thei slayn.	
7220	Full joyfull all the Ebrews arre.	

Ther wyfes then thei ta | *took [back]*
and gold full grett plenté.
And went to Cecilla; | *Ziklag*
that was ther awn cyté.

[SAUL AND JONATHAN DEFEATED BY THE PHILISTINES (31:1–4)]

603.

7225   Now at ther lyst we leve them so | *pleasure*
    with David that of were was wyse, | *war*
  And telle we of the hostes two
    on Gylboy, whore Kyng Saul lyse. | *Gilboa; remains*
  Full gretly thei togeydder go
7230   to se what syde suld wyn the price. | *win the prize (victory)*
  The Phylysteyns ware mony moo
    that wer comyn with Kyng Achys.
  Full boldly thei abyde
    and bett on with brandes bryght. | *beat; swords*
7235   And Ebrews on ther syde
    full fersly fandyd to fyght. | *fiercely tried*

604.

  To tell how all that werkyng was,
    lyne be lyne, full lang yt were. | *it would take a long time*
  The Ebrews all the overhand hays | *had the upperhand*
7240   fro morn to mydday and more; | *from morning*
  Bot at the last thei sayd, "Alas!"
    for lordes that leved ther lyfes thore,
  And most for gentyll Jonatas, | *noble*
    that David fand his frend before. | *found [to be]*
7245   He had stroyd in that sted
    Phylysteyns full gud woyne, | *in great numbers*
  And sythyn he was ded | *then*
    and his breyther ylkon. | *brothers each one*

605.

  When Saul saw that his sun was gone | *son*
7250   and chefe of all his chevalry, | *knights*
  And how he thore was leved alon | *left alone*
    and had no beld to byde hym by, | *protection to remain by him*
  Well lever he had forto have bene sloyn | *He much preferred; been slain*
    then lyfe in lawles cumpany. | *lawless*
7255   Therfor of his men bad he on | *ordered he one*
    putt hym to ded thor prevcly | *to put him to death there privately*
  So that he past no ferre | *went no further*
    with folkc of fals lyvyng. | *false belief*

7260	That man wold noyght hym marre bycause he was his kyng.	*harm*

[SAUL'S DEATH (2 KINGS [2 SAMUEL] 1:6–10)]

606.

	With his awn sword he con begyn	*did*
	to styke hymself in that stound.	*impale; place*
	So com a knave of Kaym kyn;	*Cain's kin*
	the kyng sayd, "Felow, or thou found,	*before you depart*
7265	Beyr me thrugh, for nothyng blyn,	*tarry*
	and take my crown and my be rownde!"	*my round armlet*
	The knave was glad that gold to wyn	*gain*
	and gaf the kyng his dedes wounde.	*mortal wound*
	Thus ended the fyrst kyng	
7270	that ever was of Ebrew,	
	For he brake Goddes bedyng	*broke God's bidding*
	and was not to Hym trew.	*loyal*

[THE SPOILS OF GILBOA (31:7–13)]

607.

	Swylke cayre behoved cum hym tyll	*It was fitting for such sorrow to come to him*
	for marterdoms that he dyd make —	*martyrdoms*
7275	Byschopes and prestes both he gart spyll	*did kill*
	and dekyns als for David sake —	*deacons*
	And for he wroyght not Goddes wyll	
	that cumaund hym he suld take wrake	*vengeance*
	Of Kyng Agag that greved Hym yll,	
7280	and to trews he con hym take.	*truce he did*
	That day ware Ebrews slayn,	
	als Samuel sayd before.	
	Phylysteyns ware full fayn:	*very joyful*
	mawmentes thei wrschept the more.	*idols; worshiped all the more*

608.

7285	Sone on the morn thei sessyd not yett	*Soon in the morning*
	or dede bodes spoled bee.	*before dead bodies were spoiled*
	Kyng Saul hed thei have of cutt	*head they have cut off*
	and the same of his suns all thre.	
	On ther ceté thei have sett yt	*their city*
7290	that folke on ylka syd suld see,	
	And for thei wold all the werld suld wyt	*should know*
	of ther jornay in Gylboy.	*campaign*
	To sere cytes thei sentt	*various*
	qwerters of lordes be lade	*quarters of the [bodies of the] lords [to] be laid*

7295   To mak yt be on ment   *be remembered*
         the maystrys that thei thore made.   *masteries; there won*

609.

     Bycawse Kyng Saul thus was slayn,
         Phylysteyns made grett sacrafyce.
     His armurs offerd thei ylkon   *armors*
7300   to Astrott, ther god of price.   *Astaroth (Astarte)*
     Sythyn Ebrews with grett hand ar gone   *Then; courage went*
         to tho cytes be certan spyse.   *spies*
     Both hedes and bodes have thei ton   *heads and bodies; taken*
         and bered them in ther best wyse,   *buried*
7305   With grett wrschep allways,   *honor*
         for thei so worthy wore,
     And made sorowyng sevyn days,
         als costom then was thore.   *there*

610.

     When Kyng Saul was went his way,
7310   twenty yeres then regnyd had hee.
     And whyls he lufed God and His lay,   *law*
         he had lykyng by land and see.
     Ther lyfed non ayre aftur his day;   *lived no heir*
         the prophett sayd yt suld so be.
7315   The Fyrst Boke endes in this aray
         that tels how kynges come in cuntree.   *came into the country*
     Forther who lykes to loke
         how was with David done,
     Seke in the Secund Boke;
7320   ther thei sall see full soyne.   *see it all at once*

SECOND BOOK OF KINGS (2 SAMUEL)

LIBER SECUNDUS REGUM.

[DAVID KILLS THE MESSENGER WHO HAD KILLED SAUL (1:1–15)]

611.

In the Fyrst Boke of Kynges herd have we
  how Saul was fyrst crowned kyng,
And how he dyed on Gylboy   *Gilboa*
  with his ost outrayd, old and yyng.   *defeated*
7325   Now in the Secund sall we see
  of David and of his doyng.
In Cesilla then sojornd he,   *Ziklag*
  and of that werke wyst he nothyng.   *deed knew*
Tyll aftur, on the thryd day,   *Until afterwards*
7330   then come a messynger,
And swylke saws con he say   *such news did he tell*
  that chaunged all his chere.   *his (David's) mood*

612.

"Ser," he sayd, "be mery, I rede,   *be happy, I counsel [you]*
  for gud thynges sall I tell thee.
7335   Kyng Saul thin enmy is dede;   *your*
  I saw hym sloyn and his suns thre."   *slain; sons*
Then David hert wex hevy as lede.   *David's heart grew; lead*
  He sayd, "How wott thou yt suld so be?"   *know*
He sayd, "From Jews in the same sted;   *place*
7340   the certan seygne that sall thou see.   *clear indication [of]*
Hymself he wold have slayn,
  so was he stede in nede.   *placed in desperation*
And for he had no mayn,   *because; strength*
  he prayd me do that dede.   *deed*

613.

7345   "I wyst hyt was his awn desyre;   *knew it; own*
  to beyre hym thrugh I was full bownne   *run him through; entirely ready*
And have here that I have to hyre: *what I earned as wages*
  hys bees of gold and his gud crownne.   *armlet; good*

	I wott thou sal be lord and syre	*know; sire*
7350	and rewle the reme, both towre and town."	*rule the realm*
	Then David loked on hym with yre	*anger*
	and sayd, "Thou sall have waryson.	*a reward*
	He was enoynted kyng,	*an anointed*
	that thou dyde swylke dyspytte."	*so disparage*
7355	Withowt more doyng	
	hys hede he dyde of smytt.	*head he did cut off*

[DAVID MOURNS SAUL AND JONATHAN (1:16–27)]

614.

	Full oft he syghtyd and sayd, "Alas!"	*he (David) sighed*
	that ever Kyng Saul suld ende so,	
	Bot more for gentyll Jonatas.	*noble Jonathan*
7360	When he yt wyst, then was he woe,	*knew [for certain]*
	For trewer luf in werld ne was	*there was not*
	then ever was betwyx them two.	
	Therfor slyke care in hert he has	*such sorrow*
	ne he wyst in werld what he myght do.	*[that] he knows not*
7365	He swouned, als he wold swelt,	*as if; die*
	and weped and wrang his hend:	*wept and wrung his hands*
	Lang with swylke doyles he delt.	*sorrows he dealt*
	No man myght hym amend	*cure*

615.

	Tyll at the last a duke hym dyght	*made*
7370	to bryng his bale in bettur guyse.	*present his woe in a better manner*
	He says, "Yt is no semly syght	
	men forto werke on swylke a wyse.	*in such a way*
	Yt is well fayrrer forto fyght	*much better*
	and venge us on our yll enmyse.	*evil enemies*
7375	So suld acord to ylka knyght;	*agree to each*
	with wepyng sall never wrschepe ryse.	*from weeping; honor*
	Yt falys wemen of eld	*befits old women*
	to wepe, when thei have wrang,	
	And knyghtes to fyght in feld	*field*
7380	ther foys with fors to fang."	*foes with force to catch*

[DAVID ANOINTED KING OF JUDAH (2:1–4)]

616.

	Then sayd thei so on ylka syde	
	and cachyd myrth so them amell.	*between*
	He trowed ther tayles in that tyde	*believed their tales*
	and prayd to God that He wold them tell	
7385	Whore hym ware best to beld and byd.	*Where it were best for him to live and remain*

And Goddes prophett bad hym go dwell

In Ebron, a cety long and wyd,   *Hebron, a city*
    with chosyn chylder of Israel.

The kynred of Juda   *kindred of Judah*
7390   thor chose hym forto ther kyng   *there; their*

All way well or wo   *weal or woe*
    to lyfe at his ledyng.

617.

Now wex David a man of myght   *grew*
    when he was kyng by comyn crye.   *common assent*

7395   The pure and rych he rewled ryght,   *ruled fairly*
    aftur ther werkyng was worthy.

Hys cosyn Joab, a gentyll knyt,   *noble*
    made he chefe of his chevalry

And next hym his two brether, that heyght   *brothers, who were called*
7400   Aghaell and Abaghai.   *Asahel and Abishai*

Ay the eldyst of Ebrew   *Always*
    held he of the most counsell,

Qwyll all he trest for trew   *Whom; trusted for loyalty*
    and wold not fayntly fayle.   *fail for weakness*

[Ishbosheth's rival claim to kingship (2:8–10)]

618.

7405   We told before, and not full ferre,   *and not very far away*
    how Kyng Saul was feld in feyld.   *killed on the battlefield*

At home was left Duke Abnarre   *Abner*
    his land and his welth to weld   *hold*

So that none suld with maystry marre   *harm*
7410   Ysboset, Saul sun unweld.   *Ishbosheth, Saul's helpless son*

He and that duke yll angerd arre
    that David so was broyght to beld.   *comfort*

Thei hard how he was kyng
    of the kynred of Juda;

7415   That toyght them herd hethyng   *they thought a great shame*
    and kest betwen them twa   *debated; two*

619.

How thei myght turne all that entent,
    and thus thei ordand them omell: *among themselves*

Thei sembled all to ther assent   *assembled; their agreement*
7420   that with Saul ware wunt to dwell.   *wont*

That Ysbosett then have thei hent   *summoned*
    and made hym kyng of Israel;

And forto marre so have thei ment   *to harm; intention*
    Kyng David and his force to fell.

7425	When Joab herd of tho	*those*
	and of ther purpase playn,	
	He and his breyther two	
	grathed them thor agayn.	*prepared themselves against that*

[JOAB AND ABNER FIGHT FOR THEIR KINGS (2:12–17)]

620.

	Duke Joab hath for David heyght	*promised*
7430	to feyght on feld and not to flee.	*fight on the field*
	Duke Abnarre says for Ysbotsett	
	in batell sall he byde and bee.	*remain and endure*
	Bot both ther men, when thei ware mett,	*their*
	ware Ebrews and of on cuntree.	
7435	Therfor to were wyll thei not lett	*war; go*
	tyll that thei wytt who sall wyn degré.	*know*
	Ful fersly then thei fyght.	*fiercely*
	Bot to tell at the last:	
	Abnare was put to flyght,	
7440	and Joab fowled fast.	*Joab [and his army] followed*

[ABNER KILLS ASAHEL; THE FIGHT IS BROKEN OFF (2:18–3:5)]

621.

	And als thei persewede thore,	*pursued there*
	ware mony dede withowtyn drede.	
	Bot Aghaell was ay before,	*ever in front of them*
	for thore hade he so wyght a stede.	*strong a horse*
7445	When Abnare saw he sewed so sore	*pursued so hard*
	and to his hele wold take no hede,	*safety; heed*
	He prayd hym to persew no more,	*asked*
	and he suld gyf hym gold to mede.	*for reward*
	Therfor he wold not lett,	*But for that; cease*
7450	ne for his spekyng spare.	*speaking pause*
	And Abnare on hym sett	*beset*
	and thrugh his brest hym bare.	*bore [his spear] through his breast*

622.

	When Joab saw that sory syght:	
	his brother lyg dede on the land,	*laying dead*
7455	Then dyde he all his mayn and myght	*strength*
	to venge his ded with hert and hand.	*avenge his death*
	And by that was yt nere the nyght,	
	and no tyme to be traveland.	*traveling*
	Duke Abanare toke a hyll on hyght	
7460	and gatt a strengh in forto stand.	
	And then for peyce he prayd	*peace*

to Joab and his men.
"We werke all wrang," he sayd.
    "That sall ye clerly kene.   *realize*

623.

7465   "Joab," he sayd, "full well I knaw
           a feller knyght may no man fynde.   *keener*
       With Phylysteyns to fyght thee aw,   *you ought*
           and with paynyms that thei ben pynd.   *pagans; be put to pain*
       Bot we that lyf all by a law   *by one law*
7470   and all are Ebrews of on kynd   *one*
       Ylkon to bryng other a daw,   *Each one; bring the other a day (kill)*
           we suld have God more in our mynd.
       Both cosyns and kynred
           ar sembled on ayder syde.   *assembled on either*
7475   The mo that thus ar dede,
           the more tene sall us be tyde.   *sorrowful*

624.

       "I prayd thi brother of peyce
           when he persewed me with envy.
       Bot for my saws he wold not sesse   *advice; cease*
7480   and fell so thrugh his awn foly.   *own folly*
       So myght fall the same messe   *blow*
           thiself to suffur or perchaunce I.
       Therfor yt is fayrest forto sese,
           and ylk man kepe his cumpany."   *each*
7485   Qwen Joab saw certayn
           he sayd reson and ryght,
       Hee turned his men agayn
           and rested thore that nyght.

625.

       Bot on the morn thei morwnd omell   *mourned together*
7490   for folke that thei fand fallyn in feld.
       Thei beyred the body of Aghaell   *buried*
           with all the wrschep that thei myght weld.   *honor*
       When Kyng David herd how yt fell
           that Aghael was schent on feld,   *killed on the field*
7495   His tene in hert no tong myght tell,   *grief*
           for he was all way hym to beld.   *comfort*
       Kyng David had in Ebron
           sex wyfes with hym to go,
       And sere suns: Absolon,   *many sons: Absalom*
7500   Adony, and other moo.   *Adonijah*

[Abner turns against Ishbosheth (3:6–21)]

626.

Sone aftur this then fell debate
  betwyx Ysboset and Abnare,
For he had takyn a leman latt   *Because he (Abner); woman recently*
  that with Saul before con fare.   *did go*
7505 He sayd yt fell not for his astate   *He (Ishbosheth); estate (class)*
  to use wemen that with kynges ware.
Abnare in hert then con hym hatt,   *hate*
  that chalenged hym fore swylk a chare.   *such an action*
He says, "Evyn als I broyght
7510 the folke to wun hym wyth,   *live with (be loyal to)*
So sall I sett ther toyght   *their thoughts*
  and turne them to David."

627.

And sone unto the same entent   *at once with that very intention*
  letturs dyde he to wrytyng.
7515 And messyngers sone hath he sent
  unto David, of Juda kyng.
He told hym holy how he ment   *completely*
  under his bundom forto bryng   *governance*
All the Ebrews that with Saul went,
7520 fro Ysbosett, both old and yyng.   *young*
Kyng David was full glade
  when thei told this tythyng,
And sayd with sembland sade,   *with a resolute countenance*
  "He sall have his askyng."

628.

7525 And forto prove be reson ryfe   *by ample reason*
  yf he this purpasse wold persew,
He sayd, "Send Mycoll, my fayrest wyfe,   *Michal*
  that homly is of hyd and hew.   *beautiful; skin and complexion*
I luf hyr lely as my lyfe   *loyally*
7530 sen fyrst that I that cumly knew.   *since*
Yf he do this to stynt all stryfe,
  then wyll I trest that all be trew."
The messyngers ar wentt
  to Abnare evyn agayn,
7535 And Mycoll sone was sent,   *at once*
  and David then was fayn.   *glad*

629.

Abnare this forward wold fulfyll.   *pact*
  full sone he gart togeydder call   *caused to be called together*

7540	Lordes of the land, both lowd and styll,	*publicly and privately*
	that oght myght govern, grett or small.	*anything*
	He sayd, "Sers, tentes unto my skyll;	*attend to my counsel*
	the certan soth say yow I sall.	*truth*
	I wott well yt is Goddes wyll	
	that David be kyng of Ebrews all.	
7545	The prophett Samuel	
	sayd yt suld so be,	
	And with hym wyll I dwell."	
	Thei say, "Ser, so wyll we.	

630.

	"With hym to pase ware we prest,	*live were we eager*
7550	had we not bene at thi bydyng."	
	Then twenty barons of the best	
	befor Kyng David con he bryng.	
	A fyrm sewrty thore thei fest	*firm surety there they established*
	and made hym homage, old and yyng.	
7555	So were all the twelfe kynredes kest	*twelve tribes cast*
	with hym to hold and he ther kyng.	
	Grett fest than mad he thore	*feast then he made there*
	bycause of kynredes twelfe,	
	Bot Abnare ay before	*ever before [everyone]*
7560	was honerd next hymselfe.	

[JOAB'S WRATH AGAINST ABNER (3:22–27)]

631.

	When all was wele, thei went ther ways,	
	ylkon to ther awn cuntré.	*each one; own*
	Joab, the duke, was all ther days	*these*
	for errandes fare fro that cety.	*far from*
7565	When he come and herd how men says	
	of fest and grett solempnité,	
	That purpas no thyng to hym pays:	*satisfies*
	that Abnare suld so neghtbur be.	
	He hoped he suld be nare	*close*
7570	unto the kyng all way.	
	That mater wyll he marre	*mar*
	in all that ever he may.	

632.

	Fyrst he told unto the kyng,	
	"That Abanare dose is all envy.	*What*
7575	He feynys frenschepe for nothyng	*pretends*
	bot for he wyll this land aspye	*spy out*
	How he may best hys ost in bryng	*army*

	so to persew thee prevely.	*secretly*
	And thou wyll trest to his tellyng,	*If; trust in his speech*
7580	this land may so be lost therby."	
	The kyng wyst this was wrang;	
	the case full well he knew,	
	And sayd, "Wherever he gang,	*goes*
	I trow Abnare be trew."	*trust Abner to be faithful*

633.

7585	When Joab wyst this wold not be,	
	sone hath he soyght a sotell gyne.	*cunning trick*
	Fayr letturs sent he forto se	
	with the best knyghtes of all his kyn	
	And prayd Abnare that hast suld he	*haste*
7590	to the kyng be lyve, for no thyng blyn,	*at once; delay*
	And speke with hym in specialté	
	for bourdes that thei suld begyn.	*games*
	Abnare full sone assent	*immediately*
	to werke the kynges wyll.	
7595	Wyghtly with them he went,	
	that wold sped hym to spyll.	*kill*

634.

	Then Joab con full grathly spye	*readily look out [for him]*
	and wentt to feld hym forto kepe.	*to attend to*
	He and his brother Abyghai	
7600	welcumd hym with grett wrschepe.	*honor*
	In consell thei cald hym in hy,	*council; haste*
	ryght als thei for his wo wold wepe.	*just as if they would weep for his woes*
	Joab then spake full specialli	*individually*
	and therwith wroyght hym wowndes depe.	
7605	This was an evyll corde	*plot*
	and wroyght with weked trayn.	*wicked guile*
	Alas that swylke a lord	*such*
	falsly suld be slayn!	

[DAVID CONDEMNS JOAB FOR KILLING ABNER (3:28–39)]

635.

	So prevely his sword he drogh;	
7610	the duke was dede thore sodanly.	
	Kyng David hath full mekyll woght	*much misery*
	when he herd tell this trechery.	
	Duke Joab made his tale full togh	*most arrogant tale*
	and sayd he had encheson why:	*cause why he did it*
7615	"My brother Ayghel he slogh,	
	and then I myght no wyn hym by."	*be no joy to him*

Bot als men may suppose,
    he dyd yt more for drede
The lordschep forto lose
7620   that he had forto lede.

636.

The kyng is so with mornyng mett;   *mourning afflicted*
    hym gaynes nowder game ne glee.
Unto the duke he dyd his dett: *duty*
    interyd hym in that same cyté.   *buried*
7625   Then of this lesson wyll we let   *cease*
    sen of this bale no bott may be,   *since; sadness no remedy*
And say how fell of Ysbosett,   *what befell*
    te kyng of Israel cuntré.
When he herd how men sayd
7630   that Duke Abnare was dede
And trayturly betrayd,
    he was full wyll of rede.

[ISHBOSHETH BETRAYED AND KILLED (4:1–12)]

637.

Full grett mornyng he mad amang; *mourning he made among [his people]*
    so dyd all that then wore thore.   *were there*
7635   Bot his lyfe lasted not aftur lang;
    swylke falshed was formeld therfore. *due to such betrayals mentioned before*
To hym was wroyght als mekyll wrang
    as to Abnare or ellys more,   *much wrong*
Be two tyrandes and trayturs strang: *tyrants*
7640   of Bynjamyns both born thei wore,   *Benjaminites*
Rocab and Baana,   *Rechab and Baanah*
    as beyrs wyttenese the Boke.
Thies ware the trayturs two
    that treson undertoke.

638.

7645   For none may bettur a man betray   *Because*
    then he in whom his hert is trist,   *heart is entrusted*
So prevey with the kyng war thei   *privy*
    to com in and owt at ther lyst.   *desire*
Als he lay slepand on a day
7650   in place whore non bot thei yt wyst,   *knew*
His hed thei toke and bare away
    full mony myls or thei ware myst.   *were missed*
Thei wend full well have done   *thought much good to have accomplished*
    qwen thei this falshed fand.   *labored*

| 7655 | To Kyng David full sone | *immediately* |
| | thei offerd that presand. | *present* |

639.

	With full grett gladnese thei hym grett	*greeted*
	and sone rehersed hym ther resown:	
	"Ser, here the hede of Kyng Ysbosett	
7660	that was thi foo in feld and town.	
	Now lyfes there non thee forto lett."	*obstruct*
	He sayd, "Trayturs, full of tresown,	
	Have ye no mynd how I hym mett	*treated*
	that proferd me Kynges Saul crown?	*King Saul's*
7665	His hed I gart of schave,	*head I had cut off*
	for he dyd that dyspyte.	
	The same hyre sall ye have."	*wage*
	Ther hedes he gart of smytt.	

[THE TRIBES OF ISRAEL SUBMIT TO DAVID (5:1–2)]

640.

	Unto Kyng David than thei draw,	
7670	lordes of ylka cuntré cleyne.	*every; entirely*
	And for ther kyng all thei hym knaw	*acknowledge*
	and makes hym homage all be dene.	*forthwith*
	So was he lord of hegh and law	*high and low (i.e., everyone)*
	that langed to the twelfe kynredes kene.	*belonged; (i.e., all Israel)*
7675	Then loves he God, als he well aw,	*ought*
	that so hath sett hym to be sene.	
	And full grett sacrafyce	
	to God thore con he make,	
	And ylke man on ther wyse	
7680	dyde the same for His sake.	

[THE CENSUS OF ISRAEL AND JUDAH (24:1–9)]

641.

	Sen that his enmys then ware ded	*Because*
	that lyfand wold have done hym dere,	*harm*
	And all ware sembled in that same stede,	*place*
	the kyng wyll wytt what folke thei are.	*know how many people they are*
7685	He gart cownt of ylk kynred	*caused to be counted*
	all that ware abyll armys to bere,	*able to bear arms*
	And that hade force to fend thar hede	*defend their head (leader)*
	and fals Phylysteyns forto fere.	*to frighten*
	The kynred of Juda:	
7690	sex thowsand and faur score,	*6,080*

	This was nowmer of tha	*those*
	that ware ay sett before.	*were ever*

642.

	Of the lyne of Levy, lygh als levyn,	*lineage of Levi, quick as lightning*
	faur thowsand sevyn hunderth told.	*4,700 altogether*
7695	Of Benjamyn faur thowsand evyn,	
	and then of Effraym elders old	
	Were twenty thowsand styrd be stevyn,	*moved by speech*
	and aght hunderth of berns bold.	*800 bold men*
	Of Ysacar two hunderth to nevyn	*to name*
7700	and twenty thowsand, wytt who wold.	*whoever would know it*
	Sevyn thowsand of Symeon	
	and one hunderth at hand.	
	And sythyn of Zabulon lygh als	*then; quick also*
	ware fyfty thowsand.	

643.

7705	Of Neptalim was so grett plenté,	
	to nowmer them myght no man com.	*manage*
	Of Aser faurty thowsand free,	
	of Dan twenty and sevyn thowsand sum.	*27,000 total*
	Of Ruben, Gad, and Manasse,	
7710	that ware wunnand beyond the flum,	*dwelling; river (Jordan)*
	Sex hunderth thowsand had tho thre.	
	Of all ther was a thryfty thrum.	*flourishing body of people*
	And ther ald and yeyng	
	with wrschyp on ther wyse	*honor in their way*
7715	Raysed David to be kyng.	
	then was he ordand thryse.	*ordained for a third time*

[DAVID ANOINTED A THIRD TIME, ATTACKS JERUSALEM (5:3–6)]

644.

	The fyrst tym was betwyx them two,	
	the prophett Samuel and he,	
	When God bad hym to Bedlem go,	
7720	and David keped his fader fee.	*father's flock*
	The secund was in Cecilla	*Ziklag*
	whore he wonned with his wyfes three.	*dwelled*
	Thore come the kynred of Juda	
	and made hym kyng of that cuntré.	
7725	The thryd was now hymselfe	
	in Ebron was made kyng	
	Of all the kynredes twelfe	
	that lyfyd to Goddes lykyng,	

645.

	Qwylke comynly ware cald Cananews	*Who; Canaanites*
7730	for Canan that thei dwelled in.	*they lived in*
	And for Abraham thei ware Ebrews	
	namyd with men, both more and myn.	*(i.e., all of them)*
	In Jerusalem then wonned Ghebesews,	*lived Jebusites*
	the fellest folke of Phylysteyn.	*cruelest*
7735	And for thei ware so mekyll schrews,	*great villains*
	on them to were he wyll begyn.	*war*
	The men that thus ware mett	
	and geydderd in grett rowte	*gathered in a great force*
	To that cyté ware sett	
7740	and segyd yt all abowte.	*besieged*

[DAVID CAPTURES THE CITY OF JERUSALEM (5:6–8)]

646.

	The folke within, of felows fame,	*infamous*
	saw thei had no force to fyght.	
	Thei toyght to gare them schon for schame;	*thought to make them retreat*
	this sotelty sone have thei dyght:	*subtlety immediately; made*
7745	All the lepurs and all the lame	*lepers*
	and all the blynd that wantyd syght	
	Apon the walles thei sett tho same	*those same [people]*
	and bad them crye holy on hyght:	*ordered; in loud voices*
	"David, that kyng is cald,	
7750	for all thi brag and bost,	
	This cety sall we hald	
	fro thee and all thin ost."	*army*

647.

	The kyng hard how the crepyls cryde	*cripples cried out*
	and wyst yt was done in dyspytt.	*knew; despite*
7755	Therfor he wold no langer byde	*wait*
	bot qwykly fand yt forto qwytt.	
	Thei seged yt full sadly on ylka syde	*besieged; resolutely*
	so that that cyté toke thei full tytte.	*very quickly*
	Both man and page for all ther prid	*boy*
7760	ther heddes full smartly thei of smytte.	*heads very promptly they cut off*
	The kyng thus and his ost	*army*
	dystroyd both bred and lengh.	*width and length*
	Tho that wore maysturs most	
	had takyn a towr for strengh.	*tower (citadel) for strength*

[DAVID CHALLENGES HIS MEN (1 CHRONICLES 11:6)]

648.

7765	When thei had thus that cety wun	*won*
	and broyght yt all under ther bale,	*their authority*
	Unto the towre thei have begun	
	to sett and sadly yt asale.	*beset; resolutely assail it*
	Kyng David sayd what moder sun	*mother's son (i.e., whoever)*
7770	that enturs fyrst withoutyn fale,	
	Als most frendly he sal be fun	*held most in friendship*
	and most cheve of the kynges consale.	*most chief; council*
	When Duke Joab con here	*did hear*
	the kyng gaf this decré,	
7775	He wold non were so nere	*would have none be so near*
	of his consell os he.	

649.

	Therfor he dyd his myght and mayn	*strength and effort*
	that wrschep to hymself at wyn.	*honor*
	He cast no perels ne no payn	*shunned no perils nor*
7780	tyll he that towr was enturd in.	
	And hastely he hath them slayn;	
	that boldnes gart his gamys begyn.	*caused his pleasure to be achieved*
	For so he was sett as soverayn	
	of all the kynges men, more and myn,	*more and less (i.e., all of them)*
7785	And most chefe of conselys,	*counselors*
	whore so thei gang or ryde,	*wherever*
	And ordenare of batellys	*director*
	to buske or ellys to abyde.	*hurry; wait*

[JERUSALEM RENAMED (5:9–10)]

650.

	Sen that place was ther best socour,	*haven*
7790	to byd thore ware thei not to blame.	*live there were*
	The folke then namyd yt David Towre,	*the Tower of David*
	and to this day yt beyrs that name.	*bears*
	So was the kyng sett in honour	
	and over all namyd of nobyll fame.	
7795	Phylesteyns that war styfe in stowre,	*were hard in battle*
	in this tyme thei war mad full tame	
	And flemed fro that cyté,	*driven away*
	and Ebrews thor ordand.	*set themselves*
	The kyng bad yt suld be	
7800	chefe cyté of that land.	

651.

Thos lordes then ther levys hath tane	*their leaves have taken*
when he was sett as soveran syre.	
For hym to noye then was ther none	*trouble*
bot fals Phylysteyns, fell ose fyre.	*cruel as fire*
7805 Amang all other was ther on,	*one [leader]*
Aram, that was kyng of Tyre;	*Hiram*
Of syder wod had he gud wone.	*cedar wood; plenty*
And that was Kyng David desyre	
Forto make howse in hast	
7810 his Ebrews in to abyd,	*live*
For that cyté was wast	
sere tyms befor that tyde.	*many times*

[Hiram of Tyre's offering to David; David's children (5:11–16)]

652.

When Aram, kyng of Tyre, herd tell	
Kyng David in so grett degré,	
7815 And that he dyght hym forto dwell	*desired*
in Jerusalem, that grett ceté,	
Grett syder treyse fast gart he fell,	*cedar trees did he chop down*
and bad that wryghtes bown suld be	*wrights conscripted*
And the best masons them omel	*together with them*
7820 at wend to Canan cuntré.	*that would go*
"Sekys to the kyng," he sayd,	*Seek*
"and werkes what he wyll bede."	*order*
Kyng David was well payd,	*very glad*
for of swylke had he nede.	*such [men]*

653.

7825 Then made he walles full mekyll of myght	*very great in strength*
with nobyll towrs and turettes by	
And barrys bune with yrn and dyght	*bars [on gates] bound with iron*
forto eschew all yll enmy.	*wicked enemies*
Then mad he halles and howses on heyght	
7830 for lordes and lades in to ly	*to sleep in*
With selers semly unto syght	*cellars*
pavyd and paynted with ymagry.	
Of wyfes he had gud wone,	*plenty*
that with hym wonnand ware.	*were dwelling*
7835 A wyfe bare Absolon	*Absalom*
and his suster Thamar.	*Tamar*

[PHILISTINE ATTACKS (5:17–25)]

654.

Now hath Kyng David power playn
  of Ebrews in ylk cuntree.
Bot Phylysteyns ware no thyng fayn   *in no way glad*
7840   that he suld goverand swylke degré.
Thei sembled men with all ther mayn   *their strength*
  to sege Jerusalem cyté.   *besiege*
Bot os God wold, sone was sum slayn,   *at once were some slain*
  and sum also ware fayn to flee.   *happy*
7845   That toyght them grett dyspyte;
  therfor thei wold not blyne.   *tarry*
Thei gatt mo folke full tytt   *very quickly*
  and new were con begyne.   *war did begin*

655.

Thei geydderd full grett cumpany
7850   that cyté oft sythys to assayle.   *many times*
Kyng David wold not feygh forthi   *fight at that point*
  or he of God had sum consayle   *before*
Whether he suld have the vyctory
  and bettur byd in that batell.   *perform*
7855   God warnd hym then full wyttly   *advised; wisely*
  by a sygne that he suld not fayle.
God bad he suld take tent   *take heed*
  and on the evynyng-tyd   *in the evening*
Lay his men in buschement   *ambush*
7860   under a forest syde:

656.

"On the morn then sall ye fynd
  this tokyn trew that I yow tell.
When the wod wages withoutyn wynd,   *forest shakes*
  wend thou then be lyve; no langer dwell.   *go; quickly*
7865   Your enmys sall ye bette and bynd   *beat*
  and make them flee over fyrth and fell.   *field and forest*
Thei sal be lorn that levys behynd,   *killed who are left*
  and maystry leve thi men omell."   *among*
Os God demed, David dyde.
7870   His men sone he arayde.
And all to hym betyd,   *happened*
  als God Hymself had sayd.

657.

When thei to batell bremly breyst,   *fiercely broke*
  Phylysteyns ware full fayn to flee.   *very desirous*

7875	The kyng with his folke foled fast	*followed*
	and putt them down, full grett plenté.	
	With ther pursewyt so ar thei past	*pursuit*
	to Gessore, that was ther cyté.	*Gazer*
	That thei conquerd and down yt cast	
7880	and gat gret gud of gold and fee.	*goods; livestock*
	Thei wan thor welth enogh,	*won there*
	that wold to tresour tent.	
	Hamward then thei drogh	*withdrew themselves*
	and stroyd ever as thei wentt.	

658.

7885	The godes of gold that thei gat thore,	*won there*
	that ware made for ther mawmentry,	*idolatry*
	Kyng David toke them to tresour	
	and forto menske God Allmighty.	*honor*
	So fals Phylysteyns wasted wore	*were*
7890	that thei myght make no more maystry.	
	Kyng David wex ay more and more	*grew ever*
	with wrschep, als he was worthy.	*honor*
	God wroyght for hym allway	
	and made hym mekyll in price.	*great in glory*
7895	And he honerd God ay	*always*
	with suyt and sacrafyce.	*submission*

[DAVID FETCHES THE ARK OF GOD (6:1–5)]

659.

	Then toke he purpase forto ta	*take*
	into Jerusalem cyté	
	The Arke of gold fra Gabatha	*Gibeah*
7900	and sett yt up in grett degré.	
	Thryty milia gart he ga	*30,000 caused he to go*
	with sang and grett solempnité	*song*
	Withoutyn prestes and dekyns ma	*Beyond the priests and other deacons*
	that abowt yt agh to be.	*around it ought*
7905	All maner of mynstralsy	
	was ordand for this thyng,	*occasion*
	And full fayre cumpany	
	went before with the kyng.	

[UZZAH TOUCHES THE ARK AND IS STRUCK DOWN (6:6–8)]

660.

	All loved thei God both loud and styll	*outwardly and inwardly*
7910	that His Arke suld lend in ther land.	*remain*
	The Arke, als thei went down a hyll,	

for als yt suld be falland.   *seemed as if it would be falling*
On Osay went with full gud wyll   *Uzzah; good intention*
   to hald yt up layd on his hand.   *hold it up*
7915   Sone sodan ded was sent hym tyll,   *At once sudden death*
   for he therfor was not ordand.   *for that was not ordained*
This lesson wyll us lere: *learn*
   non suld neght howled thyng   *no one should approach a hallowed*
Bot thei that have power
7920   grauntyd of Goddes gyfyng.

[THE ARK IN JERUSALEM (6:12–15, 17–19)]

661.

To Jerusalem that Arke is broyght
   with prelettes and with prophettes of price.   *prelates; renown*
A tabernakyll therto was wroyght,   *built*
   als well os werkemen cowd avyse.   *manage*
7925   On ylka syde therto thei soyght
   with sense and solempne sacrafyce.   *incense*
Als thei had God Hymself thei toyght;   *As if; thought*
   so fayn was ylkon on ther wyse.   *joyful was each one in their ways*
Kyng David was full glad
7930   that hym was sent swylke seyle;   *such good fortune*
Gud hope in hert he hade
   that God dyd ever ylk dele.   *part*

[DAVID'S PROPOSAL TO BUILD A TEMPLE DENIED (7:1–29)]

662.

And because he swylke wrschep wan   *such honor won*
   and gat to govern swylke degré,
7935   To honer God, yf that he can,
   in all his myght ymagyns hee.   *imagines*
He told to the prophett Nathan
   that he wold make of ston and tree
A chyrch that was cald tempyls then   *called a temple at that time*
7940   whorein the Arke of God myght be,
That folke may call and knell   *kneel*
   to be assoiled of ther syn.   *forgiven*
Tho prophett prayssed hym well   *That*
   swylke gud werke to begyn.

663.

7945   Bot aftur, os I understode,
   God cald unto hym on a nyght,   *him (i.e., Nathan)*
"David, my servand myld of mode,   *cheer*
   a howse to Me sall thou non dyght,   *not build*

Bycause thi handes ar full of blod
7950   of thos that thou hath feld in fyght.   *killed in battle*
I thanke thee that thi wyll is gud,
            and therfor sall thou reyng be ryght.   *reign*
And aftur thee thin hayre,   *your heir*
            that sal be Salamon,   *Solomon*
7955   He sall make well and fayre
            my howse of tree and ston."

664.
The prophett sayd the kyng certayn,
            als God had told hym under teld.   *just as; under [his] tent*
Then was Kyng David ferly fayn   *marvelously glad*
7960   that his heyre suld his welthis weld.   *heir; wield his wealth*
He honerd God with all his mayn   *strength*
            that hym had broyght unto swylke beld   *such comfort*
And mad hym kyng with power playn
            fro hyrd that keped fee in feld.   *from a shepherd who kept the flock in the field*
7965   He governd ald and yyng
            allway by consell clere;
So lyfyd he in lykyng
            in myrth full mony a yere.

[DAVID'S GOOD RULE; HIS KINDNESS TO JONATHAN'S SON (8:15; 9:1–13)]

665.
Kyng David both be nyght and days
7970   full dewly demys of ylka dede.   *duly judges every deed*
For on poynt was he worthy to prayse: *one*
            that he wold herkyn and take hede   *listen*
In ryght and reverence them to arase   *raise up*
            that helped hym when he had nede.
7975   For Jonatas waytt he allways   *Jonathan he watched always*
            yf any sewtt ware of his sede,   *offspring were; seed*
For whyls he lyfed in land,
            his luf myght nothyng lett.   *cease*
A sun of his thei fand   *found*
7980   that heygh Mifibosett.   *who was called Mephibosheth*

666.
This Mifebozett was of age,
            bot mayned and halt was he.   *crippled and lame*
Kyng David putt hym into perage   *peerage*
            of bacheler, os aght to be.   *bachelor, as it ought*
7985   In Jerusalem a certayn stage   *place*
            was made for hym and his meneye.   *company*
He held wyght men for ther wage   *strong*

	to serve hym in sere degré.	*various means*
	His steward con he make	
7990	Cyba, that soveran was;	*Ziba*
	All for his fader sake,	*father's*
	gentyll Jonatas.	

[HANUN BECOMES KING OF THE AMMONITES (10:1–2)]

667.

	When this was done sone aftur this	*immediately*
	a duke, that David trysted apon,	*trusted*
7995	Heyght Naas, kyng of Amonys,	*Called Nahash; Ammonites*
	and had an heyre, that heyght Anon.	*heir; Hanun*
	The fader was wytty and wyse,	*clever*
	bot sythyn the sun was fon a fown.	*afterwards; found [to be] a fool*
	Kyng David held hym mekyll of price	*held him in much worth*
8000	evyn as his awn son Absolon.	
	Sone when he herd of this	
	that Kyng Naas was dede,	*dead*
	He sent wysmen of his	
	the chyld to wysch and rede.	*guide; counsel*

668.

8005	He bad them tell hym how he wold	*instructed*
	mayntein hym with all his myght	
	And the same frendchep with hym hold	
	that he had to his fader hyght.	*assured*
	The messyngers, herdy and bold,	
8010	to wend this way thei war full wyght.	
	And to the yyng kyng have thei told	
	ther resons all; thei rehershed ryght	
	How Kyng David had sayd	
	his frenschepe suld not faylle.	
8015	The princes ware not payd	*satisfied*
	and cald the kyng in consayle.	*into private council*

[THE TREATMENT OF DAVID'S MESSENGERS (10:3–5)]

669.

	Thei say, "Ser, beware and wytty;	
	this is the falshed of thi foo.	*falsehood of your foe*
	Thies lordans comys thi land to spy	*little lords come*
8020	and wayte how thei may werke thee wo.	*determine*
	Therfor, ser, sett nothyng therby,	
	bot sen thou sees that yt is so,	*since*
	Lett us waytt them sum velany	*inflict [on]*
	and send them furth wher thei com fro."	

8025	The kyng was yyng of eld,	*young in maturity*
	that was sone aftur sene.	*revealed*
	He lost his bygest beld,	*greatest protector*
	and so yt turned to tene.	*grief*

670.

	Be this consell the kynges meneye	*company*
8030	this messyngers both bett and band	*these; beat and bound*
	And cutt ther cloghes up at the the,	*their clothes up to the thigh*
	als foles wer served in that land;	*as fools were presented*
	Sythyn mad ther berdes half-chavyn be	*Then caused their beards half-shaven to be*
	and the other half styll to stand	
8035	And send them so to ther cuntré	*thus*
	and bad thei suld go tell thythand.	*the news*
	Yf Kyng David for this	
	be wroth, no wonnder yt ys,	
	To see so mekyll of mys	*offense*
8040	agayns his grett gudnes.	

[DAVID RAISES ARMS AGAINST HANUN (10:6–19)]

671.

	He bad them venge this velany	*avenge*
	that under hym had his power.	
	Joab, his steward stalworthy,	
	sayd yt suld be boyght full dere.	*returned in full measure*
8045	And his brother Abbysay	*Abishai*
	sembled folk from sydes sere	*gathered; many*
	Anon, the kyng of Amonys,	
	and his cuntré forto conquere.	
	When Kyng Anon herd say	
8050	of Joab entent that tyd,	*at that time*
	His folke he gart aray	*caused to be arrayed*
	in batell hym to abyd.	

672.

	Duke Joab furth his folke he led	
	unto thei come in Amonys cuntré.	*until they came*
8055	He stroyd and brent all that was bred	*destroyed and burned; abroad*
	and nawder spared folke ne fee.	*spared neither people nor livestock*
	And als sone os thei batell bed	*offered battle*
	to loke who suld the bettur bee,	
	Phylysteyns full fast thei fled	
8060	and toke to Rabatt, thare ryche cyté.	*Rabbah, their*
	That cyté was so strong	
	with guns and other geyre,	*ballistae; equipment [of war]*

Fro thei that force myght fang,
   thei dowtt no dedes of were.   *feared no deeds of war*

[DAVID FALLS INTO ADULTERY WITH BATHSHEBA (11:1–5)]

673.

8065   Duke Joab dyght hym forto dwell
     and wyn that cyté, yf he myght.
  And in this meyntyme that I tell,
     Kyng David rewled hym all unryght.   *ruled himself*
  In awowtry fowle he fell   *foul adultery*
8070   with Ury wyf, that was his knyght.   *Uriah's*
  Swylke medyturs was mad omell   *Such mediation was made between [them]*
     that with hym was scho all nyght.
  Dame Barsabé scho hatt,   *Bathsheba she was called*
     that was tane under teld.   *taken under tent*
8075   Ser Urré at Rabat   *Sir Uriah*
     lay forto fyght in feld.   *on the battlefield*

674.

  Sone on the morn Dame Barsabé
     supposed to be with chyld in hy.   *learned at once that she was with child*
  And costom was in that cuntré:
8080   whoso was tan in avowtry   *taken in adultery*
  Suld be stoned in the same cyté.
     Therfor scho past full prevely
  And prayd the kyng hertly that he   *heartily*
     suld ordan therfor remedy.
8085   The kyng sayd, "Dred thee noyght.
     Thor sall no folke thee fyle."   *defile*
  Sone then he hym betoyght   *devised*
     of a full wekyd wyle.   *very wicked trick*

[DAVID PLOTS TO BRING URIAH AND BATHSHEBA TOGETHER (11:6–13)]

675.

  He thynkes in his awn entent   *own intention*
8090   how he suld fell all fowle defame.   *do away with all foul rumor*
  Aftur Ser Urré hath he sent
     and bad that he suld hast hym hame.   *homeward*
  And in this message hath he ment   *intended*
     so forto scheld the wyfe fro schame.
8095   Fro he with hyr alon ware lent,   *Because*
     of that barne suld he bere the blame.   *child should he bear*
  Syr Urré hast hym sone   *hastened himself immediately*
     and com the kyng untyll.   *unto*

	He wyst not what was done	*knew*
8100	and askyd what was his wyll.	

676.

	The kyng says, "Full fayn wold I fele	*gladly would I learn*
	how frendes faryn sen thei ferd us fro,	*fared since they fared from us*
	And for thin awn sake, ser, sum dele	*some part*
	that thou may rest a day or two.	
8105	Thi wyfe thynkes lang, I wott full well;	*know*
	therfor to hyr I red thou go	*advise*
	And make hyr solace for your sele.	*your own sake*
	Yt is semly that thou do so."	*advisable*
	Syr Urry sayd not nay,	
8110	bot furth he wendys his ways,	*went*
	And all that nyght he lay	
	within the kynges palys.	*palace*

677.

	Sone on the morn the kyng beheld	
	he was not gone his wyfe to glose,	*copulate with*
8115	And askyd hym why he wold not yeld	*give*
	chere to his wyfe sen he had chose.	*comfort; since he had chosen it*
	The knyght sayd he suld byde no beld,	*abide no comfort*
	ne be uncled of cotte ne hose,	*nor be unclad of tunic nor*
	Whyls all his felows lay in feld	*in the field*
8120	to wyn wrschep or lyfes lose.	*honor or lose their lives*
	The kyng saw his for-toyght	*forethought*
	myght nothyng stand in stede.	
	A lettur be lyve he wroyght,	*quickly*
	qwylke sayd he suld be dede.	*which*

[DAVID SENDS URIAH TO HIS DEATH IN BATTLE (11:14–17)]

678.

8125	That lettur he toke the knyght untyll	
	and sayd, "Ser, sen thou wyll not rest,	
	Unto Duke Joab bere this byll,	*letter*
	as man on lyve that I lufe best,	
	And byd hym faythfully yt fulfyll."	
8130	The knyght knew not his ded was kest,	*death was established*
	Bot furth he yode with full gud wyll;	*went*
	to plese Joab was he full prest.	
	That boke to hym he bede	*carried*
	and bad hym serve yt sone.	
8135	When Joab had yt rede,	
	he saw what suld be done.	

679.

And on the morn maystrys he mays
   als he Phylysteyns wold fere.   *terrify*
Syr Urré sett he in swylke place   *such a place*
8140   whore he wyst thei suld do hym dere.   *knew they would do him harm*
And sone away fro hym he gays.   *goes*
   Then thei within were wyse of were   *wise of war (i.e., veteran soldiers)*
And sees that he no help hays;   *has*
   thrugh the body thei con hym bere.
8145 Thus was he saklese slayn,   *in innocence*
   that shaply under scheld.   *fit man with a shield*
The kyng therfor was fayn   *glad*
   his wyf that he myght weld.   *use*

[DAVID MARRIES BATHSHEBA (11:27)]

680.

He wedyd hyr with mekyll wyn   *much joy*
8150 and mad hyr to be crowned qwene:
All forto cover that cursyd syn
   that thei had done them two betwen,
For the grett state God sett hym in
   mad hym kyng with crown clene.
8155 To greyve hym thus he con begyne,   *did*
   and that was on hymselfe sene.   *revealed on himself*
God toke not sone vengiance,   *immediate*
   bot fyrst he wyll assay   *determine*
Yf he with repentance
8160 wyll mend whyls he may.

[GOD SENDS NATHAN TO TEST AND REBUKE DAVID (12:1–15)]

681.

The prophett Natan sone he sent
   to Jerusalem, that ryche cyté.
Als God wold, wyghly he wentt   *desired it to be, promptly*
   both to Kyng David and Barsabé.
8165 "Ser kyng," he says, "sen God hath lentt   *since*
   that thou sall deme in ylke degré,   *judge*
A thyng that falys to thi jugment   *falls*
   am I comyn forto aske of thee.
Als the partys hath prayd,   *parties have asked*
8170 so sall I say thee sone.
And ser, when I have sayd,
   os thou demys, sal be done.   *as you judge, so shall it*

682.

    "A myghty man and mekyll drede   *much feared*

       wuned heyr besyd down in a dale.   *lived near here*

8175 His catell was so wyd spred

       that of them cowth he not tale.   *make count*

    A pure man was besyd hym sted   *dwelling*

       that had no catell, grett ne small,

    Owt takyn a schep that he had fed   *Except for*

8180   upon a lamb with corne and cale.   *cabbage*

    This rych man mad a fest   *feast*

       at home in his awn hall

    And sloght the pure mans best   *slaughtered*

       to glad his gestes with all.   *gladden his guests*

683.

8185 "This question that I of thee crave

       how this rych man is worthy mede."   *rewarded*

    The kyng sayd, "Ser, so God me save,

       this thynke me ryght to rede: *advise*

    I deme thus that the pure man have   *judge*

8190   fowr for on for his nede;   *four to one*

    And the rych man that so wold rave

       to suffer ded for that same dede."   *death*

    The prophett sayd, "Certan,   *Certainly*

       to be so best yt semyd.

8195 This dome ys noyght in vayn;   *judgment*

       thin awn ded hath thou demed,   *your own death*

684.

    "Bycawse thou gart kyll thi knyght —   *did*

       so semly er full seldom sawyn —   *such seemly [men] are very seldom seen*

    And haldes his wyf agayns the ryght

8200   because your syns suld not be knawn,

    And hath enow both day and nyght   *enough*

       lades and lemmans of thin awn.   *lovers of your own*

    A sodan deth suld on thee lyght,   *ought on you alight*

       bot God has bedyn yt be withdrawn.   *desired that it be*

8205 And thus therfor sall fall,

       os I sall say on one,   *at once*

    On of thin awn suns sall   *One of your own sons*

       defowle thi wyfes ylk on.   *every one*

685.

    "And that same sun sal be slyke,   *killed*

8210   thrugh helpe and myght of other mo,

    To cache thee owt of thi kyngryke   *kingship*

       and make thee fayn to fle therfro.   *glad to flee*

	And that ylke chyld that now is like	*very*
	to be broyght furth betwyx yow two	
8215	Dede with his strengh sall sone yt stryke	*Death; soon*
	that gain therof thou sall forgo.	
	This harme hath God thee hyght	*promised*
	forto be sent unsoyght,	*undesired*
	For thou dyssaved thi knyght	*defrauded*
8220	that to thee trespast noyght.	

[DAVID COMPOSES THE MISERERE (VULGATE PSALM 50:1)]

686.

	"And other baylys abyd thee bus	*punishments must await you*
	bot thou to God fast cry and call."	
	When the kyng herd yt bus be thus,	*heard that it must*
	down on the grownd flatt con he fall	
8225	And made *Miserere mei Deus*	*"Have mercy on me, O God"*
	with other psalmys, sum grett, sum small,	
	Qwylke ar now evydence to us	*Which*
	at say to God that goverans all	*who say [them]*
	Forgyfnes forto geyte,	*In order to get forgiveness*
8230	yf we in care be cast,	*distress*
	Als David dyd pennance grett	
	and prayd to God full fast.	

[DAVID'S SORROW FOR HIS CHILD (12:16–23)]

687.

	Sone aftur then by cowrse of kynd,	*nature*
	when Barsabé delyvered was,	
8235	A fayrer fode myght no man fynd	*more beautiful child*
	of hyd ne hew then scho now has.	*skin nor complexion*
	Kyng David was then mery in mynd,	
	bot aftur sone he sayd alas,	
	When that he saw the chyld was pynd	*afflicted*
8240	with payns of dede and myght not pase.	*mortal pains; live*
	Bot in his hert he toyght	*thought*
	that he to God wold pray	
	And mowrn all that he moght	*he could manage*
	to mend yt, yf he may.	

688.

8245	He dyde away his garmentes gud,	
	and in a seke he sett hym down.	*sackcloth*
	He weped als he wold be wod	*as if he would go mad*
	and kest powder apon his crown.	*ashes*
	Be sex days wold he fang no fode	*For; take no food*

8250	for spech of bacheler ne barown.	*baron*
	Ther myght no myrth amend his mode	*cheer*
	to tyme the barne to bere was bown.	*until; child to bier was taken*
	On the sevynt day, als swyth	*as swiftly*
	as the chyld lyf was ende,	*child's life*
8255	He bad all men be blyth	
	sen mowrnyng made no mende.	

[BIRTH OF SOLOMON (12:24–25)]

689.

	Of David sonnes before sayd we.	
	The first of all that hight Amon,	*those was called Amnon*
	A semely man in sight to se,	*beautiful*
8260	and the secund hight Absalon.	*Absalom*
	Now gate he anothre of Barsabee,	*begat*
	and he was named Salamon:	*Solomon*
	As wyse a man in his degree	
	as ever God layd life upon.	
8265	As Absalon was fair,	
	so was Salamon wyse	
	And after his fadir hair	*heir*
	and kyng pereles of price.	*unequaled in worth*

[JOAB DEFEATS RABBAH FOR DAVID (12:26–31)]

690.

	In all this tyme Duke Joab lay	*(i.e., beseiged)*
8270	the cyté of Rabaat forto wyn.	
	For fawt of fode thei fell down fay,	*lack of food; dead*
	Phylysteyns that ware within.	
	When Duke Joab saw certayn day	
	that thei thare fro suld nedly twyn,	*necessarily leave [the city]*
8275	Hee sent to Kyng David forto say	
	that himself suld com and begyn.	
	Heyrof well payd was he,	*rewarded*
	and ydder he wendes on one.	
	Thei wan sun that cyté	*won soon*
8280	and gatt ther welth grett wone.	*in great amounts*

691.

	Anon, the kyng of Amonys,	*Ammon*
	was thore owtrad and al to shent.	*defeated; destroyed*
	His crown that was of grett price	*worth*
	Kyng David has on his hed hent.	*placed*
8285	The lordschepes that abowt hym lyse	
	and burghes brode be lyve ware brent.	*towns; quickly were burnt*

And when all was wrogh on this wyse,   *wrought*
   to Jerusalem with joy thei wentt.
The kyng made all men glade
8290   with grett gyftes or thei gang.   *before they departed*
Grett joy in hert he had,
   bot yt last not lang.

[Tamar raped by Amnon (13:1–19)]

692.
He had a doyghtur his hert was on,
   heygh Thamar, os I told beforne.   *named Tamar*
8295   Scho was systur to Absolon;
   thei both ware of a moyder born.   *one mother*
Hyr eldest brother, that heygh Amon,   *Amnon*
   he mad mornyng myday and morn.   *mourning*
And fowle he began to fon   *sinfully; plan*
8300   to have hyr lufe, or els to be lorn.   *love; lost*
Hyre on so con he thynke,   *On this*
   and for he durst not say,   *because he dared*
He myght not ette ne drynke   *eat*
   bot peryst and wast away.   *perished and wasted*

693.
8305   A servant that was to hym nere
   and most of all his counsels knew,
He saw his maystur make yll chere
   and oft sythys chaunged his hyd and hew.   *times; complexion*
He sayd, "Ser, tell unto me heyre   *here*
8310   what thyng thee noys now of new.   *troubles*
Full gud legians I sall thee lere,   *allegiance; promise*
   or ellys trest never that I be trew."
He sayd, "Thus evyll I fare,
   and bot I sped, I spyll,   *unless I succeed, I die*
8315   My systur, fayr Thamar,
   bot I hyr weld at wyll."   *use*

694.
"A ser," he sayd, "Take myrth omell   *together*
   and for this ded be not adred.   *deed; fearful*
Feyn yow seke ose so befell,   *Pretend you are sick*
8320   and say thou may not pase thi bed.   *leave*
The kyng, thi fader, when he heyrys tell,   *hears tell [of this]*
   wyll come to se how thou ert sted.   *are in an ill plight*
Pray hym Thomar may with thee dwell,
   for of hyr lyst thee best be fed.   *from her you desire most to be*
8325   Full sone he wyll thee graunt   *At once*

or thou thi myrthes myst.
And so thou sall hyr hawnt *visit*
and luf evyn os thou lyst." *pleased*

695.

Thys purpase was well to his pay, *plan; liking*
8330 and sone all this was was done in ded.
So Thamar was comyn on a day
hyr brother frendly forto fede.
Then wysed he all his men away *ordered*
and bad them spere all as thei yede. *lock everything as they went*
8335 And to his systur con he say:
"My ded ys dyght withoutyn dred. *death is near without doubt*
No bettur boyt may be, *cure*
bot thou this grace wyll gyfe:
To werke my wyll with thee,
8340 I may no langer lyfe.

696.

"We ar heyr in our howse at hame, *here*
and non sall wytt this, I warrand." *know of this, I promise*
When Thamar hard, hyr hert was tame, *heard; faint*
and for ferd tremled fotte and hand. *fear [she] trembled*
8345 Scho sayd, "Brother, lett be for schame *stop this*
and for wreth of God all-weldand. *almighty*
Well leuer me ware of lyfe be lame *I would rather in life*
and lordschep lose and lefe this land.
No more this mote thou nevyn, *may you mention*
8350 that sory and synfull ys,
Bot heyve thi hert to Hevyn *heave*
and aske God forgyfnes.

697.

"And have in mynd, dere brother Amone,
how men wold marvell, both more and myn, *everywhere*
8355 To here thou suld so fowly fon: *sinfully behave*
thi systur forto seke with syn. *seek*
Grett vengians wold be tan theron *vengeance; taken*
both with the kyng and our kyn.
For wyst my brother Absolon, *If knew*
8360 full mekyll wo yt wold begyn." *much woe*
Amon wyst all was sperd; *prepared*
hyr sawys he sett not by. *advice; naught*
Fowle with hyr he ferd *Sinfully; dealt [with her]*
and forst hyr felously. *forced her wickedly*

698.

8365   The maydyn was full maysed and mate,   *dazed and dejected*
            bot of hyr bale no butt may be.   *misery; comfort*
        Son os a hownd he con hyr hatte   *As soon as a dog; hate*
            and sayd he wold not on hyr see.   *look*
        That scho suld go wyghtly hyr gate   *(i.e., quickly leave)*
8370   owt of his hows then commawnd he.
        Scho prayd of leve tyll yt ware latte
            that scho myght pase in preveté.   *secrecy*
        For spech he wold not spare,
            no lenger suffer hyr lend.   *her to remain*
8375   Evyll hurled hed and hare;
            sore wepand con scho wend.   *weeping; leave*

[ABSALOM AVENGES TAMAR (13:20–36)]

699.

        So went scho furth with mekyll wo   *much woe*
            tyll Absolon, hyr brother, hall.   *into Absalom['s], her brother['s]*
        And when he saw hyr gretand go,   *grieving*
8380   he had ferly what suld befall.
        "Systur," he sayd, "how ys it so?
            Who hath thee greved, grett or small?" —
        "My brother Amon and no mo."
            Then how betyde scho told hym all.   *what had happened*
8385   No mervell was to mene   *It is no surprise*
            yf he in mynd ware mevyd.   *moved [to action]*
        Bot sembland non was sene   *outward sign; seen*
            in hert how he was greved.

700.

        Thamar thus tuke he hym tyll
8390   and made hyr myrth with all his mayn.   *strength*
        He leytte Amon have all his wyll
            os he had noyght wyst of the trayn.   *as if; no knowledge; betrayal*
        So all this stryfe was haldyn styll   *kept quiet*
            unto two yeres was past playn.   *until two years*
8395   And then als end comys of all yll,
            befell in the seson certayn
        That men suld clype ther schepe,   *clip their sheep*
            and whore ther catell lendes   *where their*
        Suld ylk man take kepe
8400   ther for to fest ther frendes.   *feast their friends*

701.

        Fell Absolon for this same thyng   *It happened*
            ordand a grett mangery.   *arranged; banquet*

He (i.e., David)

He bad therto his fader the kyng,
 bot he excused hym skylfully.

8405 He bad hym take both old and yyng   *He (i.e., David)*
 of his breyther to be hym by,   *brothers*
And frendes, als fallys for swylke doyng.   *befit*
 And als he demed, he dyd in hy.   *haste*
He bad his brother Amon
8410 to se how frendes suld fare.
The ded ay thynkes he on   *deed always*
 that was done to Thamar.

702.

The fest was ordand fayr and fyne
 and purvayd in ylk poynt perfyt.
8415 Sone Absolon sayd unto his hyne   *servants*
 how Amon had done hym dyspytt,   *harm*
"When ye se hym well dronkyn of wyne,   *drunk*
 his hed then smertly ye of smytt.   *you must swiftly cut off*
For he mysded to me and myne,
8420 now sall I fand yt forto qwytt."   *repay*
Thei dyd als he commawnd,
 and sone was Amon slayn.
So for fowle luf in land   *Thus for foul love*
 ar men oft put to payn.

703.

8425 His brether, when thei saw this syght,   *brothers*
 and all his frendes ware fowle afrayd.
To Jerusalem thei went full wyght   *quickly*
 and told how Amon was betrayd.
Kyng David, qwen this dole was dyght,
8430 "Alas, both ware my suns," he sayd,
"Bot Absolon by reson ryght
 sall dere aby this byttur brayd."   *dearly atone for; evil*
He mornyd and mad grett mone
 for both thoo brether sake.   *those*
8435 So dyd his frendes ylkon
 and wered weked wrake.   *prepared wicked vengeance*

[ABSALOM FLEES TO GESHUR; JOAB BRINGS HIM BACK (13:37–14:24)]

704.

Then Absolon was fayn to fle
 and sojornnd for certan tyde
In Jessor with the kyng of Cirre,   *Geshur; Syria*
8440 his syb man on his moyder syde.   *kinsman*
And thore he bod by yeres thre   *dwelled*

his fader frenschep to abyd.   *await*
Then Joab toyght asay wold he   *thought he would try*
    to make acord, all harmys to hyd.
8445   He soyght a sotell gyn   *subtle guile*
    and ordand of this thyng:
A woman suld begyn
    forto carpe with the kyng.   *speak*

705.

He gart a lady go and grette   *caused*
8450   and ryve hyr hare full rewfully.   *tear her hair*
Scho fell before the kynges fette,   *feet*
    and "Mercy, lord!" lowd con scho cry.
He sayd, "My help heyr I thee hette;   *here; assure*
    tell unto me thi harmys in hy."
8455   "A mercy, lord, my bale thou bete,   *relieve*
    for dred of thi law lorn am I.   *forlorn*
I had two suns certayn;
    both ware full fayr of face.
On hath that other slayn
8460   as thei playd in a place.

706.

"My sun that dyd yt con hym withdraw
    to wyldernese, full wyll of wone,   *completely without hope*
For men says that he sall by law
    be turment, and he may be tone,   *be tortured; taken*
8465   And suffer ded; this is thar saw   *death*
    that makes me morne and make this mone.   *mourn*
That ware to me a weked thraw,   *evil time*
    ther I had two, forto have none.
Therfor this grace me gyfe
8470   sen thou all sydes may save.   *since*
Say that my sun sall lyfe,
    I kepe noyght els to crave."

707.

The kyng in hert then had pety.   *pity*
    He comforth hyr that men myght here.
8475   "Dame, thi sun sall lyf," says he.
    "Therfor of mornyng mend thi chere."
Then yt was solace to see.
    Scho sayd, "Ser kyng, with crown clere,
Sen thou hath grawnt mercy to me,   *Since*
8480   graunt thi sun on the same manere.
Sen myn sall mercy have
    and grace on ground to gang,   *walk (i.e., to live)*

Thin awn sun bot thou save,   *own son unless*
    men wyll deme thou dose wrang."   *deem you do wrong*

708.

8485   Kyng David to this tale toke hede.
    he wyst well what this woman ment,
And that yt was Duke Joab dede,
    and therfor aftur hym sone he sent.
He bad that he suld go gud sped
8490   and tell to Absolon his entent
Forto com home and have no dred.
    The messeg wyghtly is he went.
Then ware thei frendes fast,
    the kyng and Absolon.
8495   So was tho plenyng past   *mourning passed*
    for the ded of Amon.   *death*

[ON ABSALOM'S BEAUTY (14:25–33)]

709.

Of Absolon is ferly fare
    to fynd how fayr he was to syght,
And of his makyng mekyll mare;
8500   he past all other men in myght.
Of twenty libri wegh was his hare   *pounds weight*
    that he had on his hed on heyght.
And als clerkes con yt declare,
    like to gold wyre so was it bryght.
8505   To no maystrys he meved   *he stirred up no violence*
    whyls men dyd his desyre,
Bot and he ware oght greved,   *But if; in any way grieved*
    then was he fell os fyre.   *fierce as fire*

[ABSALOM'S CONSPIRACY (15:1–9)]

710.

He hath geydderd of gold and fee   *gathered*
8510   for hym and mony other moo,
And therof gafe he grett plenté   *very generously*
    and mad them frendes that ware his foo,   *foes*
That soverance of that same cyté   *rulers*
    and other cetys sere also.   *many*
8515   And the most of the kynges meneye   *company*
    ware wylly with hym forto go.   *willing*
So be faur yeres ware past,   *Thus by [the time that]*
    he had so wysly wroght:

8520	All folke ware with hym fast	*bound*
	and to his socour soght.	

711.

	So when he wyst both old and yyng	
	wold holly at his ledyng lende,	*completely*
	He asked leve at his lord the kyng	
	unto Ebron forto wende	*Hebron to journey*
8525	His sacrafyce thor forto bryng,	
	als he had heyght with hert and hende.	*promised*
	The kyng sayd, "Sun, in my blessyng."	*Son, [go] with*
	Bot of his cast nothyng he kend.	*treacherous plan he knew nothing*
	Of charys and chyvalry	*chariots and horses*
8530	grett plenté war purvayde,	*were provided*
	And furth he wendes in hy	*goes in haste*
	tyll Ebron, als he sayd.	

[ABSALOM'S REVOLT AND DAVID'S FLIGHT (15:10–16:14)]

712.

	Cytes and towns, when thei herd tell	
	that Absolon so was assent,	*determined [to go]*
8535	At home them lyst no langer dwell,	*desired*
	bot with hym holy ar thei went.	*completely*
	And mervell had thei them omell	*curiosity they had all together*
	what thyng he had in his entent.	
	Bot his cheve counsell, Archyttofell,	*Except for his chief; Ahithophel*
8540	ther wyst no mo men what he ment.	*intended*
	When he come in Ebron,	
	whor hym lyked best to be,	
	He gart tho men ylkon	*made those*
	to hymself make sewrté.	*give allegiance*

713.

8545	Thei ware full bown to his bedyng,	*prepared to [do]*
	both knyght, swyer, knave, and page.	*squire*
	Thei honerd hym over all thyng	
	and sett hym up in certan stage.	
	Then all the cuntré, old and yyng,	
8550	com to hym and made homage	
	And heyght to hald hym for ther kyng	*swore*
	and werke his wyll withoutyn wage.	*reward*
	When all ware same assent	
	and mad sewrty certayn,	
8555	Then told he his entent	
	and all his purpase playn.	

714.

"Sers," he sayd, "Sene ye deme   *Since you deem*
    me to be kyng and were the crown,   *wear*
Your land and yow well sall I yeme   *protect*
8560   and maynten yow in all reson.
My fader ys fayrest forto fleme,   *drive out*
    or yf he byde, to bryng hym down."   *remains*
Thei say, "Ser, sertes so wyll yt seme;   *certainly*
    to make this bargan ar we bown."   *agreed*
8565 This was a curssed cummand
    his fader forto spyll.   *kill*
And yett feyll foyles he fand   *many fools he found*
    that falshed to fulfyll.   *betrayal*

715.

Then Kyng David herd tythyng tell   *news*
8570   that his awn sun with sytt hym soght,   *son with trouble*
And how that fals Archytofell,
    his counsellar, was with hym broyght.
He ordand sone his men omell   *together*
    to remeve in all that thei moght.
8575 He sayd, "We be ded and we dwell;   *if we remain*
    I knaw so wele ther wekyd toyght.   *thought*
And yf thei here us toke
    or seged this ceté,   *besieged*
Then war over latte to loke   *Then would it be too late to look*
8580   to qwylke syd we suld flee."   *which side*

716.

He bad the byschop Abyathar   *Abiathar*
    and his wyfes with drere mode   *dreary cheer*
And other clerkes that with them ware   *priests*
    in ther sere state als thei stude   *bitter state*
8585 To dwell ther styll for any care,
    to kepe the Arke of God full gud,   *safe*
And send hym word ay how thei fare   *always*
    unto the flome or beyond the flode.   *river*
Ten wyfes with other frendes   *concubines*
8590   thor leves he sojorand so.   *there he leaves*
And furth then with hym wendes
    sex hunderth and no moo.   *600*

717.

Als he went apon a heght hyll,   *high*
    he saw the cyté and burghis by,   *towns*
8595 Qwylke he was wunt at weld at wyll   *accustomed to control*
    and was dyssavyd fro sodanly.   *defrauded of*

Then loved he God with stevyn full styll   *voice*
 and sayd, "This wo am I worthy."   *[Of] these woes*
So come a man mornand hym tyll,   *mourning*
8600 that cosyn was and heyght Cusy.   *close friend; Hushai*
Kyng David sayd, "I trest   *trust*
 to thee that thou be trew.
Full fayn I wold thou frayst   *glad I would [be if] you try*
 yf that thou may remewe   *move*

718.
8605 "Archytofell, that fals is ay,   *who is ever false*
 oute of the counsell of my sun.
He is abowt both nyght and day
 to werke that we in bale ware bun."
Then Cusy says, "I sall asay,   *try*
8610 for all this falshed hath he fun."   *committed*
And with this word he went his way
 to the ceté ward, as he was wun.   *towards the city*
This mater sal be ment   *told*
 more furth, als yt befell;
8615 Bot how Kyng David went
 is fyrst now forto tell.

719.
Sone on the morn with David mett
 fro the same cyté on Cyba,   *one [man named] Ziba*
Was stewerd to Mifbosett,   *Mephibosheth*
8620 that was the sun of Jonatha.   *Jonathan*
Both bred and wyn furth has he fett,
 a presand to that pepyll and ma.   *more*
David asked sone, when thei ware sett,
 "How farys our frend that thou com fra?"
8625 He says, "Ser, sen thou went,
 he is abowt to bryng
Sere folke to his assent   *Many*
 and says he wyll be kyng."

720.
Kyng David says, "Sertes, that ware schame; *For certain*
8630 thou wott well he may do no dede.   *know*
For he is lytyll, and he is lame
 and nothyng lyke a land to lede.
Me thynke that boy is forto blame;
 therfor sone sall I spyll his spede. *soon; end his success*
8635 Syba, thou sall have that same
 that I gaf hym when he had nede."
Then Syba went agayn;

                    in hert he was full glade
                    And toke all power playn
8640   that Myfbosett hade.

            721.
                    Kyng David cowd no comforth ken   *command*
                       bot cayred furth with his cumpany.   *traveled*
                    A grett mysdoer mett hym then,   *misdoer*
                       Kyng Saul cosyn Semey.   *Shimei*
8645   He werred David and all his men   *cursed*
                    and spytt on hym dyspytfully
                    And stones kest and fowles fene   *chicken shit*
                       and oft sythys sayd apon hym "Fy!"   *many times*
                    Knyghtes com fast hym to kyll,
8650   bot David bad them blyn.   *stop*
                    "I wott yt is Goddes wyll;
                       I suffer yt for my syn.

            722.
                    "What mervel ys yt of this dede   *surprise*
                       a hethyn hownd me forto hatte,   *dog; hate*
8655   Sen myn awn sun wyll have no dred   *own son*
                       me forto brew all this debate?"
                    Bot aftur sone, os men may rede,   *soon after; read*
                       this grome that greved hym in the gate   *fellow; road*
                    Be David dome he had his mede   *By David's judgment; reward*
8660   and lost his lyf, yf yt ware late.
                    In this tym Absolon,
                       as kyng with playn power,
                    Was comyn owt of Ebron
                       to Jerusalem ryght nere.

[HUSHAI DEFEATS AHITHOPHEL'S COUNSEL (16:15–17:23)]

            723.
8665   When thei ware in that cyté sett,
                    Archytofell, that curssed knyght,
                    He sayd, "Ser, and thou do thi dett,   *if; duty*
                       to David sall thou doles dyght;   *sorrows inflict*
                    Gar all his wyfes furth fast be fette   *Cause; fetched*
8670   hym to reprove by reson ryght,
                    And lyg by them — for no thyng lett —   *lie by them; delay*
                       playnly in the pepyll syght.
                    And therby sall thei wytt   *know*
                       and be exempyll se   *by*
8675   That luf sall never be knytt   *reformed*
                       betwyx thi fader and thee.

724.

Yf any gabbers wold hym glose   *gossipmongers; flatter*
   to say that he suld come agayn,
By this syght sall thei well suppose
8680   that he sall never have myrth ne mayn.   *nor strength*
So sall he all his lordschep lose
   and forto flee farre be full fayn.   *far be very glad*
Then of the chefe sall thou have chose   *the choice*
   that now ar to his bedyng bayn."   *obedient*
8685   Full wo the wemen wore
    when he so wekydly wroght.
That Natan told before
    bud unto end be broght.

725.

Cusy com, Kyng David frend,   *Hushai came*
8690   to Absolon, os I sayd ayre.   *before*
He haylsed hym with wordes hend   *greeted; courteous*
   and loved God fast for his welefare.
Absolon asked what he mende
   and sayd, "Swylke spekyng suld thou spare.
8695   With David was thou wunt to wende,
    chefe of his counsell to declare."
He sayd, "Ser, so I was
    whyls he stud in degré;
Now lyst me lett hym pase   *I desire to*
8700   and lede my lyf with thee.

726.

"I wott well yt is Godes wyll
   that thou be kyng with crown clere,
And at all pepyll come thee untyll   *that; unto*
   to serve thee in servyce sere.   *various services*
8705   That forward wyll I fayn fulfyll   *agreement; gladly*
    with hert and hand, I hett thee here."   *promise*
Absolon trowed of non yll   *believed*
   and toke hym of his counsell nere.
Cusy in cowrt sall dwell;
8710   ys non so grett to geysse
All for Archytofell
    to make his lordschep lesse.

727.

That wekyd man then went full wyght
   to Absolon and says his toyght: *thought*
8715   "Ser, thou sall have no rest ne ryght
    tyll David unto ded be broyght.   *death*

Take me ten thowsand men of myght;
   we sall not sesse or he be soyght.   *cease*
We sall be nere this ylk nyght,
8720   and bot I take hym, trow me noyght."   *unless; trust me not*
Absolon says, "Sawyns fayle,   *Without doubt*
   a fayr profer thou mase."   *you make*
Bot fyrst he asked counsell
   of Cusy in this case.

728.

8725   Cusy hath mynd both morn and noyne   *midday*
   to helpe David in his nede.
And wele he wyst, yf this ware done,
   he suld be dede withoutyn drede.
To Absolon thus says he sone,   *quickly*
8730   "Ser, this spekyng may not spede;   *succeed*
Ten thowsand folke wold be full fone   *too few*
   into a fere land forto lede.   *far*
Thi fader is wunt to fyght,   *liable*
   and his folke er full fell.   *terrible [in might]*
8735   Ordand thou have more myght   *See to it that you*
   or thou of swylke maters mell.   *before; speak*

729.

"Send aftur all thi knyghtes kene   *brave*
   and aftur keyn men of thi kyn,   *keen*
And wend thiself thore to be sene.   *go; seen*
8740   Lett non other that wrschep wyn."   *honor*
Archytofell herd how that thei mene
   that Cusy consell was cald in.
In hert he had so mekyll teyne   *anger*
   that langer he wold not byd ne blyn.   *wait or remain*
8745   Bot herd he con hym hy   *hard he did hasten himself*
   untyll his howse at hame.   *home*
In anger and in envy
   he hanged hymself with schame.

730.

On this wyse was the lordan lorn;   *villain dead*
8750   we hope he hasted sone to Hell.
And Cusy wentt sone on the morn
   to the Tempyll tythynges forto tell.   *news*
Abyathar he fand hym beforn
   with mony mo mowrnand omell.   *among [them]*
8755   He told all how he had hym born,
   that hanged was Archytofell.
And he was of consell

to byde at bed and borde.
This tale fro tope to tale   *beginning to end*
8760   he told them ylka word.   *every*

731.
"Werkes now," he sayd, "by your wysdom
that Kyng David may here in hy   *hear at once*
How I have ordand all and sum
— I wott he wyl be fayn forthi —   *glad therefore*
8765   And byde hym flee beyond the flum   *river*
for beldyng of his awn body.   *protection*
For Absolon his sun sall come
agayns hym with grett cumpany."   *against*
Letturs be lyve thei sent;   *quickly*
8770   this sand was for ther sele.   *message; good fortune*
Wyse men so warly went;
Kyng David wot ylk dele.   *knows each part*

[DAVID'S ARMY DEFEATS ABSALOM (17:24–18:18)]

732.
When David had the letturs rede,
well comforth in his hert was he.
8775   Furth over the flum his folke he led
to Manahym, a grett cyté.   *Mahanaim*
The folke that in that sted ware sted   *place were in difficulty*
welcumd hym with mekyll glee.   *[and] welcomed; much*
And all ther beld to hym thei bed   *their protection; gave*
8780   to byd whore so hymself wold be.   *stay where*
That cyté was walled so wele,   *well*
ther myght no man yt myne.   *undermine*
Ne thei dowt no dele   *Nor need they fear a bit*
for gune ne grett ingyne.   *ballista; siege engine*

733.
8785   Kyng David thore with blyse con byde   *bliss did await*
and had at wyll what so he wald.   *desired*
Faur barons wuned ther besyde   *dwelled*
that send hym vytell all unsald.   *victuals for free*
Ther helpe fro hym thei wold not hyde,   *Their*
8790   bot hertly hetes with hym to hold,   *heartily promised*
So that he had to tell that tyde
faur thowsand, that ware knytes cald.   *knights*
In this tyme Absolon
had geydderd grett plenté   *gathered*
8795   Of knyghtes that cough theron
his fader bayn to be.

734.

Thei rested nawder day ne nyght
    to thei the flum ware passed playn.   *until; river*
When thei had of that cyté a syght,
8800   whore David wuned, then ware thei fayn.   *dwelled; glad*
Bot he wyst wele thei had no myght   *knew well*
    to towch hym, bot yf it wer with trayn.   *unless; betrayal*
Therfor his men arays he ryght   *he arrays*
    them forto mare with all his mayn.   *destroy; strength*
8805   A parte to hymself toke he   *division*
    and unto Joab another,
And the thryd he bad suld be
    to Abysay, Joab brother.   *Abishai*

735.

Full fayn he wold with them have went,   *gladly*
8810   bot sone thei sayd hym this myschefe:
"Yf thou ware in ther handes hent,   *taken*
    then had thei gam us all to greve.   *would cause*
And, ser, yf sum of us be shent,   *killed*
    the remland then may thou releve.   *remnant*
8815   Therfor yt is not our assent
    that thou owt of this cyté meve."   *move*
He thanked them oft sith   *often times*
    that shewed ther luf so large.   *love so freely*
Bot he sayd, "Lordynges lith,   *Gentle lords*
8820   of a thyng I yow charge.

736.

"Yf grace fall, when ye have begun,   *If by grace it happens, once*
    that ye the vyctory may geyte,   *achieve*
Loke ye save Absolon, my sun,
    that he be nawder bun ne bette."   *neither bound nor beaten*
8825   Thei say, "And he in feld be fun,   *If he on the field is taken*
    we sall full dewly do our dette.   *duly; duty*
He sal be in no bandes bun."   *shackles bound*
    I hope thei held all that thei hette!   *hold [to]; promise*
Joab with cumpany
8830   os principall furth past.
His brother Abysay
    folod on full fast.   *followed*

737.

Absolon on that other syd
    come with his folke, fell os the fend.   *fierce as the devil*
8835   And with them was arayd to ryde
    Cusy, that was Kynges David frend.   *King David's friend*

Then was no bote to byd abyde,
  bot ylkon shope other to shend.   *planned the other to destroy*
Of all ther tolyng in that tyd   *their fighting; time*
8840   ware lang to tell bot loke the ende.   *[to] the end [of the battle]*
When David men had slayn
  twenty milia and moo,   *20,000*
The remland ware full fayn   *remnant; glad*
  with lyfes ther way to go.   *to leave with their lives*

738.

8845   Absolon, when he saw that syght:
  how that his folke ware fayn to flee,
Into a wod he rydes ryght;   *wood*
  thor trowd he best beldyd to be.   *believed; protected*
The wynd heyved up his hare on hyght   *hair aloft*
8850   so that yt cached into a tre.
His sted went furth his way full wyght,   *quickly*
  and by the hare so hang he.
Folke fowled hym to fere   *followed; defeat*
  and fand hym in the fryd.   *found; forest*
8855   Bot non durst do hym no dere   *harm*
  for dred of Kyng David.   *fear*

739.

When Joab herd tell this tythyng   *news*
  how Absolon hang by the hare,
He bede a boy fyfty schylyng   *gave; shillings*
8860   to sla hym, or he farre fare.   *slay*
Bot no man durst do swylke a thyng   *dared*
  for David dred, als I sayd ayre.   *before*
Then Joab toyght yt hard hethyng   *thought it very scornful*
  and thrugh the body ther hym bare.   *bore*
8865   Thus had this man myschaunce
  and for non other thyng
Bot for myse-governance
  and unlefull lyfyng.   *unloyal*

740.

Sone Joab herkynd and beheld
8870   all his enmys away wore gone.
To geydder his men agayn to beld   *gather*
  bugyls gart he blaw gud wone.   *trumpets he caused; in abundance*
Unto his hand all con thei held.
  That body down then have thei toyn   *taken*
8875   And beyred yt fayre in the feld   *buried; field*
  and mad a hyll of mony a ston.
Thus ended Absolon

                    so dyd Archytofell,   *as*
                    And hedyd was Amon   *beheaded*
8880   for Thamar, so we tell.

[David mourns Absalom (18:19–19:10)]

741.
                    When this batell was done ylk dele,
                       Joab sent sone a messynger:
                    Cusy, that lufed Kyng David well,
                       was full mery to mend his chere.
8885   He told hym all fro hed to hele   *beginning to end*
                       how that thies folke ware hale in fere.   *strong together*
                    The kyng sayd, "Say me for my sele,   *happiness*
                       ys my sun hole? That wold I here."
                    He sayd, "Ser, I wald byd
8890   thine enmys be tyd ylkon,
                    Als thi sun is be tyd."
                       Then wyst he that he was sloyn.   *slain*

742.
                    He syghyd sore and sayd, "Alas!
                       In werld is none so wyll of rede.   *so helpless*
8895   The wurthest wyght that ever was   *worthiest fellow*
                       this day with dole is done to ded.   *sorrow; death*
                    Wold God that I with payn myght pase   *die*
                       and to be styked thor in his stede.   *there in his place*
                    Whoso my sun dyssayved hath
8900   sall dere aby that doylefull dede."   *atone for*
                    He drowped day and nyght
                       with sorow sore and sad.
                    No myrth amend hym myght;
                       so wex he mased and made.   *dazed and mad*

743.
8905   Duke Joab and Abysay,
                       when God to them this grace had sent,
                    Went home with ryall cumpany,   *royal*
                       and wele thei trawed in ther entent   *believed*
                    Forto be welcumd worthyly
8910   sen thei for the kynges wrschep went.   *since; king's honor had gone*
                    Bot ever he drowped and was drery,
                       and for thei wyst not what he ment,
                    Thei ware full evyll apayd;   *very much disconcerted*
                       and becawse of this tythyng
8915   Ylk on tyll other sayd,
                       "He sall not be our kyng."

744.

When Joab wyst, he was full wo;
    be lyfe wentt whore the kyng lendes. *quickly he went*
"Ser kyng," he says, "why dose thou so?
8920   Thiself full shamely thou shendes. *dishonor (injure)*
Had thou lever the lyf of thi foo *Would you prefer*
    then the frenschep of all thi frendes?
Bot yf thou gladly to them go,
    all this folk fast fro thee wendes.
8925   Lett thi kyndnese be kyd *shown*
    and make mery chere."
Att his cownsell he dyde;
    so ware all fayn in fere. *joyous together*

[DAVID RETURNS TO JERUSALEM IN VICTORY (19:11–43)]

745.

The gud byschop Abythiar
8930   and Sadoch, that wytty prest be name, *Zadok*
Thei ordand clerkes that with them ware
    the Arke of God to kepe fro blame
And also wysmen, non wold them mare,
    to kepe ther kyng when he comys hame. *care for*
8935   The kynred of Juda furth con fare;
    thei war the fyrst soght to that same.
For thei fyrst made hym kyng *Because*
    at home in ther cuntré,
Thei went fyrst furth to bryng
8940   hym to his awn cité.

746.

Unto the flom have thei soyght, *river*
    thousandes mo then neyn or ten.
A bryg full wysly have thei wroyt *bridge*
    for Kyng David and all his men.
8945   Furth over the flode thei have hym broyght,
    and for ther kyng all thei hym kene. *acknowledge*
Thei that before faverd hym noyght
    ware all full fayn to folow hym then. *very glad*
The kynred of Juda
8950   ware next in cumpany.
Therfor full mony ma *more*
    ware greved with grett envy.

747.

Dukes, erlys, and knythys kene, *brave*
    that went with Absolon, his sun,

8955   When that thei wyst withoutyn wene   *without doubt*
         Kyng David suld in welthis wun,
    Unto hym then thei come clene
         and bed in bandes to be bun   *asked in feudal obligation; bound*
    And mendes make, als he wold meyne,   *amends; demand*
8960   for grevans that thei had begun.
    He forgaf all ther gylt,
         when that thei mercy craved.
    He wold that non ware spylt
         that wold themself be sayved.

748.

8965   So als thei ryde rychly arayd,
         sodanly that man thei mett,
    Semey, that had hym myssayd
         and stoned with stonys in the strette.
    He knelyd on knese and mercy prayd,
8970   and his frendes fell before ther fette.
    Joab wold full fayn have hym aflayd,
         bot the kyng sayd, "Hele I hym hete.   *Life I promise him*
    Sen God forgyfes us tyll
         and rychly us releves,
8975   So sall we with gud wyll
         forgyf them that us greves."

749.

    Furth in ther pase, als thei con passe,   *path*
         sone Mifbosett hath thei mett.   *Miphibosheth*
    He was the sun of Jonatas,
8980   that David lufed deuly be dett.   *loved truly dutifully*
    In febyll wede arayd he was,   *poor clothes*
         and all his face with hare umsett.   *was covered (i.e., his beard was untrimmed)*
    The kyng sone hym resond has   *soon asked him*
         yf any lede his lykyng lett: *man hindered his happiness*
8985   "Thou hath catell and corne   *grain*
         unto thi bedyng broyght."
    He sayd, "Lord, all ys lorn   *taken away*
         and me ys leved ryght noyght.   *to me is left nothing*

750.

    "Lord, my stewerd, ser Cyba,
8990   thou toke to me, as man most wyse;
    My lordschep hath he tane me fra,   *taken*
         ay redy agayns me to ryse."   *ever ready against*
    The kyng sayd, "Sen I see yt sa
         that he hath wun lordschep with lyyse,   *lies*
8995   Yt sal be parted betwyx yow two

to tyme that we may us avyse."   *until*
On knese then con he fall
    and sayd, "So wyll not he.
Gud lord, lett hym have all,
9000   I wyll wende with thee."

751.
So went thei furth withoutyn more,
    all that ware to his bydyng bown,   *bound*
To Jerusalem, and when thei come thore,
    thei raysed hym up with grett renown.
9005 In his astate con thei hym restore
    to reyn os ryall kyng with crown.   *reign*
Folke of Juda ware ever before
    to forther hym in feld and town.
His wo was waryschyd then   *relieved*
9010   and end mad of all,
As the prophett Natan
    sayd that yt suld befall.

752.
Unto the Tempyll then con he fare;
    grett sacrafyce thei have begun.
9015 Prestes and clerkes, that then ware thore,
    thei ware full fayn that he was fun.   *joyful*
His ten wyfes, that I told of ayre,   *before*
    ordand he wrschypfully to wun.   *honorably*
Bot with them wold he mell no mare   *deal*
9020   bycause of Absolon his sun.
Thus was he gettyn agayn
    and sesyd in his kyngdom.   *reinstated*
His frendes ware ferly fayn,   *wondrously glad*
    bot enmys had he sum.   *enemies*

[Sheba's revolt against David (20:1–26)]

753.
9025 Syr Cyba, that I of ayre sayd,   *Sheba, whom I spoke of before*
    was lord of Myfbosett land.   *steward of Mephibosheth's*
Full ryally he hym arayd   *royally*
    and full grett felnes furth he fand.   *fierceness*
A grett geydderyng sone hath he grayd   *gathering; made*
9030   of Ebrews, that he had at hand.
And felous poyntes hath he purvayd   *wicked*
    that David in strengh suld not stand.
"Was he not Gesse sun
    and of Bedlem bredyng?

9035   Whore has his fader fun   *found*
            that he suld be kyng?

754.
        "Sat he not als a sympyll page
            on feld to fede his fader fee?   *feed; flocks*
        And aftur when he come of age
9040   cayred abowt in sere cuntree?   *traveled; many*
        And sythyn in were for his wage   *then in war*
            wrogh mekyll woo, this wele wott we,   *we well know*
        Yf yt suld go by herytage,
            then am I neghbour nere then hee.   *nearer*
9045   Therfor I wold we wentt
            his forsce sone forto shend."   *power soon to destroy*
        Thei sayd all, "We assent
            evyn as thou wyll to wende."   *desire to do*

755.
        Kyng David herd tell tythyng then   *news*
9050   how Cyba soght to do hym dere,   *harm*
        And all on what wyse he began   *ways*
            to gedder folke hym forto fere.   *gather; defeat*
        He cald his cosyn Amasan,   *Amasa*
            a duke that was full wyse of were.   *war*
9055   "Wende furth," he sayd, "full wele thou can,   *Go*
            to the folke that our frendes ere,
        The kynred of Juda,
            that ever wyll us releve,
        And say them how Cyba
9060   ys ordand us to greve.

756.
        "Bot loke thou be by thre days end
            with all thi men at me agayn
        That thou then with my men may wende
            to mare that traytur of his trayn."   *harm; for his treachery*
9065   Amasan wold no lenger lend;
            he soyght on ylk syd certayn
        Folke that he wyst was David frend;
            to fech them furth he was full fayn.
        In all that ever he moght
9070   that space he sped and spend,
        Bot agayn com he noght
            when thre days was ende.

757.
The kyng toygh he dweltt full lang
 and dowt Cyba suld them schame.
9075 He bad Joab, his ste(w)erd strang,
 take the knyghtes he had at hame
Agayn Cyba fast forto gang:
 "Duke Amasan, he dose the same.
When ye ar mett your men amang,
9080 gos both togeydder in Goddes name!"
Duke Joab sone was dyght   *ready*
 in all that he myght hy,   *haste*
And furth he rydes full ryght
 with full clene cumpany.

758.
9085 So in his way, as he was sett,
 Duke Amasan sone can he see
With full fayr folke that he had fett   *fetched*
 and samned owt of sere cuntré.   *assembled; various countries*
He toyght, "Bot I this lordschep lett   *Unless; hinder*
9090 the kyng sall prays hym more then me."
Therfor he menys, when thei ar mett,   *intends*
 with sum debate his bane to be.
Duke Amasan lyght down   *dismounts*
 to com his cosyn untyll.
9095 Duke Joab mad hym bown   *ready*
 his falshed to fulfyll.

759.
In a fayr medew con thei mete.
 Joab fard all with faygyng fare.   *fared; flattery*
His sword owt of his sheth he lete,
9100 ryght os yt noyght his wytyng ware.   *knowing*
To Amasan spake he wordes swete,
 and com als he suld kyse hym thare.
He toke the sword up at his fette,
 and throgh the body so he hym bare.
9105 Two dughty dukes of dede
 so had he murtherd than,
And all for erthly mede: *rewards*
 Abnar and Amasan.

760.
When folke fand this felous thyng,   *discovered this wicked*
9110 thei weped and had full mekyll wo.   *much*
Duke Joab fenyd a fals lesyng   *falsehood*
 and bad thei suld not sorow so:

"He was traytur unto the kyng;
   and I was sent hym forto sloo.   *slay*
9115 To beryall lett his men hym bryng,   *burial*
   and hast we fast to fell our foo."
He gart a man of his   *caused*
   hyde the cors owt of the way,   *[to] hide the corpse*
So that men suld hym myse
9120 and makc no morc daray.   *disturbance*

761.

So went thei furth to seke Cyba
   and with ther forse to fell his pryd.
Thei soght in towns to and fra
   and in cytys on ylka syde.
9125 In a cyté, that heygh Abelay,   *Abel(a)*
   thore had he beld hym to abyd.   *lodged; to dwell*
For yt was wardyd and wallyd swa,
   thei dred no tene that myght betyde.   *sorrow; occur*
Joab and his meneye
9130 to wyn yt ware in no dowt.
Thei seged that ceté   *beseiged*
   with bold men all abowt.

762.

Thei sett a sawtt with gunys gud,   *began an assault; ballistae*
   with bowes and with alablawsters blend.   *arbalesters mingled*
9135 The folk within sone faled fode   *lacked food*
   and had no forse them to dyffend.
A lady that was myld of mode   *moderate of cheer*
   thore in that same cyté con lend.   *did live*
Apon the walles yeply scho yode   *quickly she went*
9140 and carped to Joab, that scho kend: *called; knew*
"Ser, thou suld with reson
   the kynges folke fend fro noe,   *harm*
And here thou makes thee bown   *ready*
   with strengh them to dystroye,

763.

9145 "Forto dere thies here thou dwelles   *discomfort*
   that suld maynteyn theym morne and none."
Joab takes tent how scho hym tellys,   *takes heed*
   and to hyr thus says he sone:
"Madame, to mare yow no man mellys.   *harm; intends*
9150 This is our wyll with wordes foyne: *few*
Forto noy Cyba and non ellys.   *destroy*
   Delyver hym us, then have we done."
That lady wysly wroyght;

scho saw qwat suld befall.

9155 Weyle lese perell, hyr toyght,   *Far less peril, she thought*
        to lose oon then all.

764.

A commyn consell cald scho tyte   *immediately*
  and told them holy as scho ment,
And how Cyba was worthy to wyte
9160   of all the harme thei had thore hent.   *suffered*
Smertly thei gart his hed of smytt,   *off*
  and unto Joab thei yt sent.
Hee remeved then withowt respytt,   *retreated*
  and to Jerusalem sone he went.
9165 The kynred of Juda,
        that were ay frendes of old,   *ever*
Went whore thei com fro   *where*
  and wrogh whatever thei wold.

[FAMINE IN ISRAEL (21:1–14)]

765.

Now is Kyng David broyght to rest
9170   and rewlys his reme with ryalté.   *realm*
He ordand all thyng at the best,
  os gud consell bad yt suld be.   *ordained*
For hym and his court he kest
  gud servytours semly to see
9175 And for his land by est and west
        gud governers in sere degree.   *various*
All folke ware fayn to plese
  and heyld unto his hand.   *submitted to*
Bot sone fell sodan dysese   *sudden famine*
9180   over all in his land.

766.

Brede and wyn both wex so dere   *grew so rare*
  that sympyll men myght no socur gete.
The pure perysched fare and nere   *poor*
  both for defawt of drynke and mete.   *food*
9185 The kyng of God oft con inquere   *did beg*
        the cause of all that hungur grete.
Natan the prophett con apere
  and sayd for forfaders forfett,
"The gud Duke Josue   *Joshua*
9190   heyght and ensured theron   *promised*
That peyse suld holdyn be   *peace should be held*
  with the folke of Gabaon.   *Gibeon*

767.

"For he ensured them on swylke wyse,
    all ware thei folke Phylisteyn.   *Philistines*

9195   He fended them from ther enmys,   *defended*
    evyn als thei Ebrews had beyne.   *as [if] they had been Hebrews*
He sayd no man suld them surpryse
    agayns the trews tan them betwen.   *compact taken*
Kyng Saul savyd not that assyse;   *preserved; agreement*

9200   therfor now comys the hungur keyne.   *sharp*
And, ser, it sall not sesse   *cease*
    bot rayke abowt be ryght   *go*
Tyll thei be sett in pese
    and mendes therfor be dyght."   *made*

768.

9205   Kyng David, when he herd of this,
    sent fast for the folke of Gabaon
And sayd, "Sers, I wyll mend all myse   *troubles*
    that ye wyll rekyn by reson."
"Syr Josue heyght for hym and his

9210   to send us pese in all seson,
And Kyng Saul, the sun of Cys,
    with his batels he bare us down.
That was noyght lafull thyng;
    therfor vengance we crave."

9215   Therto answers the kyng,
    "What vengance wold ye have?"

769.

Thei say, "Us nedes noyght of thi gud,   *goods*
    ne of thi catell kepe we none.
Bot that ar born of Saul blod,   *those [who] are*

9220   delyver us them ylk on."   *each one*
When Kyng David this understud,
    thei soyght and sone gate gud wone.   *a good number*
Tho folke, that were in wyll full wode,
    sessyd noyght tyll thei were sloyn.

9225   Ther cause then thei relessed
    and hyed them home agayn.   *hastened*
And so the hungur sessyd,
    and then the folke ware fayn.

[WARS AGAINST THE PHILISTINES AND DAVID'S HYMN OF PRAISE (21:15–22:51)]

770.

Then in the Bybyll may men see
9230   the kyng was oft in careys kest.   *troubles*

	And sythyn when he had playn pawste	*later; full power*
	and all his perels war over past,	
	Diligam te, Domine,	
	this salme he sett and sayd yt fast.	*psalm*
9235	That menes: "Lord, I sall luf thee	
	lelly whyls my lyf may last."	*loyally*
	With swylke prayers of price	
	he honerde God ever more	
	And with sere sacrafyce,	*many sacrifices*
9240	os costom was then thore.	

[DAVID'S CENSUS AND GOD'S PUNISHMENT (24:1–25)]

771.

	Bot afturward he dyd a dede	
	that was full grett for Goddes aw:	
	To nowmber, when he had no nede,	*take a census*
	the folke of God agayns His law.	
9245	For Moyses told, yf he toke hede,	
	that no man suld the nowmber knaw	
	Of Goddes folke for dowt and drede	
	that God suld vengance schaw.	
	For that law lett he noyght	*Because; hindered him not*
9250	bot gart seke on ylka syd,	*but [he]*
	Joab the nowmber broyght	
	and told to hym that tyde.	

772.

	He told hym of the kynred ten,	*ten tribes*
	that so many were sett in that syght:	
9255	Aght hunderth milia feyghyng men	*800,000 fighting*
	that ware in armys wyse and wyght.	*strong*
	Of the kynd of Juda myght he ken	*tribe*
	fyfty milia rekynd ryght;	*50,000*
	Of Levy ware non rekynd then,	*counted*
9260	for thei ware no folke forto fyght.	
	For orderd all ware thei	
	unto the Tempyll at tent	*attention*
	And for the pepyll at pray	
	that thei no harme suld hent.	*suffer*

773.

9265	When this was done, the kyng sone knew	
	that God was greved in this degree;	
	That rekynyng suld hym full sore rew,	
	and mercy oft sythys asked hee.	*ofttimes*
	Bot Gad, that was Goddes prophett trew,	

9270   he sayd hym sone how yt suld bee,
        For he had nowmberd so on new.
            God bad he suld chese on of thre: *choose one*
        Enmys on sydes sere   *many*
            sevyn yere to were allways,   *years to war against*
9275   Or have hungur thre yere,
            or pestalence thre days.

774.
        Kyng David toyght here full herd chose,   *thought; hard*
            for all thei grathed folke unto grave.   *brought people*
        Full loth he was his land to lose,
9280   and fro hungur hymself myght he save.
        And ded, he wyst wele, wold not glose,   *death, he knew well; comfort*
            ne take reward to knyght ne knave.
        And in God con he grace suppose;
            therfor ded asked he forto have.   *death (i.e., pestilence)*
9285   Sone on the morn was told
            amang the kynredes twelfe:
        The folke dyed so thyke fold
            that non myght other delve.   *bury*

775.
        Kyng David in his towre con stand,
9290   and sone he saw a selcowth syght: *strange*
        An angell in the ayre fleand,   *air flying*
            that feld the folk withowtyn fyght.   *killed*
        He hasted hym with hert and hand
            to save the cyté at all his myght.
9295   Full low he kneled down on that land,
            wheron he saw that angell lyght.   *whereon; alight*
        He prayd to God of Hevyn
            to byd that vengance blyne,   *make; cease*
        And sayd, with sympyll stevyn,
9300   "Lord, I dyd all this syne.

776.
        "The pepyll unto Thee trespast noyght
            that suffers ded thus sodanly.
        Bot I am he that wrang hath wroyght,
            and all this wo I am worthy.
9305   Let all the bale on me be broyght
            and spare them that ar not gylty."
        Then God of Hevyn, os Hym gud toyght,
            gaf them grace and graunt mercy.
        He sent His prophett Gad
9310   to say what he suld do,

And evyn os God hym bad,
   he told Kyng David to.

777.

He sayd, "Thi myse forto amend   *sins*
   God wyll that thou werke on this wyse: *desires*

9315   In the feld, wher the angell dyscend,
   thore sall thi ryghtwysnese upryse.

Thou sall do make thore with thi hend   *hand*
   an auter for prayers of price."   *altar*

In the same place, ose clerkes have kend,

9320   made Abraham fyrst his sacrafyce.

And sythyn in that same stede,   *place*
   as boke wytnese therby,   *books*

Was Jesus done to dede   *death*
   and cald the Mownt of Calvery.

778.

9325   And in that same place fyrst was fun   *founded*
   a tempyll folke in forto pray,

For the qwylke Kyng David hath begun
   in ylka poynt forto purvay

And sythyn Kyng Salamon, his sun,

9330   raysed yt up in ryght aray

And was cald Tempyll of Salomon
   and yett is so, os we here say.

Forther who likes to loke
   how all that werke was wroyght,

9335   Go to the Bybyll boke;
   thor may thei see unsoght.

[David grows old and frail (3 Kings [1 Kings] 1:1–4)]

779.

And for Kyng David had warnyng
   by sere exempyls forto see   *many signs*

That Salamon his sun suld be kyng,

9340   on mony wyse hym warned hee

To honer God over all thyng
   and to his bydyng bowsom be,   *obedient*

And forto governd old and yyng
   ylkon dewly in ther degree,   *everyone befitting their status*

9345   And sayd his lordes ylkon,
   fro tyme that he ware dede,   *dead*

To socour Salamon   *help*
   at stand furth in his sted.

780.

	Kyng David wex then all unweld,	*feeble*
9350	no wounder was withowtyn wene,	*doubt*
	For he was gone in full grett eld	*age*
	and bressed in batels ther he had bene.	*injured*
	Of kynd was his compleccion keled,	*nature; cold*
	and cold come on hym wonder kene	*very sharp*
9355	That in bed myght he have no beld	*comfort*
	for no kepyng with cloghes clene.	
	Physissiens com hym tell	
	be all the wytt thei wote	*wisdom they knew*
	That a yong damsell	*girl*
9360	ware best to hald hym hote.	*keep him hot*

781.

	And sone unto that same entent	
	to hym was soyght a madyn swete.	*virgin*
	On nyghtes he hyr in armis hent,	*held*
	and unto hym scho held gud hette.	*heat*
9365	In that maner no myse thei ment,	*sin they intended (i.e., they did not have sex)*
	for unto myrth was he not mete.	*inclined*
	Bot lenger lyf was to hym lent	
	and fuller forse fro face to fete.	*from [his] face to [his] feet*
	That byrd was not to blame,	*girl*
9370	for fawt myght no folke fynd.	
	Abysag was hyr name	*Abishag*
	and comyn of gentyll kynd.	

[ADONIJAH'S STRUGGLE TO BE HEIR (3 KINGS [1 KINGS] 1:5–53)]

782.

	He had a sun, heygh Adonay,	*Adonijah*
	that fast begane a fowle debate.	*quickly*
9375	To his brother he had envy	
	that he suld come to kynges astate.	
	He chese to hym grett chevalry,	*selected; knights*
	qwylke he hoped wold his brother hate,	
	And sayd to them, "Next hayr am I,	*heir*
9380	for I am elder, all men wele wate."	*know it well*
	Of his assent then war	
	Duke Joab, that gentyll Jew,	
	And the byschop Abyathar	
	that David trest for trew.	

783.

9385	Sadoc never to them assent,	*Zadok*
	ne Natan, ne Naomy and other ma,	*Nathan; Benaiah; others more*

Bot with Kyng David ay thei went;   *ever*
    so dyd the kynred of Juda.
Adonay to fulfyll his entent
9390   made a grett fest not fare ther fra,   *feast not far there from*
And all that of that mater ment
    war fayn unto that fest to ga.   *glad; go*
And thore assented thei
    all holy to this thyng,   *completely*
9395 In all that ever thei may,
    that Adonay suld be kyng.

784.

When Natan herd ther werkes wyld,
    he went belyve to Barsabé   *quickly to Bathsheba*
And sayd, "Thi sun sal be begylyd
9400   bot thou hym helpe by red of me.   *unless; counsel*
Go tell the kyng with wordes myld
    how Adonay ordance kyng to be   *plans*
And how he heyght unto thi chyld
    that non suld have the crown bot he."
9405 Scho went and asked this bowne   *at once*
    as woman full affrayd,
And he come aftur sone
    unto the kyng and sayd.

785.

He sayd, "Ser, is this with thi wyll
9410   that Adonay be kyng on dese?   *dais*
All yf thou wold that fare fulfyll,
    thou wot that God another chese."   *chose*
The kyng lyked his lesson yll
    and sayd, "Go sone, no lenger sesse.   *soon; delay*
9415 Tak Salamon my sun yow tyll
    with all my knyghtes hym to encrese.
Rydes throwgh this cyté
    and says with solempne crye
That Salamon sal be
9420   kyng of all the Jury!   *Jews*

786.

"Anoynt hym to that same entent
    at the well that is named Wyon.   *Gihon*
Then Adonay and his convent   *company*
    sall fynd how that thei fowly fon."   *behave foully*
9425 When Natan herd how that he ment,
    he mad no poyntyng ther apon,   *comment*
Bot aftur Sadok sone he sent

    forto anoynt kyng Salamon.   *Solomon as king*
  Barons and knyghtes kene
9430   that of that cowrt ware kende
  And burgeys all be dene   *straightway*
    full sone war aftur send.

787.
  Thurghoute that cety solemply
    thei went with cumpany full clene.
9435 At ylke corner gart thei cry
    that Salamon suld kyng be sene.
  When tho that ete with Adonay   *those who ate*
    herd nakers, trompes, and clarions keyne,   *drums; trumpets; sound*
  Thei sent fast forto spyre and spy   *look*
9440   what all that melody myght be meyne.   *might reveal*
  When Salamon was led
    and sett in the kynges stede,
  That feleschep fast fled
    for dred forto be dede.

788.
9445 Duke Joab then that fest forsoke   *feast forsook*
    and wyst wele that thei rudly rave.   *wrongly*
  Abyathar, byschope with boke,
    was then set os a sympyll knave.
  And Adonay the Tempyll toke
9450   for sewrty so hymselfe to save.   *protection*
  He held hym be the auter noke,   *altar's nook*
    for thor he hoped his hele to have.   *health (i.e., life)*
  Salamon then he knew
    for his kyng and his lord
9455 And send fast to persew
    for frenschep and acorde.

789.
  He sayd he wold amendes make
    for that wrang that he had wroght.
  Then Salamon for Goddes sake
9460   sayd no vengance suld be soyght;
  Bot unto trews he con hym take
    be this assent that he suld noyght
  Wayte hym with more wrangwyse wrake,   *Ambush; unjust vengeance*
    ne do hym dere in ded ne toyght.   *harm in deed nor thought*
9465 So Salamon was sett
    in cowrse, os kyng suld be,
  And all ware frendes mett,
    both his brether and he.

[DAVID'S DEATH (3 KINGS [1 KINGS] 2:1–12)]

790.

Kyng David then full clerly kend
   how that he chaunged hew and hyd.
9470
His messyngers full sone he send
   to cetys sere on ylka syd.   *many cities*
The lordes that in his land can lend,
   he bad thei suld not blyn ne byd   *wait*
9475
Bot hast to hym befor his end
   to here hym tell what suld be tyd.   *hear; happen*
The messyngers ar gone
   this forward to fulfyll.
And sone thei come ylkon
9480
   and thus he told them tyll.

791.

"Sers," he sayd, "the suthe ye see: *truth*
   day of my ded begynys to draw.   *death*
I have yow governyd in degree
   lely to lyf after your law,   *loyally*
9485
And ye have bene gud men to me
   and dewly done in dede and saw.   *deed and word*
Now wyll I consell here that ye
   luf ylkon other os ye aw.   *love; ought*
Yf ye be fast in fere,   *strong together*
9490
   foyce sall ye fynd bot foyn.   *foes; few*
And yf ye sonder sere,   *sunder apart*
   sone sall ye be for done.   *defeated*

792.

"With bandes of ded so am I bun   *the bonds of death; bound*
   that both me fayles flesch and bone. *I fail in both*
9495
Ye sall have Salamon, my sun,
   to govern yow when I am gone.
And as I have yow frendly fun,   *found*
   so, sers, beseke I yow ylkon
That ye wyll with hym wend and wun *live and dwell*
9500
   so that he wax not wyll of wone. *grows not dismayed*
God hath ordand hym kyng,
   therfor I pray yow all
To bow to his bedyng
   and com unto his call.

793.

9505
"He sal be wyse in werld allways
   dewly to deme of ever ylk dede,   *judge*

And peyse sall be in all his days;
   therfor to helpe hym, sers, take hede
The Tempyll of God ryght forto raise,
9510   als I have layd the lenght and brede.
I have ordand what so men says
   that of no thyng sall he have nede.
Of metall, tre, and stone
   is purvayd grett plenté
9515   And werke men full gud wone   *in abundance*
   to sett in sere degree.

794.

"He sall fynd all ordand at onys
   so that no more nedes to be boyght:
Gold enogh ryght for the noyns,   *right indeed*
9520   and sylver sall he have unsoght.
Besandes, pyrry, and prescius stonys   *Bezants, jewels*
   ar plenté to that bygyng broyght;   *building*
Swylke welth os sal be in that wonys   *place*
   ayre in this werld was never wroyght.   *before*
9525   Both wryghys and masons fyne   *wrights*
   therto have tane ther merkes   *taken their*
And taylurs of engyne   *ingenuities*
   and joners gentyll of werkes."   *joiners*

795.

When he had warned them on this wyse
9530   and ordand all in gud degree,
To God thei mad gret sacrafyce
   of bestes and gyftes full grett plenté.
And Salamon, that prince of price,
   then sett thei in his fader see,   *seat*
9535   And mad to hym sewt and servyce   *suit*
   and homage, als yt aght to be.
Kyng Salamon mad that day
   grett fest to folke in fere,   *together*
And then thei went ther way
9540   and parted to placeys sere.   *many places*

796.

Then David in his bed con ly;   *did lie*
   he had no forse to flytt ther fro.   *strength to flee there from*
He cald his sun to byde hym by   *bid him goodbye*
   and sayd to hym betwyx them two,
9545   "Sun, I sall wend heyn in hy   *go hence*
   the gate that all our elders go,
Whor we sall have, both thei and I,

als we ar worthy, wele or wo.   *weal or woe*
The law that God hath lent
9550   loke thou never yt forsake,
And trewly, sun, take tent   *take heed*
          His hows fayr forto make.

797.

"Sen God wold noyght gyf leve to me
          at make His howse and have my med,   *to make; reward*
9555   Bot sayd thou suld the maker be
          and lely lyf His laws to lede,   *loyally live*
And I have ordand in all degré
          that specially the werke may spede,
Layt no defawt be fun in thee   *Let; be found*
9560   forto make endyng of that dede.
And fand forto socour
          thi men with all thi myght.
Then wyll thei thee honowr
          and reverence in all ryght."

798.

9565   Also, he sayd, "My sun, beware
          for Joab that with fals envy
Slogh Amasan and Duke Abnar,
          the gentylest of all Jury,   *Jews*
The fals byschope Abathyar,
9570   that forsoke me for Adonay.
Take vengance, dere sun, when thou dare,
          of them and als of Symei   *also*
That agayns me con com
          and dyd me grett dyspyte
9575   Before I past the flome.   *river*
          Fand thou yt forto qwyte!   *Try*

799.

"And, sun, loke thou that thi fayth be fyne
          to oon that I then fand my frend.   *found*
That was the baron Bersylyne.   *Barzillai*
9580   When I in this land durst not lende,
He maynteyned then both me and myne
          agayns my sun that wold me shend.   *destroy*
And, sun, yf that he be ded sythyn,   *dead later*
          to the ayrs of hym loke thou be hend.   *heirs; gracious*
9585   When I was fled and flemed   *driven away*
          and all this myrth con myse,
No socur to me semed
          bot only of hym and his.

800.

"And hertly, sun, that thou thee hast
  to helpe all that of helpe has nede,
9590
So that thies wordes be not in wast
  that I have spokyn here for thi sped."   *aid*
In bandes of ded then was he brast   *[the] bonds of death; bound*
  that unto Hele he toke no hede.   *Hell; heed*
9595
So unto God he gaf the gast   *gave up the ghost*
  furt at His lykyng forto lede.   *away*
For he of mercy ment
  and end in trawth trewly,   *truth*
We trow his sawle went   *believe*
9600
  unto clene cumpany.

801.

Then the lordes and lades dere
  and all his meneye grett mornyng makes.   *company*
For he was prince withoutyn peyre
  wher so he past in ylka place.
9605
God was ay hend hym forto here,   *ever gracious*
  for yf he spend of myse his space,
He syghyd ever with sympyll chere
  tyll he had grauntyng of sum grace.
Whyls he in lyf can lend,
9610
  he ordan ylk thyng,
Begynnyng, myddes, and ende,
  alon to Goddes lovyng.

802.

A feller knyght was never before,   *braver*
  ne that fro yre so sone wold slake,
9615
Ne never man gat so grett thressour
  as he geydderd for Goddes sake.   *gathered*
Now of hym wyll we make no more;
  on mold he was withoutyn make.   *on earth; peer*
Of Salamon werkes how thei wore,
9620
  sum sall we tell who sotent wyll take.   *whoever will take heed*
And heyre our story twynes   *here; ends*
  with the Secund Boke of Kynges,
And the Thryd Boke heyre begynnys.
  God graunt us gud endyngys!

THIRD BOOK OF KINGS (1 KINGS)

LIBER TERTIUS REGUM.

[SOLOMON CONSOLIDATES HIS THRONE (2:13–46)]

803.

9625	In the Secund Boke before is told	
	how David, sun of Jesse,	
	In barnhed he began to be bold	*childhood*
	whyls that he keped his fader fee,	*father's inheritance (estate)*
	And sythyn how he had welth in wold	*then; prosperity on earth*
9630	and honerd God in gud degree,	
	And afturward how he was old	
	and went whor God wold hym to be.	*desired*
	This Thryd Boke is begun	
	when Kyng David was dede,	
9635	How Salamon, his sun,	
	was sett in that same stede.	*place*

804.

	In this same boke before is rede	
	how Adhony toyght full gret hethyng	*Adonijah considered [it a]; contempt*
	That Salamon suld so be sted	*placed*
9640	of Ebrews folke forto be kyng.	
	With all his forse fast he hym sped	
	and sett hymselfe to that same thyng.	
	Bot sythyn he and his felows fled	*then*
	becawse thei fayled of ther fowlyng.	*evil plan*
9645	For he was elder brother,	
	well knawn in ylke cuntré,	
	Hym toyght ther suld non other	*thought*
	be kyng bot only he.	

805.

	Therfor to seke sum sutell gyn	*subtle trick*
9650	he besys hym erly and late.	*busies*
	Abysag was comyn of gentyll kyn,	*Abishag; family*
	that maydyn that held his fader hate.	*kept his father warm*

He toyght myght he hyre to wyfe win,
   so suld he governd grett astate.
9655 And then he toyght forto begyn
   agayns his brother sum grett debate.
To make this bargan be
   he pursewed fast ther on
Unto the qwene Barsabé,   *Bathsheba*
9660   the moyder of Salamon.

806.
When he come thor, on knese he kneled
   full softly os a sympyll knave.
"I pray your sun to be my beld,   *protection*
   my dame," he sayd, "and ye vouchsave.
9665 I am his brother elder of eld,   *elder in age*
   all thof he all this kyngdom have.   *although*
Bot Abysag to wyfe at weld
   I kepe not ellys at hym to crave.
And ye wyll aske this bone,
9670   full mekyll yt mend me may."
Scho sayd, "This sal be done."
   And sone scho went hyr way.

807.
Unto the kyng scho come in hy   *haste*
   and haylssed hym be stevyn full styll.   *hailed; voice*
9675 He welcumd hyr full curtasly
   and sayd, "Moyder, what is your wyll?"
Scho sayd, "Sun, grett erand have I,
   qwylke I wyll pray thee to fulfyll,
Towchand thi brother Adony,
9680   and to helpe hym I hald yt skyll.
That woman wold he wed
   to wyf yf that thou wold,
That warmed thi fader bed
   and hym when he was cold.

808.
9685 "For this, sun, hath he me besogh,   *besought*
   and I beseke thee for the same."
The kyng wyst full well his toyght
   that all was forto schape hym schame.
"Moyder," he sayd, "meynys yow noyght,   *do you not remember*
9690   when we ware with my fader at hame,
How Joab and he wunders wroyght
   to make hym kyng and call be name?
And the same se I now

he purpase more and more.
9695   To God I make my vowe:
he sal be dede therfore."

809.

He cald a knyght heyght Banay,   *Benaiah*
and bad he suld tyte vengance take   *quickly*
Of Duke Joab and Adony
9700   for fals maystry that thei con make,
And sythyn also of Symey   *Shimei*
that with stonys at his fader strake.   *struck*
Tho thre so had ther hyre in hy,   *their payment at once*
aftur ther werkes ware worthy wrake.
9705   Abyathar was demed   *Abiathar*
as byschop aght to be.
For falshed was he flemed   *exiled*
and degrade of his degré.   *removed from his office*

810.

And Sadoke was made soveran hed
9710   als byschope stably forto stand.
And when Duke Joab thus was dede,
Duke Banay was thore ordand
Forto be stewerd in his sted,
and all the folke heldyd to his hand,   *inclined*
9715   And he them forto rewle and rede
agayn ther enmys in ylka land.
Then to Kyng Salamon
was all folke fayn to plese.
And in the werld was non
9720   that durst do hym dysesse.   *dared; distress*

[SOLOMON MARRIES; GOD GRANTS HIM WISDOM (3:1–15)]

811.

Kyng Salamon governd hym so
that ylk land had of hym aw.
He toke a wyfe wonder fayr hym to   *wondrously beautiful*
and that lyfed by another law.   *law (faith)*
9725   Scho was the doyghtur of Pharo,
of Egyp kyng, cumly to knaw.
Bot evyn als Salamon wold do,
assented scho in dede and saw.   *deed and word*
He lyfed withoutyn lese   *without lie*
9730   aftur the Law lely   *loyally*
That God gaf unto Moyses
on the Mownt of Synay.

812.

    Kyng Salamon then and his men
      unto Ebron ther gattes hath grayd   *their paths have taken*

9735   With sacrafyce ther God to ken,   *worship*
      and of ther purpase was God payd.   *pleased*
    Thei offerd mo then hunderthes ten   *more than 1,000*
      of calves and lambs on auters layd.   *altars*
    And on the nyght nex foloand then   *next following that*

9740   God spake to Salamon and sayd,
    "Aske of Me what thou wyll,
      and wheder thou wynke or wake,
    I graunt yt to fulfyll
      for thi gud faders sake."

813.

9745   Then Salamon aspyse gud sped
      what hym ware best of God to crave:
    "To aske ryches, that is no ned,
      I have enogh on all sydes to save.
    And power nedes me non for dred,

9750   all dowtes me boyth knyght and knave.   *fears*
    Bot wytt Thi folke by law to led   *wisdom*
      and wyll to werke wele wold I have."
    God answerd then and sayd,
      "Thou askys all skylfull thyng.

9755   This purpas mas Me payd.   *makes; happy*
      I graunt thee thin askyng.

814.

    "More wyse and wytty sall thou be
      then Jew or panym that ever er past.   *pagan; before lived*
    And ose thou trewly trestes in Me,

9760   fro thi kyngdom sall non thee kast,
    Ne thin ayres that cumys aftur thee   *Nor your heirs*
      as lang os thei in Law wyll last."
    Of this forward full fayn was he   *glad*
      and thanked God fully and fast.

9765   Then wentt thei fro Ebron
      to Jerusalem agayn.
    So was Kyng Salamon
      sett in his power playn.

[SOLOMON'S WISDOM: CUTTING THE CHILD IN TWO (3:16–28)]

815.

    In this meyn tyme that I of tell
9770   a torfer in the town betyde: *trouble; town (i.e., Jerusalem)*

Two wemen in a hows con dwell,
   and both thei ware for comyn kyd.   *known to be common (i.e., prostitutes)*
A myschef was mevyd them omell   *among*
   that myght noght then be hyld ne hyd.   *healed nor hid*
9775   Befor the kyng on knese thei fell
   forto gyf dome, and so he dyd.   *judgment*
Unto hym told the on   *one*
   the cause of ther comyng ydder: *coming there*
"My lord, we two alon
9780   dwelled in a hows togeyddyr.

816.

"And we ware both be seson ryght
   as grett with chyld os we myght go.
I was delyver thrugh Goddes myght
   of a fayr son; so ware we two.
9785   And this woman of the thryd nyght
   was delyver of a sun also.
Scho overlay yt withowtyn lyght,   *smothered*
   and when scho wakyd, then was scho wo.
Bot a fals wyle scho wroyght,   *trick*
9790   lord, os I slepand lay: *sleeping*
Hyr ded barn scho me broyght   *child*
   and toke myn qwyk away.   *my living [one]*

817.

"And when I wakynd of my slepe
   and fand a ded chyld me beforne,
9795   No wunder was yf I wold wepe,
   for that I lufed I had forlorn.
By clere lyght then toke I kepe   *notice*
   that yt was never of my body born.
My sun I saw bysyd hyr crepe;   *beside*
9800   thus has scho turment me this morn."
That other answerd agayn,
   "My lord, scho beyrs the wrang.   *bears the guilt*
Hyr awn sun has scho slayn;
   myn lyfes and may lyfe lang."   *mine lives*

818.

9805   The fyrst unto the kyng then cryse,
   hyr hert was hevy os lether or lede,   *lead*
"Ser, I say yow the sothe assyse   *truth test*
   as ever I styre owt of this stede."   *place*
That other cryd full lowde, "Thou leys,   *lie*
9810   bot my sun lyfes, and thin ys dede."
What was to werke now in this wyse,

the kyng asked all his consell rede.   *council's advice*
Thei sayd thei had not lered   *learned*
   swylke case forto declare.
9815   Then bad he bryng a sword
   belyve befor hym thare.   *quickly*

819.

"And the qwyke chyld that thei fore chyd   *living; before quarreled about*
   depart sonder here in this place   *cut in two*
And gyf to ayder of them a syd!"   *either*
9820   The pepyll then grett murmur mase.   *make*
Thei say, "Yt wele is sene this tyd
   of a new kyng a new comyn case."
Bot the moyder kneled and lowd scho cryde,
   "A mercy, lord, graunt me this grace:
9825   Gyfe my chyld leve to lyfe,   *permission*
   I make no more debate.
All hole to hyr yt gyfe   *whole*
   and lett me go my gate!"   *way*

820.

That other sayd, "So sall noyght be,
9830   bot to be departed evyn yt aw.   *ought*
And take that on half unto thee;   *one*
   that other is myn, now well I knaw."
And when the kyng this syght con se,
   syttand in dowm, he sayd this saw,   *judgment*
9835   "The moyder of the chyld hath peté.
   Delyver yt hyr; this lore ys law."   *word is binding*
Then wex the folke full fayn   *grew; glad*
   for joye of this jugment.
And that he was wyse certan,
9840   the word full wyd whore went.

[SOLOMON'S WISDOM AND ORGANIZATION (4:1–34)]

821.

Kyng Salamon then con assay   *endeavor*
   to sett Goddes servyce ever in syght
And sythyn his reme forto aray   *realm*
   and rewle his men by reson ryght.
9845   In certan placeys he con purvay
   princes to purge the pepyll plyght,
And dukes full dere be dyverse day
   dewly ther dome to dele and dyght.   *duly their judgments; make*
Of folke that to hym fell
9850   myght no man tell the teynd.   *trouble*

Of all wytt was he well
in werld, wher he suld wende.

822.

And by his wytt and his wysdom
us menes that he made bokes thre.   *we believe*
9855   Ane Cantica Canticorum,   *Canticle of Canticles (Song of Songs)*
that is a boke of grett bonité.   *bounty (goodness)*
Ecclesiastecen kennes sum   *Ecclesiastes some acknowledge*
the secund boke named sal be.
Proverbes and Psalmes then, as thei com
9860   forto be sayd in sere degree.   *various*
Who lykes of wytt to lere   *wisdom to learn*
or of counsell to crave,
In his bokes may thei here   *hear*
what so ther hert wold have.

[SOLOMON COMPLETES THE TEMPLE OF GOD (5:1–6:38)]

823.

9865   Then nyght and day was his desyre
the Tempyll of God to dyght and drese,   *make; arrange*
Als Kyng David, his soverayn syre,
had laft ther to enogh ryches.
Iram, that was kyng of Tyre,   *Hiram*
9870   sent word by letturs, more and lesse,
That he suld have withoutyn hyre   *payment*
tymber of syder and of cypresse.   *cedar*
So had he all that nedes
enogh, and wanted none.   *lacked nothing*
9875   And to do dyverse dedes
werke men had he gud woyne.   *in abundance*

824.

Kyng David, whyls he was on lyve,   *alive*
full gradly all that ground began.   *precisely; prepared*
Agayns his strykes wold no man stryve,   *lines*
9880   bot held his mesurs ylka man.   *maintained his measurements*
Than ware past to make rekenyng ryve,   *a complete reckoning*
as cunnand clerkes declare yt can,
Fawr thowssand yeres fyfty and fyve   *4,055 years*
fro this werld was begun to than.
9885   In sevyn yeres was yt sett,
the substance, tre and stone;
Bot afturward was yett
ymages of gold gud woyne.   *in abundance*

825.

Ther was never beste that man myght nevyn,   *beast; mention*
9890   ne fulle that was formed to flygh,   *fowl*
That ne yt was ther ordand full evyn   *wrought*
    of fyne gold and besandes bryght.   *bezants*
The suteltes of science sevyn
    thor ware to red on raw full ryght.   *there were to be read in order*
9895 Yt myght be lykynd unto Hevyn,
    for yt was ever lemand and lyght.   *shining*
Then was wunder to tell,
    or to declare by skyll
Of gold what grett vessell
9900   that ware ordand ther tyll.

826.

All ryches sere ther was to sett   *various*
    may no man say ne syng in sang.
Of sylver myght thei go and gete
    als men may now for marber gang.   *marble go*
9905 And gold was no more to be mett   *more difficult to find*
    then other metall ys us amang.
To tell the lele withoutyn lett   *truth without lie*
    sum suld suppose my wordes ware wrang;
Wher for who lykes to loke
9910   how all that werke was wroyght,
Go to the Bybyll boke!
    Thore sall thei se unsoght.

[SOLOMON DEDICATES THE TEMPLE OF GOD (7:40–8:66)]

827.

When all was done thus daynthyly   *properly*
    that to that Tempyll suld pertene,
9915 To halo yt thei hasted in hy   *hallow*
    that Goddes servyce myght thore be sene.
Thar congregacion of clergy
    cald thei fro all cuntré clene.
Thor was all maner of melody
9920   that men be museke myght of mene.
Sothyn Salamon the wyse
    of bestes, wyld and tame,
Made solempne sacrafyce;
    all other dyd the same.

828.

9925 To Hevyn held he up then his hend
    and prayd to God thus with gud wyll,

"Gud Lord that ylk myse may mend,   *sin*
    I love Thi love both lowd and styll   *publicly and privately*
That unto me this grace hath send
9930   my faders forward forto fulfyll
And of this hows forto make end,
    als Thou that tym told hym untyll.
And als my fader prayd,
    I pray with wyll and toyght   *heart and head*
9935 That Thou be plessed and payde
    of this werke that is wroyght.

829.
"And all that enturs in this place
    aftur Thi helpe to cry and call,
Lord, of Thi gudnese graunt them grace
9940   of all ther grevance, grett or small!"
And als he spake so in that space,
    God sent a sygne amang them all:
A flawm of fyre before ther face   *flame*
    evyn on ther sacrafyce con fall
9945 And hent yt up to Hevyn   *carried*
    with mynstralsy and sang.
The myrth myght no man nevyn   *account*
    that was made them amang.

830.
Then held thei with solempnité
9950   a fest full fyftene days be dene.   *forthwith*
The fest was named Synophogy,   *Feast of Tabernacles*
    whylke Jews maynteyns yett them betwen.
The Arke of God in grett degree
    thor sett thei up forto be sene.
9955 Thei went ylkon to ther cuntré
    to abyd before whore thei had bene.   *dwell*
Kyng Salamon con byd   *live*
    in his city at hame.
In all the werldes wyde
9960   of his wytt went the fame.

[SOLOMON COMPLETES HIS PALACE AND OTHER BUILDINGS (7:1–39)]

831.
Another hows then ordand he
    all only for his awn wonyng.   *living*
And that was mad in yeres thre,
    all of ryches and ryall thyng.   *royal things*
9965 And then the thryd in forto be   *third [building]*

when he suld deme of old and yyng.
Swylke a hows was never sett forto se
    in erth to emperour, ne kyng.
The fawrt then for his qwene   *fourth*
9970   qwer scho with blyse myght byde,   *blissfully might dwell*
And for lades be dene   *straightway*
    serely on ylka syde.   *many*

832.

That hows was paynted with peramour,   *courteousness*
    with resons ryall forto rede,   *royal pronouncements to be read*
9975   And fowls full fayre of favour,
    with sang and spekyng full gud spede,   *song*
And flours in ther kyndly colour,   *flowers*
    os thei in feld ar folke to fede,
And ylkon in the same savour
9980   as yt suld in the burgeon bred.   *bud*
All myrth that men may tell
    was mad withoutyn myse.   *flaw*
Who in that hows myght dwell
    thurt abyd no bettur blyse.   *needs await no better bliss*

[SOLOMON'S WIVES LEAD HIM INTO IDOLATRY (11:1–8)]

833.

9985   Kyng Salamon ys now certan
    that all the werld with hym wyll held,   *incline*
For all the Phylysteyns ar full fayn   *glad*
    to forther hym in fyrth and feld.   *assist*
Ther was never man so mekyll of main,   *of so much strength*
9990   ne that so grett wyt had to weld.   *wield*
Yett at the last yt is not to layn: *lie*
    with lust was all lost in his eld.   *age*
Wemen that he con take
    with lust to lyg them by,   *lie*
9995   Gart hym his God forsake   *Caused*
    and turnd to mawmentry.   *idolatry*

834.

Fyrst of his state to understand
    how he began on mys to go,   *in sin*
He wed a wyf of paynyms land,   *pagan's*
10000   was kynges doyghthur Pharo.   *[who] was the daughter of the king, Pharaoh*
For hyr this hows was new ordand
    and for other of hyr meneye mo.   *company*
Thei mad hym fond, and that he fand,
    for his best frend becom his foo.   *became his foe*

10005   Whyls he his God cowd knaw,
         all welthes he had gud woyne.
         And when he left His Law,
         God leved hym then allon.

835.
         Of qwennes then had he hunderthes sevyn   *queens (concubines); 700*
10010   to weld at wyll ay when he wold,   *use at will whenever he wanted*
         And thre hunderth of other evyn,   *others as well*
             doyghturs of dukes and barons bold,
         Ay forto stand unto his stevyn,   *Always; command*
             and all thei used crowns of gold.   *wore*
10015   Swylke howshald was noyght under Hevyn,   *[a] household*
             bot for this myse yt myght not hold.   *sin*
         Of Ebrews had he qwennes
             that full wyse wemen wore,
         Bot most part was paynyms   *[for the] most part [they] were pagans*
10020   that plessed hym mekyll more.   *pleased him much*

836.
         Thei fed hym fere in foly   *together*
             that all his forse fouly he fyled.   *strength foully he defiled*
         He made tempyls to mawmentry   *idolatry*
             and to fals goddes that hym begyld.   *that beguiled him*
10025   So he forgate God Allmighty
             that ever had bene his bote or beld,   *help and protection*
         And lyfed in lust and lechery
             aftur the wylles of wemen wyld.
         So Adam and Sampson,   *Just as*
10030   our forfaders, ware flayd,   *flayed*
         David and Salamon
             with wemen ware betrayde.

[Solomon rebuked by Ahijah (11:9–13, 29–39)]

837.
         He that so wyse and wytty was
             that under Hevyn he had no make,   *match*
10035   That he for lust suld be lorn, alas,   *lost*
             and wast his wytt for wemens sake!   *waste*
         God was greved with his grett trespase,
             for he to fals goddes con hym take,
         And sent the prophet Achyas   *Ahijah [the Shilonite]*
10040   to warn hym how he wold take wrake.   *take vengeance*
         The prophett sone was grayd,   *soon was prepared*
             and to that courte come he.

"Kyng Salamon," he sayd,
"take tent what I tell thee!   *take heed [of] what*

838.

10045   "Thou wott wele how God gafe the Law   *know well*
           to Moyses in the hyll on heyght,
         Qwylke wele thou wott all Ebrews aw   *ought*
           to maynteyn ever with all ther myght.   *power*
         And now thou wenes He con not knaw   *believe*
10050   how thou refusys yt all unryght.
         He hath me sent to say this saw: *pronouncement*
           thi synes ar fowle before His syght.
         Hard vengance wold He take
           so that thou suld be lorne,
10055   Bot for thi faders sake
           sum dele sal be forborne.   *some part shall*

839.

         "Hee honerd God erly and late.
           therfor God heyght, qwen he was past,   *promised; dead*
         That thou suld stand with his astate
10060   in lordschep whyls thi lyf myght last.
         All yf here thou wyll Hym hate,   *Even*
           that forward sal be full and fast.
         Bot thou sall have bale and debate   *sorrow*
           and with thin enmys oft be umcast.   *afflicted*
10065   And whore thou and no mo   *though you*
           ys kyng of kynred twelfe,   *twelve tribes*
         Thi sun sall have bot two
           assygned to hymselfe.

840.

         "And so mony suld he noyght have
10070   bot for David, thi fader dere,
         And als the heritage forto save
           that all sall noyght be sunderd sere.   *completely sundered*
         Jeroboam to thee is bot a knave,
           sal be kyng of ten kynredes clere.   *[but he] shall*
10075   And so for thou wold rudly rave,
           thi sun sall part fro his power,
         qwylke he suld have haly
           had noyght thi boldnese bene."
         Then Salamon was sory,
10080   no wunder was to wene.

[SOLOMON BESET WITH TROUBLES (11:14–40)]

841.

	Then gretand unto God he prayd,	*weeping*
	bot for all that note was never the nerre.	*sorrow [God]; nearer*
	All behoved be os the prophett sayd.	
	Ylk day wex with hym werre and werre.	*grew more and more wars*
10085	So owt of Egyp land was grayd	*sent*
	A cumly knyght, was cald Ader.	*Hadad*
	A ryall ost sone he arayd	*army quickly*
	Kyng Salamon of his myght to marre.	
	Duke Joab slow his syre;	*had slain his father*
10090	then myght he yt not aqwyte,	*at that time; avenge*
	Bot now he had desyre	
	to do Ebrews dyspytte.	

842.

	When Ader herd David was ded	
	and Joab, that his fader had slayn,	
10095	And Salamon als soveran hed	
	sett in all his power playn,	
	Then wold he byd no bettur bed	
	bot went to werre Ebrews agayn.	*war against the Hebrews*
	He brent and stroyd in mony a styd,	*burned; place*
10100	and therfor ware Phylysteyns fayn.	
	And on that other syde	
	Jeroboam of Joseph kyn,	
	He redyd hym to ryde	*readied himself*
	the reaume to weld and wyn.	*realm*

843.

10105	Wele-hernest men with hym he has.	*Well-harnessed*
	Jerusalem he hasted hym untyll.	
	Thore come the prophett Achias	*Ahijah*
	and warned hym what was Goddes wyll.	
	The pepyll lete he playnly pase,	*allowed him (i.e., Ahijah) to pass easily*
10110	and in a sted he stud hym styll.	*place*
	A new mantyll abowt hym was;	*cloak*
	that sped he hym fast forto spyll.	*drop*
	On the ground ther he yt spredes,	
	and his sword owt he brayd	*he took out*
10115	And schare yt in twelf shredes,	*sheared*
	and on this wyse he sayd,	

844.

	"Jeroboam, thou sall understand,	
	os thou seys me this mantyll twyn,	*you see; cut*

                  So sall the lordschep of this land
10120   be departed in sonder all for syne.
                  Ten kynredes sall held to thi hand,
                     and thou sall were them wele with wyn.   *wear*
                  And two are to the hayre ordand,   *heir*
                     that ar of Juda and of Bynjamyn.
10125   And Jerusalem cyté
                     sall he have in his wald,
                  And thiselfe sall kyng be
                     of ten. Thus hath God told.

          845.
                  "And als lang os thou lufes His Law
10130   sall grett lordschep to thee be lent.
                  And yf thou kest not Hym to knaw,
                     thi welth wyll sone fro thee be went."   *taken*
                  Jeroboam, sone aftur this saw,   *pronouncement*
                     gret heghnes in his hert he hent.   *took*
10135   The lordes he con fast to hym draw
                     and made them sone of his assent,
                  So that full sone had he
                     mo lordes at his ledyng
                  And wele mo commynté   *commonalty*
10140   then had Salamon the kyng.

[SOLOMON'S DEATH (11:41–43)]

          846.
                  Kyng Salamon then fand and feld   *discovered and felt*
                     that God was not fully his frend.
                  Qwat for grett dewle, qwat for eld,   *Whether for great grief, [or]; age*
                     in lyf he myght no langer lend.
10145   Then myght no boldnes be his beld,
                     bot fro his welth behoved hym wende.
                  All wysdom that he had to weld
                     was turned to foly befor his end.
                  Ryches rewled unryght
10150   is nothyng forto nevyn;   *mention*
                  Ne wytt may have no myght
                     withowtyn helpe from Hevyn.

          847.
                  Ne prowyse ys nothyng in prise
                     withoutyn grace of God Allmighty,
10155   Bot He that ys the Hegh Justyce
                     may mend all myse thrught His mercy.
                  So endyd Salamon the wyse;

I wott not what he was worthy.   *whether*
Thei layd hym whore his fader lyse
10160   in that same cyté solemply.
Faur score yeres ware past our   *eighty*
   whyls he had kynges power.
And nyne score yere and faur   *184 years*
   was all his wonnyng here.   *living*

[Rehoboam crowned; Israel divided (11:43–12:24)]

848.
10165 When Salamon thus had mad end
   and gyfyn his gast to Goddes grace,   *soul*
The lordes that in that land con lend;   *gather*
   thei toke ther counsell in that case
Who suld have force them to dyffend
10170   agayns the Phylysteyns, ther fase.   *foes*
And Roboam, his sun, thei kend   *Rehoboam*
   for myghty man and most ryght has.
Thei sembled in Sychem,   *Shechem*
   a cyté of grett renown,
10175 Nere to Jerusalem,
   a kyng ther forto crown.

849.
When thei ware geydderd grett and small,
   unto ther werke sone thei went.
An alderman spake for them all
10180   and told to Roboam ther entent
And sayd, "Ser Roboam, thou sall
   be our sufferan, so have we ment.   *sovereign*
And we sall com unto thi call
   so that thou tyll our sawes assent.   *words*
10185 We ware fayne forto plese   *glad*
   thi fader, ose for our kyng.
And he dyd us dysesse   *But; caused us anxiety (dis-ease)*
   and wrang in sum werkyng.

850.
"Thou wot full wele Ebrews ar we
10190   to lyf be the maners of Moyses.
Thi fader greved us in degré;
   of our assyse he made us sesse   *cease*
And to be thrall, whore we ware free,
   agayns the Law; this ys no lese.   *lie*
10195 Of all swylke poyntes aske we thee
   all holy forto have releyse.

And yf thou graunt this thyng,
    then wyll we graunt agayne
That thou be crowned kyng
10200   and we thi pepyll playn."

851.
When Roboam herd how he says,
    he thynkes the pepyll rudly rave.
That purpase nothyng to hym pays
    forto graunt them so that thei crave.
10205 He sayd, "Ser, respeytt of thre days,
    and then your answer sall ye have."
Them toyght he suld make no delays,
    bot neverthelese thei vouchsave.
And in thies thre days then,
10210   whyls thei this convent held,
He asked red at old men   *counsel*
    that with his fader dweld.

852.
Thei sayd, "Ser, we assent ther tyll   *to that*
    that thei be als there elders wore
10215 And have ther fredoms to fulfyll,
    als ther faders had before.
Yf thou wyll graunt them with gud wyll,
    then wyll thei lely luf thi lore.   *loyally love your wisdom*
And yf thou part from them with yll,
10220   of counsell then can we no more.
Syr, yt is wysdom,
    and wys men hath bene lefe   *spared*
To suffer a lese yll com   *lesser ill*
    and lett a more myschefe."   *stop a greater*

853.
10225 When Roboam thies wordes hers,   *hears*
    this purpase was not to his pay.   *satisfaction*
He cald to hym yyng bachelers   *young*
    that he was wonnt with forto play.
He says, "Omys this men me lerys   *I've learned these men aim*
10230   to make my lordschep les for ay.   *less for ever*
Wyll ye assent to swylke maners?"
    Thei answerd and sayd schortly, "Nay!
Bot os thei boun have bene   *were sworn [to]*
    to thi fader before,
10235 The same sall thou maynteyn
    and make them sugettes more.   *subjects*

854.

"And tell them this to understand:
   thou hath more strenght maystrys to make   *masteries*
In the lest fynger of thi hand   *smallest*
10240   then was in all thi fader bake.   *back*
And whore he bett them with a wand
   to hold them law withoutyn lake,   *in line without fault*
Bett thou with scorpions, we warand."
   All thus dyspytfully thei spake.
10245 Then Roboam was well payd;   *pleased*
   hym lyked to frayn no ferre,   *inquire no further*
Bot to the pepyll he sayd
   he suld do so or warre.

855.

Thies wys men red refused he has,   *The counsel of these wise men*
10250   and aftur yong men ways he went.
Therfor the pepyll fast fro hym pas;
   Non bot two lyneg with hym lent.   *tribes; remain*
So was the wordes of Achyas   *Ahijah*
   fullfylled that told thus his entent:
10255 Ryght ose his mantyll revyn was,   *cut*
   so suld the reme be raysed and rent.   *realm*
The same was sen that day;   *seen*
   God wold that yt ware so.
Ten kynredes turned away
10260   and with hym left bot two.

856.

A redlese man was Roboam   *An unwise*
   when the pepyll went ther ways.
He sent a prince heyght Adoram,   *called Adoram*
   and to the pepyll full fayr he prays.
10265 And lordes ylkon he nevynd by name.   *invoked*
   "Comys agayn, gud sers!" he says.
"My lord says ye sall have the same
   that ye had in your fader days
Or bettur, yf that he myght;
10270   I undertake to yow."
That spekyng was for noyght;
   his tayles thei wold noyght trow.   *stories; trust*

857.

Them lyst not bow, ose he them bade,   *desired not [to]*
   bot with dyspytt hym to dyspyse.
10275 His messynger thei stoned to ded   *(i.e., Adoram)*
   and send hym word on this kyn wyse: *in just this way*

Thei wold never hald hym for ther hede   *king*
    that made them fayle of ther fraunchese.
Then Roboam was full wyll of rede;
10280   he went whore no relevyng lyse.
So folke may frenschepe fayle
    and oft sythys harmes hent   *often times receive harm*
Because of yll counsell,
    yf thei sone wyll assent.

858.

10285 He saw the pepyll ware past hym fro
    And Adoram his cosyn slayn.
Fro Sychem then fast con he go
    unto Jerusalem evyn agayn.
And with hym went the kynredes two
10290   that ware ever to his bedyng bayn.   *command obedient*
Of all the twelfe he had no moo;
    so ware thei sonderd for certayn.
Tho kynredes mad hym kyng
    of them and ther cuntré
10295 And oblyst, old and yyng,   *promised*
    at his bedyng to be.

859.

Then is yt tym furth forto tell
    what betyd of the other ten.   *occurred with*
Jeroboam was ferse and fell   *fierce and hard*
10300   and the most cumly that thei ken.   *fair; knew*
Thei mad hym kyng of Israel,
    and holy thei become his men.
Thore was no more ther kynges omell   *among [them]*
    bot Roboam and Jeroboam then.
10305 Both byschopes, prestes, and clerkes
    with all ther barn teme   *their children*
That gaf them to Goddes werkes
    wuned all in Jerusalem.

[REHOBOAM'S REIGN (14:21–24)]

860.

Now ware ther two kynges in a cuntré,
10310   and so the folke ware sunderd sere.   *apart*
Jeroboam now lett we be
    that hath to hym ten kynredes clere.
Of Roboam furth speke wyll we
    more of his lyfyng forto lere.   *learn*
10315 He sojorns in his awn cyté

and full fayr folke with hym in fere.   *together*
Aght milia knyghtes kene   *8,000*
  had he of his assent
And other folke full clene
10320 that to hym wold take tent.   *take heed*

861.

He made in the cuntré of Juda
  a dossan cytes stif of stone.   *dozen*
To Bynjamyns he made wele ma,   *Benjaminites*
  for gold ne werkmen want he none.   *lacked*
10325 And wele he ordand in all tha
  of whett and oyle and wyn gud woyne   *in abundance*
And armours both to frend and fa   *friend and foe (i.e., to everyone)*
  to have new when old ware gone.
Aghtene qwenes with hym ware   *Eighteen queens*
10330 and of other thryty and one;   *others (concubines)*
Bot the chefe yett was Thamar,   *Tamar*
  the doyghtur of Absolon.   *Absalom*

862.

He spake with hyr most specially,
  for scho was of his kyn most nere.
10335 His ayre was born of hyr body,   *heir*
  heyght Abyam, ose men may here.   *Abijam*
He had of qwenes and other by
  twenty and aght sons all sere,   *twenty-eight sons all together*
And sexty doyghturs, I dar not ly.
10340 The feleschep was fayr in fere.   *altogether*
No man on mold myght knaw
  of his tresour the tend.   *amount*
Ay whyls he lufed Goddes law,
  all folke ware fulli his frend.

863.

10345 Bot oft sythyes have we sene the same: *often times; seen*
  grett ryches makes men myse to spede.   *sin*
So ferd yt with Kyng Roboam,   *So it was*
  als wyttenes boyth his word and dede.   *witnessed in*
He was so ryche in hows at ham   *home*
10350 that unto Hevyn toke he no hede.
He loved noyght nevyn God by His name,   *invoke*
  for of His helpe he had no nede.
He forgatte God Allmighty
  that all his sele had sent.   *happiness*
10355 In prid and lychery
  was all his lykyng lent.

864.

    So lyfed lordes of his land be dene,   *forthwith*
        and aftur all the pepyll playn.
    By yll exempyls oft tyms is sene
10360   full mony sawlys with syns slayn.   *souls with sin [are]*
    Also we se sum men wyll wene
        thei be noyght sure with ther sufferayn
    Bot yf thei of his maners mene
        and maynten them with all ther mayn.   *strength*
10365 Foule syn of sodomyte   *sodomy*
        used thei ever ylk man.
    God was noyght worthy to wyte
        yf he toke vengance then.

[EGYPT SACKS JUDAH AND JERUSALEM (14:25–28)]

865.

    Kyng Sysoc come to that cuntré;   *Shishak*
10370   fro Egyp broght he his baytell.
    A mille charyottes had he,   *1,000 chariots*
        all full of armours and vytall,   *provisions*
    And knyghtes full semly forto se
        sexty milia trew to trayvall,   *60,000*
10375 And folke on fote full fayre plenté
        faurty milia that wyll noyght fayle.   *40,000*
    Thei wasted all that was wroyght
        in burghes abowt Sychem.   *towns*
    And so sadly thei soyght
10380   ryght to Jerusalem.

866.

    The cyté thynke thei sun to wen   *win*
        and conquere yt be clene maystry.
    Kyng Roboam that was within
        to see that syght was full sary.   *sorry*
10385 Then forto grete he con begyn   *weep*
        and unto God fast call and cry.
    He sayd, "This sorow is for my syn,
        and all this wo am I worthy."
    To the Tempyll went thei all
10390   that in that cyté ware,
    And thore on knese thei fall,
        gretand to God full sore.

867.

    God sent word with his prophett playn
        when thei so ther defawtes feld,

10395 And sayd that thei suld noght be slayn,
           bot that thei suld that cyté yeld
       To Sysoc als ther soyverayn,
           and that he suld ther wrschep weld
       And that thei suld serve hym for certayn.
10400   Of God thei gate no bettur beld.   *better cure*
       He sayd, "So sall ye see
           wheder yt be more honoure
       Sisoc servandes to be
           or Goddes, your Cryature."   *Creator*

       868.
10405 Then had Kyng Roboam mekyll kare,   *much woe*
           for this forward bus hym fulfyll.
       The cyté he delyverd thare,
           bot this connand he toke ther tyll   *covenant*
       So that thei suld the pepyll spare
10410   and do no greve to gud ne yll.
       Kyng Sysoc and all that with hym ware
           enterd then at ther awn wyll.
       Thore fand thei grett ryches
           that Salamon sett to save.
10415 How so ther connand is,
           that thynke thei forto have.   *keep [the city]*

       869.
       Thor thurt no man ther traveyll tyne,   *There needs; their work lose*
           for thresour thei fand full gud woyne   *found in abundance*
       All vesels mad for mete and wyn
10420   ware pyght with mony a prescius stone,   *adorned*
       And all of gold full fayr and fyne
           and well enamyld ylkone.
       Potes, pans, and caldrons in kechyn,   *kitchen*
           wars then of sylver was ther none.   *were made of silver or not at all*
10425 Within the kynges palyse,
           of all that thei ther fand,
       Thei left noyght forto prays   *praise*
           to valow of a besand.   *value; bezant*

       870.
       Then to the Tempyll past thei playn
10430   and spoled yt full dyspytfully.   *despoiled*
       Ther gate thei gold that wele myght gayne
           grett cytes forto byg and by.   *build and buy*
       The folke was of that fare full fayn,
           als thei had grett encheson why.   *reason*
10435 Kyng Sysoc went so home agayn,

grete mirth mad all that cumpany.
For was never folke befor,
    als ferre os men may thynke,   *as far as; remember*
That wan so grete tresour
10440   and with so litle swink.   *toil*

[DEATH OF REHOBOAM (14:29–31)]

871.

Kyng Roboam then in kare was cast;   *sorrow*
    no comforth in this case he kend.
In aghtene yeres his lordschep last,   *eighteen years*
    God lyst no langer to lett hym lend.   *desire*
10445   When fyfty yeres ware fully past
    fro his begynnyng untyll his ende,
Then seknes fell on hym so fast
    that no fysyke myght hym dyffend.   *doctor*
Bot sone enturd he was
10450   wher his elders lay,
And his sun Abias   *Abijah*
    was kyng aftur his day.

[JEROBOAM'S IDOLATRY (12:25–13:34)]

872.

Now of Abyas lett we be
    forto be yemyd whyls he be yyng,   *looked after; young*
10455   And of Jeroboam speke we
    that of ten kynredes then was kyng.
He had slyke prid for his pausté   *power*
    that he sett by none erthly thyng;
Ne unto God no hede toke he
10460   that gaf hym all that governyng.
The Law that God had lent,
    that lykes hym noyght to lere,
Bot brake His Commawndment,
    and how sone sall we here.

873.

10465   The Jews used forto make a fest
    at the Tempyll ylke yere onys or twyse.
And ydder suld come both most and lest
    and make thore solempne sacrafyce,
Sum with fowle and sum with best   *fowl; beast*
10470   to offer ylkon on ther wyse.   *in their ways*
Jeroboam was so with prid encrest
    he wold not seke to that assyse.

Sone in his hert he cast
    a wylle with wekyd wyll,   *wile; will*
10475   And hasted hym full fast
    that falshed to fulfyll.

874.
"To Jerusalem yf I suld ga
    and all my frendes with me in fere,   *together*
The Bynjamyns and of Juda
10480   suld make my men so mery chere,
And thei suld there be charest swa   *entertained*
    with servyce and with solace sere   *many solaces*
That full fell folke suld turne me fra.
    Therfor a new law wyll I lere."
10485   In Bethel so he spake,
    a cyté of grett pryse,
A calf of gold to make
    evyn at his awn devyse.

875.
He cyted to that same cyté
10490   all that come of kynredes ten,
And unto them than thus sayd he,
    "Sers, our costom wele ye ken: *know*
How our hye fest sall halowd be
    ever ylk yer, ye wot wele when.
10495   And als ye wott, we are as fre
    as Bynjamyns or Judeys men.
And Jerusalem is farre
    als febyll folke suld fele.
I have ordand uus nerre   *nearer*
10500   to hald our fest full wele.

876.
"For wele we wott, els wene we wrang,
    God hath power in ylka place.
Ye sall have here a god full strang
    to governe you and graunt yow grace.
10505   We sall ordand our self amang
    prestes and dekyns in dyverse space.
And I myself befor sall gang
    forto gyf sense befor your face."   *incense*
This poynt the pepyll plese.
10510   Thei say, "Assent wyll we;
So sall we have more ese
    then kayre to farre cuntré."

877.

Then with all craftes he cowth controve
    a tempyll sone he hath ordand
10515 And made an auter noyght to move   *permanent altar*
    bot stably in that sted to stand.
The calf of gold he sett above,
    and all the folke then he commawnd
Ryght os ther Lord yt forto love
10520   that led them owt of Egyp land.
He says, "This same is He
    that our formfaders led
Safe throwghowt the se
    when thei fro Pharo flede."

878.

10525 Fals prophettes wund in that toun   *lived*
    that of this fare was ferly fayn   *extremely glad*
And sayd thei suld be ryght resoun
    maynteyn all that purpase playn.
Thei went and dyd devocion
10530   to that mawment with myght and mayn.   *idol; power*
The kyng arayd thei redy boun
    forto gyfe sense als ther soyverayn.
Als thei with werke and wyll
    thor mad ther mawmentry,
10535 A prophett com them tyll,
    was sent from God Allmighty.

879.

To greve them thus he can begyn
    that all the folke myght here on hyght,
"Thou auter that is sollyed with syn,   *Your altar*
10540   I warne thee here and ylka wyght:
Ther sall spryng owt of David kyn   *David's line*
    a kyng, Joas his name full ryght.   *Josiah*
He sall dystroye both more and myn
    that mayntenys thee with any myght.
10545 Both prophettes, prestes, and clerkes
    that now are mad on new:
He sall wast all ther werkes.
    And that this tale be trew   *be seen as truthful*

880.

    "A sygne here sal be redy grayd: *made*
10550   all this fals fare sall fall as fast.
Thou and all that on thee is layd
    sodanly sall doun be cast."

And als sone as this word was sayd,
   all syd fro syd in sunder brast.   *broke*
10555 Then ware tho folke full yll affrayd
   and Jeroboam gretly agast.
He turned hym in grett tene,   *anger*
   for the prophett harme suld have.
Bot vengance sone was sene;
10560   God wold His servand save.

881.

Evyn os he ryched owt his ryght hand
   and presed the prophett forto sloo,   *approached; slay*
Starke ase a stafe his arme con stand   *Withered*
   and wold not bow his body to.
10565 So all his falshed sone he fand,
   and fayn he was to flee ther fro.   *glad*
He cryd mercy to God Weldand   *All-ruling*
   and prayd the prophett he suld do so.
The prophett for hym prayd,
10570   als all the pepyll hym prays.
And sone by he had sayd,
   his arme was all at eys.   *cured*

882.

Then had the kyng comforth full grett
   and prayd to the prophett specially
10575 That he wold dwell with them to mete.
   Therto the prophett sayd in hy,   *at once*
"God bad I suld noyght drynke ne ette
   with none of all this cumpany.
His bedyng wyll I not forfeytt;
10580   therfor my way fast wend wyll I."
He left that folke in fere,   *together*
   and furth he wentt them fro.
Then was the kyng in were
   what hym was best to do.

883.

10585 A fals prophett thor wonnand was   *dwelling*
   that had rewled all that yll aray.   *wicked people*
When he wyst how the prophett pas,   *passed*
   he thynkes to marre hym and he may.   *if he might*
Fast aftur hym hasted he has
10590   and overtoke hym by tym of day.
And hertly cause of hym he as   *asks*
   why that he went so sone away,
And sayd, "Ser, certes, I wend

that thou wold dyne with me."

10595   He sayd, "God me dyffend
        to dyne in this cuntré."

884.
    The fals prophett sayd, "Ser, certayn
        I am in message sent Hym fro.
    He bydes that thou sall turn agayn
10600   and dyne with me, now or thou go." *before you leave*
    So sayd that traytour for this trayn *treachery*
        to gare hym breke Goddes bedyng so *to cause him [to]*
    That thei myght have ther purpase playn.
        To Bethell then turned thei two.
10605   That fals prophett hym plese
        and mad grett myrth omell, *among [them]*
    Bot sone amang ther meses *meals*
        he had messag more fell. *terrible*

885.
    God sayd hym in that same sesoun,
10610   "For thou so sone was of assent
    Att turn agayn unto this toun
        and dyne agayns My commawndment,
    Thou sal be slayn with a lyon,
        and to thi cors he sall take tent." *take possession*
10615   All this he fand full redy boun *prepared*
        or he ferre fro that cyté went. *before he far*
    A lyon hym devored,
        and other bestes to lett
    Styll be the cors he cowred
10620   tyll folke com yt to fett. *fetch*

886.
    By men that kayred thore in cuntré *traveled*
        sone ware ther tydynges told that tyd.
    The fals prophett then hasted he
        aftur that cors to ryn and ryd.
10625   And be lyve in that same cyté *quickly*
        to byre yt he wold not abyd, *bury; wait*
    And bad his barns that he suld be *children*
        beryd that same body besyd.
    For wele he wyst that noe *trouble*
10630   suld fall aftur therfor,
    When Joas suld dystroy
        that lynag, lese and more. *(i.e., entirely)*

887.

Bott yett his lyes he wold not layn;
　　full wyghtly with the kyng he mette
10635　And sayd, "Ser, a lyon hath slayn
　　that lurdan that our servyce lett.　　　　　　　　　*villain; ceased*
All that he told was bot a trayn;　　　　　　　　　*betrayal*
　　therfor he hath his dome by dett.　　　　　　　*judgment*
Be lyve gete up our geyre agayn　　　　　　　　　*Quickly*
10640　and lett us hald that we have hett.
Our auter was full strang;　　　　　　　　　　　*altar; heavy*
　　over grett charge gart yt fall.　　　　　　　　*weight*
And ser, thou sensed over lang　　　　　　　　　*incensed*
　　and noyed thin arme with all.　　　　　　　　*troubled*

888.

10645　"Ser, thou suld leve thi frendes of old
　　bettur then a boy for swylke a brayd."　　　　*[no] better; trick*
The kyng then trowd all that he told　　　　　　*believed*
　　and sone assent evyn ase he sayd.
The auter up fast con thei fold;　　　　　　　　*altar*
10650　gayly agayn sone was yt grayd
And honerd thore the calf of gold.
　　Thus ware thos folke foly betrayd.　　　　　　*foully*
The kyng ay more and more
　　kest hym Goddes men to mare.　　　　　　　　*harm*
10655　Yf he dyd yll before,
　　then wold he werke wele werre.　　　　　　　*worse*

[AHIJAH'S WORDS AGAINST JEROBOAM (14:1–18)]

889.

A holy prophett that heght Achy　　　　　　　　*Ahijah*
　　sent hym word with his awn qwene
That his falshed and his foly
10660　with sorows suld on themself be sene,
And that his ayrs suld have forthi　　　　　　　*heirs; therefore*
　　aftur his tyme full mekyll tene.　　　　　　　*sorrow*
Jeroboam sett noyght ther by
　　bot wex wers then he ayr had bene.　　　　　*grows worse; before*
10665　The folke full fast can fayle
　　als thei ther soyverayn saw.
Thei made goddes of metall
　　and left all Moyses Law.

[JEROBOAM DEFEATED BY ABIJAH (13:19; 2 CHRONICLES 13:1–20)]

890.

 He had no mynd of Goddes myght;
10670 so fell he fowly in dyspare.
 And by Goddes Law he sett full lyght;
  therfor he fell fowle and noyght fayre.
 He sembled men full wyld and wyght;   *strong*
  to Jerusalem he cast to kayre
10675 Abiam forto fell with fyght
  that of that reme was ryghest ayre. *realm was the true heir*
 Bot sone when the yyng kyng   *young*
  herd tell of that tythand,
 He had at his ledyng
10680 fayr folke fawrty thowssand.   *good men*

891.

 To Jeroboam sone he remewes,   *engages*
  and both thei mett apon a playn.
 He carped to hym and told in trewes,
  "Ser, thou wott thiself certayn
10685 We are one men and all Ebrews;
  therfor yf auder syd be slayn,   *either*
 That other syde full sore yt rewes.
  Therfor is gud to turn agayn.
 And als thou hath no ryght
10690 by no cause thou con fynd
 Agayns me forto fyght,
  for I am ayre of kynd.   *heir by birth*

892.

 "Kyng Roboam by yll counsell
  he forfett yt; bot noyght forthi
10695 He was my fader, this is no fayle,
  and thou his servand sothly.
 And my God may me mekyll avayle
  and make me have the vyctory.
 And thi goddes ar made of metayle;
10700 thou may not be beld them by.   *protected*
 All yf thi folke be fell,   *many*
  our God ther forse may fele.
 Forto hald all in hele   *health*
  I rede no more we mell."   *fight*

893.

10705 Jeroboam soyght a sutell gyn   *trick*
  in his carpyng with kynredes ten.

Prevely he parted his pepyll in twyn   *in two*
   so that non suld ther cowntenance ken,
And bad them warly thei suld wyn   *quietly*
10710   behynd Abyam and his men.   *Abijah*
Bot God that all his treyst was in
   wold noyght suffer hym be dyssayved then.
Thar falshed he aspyed
   how thei hym umbecast.   *surrounded*
10715 "As armes!" be lyve he cryde   *quickly*
   and fowled them doun full fast.

894.

Thor was talkyng of no trews,   *truce*
   full styfly strake thei in that stoure.   *hard they struck; place*
Jeroboam had mony Jews,
10720   bot God was noyght ther governoure.
Therfor that semble sone he rews,   *gathering; rues*
   and sadly sekes he to socoure.   *he seeks to [find a] refuge*
Kyng Abiam prestly persewes   *rapidly*
   and wan ther gold with grett honoure.
10725 Jeroboam folke thei fynd
   in feld fyve thowssand sloyn.   *slain*
Tho leved he hym behynd,   *Those he (Jeroboam) left behind*
   and Abiam noyght on.   *while Abijah [left] not one*

[Abijah's death; Asa crowned in Judah (15:8)]

895.

When Kyng Abiam had his wyll,
10730   to Jerusalem he turned agayn.
In that cyté he sojornes styll
   with mekyll solace for certayn
Thre yeres his tym forto fulfyll
   and honerd God with all his mayn.   *strength*
10735 And then he dyed with angers yll,
   als ylka man bus pase with payn.   *must*
And sone when he was dede,
   his eldest sone Asa
Was crowned in his sted
10740   and cald kyng of Juda.

[Jeroboam's death; Nadab crowned in Israel (15:25–26)]

896.

This yyng kyng Asa lett we dwell
   styll in strengh, os he is stad.
Jeroboam, kyng of Israel,

	dyed aftur sone with sorows sade.
10745	And then was crowned in Bethell
	his eldest sun, that heght Nabad.	*Nabad*
	Thre yere was all his tym to tell;
	in lyfe no langer hele he had.
	On Baasa hym betrayd	*Basha*
10750	that he was done to dede,	*death*
	And hymself he arayd
	to stand kyng in his stede.

[NADAB KILLED BY BAASHA; JEROBOAM'S FAMILY ERADICATED (15:27–31)]

897.

	Baasa began to styre swylke stryve,
	for he wold gofern grett degré.
10755	And for Jeroboam sede suld noyght thryve,	*family*
	Nabad his sun dyssayved he.
	Sythyn stroyd he up man, chyld, and wyve	*Then; every*
	of his kynred in that cuntré.
	Of that lyne leved he none o lyve.	*he left not one alive*
10760	The prophett said yt suld so be.	*(i.e., Ahijah)*
	Thas that in towns war dede	*Those; were*
	howndes laped ther blode.	*lapped their blood*
	That dyed in other sted
	ware leved to foyles fode.	*carrion good*

[BAASHA'S IDOLATRY (15:32–16:4)]

898.

10765	Thei ware dystroyd both yyng and old,
	and all that sorow was for syne.	*due to sin*
	Kyng Baasa then was brym and bold;
	bale forto brew wold he not blyne.	*sorrow; stop*
	He was rych of gud and gold.
10770	To mak hym goddes he con begyn
	And sayd thei suld werke ase he wold,
	and so he suld all wrschep wyne.
	He forgatt God of Hevyn,
	that hath all hele in hand,
10775	And his condicions evyn
	held the lordes of his land.

899.

	He lyfed in lust and lechery,
	in hatred and in hertly pryde.
	To gud men had he grett envy
10780	that served God on any syde.

And for he wroyght so wekydly,
   God wold not lett hym lang abyd.
A prophett Jew he sent in hy
   to tell hym all what suld betyd.   *happen*
10785 He sayd bycause he dyd
   like to Jeroboam,
Evyn als him betyd,
   so suld he have the same,

900.

He and his kynred ever ay whore   *kindred everywhere*
10790   be dystroyd, in what eld so thei ere.   *regardless of age*
Then wex his malyce mekyll more;   *grew*
   that mater meynys he forto mere.   *stop*
The prophett gart he slay ryght thore,   *did*
   for this tale suld be told no fere.   *further*
10795 And yf he had done yll before,
   then kest he forto werke mekyll werre.   *much worse*
He honerd goddes of metall,
   that mystrewth hym betrayd,
for all behoved befall
10800   als Goddes prophett had sayd.

[BAASHA AT RAMAH; ASA TURNS TO BEN-HADAD (15:16–22)]

901.

Bot fyrst he wroyght full mekyll wa   *woes*
   be were and be wyked wyle   *by war; wicked deceits*
And most unto the kyng Asa,
   that honerd God in all that whyle.
10805 He had a cyté heyght Ramatha,   *Ramah*
   from Jerusalem full fawrty myle
And langed to the lynage of Juda.   *belonged*
   That cyté gatt he sone with a gyle.   *obtained; guile*
Thore thynkes he forto dwell
10810   and do Kyng Asa skathe.   *harm*
The land of Israel
   so myght he were fra wathe.   *danger*

902.

He meneys to make that cyté strang   *intends*
   for hym and for his frendes ylkone.
10815 Wyght men on ylka syd gart he gang
   and broyght ydder both tre and stone.
Kyng Asa toyght that layke full lang,
   and power to hym had he none.
Therfor to wreke hym of that wrang   *avenge*

10820	a purpase playnly hath he tone.	*taken*
	He sentt sone for socours	
	wher the hethyn holdyn ther hame,	*pagans held their home*
	To the kyng of Matenours,	*Damascus*
	Benedab by name.	*Ben-hadad*

903.

10825	Bycause he was his fader frend,	
	in hym full fast he con affy.	*trust*
	That Kyng Baasa suld not hym shend,	*overcome*
	of helpe he prayd hym specially.	
	Kyng Benedab with wordes hend	*courteous*
10830	sayd he suld have helpe in hy	*at once*
	And wyghtly ordand hym to wend	
	to Israel with grett cumpany.	
	Cytes and burghes thei bryntt	*burned*
	and slow men lese and more.	
10835	Cornys and wynys thei shent,	*Crops and vineyards; destroyed*
	all that thei fand before.	*found before [them]*

904.

	When tythynges com to Kyng Baasa	
	of the Phylesteyns ferse and fell,	*fierce and cruel*
	Then bud hym refuse Ramatha	
10840	and wend to rescow Israel.	
	Els wold the enmys byrn and sla	*Otherwise*
	and dystroye the burgh of Bethell.	
	Lo, how God comfort Kyng Asa,	
	and he meved hym nothyng omell.	*among [them]*
10845	To Rama he con repayre	
	and toke yt into his hand.	
	He byged yt wele and fayre	*fortified*
	with store that he thore fand.	*[the] stores; found there*

[BAASHA'S DEATH; REIGN AND DEATH OF ELAH (16:5–10)]

905.

	Kyng Benedab grett welth had wun,	
10850	and home he wentt warly and wele.	
	Kyng Baasa sone in bale was bun	*sorrow was bound*
	and dyed with dole and dred sum dele.	
	And aftur regnyd Helam, his sun,	*Elah*
	and mad maystryce and mekyll unsele;	
10855	For yf the fader fell was fun,	*was found cruel*
	the sun was feller be fere to fele.	*more cruel by far*
	Therfor he last not lang:	
	within two yeres sesoun	

An Agary heyght hym wrang,   *A [man] named Agariah (i.e., Zimri)*
10860   slogh hym and toke the crown.

[Reigns of Zimri, Omri (16:11–28)]

906.
This new kyng then, Agary,
    wuned in a town was named Tharsa.   *Tirzah*
He stroyd all the progeny
    that ware comyn of the kyng Baasa.
10865   Then had the folke to hym envy
    that ware wonnand in Gabatha.   *dwelling in Gibbethon*
Thei mad them a kyng heyght Ambry;   *Omri*
    then had Israels kynges twa.   *Israelites two kings*
Kyng Ambry mad hym boun
10870   that other new kyng to noye.   *trouble*
He beseged Tharsa toun
    Kyng Agary to dystroy.

907.
Kyng Agary knew them full of yre,
    and he had no forse hym to fend.   *to defend himself*
10875   His awn palyse he sett on fyre,
    for bettur comforth none he kend.
He brent hymself both bone and lyre;   *burned; flesh*
    on this wyse was his wreched ende.
Then had Kyng Ambry his desyre,
10880   and furth in lordschep con he lend.
Twelfe yeres furth and no ferre   *more*
    lasted his lordschep thore,
Als yll of werkes or warre   *wicked*
    as any was hym before.

[Ahab made king of Israel (16:29–34)]

908.
10885   When twelfe yeres ware done be dene,   *forthwith*
    he dyed with wo, that I warrand.   *promise*
Acab, his sun, was sythyn sene   *Ahab*
    kyng and lord of Israel land.
And yf his elders yll had bene,
10890   he was the warst of hert and hand.   *worst*
That aftur turned hymselfe to tene,   *grief*
    bot fele folk fyrst his fawtes fand.
Thus ferd yt of fyve kynges
    in schort tyme forto tell.

| 10895 | For thei brake Goddes bydynges, | *Because* |
| | thei have ther hame in Hell. | |

[ASA'S REIGN (15:23; 2 CHRONICLES 16:7–12)]

909.

	Bot Kyng Aasa of Juda land,	
	he lyfed in luf and chareté.	
	Full fawrty yeres was he renand	
10900	and rewled his reme in gud degré.	*realm*
	He honerd God with hert and hand	
	so that no man myght say ne see	
	Wherfor God suld be oght grochand,	*grumbling in any way*
	bot yf yt ware for thynges thre.	*unless*
10905	And on was for he send	*one*
	unto a paynym kyng	*pagan*
	Fro his fase hym to fend,	*foes; defend*
	and asked not Goddes helpyng.	

910.

	Another was when a trew prophet	
10910	fro God of Hevyn to hym was grayd	*sent*
	And told hym how he had forfett	
	and owt of reson myse arayd.	
	In stokkes full sore he gartt hym sett,	*stocks; caused him to be set*
	for he the sothe unto hym sayd	*truth*
10915	Of evill lyvyng hym forto let,	*cease*
	and of that warke God was not payde.	*pleased*
	The thryd: of seknes sore	
	forto have help in hy	
	In lechys he trest more	*doctors*
10920	then in God Allmighty.	

[JEHOSHAPHAT MADE KING OF JUDAH (15:24; 2 CHRONICLES 16:13–17:5)]

911.

	Kyng Asa dyed in gud degré,	
	for in all his werkes was he trew.	
	He had a sun semly to see,	*fair to look upon*
	heyght Josaphat, a gentyll Jew.	*Jehoshaphat*
10925	Aftur his fader regned he	
	in Jerusalem os gud Ebrew.	
	He was the best of all bounté	
	aftur Kyng David that men knew.	
	Unto Goddes Law he tentes	*attends*
10930	both by nyght and day	

And kepes His Commawndmentes
    in all that ever he may.

912.

He was full buxum and full bayn   *humble; ready*
    to beld all that in bales ware bend,   *protect; troubles*
10935   And forto put the pure fro payn   *keep*
    wold he hym hast with hert and hend.   *haste*
The fals Phylysteyns ware full fayn
    ther servyce both to say and send,
So that all folke of hym ware fayn   *glad*
10940   with all ther myght his mys to mend.
The prophettes, prestes, and clerkes
    that mayntened Goddes servyce
Both with wordes and werkes
    he wrschept in all wyse.

913.

10945   The Tempyll of God he can restore
    with reverence and with rych aray,
Qwylk fals Phylesteyns lang before
    had brokyn doun and born away.
Ever ylk thyng he ordand thore
10950   that he hoped myght plese God to pay,   *worship*
And so increyst ay more and more
    in gud maters all that he may.
Now Josaphatt lett we dwell
    lyfand to Goddes lovyng,
10955   And of yll Acab tell
    that was of Israel kyng.

[Ahab marries Jezebel and provokes God (16:29–34)]

914.

We told how fyve before had bene   *five [kings in Israel] before him*
    that yll began and als yll end.   *ended*
This was the werst withoutyn wene,
10960   for of more malyce ever he mend.
He toyght no myrth was more to mene
    then Goddes folke scham and shend.
And lyke to hym he toke a qwene
    of Phylysteyns, full of the Fend.   *Devil*
10965   Hyr name was Jesabell,   *Jezabel*
    the kynges doyghtur of Tyre.
Malyce to meve and mell   *interfere*
    that was hyr most desyre.

915.

Kyng Acab mad goddes of metall
10970   and gaf to them wele gud woyne.   *wealth in abundance*
Bot scho mad hym more fouly fall   *she (i.e., Jezebel)*
    then forto wrschepe tre or stone.
He made a tempyll to Beall,   *Baal*
    was god of Tyre and Sydone.   *Sidon*
10975 On knese to hym thei cry and call
    and says he ys ther lord alon.
Scho ordand for tho werkes,
    als woman wardly wyse,   *worldly*
Fals prophettes, prestes, and clerkes
10980   evyn at hyr awn devyse.

[ELIJAH REBUKES AHAB (16:35–17:1)]

916.

And trew prophettes of God Allmighty,
    prestes and clerkes and byschopes bathe,
Them gart scho spyll dyspytfully;   *she caused to be killed*
    ther none myz skape withowtyn skathe.   *harm escape; harm*
10985 Kyng Acab faverd hyr forthi
    in all hyr werke, yf yt ware wath.   *dangerous*
Therfor God send his sand in hy   *message at once*
    to make hym wytt how He was wrath.
Ely the prophet trew   *Elijah*
10990   fro God to hym was grayd.   *sent*
He told hym tythyng new,
    and on this wyse he sayd:

917.

"God sendes thee word by me certayn,
    for thou mayntenys on yll maner
10995 Thi wyf that has His servandes slayn
    and makes the goddes of fendes unfere.   *weak devils*
Within thi reme sall fall no rayn,
    ne dew sall now fro hevyn apeyre   *the heavens*
To tyme that I com here agayn,   *Until the time*
11000   and that bees noyght of all this yere."
The kyng then toke gud tent   *careful care*
    and hopes he be begyld.   *is beguiled*
And the prophett so went
    his ways unto the woddes wyld.   *wild forests*

[ELIJAH IN THE WILDERNESS AND ZAREPHATH (17:2–24)]

918.

11005	He logeed hym in a forest fayr	*lodged himself*
	whore erbs ware grouand full grene,	*herbs were growing*
	And thor he fand low in a layre	
	a spryng with watur fresch and clene.	
	God sent hym breyd owt of the ayre	*bread; air*
11010	thore whore none before had bene	
	With rayvyns that cowd to hym kayre.	*ravens; travel*
	So selcoth syght was seldome sene.	*amazing a sight*
	Alon so lyfed he thore,	
	to none his nedes to nevyn,	*mention*
11015	Well sevyn monthes and more	*months*
	with helpe of God of Hevyn.	

919.

	In the meyn tyme betyd yt swa	*it happened such*
	that all the erth was dry be dett.	*duty bound to be dry*
	And his fresch watur fayled hym fro;	
11020	then was his lyst of lyfyng lett.	
	Then bad God hym that he suld ga	
	for that defawt his fode to gete	
	Into a cyté heyght Sarepta,	*Zarephath*
	in the syd of Sydone was sett:	
11025	"To a wedow ther I spake,	
	qwylk to My bedyng is bayne	*obedient*
	To fede thee for My sake.	
	Thus sall thou fynd certayn."	

920.

	Then was Ely in stallworth state	
11030	when he the bote of God con here.	*command; hear*
	To Sarepta he toke the gate,	*road*
	als his Lord con unto hym lere.	*instruct*
	The wedow was withoutyn the gate	*gate*
	and geydderd wod with sympyll chere.	
11035	He prayd hyr hys threyst to abate	
	to helpe hym with sum watur clere.	
	Scho sayd, "Styll here abyd!	*await*
	I sall sone do thi rede."	*bidding*
	Bot aftur hyr sone he cryde	
11040	and bad hyr bryng hym bred.	

921.

	The wedow was then more affrayd
	and scho had mervell how he wold mene.

"Syr, God of Hevyn He wott," scho sayd,
   "I am bredles and lang hath bene.
11045   Slyke drynes over this land is layd
    for hungur dye the folke be dene.   *forthwith*
And for that poynt I have purvayd,
    the same sall on myself be sene.
I have within my bowre,
11050   I wyll thou wytt all wele,
Bot a handfull of floure
    and a lytyll oyle in a skele.

922.

"I geydder wod, os thou may see,
    for aftur Goddes wyll wold I yt wore.
11055   I sall make to my sun and me
    a lytyll cake of all our stoure.
That sall we ete, and it sall be
    our last fode; so wyll fall therfore.
Then bus us dye both I and he,   *must*
11060   for to our mete have we no more."   *food*
He sayd, "I pray thee, dame,
    sen that the soth is so,   *since; truth*
make me fyrst of that same
    and sythyn make to yow two.

923.

11065   "And thou wyll tent to my consell   *If you will listen*
    and traw yt to the utterest end,   *believe*
I say thi flour it sall not fayle,
    bot fro defawt yt sall thee fend.   *starvation; defend*
And als thin oyle sall thee avayle   *also*
11070   to tym that God sum socour send."
Scho wold noyght fyne then forto trayvell   *finish*
    bot kyndly dyd os he hyr kend.
Hyr flour then fayled noyght,
    ne hyr oyle wex not to wast
11075   Tyll God, ose Hym gud toyght,
    heyght them His helpe in hast.

924.

Aftur this tyme betyd yt so: *it happened thus*
    the wedow sun was ded with payn.
Then was that wedow wonder wo
11080   and mad grett sorow for certayn.
To Ely gretand con scho go   *weeping*
    and sayd, "Yf thou be prophet playn,
Schew now thi myght to me and mo

and gayre me have my sun agayn!   *cause*

11085   Then wyll I trewly trow
             that thou be the prophett strang.
         And els I say that thou
             hath slayn my sun with wrang."

925.
         When Hely saw hyr sorow sere,   *many sorrows*

11090   he sayd, "Dame, sese! All sal be wele."
         He raysed hym that was bun to bere   *resurrected*
             fayr in forse fully to fele.
         Then made the mother mery chere
             and sayd, "Thi God may send all sele.

11095   Now wot I wele withowtyn were:
             thou ert His prophett trew as stele."
         Full holy then scho hym held,
             as thor was schewed to syght.
         And ay whyls he thor dweld,

11100   scho esed hym at hyr myght.

[ELIJAH RETURNS TO ISRAEL AND MEETS OBADIAH (18:1–16)]

926.
         God began then to have peté,
             for pepyll peryscht in mony a place.
         To the prophet Ely commawnd He
             them forto comforth in this case

11105   And say they shal have rayne plenté
             and be releeved in litle space.
         Ely was glad yt suld so be.
             to betell ward be lyve he gase.   *towards Bethel quickly he goes*
         He had bene thore before;

11110   full well knew he the strette.
         Bot fyrst, or he com thore,   *before*
             sum mervels con he mete.

927.
         With Kyng Acab then wonnand was   *dwelling*
             a prowd prince with armys clene,

11115   That named was Obedyas.   *Obadiah*
             he served God and that was sene
         When prophettes and prestes to payn con pase   *did succumb*
             through Jesabell, that fellows qwene.   *evil*
         Sum of them helped he has

11120   that the same day ded suld have bene.   *dead*
         In hid place he them sett   *a hiding place*
             and sayved them fro the chaunce

And broyght hymself in dett   *into debt*
   to fynd them sustinance.

928.

11125   Kyng Acab bad hym wend in hy   *ordered him to go at once*
   to seke yf he myght fynd herbe or grese   *grass*
That ther bestes myght lyfe ther by   *their beasts*
   that dyes for defawt, more and lese;   *starvation*
Or yf he myght awr spyre or spy   *either find or spy*
11130   whore that warlow wonnand es   *where that powerful sorcerer is dwelling*
That proved them by his prophecy
   that thei suld dwell in swylke drynes   *such a drought*
To tyme he come agayn.   *Until the time*
   "And yf thou may hym bryng,
11135   Als sone he sal be slayn,   *Immediately*
   for he told swylk tokynyng."   *foretold such signs*

929.

Obedyas wold no langer lett;   *delay*
   he was full boun all bale to bete,   *very ready all misery to relieve*
For herbys or gryse, yf he myght gete,
11140   bot he fand nawder sawre ne swete.   *sour nor sweet (i.e., none at all)*
Bot in the way, as he was sett,
   with the prophett Ely con he mete.
When he hym saw, for joy he grette   *greeted [him]*
   and fell doun flatt before his fete.
11145   He fraynd als man afrayd,   *acted*
   "Es this my lord Ely?"
He answerd sone and sayd,
   "Goddes servand here am I."

930.

"Ser," he sayd, "thus I am sent
11150   thee forto seke, os thou may see.
Kyng Acab hath gyfyn his jugment
   that for this dry ded sall thou be,   *drought*
And bot I bryng thee, I be shent.   *unless; killed*
   Therfor sum consell ken thou me."   *teach*
11155   He says to hym, "I wold thou went
   and tell hym os I tell thee:
Styll here I sall abyd   *await*
   and no fote ferther flee.
And say for all his pryd
11160   God sall my belder be.   *protector*

931.
"And I sall warrand thee full wele   *assure*
    and fro his felnes thee dyffend."   *wickedness*
Obedias went and told ylk dele   *each part*
    unto Acab as Ely hym kend.   *instructed*
11165 He sayd, "Ser, seke we for our sele   *we [should] seek [Elijah]; safety*
    and pray hym sum socur to send!"
And for the folke swylke fawtes fele,   *such starvation feel*
    unto hym both wyghly thei wend.   *quickly they go*
Then sayd the kyng for scorn,
11170   "Ys thou not he, that same
That gayrs my land be lorn   *causes*
    and wastes both wyld and tame?"   *(i.e., everything)*

[The contest at Mt. Carmel (18:17–46)]

932.
Then sayd Ely, "Ser, I thee tell:
    this sorow is sent all for thi syne.
11175 Bryng same the best of Israel,   *together*
    yf that thou wyll this baret blyne,   *trouble cease*
And the fals prophettes of Jezabell
    and prestes and dekyns, more and myn,
And comys all to the Mownt Carmell!
11180   Ther sall I tell them, or I twyne,   *before I depart*
The cause of all this kare   *sorrow*
    and what may most amend."
Forto fulfyll this fare
    the kyng full sone hath send.

933.
11185 Unto the lordes of his land
    and most clene of the comonalité,
Prophettes that Jezabell ordand,
    prestes and dekyns in ther degré,
Unto them all he thus commawnd,
11190   "Comys to the Mount of Carmell with me!
Thore sall ye se the prophett stand
    that mad us in this bale to be."
Sone on a hyll on heyght
    this pepyll was purvayde.
11195 Then Ely stud up ryght
    amang them all and sayd,

934.
"Lordynges, your lyfes thus worthys to lake   *changed to waste*
    that levys the Law that Moyses lent.   *who leaves; gave*

Grett God that to your faders spake,
11200   Hym suld ye trow with trew entent.   *believe [in]*
God of Abraham and of Ysac,
   unto His saws ye suld assent,   *words*
And leve Beall that ever is blake,
   or els in bale ye mon be brent.   *sorrow; tormented*
11205 Yf ye may prove by skyll
   that he may helpe yow oght,   *any*
Tell yt this pepyll untyll!"   *unto*
   To this thei answer noght.

935.

"Now sers," he says, "asay we sall   *test*
11210   whedder of our goddes hath more power.   *which*
Rayse up an auter amang yow all,   *altar*
   and I sall rayse another nere.
Takes then an ox owt of a stall
   and part yt in sunder in peysese sere.   *many pieces*
11215 And on your auter lettes yt fall,
   and I sall do the same ryght here.
To God then sall we pray,
   and qwylk so fyrst is brent,   *burned*
Hald hym for God verray."   *verily*
11220   To this thei all assent.

936.

Fals prestes, clerkes of Jezabell,
   and prophettes, faur hunderth and mo,   *more*
Raysed up an auter them omell,   *altar among them*
   for so thei wene to wast ther wo.   *hope to end their woe*
11225 Thei leide theron full fayr fuell,   *a great deal of fuel*
   and then a gret ox con thei slo   *slay*
And layde furth both flesch and fell;
   and Ely dyd another also.
Then prestes and prophettes kneled,
11230   ylkon aftur ther state,
And prayd Beall forto beld,   *protect [them]*
   bot his comforth com late.

937.

Full rudly then thei rope and rare   *Very violently; cry out; roar*
   on ther mawment to mend ther mode.   *idol*
11235 Bot ther offerand moved never the mare,   *more*
   bot in a state full styll it stod.
Thei rent ther face and rave ther hare   *their faces and tore their hair*
   and weped for wo, ose thei ware wode.   *crazy*
Ely stud styll on them to stare,

11240   hym toyght that game was wounder gud.
         He says, "Your god is on slepe
             or els went ferre fro hame: *far from*
         To yow he takes no kepe.
             Crys on hym fast for schame!"   *Call upon*

938.
11245   So dyd thei holly half a day,   *wholly*
             to cry and rare thei wold not rest.   *roar*
         Ther offerand on the auter lay,   *offering; altar*
             and no kyns fyre wold in yt fest.   *no kind of fire; alight*
         Then Ely bad them wend away,
11250   God was not to ther prayer prest,
         And sayd, "For soth, I shall assay
             yf my God wyll be bettur gest."
         His auter and ylk dele   *altar*
             in Goddes name was agrayd.
11255   His flesch was weschen wele   *washed well*
             and on the auter layd.

939.
         On both his knese then knelse he doun
             and prayd to God with stabyll stevyn   *steady voice*
         To send sum segn in that seson
11260   that His name myght be new to nevyn.   *invoke*
         Or he had endyd his oryson,   *prayer*
             a fyre dyscended doun fro Hevyn.
         Yt brent all up that he mad boun
             and went up into the ayre full evyn.
11265   Then ware tho folke full fayn,
             and lowd thei cast a crye:
         "Ther is no god may gayn
             bot the God of Ely!

940.
         "We wot Beall ys bot a fend,   *fiend*
11270   and fals prophettes, foull mot them fall!"   *must*
         Ely bad that thei suld shend
             prophettes and prestes that on hym call.
         Of all the meneye mad thei end   *company*
             that governd hym, both gret and small.
11275   Then Ely heygh with wordes hende,   *called*
             "Sum socur yow God send sall."
         The Ebrews went at wyll
             and toyght ther werkyng wele.
         And Ely loged hym styll
11280   apon the Mount of Carmele.

941.
To God fast con he call and crye
 of His pepyll forto have pyté
And bad his servand spyre and spye   *look and see*
 yf any clowd com fro the see.
11285 At last he sayd, "Ser, certanly
 the ayre begynys all brown to bee."
God send helpe then sone in hy: *haste*
 rayn fell over all that cuntré.
Then love thei God allways
11290 with wyll, word, and dede.
And the prophett thei prays
 that so spake for ther sped.

[JEZEBEL SWEARS VENGEANCE; ELIJAH FLEES TO BEERSHEBA (19:1–3)]

942.
Bot Jezabell, that cursed qwene,
 when scho herd tell of this tythyng,   *news*
11295 How all that had with Beall bene
 ware ded and thrugh Ely demyng,   *deeming*
Then in hert scho had grett tene   *anger*
 and sayd ther suld non erthly thyng
Save hym, and he myght be sene,
11300 that he ne suld have the same endyng.
Ely herd hyr swere swa;   *swear this*
 therfor fast con he flee
Tyll a cyté of Juda,
 that named was Barsabé.   *Beersheba*

[ELIJAH'S REVELATIONS IN THE WILDERNESS AND HOREB (19:4–21)]

943.
11305 Lang sojornyng ther saw he none,
 for he was ferre from ylka frend.   *far*
To wyldernese he went alone,
 and in a loge ther con he lend.
To myghty God he mad his mone
11310 and prayd Hym that he myght make end,
"Als myn elders ar ded ylkon,
 Lord, suffer me that way to wend!   *go*
Sene them no lyffe ys lent   *Since in; life*
 that wore more of wrschepe,   *honor*
11315 Lett me wend os thei went!"
 With thys he fell on slepe.

944.

He was wery and myght not wake,
    for he had wentt be ways sere.   *many roads*
An angell come and to hym spake
11320   and sayd he was Goddes messyngere.
Mete and drynke he bad hym take   *Food*
    so forto hold hym hoyle and fere.   *healthy and strong*
Then at his hed he fand a cake
    and a vessell with watur clere.
11325 And for hym fayled fode,
    of that fayre was he fayn.
He ete and dyd hym gud,
    and sone he sleped agayn.

945.

The secund tyme the angell sayd,
11330   "Wake, wake, Ely, and no more thou wynke!   *sleep*
Swylke ose ys in this place purvayd   *Such [stores]*
    God byddes that thou sall ete and drynke.
A grett way is before thee grayd   *prepared*
    that thee behoves both swett and swynke."   *sweat and toil*
11335 He rayse and rathly hym arayd.   *arose*
    his lymys ware then full lyght, hym thynke.
By the myght of that same mete   *food*
    he trayveld fawrty days
The hyll of God to gett,
11340   heyght Oreb the story says.   *Mt. Horeb*

946.

God spake to hym in that space
    and sayd, "What sterd thee into this stede?"   *brought; place*
He sayd, "Lord, for ferd of my fase.   *fear; foes*
    For and I byd, I ete never bred.
11345 Thi prophettes in evere ylk place
    by Jezabell ar putt to ded,
And the same to me heyght scho has.   *promised*
    That dose me flee fro hyr hatred."
God sayd, "Go ydder agayn
11350   and do message of Myne!
I sall thee sayve certayn
    fro hyr and all hyr hyne.   *servants*

947.

"Take tent to tales that I thee tell   *Take heed*
    and trewly trest that thei are trew!   *truly trust; true*
11355 Ordan for kyng of Israel   *Ordain*
    aftur Acab on that named ys Jew!   *(i.e., is a Jew)*

And kyng of Syre make Azaell   *Syria; Hazael*
    that ever has bene a gud Ebrew!
And when thou may no langer dwell,
11360   for thiself then set Elysew!   *Elisha*
He sall be prophett playn,
    wysest when thou ert wentt
And man full mekyll of mayn   *power*
    to mustur Myn entent.

948.

11365   "Thei sall Me venge with hert and hand
    of them that hath forsakyn Me."
So went he furth and sone he fand   *(i.e., Elijah)*
    Elysew in feld kepand his fee.   *field; flock*
He told unto hym new tythand,
11370   all how God bad that he suld bee.
Then Elysew left lord and land
    and went with Ely os menyhe.   *follower*
So same we lett them dwell,
    two gud servandes to God,
11375   And of Kyng Acab tell
    and of his neghtbour, Nabod.   *Naboth*

[NABOTH'S VINEYARD (21:1–29)]

949.

Kyng Acab wuned in Jezerael,   *lived in Jezreel*
    a cyté that was long and wyd.
And also his qwenne Jezabell
11380   was wonnand thore with mekyll pryd.   *dwelling*
And this Nabod that I of tell
    sojornd als a neghtbour nere besyd.
He had a feld that to hym fell
    whore wynes full mekyll multyplyd.
13385   The kyng oft yt beheld,
    for yt was large and lang.
He thynkes to have that feld
    awder by ryght or wrang.   *either*

950.

And to fullfyll this purpase playn
11390   to Nabod sent he message thore.
To by hys feld he wold be bayn   *buy*
    and to gyf gud fully therfore.
Bot Nabod sent hym word agayn
    that yt fell to his ayrys ever more.   *heirs*
11395   He wold noyght sell yt for certayn.

Then was the kyng greved full sore.
So grett dyspytt hym thynke,
  his hert he myght not meke.
He myght nawder ete ne drynke
11400   bot layd hym doun sore seke.

951.
No sang, ne solace myght hym save,
  ne no helpyng to hym avayld.
Qwene Jezabell the cause con crave
  and asked hym hertly what hym ayled.
11405 He sayd, "For Nabod feld I crave,
  and therof have I fowly fayled."
Scho says, "That hette I thee to have,   *promise*
  all be yt never so trewly tayled."
Scho gart hyr rebels ryse
11410   that tyll hyr bode was bayn,
And charged them on all wyse
  that Nabod sone ware slayn.   *Naboth's sons*

952.
Scho bad that thei suld bere hym on hand
  that he had sclaunderd God of Hevyn,
11415 And lett hym so no langer stand.
  And at hyr wyll thei went full evyn.
Thei wold noyght fyne or thei hym fand,   *stop before*
  and then thei wold not here his stevyn,   *hear his speech*
Bot slow that lele man for his land.   *law-abiding*
11420   This was a cursed note to nevyn.   *mention*
When this yll ded was done,
  the kyng was hole, hym toyght.
Bot God sent message sone
  that sayd yt suld sore be boyght.

953.
11425 Gud Ely to the kyng con tell,
  "For thou hath wroyght thies werkes wode,   *insane deeds*
In that same feld that Nabod fell
  sall thou be slayn for all thi gud.
Wyld bestes sall with thi body mell,   *meddle*
11430   and thi flesch sal be fowles fud.
And say to thi wyfe, Jezabell,
  in this cyté sall houndes lape hyr blud.   *lap her blood*
Als Kyng Jeroboam kyn
  dyed all withoutt bereyng,   *bearing [further generations]*
11435 So thi frendes for thi syn
  sall fall to fole endyng."   *foul*

954.

Kyng Acab then was cast in care.
  to God fast con he call and crye
And heyght that he suld never mare *promised; more*
11440   werke to wrath hym wylfully,
So that he wold of vengance spare
  and of his synys then have mercy.
And when God saw his sorows sare, *sore*
  agayn to hym he sent Ely. *Elijah*
11445 He says his kynred sall
  be saved whyls he has myght,
Bot all ellys suld befall
  as he before had heyght.

955.

The prophett then his way is went
11450   whore God wold governe hym to gang.
The kyng then toke full gud tent *reflected very carefully [upon]*
  what tales ware thore them amang. *were said there among them*
And Jezabell, that lady gent, *well-born*
  was ever in wyll to werke wrang. *wanting to do evil things*
11455 In grett lykyng now ar thei lent; *happiness*
  we sall leve that yt lastes not lang.
The kyng of Syre, Benedab, *Syria, Ben-hadad*
  with kynges thryty and two
Soyght unto Kyng Acab
11460   with were to werke hym wo. *war*

[BEN-HADAD AND THE SIEGE OF SAMARIA (20:1–22)]

956.

When Kyng Acab persaved in hy *at once*
  how enmys enturd intyll his land, *enemies entered into*
And wyst with swylke a cumpany *knew [that] with such*
  to fyght in feld no folke he fand, *field; folk [could] he find*
11465 He clossed hymself in Samary; *closed himself [up] in Samaria*
  was full wele walled hym to warrand. *very well fortified*
Bot Benedab sett not therby; *thought nothing of this*
  ther myght no strength agayns hym stand.
That cyté large and wyd,
11470   that semly was to see,
Seged he on ylka syd *He besieged on every side*
  with paynyms grett plenté. *a great many pagans*

957.

Unto Kyng Acab word he send,
  "Yf that thou wyll take me untyll *Unless; give unto me*

11475	Both wyves and chylder into myn hend,	
	at my lyst forto spare or spyll,	*desire*
	And all that is for thresour kend	
	within the cyté, lowd and styll,	*publicly and privately*
	To have with me, then wyll I wend."	*cause [to happen]*
11480	Kyng Acab answerd to that skyll,	
	"Of myn all that men kens	
	wyll I lefe forto lyfe.	*leave [you]*
	Bot gudes of other mens	
	have I no ryght to gyfe."	

958.

11485	Kyng Benedab then was not payd;	*pleased*
	therfor he answerd wordes fell.	*terrible*
	"I have here sembled men," he sayd.	
	"So mony that yf I them omell	*among*
	Ylkon a handfull had purvayd	
11490	of erthe to lay here whore we dwell,	
	Of that same erthe suld be grayd	*created*
	a hyll os hegh os a castell.	*as*
	And fare thei sall not fare	
	or all this burgh be brent."	*burned*
11495	Then Kyng Acab had care,	*sorrow*
	bot socour sone was sent.	

959.

	God to his helpyng has tane hede	*taken heed*
	and send His prophett hastely.	
	He sayd, "Kyng Acab, have no dred!	
11500	God says thou sall have vyctory."	
	The kyng askys, "Who sall do that ded?"	
	He says, "Chylder and no chyvalry."	*Servants*
	Then gart the kyng geydder full gud sped	*caused; to gather*
	of chylder a full fayre cumpany,	
11505	Swylke os myght wepyns weld	
	faur hunderth furth he fand.	
	Thei wentt before to the feld.	*in front; battlefield*
	He sued with sevyn thowssand.	*came forth*

960.

	Thei musterd them with myght and mayn;	
11510	God mayntend all that meneye.	*company*
	The paynyms sone ware put to payn,	*pagans*
	all ware thei never so grett plenté.	
	Fyve thowsand sone of them ware slayn,	
	and all the remnand fayn to flee.	*remainder glad*
11515	Bot sone thei sembled mo agayn	

and sayd that thei suld venged bee. *avenged*
Kyng Benedab asked consell *[his] council*
   what thyng that most myght noye,
And what myght most avayle
11520   the Ebrews forto dystroye.

[BEN-HADAD DEFEATED ON THE PLAIN (20:23–34)]

961.
Thei answerd sone unto his saw *words*
   and sayd, "For this fare that thou frayns *you ask about*
Condicion of ther God we knaw.
   His helpe is all in hegh mountayns.
11525 Therfor to dales I red we draw, *low places (the plains) I advise we withdraw*
   for ther our god most to us gayns. *there*
And ther God wyll not lyght so low, *their*
   so sall thei sone be put to payns."
This consell toke he tyll
11530 and held yt gud and hale.
Evyn under Japhet hyll *Aphek*
   he loged hym in a dale.

962.
Kyng Acab herd tell how ther hales *tents*
   was sett to sojornd in certayn space.
11535 Bot for he suld noyght trow ther tales, *believe*
   fro God full gud warnyng he has.
A prophett bad go bede them bales,
   for God wold schew of His gud grace
That he myght ese als wele in dales *help as well*
11540 as in hylles or in hy places.
Kyng Acab assayld them sone,
   as God gaf hym to red, *be ready [to do]*
And als God demed, was done:
   paynyms ware done to ded.

963.
11545 A hunderth thowssand and wele mo
   of hethyn folke ware feld in feld *were killed in the field*
That come with thrytty kynges and two.
   ther scaped non that suld wepyns weld. *escaped*
Kyng Benedab he wan with wo *went*
11550 to a cyté hymself to beld. *protect*
He wyst not what was best to do:
   to byd or his body to yeld, *remain*
For wele he wyst certayn
   Kyng Acab wold not fayle

11555   Or he ware soght and slayn.
      Bot thus spake his counsell:

964.
    "Ser," thei say, "suffer sall we
      a lese harme forto lett a more.   *stop a greater [one]*
    Ebrews ar men of mercy free;
11560   wend we unto them fast therfore   *go*
    And pray ther kyng to have pyté
      for his goddes sake with syghyng sore,
    And profer us his bond men to be
      and also that we sall restore
11565   All that our elders wan
      fro his elders and fro hym.
    So sall he graunt uus than
      forto have lyf and lym."

965.
    Unto this counsayle have thei tone,   *taken [heed]*
11570   and sone ther gatte thei have begun.   *journey*
    Barfote, in ther serkes alon,   *Barefoot; shirts*
      with cordes abowt ther halse bun,   *necks bound*
    To Kyng Acab thei kneled ylkon
      and fell doun flatt when he was fun.   *reached*
11575   When he saw them wyll of woyne,   *without hope*
      grett rewth to his hert is run.
    He forgaf all his grefe
      and graunt them pardon playn.
    He mad hymself myschefe
11580   and the hethyn folke full fayn.   *glad*

[Ahab's mercy on Ben-hadad; the prophet's rebuke (20:35–43)]

966.
    Kyng Benadab by the hand he hent   *took*
      and kyssed hym and become his frend,
    So thai that hoped to be shent
      now in this tyme no more were tend.   *troubled*
11585   Kyng Acab with his Ebrews went
      to Samary fayr forto lend,
    Bot message sone to hym was sent
      that God was yll payd of ther end.
    A prophett, Machias,   *Micaiah*
11590   thor lendyd in that land.   *dwelled*
    To Samary con he pase
      with his staf in his hand.

967.

To that cyté so as he yode,
　　Ebrews mett hym in the way.
11595　To on of them he spake gud sped,
　　"Have here my stafe, I thee pray,
and breke my hed and gare yt bled!"　　　　　　　　　*strike; cause it [to] bleed*
　　The Ebrew answerd and sayd, "Nay!
Why suld I do to thee that dede
11600　　that greved me never be nyght ne day?"　　　　　　　*who*
The prophett sayd, "Forthi　　　　　　　　　　　　　　　*Because*
　　that thou dose noyght my wyll,
Thou sall dye sodanly,
　　and bestes thi sped sall spyll."　　　　　　　　　　*success (life)*

968.

11605　A lyon come with byttur brayd
　　and wowred hym amang them thore.　　　　　　　　　*devoured*
The prophett to another sayd,
　　"Have here my staf and smyt me sore!"
That other saw his felow flayd,
11610　　that made hym buxum mekyll more.　　　　　　　*much more humble*
His awn stafe on his hed he layd
　　that blud fell over the face before.
A cloght abowt he band　　　　　　　　　　　　　　　　*cloth*
　　to be owt of knawyng.　　　　　　　　　　　　　*(i.e., disguised)*
11615　His stafe he toke in hand
　　and come so to the kyng.

969.

"A, lord," he says, "this herm I hent
　　in the batell, for I wold not fle.
The stewerd toke me forto tent　　　　　　　　　　　　　*take care of*
11620　　a man that had mysdone to thee.
To kepe hym safly I assent.
　　He ys away; full wo is me,
For I be tane to grett turment　　　　　　　　　　　　　*taken*
　　bot yf thou my beldyng be."　　　　　　　　　　*unless; protector*
11625　The kyng sayd, "Sine he was　　　　　　　　　　　*Since*
　　worthy forto be ded
That thou has lettyn pase
　　and standes in that same sted,

970.

"For bettur beld thee thar not byde　　　　　　　　　　*comfort*
11630　　bot ded for ded, this is the law."　　　　　　　*death*
The prophett sone his hed unhyd,
　　bycause the kyng then suld hym knaw.

"Ser kyng," he says, "this same thou dyd   *judgment; ought*
     and this same dowm to have thou aw.
11635   For Benadab that ever is kyd   *known*
     enmy to God in dede and saw,   *deed and word*
     God gaf hym in thi hend
     forto venge ylk dele.
     And thou has lettyn hym wend;
11640   therfor I warn thee wele:

971.

     "For thou wold not putt hym to pyne   *Because*
     when he was putt in thi pawsté,   *power*
     And wyst yt was Goddes wyll and myn
     of hym and his venged to be,
11645   For his lyfe thou sall lose thin
     and all thi kyn in this cuntré,
     For socur of God now sall thou tyne.   *lose*
     Thus sall yt wurth, thus warne Y thee."
     Then was Kyng Acab kene.   *bitter*
11650   In preson he dyd hym cast
     And sayd he suld be sene
     a lyer at the last.   *liar*

[Jehoshaphat and Ahab at peace (22:1–4)]

972.

     In preson now lett we hym dwell
     and Acab in his yll lyfyng.
11655   Of Josaphat furth wyll we tell   *Jehoshaphat*
     that of Jerusalem was kyng.
     He musterd mercy ever omell   *among [them]*
     and honerd God over all thyng.
     Therfor all frendschepe to hym fell
11660   and beldyng both of old and yyng.   *comfort*
     Both by est and west
     he mayntened Moyses Law,
     And paynyms ware full prest
     to wrschepe hym all way.   *honor*

973.

11665   Kyng Josaphat had with his quene
     mony suns, semly to syght.
     The eldyst of them all be dene   *straightway*
     heyght Joran, a full gentyll knyght: *Jehoram*
     He toke a wyfe withoutyn wene,   *doubt*
11670   Kyng Acab doyghtur, Godely scho hyght.   *Athaliah*
     Scho had of kynd forto be kene   *nature; angry*

by Jezabell, hyr moyder, ryght.   *through*
To wayte be est and west   *look*
    so worthy was no moo.

11675   That marage mad grett rest   *peace*
    betwyx the kynges two.

974.
Befell aftur the thre yeres end:
    Kyng Josaphat went to Samary
To Kyng Acab, his fader and frend,   *father[-in-law]*
11680   to conferm cours of cumpany.
Thei welcumd hym with wordes hend   *courteous*
    and wrschep, os he was worthy,   *honor*
And als lang os hym lyked to lend,   *remain*
    for hym was mad grett mangery.
11685   Kyng Acab towched hym tyll
    what hast he had on hend,
And sayd, "Ser, and thou wyll,
    thou may me mekyll amend.

975.
"Benedab, the kyng of Syre,
11690   hath angerd me and all my kyn.
My cetys hath he sett on fyre
    and bene full boun in burghes to bryn.   *burn*
And Ramatha, price of my empyre,   *Ramoth-Gilead, crown jewel*
    that has he wun and dwels ther in.
11695   Therfor is now my most desyre
    to wast hym and that cyté to wyn.   *defeat*
With both our power playn
    sone sall we dyng hym doun."
Josaphat says, "Certayn,
11700   I sal be redy boun.

[The kings ask Micaiah about attacking Ramoth-Gilead (22:5–28)]

976.
"Bot fyrst I wold now or we went   *before*
    we pray sum prophett us to tell
Whedder we in werys sall harm hent   *war shall suffer harm*
    or els our foyse in feld to fell."   *foes*
11705   Faur hunderth sone ware aftur sent,   *[prophets] were soon*
    and all cord thei them omell   *agreed; together*
And says ther enmys sall be shent   *destroyed*
    and vyctory with them sall dwell.
Kyng Josaphat trowd all tho   *believed all those*
11710   fageed the kyng for dowte.   *flattered; fear*

He asked yf any moo
  ware wonnand ther abowt.   *dwelling*

977.
Kyng Acab says, "Ya, ther is one
  in my preson, a prophett strang.
11715 Gud word of me spake he never none;
  he noyght sall, lyf he never so lang."
Machyas was fro preson tone,   *Micaiah; taken*
  and thus he sayd them all amang,
"Acab hymself he sal be sloyn.
11720 All other sall savely come and gang."   *safely*
Then sayd Kyng Acab, "Loe,
  this told I yow beforn,
He sall never say ne do
  bot yll both evyn and morn."

978.
11725 Kyng Josaphatt says, "Forsoth us aw   *Truly we ought*
  to trow all that he says sall be.
Swylke case before may he not knaw
  bot only of Goddes privaté."
Up stert a lordan of ther law,   *villain*
11730 heyght Sedechy, and this sayd hee: *Zedekiah*
"Sers, sett not by this segger saw;   *soothsayer's words*
  he says noyght sothe, that sall ye see.
I sall hym stryke in the face
  to gare hym staker and stand.   *cause him [to] stagger*
11735 And yf I pase the place
  withoutyn harme of my hand,

979.
"Then sall ye trest that I am trew,
  and that his tales es bot a trayn.   *are; trick*
And yf my hand fayle hyd or hew
11740 or stand noyght in yt power playn,
Supose ye then that all sall sew   *take place*
  as he has sayd yow for certayn!"
The kynges assented, no soth thei knew,
  and he stroke hym with all his mayn.   *strength*
11745 His hand was never the warre,   *worse*
  and that was for this skyll: *reason*
For no mirakle suld marre
  the prophett spech to spyll.

980.

Ware hurtyng on his hand to schew,   *ensue*
11750   then wold the kyng not pase that sted,
And so suld not the prophett saw   *prophet's speech*
    be soth that sayd he suld be ded.   *dead*
Then says the kyng, "Now may we knaw
    not for trew this rybald red.   *advice*
11755   Gose putt hym in my preson low   *Go*
    and gyf hym noyght bot watur and bred!"
So for trew entent,
    through the sawys of Sedechy,   *words*
To were so ar thei went   *war*
11760   with full clene cumpany.

[THE KINGS ATTACK RAMOTH-GILEAD; AHAB KILLED (22:29–40)]

981.

When thei come whore ther enmys ere,   *enemies are*
    Kyng Acab then this poynt purvayde,
For he hymselfe fro wa wold were.
    "Josaphat, my sun, take hed," he sayd,
11765   "Myn armys in batell sall thou bere
    and all my ryches ryght arayd.
Thin armes and thi wede sall I were;
    so sall our enmys be betrayd."
On that other syde Kyng Benedab
11770   warned his men, lese and mare,
To kyll the kyng Acab
    and all other forto spare.

982.

Thei rewled them trewly in that tyd
    fro erly at morn tyll evynsang.   *evensong*
11775   Kyng Josaphat con boldly byd,
    he presed full fast paynyms amang.
Thei knew hym wele by hew and hyd;
    therfor at lyst thei lete hym gang.
Kyng Acab soght thei on ylka syde   *each*
11780   and full throly to hym thei thrang.   *violently*
A paynym spened a spere   *clasped a spear*
    and stert to hym that stownd.
Thurght the body he con hym bere
    and gaf hym dedes wound.   *a mortal wound*

983.

11785   When Kyng Acab doun was cast,
    his men ware bayn hym forto beld   *protect*

	And hamward hyed them with hym full fast	*hastened*
	whyls he myght any wyttes weld.	
	With mekyll payn so are the past	
11790	to thei come evyn in Nabod feld.	*Naboth's vineyard*
	Then myght his lyf no langer last,	
	bot ther the gast behoved hym yeld.	*spirit*
	Als Mychias prophesyd,	
	in the batell he was turgh born	*struck through*
11795	And in Nabod feld he dyed,	
	os Ely sayd beforn.	*Elijah*

984.

	In that same feld doun he fell	
	that he before had wun falsly	
	Be counsayle of Quene Jezabell,	
11800	that mad Nabod therfor to dy.	
	Hondes laped his blud, whor thei dwell,	*Dogs lapped his blood*
	als yt was sayd be prophecy.	
	Thei bered the body them omell	*buried; together*
	in his awn cyté of Samary.	*own*
11805	Because he was a kyng,	
	his body honerd ys,	
	Bot for his yll lyfyng	
	men mened hym mekyll the lese.	

[JEHOSHAPHAT, REBUKED, RULES WISELY (22:40; 2 CHRONICLES 19:1–20:30)]

985.

	When that Kyng Acab thus was slayn,	
11810	as prophettes sayd that yt suld be,	
	And Occozi, his sun certayn,	*Ahaziah*
	was crowned kyng of that cuntré,	
	Kyng Benedab went home agayn	
	with his paynyms full grett plenté.	
11815	Kyng Josaphat, he passed playn	
	to Jerusalem, his awn cyté,	
	And all his folke in fere	*together*
	ware scaped withoutyn scathe.	*injury*
	God sent His messyngere	
11820	to warn hym from all wathe.	*danger*

986.

	A prophett com and to hym sayd,	
	"Ser, for thou went in cumpany	*because*
	Of Kyng Acab that ys owtrayd,	
	and wyst that he was Goddes enmy,	
11825	I warn thee wele God was not payd,	*pleased*

and vengance suld be sent forthi   *therefore*
Bot that thi dedes ware gudly grayd.
   Bot yett He bydes: beware therby
That thou trespase no more
11830   in swylke maner of thyng,
For dred yt happyn to sore
   to thee or thin ofspryng."

987.
Then loved he God with hert and hand
   and honerd Hym in all kyn wyse.   *kinds of ways*
11835 And sone was told to hym new tythand
   of grevance that began to ryse:
How thei enturd into his land,
   mystrowand men that heyght Moabyse;   *misbelieving; Moabites*
And full grett ost thei had ordand   *army*
11840 with mony other of Amonyse.   *Ammonites*
Thei say non sall them tene
   ne wrath owt of ther wyll
To stroye Jerusalem
   and all that langes ther tyll.

988.
11845 Kyng Josaphat full sone hath he sent
   for prophettes, prestes, and dekyns dere,
For dukes and erles; all thei went
   to the Tempyll to make ther prayer.
Thei prayd to God with gud entent
11850   that He wold helpe that stoure to stere   *battle to guide*
So that His men no harmes hent   *received*
   with hethyn folke that fowled nere.
And as the pepyll prayd
   with word, wyll, and toyght,
11855 A prophett come and sayd,
   "Kyng Josaphat, dred thee noyght!"

989.
Then was Kyng Josaphat full fayn   *glad*
   when he had swylke hertyng fro Hevyn.   *such encouragement*
He sembled men with all his mayn
11860   and comforth them wele with his stevyn.   *voice*
Out of the cyté past thei playn
   and busked unto the enmys evyn.   *hurried*
Bot the paynyms com prowdly them agayn
   with nowmmer mo then men can nevyn.   *numbers; express*
11865 Bot God swylk socour sent
   os none of them other knew,

Bot ylk paynym wend
  his felow had bene an Ebrew.

990.
And so ylkon over other dang
11870   as thei had with ther enmys bene.
Thei wold not sese bot thryst and thrang   *cease but thrust and struck*
  tyll thei ware dongyn to ded be dene.   *beaten to death forthwith*
Ther had non hele home forto gang   *health*
  to say what syght he thore had sene.
11875 So con God ordan murth amang
  to men that on His myght wyll mene.
Kyng Josaphat come then
  with his men to that place.
Grett wardly welth thei wan   *worldly*
11880 with spolyng in that space.   *despoiling*

991.
Thore was ryches and ryalté,
  wyn and oyle and all kin store.
The Ebrews gatt thor gold and fee
  to mend ther myrth forevermore.
11885 Then went thei to ther awn cuntré.
  Kyng Josaphat, when thei come thore,
Bad that all men suld buxum be   *obedient*
  to wrschep God as worthy wore
That ever in ded and saw
11890 to His pepyll tentes   *listens*
That lelly lufes His Law   *loyally loves*
  and kepes His Commawndmentes.

992.
Kyng Josaphat now lett we ly
  in Jerusalem with joy to dwell.
11895 So the Thryd Boke of this story
  is broyght to end, evyn os yt fell.
The Fawrt begynys of Occozi,   *Ahaziah*
  that then was kyng of Israel,
How he sojornd in Samary
11900 with his moyder, Qwene Jesabell.
God graunt us to begyn
  our dedes in gud degré
And end them owt of syn!
  Amen, so mott it be!

FOURTH BOOK OF KINGS (2 KINGS)

LIBER QUARTUS REGUM.

[AHAZIAH TURNS TO IDOLATRY, IS REBUKED BY ELIJAH (1:1–18)]

993.

11905	In this Faurt Boke of Kynges to ken	*make known*
	wher lykyng and wher luf lyse,	
	Us nedes to nevyn the names of men,	*invoke*
	of kynges, of dukes, of prinsese of price,	
	And of ther werkyng wher and qwen	
11910	by dyverse dedes forto devyse.	
	Insampels sere sall we se then	*various*
	how grett relefe therof may ryse;	
	For as lerned men may loke,	
	Sant Paule telles old and yyng:	
11915	"All that is wryttyn in boke	*books*
	is lefed for our lernyng."	*left*

994.

	Kyng Occozi was Acab sun	*Ahaziah; Ahab's*
	and had his welthis all in his weld.	*control*
	And yf the fader a foyle war fun,	*fool was found [to be]*
11920	the sun was more fole, and that he feld.	*foolish; suffered*
	To make hym godes he has begun,	*himself gods*
	os paynyms used in yowth and eld.	*pagans used [to do] all the time*
	To gud God wold he not be bun,	*bound*
	bot Belsabub he made his beld,	*Baal-zebub; comfort*
11925	Was god of Acaron,	*Ekron*
	a nacion not to nevyn.	*mention*
	Hys hope was all hym on.	
	He toke no hed to Hevyn.	

995.

	So lang in lust his lyfe he lede	
11930	hym lyst to lere no lefull layre.	*desired to learn no lawful lore*
	The dome of God nothyng he dred,	*judgment; feared*
	bot ever he dyd myse more and more.	*sin*

Fro a hegh sted — thor was he sted —   *place; placed*
    he fell and hurt hymself full sore
11935 So that he lay seke in his bed,
    and fast thus ordand he therfore:
His messyngers he send
    to Belsabub at wytt
Whedder his seknes suld mend,
11940   or he suld dy on yt.   *die of it*

996.
And als thei went, befor fand thei
    the prophett Ely in a playn.   *Elijah*
He asked wheder thei ware on way,
    and thei sayd hym the soth certayn
11945 All how ther lord in langur lay.   *illness*
    He bad them boldly turn agayn:
"And to your lord salfly ye say:
    of this seknes he sall be slayn,
Bycause he hopes his hele   *health*
11950   of Belsabub forto have
And leves Hym that is lele   *true*
    and all seknes may save."

997.
The messyngers agayn con wend
    this bodword boldly forto bere.   *pronouncement*
11955 Thei told hym all that tale tyll end
    as thei with Ely warned were.
Then was Kyng Occozi yll tend;
    full grett othes then con he swere   *oaths*
Old Ely with shame forto shend   *kill*
11960   so that his demyng suld noyght dere.
He cald his steward strang
    this forward to fulfyll
And bad hym wyghtly gang
    and bryng Ely hym tyll.

998.
11965 "He sall be pyned in my palas   *tortured*
    and lernyd swylke lesynges forto tell."
The steward hastely sembled has
    fyfty folke, both ferse and fell.   *fierce and cruel*
To Ely playnly con he pase
11970   and moved this mater them omell   *among them*
How that the kyng yll angred was,
    and that he myght not byd ne dwell
Bot wyghtly wend hym to

and fand to ese his hert.
11975 "And yf thou wyll not so do,
   with greve thou sall be gert."   *grief; afflicted*

999.
The prophett answerd sone and sayd,
   "Thi manase may not marre to me,
For all thi fayre I am not flayd;
11980   therfor a fote I wyll not flee.
And that God is with me wele payd,
   ensampyll here sone sall thou see.
Thou sall be brent for all thi brayd   *burned; evil*
   and all this cowrt that come with thee."
11985 By this word was end,
   God wold do hys desyre.
A fyre from Hevyn dyscend
   and brent them bone and lyre.   *flesh*

1000.
Unto the kyng com non of tho
11990   to tell hym how this werke was wroght.
Bot when he wyst, he was full wo
   and sayd yt suld be full dere boyght.
He ordand men ose mony moo
   and bad the prophet suld be broyght.
11995 Bot thei ware ryght sone served so
   as the fyrst fyfty that hym soyght.
Thei ware brent ylkon
   with fyre that on them fest.
Then was the kyng wyll of woyne;   *perplexed*
12000   he wyst not what was best.

1001.
Thore in that cyté wonned a man   *dwelled*
   that Moyses Law wold never lett.   *disobey*
The kyng to hym commawnd then
   the prophett with fayrnes to fett.   *fetch*
12005 He went and warly to hym wan
   within his sell whore he was sett.   *cell*
As curtasly ose ever he can
   and with grett gladnes he hym grett   *greets*
And sayd, "Ser, have mercy
12010   on me and my meneye!"   *company*
Then to hym sayd Ely,
   "What is thi wyll with me?"

1002.

    "A, ser," he says, "full wele I knaw
        God goverence thee in word and dede.

12015 We ar charged with full grett aw   *fear*
        unto the kyng thee forto lede.
    And thou wyll se tyll our saw,
        so may thou make us mekyll mede;
    And yf thou wyll not ydder draw,

12020   we mun be ded withoutyn drede.
    We sall noyght do ne say
        in this gate thee to greve.
    Bot, gud ser, and thou may,
        have mynd of our myscheve!"

1003.

12025 The prophett saw thei sorewd so
        and herd them carpe so curtasly.
    He graunt hym with them to go.
        so wentt thei same to Samary.
    Then went Ely with other mo

12030   to carpe with the kyng Occozi.
    He fraynd yf he suld flyt ther fro
        or els of that same sekenes to dy.
    He sayd, "Sen thou takes rede   *(i.e., Elijah); counsel*
        of Belsabub, the fend,

12035 Als sone thou sall be ded
        and with that warlow wend."   *devil*

1004.

    So sodanly he mad endyng
        aftur his werkys wele worthy wore.
    He had non ayre, old ne yyng,   *heir*

12040   his state ne his sted to restore.
    His brother Joram was crowned kyng   *Jehoram*
        and lord of Israel, lese and more.
    He was wele wars in all thyng   *much worse*
        then any had bene hym before.

12045 He melled with mawmentry   *meddled in idolatry*
        and lyfed in lust of flesch.
    Acab ne Occozi
        was never to fylth so fresch.

[Elijah taken into Heaven (2:1–25)]

1005.

    In this mene tyme that I of tell
12050   was gud Ely, Goddes prophett trew,

Rayvesched up in flesch and fell *flesh and skin (whole body)*
 in a chare byrnand, bryght of hew, *burning chariot*
And in Paradyse dyght to dwell *placed*
 with Eunoke that our elders knew. *Enoch*
12055 With Antecryst sall the mete and mell. *they meet and fight*
 and aftur hym leved Elysew, *Elisha*
A prophett proved of price,
 to nevyn in ylk nede, *mention*
In word and werke full wyse,
12060 als we sall aftur rede.

[JEHORAM AND JEHOSHAPHAT'S WAR AGAINST MOAB (3:1–27)]

1006.

 Kyng Joram was a gentyll knyght,
 all yf he lyfed unlafully, *even if; unlawfully*
Aftur his fader, that Acab heygh,
 and aftur his brother, Kyng Occozi.
12065 He geydderd folke, for he wold fyght
 agayns the kyng of Moaby *Moab*
Of hym forto recover his ryght,
 and this was his encheson why: *reason*
The Moabyse ware bun *Moabites were required*
12070 to gyf Kyng Acab clere,
For thei in pese suld wun, *peace should live*
 two hunderth shepe be yere. *sheep each year*

1007.

 And now thei say, what so yt ment,
 that thei wyll pay swylk payn no more. *tribute*
12075 The kyng thynkes loth to lose his rent,
 wher his fader was fest before.
Unto Jerusalem has he sent
 to Josaphat, that was kyng thore, *Jehoshaphat*
And prayd hym forto take entent
12080 and help his ryght forto restore.
Josaphat says, "I sall
 helpe all that ever I may."
And same so went thei all
 in full ryall aray.

1008.

12085 Bot qwen the gayre was gudly grayd *gear; prepared*
 and thei all redy forto ryde,
Kyng Joram then the prophett prayd
 forto tell them what suld betyde. *occur*
Elysew answerd hym and sayd, *Elisha*

12090	"I am not sent to save thi syde.	
	With Josaphat is God wele paid;	*satisfied*
	His helpe fro hym He wolle not hyde.	
	I say yow sothfastly	
	that for his luf alone	
12095	Ye sall have the vyctory	
	of your enmys ylkone."	

1009.

	Then went thei furth with mekyll glee.	
	syght of ther enmys sone thei have.	
	Als the prophett sayd that yt suld be,	
12100	sone ware thei skomfett, knyght and knave.	*they were discomfited*
	Thei conquerd sone all that cuntré	
	and mad ther rebels to ryn and rave.	
	The kyng for ferd was fayn to fle	
	tyll a cyté hymselfe to save.	
12105	And ther he wund with wo,	
	for Ebrews all abowt	
	Besegede that cyté so	*Besieged*
	that he suld never wyn owtt.	*win [a way] out*

1010.

	And when he saw he suld be shent,	*destroyed*
12110	a sotelté full sone he dyght.	*trick*
	Unto the walles wyghly he went	
	wher Ebrews of hym myght have syght.	
	His eldest sun in hand he hent	
	and heved his sword hegh apon hyght.	
12115	He bretynd hym forto be brynt	*cut him into pieces to be burned*
	als sacrafyce to God Almyght.	
	Ebrews con on hym loke;	
	in hert thei had pyté.	
	That sege sone thei forsoke	
12120	and went to ther cuntré.	

[JEHOSHAPHAT DIES; ANOTHER JEHORAM REIGNS (8:16)]

1011.

	Kyng Josaphat agayn ys gone	
	to Jerusalem the redy way.	
	Sone aftur seknes has hym tone	*taken*
	so that he dyed that aghtdane day.	*on the eighth day*
12125	For hym was mad full mekyll mone,	
	for lely lufed he Godes Lay.	*loyally; Law*
	Joram, hys sun, full sone on one	*Jehoram*
	resaved his reme by ryght aray.	

	Now be we ware for wathe	*aware to be cautious*
12130	to tell thire kynges twa,	*these kings apart*
	For Joram heygh thei bathe,	*named*
	of Israel and of Juda.	

1012.

	Bot this Joram that I now of tell	
	had wedded a wyf heyght Godolé,	*Athaliah*
12135	Doyghhtur of Kyng Acab and Jezabell	
	and systur unto Kyng Occozé.	
	And Joram, the kyng of Israel,	
	brother unto hyr was he;	
	Therfor was frendschep them omell	*among them*
12140	with beld os brether aght to be.	*comfort*
	Now leve we ther two kynges	
	that governd all Ebrew,	
	And tell furth ferly thynges	*wondrous*
	of the prophett Elysew.	

[ELISHA'S MIRACLE TO HELP THE WIDOW OF OBADIAH (4:1–7)]

1013.

12145	He sojornd then in Samary,	
	and mony of seknes con he save	*illnesses*
	And be poyntes of prophecy	
	what any man wold aftur crave.	
	A woman come with carfull crye	
12150	that hoped of hym helpe to have.	
	Scho sayd, "Ser, have of me mercy!	
	Bot thou me red, els may I rave."	*Unless; advise, I may go mad*
	"Dame," he sayd, "be styll	
	and putt wepyng away!	
12155	Say me what is thi wyll,	
	I sall helpe and I may."	*if*

1014.

	"A, ser," scho says, "full wele thou knew	
	my husband that heyght Obedias,	*Obadiah*
	That in his tyme to God was trew,	
12160	now is he ded, my lord, allas!	
	When Jezabell Goddes prophetes slew	
	that in this land then wonnand was,	*dwelling*
	One hunderth held he hale of hew	*[of them] he kept healthy of skin (i.e., alive)*
	whyls all perels con overpase.	
12165	He sold up all his gud	
	and broght hym in grett dett	*put himself; debt*

For to fynd them ther fode
   and fro greve them to gete.   *keep*

1015.
"In a seler he dyd them sytt   *cellar*
12170   whore that non sargandes suld them see.   *officials*
Now is he ded and the dett unqwyte,   *unpaid*
   and ylka man askes his dett of me.
And wele wars tythandes tell thei yett: *news*
   my sun that is full fayr and free,
12175 Thei say thei sall have hym forfett.
   Then are we lorn, both I and he.   *lost*
And, ser, sen all this dede
   was done for our Goddes sake,
Unto my harme take hede
12180 and help my sytt to slake!"   *grief*

1016.
"Dame," he sayd, "I sall thee tell
   thrugh myght of God to mend thi mode.
What has thou in thi howse at sell?"   *to sell*
   "Sertes, ser," scho sayd, "non erthly gud
12185 Bot a lytell oyle in a vessell
   to fynd me and my chyld oure fud,
Als lang os we sall same dwell."
   He says, "I wold thou understod.
Go home and fand to gete
12190 into thin howse this day
Of vessell small and grett
   ose mony as ever thou may.

1017.
"Borow of thi neghtbours nere and ferre
   all that ar tume, both tub and tune.   *empty; barrel*
12195 Wend into thi hows, thi dore thou spare   *lock*
   and be within, thou and thi sun.
When that thi vessell ordand are,
   lett sum oyle into ylkon run,
And sone thou sall thi mornyng marre,   *mourning cease*
12200 for Goddes fuson sall thore be fun."   *abundance; discovered*
Scho wroyght, and als God wyld
   hyr kare full kyndly cover,
All tho vessels ware fyld
   so full that oyle went over.

1018.

12205   Then was the woman ferly fayn,   *wondrously glad*
  And to the prophett fast scho rane.
Scho sayd hym all the soth certayn,
  and to hyr he commawnd thane,
"Wend home unto thi howse agayn,
12210   sell oyle and pay ever ylk man.
And lyf thou and thi lytyll swayn
  furth of the remnand as ye cane."   *remnant*
Thus was hyr oyle encrest
  that all hyr dett was payd,
12215   And so hyr sorow sest
  als Elysew had sayd.

[ELISHA'S MIRACLES OF A CHILD IN SHUNEM (4:8–37)]

1019.

  A man wunned with his wyf to weld   *dwelled; live*
    besyd that cyté of Samary   *(i.e., Shunem)*
Whor Elysew oft toke his beld;   *took his rest*
12220   and his wyf drowped oft drerely   *fell often into depression*
Bycawse scho was gone in gret eld   *great age*
  and had no barn hyr husband by.   *children*
When Elysew to hyr beheld,
  he sent his servant Gyezi   *Gehazi*
12225   And bad bryng hyr hym tyll
  hyr sorowyng forto say,
For he wold with gud wyll
  amend yt yf he may.

1020.

  Scho come to hym os he hyr bad,
12230   and told hym all hyr purpase playn:
"Chyld with my husband never I had,
  therfor my hert hath mekyll payn."
"Dame," he sayd, "be blyth and glad,
  and here I hete thee for certayn   *promise*
12235   That with a sun thou sal be sted
  or tyme I com eft here agayn."   *before the time*
Scho sayd, "For grett Goddes sake,
  gud ser, dyseve me noght!"
He says, "I undertake
12240   God wyll that this be wroyght."

1021.

  Gud hope in hyr hert scho hang
    that all his saws suld suth be fun,   *words should be found truthful*

	And with hyr husband or oght lang	
	consayved scho and bare a sun.	
12245	Then mad thei grett myrth them amang	
	and kepyt yt warly whor thei wun	*safely*
	To tyme that it couth speke and gang,	*go*
	and then new grevance is begun.	
	The chyld toke evyll and dyed	*ill*
12250	thre yeres fro yt was born.	
	The mother wept and cryd,	
	"Alas, now am I lorn!"	*lost*

1022.

	Scho went furth als a wod woman	*as a mad woman*
	for the prophett by fyrth and fell,	*(i.e., everywhere)*
12255	And at the last to hym scho wan	
	whore he wund on the Mount Carmele.	*lived*
	"A, ser," scho sayd, "no red I con;	
	my myschef now may no man tell.	
	Alas, the whyle that I began	
12260	to aske a chyld with me to dwell!	
	I wened when I yt bare	
	to make me myrth ever more.	
	Now is my mornyng mare	
	then ever yt was before.	

1023.

12265	"Ser, for a chyld I con thee pray,	
	noyght forto gab me ne begyle.	*mock me*
	Then wold I thou had sayd me nay	
	lever then to lyf so schort a whyle.	*rather than*
	And yf thou be prophett verray,	*a true prophet*
12270	as schews thi mervelys mony a myle,	
	Geyte me my sun; els wyll I say	
	that yt was wroyght with wekyd wyle."	
	The prophett had pyté,	
	swylk mone that woman ment.	
12275	To his servant sayd he,	
	"Gyezi, thou take entent!	

1024.

	"Have here my stafe and wend thi way	
	with this woman fast on thi fete.	
	Apon hyr sun doun thou yt lay	
12280	and fand yf thou fele any hete.	
	Yf he ryse noyght by this aray,	
	com thou agayn me forto mete;	
	And then sall I myself assay	

on Goddes behalf hyr bale to bete."   *misery to relieve*
12285   He wentt with pase full playn,
            and aftur his word he wroyght;
        Bot sone he come agayn
            and sayd he rose noyght.

1025.
        Then Elyse this pase thus purvayd.   *course; prepared*
12290   he voyde all pepyll owt of that place.
        The chyld unto his body he layd,
            hand to hand and face to face,
        And unto God hertly he prayd.
            The chyld has lyf in lytyll space.
12295   "Have here thi sun, dame, now," he sayd,
            "and love God gudly of grace!"
        Then was hyre hert full lyght,
            to love Hym was hyr lyst.   *desire*
        So con God schew His myght
12300   to them that in Hym tryst.

[ELISHA'S MIRACLES OF THE LOAVES AND THE HEALING OF NAAMAN (4:38–5:19)]

1026.
        Aftur this tym began to be
            grett hungur over all that land
        And pestilence in sere cuntré   *many countries*
            for fawt of fode that no man fand.   *lack*
12305   And Elysew that tym was he
            in wyldernese allway wonnand.   *always dwelling*
        To hym soyght pepyll grett plenté;
            fro Hevyn helpe was in his hand.
        With erbys and other gud   *herbs*
12310   God ordand for that spence,   *expense*
        So that non fayle fode
            in that prophett presence.

1027.
        A man that wonned that forest by
            purvayd the prophett to rehete.   *nourish*
12315   To his fode ordand he forthi   *therefore*
            a lytell seke full of fayr qwete,   *wheat*
        And ten lovys bare he hym in hy   *loaves; in haste*
            of the same flour for his awn mete   *food*
        And twenty other of barly.   *other [loaves]*
12320   We may wele wytt thei ware not grette.   *large*
        "Vowchesave, gud ser," he sayd,
            "to take this gyft of me."

The prophett was wele payd,   *glad*
     and thus then ordand he.

1028.

12325   His servant to hym con he call
     and bad hym gare the folke go sytt
And part this bred amang them all
     so that ylkon have sum of yt.
The servant sayd, "Ser, so I sall,
12330   bot in that werk wyll be not wytt.   *wisdom*
To swylk a pepyll yt is full small
     yf ylkon suld have bot a bytt.
Me thynke, ser, yt ware nede
     to take sum other red,
12335   For here is folke to fede
     a hunderth that fayles bred."   *who need bread*

1029.

The prophett sayd, "Go herdely,   *boldly*
     for yf thei hungur never so yll,
God is of myght to multyplye
12340   to ylk man his mete at wyll."
Als he commawnd, dyd Gyezi;   *Gehazi*
     he served them full fayr and styll.
When all war fed, ther leved by
     als mony folk mo forto fyll.
12345   Thus sendes God socur sone
     to them that His Laws wyll lere.
Bot mekyll more was done,
     als men may aftur here.

1030.

In Syry landes of Sarsynes   *Syria; Saracens*
12350   wund a kyng, Benadab his name,   *lived; Ben-hadab*
And a prince proved of grett prowes,
     Naman nevynd, of nobyll fame.   *Naaman called*
He was renownd of grett ryches
     and non so hend haldyn at hame.   *courteous*
12355   Bot defawt felyd he in his flesch,
     with lepur was he lath and lame.   *leprosy*
That was grett harm to here,
     for his lord lufed hym wele
And folk both ferre and nere
12360   grett helpe on hym con fele.

1031.

His wyfe was fayre of flesch and fell
   and of gud maners mekyll more,
And with hyr wund a damsell   *lived*
   that fro Ebrews was stolyn before.
12365   Scho sayd, "Thor wuns in Israel
   a prophett that may sayfe all sore."
This tale oft tyms con scho tell
   and sayd, "Wold God my lord ware thore!
For certes he suld be hale   *[made] whole*
12370   or he past that provynce."   *before he left*
The lady told this tale
   untyll hyr lord the prince,

1032.

On qwat maner the maydyn yyng   *young*
   sayd how that his bote suld be.   *remedy*
12375   When he herd tell of this tythyng,
   full mekyll myrth in hert had he.
He went and told unto the kyng
   and sayd, "Lord, yf thi lykyng be
To gyf me leve a lytyll thyng
12380   that myght be medcyn unto me!"
The kyng sayd, "Tell us tyll
   what consell that thou hath kend.
I sall help with gud wyll
   thi myrth forto amend."

1033.

12385   He says, "Ser, with my wyf at hame
   dwellys a lytyll damsell,
And scho hath told unto hyr dame
   a prophett is in Israel
That be nevynyng of his goddes name   *invoking*
12390   hath myght of maystres forto mell   *exercise*
And forto lech ylk lame,   *heal*
   whedder yt be maynd or mesell."   *maimed or leprous*
Kyng Benedab says, "I am kend
   with Joram, kyng of Jews.
12395   Unto hym sall I send
   to traw thi tales in trews."   *believe*

1034.

He mad a lettur to be lele   *legal*
   in thies wordes wrschypfully:
"I, kyng of Syry, under my seall   *seal*
12400   sendes worschep, os wele is worthy,   *honor*

To Joram, the kyng of Israel,
    as frend that I fast in affy   *in trust*
At helpe my servand to have hele,   *cure*
    Naman, chefe of my chyvalry.
12405 Of his lepur leche hym so   *heal*
    faythfully withoutyn fayle
As thou wyll ever I do
    thyng that may thee avayle."

1035.

Naman ordand full rych aray:
12410 somers with cloghes, sylke and satayn,   *packhorses*
Ten payr of garmentes gud and gay
    with pyrry and with pure ermyn,   *precious stones; ermine*
Talentes of sylver of assay,
    sex milia besantes of gold fyne,   *6,000*
12415 The prophett forto plese and pay.
    He hoped to have his medcyn.
With full clene cumpany
    that he had ever at hand
He soyght to Samary,   *journeyed*
12420 ferre owt in Ebrews land.

1036.

So with this letters is he went
    full wrschypfully, this may we wene.
Kyng Joram told he his entent
    and toke hym letturs them betwene,
12425 And sone in hand he has them hent.
    And when he all the suth had sene,
His ryche robes he rofe and rent   *ripped and tore*
    and sayd, "Alas! what may this mene?
Wenes the kyng of Syry   *Believes*
12430 that I have God at wyll
To do all my desyre
    men forto spare and spyll?

1037.

"Occasions sekes he now, I se,
    how he may make my lordschep lese,   *lessen my authority*
12435 And thus he says be a sotelté
    so for to dryfe me to dystres."
When Elysew herd how that he
    had ryfyn his wedes so in wodnese,   *clothes; madness*
He sayd, "Send Naman unto me,
12440 then sall thei se that suthnes.
In Israel er prophettes lele,   *are true prophets*

mo then is ned to nevyn,   *more; mention*
  That his seknes sall hele
    thrugh the helpe of God of Hevyn."

1038.
12445 Kyng Joram that before was rad
    now wex he lyxsom of his late,   *cheerful in his mood*
  And the prince Naman was full glad
    that the prophett heyght to amend his state.   *promised*
  With all the harnays that he thore had
12450   to hym he toke the gayneste gatte.   *straightest road*
  Then Elysew to his servand bad
    go speke with hym withoutyn the gatte.
  "And when thou sees hym com,
    say I tell hym this tale:
12455 To wasche hym in the flom   *river*
    sevyn sythys, he sal be hale."   *seven times*

1039.
  Then com this nobyll prince Naman
    full playnly to the prophett place.
  Bot Gyezi sone unto hym wan
12460   and sayd, "My maystur this message mase: *makes*
  Go wesch thee in the Flom Jordan
    sevyn sythys in certayn space,
  And so he says thou sal be than
    salved of seknes that thou hase."   *healed of the sickness*
12465 Then was the prynce not payd.   *pleased*
    He cald his men togeydder,
  And to them thus he sayd,
    "Wherto ar we comyn hydder?

1040.
  "Ar not at hame in our land
12470   als clene waturs that we com fra,
  In Damaske and in Syrry rynnand,
    both Farfar flud and Abbana?   *the Pharpar and Abana rivers*
  I wened the prophett with his hand   *thought*
    suld have helyd me betwyx us twa.
12475 His warke ys noyght, now I warrand,   *naught*
    therfor agayn fast wole we ga.
  Folke sayd, or we come here,
    that he cowth bete all bales.   *triumph over all ills*
  Thus may men lyghtly lere   *learn*
12480   forto trow wemens tales."   *believe women's*

1041.

He removed sone all his aray,   *company*
    for in hert was he angerd yll.
Sum of his men can to hym say,
    "Ser, yf that yt ware thi wyll,
12485 Of this poynt we wole thee pray:
    the prophettes consell to fulfyll.
For thrugh his myght, mend yf it may,
    harme may non towch thee untyll.
Yf he had gyfyn grett thyng   *difficult*
12490   to do for thi releve,
Thou suld noyght make grochyng
    for dred his god to greve.

1042.

"And this thyng that he now of ment
    is lytyll and may be for the best."
12495 Unto ther sawes then he assent,   *their words; assented*
    and to the flom the cowrse thei kest.   *took*
He wesch hym ther with gud entent
    sevyn sythes or ever he rest,
And hertly hele sone has he hent,
12500   that no fowle fylth on his flesch was fest.   *remained*
Bot evyn os a yyng chyld
    ys soft and semly sene,
So was his flesch unfyled   *undefiled*
    of all that corupcion clene.

1043.

12505 Thus when he was be sythes sevyn
    weschyn clene both flesch and fell,
So mekyll joy myght no man nevyn   *mention*
    os ther was mad them omell.   *among*
He cryd and sayd with stabyll stevyn,   *steady voice*
12510   "Now wyll I say wherso I dwell: *wherever*
Ther is no god in Erth ne Hevyn
    bot only God of Israel,
Ne non that myght may schew   *power*
    to save men of sekenes
12515 Bot only Elysew.
    A prophet proved he es."

1044.

Than counsayld all that cumpany,
    because that thei so comforth ere,
At wend agayn to Samary
12520   the prophett presand forto bere.   *gifts*

The prince proferd hym in hy *at once*
    sylver and gold and other gere.
The prophett sayd, "Gramercy, *Thanks*
    bot swylke welthes aw us non to were. *ought; accept*
12525 Sen God heled thee thus,
    thanke Hym of His gud dede!
Yt falys noyght untyll us
    therfor forto take mede. *reward*

1045.
"And, ser, I say thee for certayn:
12530   the werkes that God here wyll have wroyght
By His myght and His power playn,
    aw nawder to be sold ne boyght.
Sen thou ys hale, wend hom agane,
    and thanke Hym hertly in thi toyght!"
12535 The prince says, "Certes, so wyll I fayn;
    all other goddes to nevyn ar noyght. *name*
His trewth I take me tyll
    als lang os I may lyfe;
And, ser, for that same skyll
12540   I pray thee me to gyfe

1046.
"Two horssus lade of erth of this land *burdened*
    in privay place yt forto lay.
That I theron may stably stand
    my Cryatur when I sall pray.
12545 For I wott He is all-weldand
    and that His lordschep sall last ay
That me hath heled both hede and hand.
    Ther ar no mo that men mend may.
Bot when the kyng of Syry
12550   sees this werke on this wyse,
I wott he wyll desyre
    forto make sacrafyce

1047.
"To Beall that is blake and blo,
    in whom he hopes to have releve.
12555 And bot I gladly with hym go, *unless*
    agayns me wyll he malyce meve.
Then yf I wend with other mo
    forto eschew a more myschefe, *greater*
Pray thou thi God betwyx yow two
12560   so that He take yt not to greve.
Fore my hert sall be hale *wholly*

to hym that salves all sare."
The prophett says, "I sall
    pray fast for thi wele fare."

[GEHAZI'S GREED AND PUNISHMENT (5:20–27)]

1048.

12565	The prince so turnes hym home in hy;	*in haste*
	full mery ware his men ylkon.	
	Elysew convayd hym curtasly,	
	bot ryches wold he resave none.	
	Therfor his servant Geezi	
12570	toyght yt was ungraydly gone.	*improperly*
	Full fast he ordand hym forthi	
	at have sum to hisself alon.	
	Aftur them radly he ran;	
	hym had bettur bene styll.	
12575	The prince persayved hym than	
	and sayd, "What is thy wyll?"	

1049.

	"A, ser," he sayd, "sen ye con wend,	
	ar new men with my maystur lyght,	
	Two of his kyn of lang tym kend,	*kinsmen; acknowledged*
12580	and both thei byde with hym all nyght.	*stay*
	And for he wold ther myrth amend,	
	he bad me ryn aftur yow ryght,	
	And prays yow that ye wold hym send	
	two cloghes and two besandes bryght	
12585	His frendes with forto plese.	
	This may hym gretly gayn."	
	To do that hym myght ese	*what might ease him (Elisha)*
	the prince was farly fayn.	*very glad*

1050.

	Two somers charge be lyve he bad	*packhorses quickly*
12590	with dyverse drewres forto dele.	*gifts*
	"Bot I hym mensk, els am I mad,	*honor*
	and thanke hym hertly of myn hele."	
	Then Gyezi was wunder glad	
	for wynyng of this werldly wele.	*wealth*
12595	Unto his awn howse he yt had	
	so fro his maystur yt forto fele.	*hide*
	For prively he yt keped	
	and wend all had bene wele.	
	Bot bettur hym ware have slepyd,	
12600	his maystur wyst ylk dele.	*knew every part of it*

1051.

And sone his knave to hym he cald:
    "Gyezi, whore has thou bene?"
"Maystur," he sayd, "here I me hald
    to wayte your wyll, wele may ye wene."   *know*
12605   "Bewsir," he sayd, "Thou ert to bald   *Fair sir*
    and says not soth, that sal be sene.
I herd the tales all that thou told
    unto the prince yow two betwene.
I saw ferre in the feld   *far; field*
12610   when thou toke gold and fee.   *payment*
Bot thou sall never yt weld
    with wyn, I warn yt thee.   *joy*

1052.

"Thou wyst I wold no welthys wyn
    when he swylke bewtes to me con bede.   *extend*
12615   Thou herd me say how yt was syn
    for Godes werke to take mede.
The same seknes that he was in,
    for thou hath done swylk dede,
Sall come to thee and all thi kyn
12620   ever more persewand in thi sede."
Full sone was Gyezi
    then aftur his maystur dome   *master's doom (proclamation)*
Maynhed with mesellri   *Crippled with leprosy*
    and all that of hym come.   *are descended*

1053.

12625   We have herd how that prince Naman
    was saved of all seknes sere,
And Gyezi was mad messell than
    and aftur hym all his kyn clere.
So se we how God wyll and con
12630   ordand well for His frendes dere,
Als He with Elysew began.
    Bot mekyll mor yett men may here.
And sen sere ferles fell,   *since such wonders occurred*
    yt is gud to saye sum.
12635   Of on wyll we tell,   *one*
    was sene besyd the flum.   *river*

[ELISHA'S MIRACLE OF THE AXHEAD (6:1–7)]

1054.

Sant Elysew, Goddes prophet gud,
    and other that wold with hym byde,   *others who; dwell*

Toyght fayre forto be nere the flud
12640   to soyjorn in that somer tyd.
He ordand wryghes and ydder yode   *carpenters; there went*
      and chese ther place by the flome syde
And hewed down trese swylk os thor stod   *trees such as there*
      to make a howse them forto hyde,
12645 Whore thei myght wynly wun   *live*
      fro wynd and wedders wete   *damp weather*
And also fro the sun,
      that thor gafe full grete hete.

1055.

A tree ther on the banke con stand
12650   that to a balke was bowand best.   *for a beam was very suitable*
A wryght when he that faceon fand,   *shape found*
      to hew yt down wold he have no rest.
His ax, that he ther had ordand,
      fayled and was noyght fully fest.   *held fast*
12655 Therfor the hed owt of his hand   *axhead*
      fell whore the watur was depest.
Then was he wyll of wytt,
      so all his felows wore.
Bot he had borowd yt,   *Because*
12660   his mornyng was the more.   *mourning*

1056.

Unto the prophett fast he hym ment,
      at fall to fete he wold not fyne.
"Maystur, mercy, I mun be shent
      bot yf I have Goddes helpe and thin.
12665 Myn ax hed in the watur is went,
      therfor my tym now mun I tyne,   *may I lose*
And like more harme forto hent   *suffer*
      becaws I wot yt was not myne.
I borowd yt at my frend,
12670   and bot he may it have,
He wyll hold me unhend.   *unworthy*
      Gud ser, helpe me to save!"

1057.

The prophett sayd, "Con thou me tell
      about the place betwyx us two?"
12675 "Yay, ser, forsoth," he says, "yt fell
      in the myddes of the flud o ferre me fro."
Thei went and wold no lengur dwell,
      the prophett prayd ever os thei go.
The watur boyld up os a well;

12680	the hevy yrn com up also	*heavy iron*

12680   the hevy yrn com up also   *heavy iron*
          Evyn unto the prophett hand.
               Then was the wryght full glade.
          The word went all that land
               how he his axhed hade.

[ELISHA THWARTS AN ARAMEAN ATTACK (6:8–23)]

1058.

12685   Sone aftur this the kyng of Syry,   *Syria*
               Ser Benedab, that we of tell,
          Was moved in anger and in yre
               agayns the kyng of Israel.
          He cald Phylysteyns fell ose fyre   *fierce as fire*
12690   and moved his malyce them omell.   *among*
          To stroy Joram was his desyre,
               bot with quayntyse he wold hym quell.   *cunning*
          He wyst a privay strayt   *knew; path*
               wher Joram oft con gang.   *did go*
12695   Ther bad he them go wayte   *ordered*
               and murther hym them amang.   *murder*

1059.

          Forto fulfyll this fals entent
               his kenest knyghtes he cald by name.   *bravest*
          Unto that way wyghtly thei wentt,
12700   als he had sayd to do that same.
          Sant Elysew wyst how thei ment.   *what they meant to do*
               Kyng Joram forto sheld fro shame
          His message sone to hym he sent
               and bad he suld hold hym at hame
12705   And pase noyght owt of toun
               fro dred of more myschefe,
          For his enmys ware bown
               with hatred hym to grefe.

1060.

          When Kyng Joram wyst of this wrang,
12710   that he was warned, he was full fayn.   *very glad*
          The knyghtes when thei had lygen lang   *lain long*
               in wayte, then went thei hame agayn.
          Kyng Benedab of sorow sang
               when he wyst his warke was in vayn,
12715   And sayd his men themself amang
               his privay consell couth noyght layn.
          He sware who yt ascryd   *revealed*
               that his wyll was unwroyght,

Fro yt myght be aspyd
12720   with bale yt suld be boyght.

1061.

The knyghtes themself sakles knew   *knew they were innocent*
    and herd hym make slyke manasyng,   *threats*
Sayd, "Ser, we sal be fown trew   *found*
    and no consell to bere ne bryng.
12725   Thor is a prophett Elysew
    that at his wyll may wytt all thyng.
And thei both are of Ebrew,
    we wott well he hath warned the kyng.
He dwels in Dotaym,   *Dothan*
12730   a cyté here nere besyde.
Bot yf yt ware by hym,   *Unless it was through him*
    thi spech myght never be spyde."   *spied*

1062.

Then bad the kyng go grett plenté
    and that this fatur fast ware feld.   *traitor quickly was killed*
12735   "Sett a sege to that same cyté
    whore in thei sayd the prophett dweld,
And bryng that mawment unto me   *idolater*
    that of swylke maystres has hym meld.
He sall be hanged heygh on a tre
12740   bycause he has our consell teld."
To Dataym then thei soyght,
    and seged yt sone thei have.
Bot all ther werke was noyght,
    God wold His sonderman save.   *messenger*

1063.

12745   Fell on a morn the prophett man   *[It] befell; prophet's servant*
    luked furth, and in the feld he fand
Wele mo men then we nowmer can,   *can count*
    harnest full wele both heuyd and hand.   *armed*
Unto his maystur fast he ran,
12750   "Alas, alas!" full lowd cryand,
"That we ware born, now may we ban
    bot we be lyve may lefe this land.   *quickly*
For sertes sone we be ded,
    our enmyse are so nere."
12755   The prophett says, "I red   *advise*
    that thou mend thi chere.

1064.

"Hopes thou not that I may have   *Believe*
   os mony men and more of myght
Fro all Sarsyns me forto save   *Saracens*
12760   and forto maynten me in my ryght?"
Then forto loke he led his knave:
   on that other syd a selcowth syght.   *side [they saw] a strange*
He saw no sted to styre his stave
   for baners and for basnettes bryght.   *helmets*
12765 Then sayd the prophett, "Loo!
   Thies men are at my wyll
Whatso I byd them do
   with forse yt to fulfyll."

1065.

His servant sayd, "The kyng of Syre
12770 myght never rayse so rych aray."
The prophett says, "Wele mo then thire   *Many more than these*
   may I have redy ylka day
To do whatever I wyll desyre."
   Then unto God thus con he pray
12775 Thyr hethyn folk, fulfylled of yre,
   sone of ther syght be tane away.   *taken*
Hastely he had his bowne: *boon*
   God so his sand has sent.
Thei fayled syght as sone
12780 and wyst not whore thei went.

1066.

The prophett then began to go
   to them that waytt hym with wrang.   *awaited*
He and his man withoutyn mo   *delay*
   went all ther enmys evyn amang.
12785 He sayd to them, "Who seke ye so?"
   Thei sayd, "To take a traytur strang,
On Elysew, hym sall we slo."   *slay*
   He says, "So may ye lygg full lang!   *remain*
He went fro this cyté
12790 sythyn a sevyn nyght past.   *a week ago*
And ye wyll wend with me,   *If*
   we sall fynd hym at last.

1067.

"Yow forto led I sall not layn   *deny*
   tyll ye se hym all opynly."
12795 Thei say, "We sall ye sew certayn,   *follow*
   for that carll we wold fayn com by."

He led them furth with pase full playn   *a very quick pace*
   into the cyté of Samary.   *Samaria*
Of that fayr was Kyng Joram fayn,
12800   for thei had wayte hym with envy.
The gates full sone ware sperd,   *bolted*
   thei wend all had bene feld.   *knew; hidden*
Of Ebrews noyce thei hard,   *sounds they heard*
   then was ther comforth keld.   *dashed*

1068.
12805   The prophett then Sant Elysew
   prayd God to graunt agayn ther syght.
Sone ylkon of them other knew;
   then ware thei mased all owt of myght.   *astonished*
Ylkon trowd other was untrew
12810   to lede them so withoutyn lyght.
Abowt was mony bold Ebrew
   to welcom them, os yt was ryght,
With mony upbraydynges brayd   *outspoken*
   and skornyng wordes gud wone.   *aplenty*
12815 In bale thore thei abade,
   and comforth kene thei none.

1069.
Thei saw how thei ware broyght in bale
   and clossed evyn in ther enmys hend.   *trapped*
The kyng asked the prophett counsayle
12820   how thei myght best of them make end.
Sant Elysew con say, "Sauns fayle,   *Without doubt*
   that thei be dede, I dyffend.   *forbid*
Thou hath noyght wun them in batell,
   ne aftur them no sand thou send.
12825 Sen God thus hath them sent
   by His myght us amang,
Yf thei suld here be shent,   *destroyed*
   me thynke then werke we wrang.

1070.
"And, ser, also thei trespast noyght
12830   sen tyme thei com to this cuntré.
Aftur myself thei say thei soyght,
   that mater lyges alon to me.
I red thei be to beldyng broyght   *advise; protection*
   for this nyght in this same cyté,
12835 And to morn mete unto them boyght,   *tomorrow food*
   and aftur fode lete them go free.
So sall we wrschep wyn   *honor*

of all thir men ever more,
    And other all of ther kyn
12840   to do us favour therfor."

1071.

The kyng sayd, "Ser, I vouchsave
    that thei be led os thou wyll lere."   *instruct*
The prophett gart them herber have   *safe harbor*
    and bad no noye suld neght them nere,   *trouble come near them*
12845   And on the morn both knyght and knave
      had mete and drynke and meré chere,
    And nothyng for ther cost to crave,
      bot bad them wend furth all in fere.   *all together*
    To ther cuntré thei come
12850   withoutyn lake of lym.   *without injury*
    The prophett went hym home
      agayn to Dotaym.

1072.

Thei went full fast unto thei fynd   *until*
    Kyng Benedab with dukes hym by.
12855   Thei told hym how thei ware mad blynd
      with Elysew, the prophett myghty,
    And how he them as presoners pynd   *pinned*
      within that cyté of Samary.
    And sythyn he held them noyght behynd,
12860   bot convayd them all curtasly
    And so with beld them broyght   *help*
      owt of ther enmyse hand.
    The kyng grett wounder toyght
      that thei slyke frenschep fand.

1073.

12865   He sayd, "The prophett is myghty
      that so wele owt of wo may wyn.
    Bot Kyng Joram, our yll enmy,
      he sall aby or ever we blyn.   *suffer; cease*
    Yf we persew hym prevely,
12870   the prophett sall sett debate therin.
    With opyn batell wende wyll I
      and dyng hym doun for all his dyn."   *strike; sorrow*
    His barons sayd also,
      "We sall ye never forsake.
12875   Full gladly wyll we go
      this vyag forto take."   *expedition*

[ARAMEAN SIEGE OF SAMARIA (6:24–7:20)]

1074.

	So sayd his Sarsyns all be dene	*straightway*
	that fro that ded thei wold not dwell.	*deed*
	So grett an ost was seldome sene	
12880	os thei sone ordand them omell	*together*
	Of erlys, barons, and knyghtes kene,	
	and commyn folk full ferse and fell.	*fierce and strong*
	So went thei furth by cuntres clene	
	unto the land of Israel.	
12885	And charyottes with vytale	
	gate thei full grett plenté,	
	For that thei wold noyght fayle	
	of Samary cyté.	

1075.

	Unto the cyté rayked thei ryght	
12890	and sone enseged yt all about.	*besieged (encircled)*
	Kyng Joram when he saw that syght,	
	forto be ded he was in dowtt.	
	His enmyse dered hym day and nyght	*harmed*
	with full scharpe shetyng and with schowt.	
12895	Unto tho men he had no myght,	
	ne to no place he myght pase owt.	
	When ther vytels ware gone,	
	began hungur full grett.	
	Then ware thei wyll of wone,	
12900	for no more myght thei geytt.	

1076.

	When whette and wyn and oyle con pase,	*did pass away*
	then ete thei up all ther fee.	*cattle*
	Thei myght sell the hed of an asse	
	for aghtene pennys of moné.	*eighteen pence; money*
12905	Of two wemen grett pyté was	
	that samyn wund in that cyté.	*together dwelled*
	That on of them cryd, "Alas!"	
	fell doun before the kynges kne.	
	The kyng wened that hyr wyll	
12910	had bene mete forto crave.	
	He sayd, "Woman, be styll!	
	of me thou may non have.	

1077.

| | "Yt may not helpe on me to crye, | |
| | I have no mete to mend thi chere." | |

12915 "A, lord," scho sayd, "I aske mercy
           and a ryghtwyse dome for Dryghten dere.   *judgment from the Lord*
       Another woman, lord, and I,
           when fode fayled both ferre and nerre,
       We made connand of cumpany   *agreement*
12920   to ete our barnys both in fere.   *eat our children all together*
       And, lord, my barn is etyn,
           and I for hungur spyll.
       Away hyrs has scho gettyn
           and wyll noyght forward fulfyll."   *[the] covenant*

1078.
12925 When Kyng Joram herd hyr thus say,
           that care com to his hert full cold.   *sorrow*
       He says, "Woman, wend hens away!   *go*
           My sorow is more by mony-fold.
       The prophett that wyll noyght for us pray
12930   and myght amend us and he wold,   *if*
       He sall be done to dede this day   *(i.e., executed)*
           for all the tales that he has told."
       Wyght men he bad furth wend
           stryke of his hed at home.   *off*
12935 Bot God was ever his frend
           and warned hym or thei come.   *before*

1079.
       He told to other prophettes mo
           that samyn ware wonnand with wyn: *together were dwelling with joy*
       "The kyng hath sent men me to slo,
12940   bot when thei come this close within,
       Spere our gattes, lett them not go!   *Bar*
           Thei sall not dere us with ther dyn.   *injure*
       The kyng sall sone come aftur so,
           and then sall we make his bale to blyn."   *sorrow to cease*
12945 Evyn als he sayd was done:
           tho men ware haldyn styll.
       The kyng com aftur sone
           and sayd the prophett untyll:

1080.
       "Us thynke, ser, thou dos noyght thi dett,   *duty*
12950   that wyll not pray to God for me
       And sees how that I am umsett   *beset*
           with fellows folke and may not flee."   *fierce*
       And with tho wordes for gref he grett,   *wept*
           the prophet of hym had pyté.
12955 He sayd, "Ser kyng, thi mornyng lett!   *cease*

      To have helpe hastely I hete thee.   *assure*
      Befor this tym to morn,
          here in this same cyté,
      Of wyn and oyle and corn
12960   sall all men have plenté."

1081.
      The kyng was of that word full fayn
        and his gud Ebrews yyng and old
      Bycause thei had oft sene certayn
        all trew that he befor had told.
12965   Bot on ther was spake ther agayn
        and brast owt with thir wordes bold.
      He sayd, "Bot God fro Hevyn yt rayn,   *Unless*
        slyke welth may not com in our wold."   *such*
      The prophet says, "Thou sall se
12970   this same that I of mell.   *speak*
      Bot for thou trows noyght me,   *because; believe*
        ther with thou sall not dele."

1082.
      Als the prophett sayd, sone aftur fell,
        for he askyd nothyng God to greve.
12975   Besyde that same cyté con dwell
        faur messell men in gret myscheve.   *leprous*
      Ylkon con to other tell,
        "We wun here owt of all releve.
      The hethyn men is myrth omell,   *among [themselves]*
12980   to them for mete is best we meve.
      For yf thei wyll us slo,
        that suld to us be levere   *preferable*
      Then thus to wun in wo
        and fele defawt forever.   *feel emptiness*

1083.
12985   "And yf thei with mete mend our chere,
        then have we not wast all our way."
      So went thei furth all faur in fere   *together*
        agayns the evyn on the sam day.   *evening*
      The hethyn oft, or thei com nere,
12990   ylkon con untyll other say,
      "The Ebrews comys in armys clere.
        The feldes ar full of rych aray."   *fields*
      And sone sum other sayd,
        als yt semed unto ther syght,
12995   "All Ebrews ar arayd
        us forto fell with fyght."

1084.

Kyng Benedab fast mad hym boun
    to lett all be withoutyn beld.   *courage*
He sayd, "I hard never swylke a sownd   *heard*
13000   of folke sen fyrst I was a chyld.
I warrand Egyp is comyn doun
    with Arabys full wod and wyld.   *Arabs*
Fast wyll I flee and take sum toun,
    for, and we byde, we be begyld."   *if we remain; deceived*
13005   He hyed hym fast before
    and left all his aray.
Them toyght thei wysest ware
    that fyrst myght wyn away.

1085.

Thei ware so mased in ther mode
13010   that of ther tressour toke thei none.
Thei forgatte all ther erthly gud,
    that greved noyght when thei ware gone.
The faur seke men full softly yode,
    thei wend have fon men mony one.
13015   Ther lyst was most to lyfes fode,   *pleasure*
    and therof fand thei full gud wone.   *they found a great amount*
Thei ete and dranke ther fyll,
    to warn them was no wyght.
And thore thei held them styll
13020   and rested all that nyght.

1086.

Thei ware up erly on the morn
    and trussed togeydder gold and fee.   *packed up*
And to ther howse thei have it born
    with other gud full grett plenté.
13025   Then went thei furth the gattes beforn
    and told semers of that cyté: *[the] gatekeepers*
"The hethyn has ther loges lorn,   *abandoned*
    and thei ar went, this warrand we."   *attest*
Tho kepers told the kyng
13030   how the faur seke men sayd.
He was glad of that tythyng,
    and hastely he purvayd.

1087.

The chef of all his chevalry
    he bad then wend in wyll and toyght
13035   Aftur this spech forto spyre and spye   *look and see*
    whedder thies sawes bene soth or noyght.   *truth*

"Thay may lyg in a buschement by   *ambush nearby*
    tyll we out of our beld be broyght,   *shelter*
And fall on us so sodanly.
13040   Therfor is gud the soth be soyght."
His knygh went and fand,
    als the seke men con say,
All welthes wele ordand
    and the men went away.

1088.

13045   Thei fand in chambers and in hall
    sylver and gold and garmentes gud
And garners full, both grett and small,   *granaries*
    with whette and flour for mannys fode.
Grett vessels in ther cayves we call,   *cellars*
13050   with wyn and oyle full styll thei stod,
And stalworthy stedes in ther stall
    with charyottes charged as thei yode.
Thei fand ther vitaylyng
    to releve all that land.
13055   Unto Joram the kyng
    this was joyfull tythand.   *news*

1089.

Kyng Joram wyst by sawes sere   *many signs*
    that his enmys war went away.
No mervell yf he had gud chere
13060   that lang had fun so fell affray.   *long; experienced such terrible fear*
Sone gart he crye be clarions clere
    and to his Ebrews con he say
That thei suld pase furth fast in fere   *as one*
    and ylkon geyte gud that he may.
13065   Then, both by hors and man,
    grett ryches have thei broyght.
Every on had plenté then
    that befor had ryght noyght.

1090.

No ferly yf tho folke ware fayn,
13070   and thei thanked God, os was worthy.
And als thei enturd in agayn
    into the cyté of Samary,
The man that sayd, bot God yt rayn,
    ther mete suld never so multyply,
13075   Evyn in the entryng was he slayn.
    So was fulfylled the prophecy
Qwylk Elysew by word wroyght,

that sayd he suld yt se,
   Bot for he trowd yt noyght,
13080   no help therof had he.

[A DIGRESSION ON DESPAIR, AND THE EXAMPLE OF JUDAS]

1091.
   Heyre may we fynd by fygur fayre   *figuration*
      exsempyll schewd to our syght
   That no man suld be in dyspare
      of Goddes mercy, ne of His myght.
13085 For als He made both erth and ayre
      and with His Word all wardly wyght,
   So is His myght to amend or payre   *harm*
      aftur ther wyll is wrang or ryght.
   Who in dyspare makes end
13090   so fro all fayth to fayle,
   Thei fayr furth with the Fend   *the Devil*
      to byde ever in his bayle.

1092.
   This case was kend by cursed Judas,
      qwylke sold his Lord that all may sayve.
13095 He trowd not trew for that trespase,
      therfor he wold no mercy crave.
   He was so sett with Satanas
      that with a cord that cursed knave
   Hanged hymself. And so he has
13100   his home in Hell and ever sall have.
   What syn so we have done,
      yf we to trowth wyll tent,   *listen*
   God wyll forgyf als sone
      as we wyll ryght repent.

1093.
13105 Also we may exempyll se
      and by swylke case have knawyng clere:
   All yf ourself so synfull be   *Even*
      that God wyll not our prayers here,   *hear*
   Of holy men then here wyll He
13110   that for us profers ther prayer.
   Then is yt gud wysdome that we
      send our saynges by sanctes sere   *prayers by many saints*
   And speke, whyls we have space,   *(time on earth)*
      to them we wott are wyse,   *know*
13115 Of God to gett us grace
      sone of our syns to ryse.

1094.

The Fend is qwaynt us forto qwell   *cunning; destroy*
   bot yf we lefe his lare lyghtly.

For and we in his donger dwell,   *if we; power*
13120   he makes our myse to multyply,   *errors*

As yt with Judas fyrst befell.
   For he mystrest in Goddes mercy,

He hanged hymself and is in Hell
   with wo, as his werke was worthy.

13125   God graunt us spech and space
   sone to forsake our syne,

And so to gete His grace
   that we to welth may wyne!

[The death of Ben-hadad (8:7–15)]

1095.

Now forthir of this same to see
13130   our processe playnly to declare:

Kyng Benedab com to his cuntré
   and herd tell of this ferly fare,

How four messell mad hym to flee   *lepers*
   and all wyght men that with hym ware.

13135   Swylk schame ther in his hert had he
   no comforth myght hym cover of care.   *relieve of sorrow*

For he so fayntly fled
   and lefed all in that sted,   *left; place*

He lay seke in his bede
13140   in dowt forto be ded.

1096.

With no kyns medcyns wold he mell,   *deal*
   so was he angred inwardly.

He cald a prince heygh Azabell,   *Hazael*
   and bad hym take tressour and cumpany,

13145   And wend furth fast, for nothyng dwell,
   unto that cyté of Samary,

And pray the prophett hym forto tell
   whedder he sall lyfe or dy.

The prince the cuntré knew;
13150   he went, and sone he fand

The prophett Elysew
   and proferd hym his presand.

1097.

"Syr, the kyng of Syry certayn
   is seke, and hydder he hath me send

13155   To wytt sum certayn of his payn,
            wedder yt sall sesse or sone make end.
         He prays thee take this presand playn."
            The prophett says, "That may not me amend.
         Bot have yt home with thee agayn
13160   and say hym als thou sall be kend.   *told*
         Lere hym that he sall lyfe   *Instruct*
            and in that poynt hym plese;
         Els may thou mater gyf
            to do hym more dysese.   *discomfort*

1098.

13165   "Bot hardely I to thee hete: *firmly; assure*
            within few days his ded is nere."
         The prophett then began to grete   *weep*
            and forto mon and make yll chere.   *moan*
         When Azaell saw hym so lete,   *behave*
13170   the cause full fast he con enquere.
         He sayd, "For thou sall make thee mete   *yourself fit*
            to wayte Ebrews with sorows sere."   *ambush; many*
         Azaell answerd ryght,
            "That ded I wyll deny.
13175   I am no man of myght
            forto make swylke maystry."

1099.

         The prophett hert was hevy os led.
            He sayd, "In thiself this I se.
         The kyng of Syry sall sone be ded,
13180   in lyfe no langer last sall he.
         And thou sall stand furth in his sted
            as crownd kyng of that cuntré.
         Then sall thou werke by weked red   *through wicked advice*
            and stroy this reme, that rewys me.   *realm; rues*
13185   Bot I am fayn forwhy   *glad because*
            I sall noyght se that syght.
         For of grett eld am I,
            me fayles both mynd and myght."

1100.

         The prince agayn his gate has grayd   *road has taken*
13190   als glad a man as he may gang.
         Unto the kyng of Syry he sayd,
            "Ser, thou sall fare well and wax strang."
         Bot yll lechyng for hym he layd   *doctoring*
            so that his lyf last not lang,
13195   And with the paynyms so he purvayd   *pagans*

        that he was mad kyng them amang.
        He rewled them so in rest
           and mad ther myrthes more.
        Thei sayd he was the best
13200   of all that had bene before.

[REIGN OF JORAM OF JUDAH (8:16–24; 2 CHRONICLES 21:4–20)]

1101.

        Now lefe we this Azaell
           that kyng of Syré hymself con ma,   *did make*
        And Joram, kyng of Israel;
           a lytyll tyme we lefe them twa.
13205   Of that other Joram wyll we tell,   *(i.e., Jehoram)*
           kyng of Jerusalem and of Juda.
        He wedded the doyghtur of Jezabell
           and Kyng Acab doyghtur alswa.   *also*
        Hyr name was Godolé,   *Athaliah*
13210   als clerkes may clerly knaw.
        Thrught hyr ordanyng was he
           to lef God and His Law.

1102.

        For scho was comyn of paynyms kyn,
           scho mad hym on hyr mawmentes mene.   *to practice her idolatry*
13215   When he to govern con begyn,
           he slogh up all his kynred clene,   *murdered*
        Fyrst his brethyr, he wold not blyn,   *brothers*
           and sythyn his dukes dughty be dene.   *brave dukes forthwith*
        Hym toyght no wrschep more to wyn   *honor*
13220   then greve them that gud men had bene.
        Thus may gud womans wyll
           to God full gretly plese,
        And als whore thei ar yll
           gare do full grett dysese.

1103.

13225   To tyrantré so con he tent,   *tyranny; attend*
           no gaine myght hym bettur glad.
        Sant Elysew unto hym sent   *Elisha*
           a byll that his maystur had made.
        Ely, whyls he in land was lent,   *Elijah; remaining*
13230   mad prophecy in bokes brad,
        And of this mater then he ment
           to bye, all yf yt long abad.   *tarried long (took a long time to occur)*
        For all behoved be done,
           poyntes of ther prophecys,

13235 Auder sythyn or sone.   *Either then*
    The wrytt was on this wyse:

1104.
    "Joram, for thou has left the Law
     that Moyses in his lyf con lere,   *teach*
    And unto dewlys thi dedes doos draw   *devilry*
13240 and of Hevyn has no hast to here,   *hear*
    And for thou has kylled, as we knaw,
     thi brethyr and thi dukes dere,
    Her is assygned in this saw
     how thou sall suffer sorows sere.   *many*
13245 Enmys sall on thee fall
     and defoule thee before
    Thi wyfes and wemen all
     that thou wold wrschept wore.   *desired to be honored*

1105.
    "Thi suns and thi doyghturs sall be slone,   *slain*
13250 als thou hath kyld other of thi kyn,
    And sythyn thiself sall be tone   *taken*
     with wo that thou sall never owt wyn.
    Thi lygham and thi lyms ylk one   *body*
     sall rankell and thou royte within,   *fester; rot*
13255 And medcyn sall thou never have none
     bot fall to fylth for thi syn.
    And so sall thou make end
     with wo, as ys worthy."
    All this care was contened
13260 with poyntes of prophecy.

1106.
    And for all suld wurth on swylke wyse   *happen in such ways*
     as God by prophettes purvayd has,
    With Ethyopes and Arabyse   *Ethiopians and Arabs*
     sone all his wyfes unwrschept was.   *dishonored*
13265 And all his suns with doles dyes   *sorrow died*
     bot one, the eldest, Occozias.   *Ahaziah*
    Hymself royted and myght not ryse, *He himself (i.e., Joram) rotted*
     with hydows payn so con he pase.   *die*
    For unlafull lyfyng   *(i.e., contrary to the Law)*
13270 thus was his endyng vyle.
    Then Occozi was kyng,
     bot he lest lytyll whyle.   *lasted*

[JORAM OF ISRAEL WOUNDED (8:25–29; 2 CHRONICLES 22:4–6)]

1107.

	Now lefe we the kyng Occozi.	*Ahaziah*
	of other Joram wyll we tell	
13275	That soyjornd kyng in Samary	*remained*
	and led that land of Israel.	
	He geydderd hym grett cumpany	
	with Kyng Benedab more forto mell,	*Ben-hadad (see note); interfere*
	Bycause he had wun with maystry	*violence*
13280	Ramatha and thor con he dwell.	*Ramoth-Gilead*
	Joram wold wyn agayn	
	that cyté yf he myght;	
	Bot his werke was in vayn,	
	that boldenese dere he boyght.	*cost him dearly*

1108.

13285	To Ramatha he con persew	
	and seged yt on ylka syd.	*besieged*
	And sone ther had he note all new:	*troubles*
	with a dart a wound full wyde.	
	He feled yt so that few yt knew,	*received it [in such a way]*
13290	bot ther he myght no langer byde.	*stay*
	He had a steward that heyygh Jew,	*who was named Jehu*
	to hym he toke his ost that tyd.	*host at that time*
	He went to Jezeraell	*Jezreel*
	softly, for he was sare.	*injured*
13295	Thore wonned Qwene Jezabell,	*dwelled*
	his moyder we ment of are.	*spoke of earlier*

1109.

	With hyr with lechyng thor he lay,	*medical help*
	for nerre home he myght not pase.	*closer to home*
	Kyng Occozi, his cosyn, herd say	
13300	how that his eme yll wounded was.	*uncle*
	He ordand hym full rych aray	
	of hors and harnes that he has.	
	To Jezeraell he toke the way,	
	and of his fare full fast he as.	
13305	So sojorn thei in fere	*together*
	with Jezabell, the qwene.	
	Full sone ther sall thei here	
	that sall turn them to tene.	*what shall; sorrow*

[JEHU PURGES ISRAEL'S ROYAL HOUSE AND RELIGION (9:1–10:36)]

1110.

	The nobyll prophett Elysew,	*Elisha*
13310	als God ordand them two omell,	*together*
	He sent another prophet trew	
	and bad hym go and tythynges tell	
	Unto the dughty duke ser Jew	*brave; Jehu*
	in the ost whore he con dwell,	*company*
13315	And that he suld anoynt hym new	
	forto be kyng of Israel:	
	"Say God hath ordand so	*thus*
	that he that forse sall fell	
	And venge hym on them two:	
13320	Joram and Jezabell.	

1111.

	"And bad hym stroy up all the kyn	*family*
	of Kyng Acab in elka eld,	*of every age*
	For he to Nabot dyd grett syne	*Naboth*
	that slogh hym falsly for his feld.	*vineyard*
13325	And Jesabell gart all begyn,	*caused all to begin*
	and sythyn scho gart with spere and scheld	*made*
	A hunderth prophettes lyfes to twyn	*end*
	for all the welth that thei had in weld."	*in possession*
	The prophett went to Jew	*Jehu*
13330	and told hym all this chaunce,	
	How the prophett Elysew	
	bad hym go take vengance.	

1112.

	And when he had sayd his errand	
	betwyx them two full prevely,	
13335	Thore he anoynt hym with his hand	
	and cald hym kyng of Samary	
	And of all els in Israel land,	*the land of Israel*
	and then he wendes his way in hy.	*goes; haste*
	The pepyll asked to understand	
13340	what this sendyng suld sygnyfye.	
	The duke told them tythyng	*the news*
	how Joram suld be ded,	
	And how he suld be kyng	
	and stand furth in his sted.	

1113.

| 13345 | Then was grett myrth to see them mete, | *gather* |
| | so wylly to that warke thei wore. | *willing* |

Thei spred ther cloghes befor his fete
   and raysed hym kyng, ose fell therfor,
And holy unto hym thei hete   *promised*
13350   to be his men forevermore.
And then thei gate the gaynest strett   *took the most direct route*
   to Jezarell, for Joram was thore.
When Kyng Joram hard say   *heard how*
   hys ost com on swylke a wyse,   *in such a way*
13355   He wend full wele that thei   *knew*
   had overcomyn his enmyse,

1114.

And therfor was he ferly fayn.   *wondrously glad*
   All yf his wound werkyd hym yll,   *Even*
He rayse and went Duke Jew agayn   *rose; [to meet] Duke Jehu*
13360   to welcom hym with word and wyll.
Tyll Nabod feld he passed playn,   *Naboth's field*
   and in that sted then stod he styll,
And with a dart thor was he slayn
   the propfecy to fulfyll.
13365   Lyke to his fader before,
   forto venge Nabod blod
Hys body left thei thore
   to bestes and foules fod.   *as food for beasts and birds*

1115.

Kyng Occozi, his cosyn, saw
13370   how that his eme to ded was dyght.   *unto death was struck*
Therfor on dregh he con hym draw
   and ordand hym full fast to flyght.
Bot als he rayd furth by a raw,   *hedgerow*
   the dukes men of hym had syght,
13375   And to hym thrast thei in a thraw
   so that he lost his lyves lyght.
Hys men his body bare
   to Jerusalem cyté.
That comyng was grett care   *sadness*
13380   to his moyder Godolé.   *Athaliah*

1116.

Duke Jew with his clene cumpany
   enturd the cyté of Jezeraell.
"Welcom, our kyng!" the folke con crye
   and mad hym homeg them omell.   *homage among them*
13385   All this was care and contrarye
   unto the fals Quene Jezabell.
To a hygh tour con scho hy,   *haste*

	and thore scho cast out wordes fell.	*fierce*
	Scho cryd to the duke, "Ser Jew,"	
13390	and oft scho con record,	*repeat*
	"Thou fals traytur untrew	
	sakles hath slayn thi lord."	*without cause*

1117.

	Scho wered hym with wordes kene.	*worried*
	He spyrd who spake tho wordes bold.	*asked*
13395	Thei sayd, "Ser, Jezabell, the quene,	
	Kyng Acab wyf ye knaw of old."	
	Then at hyr wordes he was full tene.	*very angry*
	He bad two men that wyghtly wold,	
	"Go cast hyr down yow two betwene,	
13400	so sall hyr sayng sowr be sold."	*talking be bitterly rewarded*
	To that werke ware thei prest	
	and hasted them full fast.	
	Over the wall thei hyr kest	
	that all hyr bowels brast.	*burst out*

1118.

13405	The duke was sett in Joram se,	*Joram's seat (i.e., throne)*
	resavyd with alkyns reverence ryfe.	*every kind of*
	Thei mad grett fest with mekyll gle,	
	and all thei love God of His lyfe.	
	On Jezabell yett mynd had he,	
13410	all yf scho had styrd mekyll stryf.	*even though she had stirred*
	He bad hyr cors suld bered be	*ordered that her corpse; buried*
	because scho was a kynges wyfe.	
	Bot with hundes was scho etyn	*dogs*
	or any man com thare.	*before*
13415	To bereyng was noyght gettyn	*burying; retrieved*
	bot nayles and banes bare.	*[anything] but; bones*

1119.

	Kyng Jew then cald his princese of price	*honored princes*
	and sayd, "Sers, loke ye mervell noyght	
	That I have wroyght now in this wyse,	
13420	both kyng and qwene tyll end broyght.	
	This is for nokyns covetyse,	*no kind of covetousness*
	that sall ye wyt wele in your toyght.	*know well; mind*
	Bot God in whom all lordschep lyse,	
	He wold that vengance suld be soyght	*desired*
13425	For Nabod, that nobyll man,	
	that was slayn for his feld.	
	For Sant Elysew sayd then	*Elisha (see note)*
	bestes suld ther bodes weld."	

1120.

Then answere all that folke in fere,	*people as one*
13430	"Ser, of this fare ar we full fayn.	
For sen God wold that yt so were,	*since*
no gud man suld say thor agayn."	*speak against it*
Then sent he folke both fere and nere	*far and near*
to seke on ylka syd certayn	*every*
13435	Kyng Acab kynred to conquere.	*Ahab's family*
Thei sessyd not or all ware slayn.	*until*
Both man and chyld and wyfe	
full wyghtly had ther wage.	*reward*
Thei left not on on lyfe	*one alive*
13440 | that langed to that lynage. | *belonged* |

1121.

To hym was told then prevely	
that ther was sexty chylder yyng,	
Kyng Acab suns, in Samary	
to soyjorn thore in save kepyng.	
13445	And to that cyté he sent forthy	*therefore*
and bad men suld byd for nothyng	*not delay at all*
Bot stryk of all ther hedes in hy	*strike off; haste*
and unto hym be lyve them bryng.	*quickly*
To hym tho hedes ware fette,	*brought*
13450	and sone he wold not blyn	
Bot on the walles them sett	
in sygne of Acab syn.	*sign*

1122.

Kyng Jew then wold no langer lend	*remain*
in Jezeraell so styll to stand.	
13455	To Samary then wold he wend,	*go*
the chefe cyté of Israel land.	
All folke that were to Acab frend,	
he feld them down wher he them fand,	*killed*
And all fals prophettes he schope to shend	*caused to die*
13460	that Jesabell thor had ordand.	*ordained (i.e., by her actions)*
And all by a sotell sleght	*cunning trick*
ordand he yt suld be.	
He gart cry all on heght	*caused it to be cried out*
throught owt all that cuntré	

1123.

13465	That he wold make thor sacrafyce	
to Beall, that was god of Tyre.	*Baal*
And all that wold werke on that wyse	*worship*
he sayd suld have his helpe to hyre.	

The fals prophettes full fast con ryse,
13470   to do that ded was ther desyre.
And sone thei soyght for that assysse
    to Samary, both sun and syre.   *son and father (i.e., all of them)*
The kyng this forward fest,   *agreement made*
    when thei ware samned so,   *gathered*
13475 Who so lufed Beall best
    into the tempyll at go.

1124.

He sayd, "Tho that have bene abowt
    to wrschep hym with word and wyll,
Within the tempyll sall thei hym lowt   *submit to him*
13480   and all ther sacrafyce thor fulfyll.
All other folk sall byd ther owt
    and pray to hym be stevyn full styll."   *words*
All this was done withoutyn dowt.
    Who lufed hym best sone lyked yll.   *pleased*
13485 The fals prophettes ylkon
    with wyfes and chylder yyng
Into the tempyll ar gone
    at bydyng of the kyng.

1125.

When all the fals prophettes ware past
13490   into the tempyll of ylk eld,   *every age*
The dures and wyndows spered he fast,   *doors; barred*
    and when he them wele festyd feld,   *he had them well enclosed*
Att ylka corner gart he cast
    als mekyll wod os men myght weld,   *as much wood*
13495 And brynt all up with wyndes blast
    that non myght be tyll other beld.
Yf any withoutt ware leved   *remained*
    that to Beall had tone,   *given [honor]*
He gart strykke of ther hed.
13500   so ware thei stroyd ylkon.   *destroyed every one*

1126.

Then gart he layte thurgh all that land   *searched*
    who wold be boun unto Beall,   *loyal*
And mawmentes, that ware made with hand   *idols*
    of sylver and gold and gud metall,
13505 He stroke all down and lete non stand
    with the belders in bowre and hall,   *dwellers*
So that the folke no favour fand
    bot in grett God that governs all.   *except*
Both be est and west

13510   thei wrschept God allway.
            Then regned he in gud rest
            and rewled in ryght aray.

[ATHALIAH'S REIGN OVER JUDAH (11:1–3; 2 CHRONICLES 22:10–12)]

1127.
            Kyng Acab doyghtur Godolé   *Athaliah*
            held all Juda in hyr awn power.
13515   Yt was grett sorow hyr forto se
            hyr sun body broyght on bere.   *son's body; bier*
            Hyr brother Joram, ded was he,
            and Jezabell, hyr moyder dere,
            And all hyr kyn in that cuntré.
13520   This was full herd to hyr at here.   *very hard for her to hear*
            Therfor grett athes scho sware   *oaths*
            to venge hyr vilansly   *villainously*
            And to stroy les and mare   *(i.e., everyone)*
            the kynred of Kyng Davy.

1128.
13525   Scho sayd, "Sen thei thus begyn
            Kyng Acab kynred forto sla,   *Ahab's family*
            Ther sall never none of David kyn
            lyf to be kyng of Juda."   *live*
            Scho gart dystroy both more and myn
13530   that scho wyst ware comyn of that kyn swa.
            Bot a yyng chyld away con wyn
            by helpe of Byschop Joiada.   *Jehoiada*
            He was hyd with his wyf   *(I.e., the boy); his (Jehoiada's)*
            in a chamber full fast,   *bedroom*
13535   And so thei sayved his lyf
            unto sex yer was past.   *six years were*

[JOASH ANOINTED AND ATHALIAH OVERTHROWN (11:4–21; 2 CHRONICLES 23:1–27)]

1129.
            The chyldes name was cald Joas,   *Joash*
            Kyng Acaze sun forsoth was he.   *Ahaziah's son truly*
            Bot thore wyst no mo how yt was
13540   bot Joiada and his mene.   *company*
            He thynkes with all the helpe he has
            to sett hym in Kyng David se   *David's throne*
            Over Juda with power to pase,
            qwylke that tyme governs Godolé.
13545   He sent clerkes that he knew
            thurghowt all that cuntré

To prestes and prophettes trew
   and dekyns in sere degré.   *deacons of every rank*

1130.

        He bad thei suld com certan day
13550   to Jerusalem at make offerand.
        Unto hys sand durst non say nay,   *message dared*
          for he was byschop of that land.
        To Jerusalem the toke the way,   *they took*
          redy to do all his commawnd.
13555   When all ware geydderd in gud aray,
          he sayd, "Sers, ye sall understand:
        God heyght to Kyng David   *promised*
          and furth to hys barn teme   *children's offspring*
        To be kynges of this kyth   *land*
13560   of Juda and Jerusalem.

1131.

        "And in this tym is so betyd
          als Godlé hath ordand evyn: *Athaliah*
        Of David kyn may non be kyd,   *known*
          bot thei be stroyd aftur hyr stevyn.   *command*
13565   Here is a chyld that I have hyd
          and noryscht now yeres sevyn.
        That he be kyng, this wold I byd,
          for nere that kyn is non to nevyn.   *mention*
        And so sall God be payd,   *pleased*
13570   for els is all owt gone."
        Be all assent thei sayd,
          "Ser, we ar payd ylkon."   *pleased each one*

1132.

        Into the Tempyll thei toke the gate,
          and Joas for ther kyng thei ken.   *acknowledged*
13575   Thei raysed hym up in kynges astate,
          in David se thei sett hym then.   *throne*
        The byschope bad men yeme the gate   *watch*
          for Godolé and for hyr men,
        And, yf thei com to make debate,
13580   to slo them and thei ware slyke ten.   *such*
        Scho gate hyr men of myght
          unto the Tempyll to gang.
        To ded thore was scho dyght;   *death*
          sum toyght scho lyfed overlang.

1133.

13585	The gud byschop than Joiada	
	cast down the tempyll of Beall	
	And other mawmentes mony ma	*idols*
	that men had mad of sere metall.	*much metal*
	Then all the kynred of Juda	
13590	gart he sone togeydder call,	
	And Joas for ther kyng thei ta	*took*
	and sett hym in Kyng David stall.	
	He lyfed in pese and rest	
	and wed a worthy wyfe.	
13595	To pay God was he prest	*please; eager*
	whyls Joiada last in lyfe.	

[HAZAEL THREATENS JERUSALEM; JEHOAHAZ REIGNS IN ISRAEL (12:17–13:9)]

1134.

	Bot aftur sone so yt befell	
	that in his trewth he wex untrew,	*grew*
	Als we sall sone here aftur tell,	
13600	bot fyrst we wyll nevyn noyes new.	*mention*
	The kyng of Syre, ser Azell,	*Hazael*
	with mony Sarsyns con persew	*Saracens (i.e., pagans)*
	To stroy Kyng Jew of Israel	*Jehu*
	by the prophecies of Elysew.	
13605	Thei brynt town and cyté	*burned*
	to Samary on ylka syde.	
	Kyng Jew was fayn to flee	
	and fro ther harm hym to hyd.	

1135.

	He regned twenty-sevyn yer,	*years*
13610	full ryall kyng in rych aray,	
	And then he dyed with sorows sere,	
	when all his welth was went away.	
	And Joacas, hys sun so dere,	*Jehoahaz*
	was crowned kyng aftur his day.	
13615	Bot he was noyght, als men may lere,	
	lyke to his fader in lefull lay.	*lawful loyalty*
	Kyng Jew sun Joacas	
	now leve we renand thore,	*reigning*
	And of yyng Kyng Joas	*Joash*
13620	now wyll we muster more.	

[DEATHS OF JEHOIADA, HIS SON, AND JOASH (12:19–21; 2 CHRONICLES 24:15–27)]

1136.

Grett wrschep in his yowth he wan	*honor*
ay whyls he in God con trow.	*ever while*
Bot Joiada, that nobyll man,	*Jehoiada*
dyed aftur then in lytyll thraw,	*in a short time*

13625 And Zacary, his sun, was than   *Zechariah*
   ordand byschop of ther law.
  Kyng Joas sone aftur begane
   to yll dedes hym forto draw.
  He forsoke Goddes servyce
13630   and lyfed in mawmentry.   *idolatry*
  All wroyght on that same wyse
   that used hys cumpany.

1137.

  The laws of God hym lyst not lere. *it pleased him not to follow*
   That was foly, and so he fand.
13635 Bot for hys werkes to God ware dere *But because*
   whyls Joiada had lyf in land,
  He warned hym by prophettes sere   *many*
   his yll lyf to lef of hand.   *to let go*
  And Zacary was byschop nere;
13640   he styrd hym most, I understand. *stirred*
  And for he proved hym playn
   how he his myse suld mende,   *sins*
  In the Tempyll was he slayn
   evyn at the auter ende.   *altar*

1138.

13645 To serve God as he con stand,
   so was he kyld with Kyng Joas. *killed by*
  All the grett favour that he fand
   in Joiada forgettyn he has.
  And for he was to God grocheand, *insulting*
13650   his powere sone gun payre and pas, *disintegrate*
  And full hard hape com hym on hand *fortune*
   with grett were, os he worthy was. *uncertainty*
  The kyng of Syre, Azaell,
   that we spake of before,
13655 With grett ost on hym fell
   and stroyd up all that store. *destroyed all that possession*

1139.

  He cast down castels, townes, and towrs,
   ther myght no strenght agayn hym stand.

He brynt ther burghes, hales, and bowrs	*halls, and homes*
13660 and all ther frutt wher he it fand.	*their fruit*
Kyng Joas than full lowly lowrs,	*frowns*
and lever he was to lefe of hand	*leave behind*
All ryches and erthly honowrs	
then forto lose his lyf in land.	
13665 He gafe them all the thressour	*treasury*
and all the vessel of price	*worth*
That his elders before	
had sett to Godes servyce.	

1140.

Phylysteyns then ware ferly fayn	*very glad*
13670 for goddes that thei togeydder brast.	*goods; packed up*
Kyng Azaell went hom agayn	
with tressour all withoutyn taste.	*without difficulties*
Kyng Joas lyfed with mekyll payn,	
for Jerusalem was roved and rast.	*plundered*
13675 Sythyn with hys awn men was he slayn,	*Then*
for all that cyté so had he wast.	*laid waste*
Of yeres aght and fawrty	*forty-eight years*
regned he befor his dede.	
Then his sun Amazi	*Amaziah*
13680 was crownned in his sted.	

[ELISHA'S DEATH AND HIS FINAL MIRACLE (13:10–21)]

1141.

Long aftur this so yt befell:	
another kyng that heygh Joas	*Jehoash*
Governd that land of Israel	
aftur his fader, Kyng Jocas.	*Jehoahaz*
13685 Sant Elysew then thor con dwell,	*Elisha*
and in that same tyme seke he was.	*sick*
Kyng Joas when he herd so tell,	
to vysett hym grett hast he has.	*visit*
His seknes so sore he plenyd	*mourned*
13690 and sayd, "Ser, and thou dy,	*if you die*
My strenght mon be restrened;	
therfor I am sory."	

1142.

The prophett comfort than the kyng	
and sayd, "The soth we sone sall knaw	
13695 Wher thou sall lang lyf in lykyng	*Whether*
and be owt of thi enmys aw."	*fear*
A bow he gart unto hym bryng	

and bad the kyng bend yt and draw
And schote arows at his desiring
13700   evyn as hym lyst both hegh and law.
Thre arows schott he sone,
    the bow than down he layd,
And when he so had done,
    the prophet was noyght payd.   *pleased*

1143.
13705 He sayd, "Ser, had thou schott all thies,   *all these [arrows]*
    thou suld have had lordschep in land
And overcomyn all thin enmyse,
    the Phylysteyns, whore thou them fand;   *wherever*
And now bycause thou schott bot thryse,
13710   bot thre tyms thou getes the overhand."   *you will get the upper hand*
When he had sayd on this wyse,
    the kyng went home full sore wepand.
Then dyed Sant Elysew,
    and for he lufed His Lay,   *God's Law*
13715 God sent full grett vertu
    for hym aftur his day.

1144.
When he was dede, his cors thei dyght   *corpse*
    in a grave stalworthy of stone.
A man was murdred on a nyght
13720   with thefes that had his tressour tone.   *thieves; goods stolen*
And for he suld be owt of syght
    that of ther werkyng wytt suld none,   *none should know*
That ded cors thei had hid full ryght   *dead body*
    thor Elysew was layd alone.   *where*
13725 And when yt neghted nere   *approached near*
    to the cors of Elysew,
Yt rayse up hole and fere   *rose; whole and healthy*
    and told this tale for trew,   *truth*

1145.
How that he was with enmys slayn
13730   and stylly stokyn under the stones,   *quietly stuck*
And how God gaf hym lyf agayn
    by vertu of tho blessed bones.
So may men see yt was certayn
    that he lyfed nobly for the nones,   *all the time*
13735 When God wold schew swylke power playn   *openly*
    aftur his ded ofter then ones.   *more often than once*
For oft tyms seke and sore
    that to that place persew,

13740	Full wele waryscht thei wore	*relieved*
	and hole of hyd and hew.	*made completely whole*

[JEHOASH AGAINST ARAM; AMAZIAH OF JUDAH (13:22–14:22; 2 CHRONICLES 25:1–28)]

1146.

	The kyng of Syre, Ser Azaell,	
	that named was an nobyll man,	
	Dyed aftur sone, and so befell	
	that aftur hym regned his sun Adan.	*Ben-hadad*
13745	Joas, the kyng of Israel,	
	wered on hym and thryse wrschep wan,	*warred upon*
	Als Elysew before con tell	
	by thre arows that ware schott than.	
	All that was lost before,	
13750	both cytés, town, and toure,	
	By strengh he con restore	
	and gate full grett honoure.	

1147.

	The kyng of Jerusalem Amasy,	*Amaziah*
	a herdy man of hert and hand,	
13755	Toyght he wold have the maystry	
	of hethyn folke whore he them fand.	
	He sembled sone grett cumpany	*assembled*
	of harnest men thryty thowssand,	
	And to Kyng Joas of Samary	
13760	sent he a full fayr presand	
	Of sylver and of gold,	
	a thowsand besandes bryght,	*bezants*
	And prayd hym that he wold	
	help hym with folke to fyght.	

1148.

13765	Kyng Joas was of this presand payd.	*gift glad*
	Therfor be lyve to hym he lent	*quickly*
	A thowsand men ryght wele arayd	
	to wend with hym whorso he went.	*wherever*
	And when thei ware full redy grad,	*fully made ready*
13770	God told Kyng Amazi His entent:	
	The folke that Kyng Joas had purvayd,	*provided*
	He bad thei suld agayn be sent.	*should be sent back*
	For and thei with hym yode,	*if; went*
	He sayd yt suld bewarre:	
13775	"Ther lyfyng is not gud,	
	therfore led them no ferre."	*farther*

1149.

This commawndment fro he had knawn,
    for he wold gare no grevance grove,   *cause; [to] grow*
Tho men he dyd sone be withdrawn;   *caused quickly to be*
13780   that toyght them was grett reprove.
And furth he went than with his awn,
    to Moabyse fast con he move.   *Moabites*
He stroyd all that was sett or sawn   *sown*
    and gatt gold to his awn behove
13785 More then men myght tell,
    and went home agayn.
The folk of Israel
    therfor ware nothyng fayn.   *not glad*

1150.

Bot grett dyspyte them toyght therby
13790   that he had swylke hape in his hende,   *such fortune*
For he refused ther cumpany
    and wold not lett them with hym wend.
Then this prowd Kyng Amazi,
    when God had hym swylke socur send,
13795 He lad his lyf in lechery   *led*
    and in Goddes Law hym lyst not lend.   *he cared not to follow*
And when prophettes hym blamed,
    in tene he told them tyll
Thei suld be shent and shamed   *destroyed*
13800   bot yf thei held them styll.   *unless*

1151.

So hegh pride in his hert he has
    hym thynke no prince suld be his peyre.   *peer*
He sent unto the Kyng Joas
    letturs mad in this manere
13805 That he and all that with hym was
    suld serve hym on sydes sere;   *every side*
Or els with playn ware wold he pas   *war*
    hym and his kyndome to conquere.
Kyng Joas sent agayn
13810   he was noyght ferd therfore;   *afraid*
Yf he ware mekyll of mayn,   *great in strength*
    he sayd Goddes myght was more.

1152.

To tell of all ther toyle that tyd   *struggle at that time*
    wold take long tym or all ware told.   *before*
13815 Kyng Amazi for his grett pride
    was putt to myschef mony-fold.

How he had herme, is not to hyde,	*harm*
when Kyng Joas had hym in hold.	*in his control*
His awn men gatt hym so on syd	
13820 that he was kylled with cares cold.	
Thei broyght hym to bereyng	*burying*
in Jerusalem wrscheply,	*honorably*
And after hym was kyng	
his sun that heyght Ozi.	*Uzziah*

[JEROBOAM II BECOMES KING OF ISRAEL (14:23–28)]

1153.

13825 Sone aftur this the kyng Joas	
dyed in the cyté of Samary.	
Jeroboam, his sun, than was	
kyng crowned of that cumpany.	
Unto hym come a prophett Jonas	
13830 and told to hym by prophecy	
Agayns the kyng of Syre to pase,	*go*
for sone he suld have vyctory.	
He ordand hym and yode	
with baytell ryght arayd,	
13835 And all was done in dede	
evyn als the prophet sayd.	

[STORY OF JONAS (JONAS 1:1–4:11)]

1154.

Now in this tym is forto tell	
how God to men musters his myght,	
And of grett ferlys that befell	*wonders*
13840 to this prophet that Jonas hyght,	*is called Jonas*
And how God unto hym con tell	
of Ninivé that day and nyght	*Nineveh*
Unto His resons ware rebell.	
And for He wold rewle them ryght,	
13845 He bad Jonas go preche	
to tho men evyn and morn	*those*
And His Law to them teche	
so that thei ware noyght lorn.	*abandoned*

1155.

Jonas herd tell of Nynyvé	
13850 and of the folke so fell thei wore	*fierce*
And yll-doers in all degré,	*evildoers in every way*
therfor he dred hym to come thore.	
He gate hym schypmen over the se	*hired for himself shipmen*

and ordand hym full fast therfore
13855   In sum fere cuntré forto be,   *far*
        that God and he suld mete no more.
     This was a foull foly   *folly*
        when he so fondly dyd.
     God ys ever Allmyghty,
13860   from Hym may noyght be hyd.

1156.

     With maryners full sone he mett
        that sayd thei suld sayle to Cecile.   *Sicily*
     Gud hyre to have thore he them hett   *Good wages; promised*
        to helpe hym to that uncouth yle.
13865   Bot in the se when thei ware sett
        and fro the land full mony a myle,
     Swylke stormes blew and on them bett   *Such; beat*
        thei wened to be lorn in lytyll whyle.   *believed they would be dead*
     The merchandes them amang
13870   cast owt the ryches fele,   *many*
     Bot the storme was so strang
        thei had no hope of hele.   *living*

1157.

     So when thei ware thus stratly sted   *in dire straits*
        in poynt that perell never to pase,   *amid indications*
13875   Thei kest lotes als ther counsel red,   *cast lots as their beliefs advised*
        and sone the lote fell on Jonas.
     Thei layted whore he lay on a bed,   *searched*
        and asked hym what he done has.
     He sayd, "Fro God thus am I fled,
13880   and all this wo for me yt was.
     I knaw to God my gylt
        and all my weked toyght.   *thought*
     Bettur ys that I be spylt
        then tho that trespast noyght."   *those who*

1158.

13885   When thei this herd, thei had pyté
        that his lyf suld no langer last.
     Bot for yt myght no bettur be,
        into the se thei have hym cast.
     Then sayled thei fast to ther cuntré,
13890   and fro all perels are thei past.
     And with a whalle sone hent was he   *whale soon seized*
        that nawder flesch ne bon brast.   *nor bone were broken*
     Thre days and thre nyghtes
        was he within that whalle.

13895   So con God schew His myghtes
       apon His frendes to fall.

1159.
     When thre days and thre nyghtes ware gone,
       that fysch unto the banke hym broyght
     And in that land leved hym alon   *left*
13900   whylke God bad fyrst he suld have soyght.
     With mornyng then he mad his mone   *mourning; moan*
       and wyst he had unwysly wroyght.   *knew; worked unwisely*
     Another tyme God hath hym tone   *Once more; taken*
       and told unto hym eft His toyght:
13905   "Wende unto Nynyvé
       and tell to more and myn: *more and less (i.e., everyone)*
     Both thei and ther cyté
       sall synke down for ther syne

1160.
     "In faurty days bot yf thei pray   *unless*
13910   and do swylke penance as to Me pays."
     Then Jonas went wyghtly his way,
       he durst no langer make delese.   *delays*
     That cyté was, als we here say,
       so mekyll and so wyde of ways   *great*
13915   That unethes that any man may   *scarcely*
       a fote pase thrugh yt in thre days.   *on foot*
     Jonas enturd within,
       als God had hym purvayd.
     To preche con he begyn
13920   and thus to them he sayd:

1161.
     "Your Savyour thus has me send
       to warn yow how His wylles wore:
     'Bot yf ye wyll your myse amend   *Unless; sins*
       and graunt to greve your God no more,
13925   Or faurty days ben comyn tyll end,   *Before; are come to an end*
       sall ye have sorows sere and sore.   *many*
     To Hell your cyté sall dyscend,
       als other fyfe hath done before.   *five*
     Thei used unkyndly syn,   *unnatural*
13930   als ye werke now all ways.
     Be lyve bot yf ye blyn,   *Unless you quickly cease*
       your cyté synkes,' He says."

1162.

Sone all tho folke of Nynyvie,
   qwen thei herd of this carfull cry,   *sorrowful*
13935   Graunt ther gylt with grett pety   *pity*
   and mekly asked of God mercy.
And the kyng of that same cyté,
   the qwene, and all ther cumpany
Laft all ther ray of ryalté,   *Abandoned; array of royalty*
13940   and sekes and hayres thei hent in hy.   *sackcloth and hairshirts they seized in haste*
And so cled sat thei down
   full low both more and lese,   *(i.e., everyone)*
And cast powder over ther croun   *ashes*
   in maner of meknese.

1163.

13945   When thei ware then thus stratly sted,
   the kyng gart be his commawndment   *caused*
That all folk suld in sekkes be cled   *be clad in sackcloth*
   and to mete suld thei take no tent.   *food; heed*
Yyng barns also suld not be fed   *Young children*
13950   bot that the lyf ware in them lent,   *unless*
Nore bestes also suld not be led
   to fude or faurty days ware went,   *before; spent*
So that both man and best
   suld pray and fast fro mete
13955   Of syns to be releschest   *released*
   and forgyfnes to gete.

1164.

When God saw them so benly bow   *obediently*
   and do His bedyng bowsomly   *humbly*
And holly heyght in Hym to trow   *wholly promise; trust*
13960   and forsake all ther mawmentry,   *idolatry*
Ther lyfyng then He con alow
   and graunt them grace and gud mercy.
This schewys to uus all holly how   *show to us*
   all sall have welth that are worthy.   *bliss*
13965   As the prophet Jonas
   was thre days in the se,
So Cryst in erthe here was
   bered be days thre.   *buried*

1165.

Then stalked he fro that cyté styll,
13970   and the pepyll fast with penance prayd.
He luged hym heyght under a hyll   *set himself high*
   to se what suld be aftur grayd.

And ay he loked that cyté untyll   *ever; unto that city*
    when yt suld synke, os he had sayd.
13975   And for yt stud, hym angerd yll,
    bot God was of ther pennance payd.   *gladdened*
And thayr prayer Hym plessed,
    therfor had thei ther boune.   *reward*
Jonas was yll dysplessed
13980   with hete of the sun full sone,

1166.

Als yt in somer seson is sene.
    Bot God, that sone may send all seele,   *happiness*
He mad an yvyn grofe grene,   *ivy grow green*
    that umbrayd hym ever ylk dele.   *covered; every part*
13985   So sat he styll two hyllys betwen;
    that all suld wast, he wend full wele.   *knew full well*
And to hymself he sayd in tene,   *grief*
    "This fayr is fals, fully I fele."
Bot on the morn be prime   *by [the hour of] prime*
13990   then wex his mervell more.
The son was clere that tyme,
    and the yvyn was noyght thore.

1167.

Then had he tene for that the tre
    was so away went on that nyght.
13995   God sayd to hym, "Why greves thou thee
    for thyng that is not in thi myght?
Me lykes to sayve now Nynivé   *It pleases me*
    because thei ar repentand ryght."   *repenting*
Then sayd he, "Lord, have mynd of me
14000   that I myght sone to ded be dyght   *death be taken*
And fro this lyfe be reft!"
    Thus leve we of ther thynges
And tell furth whore we left
    to end the Boke of Kynges.

[Zachariah and Uzziah (14:29–15:7; 2 Chronicles 26:1–23)]

1168.

14005   Kyng Jeroboam we told of before
    of Israel and of Samary,
He dyed when he myght lyf no more,
    when faurty yeres ware gone fully.
And in his sted was crowned thor   *place*
14010   his eldest sun heyght Zacary.   *named Zachariah*
Hym wyll we lefe now styll in store

and carpe furth of Kyng Ozi.   *speak forth; Uzziah*
Jerusalem and Juda
    begane he to governe wele.
14015 Bot sythyn he fayled ther fra
    with foly, that con he fele.

1169.

Ay whyls he was a nobyll man,
    all had daynteth with hym to dele.   *pleasure*
He wered on Sarsyns and so wan   *warred against the Arabs*
14020 grett wrschep and grett werdly wele.   *honor; worldly wealth*
To by and byg fast he began
    borows fayre and cetys fele,   *towns; cities strong*
And wele lufed was he than
    ay whyls he was of lyvyng lele.   *loyal [to God]*
14025 Goddes Tempyll ryght he arayd
    and mad gret cost theron,
Evyn as yt was purvayd
    in tyme of Salamon.

1170.

He was chefe of all chevalry
14030 whore so he come in all cuntré.
On mold was no man so myghty,   *On the earth*
    ne none so grett of gold ne fee.
So was he sett in surquidry
    he held non half so gud os he.
14035 Therfor he fell in fond foly
    and past all over his awn degré.
The Jews used ylk yere
    to make a fest of price
And hald that day full dere
14040 with solempne sacrafyce.

1171.

And so befell on that same day
    Kyng Ozi wyll no langer byd.   *wait*
Into the Tempyll he toke the way,
    and to the auter he hym hyed.   *altar; hastened*
14045 He revescht hym in ryche aray,   *ravished himself*
    as byschopes used in that tyd.   *in that time*
"I sall gyf sens," thus con he say,   *give incense*
    so was he sett in pomp and prid.
To the sensurs he brayd   *rushed*
14050 and gaf sens full gud sped.
The prestes ware not apayd   *pleased*
    and blamed hym for that ded.

1172.

"Syr kyng," thei say, "to sayve thi grace,
    swylk offyce is not unto thee.

14055   Non aw at entur into this place   *None ought*
    bot connand clerkes of dygnyté,   *knowledgeable*

As prelates that the power has
    and prestes and dekyns of degré."

Unto ther tales no tent he tas;   *he takes no heed*

14060   that boyght he sone, all men myght se.

God toke vengance in hye
    and sent on hym ryght thore

The evyll of meselry.   *leprosy*
    so foule was none before.

1173.

14065   He was so lothly on to loke   *loathly*
    that none had lyst with hym to lend.   *desire*

Bot frendes and felows hym forsoke
    themself fro seknes to dyffend.

The lordes and knyghtes that counsell toke   *decision made*

14070   owt of the cyté hym to send.

And thor he wonned with wo and woke   *dwelled; misery*
    and so in myschef mad his end,

For he tent not to   *he does not listen to*
    presthed ne to prelate,

14075   And putt hymself to do
    that fell not for his astate.   *estate*

1174.

Be this ensampyll may we se,   *example*
    sen vengance thore so sone was sene,   *since; there; soon; seen*

Us ow to honour ylke degré   *We ought; each rank*

14080   of Holy Kyrke that kept is clene,   *Church; pure*

And noyght to wene ourself that we   *think*
    be worthy swylk maters to mene,   *consider*

Bot als thei deme in dew degré   *Except as they judge; manner*
    to drese our dedes on days be dene.   *arrange; deeds; straightway*

14085   God graunt us well to werke
    and so to lyfe and end

In trowth of Holy Chyrche
    that we to welth may wend!   *bliss; journey*

EXPLICIT LIBRI REGUM.

IOB.

[JOB'S UPRIGHTNESS (1:1–6)]

1175.

Job was a full gentyll Jew,
14090   of hym is helfull forto here.   *salutary to hear*
For whoso his condicions knew
    of meknes myght fynd maters sere.
Ever in his trewth he was full trew,
    os men may in his lyfyng lere.
14095 He lyfed ever als a lele Ebrew,   *loyal Jew*
    in the land of us he had no pere.   *(i.e., on earth)*
All yf he ware to knaw
    full mekyll in erthly myght,
In hert he was full law   *very humble (low)*
14100   and dred God day and nyght.

1176.

He honerd God in all degré
    and ever was dredand to do yll.   *afraid; evil*
Fro foyles was he freke to flee   *fools; eager*
    and fayn all frenchep to fulfyll.   *glad*
14105 He had a wyfe both fayr and free
    that redy was to werke his wyll,
And sevyn suns semly to se   *sons handsome*
    and doyghturs thre full stabyll and styll.
Of gold God had hym sent
14110   to mend with mony a store,   *great supply*
Rych robys, and ryall rent.
    Myrth myght no man have more.

1177.

He had hymself sevyn thowsand schepe   *sheep*
    in flokkes to flytt both to and fro,   *flocks to go*
14115 Thre thowsand camels forto kepe,
    and fyve hunderth asses also.   *donkeys*

He had in hyllys and daylys depe   *deep dales*
  fyfty yoke of oxyn in ylkon two
And servantes wele to wake and slepe
14120 in dyverse werkes with them to go.
For plowes he had plenté
  his land to dele and dyght.
In all the Est cuntré
  was non so mekyll of myght.

1178.
14125 All yf he regned in rych aray,   *Although*
  of his gud rewle thus men may red: *good rule [of himself]; read*
He lyfed full lelly in His Lay
  and to grefe God he had grett dred.
His sevyn suns, als I herd say,
14130 mad ryall festes ther frendes to fede   *feasts*
Ever ylkon sere be dyverse day,
  and ther thre systers con thei bede
Ther fest so forto fyll
  with frendes old and yyng.
14135 Ther fader com them tyll
  and gafe them his blessyng.

[SATAN ASKS PERMISSION TO ATTACK JOB (1:7–12)]

1179.
The Fend that is our fals enmy   *(i.e., Satan)*
  to payr them putt hym furth in prese.   *injure; the throng*
Unto them had he grett envy
14140 and care to se them so wele encrese.   *sadness*
He come before God Allmighty
  to gette hym leve, this is no lese,   *lie*
With tene to turment Job body   *injury*
  so forto make his solace sese.   *end*
14145 All yf our Lord wele wyst   *Even though; knew well*
  of all his purpase playn,
Nerthelese yett als Hym lyst   *pleased*
  the Fend thus con He frayn: *ask*

1180.
"Whens comys thou, tell me in this tyd,   *From where*
14150 and whore abowt now has thou bene?"
He sayd, "Ser, I have walked wyd
  over all this werld withoutyn wene   *without doubt*
So forto seke on ylka syde
  for syners, and sum have I sene.   *sinners*
14155 Thor is my bourd to gare them byd   *game to cause; wait*

tyll I may turment them with tene."
God says, "Takes thou no hede
   to Job, My trew servand,
How he of God has dred,
14160   non lyke hym in no land?

1181.

"In mynd hc is full mckc and law,   *low*
   both sobour and sothfast for certayn."   *truthful*
Then sayd the Fend unto that saw,   *those words*
   "That Job Thee dredes ys all in vayn.
14165   Thou has so clossed hym, well I knaw,   *protected*
   that no grefe may go hym agayn.   *against*
Bot and Thou wold Thi hand withdraw   *if*
   and putt hym in my power playn,
Full sone then sall Thou se
14170   how he suld turn full tyte.   *very quickly*
He suld not sett be Thee
   the mountynance of a myte.   *value of a mite*

1182.

"Thou makes his catell forto creve   *grow*
   and so Thou rewardes hym with ryches
14175   That he may mene of no myschefe.
   What ground is then of his gudnes?"
Then sayd our Lord, "I gyfe thee leve
   of all his mobylles more and lese;   *movable goods*
Bot loke that thou no malyce meve   *stir up*
14180   his body to do any dystrese.
I graunt thee power playn
   of all his erthly gud."
Then was the Fend full fayn
   and fast fro God he yode.   *went*

[JOB LOSES HIS CHILDREN AND HIS RICHES (1:13–22)]

1183.

14185   So when tho two ware fayren in twene,
   the Fend sone putt furth his power.
Job chylder then a howse within
   ware bresed to ded and broyght on bere.   *beaten to death; biers*
Sythyn all his bestes he wald not blyn   *his (Job's) beasts he (Satan); cease*
14190   to slo them and his servandes sere.
And how this batell all con begyn,
   berys wyttenese mony a messynger
That unto Job con tell,
   syghand with sympyll chere,

14195   How all this fayre befell.
    Who wyll take hede may lere.

1184.
Fyrst com in on, wepand with wogh,   *weeping with woe*
    to Job whore he in blys con byd: *did live*
"Thin oxin went in wayn and plogh;   *went out with wagons and plows*
14200   thin asses pasturd them besyd.
Com folk fro Saba and theyn them drogh   *drew them off*
    and slogh thin hyne, is not to hyd.   *slew your servants*
I wan away with noy enogh
    to tell thee tythynges in this tyd."
14205   Unethes had he thus sayd   *Scarcely*
    when another com in
With a full balfull brayd,   *sorrowful rush*
    and thus he con begyn.

1185.
"A, ser," he sayd, "to me take tent,   *take heed*
14210   for I may tell of mekyll tene.   *sadness*
Thi sheperds and thi shepe ar shent,
    and all ther welth is wastyd clene.
A sodan fyre was on them sent,
    so brym before had never bene.   *such brim(stone)*
14215   To bare bones all ar thei brent,   *burned*
    bot I that was not nere them sene,
I com thee forto tell
    how all this tene betyd."   *happened*
Then langer he wold not dwell,
14220   bot sone com in the thryd.

1186.
"Ser," he sayd, "our yll enmyse,
    the Caldews, that we ever hath dryd,   *Chaldeans; dreaded*
Thei come with thre grett cumpanys
    of men of armys in yrne cled.
14225   The camels all withoutyn price
    have thei tone and furth with them led,
And sloyn thi servantes in the sam wyse
    bot me allon, that fro them fled.   *except*
I was full fayn to fle
14230   and sythyn full fast to go
Hyder at tell to thee
    of all this were and wo."

1187.

The ferth com then with febyll chere,   *fourth*
   the hardest hap in hand had he.
14235   "Alas," he sayd, "for sorows sere,
   that I suld ever sych syghtys se!
Thi sevyn suns and thre doyghturs dere
   ar ded, therfor full wo is me.
I sall thee say on what manere,
14240   for now ther may no mendes be.
Thei spake in certayn space
   to ete and drynke togeydder
In the eldest brother place,
   and ylkon come thei ydder.

1188.

14245   "And als thei ware within the wonys,   *building*
   sett at ther fest full fayr and fast,
A wynd com on them grett for the noyns   *at once*
   and all the howse sone down yt cast.
Yt bressed the barns both flesch and bons   *bruised the children*
14250   so that thei myght no langer last.
I fled and was full wyll of wons   *despair*
   tyll I was fro the perels past.
And, ser, sen thus is kend,
   I red yow werke als wyse.
14255   Grett mornyng may not amend
   wher no relefe may ryse."

1189.

When Job had herd of all this care   *sadness*
   and saw yt myght no bettur be,
His sorows ware so sere and sare   *varied and profound*
14260   that non for syte may on hym see.   *grief; look*
He rafe his cott and rent his hare,   *tore his coat; hair*
   swylke hevenes in hert had he.
Full well he wyst tho werkkes ware
   of the Fend and of his fals meneye.
14265   Down on his knese he kneled
   full low by hym alon,
And to Hevyn he beheld,
   and thus he made his mone: *lament*

1190.

"Lord God," he sayd, "mekyll is Thi myght
14270   amang mankynd here forto knaw,
That rewls all thyng be reson ryght
   Thi ryalté forto rede by raw.   *to rule properly*

Thou dos nother be day ne nyght
　　bot dewly evynhede, os Thee aw.　　　　　*proper justice; ought*
14275　Thou ponysch men here for ther plyght
　　at lern them forto luf Thin Law.
Thou kens me curtasly　　　　　　　　　　　*show*
　　of my defawtes before.
I wott I am worthy
14280　for syn to suffere more.

1191.
"Thou gafe me of Thin awn gudnese
　　all werldly welth to weld at wyll,
All ryall rentes with grett ryches,
　　all folke to be tendand me untyll.
14285　Now se I welle Thi wyll yt es
　　that fare no ferther to fulfyll.　　　　　*such things any further*
Blessed Thou be with more and lese!　　　　*in every way*
　　I love Thi layn both lowd and styll."　　*laws; publicly and privately*
When all this werke was wroyght,
14290　als men full ryght may rede,　　　　　　　*read*
That Job yit trespast noyght
　　nother in word ne dede.

[JOB LOSES HIS HEALTH (2:1–10)]

1192.
Bot when the Fend saw for certayn
　　that Job wold not unbowsom be,　　　　　　*disobedient*
14295　He hyde hym fast to God agayn　　　　　　*hastened himself*
　　to greve Hym in gretter degré.
Bot God than to reprove hym playn
　　sayd, "Satanas, now may thou se
That Job dredes me not all in vayn
14300　bot in lele luf and charité.　　　　　　*loyal*
All wo that thou hath wroght
　　both to hym and hys hyne,　　　　　　　　*household*
Thou may not chaunge his toyght
　　to skyft fro Me and Myne."　　　　　　　　*shift*

1193.
14305　Then sayd the Fend, "For all this fare
　　wyll he not waynd in warld to wend.　　　*shrink from*
For catell wyll he have no care,
　　he trows his frend wyll hym dyffend.　　*believes*
Bot wold Thou towch his body bare
14310　and suffer seknes on hym be send,　　　　*allow sickness*
So suld Thou wytt yf that he ware

lele lastand in Thi Law to lend."
God sayd, "I gyfe thee leve
   of his body all be dene.   *forthwith*
14315 Bot luke that thou not greve
   his sawle bot kepe yt clene."   *soul*

1194.
The Fend was then full fayn forthy   *therefore*
   that he of Job had swylk powsté.   *power*
He mared hym sone with meselry,   *leprosy*
14320 fro hed to fote nothyng was fre,
Bot blayns and bledders all his body   *pustules and blisters*
   and scabbes whor skyn was wonnt to be.   *supposed*
So satt he syghand sorely,
   grett sorow yt was that syght to se.
14325 All folke then hym forsoke
   that was his frend before.
Men lathed on hym to loke   *were loath*
   and ylk day more and more

1195.
The Fend more care unto hym cast   *grief*
14330 to make hym wake and wyll of wone.   *helpless*
Thys blayns and bleders bolnd and brast   *swelled and burst*
   and mad the flesch flytt fro the bone.
His servandes, that before ware fast,   *beside him*
   ware fayn to fle and leved none.
14335 Bot so he was kest at the last
   in a mydyng sett allone.   *midden (dunghill) chair*
He that no man wold greve
   befor for his ryches,
Now was muke most his releve   *muck (dung)*
14340 forto inforse his flesch.

1196.
He had no howse in forto dwell,
   ne cloghes for cold his cors to hyde,
Bot in that mydyng muke omell   *midden muck together*
   thor was his toure als for his tyd.   *palace*
14345 With a pott-scarth or with a schell   *potsherd*
   he scraped the scabys on ylka syde.
For yll are and unhonest smell   *sick air*
   ther wold non buske with hym to byde.   *no one would meet with him for long*
Bot in all his myschefe
14350 full trew was his trowyng   *belief*
That God suld hym releve
   and owt of bale hym bryng.   *suffering*

1197.

So os he rested in yll aray,
   his wyf turment hym more to teyne.   *tormented; anger*
14355   "Now may men se," thus con scho say,
    "of what condycions thou hath bene.
Blyse God and dy and wend thi way,
   for other welthys is none to wene.
Thou has not plessed Thi God to pay,
14360   that is wele by thi sorow sene."
"Alas," he sayd, "for dole,
   why frays thou me with flytt?   *insults*
Thou spekes evyn als a foyle   *fool*
   that hath no womans wytt.

1198.

14365   "Thier wordes thou werkes, we may warrand,   *These*
   thei are not rewled by ryght ne skyll.
Sen that we take here of Goddes hand   *Since what*
   all werldly welth to weld at wyll,
Why suld we not als stably stand
14370   when tenys and turfurs tydes us tyll,   *sorrows and misfortunes happen to us*
And love that Lord on ylka land,
   sen He governs both gud and yll.
God gyfes us here certayn
   to weld both wyld and tame
14375   And takes yt agayn.
   blest mot ever be His name!

1199.

"Of erth I wott I was furth broyght   *From dust I know*
   naked, yt nedes not at layn,   *be denied*
And, when my werldly werkes ar wroyght,
14380   with teyne then sall I turn agayn.
To bale or blyse wheder we be broyght,
   to Goddes bedyng we suld be bayn."   *obedient*
In all ther tales Job trespast noyght,   *these*
   ne spyd to spend his spech in vayn.
14385 So, als he lothly lendes   *loathly remains*
   alon in low degré,
Thre of his faythfull frendes
   soght fere his syte to se.

[Job's three friends (2:11–13)]

1200.

Thei come ylkon fro dyverse place,
14390   now wyll we here how that thei heyght: *are called*

Elyphath and Baladach toke that trace,   *Eliphaz; Bildad*
   and Sothar soyght to se that syght.   *Zophar*
For ylkon spake in dyverse space,
   so sall we wytt ther resons ryght.
14395 Bot when thei come before his face,
   to mell with mowth had thei no myght.   *speak*
Thei saw his syte so sad,
   for bale ther hertes myght breke.
Thei ware so mased and mad,
14400   a word thei myght not speke.

1201.

Bot on the erth then fell thei down
   and bett apon ther bodes bare.   *beat; bodies*
Thei rafe ther robes of rych renown,   *tore*
   and als rude bestes oft thei rare.   *roared*
14405 Thei cast powder on ther crown,   *ashes*
   as foran folke febylly thei fare.   *foreign*
And so thei satt in that sessown,
   syghand sex days with sorow sare.   *sighing six*
Job saw that thei sayd noyght,
14410   bot sat so lang alone
With mornyng as he moght.
   to God he mad his mone:

[JOB LAMENTS HIS PITIFUL EXISTENCE (3:1–26)]

1202.

"Alas," he sayd, "Lord, with Thi leve,
   why ledes Thou me thus to be lorn?   *forlorn*
14415 I have not gone Thee forto grefe,
   ne forfeytt so felly here beforne.   *transgressed so terribly*
Why suld I suffer swylke myscheve
   of all men to have scath and skorn?
Thi mercy, Lord, unto me Thou meve,
14420   els may I ban that I was born.   *otherwise; curse*
And wold God that I had bene
   fro bryth broyght to my grave.   *birth*
Then suld non me have sene
   swylke hydows harm to have."   *hideous*

[ELIPHAZ SAYS JOB HAS SURELY SINNED (4:1–5:27)]

1203.

14425 Elyphath herd then how he ment,
   and saw how he in bale was boun
And loved not God that it had lent,

bot more to blame he has begun.
"Job," he says, "thou takes no tent   *you take no heed*
14430   to wrschep God als thou was wun.   *you were meant to do*
Thou makes thiself an innocent,   *fashion yourself*
     as never defawt in thee was fun.   *found*
Thou was wonnt to wysch   *teach*
     how we suld suffer wo.
14435   Now thynke me wele be this
     thiself con noyght do so.

1204.
"To ruse thiself I red thou blyn,   *praise; advise you cease*
     yt dose us harme swylk wordes to here.
Wytt sothly it is for thi syn   *Know truly*
14440   that thee is sent thies sorows sere.   *you are sent these many sorrows*
Sen ther wunys none this werld within   *Since there lives*
     that in ther consciens are all clere.
How dare thou so boldly begyn
     to maynten mys on this manere,   *misdeed*
14445   To say thou has noyght done
     slyke fellows fandynges to fele!   *trials*
Man, knaw thiselfe ryght sone!
     Els wyll yt not be wele."   *Otherwise*

[JOB SAYS HIS COMPLAINT IS JUST (6:1–7:21)]

1205.
Then answerd Job with drery toyght
14450   and sayd to them that sat besyd:
"Wold God all yll that ever I wroyght   *everything I have done*
     and ther bales that I here byd   *these sorrows; suffer*
Ware both in a payre of balans broyght   *pair of balancing scales*
     forto be wowed and well dyscryd.   *weighed; judged*
14455   Then suld ye se yourself unsoyght,
     for all that ye can tell this tyd,
That my payns ar wele more   *are far more*
     and feller by sythes fyve   *more cruel by five times*
Then ever I synd before   *sinned*
14460   in lengh of all my lyf.

1206.
"My flesch is nother of yrn ne styele,   *iron nor steel*
     ne my banes ar not mad of brase   *bones*
Bot of freyle mater ylk dele   *frail; each part*
     that with full lytyll payn may pase.   *may pass [away]*
14465   And ye had faurth part that I fele,   *If; a quarter of what I feel*
     sore suld ye sygh and say, 'Alas,'

For I fayr werse, I wott full wele,
    then any wrech that ever was.
And ye myght wytt my wogh,   *If; know my woe*
14470   then suld ye fynd before
That I have sorow enogh
    yf ye make me no more.

1207.

"For so carfull sorows ware never sene,   *such*
    ne so saklese, and I durst say,   *causeless, if I dare say*
14475   And your tales tempyse me to tene   *tempt; anger*
    more then doles that I dre ylk day.   *suffer*
To Myghty God I wyll me mene,   *complain*
    ther is no mo that mend me may: *no other who*
Lord, lege me of thies carys keyn   *relieve; these sharp pains*
14480   or wyn me fro this werld away.   *take*
Sen servantes, frendes, and wyfe   *Since*
    are glad fro me to gang,   *go*
My saule laythes with my lyfe,   *is disgusted*
    Thou lattes me lyfe over lang.   *allow me to live too long*

1208.

14485   "And certes, Lord, with lefe of Thee,   *for certain; leave*
    in my mynd mervayle have I
That thou wyll putt furth Thi powsté   *power*
    and muster so Thi grett maystry   *mastery*
In swylke a wofull wreche as me
14490   that hath no strengh to stand therby,
And lettes full fellows folke go free   *very evil people*
    that mekyll mo wo ware worthy.   *of much more woe*
That suld be sene full sone   *very quickly*
    and penauns ordand wore   *if penance*
14495   Eftur mens dedes wore done,
    and nother lese ne more.   *neither*

1209.

"A, Lord, as Thou me mad with myght,
    so may Thou make me to have mede,   *reward*
And Thou may loyse with labour lyght   *destroy*
14500   my lyfe and all that lyfes in lede.   *in the nation*
Bot when the Day of Dome is dyght   *Judgment Day comes*
    men to be demed aftur ther dede,   *judged according to their deeds*
I sall be fun befor Thi syght   *found*
    sothfast enogh for any nede.
14505   For I wroght never swylke wrang,
    ne served never so unsele   *deserved such misery*

Forto have half so lang
   so fell payn als I fele."

[BILDAD SAYS JOB SHOULD REPENT (8:1–22)]

1210.

       Then Baldath myght no langer byde,   *wait*
14510   hym toyght this tale last to lang.
       He sayd, "Job, for thi pomp and prid
          is thou put in payns strang.   *are you*
       How dere thou thusgayte with God chyd   *in this way; quarrel*
          and deme that His werkyng ys wrang!   *judge*
14515   Thi dedes here has thou justyfyed
          als thou had never wonned men amang.   *as if you; dwelled*
       And, sertes, yf thou had bene   *[even] if*
          ay styll stokyn in a stone,   *ever stuck under a rock*
       Yytt suld thou not be sene   *judged*
14520   withowtyn syn gud wone.   *plenty*

1211.

       "For thou may here wysmen say thus,
          als Holy Wrytt wytnese allway:
       Septies in die cadet iustus —   *"Seven times the just will fall in a day"*
          he says that sevyn sythis on a day   *times*
14525   Syns ryghtwys men here amang us.   *sins*
          What sall then wreched syners say
       That ever are yll and vycyus   *vicious*
          and non bot God mend us may?
       Sen non may helpe bot He
14530   our myse forto amend,   *misdeeds*
       Mekly suffer suld we
          what saynd that He wyll send.   *trial*

1212.

       "And thou makes proveys here playnly   *If; proofs*
          that Goddes ordynance ys owt of skyll —   *reason*
14535   When thou thiself wyll justyfye
          and deme that thou hath done none yll —   *judge*
       Thore takes thou fro God Allmighty
          the fredom that falys Hym untyll.   *falls*
       For dome is His forto dystrye   *judgment; compel*
14540   both word and werke at His awn wyll.
       Thou demys God is not stabyll
          to stand as hee justyce,   *high*
       Or els unresnabyll,
          when thou says on this wyse   *manner*

1213.

14545 "That thi penaunce is mekyll more   *felt*
    then other folke before have feld,
   Or els thi werkes worthy wore   *were*
    that thou has wroyght in yowth or eld.
   I red thou sese and rew yt sore   *advise you cease*
14550   and beseke God to be thi beld,   *protector*
   Lese that thou fare no warre therfor,   *Lest; worse*
    for thou no thankyng to Hym wyll yeld.
   Yf God ware in gud wyll
    thi comforth to encrese,
14555 Swylke spech thi spede may spyll,   *relief*
    and therfor hald thi pese."   *hold your peace*

[JOB RESPONDS TO BILDAD (19:1–29)]

1214.

   Then answerd Job unto tho thre,
    and mekly thus he con hym mene.   *moan*
   "Alas," he says, "how lang thynke ye
14560   to turment me thus yow betwene?
   Of my payn suld ye have pety   *pity*
    that my frendes ay before hath bene.   *who*
   Vengance of God hath towched me,
    that is with sorow on me sene.
14565 And sen ye see my sore   *since*
    and castes yt not to keyle,   *relieve*
   Yowr gabbyng greves me more   *talking*
    then all the fawtes I fele.

1215.

   "Ye sett my fare bot als a fabyll,   *doings; fable*
14570   and my wordes tell ye wroyght in vayn *you say are*
   And says that I make God unstabyll,
    for that I pleyn me of my payn.   *complain*
   I say yt is unmesurabyll
    forto sett for my syn certayn,
14575 Bot God that kast me in this cabull   *this bondage*
    may, when Hym lyst, lawse yt agayn.   *loose it*
   Wold God my wordes ware wryttyn,
    that thei ware not tynt,   *lost*
   With a poyntyll of steylle   *stylus of iron*
14580   in a hard stone of flynt   *on*

1216.

   "So that thei myght ever more be ment *remembered*
    and made in mynd all men emang.

Then suld all wytt whore so thei went   *everyone know wherever*
  wheder my wordes ware wele or wrang,   *right*
14585 And yf I ever to syn assent
  to be putt to slyke payn strang.
God knaws my mynd and myn entent
  yf ye go whore ye have to gang.   *go*
And, sertes, yf ye me slo,
14590   my fayth sall ever be fast   *strong*
And never depart Hym fro,
  als lang os my lyf may last.

1217.

"My wytt is allway in this wyse,
  and so my trowth sall evermore be.
14595 My Sayvyour lyfes and never more dyse,   *dies*
  and on the last day deme sall He.   *judge*
Then fro the erth sall I upryse,
  both bone and flesch, in faccion free,   *fashion*
And with myn eyne in that assyse   *eyes; assize*
14600   my Sayvyour then sall I see.
All yf I byde in bale   *Even if I endure in grief*
  and be here bressed and brokyn,   *bruised*
Thor sall I ryse all hale   *There (i.e., at Doomsday); whole*
  when all your speche is spokyn.

1218.

14605 "And there shal ye allso be sene
  for all youre saunttering and your saws.   *hypocrisy; words*
And then sall I be fun als clene
  as ye that all this bostes blaws.   *who blows hard all these boasts*
Ye come als men me to mene   *as men to pity me*
14610   and seys me suffur so sore thraws,   *such sore wounds*
Bot more ye tempe me unto tene.   *sorrow*
  and God that all our conciance knaws,   *inner thoughts*
He wott I have not wroyght
  so gretly Hym agayn
14615 Wherfor I suld be broyght
  to fele slyke perles payn."   *feel such painful perils*

[ZOPHAR SAYS JOB IS WICKED (20:1–29)]

1219.

Sophar says then, "For soth I trow,   *truth I believe*
  Job, thou justyfyse thiself overlang.   *too much*
Yf thou had never done yll or now,   *before*
14620   thou servys to suffer sorows strang.   *you deserve*
For all thi werkes thou wyll avowe

whedder so thei were wele or wrang.
Wele bettur ware thee forto bow
   and graunt thi gylt now or thou gang.   *·before you go (die)*
14625 Thou wenes so all be wun   *think; accustomed*
   thi dedes to justyfye.
Bot that fare sall be fun   *revealed [to be]*
   full fals ypocrysie.

1220.

"For in this werld werkes none so wele
14630   that wott wheder his werke be wroyght   *knows whether*
Unto his sorow or to his sele.   *happiness*
   For, when the soth is all up soyght,
Of gud werke God dose ylk dele.   *does each part*
   Bot He yt werke, the werke is noyght.   *Unless*
14635 And of the Fend, als folke may fele,   *Devil*
   full yll bargans ere furth broyght.
Sen non ther werkes may wytt   *Since no one their*
   qwylk is trew forto treyst,   *trust*
Pray God to ordand yt
14640   and reward als Hym lyst.   *desires*

1221.

"Thou hath governd so grett degré
   and had this werld all at thi wyll.
Yf thou trespast to two or thre,
   ther durst none say that thou dyd yll.   *dared*
14645 And yf on trespast unto thee,
   all had he never so opyn skyll,   *even if; such evident reason*
Auder thou or other of thi meneye   *Either; company*
   wold nothyng spare his sped to spyll.   *advantage*
So for thi grett ryches
14650   that God gaf of His grace,
All men both more and lese
   ware fayn to take thi trace.   *glad to follow your lead*

1222.

"And now wyll non sett by thi saw   *message*
   als wytty os thi wordes wore.
14655 God wyll that thou of Hym have aw   *desires*
   and sett His honoure ever before.
And for thou sall thiself knaw,
   He sufferd to dystroy thi store,
And all thi guddes He con withdraw   *goods*
14660   and sent thee sekenes sad and sore
Thi pacience so to prove
   and thi sadnese assay,

Wheder thou wyll last in love
  or fayle for lytyll affray.   *fail for a little fright*

1223.
14665 "Thou may wele wytt that wrang thou went
  and thi wordes ware not wyty   *wise*
To say thiselfe an innocent,
  as he that ware no wo worthy.
Therfor I rede thou thee repent   *advise*
14670 and mekly aske of God mercy
And say this sekenes that is sent
  is for thi mysrewle ryghtwysly.
And lett no rusyng ryse,   *boasting*
  ne graunt of thi gud dede.
14675 Thiself thou suld dyspyse,
  then wyll God make thi mede."   *reward*

[JOB REAFFIRMS HIS FAITH; RESPONDS THAT THE WICKED CAN GO UNPUNISHED (21:1–34)]

1224.
Job then for bale began to qwake,   *grief; shake*
  swylk angers in his hert had he.
"Alas!" he sayd, "When sall ye slake   *cease*
14680 with tene thus forto turment me?   *insult*
Yf God more vengance on me take   *[Even] if*
  to make me turment on a tre,   *tormented on a tree*
My ryghtwysnes sall I never forsake,
  therin I hope my helpe sall be.   *in that*
14685 When ryghtwyse Juge sall sytt
  to deme ever ylka dele,   *pass judgment over everything*
Then all the werld sall wytt   *know*
  who dyd wrang and who wele.

1225.
"Bot, sertes, ther is a comyn case   *certainly*
14690 that trobyls me in wytt allway: *troubles my mind*
A man that spendes his lyfes space
  in syn that sorow is forto say,
And to no man amendes mase   *makes amends*
  bot dose ever yll all that he may,   *does wickedness in every way he can*
14695 And evermore hape and hele he has   *happiness and health*
  and gud enogh both nyght and day;   *wealth*
And he that rewls hym ryght   *rules himself rightly*
  mydnyght, morn, and noyne,   *noon*
He has dole day and nyght.   *sorrow*
14700 How ys this dewly done?"

[Eliphaz says Job must be wicked (15:1–35)]

1226.

 Elyphath then answerd agayn
  and says, "Then, man, grett ferly have I   *wonder*
 That thou labours thi wytt in vayn
  and fyllys thi toyght with fantasy.

14705 Tho that lyfes wele, thei ar certayn   *Those who live well*
  forto have blyse how so thei dy.   *however they die*
 Tho that lyfes yll to thei be slayn
  sall wun in wo, as yt is worthy.   *dwell*
 And if thei syn forsake
14710 and mend whyls thei have myght,
 Thei may als wynly wake   *pleasantly awake*
  als thei that lyfes full ryght.

[Parable of the rich man and the leper (Luke 16:19–31)]

1227.

 "To this may men in sampyll tell   *example*
  and lyghtly lere, yf yt be late,   *learn, even if it is late*
14715 Of the ryche man how yt fell,   *happened*
  and of a lazar that lay at his gate.   *leper*
 The ryche wold with no mercy mell   *speak*
  bot lyf in lust erly and late.
 Therfor he had his hame in Hell
14720 with fendes foule and fyre full hate.   *devils*
 With fylth ther was he fed   *dung*
  for all his fare before,
 And the lazar was led
  to wun in myrth evermore.   *dwell*

1228.

14725 "Forthi I rede thou thee avyse
  and that thou of slyke bostyng blyn,   *such boasting cease*
 When thou thiself so justyfyse
  to say thi payn passys thi syn.   *surpasses*
 For whoso wyll with rusyng ryse   *boasting*
14730 and wenys so wrschep forto wyn,   *intends thus honor*
 Thei sall be sett in law assyse   *legal assize*
  and haldyn down for all ther dyn.   *held*
 Then is it wytt to bewarre
  for ferd of slyke a fall.   *fear*
14735 Yll or wele yf we fare,
  evermore love God of all."

[Job responds declaring his innocence (16:1–17:16)]

1229.

	Job then says, "Forsoth I trow	*Truly I believe*
	for all the kavtels that ye can	*cunning devices*
	That yt sall fall by me and yow	
14740	als yt fell by the pepyll than.	
	For ye lend in your lordschepes now	*remain*
	and weldes the welthys your faders wan,	*wield; won*
	And yow lyst nawder bend ne bow	*desire neither*
	ne graunt servyce to no gud man.	
14745	To me ye con take tent	*take heed*
	and turment yow betwene	
	A sely innocent,	*pitiable*
	that may no malyse mene.	*intends*

1230.

	"And yf yt sall be als ye say,	
14750	that tho in Hell sall have ther hame	
	That lyfes in lust and lykyng ay	*pleasure always*
	and hath all welth of wyld and tame	
	And none anoye be nyght ne day,	*trouble*
	then to yourself sall fall the same.	
14755	Therfor I wold ye wentt your way	*wish you*
	and lett me lyg here law and lame.	*lie here low*
	And when ye part me fro,	
	I aske of God this boyne,	*boon*
	That here come nevermo	
14760	to dere me als ye have done."	*harm*

[Bildad insists Job must have sinned (18:1–21)]

1231.

	Baldach brast owt with wordes breme	*rough*
	and says, "Thou doytes in this degré,	*You are foolish*
	When thou dare take on thee to deme	*judge*
	what werkyng sall worth of us thre.	*is proper to*
14765	To God allon that same suld seme,	*alone*
	for demer of all erth is He.	*judge*
	Unto thi yowth thou suld take yeme,	*pay attention*
	and in thiself then suld thou se	
	That thi werkes hath bene warre	*worse*
14770	forto deme al by dene	*altogether*
	And febyler be fare	*worse by far*
	then any of ours have bene.	

1232.

"For thou had yemyng in thi yowthe   *care*
  and fyndyng of thi frendes in fere,   *together*
14775 When we trayveld by north and sowth
  to seke our sele on sydes sere.   *happiness in every place*
God gaf thee myght to mell with mowth   *speak*
  befor all folk both fere and nere,   *far and near*
And sotell carpyng non we cowth   *subtle argument*
14780   bot comyn course of craftes clere.
Thou had of frendes before
  swylke fee os myght not fayle,   *property*
And all our erthly store
  gatt we with grett travayle.

1233.

14785 "Thou trespast never in no degré
  by ther tales that we here thee tell,   *these*
And forto nevyn no more dyd he   *mention*
  that clerkes says had his hame in Hell.
Bot for he was of gold and fee
14790   rychest that in his land con dwell   *did*
And of the pore hade no pyté,
  for that defawt full fowle he fell.
And so sall all tho do   *those*
  that has here welth gud woyne   *in plenty*
14795 And takes no tent therto   *takes no heed*
  to helpe them that has none.

1234.

"Whyls thou myght in thi lordschepe lend,
  forto have wo thou wold not wene.
That thou was ryche, full wele was kend,   *well was known*
14800   thi catell in all cuntreys clene.
Bot wher thou auder gaf or send   *either*
  to solace the seke, that was not sene,   *sick; seen*
Or any man in myschef mend,
  ther is non swylke maters to mene.   *mention*
14805 When thou so lordly foyre,   *lived*
  then suld thou have had toyght
Forto part with the pore   *divide; poor*
  and nede that had noyght.   *needy*

1235.

"Yf thou were meke and myld of mode,
14810   what mend that to other men
Bot so with gawdes to gett ther gud   *tricks to take their goods*
  as he that cowd no cawtels ken.   *trickeries know*

	So in thi strengh when that thou stud,	
	thou suld wysly have wayted then	*attended*
14815	To febyll folke that wanted fode	
	and fast ware fest in fylth and fen.	*bound; shit*
	Thou suld have loked to lawse	*release*
	tho that ware bun and thrall.	*bound and enslaved*
	Meknes is lytyll at prays	
14820	bot mercy be mengyd with all.	*unless mingled*

1236.

	"Thou rusys thiself of ryghtwysnes;	*boasts*
	what favour suld thou therfor fang,	*get*
	When no man durst do thee dystreyse,	*dared*
	wheder thi werkes ware wele or wrang,	
14825	Bot ylka man, both more and lese,	
	ware glad fro thi grevance to gang.	
	Thi pompe and pride wyll prove exprese	
	thou has bene an yll levere lang.	*long been a sinful person*
	Therfor aske God mercy	
14830	that thou has sayd of myse,	*sin*
	And wytt thou is worthy	
	forto fele warre then this."	*feel far worse*

[JOB OBSERVES THAT GOD ALONE KNOWS THE REASON (9:1–22)]

1237.

	Job says then with sympyll chere,	
	"Alas, this lyf lyges yow full lyght,	*concerns you very little*
14835	And wold God that ye thre in fere	*together*
	suld fele yt both day and nyght,	
	Or that my domysman wold apere	*judge*
	my dedes dewly to deme and dyght.	*determine and judge*
	Then suld ye se yourselfe all sere	*in various ways*
14840	that your reprovyng is unryght,	*reproof is unjust*
	Ne that this grete vengaunce	
	is noght thus on me tone	*taken*
	For my mysgovernaunse,	
	ne for my syn alon.	

1238.

14845	"Bot ather yt is to this entent	*either*
	that God wyll schew His grett maystry	
	In me, a wofull innocent,	
	to make other beware therby;	*other [people]*
	Or els for ye suld yow repent,	*yourselves*
14850	that wrethes me thus wrangwysly,	*who chastise*
	Or sorow sere be to yow sent,	*various sorrows*

so worthy wore als wele os I;
Or els unto this end
   may seknes oft be sawyn,   *sickness; sown*
14855   For falshed of the Fend   *Devil*
   amang men suld be knawn.

1239.
"And yf the Fend this wo hath wroyght
   and mad me to have this myschefe,
I have gud mynd his myght is noyght
14860   ferrer then God wyll gyf hym lefe.   *more; leave [to have]*
And when the soth is all up soygt,   *truth*
   yf God have graunt hym me to grefe,
My body he has in balys broyght,   *sorrows*
   bot to my saule he may not mefe.   *interfere*
14865   Therfor I hym defy
   and all his felows fare
And als your cumpany   *also*
   that encressys all my care.   *grief*

1240.
"For, sertes, ye sall have syn and shame
14870   to wreke yow so in wordes vayne,   *wreak*
So bytterly me forto blame
   for that I pleyne me of my payn.   *lament*
And, sertanly, feld ye the same,   *if you felt*
   to say fowler ye suld be fayn.   *fouler; ready*
14875   Therfor I pray yow hast yow hame;   *haste yourselves homeward*
   God leyn that ye com never agayn!   *grant*
For your unfrendly fayre
   with your carpyng so keyn   *sharp*
Has made my myschef mare   *more*
14880   then yt suld els have bene."   *otherwise*

[ZOPHAR REPEATS HIS CHARGE THAT JOB IS GUILTY (11:1–20)]

1241.
Sother says, "Forsoth I fele,   *Truly I feel*
   when all thi tale is told tyll end,
Thou says thi sorow and thin unsele   *innocence*
   comys ather of God or of the Fend
14885   And for thin awn dedes never a dele.   *never a part*
   This mater is of myse remynd,   *wrongly interpreted (recounted)*
For and thou wold avyse thee wele,   *if you would think rightly*
   I trow thou cowd not tell the tend   *tenth [part]*
Of werkes that thou has wroyght
14890   agayns Goddes Commawndment,

And now wyll graunt ryght noyght
    bot als an innocent.

1242.
"An innocent in erth is none,
    ne never was, ne never sall be,
14895   That dyd never grefe bot God alon
    and Mary His moyder, a maydyn free.
And thou rekyns thiself for on
    and makes thee thore als holy as He!   *therefore*
And we wott wele thou hath mysgone   *know well*
14900   and greved thi God in sere degré.   *various ways*
Sen we have sayd thee lang   *Since; spoken to you long*
    and thou no myse wyll mend,   *misdeeds*
Fayrwele! For we wyll gang;
    us lyst no lenger lend."   *we desire no longer to stay*

[ELIPHAZ REMINDS JOB THAT TIME IS SHORT (22:1–30)]

1243.
14905   Then Elypach with wordes hend   *courteous*
    sayd, "Job, thou spendes thi spech in vayn
To say thi care comys of the Fend,   *sorrow*
    for of that fare is he full fayn.   *glad*
When thi wo at his wyll sall wend,
14910   that settes hym thore als thi soverayn.
Dyfye hym and make God thi frend
    and fand his frenschep forto frayn.   *busy yourself; question*
For thi care comys of kynd,   *sorrow; by nature*
    yf thou thee wele avyse,   *unless you rule yourself well*
14915   Als bokes makes in mynd   *As books*
    and wyttenes, ser, on this wyse:

1244.
"*Homo natus de muliere,*   *Man born of a woman*
    he says a man of a woman born,
Hic breui vivens tempore,   *Here living for a short time*
14920   in lytyll tym his lyf is forlorn,   *lost*
And fylled with fayndyngs sall he be   *hardships*
    and with myschefes mydday and morn,
Ryght os a flour is fayr to se   *flower*
    and sone wast als yt was beforn.   *wasted*
14925   So ere we ylkon wroyght   *are we each of us*
    to trayvell, tray, and teyne   *travails, struggles, and grief*
And sorows sere unsoyght,   *many*
    als our elders have beyne.

[THE FRIENDS LEAVE; JOB ADDRESSES GOD]

1245.

"And sen thou says thiself is on   *since*
14930   that never greved in no degré,
Fayrewele, we lefe thee here allone,
    for other ways to wend have we."   *go*
Job says, "Wold God that ye ware gone
    so that ye mett never more with me.
14935   Then to God may I make my moyne;   *complaint*
    ther is none that may helpe bot He.
All erthly frendes are faynt   *weak*
    and fals into affye.   *trust*
Now wyll I make my playnt
14940   to god God Allmighty.

1246.

"*Nunc parce mihi, Domine*!   *Now spare me, Lord!*
    Lord God that gyfes gudnes and grace,
Lord, in Thi myght have mynd of me
    and spare me, Lord, a lytyll space;
14945   And of my payns, Lord, have pyté
    and teche me forto take Thi trace,   *path*
So that I myght have mynd of Thee
    to tell my counsayle in this case.   *clarify my opinion*
Lord, thou makes men to encrese
14950   with corn and catell clene
And sodanly to sese,   *end*
    als by myself is sene.

1247.

"A, Lord, sen thou may at Thi lyst   *since; desire*
    and at Thi lykyng lowd and styll   *publicly and privately*
14955   Make men in erth forto be blest   *blessed*
    and have all wardly welth at wyll,   *worldly*
And sythyn in wo, or ever thei wyst,   *then, before they are even aware*
    forto have evyll and angers yll —
Sen I so lang have myrthes myst —   *joy missed*
14960   Lord, spare me now that I not spyll.   *be destroyed*
Thei have made me debate
    that ware my frendes before.
I am so mased and mate   *amazed and dejected*
    that I may now no more.

1248.

14965   "*Memento, queso, Domine*,   *Remember, I beseech Thee, Lord*
    umthynke Thee, Lord that last sall ay,   *recall to Yourself*

	Quod sicut lutum feceris me,	*That Thou hast made me as the clay*
	that Thou mad me of erth and clay	
	With bonys and synows semly to se,	*bones; fair to look upon*
14970	with flesch and fell in ryght aray	*skin*
	In bale awhyle here forto be	*grief*
	and sythyn as a wed wast away.	*then; weed*
	Bot my saule forto save,	
	that lyges in Thin awn chose,	*lies in Your own choice*
14975	That hope I Thou wyll have	
	and lett no lust yt lose.	*allow; [to] lose it*

[PROOF OF GOD'S POWER: THE RAISING OF LAZARUS (JOHN 11:38–44)]

1249.

	"Lord, Lazar that lay low os led,	*Lazarus*
	dolven as the ded suld be dyght,	*buried*
	Full faur days stynkand in that sted	*rotting in that place*
14980	and lokyn fro all erthly lyght,	*locked*
	Thou raysed hym up to lyf fro ded	
	and mad hym man in erthly myght.	
	So may Thou rayse me be Thi red	*word*
	fro dole that I dre day and nyght.	*from the sorrow; suffer*
14985	Thou wot, and Thi wyll wore,	*know, if*
	for fro Thee is noyght hyd,	
	That my payns ere wele more	*are far more*
	then yll that ever I dyd.	

[PROOF OF GOD'S POWER: THE THIEF ON THE CROSS (LUKE 23:39–43)]

1250.

	"And the thefe that on the Crose hang,	*Cross*
14990	that in lust had led all his lyfe	
	And manys murtheryng mad oft amang	*murdering of men*
	and styrd men unto mekyll stryfe,	*much*
	Thou gaf hym grace with Thee to gang	
	in Paradyse with ryotes ryfe.	*many joys*
14995	And thou wott I wroght never swylke wrang	
	to murther nother man ne wyfe,	*murder neither*
	Ne never manys gud I stale	*men's goods I stole*
	nother in stall ne in stabyll.	
	Why I suld byd this bale?	*suffer this grief*
15000	This is unmesurabyll.	

[JOB GIVES HIMSELF OVER TO GOD'S POWER]

1251.

    "Bot, Lord, in comforth to encresse

        this wold I wytt, and Thi wyll wore,   *would I know, if*

    Wheder my sorow sall ever sesse

        or yt sall last thus evermore.

15005   I wyle not pray for pride ne pese,   *nor peace*

        ne guddes agayn forto restore,

    Bot yf thou wold of Thi gudnes   *unless*

        be my frend als Thou was before.   *as*

    For whyls Thou was my frend,

15010   all folke ware than full fayn   *very glad*

    Att my wyll forto wend

        and non to gruche agayn.   *grieve against me*

1252.

    "Whyls I moght governd grett degré,

        all daynthes dere to me wold draw.   *pleasant things*

15015   All men and wemen wrschept me   *honored*

        in servys both in ded and saw,   *service; deed and word*

    Both dukes and erlys in ylk cuntré,

        and lordes that led ther landes law.   *lawfully*

    Os I wold byd, so suld yt be

15020   fro tyme thei couth my consayll knaw.

    And now lyfes ther no lad

        that me wyll loke ne lufe,   *look upon nor honor*

    Bot all folke are full glad

        to put me to reprove.   *reproof*

1253.

15025   "My catell cayred in mony a clough   *traveled; valley*

        with mekyll myrth myd day and morn.

    Myn oxyn went to wayn or plough   *cart or plow*

        with hyne to herber hay or corn.   *servants to gather*

    Now have I noyght bot noy enogh;   *harms*

15030   all folke ere fayn me forto scorn.   *are glad*

    So all my welth is turned to wogh;   *woe*

        was never swylke wrych of woman born.   *wretch*

    I had all daynthes dere   *delicacies*

        that men myght aftur thynke.

15035   Now wyll non negh me nere   *come near me*

        for fylth and for fowle stynke.   *foul*

1254.

    "And therfor, Lord, have mynd amang

        of me, Thi man ay whyls I moght.   *always while I might [remain so]*

	Have pety of my payns strang	
15040	that sakles ere to me soght.	*innocent*
	For thou wott wele I wroght never wrang	*know well*
	why I suld in swylke bale be broyght.	*such sorrow*
	Bot at Thi lyst, schort or lang,	*desire*
	and at Thi wyll all bus be wroyght.	*must*
15045	In Thee I trow and trest	*believe and trust*
	that Thou my sawle sayve.	
	Lord, led me als Thou lyst.	*desire*
	I kepe noyght els to crave."	

[GOD RESPONDS TO JOB'S APPEAL (38:1–41:34)]

1255.

	When Job had thus apertly prayd,	*openly*
15050	God, that is ever of mercy free,	*generous*
	Of his prayers was noyght well payd	*not well pleased*
	and unto hym all thus sayd He:	
	"Thi prayers, Job, of myse er grayd	*wrongly are sent*
	so forto make thi playnt of Me.	*thus*
15055	I have herd all how thou hath sayd	
	that I have done grett wrang to thee	
	To make thi penance more,	
	als thee thynke in thi toyght,	
	Then thi werkes worthy wore	
15060	that thou in werld hath wroyght.	

1256.

	"Thou rusys thiself of ryghtwysnes	*boasts*
	als thou in werld ware never gylty.	*as if*
	So by thi playnt thou proves exprese	
	that thou is God als wele os I.	*as well as I*
15065	For I am He that ryghwyse is	*righteous*
	and ryghtwyse Juge to justyfye	
	All erthly men, both more and lese,	
	aftur ther werkyng is worthy.	
	I gafe thee power playn	
15070	to be all other abufe.	
	Thou gyfes to Me agayn	*in return*
	bot plenyng and reprofe.	*complaining and rebuke*

1257.

	"Thou says thiself an innocent,	*call*
	als he that never couth do none yll,	
15075	And wele thou wott how thou has went	
	in werdly welth ever at wyll.	
	Thou wyst never what myslykyng ment,	*discomfort*

for non durst trespase thee untyll. *dared*
Now rede I that thou thee repent *I advise*
15080 and love thi Lord, both lowd and styll, *publicly and privately*
That may putt thee to payn
and sythyn flytt yt thee fro, *then remove*
And gyfe thee gudes agayn *goods*
yf thou can serve hym so.

1258.
15085 "For and thou had never done mys *if; misdeed*
bot greved thi God in this aray,
Thou ware not worthy to be in blyse *bliss*
bot thou amend yt whyls thou may. *unless*
Yf thou wyll werke ase I thee wysse, *direct you*
15090 putt thi wyt in His wyll allway,
Then wyll thi God forgyfe thee this
and lett thee be in blyse for ay. *forever*
Knaw thiselfe for unclene
and evyll in all degré,
15095 And thynke what ayre hath beyne *earlier*
and what sall aftur be.

1259.
"And yf thou wyll werke on this wyse,
graunt to God that thou is gylty.
Then wyll He graunt thee grace to ryse
15100 and mend thee of thi meselry. *leprosy*
Therfor I rede thou thee avyse
and mekly that thou aske mercy,
And then that thou make sacrafyce
for thi gylt to God Allmighty."
15105 When all ther saws ware sayd, *these*
then God away was gone,
And Job als man amayde *as a man dismayed*
full mekly made his mone: *meekly*

[JOB'S HUMBLE PRAYER (42:1–6)]

1260.
"I love Thee, Lord of ylka lede, *every nation*
15110 that me has lerned to lere Thi Lay. *taught to follow; Law*
I wrschep Thee in word and dede *honor*
in all the myght that ever I may. *power*
Of no kyns thyng now I have nede,
for all my wo is went away.
15115 Bot of that dome now have I dred *judgment*
that sall be done on the last day,

How I sall answer thore
   of the dedes in my yowthe
That I have done before,
15120   sen tym I counsell couthe.

1261.
"What sall I do, wrech wyll of wone?   *wretch without hope*
   Whore sall I hye me forto hyde   *haste*
Unto Thi dredfull dome be done
   and all by jugment justyfyed?
15125   I have no gatt bot to God allon   *course*
   to teld me under in that tyde,   *protect*
And His gudnes beys never gone,   *goodness is*
   in His beld is me best to byd.   *shelter; dwell*
Bot God that all gud is
15130   sall deme then all be dene   *forthwith*
By rewle of ryghtwysnes
   and of no mercy mene.

1262.
"*Dimitte ergo me, Domine,*   *Thus suffer me, Lord*
   ut ego plangam paululum.   *that I may lament a little*
15135 A lytyll whyle, Lord, suffer me,
   that lang hath bene both def and dum,   *deaf and mute*
That I may meyne me unto Thee   *address myself toward*
   and schew my syns all and sum.
And lett my corse here clensed be   *body*
15140   so that my sawle, Lord, never come
In the land of dole and dyn
   qwylk I wott ordand is   *which I know*
For them that endes in syne
   and geytes no forgyfnes.

1263.
15145 "Lord God, that governs hegh and law,
   I love Thi sand both lowd and styll. *words; publicly and privately*
My wekydnese now well I knaw
   that I have wroyght agayns Thi wyll.
For I have oft sayd in my saw   *speech*
15150   that I dyd never so mekyll of yll,
Ne never greved agayns Thi Law
   lyke to the payns ware putt me tyll.
I wott I have done wrang;
   that sayng rewys me sore.   *speech I rue greatly*
15155 Lord, mell mercy amang,   *show*
   I wyll trespas no more.   *sin*

1264.

"And that I have done day or nyght
    agayns wrschep or wyll of Thee,   *honor*
I wyll amend yt at my myght
15160   whyls any lyfe lastes in me;
    So, Lord, that, when Thi dome is dyght   *judgment is ready*
    that Thou sall deme ever ylk degré,
That I be sene then in Thi syght
    amang them that sall saved be.
15165   For in that otterest end   *uttermost*
    helpe forto nevyn is none,   *invoke*
Ne medcyn that may mend
    bot Thi mercy allon."   *except*

[ALL IS RETURNED TO JOB (42:10–17)]

1265.

When Job had thus made his prayer,
15170   then was his grefe all gon, I geyse.   *I understand*
His wyfe com than with woman chere   *feminine cheer*
    and askyd hym gudly forgyfnes.
His servandes come on sydes sere   *many sides*
    and asked hym mercy more and lese.
15175   Hys neghtbours and his frendes in fere   *together*
    releved hym with full grett ryches,
So that in lytyll space
    God made hym to be more
Of power in all plays   *all places*
15180   then ever he was before.

1266.

Hys ryches and his ryalté,
    as robes and rentes and other aray,
Hys waynys and ploughys and foran fee   *carts; imported livestock*
    were all dobyll by dyverse day.   *doubled*
15185   And aftur with his wyfe had hee
    sevyn semly suns, the sothe to say,   *handsome sons*
And thre doyghturs; in ther degré
    were none fundon so fayre os thei. *found so beautiful as*
He had all welth at wyll
15190   and hele fro hede to heyll.   *health; heel*
He loved God lowd and styll   *publicly and privately*
    als worthy was full wele.

1267.

When he was sett in this assyse
    and waryscht well of all his wo,   *was relieved*

15195   To God than mad he sacrafyce
             als He before had bydyn hym do.   *commanded him [to] do*
         He saw his suns full rychly ryse
             in grett degré to ryd and go,
         And his doyghturs als wemen wyse
15200   to grett wrschep wed also.   *honor wedded*
         He teched them to take hede   *taught*
             in ther werkyng allway
         Ther God to luf and dred
             both by nyght and day.

         1268.
15205   Then lyfed Job aftur his grett dystresse
             one hunderth wynters and fawrty   *140 years*
         And loved God ay of more and lese   *always*
             that so his myrth wold multyplye.
         Thus lykyd God forto prove exprese
15210   his grett meknes with messelry;   *leprosy*
         And for He fand his fayth ay fresch,
             he wuns in welth, als is worthy.   *lives*
         God graunt us grace to lyfe
             in luf and charité,
15215   That we our gast may gyfe   *souls*
             to myrth. So moyte yt be!

AMEN DE JOB.

THOBIE.

[TOBIT'S BACKGROUND, FAMILY, AND CHARITY (1:1–22)]

1269.

	Of trew Thoby now tell wyll we,	*Tobit*
	of whom the word hath went full wyd,	*fame*
	How he was born in Galalé,	*Galilee*
15220	a cuntré nere the est seesyd,	*eastern seaside (i.e., Dead Sea)*
	And noryscht in a ryche cyté	*brought up*
	that Neptalym was named that tyde;	*Naphtali*
	And of that same kynred come he,	*family (the Naphtali)*
	als connyng clerkes hath clarefyde.	
15225	Who wyll take tent ther tyll	*Whoever will also listen*
	by this tale may be kend	*shown*
	To love God lowd and styll,	*publicly and privately*
	what soynd so He wyll send.	*whatever message*

1270.

	Jeroboam we have herd tell	
15230	of the Ebrews was crowned kyng,	
	And all the land of Israel	
	had he to led at his lykyng.	
	And whyls he wold with God dwell,	
	he had welth of all werdly thyng;	
15235	Bot sythyn in fowle folys he fell,	*then in foul foolishness*
	so dyd his pepyll, old and yyng.	
	He made them calfys of gold	
	and sayd tho myght them mend,	
	Bot sythyn that bargan bold	
15240	broyght hym to have yll end.	

1271.

	Jeroboam wyll we leve at hame	
	and nevyn another nere therby.	*mention; near*
	Salmanaser was his name,	*Shalmaneser*
	and he was kyng of all Assery.	*Assyria*

15245	Als Jeroboam dyd, he used the same,	
	maynteinyng his men in mawmentry.	*idolatry*
	Therfor gud folke he shent with schame,	*destroyed*
	bot God saved His servant Toby.	
	Thys ylk Kyng Salmanaser,	
15250	his foylies to fulfyll,	*follies*
	Wold wyt yf any were	*know*
	that wold not werke his wyll.	

1272.

	He commawnd all men lese and mare	
	that hym with sewt or servyce soght	*suit*
15255	That thei suld cum furth hym before	
	and wrschep goddes that he had wroght.	
	Bot Toby kyn wold not come thore,	*Tobit's family*
	therfor in bondag were thei broyght.	
	And he, all yf he yongest wore,	*even if*
15260	ever wrschept God with wyll and toyght.	
	He fled fro his enmys	
	to Jerusalem in hye	*haste*
	And made therfor sacrafyce	
	to God Allmightye.	

1273.

15265	The kyng of wyll was so otrayge,	
	all tho that wold groch hym agayn,	*work against him*
	All wore yt man or woman or page,	*Regardless if it were; child*
	he commawnd that thei suld be slayn.	
	Then Toby went withoutyn wage,	*payment*
15270	to bery them he was full bayn,	*ready*
	And all that lyfes of his lynag	
	forto dyffend was he full fayn.	*glad*
	Bot sone fro frendes he fled	
	of ferre for dred of dede,	*of fear for dread of death*
15275	And thore a wyf he wede	
	comyn of his awn kynred.	*own kindred*

1274.

	That wyfe heyght Ana, as I herd say,	*was called Anna*
	that ever in hyre trewth was trew,	
	And unto God so con thei pray.	
15280	scho bayre a sun semly of hew.	*beautiful of appearance*
	The fader, that lyfyd by Moyses Lay,	*Mosaic Law*
	wold make his sun aftur hym to sew	*follow*
	And named hym Toby; then ware thei	*Tobias*
	two of an name, both old and new.	
15285	The fader with luf and aw	*fear*

lernd hym, whyls he was yyng,   *taught*
To lyfe by Moyses Law
   and luf God over all thyng.

1275.

Sythyn was the kyng assent certayn,
15290   ryght evyn als God wold that yt were,
That Toby suld com home agayn
  and have his sted and all his store.   *home; goods*
Of that fayre was his frendes full fayn,
  and Toby ordand fast therfore.
15295 So was he putt in power playn
  als mekyll os he ever was before.
The kyng commawnd to loke
  that he had his all hale,   *his [old goods] in full*
And unto hym he toke
15300   tresour withoutyn tale.   *beyond measure*

1276.

When Thoby thus had gettyn grace
  and gold was gyfyn hym grett plenté,
He went abowt fro place to place
  to cumforth folke of his cuntré.   *comfort*
15305 And no spense spared he in that space   *expense*
  to tho that ware thrall to make them free.   *slaves*
Tho folk ware fayn to folow his trace,   *path*
  for all that sorow had socurd he.   *succored*
He beryd all that ware ded   *buried*
15310   whore he them fand before;
Into the provynce of Mede,   *[Even]; Media*
  and thus befell yt thore,

1277.

In the rych cyté of Rages,
  a frend of his before he fand
15315 That lely lyfyd withoutyn lese.   *loyally; lies*
  Than had he lorn both lyth and land.   *lost; people*
Toby hym saw and myght not sese,   *delay*
  bot for his sake he was sorowand   *sorrowful*
And bed his comfort to encrese   *determined*
15320   at his power with hert and hand.
Gabell heyght that gud man   *Gabael*
  that was so stratly sted.   *placed in such straits*
Tyll Thoby told he than   *To*
  how his land was layd in wede,   *was mortgaged*

1278.

15325　And he had noyght therfor to pay,　　　　　　　　*believed it to be lost*
　　　　wherfor he trowd yt forto tyne.
　　Then to Toby thus con he say,
　　　　"Ser, save me and yt sall be thine."
　　Thor Toby toke to hym that day
15330　　ten talentes of gold fayr and fyne.
　　Sevyn hunderth and twenty libras weyd thei　　*720 pounds weighed*
　　　　forto be wayred in wax and wyne.　　　　　　*converted into*
　　For ylke talent of tho,
　　　　forto tell by trew payse,　　　　　　　　　*accurate weight*
15335　Weyd twenty libras and two;　　　　　　*Weighed twenty-two pounds*
　　　　Catholicon yt so says.

1279.

　　This gud toke Toby to Gabell　　　　　　　　　*These goods*
　　　　by sewrty mad betwyx them two,　　　　　　　*agreement*
　　And Gabell sett therto his seall　　　　　　　　*seal*
15340　　by wyttenesyng of mony moo.
　　Both in ther law thei ware full lele,　　　　　　*loyal*
　　　　as afturward was fundun so.　　　　　　　*shown clearly*
　　Than wund Thoby with werdly wele　　*departed; worldly possessions*
　　　　and warescht all that ware in wo.　　　　　*protected*
15345　And so betyd that tyd,　　　　　　　*it happened at that time*
　　　　als God ordand therfore,
　　Kyng Salmanaser dyed
　　　　and past with payns sore.

1280.

　　When Salmanaser so was deyd
15350　　and broyght unto his bereyng bowne,　　　　　*burying place*
　　Hys sun Senacheryb on hed　　　　　*Sennacherib precipitately*
　　　　resayved the kyngdom and the crowne.
　　Tho that the fader with wekyd red　　　　*Those; wicked counsel*
　　　　mad to be ponyschyd in presown,　　　　*punished in prison*
15355　The sun wold byd no bettur bede,　　　　　*allow; reward*
　　　　bot bad that men suld dyng them down.　　*ordered; strike*
　　So ware full mony slayn
　　　　of Ebrews old and yyng,
　　And Toby was full bayn　　　　　　　　　　*ready*
15360　　at bere them to bereyng.　　　　　　　*bear; burial*

1281.

　　When the kyng herd that he dyd so,
　　　　he had no daynteth of that dede.　　　　　　*pleasure*
　　He commawnd that men suld hym slo
　　　　and all that Ebrews lyf con lede.　　　　　　*left alive*

15365	Bot Toby was wernd of that wo	*warned*
	and conseld forto flee for dred.	
	So was he fayn to flytt them fro;	*flee*
	his wyfe and his sun with hym yede.	*went*
	And allway was he bowne	*prepared*
15370	to helpe all that had nede,	
	And namly his nacion	
	both forto cloght and fcdc.	*clothe*

1282.

The kyng persewyd with payns strang
    all Ebrews kynd, wher he them kend,   *wherever he knew of them*
15375 That to his fals goddes wold not gang   *go*
    to wrschep them with hert and hend.
Therfor God wold not suffer hym lang
    in wekyd lyf so forto lend.
He mad hym with his warkes wrang
15380 at pase to wo withoutyn end:
With his suns was he slayn.
    Than be commun acorde
Was Thoby gettyn agayn
    and of hys guddes restored.

[TOBIT'S CHARITY RESULTS IN HIS BLINDNESS (2:1–10)]

1283.

15385 Then was he sted withoutyn stryf;
    full fayn were all his frendes fre
With his yyng sun and with his wyfe
    and other mo of his awn meneye.   *own company*
He rewled them by reson ryfe
15390 and governd them in gud degré
Aftur the law to lede ther lyfe
    and to Goddes bydyng bowsom to be.
So fell on a dere day   *it befell*
    Thoby ordand to make
15395 A fest of gud aray
    for his gud frendes sake.

1284.

Thei had daynthes of drynke and mette;   *pleasures; food*
    he mad them myrth with all his myght.
Hymselfe wold ocupye no sett,
15400 bot to his sun thus sayd he ryght,
"Gud sun, go loke yf thou may geyte
    any of our lyne to make us lyght,   *kin; merry*
And bryng them in with us to ete."

	The chyld to werke his wyll was wyght.	*glad*
15405	He went and com agayn	
	and sayd he fand ryght none	*found*
	Bot on sodanly slayn	*one [man]*
	and levyd lygand alon.	*left lying alone*

1285.

	"And, ser," he says, "I herd men tell	
15410	that he of myse nothyng had made,	*wrongdoings none*
	Bot for he was of Israel,	
	with fals Phylysteyns was he fade."	*slain*
	Then Thoby wold no langar dwell.	*remain*
	He left gud men his geystes to glade.	*guests to gladden*
15415	He and his sun, them two omell,	*together*
	toke the body withoutyn bade.	*delay*
	In a howse thei yt hyde	
	and mad ther geystes gud chere.	
	At evyn dewly thei dyd	*eventide dutifully*
15420	to bery yt in best manere.	

1286.

	Allthof Thoby were well ocupyd,	*Although*
	yett other wayte to werke hym wo;	*others waited*
	And all his counsell thei ascryd	*reported it*
	and in grett teyn thei told hym to,	*distress*
15425	"This ylk that thou helpes to hyde,	*This man*
	he had his ded for he dyd so;	
	And thou was fayn before this tyde	*occasion*
	therfor to flee thi frendes fro.	
	And yett thou dose the same;	
15430	and bot thou lefe yt soyne,	*unless you stop it soon*
	Thou sall beyr byttur blame	*bear*
	for dedes that thou has doyne."	

1287.

	Bot for oght thei cowth to hym say,	*could*
	to bery this ded ay toyght hym best.	
15435	And so fell on a somers day,	
	when he of swylke werke was werest,	*weariest*
	In his howse syd a lytter lay,	
	theron he reid hym forto rest.	*arrayed himself*
	And thor hym fell a full grett affray:	*terror*
15440	abowve hym was a swolws nest.	*swallow's*
	Als he lyft up his eyelyddes	
	to loke agayns the lyght,	
	Hate fylth of swolows brydes	*Hateful filth; birds*
	fell down and lost his syght.	*took*

1288.

15445   This werke was wroyght withoutyn wene,   *without doubt*
             for God wold so his pacience prove,
         Wheder he wold turn for any teyne   *sorrow*
             or to be lastand in hys love.   *lasting (faithful)*
         Sum of his frendes fast con hym meyne,   *pity*
15450   and sum to malyce wold hym move.
         Thei sayd, "Now is thi servyce sene
             that thou the ded so gladly grove   *dead; buried*
         And dyde grett almus dede   *alms deeds*
             tyll all folke that wold frayn.   *ask [for it]*
15455   Lett se now in thi nede
             who gyfes thee oght ogayn!"   *anything in return*

1289.

         Thei say, "We hald them wers then wode —   *worse than crazy*
             and so thiself sall say certayn —
         That gyfes away his werldly gud   *worldly possessions*
15460   and puttes hymself to povert playn."
         Bot Thoby ever full stably stud,
             of ther faygyng he was not fayn.   *attention; glad*
         Ther malyce moved nothyng his mode;
             he loved ay God with all his mayn.   *strength*
15465   He sayd, "Ye do on myse   *do amiss*
             in vayn your speche to spend.
         My Lord that sent me this
             has myght me forto mend.

1290.

         "This wo I wott I am worthy   *know*
15470   for weked werkes that I have wroght.
         I do me hale in his mercy   *put myself completely*
             that mad me new when I was noght."
         Thei left hym thore and lett hym lye.
             He thanked God with wyll and toyght.   *heart and head*
15475   His wyfe and his sun were redy
             to mend his myrth all that thei moght.
         Thus when men have dysesse,
             both kynred and counsayll
         That in welth wold them plese
15480   wyll then full fayntly fayll.

[TOBIT SENDS HIS SON TOBIAS TO GABAEL (4:1–5:3)]

1291.

         Thus was Thoby in langor lent.   *remaining in illness*
             He loved ay God both lowd and styll   *publicly and privately*

Of all the saynd that He to hym sentt,   *trials*
  and groched never in word ne wyll.   *complained*
15485 Then on that mone has he ment   *remembered*
  that Gabell borowd of hym by byll.   *Gabael; bill (promissory note)*
Therfor he wold that sum man went
  to feche yt and forward to fulfyll.
He cald Thoby hym to,   *Tobias*
15490   his sun, and sayd thus suyn,   *quickly*
"I have errandes to do
  qwylke I wold were wele doyne."   *which; done rightly*

1292.

The sun answerd full curtasly
  and sayd, "Fader, I am all bown   *ready*
15495 To werke your wyll, als is worthy,
  bothe nere and fere, in feld and towne."
The fader was full fayn forthi   *very glad therefore*
  and sayd, "Sun, in my benesowne   *benison*
All myn entent tell thee sall I,
15500   take gud reward to my reson.
Sun, Salmanazer the kyng,   *Shalmaneser*
  or tyme that thou was born,   *before the time*
He ordand in all thyng
  to have our lynge lorn.   *lineage destroyed*

1293.

15505 "Thore saw we mony sakles slayn,   *innocents*
  for of sere sydes thei ware out soght.   *from many sides*
To bery them I was full bayn,   *bury; prepared*
  bot to the lordes that lyked noght.
Then forto flee I was full fayn
15510   tyll all that bale tyll end was broyght.
Then gatt I gud enoght agayn;   *goods enough*
  evyn als God wold, so was yt wroyght.
Full yapely then I yode   *promptly; journeyed*
  abowt to cytes sere
15515 To helpe them that had nede
  and of our nacion nere.

1294.

"And sone aftur thi bryth yt befell   *birth*
  I fand on in a fare cuntré,   *a man*
Born of our blod and heyght Gabell.
15520   In preson herd haldyn was he.   *prison*
Thore made we menyng uus omell   *among ourselves*
  how my monay myght make hym free.
Ten talentes con I to hym tell

                to gyf agayn by gud sewrtyé.   *firm assurances*
15525   He made a lettur lele   *legal letter*
                of that payment exprese,
          And selyd yt with his seall   *sealed*
                befor full gud wyttenese.

1295.
          "That same lettur withoutyn lese   *without a lie*
15530   have I here forto send certayn.
          I wott full wele he wyll not sese
                thorwith to make my payment playn.
          For I here tell of his encrese,   *hear*
                how he hath gotyn his gud again.
15535   In a ryche cyté, Rages,
                ys his wonnyng withoutyn trayn.   *dwelling without doubt*
          Thidder wold I that thou wende   *There I want*
                and thou couth ken that place.   *know*
          That monay now myght mend
15540   to spend whyls we have space."

1296.
          The sun sayd, "Ser, so God me sayve,
                I wold full gladly do this dede.
          Bot aftur that cuntré forto crave
                I wott not whore my spech suld spede."
15545   "Gud sun," he sayd, "go seke sum knave
                that wyll wend with thee for his mede,   *payment*
          That thou of hym may helpyng have
                into that land thee forto lede,
          And that con understand
15550   the way tyll ye come thore."
          Thoby went furth and fand
                a fare chyld hym before.

[RAPHAEL WILL GUIDE TOBIAS TO GABAEL (5:4–6:1)]

1297.
          Iff he ware fare of flesch and fell,   *fair; skin*
                no ferly, for God had hym sent,   *wonder*
15555   His awn archangell, Raphell,   *Raphael*
                tyll yong Toby to take entent,
          And mornyng that was them omell   *among them*
                forto amend, so has he ment.   *told*
          He sayd, "I knaw full wele Gabell,
15560   for to Rages oft have I wentt."
          Yong Toby was fayn than,   *glad*
                and to his fader he sayd,

"Fader, I have fun a man   *found*
    to gang all redy grayd.   *go; prepared*

1298.
15565   "He says he knaws that cuntré clere
            and the gud man and that same cyté,
        And all the way he wyll me lere."   *guide*
            Toby sayd, "Sun, God leyn so be!   *grant [it] so [to] be*
        Bot sen thou says he is so nere,
15570   pray hym come and speke with me,
        So that I may the sothe enquere   *truth*
            of this that he hath told to thee."
        Yong Thoby saw unsoght
            the angell hym to byd,
15575   And so in he hym broyght
            to his fader bed-syd.

1299.
        So als thei stod that bed before,
            the angell thus unto Toby bade,
        "Be myrry, man, and mowrne no more,   *mourn*
15580   bot in thi God thou suld be glad.
        All yf thou sytt and sofer sore,   *Even; suffer sorely*
            sone may He seyse thi sorow sade   *end*
        And to thi state thee wele restore
            to have more hele than ever thou had."
15585   When the angell thus had sayd,
            yf Thoby febyly ferd,
        In hert he was wele payd,   *pleased*
            bot all thus he answerd:

1300.
        "What myrth may unto me avayle
15590   that syttes in derknes evyn and morn?
        I byde here blynd as best in bale   *live; beast*
            that bettur ware have bene unborn.
        All folke I fele now fayntly fayle
            that ware my frendes full fast beforn.
15595   Tho that then com me to consayle,
            now come thei more me forto scorn.
        Thus am I sett certayn
            in dole both nyght and day;   *sadness*
        Therfor I wold full fayn
15600   be fro this werld away."

1301.

The angell sayd, "Thoby, take tent,   *pay attention*
  swylk maters may non mend to move.   *such matters (complaints)*
God hath this seknes to thee sent
  thi pacience so forto prove.
15605 Yf thou Hym love that it has lent
  and be lele lastand in His love,   *faithfully loyal*
I hette thee than in hast to hent   *assure*
  full gud hele to thi sawle behove."
Thoby sayd, "Graymercy!
15610   This is full frendly red,   *advice*
Bot grett hast now have I
  of thyng I wold wore sped.   *done quickly*

1302.

"My sun says that thou wyll wend
  and teche hym to the land of Mede.   *guide*
15615 Thor dwels Gabell, my faythfull frend,   *Gabael*
  and unto hym I wold ye yede."   *went*
The angell then with wordes hend   *courteous*
  sayd, "To that land I sall hym lede.
For in Rages thor can I lend,
15620   and to Gabell than toke I hede.
I sall bryng thi sun ydder   *there*
  and sayve hym sownd in qwerte,   *health*
To he com agayn hydder.   *Until; here*
  This hete I here with hert."   *promise*

1303.

15625 Than Thoby says, "Ser, yf thou may
  bryng me my sun withoutyn blame,   *blemish*
I hete thee trewly forto pay   *promise*
  thi hyre in hand when thou comys hame.   *wages*
And also, ser, I wold thee pray
15630   that thou wold tell to me thi name,
That I may, whyls ye dwell away,
  thynk on my sun and on that same.
And thi kyn more and lese   *family*
  wold I have in my mynde.
15635 For wele I wott thou ys   *know you are*
  cumyn of full curtase kynd."   *courteous (noble) family*

1304.

The angell sayd, "Ser, for certayn,
  now thynke me selcowth of thi saw,   *I think your speech strange*
And thi wordes thynke me wroyght in vayn
15640   by sere resons to red by raw.   *many; counsel in turn*

I hette to bryng thi sun agayn   *promise*
  werly and wele withoutyn aw.   *worldly; fear*
Thee nedes no ferther forto frayn   *question*
  my kynred, ne my name to knaw.   *family*
15645   Bot neverthelese yett,
  ser, to fulfyll thi fantasy,
I reke not who yt wytt: *care; knows it*
  my name is Azary.   *Azaraiah*

1305.

"My fader in his lyfe was leve   *glad*
15650   to love his lord both lowd and styll."   *publicly and privately*
Toby says, "Take yt to no greve,
  for sertes I asked yt for non yll."
He toke them a boyst with that brefe   *box; letter*
  that thei suld beyre Gabell untyll,   *carry*
15655   And sayd, "God sayve yow fro myschefe!
  Wendes now furth when so ye wyll."   *Journey*
Yong Thoby than kneled down;
  his fader and moyder he prays.   *prays [for]*
To blese hym were thei bown,   *bless; ready*
15660   and so thei wend ther ways.

1306.

A lytyll hund at hame thei had   *dog*
  that went abowt not bun in band.   *not bound in confinement*
What yong Toby unto hym bad   *instructed*
  he wold take hed unto his hand;
15665   And to wend with hym was he glad
  bycause that he hym frendly fand.   *found*
In ylka a stede wher thei ware sted   *each place; lodged*
  the hound wold stably with hym stand.   *faithfully*
Now leve we Raphaell,
15670   that yong Thoby furth lede,
And of old Thoby tell,
  that was full stratly sted.   *in such straits*

1307.

The moyder drowped ever ylka day   *drooped*
  when scho wyst wele hyr sun was went;   *knew well*
15675   And to Thoby oft con scho say,
  "All our sele has thou fro us sent,   *happiness*
Our sun, that suld us wysch all way   *direct*
  when we in any bales war bent.   *with any problems are humbled*
Thou told ther was monay to pay,
15680   bot other maters has thou ment.
Yt was never for moynay   *money*

that thou so sone suld send   *quickly*
Hym that our beld suld be   *comfort*
    and fro fawt us defend.

1308.

15685   "Alas, that ever thou lerned that lore
             at send our sun so to Gabell!   *that sent*
         That man may say, when he comys thore,
             he knaws of thi noyte never a dele."   *no part of your troubles*
         Thoby sayd then, "Wyfe, mowrne no more,   *mourn*
15690   for sertanly all sall be wele.
         He sall fynd gud frendes hym before,
             so that he sall no fawtes fele.
         I trow withoutyn trayn   *believe without doubt*
             that Goddes angell sall hym lede
15695   And bryng hym save agayn
             full fayre als thei furth yode."

[ANNA AND THE GOAT (2:19–3:6)]

1309.

         Thus mekly mesyd he hyr mode   *calmed*
             and was full fayn hyr forto styll;   *very glad*
         And ever he thanked God of all gude
15700   and of all the saynd He send hym tyll.   *trials*
         The wyf to wefyng craft scho yode   *women's work she went*
             and wroyght that werke with full gud wyll;
         And thorwith fand scho thayr fode   *thereby she found there food*
             hyr husband and his folke to fyll.
15705   So in a tyme betyde,   *it happened*
             for monay evyn to marke,   *(i.e., in lieu of money)*
         Hyr was gyfyn a yong kyd   *young kid (goat)*
             in reward for hyr werke.

1310.

         That broyght scho home unto ther mette   *food*
15710   in hope to have gud thanke forthi.   *therefore*
         Thoby lay blynd and herd yt blette,   *heard it bleat*
             and in his hert had he grett ferly.   *wonder*
         "Bese ware," he sayd, "both small and grett,   *Beware*
             of that best how ye com ther by.   *beast*
15715   Yt is not lefull us to ete   *lawful*
             nothyng that falys to felony.   *is stolen*
         I warn yow yt is full wath   *dangerous*
             with stolne fode forto dele."
         Than was the wyfe full wrath,
15720   and langer hyr lyst not hele.   *she desired to keep silent no longer*

1311.

Bott out scho brast with byttur brayd   *burst; anger*
  and sone begane barett to brew.   *trouble*
With a sowre sembland scho sayd,   *bitter countenance*
  "Aftur thi dedes thi saws persew
15725 That trowes that we have thee betrayd,   *beliefs*
  whom thou has fun full trest and trew.   *found; trustworthy*
And God ware of thi pennans payd,   *If; pleased*
  thou wold nevyn non swylke note of new.   *speak no such words anew*
Bot be thi sawys is seyn,   *by your words is seen*
15730 aftur this tale is tald,
That thou before has bene
  mystrowand yong and ald.   *mistrusting*

1312.

"Thou releved all men lese and more,
  now hath thou mornyng to thi mede.   *for your reward*
15735 For all folke that thou fed before
  now fyndes thou few thee forto fede."   *few to feed you*
When Thoby this herd, his hert was sore,
  bot softly spake he for his spede,   *advantage*
"Sertes, woman, and thou wytty wore,   *if you were smart*
15740 thou wold not deme so of my dede.   *judge*
For yf I wroyght Goddes wyll,
  to welth He wyll me wys,
And all thof I dyd yll,   *if instead*
  He may amend all myse.   *sin*

1313.

15745 "And, Lord," he sayd, "sen Thou me wroyght
  to wander in this werld so wyde,
Now in myn eld forsake me noyght,   *old age*
  bot take entent to me this tyd.   *heed to me at this time*
Sen sorows sere ar to me soyght   *Since many sorrows*
15750 with sere assawtes on evere syd,
Vochsave that I myght sone be broyght
  out of this bale that I in byde.   *abide*
I wott I am worthy   *know*
  with more dole to dele,
15755 Bot, Lord, in Thi mercy
  ys all my hope of hele."

[SARAH AND THE DEMON (3:7–17)]

1314.

Now in the same tyme so befell,
  als men may rede by resons ryfe:

Sara, the doyghtur of Raguell,
afterwards; Tobias' wife
15760   that aftur was yong Thoby wyfe,
With hyre than dwelled a damsell
stirred her mistress
   that styrd hyr maystryse oft to stryfe
By tenfull tayles that scho wold tell
harmful tales
   of hyr that lad ever honest lyfe.
who led
15765 For sevyn husbandes all sere
altogether
   weded that worthy wyyght,
wedded that worthy person
And or thei neghed hyr nere,
before they had sex with her
   thei ware ded the fyrst nyght.
dead

1315.

And this was the encheson why
explanation
15770   the fend of them had swylke pausté:
demon; such power
Thei wede for lust of lechery,
They wedded
   and in that sted them strangeld he.
place
Hyr servant was full fell forthi.
cruel therefore
   "Thou sall," she sayd, "not fare with me
15775 Als thou has done sevyn husbandes dy,
[to] die
   qwylk I wott wele were wed with thee."
And clarkes declarys yt thus:
   that fend that foles so fels
demon that so killed the fools
Ys named Asmodyus.
Asmodeus
15780   of swylke maters he mels.
deals

1316.

Bot Sara was full sory then
   that hyre servand so to hyr sayd.
Into a prevay place scho wan.
secret; went
   Ther prevely to God scho prayd:
privately
15785 "Lord God, of whom all gud began,
   Thou bryng me owt of this upbrayd,
reproach
Als I never cofuett erthly man
coveted
   with me in lust forto be layd.
Have mercy, Lord, on me
15790   to sese my grevance grette."
end
Thus dyd scho days thre
   withoutyn drynke or mette.
food

1317.

So when thre days tyll end war went,
had passed
   full sore wepand withoutyn weyne
weeping without doubt
15795 To Myghty God hyr mayne scho ment:
moan
   "Lord, sen Thou has ay keped me clene,
always; pure
Lett never my sawle to syn assent
   bot als Thi servand to be seyne
unless; seen
And to Thi Laws trewly to tent,
listen

15800	or to take me sone owt of this teyne."	*difficulty*
	Thus ware thei sore assayd,	*sorely tested*
	both Sara and trew Thoby.	
	Therfor God has purvayd	
	to mend them with mercy.	

[Tobias at the river Tigris (6:1–9)]

1318.

15805	To them He sent His archangell	
	als a man semand to ther syght.	*looking like a man*
	Bot in ther dole we lett them dwell	*grief*
	to aftur that we rehers them ryght;	*until*
	And of yong Thoby wyll we tell,	
15810	how he went with the angell bryght,	
	And what ferlys to them befell,	*marvels*
	whore thei ware loged in the fyrst nyght.	*lodged*
	Thei had harber full gud	*shelter*
	and beld, whyls thei wold abyd,	*protection*
15815	Evyn fast besyd a flode	*river*
	that heyght Tygres that tyde.	*Tigris*

1319.

	Thor went Thoby to wesch his fete;	*There (into the river); wash his feet*
	his felow folowd full fast in fere.	*together [with him]*
	A mekyll fysch thore gart hym grette,	*A mighty fish; did him greet*
15820	that rose up owt of that ryver.	
	That it wold lose that chyld yt lette.	*destroy; intended*
	He cald fast, "Azari, com nere!	
	Bot yf thou helpe my bale to bette,	*Unless*
	this fysch is lyke to lose me here."	
15825	The angell sayd, "Be styll!	
	Wherfor is thou dredand?	*fearful*
	Take hym boldly by the gyll	*gills*
	and lay hym up to the land."	

1320.

	Als the angell bad he dyd ylk dele;	*instructed; each part*
15830	ane other craft than he hym kend:	*another; showed him*
	"Undoo his wome warly and wele	*gut carefully*
	and take hys hert owt in thi hend.	*heart*
	His gall and his maw men may fele	*gall; stomach; eat*
	for medsyns may thei mekyll amend.	*many things*
15835	Salt the fysche than for thi yele	*welfare*
	furth in our fare forto be spend."	
	All this was done in dede,	
	and thore thei rest that nyght;	

And on the morn thei yede   *journeyed*
15840   the way to Rages ryght.

[RAPHAEL INSTRUCTS TOBIAS AS THEY JOURNEY (6:10–22)]

1321.
And als thei cayred so in cuntré,   *traveled*
    Thoby sayd, "Tell me, I thee pray,
The vertu of ther thynges thre   *these three things*
    thou bad me yeme yisterday."   *look after*
15845   The Angell says, "Thiself sall see
    in what maner thei medsyn may
Both to thi fader and to thee
    and to Sara, als I sall say,
And to hyr fader Raguell,
15850   that wuns here fast beforn;   *dwells; close before [us]*
For with hym wyll we dwell
    this nyght or els tomorn.   *tomorrow*

1322.
"Thor be we sted withoutyn stryfe   *dwelling*
    and ryght welcom, I wot full wele.   *know [it] very well*
15855   For he has rent and ryches ryfe
    and hape and hele fro hed to heyle.   *happiness and health from head to toe*
His doyghtur sall thou take to wyfe
    and be his heyre of ylka dele.   *heir of every part*
And same sall ye lede your lyfe
15860   with mekyll myrth at ylka mele.   *every meal*
I undertake to thee
    this forward sall not fayle,
And, ser, than sall thou se
    qwat medsyns may avayle."

1323.
15865   Thoby than hard and thynkes in hye   *haste*
    this bargan all tyll end is broyght.
He says, "My brother Azari,
    this is nedlese, nevyn yt noyght.   *unnecessary, mention*
For of that woman hard have I   *heard*
15870   what wo be hyr wedyng was wroyght.
I pray thee, gud felow, forthi: *therefore*
    putt all swylk thyng outt of thi toyght.
Yt is not myn entent
    forto be weded so sone.
15875   Thynke that we ware for sent,   *Things*
    that wold I fyrst ware done.

1324.

"This woman that I here thee nevyn   *hear you name*
   at fang to fere wold I be fayn.   *that catch to espouse; glad*
Bot scho was wed with husbandes sevyn,
15880   and sodanly all were thei slayn.
And thou hath heyght with stabyll stevyn   *have promised; speech*
   at bryng me to my fader agayn.
Me thynke thou ordance all unevyn
   that wold I were put to slyke payn.
15885   I knaw not that man
    that hyr fader suld be."
The angell answerd than
    and full sothly sayd he: *very truthfully*

1325.

"Thoby," he sayd, "to me take hed: *heed*
15890   thi fader sall no fawtes fele,
For safe agayn I sall thee lede
   and do his desyre ylka dele.   *each part*
My spekyng is all for thi spede   *safety*
   and sal be for thi soveran sele.   *good fortune*
15895   For all that weddes with luf and dred   *for love and fear*
   withoutyn fayle thei sall fare wele:
With lufe both lowd and styll   *public and private*
    to lyf in Goddes Lay,   *Law*
And with dred to do yll   *evil*
15900   both by nyght and day.

1326.

"Of hyr sevyn husbandes wele wott I   *I know well*
   how thei were for done with a fende.   *demon*
And his ryght name is Asmody;
   he has power swylke scherwes to shende   *such rogues to destroy*
15905   That weddes for lust of lechery
   and takes weddyng unto non other ende.
For that werke ware thei wele worthy
   furth with that warlow forto wende.   *warlock (demon)*
Of thos sevyn was none seyn   *seen*
15910   in bed with hyr to be.
So God has keped hyr cleyne   *pure (virginal)*
    to be weded with thee.

1327.

"Therfor take kepe to my counsayle,   *heed*
   and styth than sall thou graydly go.   *undeterred; quickly*
15915   When thou is broyght within hyr bale   *room*
   and non togeydder bot ye two,

To have a fyre lok thou not fayle,   *start a fire*
    and loke that thou flytt not ferr therfro.   *leave not far from it*
Thor sall my medsyn mekyll avayle,
15920   and therfor take gud tent therto.   *take good heed*
Take the hert and the maw,   *stomach*
    of ather a remnand ryght,   *remnant*
And in the fyre them thraw
    when yt is byrnand bryght.   *burning*

1328.

15925   "And the vertu sall I thee tell,
    how yt sall be beld to yow bathe: *protection*
The smoke therof and als the smell   *also*
    with reke that sall ryse up full rath,   *reek; quickly*
May dryfe owt all the dewls of Hell,   *devils*
15930   that thei do nother scorne ne scath.   *harm*
Dewle Asmody then may not dwell;
    so sall ye wun withoutyn wath.   *live; danger*
And what ye sall do more,
    now sall I tell thee tyll.
15935   And loke, when thou comys thore,
    that ye both yt fulfyll.

1329.

"When this is done thus als I say,   *also*
    owt of all bale ye both ere broyght.   *tragedy; are*
Then sall ye go your God to pray
15940   with hertly wyll and stabyll toyght   *faithful thought*
That He ordand your werke all way
    aftur His wyll forto be wroyght.
Comforth that maydyn now wele thou may,
    bot loke yett at thou neght hyr noyght.   *take care not to have sex with her yet*
15945   Thre nyghtes ye sall lyf chast
    and be in prayers prest   *eager*
Evyll wyghtes away to wast,
    and God sall be your gest.

1330.

"Sythyn may ye do all lefull dede,   *lawful deeds*
15950   as course of matrimon hath kend.   *matrimony*
Whyls ye your God wyll lufe and drede,
    fro all defawtes He wyll yow fend.   *defend*
Then sall He multyplye your sede   *seed*
    and in this erth slyke socour send
15955   To have enogh and never nede
    and sythyn the welth withoutyn end."
When Thoby herd this tale,

	hym lyked yt wounder wele	*wondrously well*
	And sayd, "Forsoth I sall	
15960	do this ever ylka dele."	*each part*

[TOBIAS, WELCOMED BY RAGUEL, DEMANDS SARAH AS HIS WIFE (7:1–20)]

1331.

	To Raguell howse thei com in hye	*Raguel's house; haste*
	whore the angell sayd thei suld be.	
	He cald them in full curtasly	*courteously*
	and welcomed them with wordes free.	*generous*
15965	And als sone as he saw Thoby,	
	unto his wyfe sothly sayd he,	
	"This chyld be face forto dyscrye	*by the face to be described*
	is lyke to Thoby of Nynevé,	
	My cosyn. And he lyf yytt,	*If he still lives*
15970	than wold I be full fayn,	*very joyful*
	And, sertes, the sothe to wytt	
	his felow sall I frayn."	*inquire*

1332.

	He toke the angell on the morne	
	and sayd, "Sun, tell me, and thou may,	*if you can*
15975	Of what kynred this chyld was born,	
	and als wher he hath wund allway."	*also; lived*
	The angell sayd, "His frendes beforn,	
	in Nynevé wunand wer thei.	*living*
	Thor were thei lyke forto be forlorn,	*destroyed*
15980	for thei wold maynteyn Moyses Lay,	
	His fader befor hym	
	and other of his kynred.	
	Of the lyne of Neptalym	*Nepthali*
	ware thei both born and bred."	

1333.

15985	Raguell says, "Sen ye thore wun,	*lived*
	knaw ye oght on Thoby be his name?"	*by*
	The angell says, "That bus uus kun,	*[one] must be our kin*
	for we dwell in his howse at hame.	
	The chyld ye se here ys his sun,	
15990	and I am servand to that same."	
	Then Raguell thynkes here ferleys fun	*astonishments*
	and cald his wyf, "Com hydder, dame!	*hither*
	Our cosyn have we here,	
	the sun of Thoby trew."	
15995	Then made thei all gud chere	
	when thei ther cosyn knew.	

1334.

Sara was ever of sembland sad *countenance*
  for grevance that scho had full grette.
Bot of this gam scho was full glad, *amusement*
16000   and ylkon hertly con other rehete. *each one heartily did the other cheer*
Then Raguell to his servand bad *ordered*
  to sett up bordes and go to mette. *tables; meal*
Bot Thoby sayd other hast he had
  "That bus be done or ever I ete." *must; before*
16005 Raguell says, "Tell me!
  Yt sall be done be lyve." *quickly*
He says, "Then aske I thee
  thi doyghtur to be my wyfe."

1335.

Raguell unto hym answerd noyght
16010   bot stod styll stodeand in that sted. *perplexed*
He wold full fayn his doyghtur myght *glad*
  be maryed in hyr awn kynred. *wedded; kindred*
Bot on that other syde he toght
  he wold not yong Thoby were dede.
16015 For and thei were togeydder broyght, *if*
  he trowed to here no bettur bede. *hear no better news*
And when the angell saw
  how that he stud so styll,
He sayd, "Ser, have non aw, *awe*
16020   for yt is Goddes wyll

1336.

"That this man sall thi doyghtur wedd
  and weld hyr wynly to his wyfe. *take; pleasantly*
Full blessed frut bees of them bred, *will be from them bred*
  als men sall red be reson ryfe. *counsel*
16025 Tho sevyn that fyrst with hyr ware sted, *Those seven [men]*
  no wounder yf thei went with stryfe,
For dome of God nothyng thei dred *judgment*
  bot ever in lust to lede ther lyfe.
That was wele on them seyn. *revealed*
16030   God wold that yt ware so,
And He hath keped hyr cleyn
  in maydynhede this man unto." *maidenhood (virginity); until*

1337.

Then were thei full fayn all in fere *together*
  that God wold gare ther grace so grove. *cause; grow*
16035 Bot Sara mad most mery chere
  to be relessyd of hyr reprove.

Raguell bad them both com nere.

  He layd hyr hand in Thoby love   *Tobias' palm*

And sayd, "Fully I feyst yow here   *pledge*

16040   to wun same for your sawles behove.

Grett God, that sum tyme spake

  tyll our elders beforn,

To Abraham and to Ysaac,

  He yeme yow evyn and morn   *protect*

1338.

16045   "And bynd yow same in His blessyng

  lely to lyf aftur His Law   *loyally*

And thrugh this blessed band yow bryng

  His Commawndment clerly to knaw."

Then were thei blyth, both old and yyng,   *joyful*

16050   and sayd Amen all to that saw.   *that speech*

When thei had endyd all this thyng,

  to mette than satt thei ryght by raw.   *meal; as was proper*

With all kyns daynthes dere   *delicacies*

  full fayre thore were thei fede,

16055   And sone aftur sopere

  ylkon busked to bede.   *prepared themselves for bed*

[TOBIAS AND SARAH, WITH RAPHAEL, DEFEAT ASMODEUS (8:1–24)]

1339.

A chambre was wynly wroyght   *pleasantly*

  for Thoby and for his wyf in fere.   *together*

And when thei were togeydder broyght,

16060   he mad hyr myrth on his manere,

And sone he told to hyr his toyght,

  how that his gud frend con hym lere   *did him instruct*

The fyrst thre nyghtes to do ryght noyght

  bot be in pennance and prayer.

16065   In hert grett joy scho hade

  when scho herd hym say so.

For Goddes sake was scho glad

  to do that and swylke two.

1340.

He toke the hert then in his hend   *the [fish's] heart*

16070   and furth also of the fysch maw.   *stomach*

In myddes the fyre he lett them lend,   *be set*

  and to Sara he sayd this saw: *speech*

"This medsyn is made us to mend

  all dewls werke away to draw.   *devils'*

16075   Fro all ther fare yt wyll us fend   *their fare; defend* ay whyls we luf God and His Law."

That nyght thei ware full prest   *eager*
   to do pennance and pray.

In schort tyme toke thei rest   *For [a] short time*
16080   noyght fere befor the day.   *long*

1341.

Bot als the fend so fled for schame,   *demon*
   the angel werly with hym mette

And asked hym what was hys name
   and for what servyce he was sett.

16085 "Asmodeus we hatte at hame,   *are called*
   a multitude when we are mett.

Our offyce is of wyld and tame   *over everything*
   that wedes for lust ther lyfes to lett,   *desires*

And shamly them to shende   *destroy*
16090 that ar noyght ferd therfor."   *afraid*

Then the angell gart hym wende   *made him leave*
   never forto noye man more.   *trouble*

1342.

Bot Raguell, that gentyll Jew,
   and his gud wyfe sore hertes thei have   *sore hearts*

16095 For yyng Thoby, ther cosyn trew,
   for thei wyst not what suld hym save.   *knew*

And als sone as the kok crew,   *cock*
   he gart his men go make a grave

To hyd hym als thei costom knew;
16100 non other counsayle cowd he crave.   *imagine*

Evyn as he demed was done;
   the costome wele thei knaw.

And aftur then full sone
   the day begane to daw.

1343.

16105 The mother sent then prevely   *secretly*
   unto the chambre a fayr servand

Ther countenance thor forto spy
   and tell to hyr what fare scho fand.

Scho went and com agayn in hy   *haste*
16110 and sayd scho saw them sownd slepand.   *sleeping soundly*

The wyf then was full glad forthi   *therefore*
   and told that tale to hyr husband.

Then Raguell was full fayn
   and bad, whyls yt was derke,

16115 "Go fyll the grave agayn
   that none wytt of our werke."

1344.

Then loved all God with hert and hend
    that fro the fend had mad them free.   *demon*
Then Thoby lykyd thor forto lend   *remain*
16120   and lyf in prayers tho nyghtes three.
He prayd his felow forto wende   *journey*
    unto Rages, that ryche cyté,
And to Gabell, that he wele kend,   *well knew*
    to foche home his fader monye.   *fetch; father's money*
16125   The lettur he toke hym tyll
    how all ther maters ment.
The angell with gud wyll
    that way full wyghtly went.

[RAPHAEL BRINGS GABAEL TO TOBIAS (9:1–12)]

1345.

To Gabels howse full herd he hyde,   *hastened*
16130   and to hym sone he bed his boke.   *offered his letter*
Then Gabell wold no langer byde,   *delay*
    bot ten talentes to hym he toke.
The angell told to hym that tyde   *time*
    how yong Thoby was wed that woke.   *week*
16135   Then radly he rayd hym to ryde   *quickly he arrayed himself*
    and sayd he suld onys on them loke.   *once*
And so ryght furth he rode
    evyn with the angell ydder.   *together; there*
Full mekyll myrth thei made
16140   when thei were all togeydder.

1346.

And Raguell made grett fest forthi   *feast therefore*
    with mette and drynke when thei ware mette,   *food*
With all maner of mynstralsy
    and other game that thei myght gete.   *entertainments*
16145   Then to the angell sayd Thoby,
    "Sen we have done dewly our dette,   *duly our duty*
My fader wyll have full grett ferly   *astonishment*
    and we oversytt the tyme that was sett.   *if we overstay*
I wold we hasted us hame
16150   for ferd hym forto greve."   *for fear; upset*
The angell sayd the same:
    "Sone sall we take our leve."

[TOBIAS TAKES HIS LEAVE WITH SARAH, RAPHAEL, AND NEW RICHES (10:1–13)]

1347.

Sone on the morn thei made them bown,   *ready*
  no lenger forto lend thei lete.   *remain*
16155 Then Sara softely kneled down
  befor hyr fader and moyder fete   *feet*
And mekly asked ther benysown.   *benison*
  Then other frendes full fast con grete,
Bot Raguell, or thei trusse of town,   *before they left the town*
16160 ordandes bettur ther bale to bete.   *sorrows to beat down*
Thresour withoutyn tale   *treasure uncountable*
  he toke them or thei yode,   *before they went*
And muls with mony a male   *mules*
  with them furth forto lede.

1348.

16165 He gaf them catell, schepe, and nete   *cows*
  and all maner of foran fee,   *exotic livestock*
And servantes graydly them to gete
  and bryng them safe whor thei suld be.
With all ryches thei them rehete,   *comfort*
16170 and unto Thoby all thus says he,
"Sun, all my gudes, both small and grette,   *possessions*
  when I am gone I gyf them thee,
And my blessyng allwas
  in werld myght with yow wend."   *go*
16175 "Graymercy, ser," he says,   *Thank you*
  "and fayrs wele, ylka frend."

1349.

Now here we how this angell,   *hear*
  that Azary to his name chese,   *Azariah for; chose*
Of whom the ryght name is Raphaell,
16180 send fro his Lord withoutyn lese   *without lies*
Forto bryng yyng Thoby unto Gabell
  in the ryche cyté that heyght Rages   *was called*
And forto releve gud Raguell   *relieve*
  and sett Sara in parfytt pese,   *perfect peace*
16185 Now sall we here in hy   *haste*
  how he, or ever he sese,   *before he ceased [his work]*
Ordand for old Thoby
  his comforth to encrese.

1350.

Als thei went furth in ther jornay
16190 with wyf and servandes and ther store,   *goods*

The angell con to yyng Thoby say,
  "I rede we two wende home before,   *advise; go; before [the others]*
For yt is sum dele past the day   *some time*
  qwylke we heyght forto have bene thore.   *which; promised*
16195 Lett our meneye com als thei may,   *company*
  for that may ese them mekyll more."
Then Thoby was wele payd,   *very glad*
  and for he wold sho wyst,   *understood*
Unto Sara he sayd,
16200   "Cums aftur als yow lyst."

[RAPHAEL ADVISES TOBIAS; THEY RETURN HOME (11:1–21)]

1351.

The angell says, "Thoby, thou sall
  tent to my sawys now for thi sele.   *listen to my words now for your own sake*
Now is tyme to take the fysch gall,
  thi fader of yt sall favour fele.
16205 Enoynt his eyne wele ther with all,   *Anoint his eyes*
  so by Goddes saynd he sall se wele."   *God's grace; see well*
He was full fayn so suld be fall,
  and sayd yt suld be done ylk dele.   *each part*
His lytyll hund toke hede   *dog*
16210 his herber was nere hand.   *home was near at hand*
Before full fast he yede   *Before [them]; went*
  and wold no lenger stand.

1352.

Old Thoby lay and lyked yll
  because that tyme was so overpast.
16215 The wyf was wrast outt of hyr wyll   *wrested out of her wits*
  and sayd hyr welth away was kast.
Ylk day sho went to a hegh hylle
  to loke als lang os scho moght last.
Ther come the hund evyn hyr untyll   *unto*
16220 and fayned hyr with his tayle full fast.   *fawned*
Then gradly sho aspyde   *promptly she looked*
  and saw wele how thei come.
To hyr husband sho hyed   *hastened*
  and sayd, "Our sun cums home."

1353.

16225 Than was that husband hert full glad   *husband's heart*
  and for gladnes begane to wepe.
"Do lede me furth belyve," he bad,   *quickly*
  "my blessed sun I wyll go kepe."   *attend*
Thei mett als thei ware massed and made, *amazed and astonished*

16230	so ylkon wold on other crepe.	*embrace*
	So sone was all ther sorows sad	
	turned unto wele and to wrschepe.	*happiness; honor*
	The sun his medsyn layd	
	unto his fader eyne in hy.	*eyes in haste*
16235	Than had he syght and sayd,	
	"I love God Allmighty,	

1354.

	"That ay sall be, and ever was,	
	fulfylled of gudnese and of grace.	
	I have not lufed Thi Law, alas,	
16240	ne trewly tent to take Thi trace.	*attended; path*
	And Thou mekly for my trespase	
	hath ponyscht me here in this place,	*punished*
	And now thus hendly heled me has	*nobly healed*
	forto loke in my lyfes space	
16245	On my sun that was sent,	
	and here his course declared,	*set forth*
	And the man that with hym wentt	
	forto be wele reward."	

1355.

	Full mekyll myrth thei mad omell.	*together*
16250	then the sun to his fader sayd	
	Of all ther fare how yt befell:	
	fyrst with the fysch how he was flayd;	
	And sythyn of the gud man Gabell	
	how he ther monay full prestly payd;	
16255	Then how thei rested with Raguell	
	and how ther wedyng was arayd.	
	"Thus all that myght avayle	
	was done withoutyn dystance	*dispute*
	By my felows consayle	
16260	and his gud governance,	

1356.

	"Wherfor he is wele worthy his wage."	
	The fader sayd, "Els God forbede!"	*God forbid [it be] otherwise*
	Sone aftur then come ther careayge	*carriage*
	with the yyng wyf worthy in wede,	*young; worthily clothed*
16265	With charged mulys and mony a page	*laden mules*
	ther catell forto fend and fede.	
	Thei ware mendyd by this message	
	in grett lykyng ther lyf to lede.	
	So when thei neghed nere	*came near*
16270	with all this ryches ryght,	

The fader and all in fere   *together*
   had ferly of that syght.   *wonder*

1357.

Bot sone als he couth Sara see,
   he welcomd hyr and with hym lede.
16275   Grett gladnes in his hert had hee
   that his yyng sun so wele had spede.   *prospered*
Scho had servandes in sere degré   *of many kinds*
   that wund with hyr or sho was wede,   *dwelled; before she was married*
And with hyr come to that cuntré
16280   to beld hyr both at burd and bede.   *comfort; table*
Old Thoby wyfe, Dame An,   *Anna*
   that are lyfyd full heve lyf,
With all comforth sho can
   welcomyd sho hyr sun wyfe.

1358.

16285   And derly dyght sho them to dyne,   *prepared*
   ther travell toke sho tent untyll.   *travails; attention unto*
Sho broyght them furth both bred and wyne
   and other fode all folke to fyll.
Old Thoby asked of his sun syne   *ten*
16290   who aght tho guddes by ryght and skyll.
He sayd, "Ser, thei ar Goddes and myne
   and sall be yours evyn at your wyll."
Then on his knese he kneled
   and loved God of all thyng,
16295   That so wold be his beld   *protection*
   and owt of bale hym bryng.

1359.

And for he wold Sara were seyne   *revealed*
   and knawn with all his kynred clere,
He gart make a fest fayr and cleyne   *feast*
16300   and bad therto his frendes in fere.   *altogether*
The angell ordand all be dene,   *straightway*
   both mete and drynke with meré chere.
Thor wanted noyght, wele may we weyne,   *believe*
   qwer swylke stewerd was to stere.   *when such a steward; direct [matters]*
16305   And when this fest was done
   dewly in all degré,
Ylkon were ordand sone
   whore them likyd best to be.

[RAPHAEL REVEALS HIMSELF (11:1–22)]

1360.

Then sayd old Thoby, "My sun, take hede

16310   and tell me now betwyx us two

What we may gyf this man to mede   *reward*

    that went with thee thus to and fro."

Yyng Thoby sayd, "For his gud dede   *good deeds*

    he hath servyd ther gudes and mo.   *these*

16315 Bot the on halfe we wyll hym bede   *the one*

    and vowche them safe yf he wyll so,

My wyfe and hyr meneye   *company*

    to have the tother half clere.

That is enogh for me

16320   to fynd them fayre in fere."   *together*

1361.

Thei cald the angell prevely,

    and old Thoby thus to hym sayd,

"We thanke thee hertly, Azary,

    for all our hele has thou purvayd.

16325 We wott that thou were worthy

    to have all guddes that here ar grayd,   *prepared*

Bot we pray thee, my sun and I,

    to take thee half and hald thee payd.

And all that fallys us tyll

16330   of mobyls more and lese   *movable goods*

Sall ever be at thi wyll,

    als full wele worthy ese."

1362.

The angell then with wordes playn

    sayd, "All the soth I sall yow tell,

16335 Me lykes no langer forto layn: *hold back*

    wytt ye wele I am an archangell.

Fro God thus was I send certayn

    to mend all myschefes yow omell.   *among you*

Now is tyme I turn agayn   *return*

16340   in blyse of Hevyn with Hym to dwell.

I sayd yow here at hame

    my name was Azary.

Raphaell is my ryght name,

    this sall ye trow trewly.

1363.

16345 "In all aray I have bene ryght

    als erthly man of flesch and bonne

To ete and drynke both day and nyght,
  bot of your mete I ete ryght none. *food I ate*
For my mete is the verray syght
16350   of the Godhed that sall never be goyne, *gone*
And my cloghyng is hevenly lyght, *clothing*
  and my werke is lovyng allon.
All that lelly lyfe has led *loyally life*
  and endes in Goddes servyce,
16355 Thei sall be cled and fed
  and werke in that same wyse.

1364.

"And for thi werkes were to His pay, *because; satisfaction*
  in all wathes was He thi warrand *dangers; defender*
And sent His saynd thee to assay *trial; test*
16360   yf thou wold fayle or stably stand.
And for thou groched noyght nyght nor day *complained*
  when thou sych fell defautes fand,
Now has He wast thi wo away *taken*
  and sent thee welth to weld in land.
16365 Do os thou dyd beforne:
  gyf almus with gud chere *alms*
And that yt be up born
  with pennance and prayere.

1365.

"Also, yyng Thoby, to me take tent, *take heed*
16370   sen thou has wyf and welth at wyll. *since*
Luf thou thi Lord that yt has lent,
  and love His Law both lowd and styll. *publicly and privately*
And loke that thou never to syn assent
  bot ever have drede forto do yll,
16375 And kyndly kepe His Commawndment,
  els may thou sped thiself to spyll."
Thus lernd he als hym lyst *taught; desired*
  how thei suld trewly trow,
And then he was ravyschett *ravished*
16380   away, thei wyst not how.

[TOBIT LIVES WELL AND DIES HAPPY, AS DOES TOBIAS (13:1–14:17)]

1366.

Thoby was sevynty yeres of eld *Tobit; years of age*
  when he began blynd to be.
That same defawt then furth he felyd *felt*
  all fully fyfty yere and thre.
16385 Then was he broyght to bettur beld

	in two and faurty forto wele see.	*to see well*
	So in this werld he myght hym weld	
	fyfe score and two in sere degré.	*102 [years]*
	Then saw he that he suld dy	
16390	and the tyme to fulfyll.	
	He cald his sun Thoby,	*Tobias*
	and thus he told hym tyll.	

1367.

	He sayd, "Sun, I sall sone make end,	
	to bere me loke thou not byd.	*bury; delay*
16395	Thi moyder, sun, sall eftur wende,	*go*
	and bere hyr then me fast besyde.	*bury*
	Pray thou then God with hert and hend	
	that He fro harme thee hape and hyde.	*protect and conceal*
	And kepe His Law als I have kend,	*taught*
16400	then sall no torfure thee betyde.	*hardship; befall*
	Full grett defawttes sall fall	
	to folke of Nenevyé,	
	And therfor, sun, thou sall	
	do als I consayle thee.	

1368.

16405	"This cyté sone sall synke certayn	
	for syn bot thei ther myse amend.	*unless; sin*
	Therfor, when we ere past with payn,	
	no lenger here loke that thou lend,	*remain*
	Bot wende unto Raguell agayn	
16410	with all the gudes that God has yow send.	
	All Israel folke wyll be ful fayn	
	that our kynred with them be kend."	
	Old Thoby and his wyfe	
	thus ferd als folke may fynd.	*fared*
16415	His tym and his trew lyfe	
	mun ever be made in mynd.	*must*

1369.

	Yyng Thoby wold no langer dwell	
	for tayls his fader told hym to.	
	He dyd to carry all his catell,	
16420	his wyf, and ther servandes also,	
	And all that to his fader fell	
	were then his awn, so were thei mo;	
	And raked ryght to Raguell,	*went*
	his wyfe fader, that thei went fro.	
16425	Thor ware thei welcomd fare,	
	both man, wyfe, and page.	

Then was Thoby sun and ayre   *heir*
   of all ther herytage.

1370.

   For Raguell be reson ryfe
16430   sone aftur out of this werld was tone.   *taken*
   Then Thoby and his worthy wyfe
    had chylder fayr and welth gud woyne,   *in plenty*
   And when he had lyfed in his lyfe
    one hunderth wyntur all bot one,   *ninety-nine winters (years)*
16435 He went away withoutyn stryfe.
    We trow he had full graythly goyne.   *believe; a very quick passing*
   His wyf sone aftur sesyd,   *ended (died)*
    als God wold behoved to be.
   His chylder furth encressed
16440   and governd grett degree.

1371.

   Full blessed barns furth of them bred,   *children*
    als sythyn was sene on ylka syde.   *then*
   And so ther lynag sprang and spred,
    als ys wyttenest in werldes wyde.   *witnessed*
16445 This story is rehersed and red   *read*
    us forto tech in ylka tyde,   *to teach in each place*
   Yf we in stourys be stratly sted,   *hardships; placed in straits*
    all bowsomly all bale to byde   *obediently; grief to endure*
   And love God of His grace,
16450   what saynd so He wyll send.   *whatever trial*
   God graunt us spech and space
    our myse here to amend!   *misdeeds*

BOOK OF ESTHER

HESTER LIBER.

[KING AHASUERUS' FEAST AND QUEEN VASHTI'S DEPOSITION (1:1–22)]

1372.

	Here may men loke who lykes to lere	*learn*
	of solace and of sorowyng also;	
16455	How that this werld wuns ever in were	*exists; strife*
	fro wo to wele, fro wele to wo;	
	Of a rych kyng heyght Assuere,	*called Ahasuerus*
	and of his wyfes, for he had two.	
	Both were thei qwenys by seson sere.	*in various times*
16460	Qwene Vasti heyght that on of tho,	*Vashti*
	That other Hester heyght;	*Esther*
	and als lernyd men may loke,	
	Aftur hyr name full ryght	
	this ys cald Hester Boke.	

1373.

16465	This mater more to make in mynd,	
	this myghty man that I of meyne,	*speak*
	Fro Ethiope unto grett Iend	*Ethiopia; India*
	was he kyng of all cuntré cleyne.	
	He mad a fest, als folke may fynd,	
16470	of dukes, erles, and knytes kene,	*brave knights*
	And bad that none suld leve behynd,	*ordered*
	because he suld be soveran sene	*seen as sovereign*
	And knawn for kyng and prince	
	of castels, towre, and town.	
16475	Sex score and sevyn provynce	*127 provinces*
	were to his bedyng bown.	*bidding obedient*

1374.

	And all he bad that thei suld be	
	ylk man in ther rychest arays	
	At Susa, in his awn cyté,	*Susa*
16480	for thor was purvayd his paylays.	*palace*

And to his kepers commawnd he
   that his fest suld last faurty days
With all ryches and ryalté
   that any man couth poynt or prays.   *appoint*
16485 The chambers dyd thei dyght   *construct*
   so that noyght suld be sene   *nothing*
Bot of gold burnyscht bryght
   and pyrry couchyd full clene.   *precious stones*

1375.
Ther bordes ware sett of sylver syne,   *tables; then*
16490   and trystes of the same ordand ere;   *trestles; are*
Ther vessell all of gold full fyne
   that any man to bord suld bere;
And kokes that were in kechyn   *cooks; kitchen*
   of sylver and gold was all ther geyre.   *gear*
16495 Ther was no wantyng of no wyn,   *lack; any*
   ne of no welth that lordes suld were.   *wear*
All maner of mynstralsy   *entertainment*
   wore thore them forto glad.
Ther myght no man dyscrye
16500   more myrth then thore was made.

1376.
In this meyne tyme that I of tell,   *same time*
   Qweyne Vasty made full grett gedderyng
Of all the lades that con dwell
   abowt hyre nere, both old and yyng.   *her near*
16505 And on the aghtyn day befell   *eighth*
   that Assuer, this ryall kyng,
Wold schew his myght thos men omell   *among those men*
   and his power of erthly thyng.
And of more myrth to meyne,
16510   because sho was semly,   *beautiful*
He sentt aftur the qweyne
   to glad that cumpany.

1377.
Sevyn eunokes of his chambre chefe   *eunuchs*
   that to lades that tym toke tent   *ladies; took heed*
16515 Wentt to the qweyn with wordes brefe
   and sayd how the kyng for hyr sent.
Sho toke yt gretly unto grefe
   that swylke men on that errand wentt;
For worthy lordes that were hyr leyfe   *dear to her*
16520   suld make sych message, so sho ment.
Scho gart them wend agayn   *She made; go back*

withoutyn motyng more | *arguing*
And say the kyng certayn
    that sho myght not come thore.

1378.

16525 Swylke eunockes both north and south
    ware wont then lades forto lede. | *ladies*
Forto kepe ther counsayll welc thci couth
    and no thyng speke bot that myght spede.
And thei were ordand in ther yowth
16530   that thei myght do no manly dede, | *deed*
Bot ever more meke and myld of mouth
    servandes als maydyns for ther mede. | *service*
The queyne toyght ther servyce
    fell not for hyr degré,
16535 Whyls mony princes of price | *renown*
    ware in that same semlé. | *assembly*

1379.

The kyng toke yt to grett dedyne | *disdain*
    that his wyf wold not werke his wyll;
And to princes he con hym pleyne | *[the] princes; complain*
16540   and bad thei suld take tent thertyll | *take heed thereto*
How that the qweyne so wold hyr feyne | *shirk*
    his commawndment not to fulfyll,
And that thei suld, or thei went theyne, | *before they departed*
    be wele avysyd of that same skyll | *advised; happening*
16545 And ordan them amang
    what were best forto do;
And were yt wele or wrang, | *good or bad*
    he wold assent therto.

1380.

Thos princes, als the kyng purvayd,
16550   assembled all into a halle,
And thore ther resons thei arayd | *there their*
    for swylke a fare what suld befall.
And all samyn to the kyng thei sayd: | *as one*
    "Ser, our assent say thee we sall:
16555 Us thynke this lake is not layd | *affront; directed*
    to thee allon bot to us all; | *alone*
For swylk maters to move,
    bot boyte be sett therin, | *unless solution*
Yt may be grett reprove
16560   to us and all our kyn.

1381.

"For yf this noyte were noysed in land,   *trouble; widely known*
    yt suld make lades be more kene   *women; bold*
And noyght to be to ther husband
    bowsom als thei are hath bene.   *obedient as they have been*
16565   Ther commawndmentes thei suld gayn stand   *turn against*
    and sett exempyll of the qwene.   *follow*
And therfor, ser, we have ordand
    that swylke maters no more be sene;
And for this dede is demyd
16570   so that thi qwene Vasty
For hyr defawt be flemed   *driven away*
    fere fro thi cumpany.   *far*

1382.

"And then do crye in ylk cuntré
    and byd all wemen to be bown   *obedient*
16575   To ther husbandes in all degré
    to save his ryght and his renown.
And sone do seke in ylke cyté   *soon*
    fayre maydyns both in feld and town,
And chese on of them to thee   *choose*
16580   forto be qweyne and were the crowne,   *wear*
Qwylke thee thynke best wyll seme
    a lades lyf to lede."   *ladylike life*
Evyn als tho princes con deme   *did advise*
    gart he be doyn in dede.   *he caused to happen in deed*

[AHASUERUS SEEKS A NEW QUEEN, MARRIES ESTHER, A JEW (2:1–18)]

1383.

16585   Thei soyght in towns to and fra,   *fro*
    and all fayre maydyns that thei fand   *found*
To the kynges court thei gart them ga   *made them go*
    to se who suld be qweyne ordand.
In that same cyté of Susa
16590   a gentyll Jew then was dwelland   *dwelling*
That manly durst no maystrays ma,   *dared make no revolt*
    for paynyms law used all that land.   *against the pagan*
The Bybyll tellys to us
    this man that I of meyn   *speak*
16595   Was named Mardochius,   *Mordecai*
    that before bold had beyn.

1384.

Mardochius was dyght to dwell
    als neghtbour nere to the kynges gate,

And with hym wund a damsell, *lived*
16600   his brother doyghtur leved o late. *left [to him] recently*
Hester scho heyght, os I herd tell; *Esther she as called*
   of a fayrrer woman no man wate. *knew*
Mardochyus meneys hym forto mell *intends; inquire*
   yf sho mygth stepe unto the qweynys astate.
16605 Rychly he hyr arayd *adorned*
   that wrschep forto wyn, *honor*
And for hyr parte he purvayd,
   so that sho was takyn in

1385.

And ordand to be on of sevyn
16610   that with the kyng suld ryse and rest,
Of whom on suld be ordand evyn
   with hym in fayth forto be fest. *married*
When he had purvayd them state and stevyn *places and the right of speech*
   ylkon abowt to be his gest,
16615 Als God wold send hyr helpe fro Hevyn,
   Hester to luf hym lyked best.
The other wentt home be deyne *straightway*
   bot hyr that hym was levere. *except her that he preferred*
Hester was crowned qweyne
16620   and Vasty voyde forever.

1386.

Mardocheus was full mery in mynd
   when he hard how this fare fell in.
He sent his frendes, als folke may fynd,
   to say hyr how sho suld begyn,
16625 That sho suld noyght carpe of hyr kyned *speak of her kind*
   that scho was comyn of Jewys kyn; *of a Jewish family*
For paynyms had lever had them pyned *would rather; tortured*
   then wytt that thei suld to welth wyn. *know; they (Jews)*
The kyng made festes thre *three feasts*
16630   with lordes and knyghtes keyne,
And bad all folke suld be
   bowand to his new qweyne. *obedient (bowing)*

[HAMAN SEEKS TO DESTROY THE JEWS (3:1–15)]

1387.

The qweyne in lykyng leve we than *joy*
   in ryall state so styll to stand,
16635 And of the kyng carpe, yf we can, *speak*
   a farly fare that he furth fand.
He had a stewerd, that heyght Aman, *Haman*

that was leder of all his land;
And what the kyng with wrschep wan,   *honor won*
16640   all had he holly under hand.
The kyng lufed hym so wele
his hert he con hym hete,   *promise*
And commawnd all men to knele
whore so thei suld hym mete,

1388.
16645   And that men suld hym honour ay   *always*
evyn als hymself in gud degré.
And yt befell so on a day
Aman went so unto his meneye.   *company*
Mardochyus satt evyn in his way
16650   on benke whore he was wonnt to be.   *bench*
To Aman wold he no word say,
bot styll in sted evyn ther satt he.   *place*
Aman for his behove
be that same way oft yode.   *went*
16655   Mardochyus wold not move
to hym nauder hat ne hode.   *neither hat nor hood (i.e., he would not bow)*

1389.
So Aman noyes were ever new   *Haman's annoyance*
for this same cause when he com thore.
Sum enmyse that Mardochyus knew   *enemies*
16660   sayd he and his kyn Jewys thei wore.
When Aman wyst he was a Jew,
then was his malyse mekyll more   *much*
And sayd full sone yt suld hym rew,
for he wold not fale hym before.   *bow before him*
16665   He askyd leve of the kyng
all for Mardochius sake
All Jews to draw and hyng   *hang*
whore so men myght them take.

1390.
Aman gart wrytt this ylke warrand   *caused to be written; warrant*
16670   in all the hast that ever he may.   *haste*
The kyng yt seled with his awn hand,   *sealed*
and then Aman went fast his way.
He sent letturs thrugh all that land
that all tho that lyfyd by the Jewys lay
16675   Sall com, als the kyng hath commawnd,
tyll Susa cyté a certan day.
He bad both wyf and chyld
suld bow to this bydyng

| | And thare gudes tame and wyld | *all their goods* |
| 16680 | befor feyt to the kyng. | *fetched* |

[MORDECAI SEEKS ESTHER'S HELP TO SAVE THE JEWS (4:1–17)]

1391.

	When this word to the Jewys was went,	
	to Susa soyght man, wyf, and knave.	
	Mardochyus herd then how thei ment;	
	for reuth he remed als he suld rave.	*ruth he cried out; be mad*
16685	For wele he saw he suld be shent	*killed*
	yf Aman so his hele myght have.	
	Unto the qweyne softly he sentt	
	and prayd hyr help hyrselfe to save.	
	He made hyr understand	
16690	and all the soth suppose	
	How Aman had ordand	
	all hyr lynage to lose.	

1392.

	So qwen the qweyne this consell kend,	*when; counsel knew*
	scho syghyd sore with sympyll chere.	
16695	This myschefe wold scho were mend,	
	bot sho wyst not on what manere.	
	Hyr folke sho wold full fayn dyffend	*very gladly*
	so that thei myght lyf furth in fere,	*together*
	And hald hyr eme owt of ther hend,	*uncle; hands*
16700	forto be noyd was non so nere.	
	Sho wyst wele of this thyng	
	was no counsayle to crave	
	Bot thrugh helpe of the kyng,	
	and that was hard to have.	

1393.

16705	Unto hyr eme sho sent in hy	*haste*
	that he suld take no grevance grett,	
	Bot trest wele in God Allmighty	
	and thre days fast fro drynke and mette	*food*
	And pray to God all specially	
16710	Hym forto helpe owt of that hette.	*difficulty*
	"And so sall my maydyns and I,	
	for so I trow gud grace to gette."	*thereby I believe*
	Thus dyd thei tho thre days,	*those*
	and than withoutyn more	
16715	Rychly sho hyr arays	*adorns herself*
	to com the kyng before.	

[ESTHER SETS A FEAST FOR THE KING AND HAMAN (5:1–8)]

1394.

Als he was sett in solace sere
 with other maysters full mony moo,   *lords*
In his presens sho con apeyre   *did appear*
16720 full ferdly all of ferrom hym fro.   *coldly; far from him*
He made hyr tokyns to come nere,   *signs*
 and when sho saw that he dyd so,
Scho menskyd hym with full meré chere;   *honored*
 yt was solace to se them two.
16725 He sayd, "Welcom, my qweyne!
 Thou comys sum thyng to crave.   *ask for*
Say what thou wyll of meyne,
 and, sertes, thou sall yt have."

1395.

"A, lord," sho sayd, "and thi wyll be,   *if you desire it so*
16730 my myrth yt myght full mekyll amend
And thou wold this day dyne with me   *If*
 in lufly loge that I in lend,   *the beautiful home; live*
And byd Ser Aman com with thee,   *command*
 that is chefe of thi counsell kend."
16735 "My wyfe," he says, "gladly wyll we.
 For Aman sall we aftur send."
That fest was gudly grayd   *well prepared*
 with all gamys that myght glade.   *entertainments*
Sho toyght more then scho sayd,
16740 bot mekyll myrth thei made.

1396.

The kyng come namly at the noyne,
 and Aman, that grett favour feld.
Sho welcomd them, yf thei were sone,
 with all wrschep that scho couth weld.
16745 And when the dyner was all done,
 the kyng unto his qweyn beheld
And bad hyr boldly aske hyr boyne,   *reward*
 for he was bowne hyr forto beld.   *comfort*
Sho sayd then to the kyng,
16750 "My lord, be leve of thee,
This day I aske nothyng
 bot glad and blyth to be.

1397.

"And ferrer, lord, now wold I frayn,   *further*
 sen ye to speke hath graunt me space,

16755	That ye to morn wold come agayn
	to dyne with me in this same place,
	And of Aman als I am fayn
	that he playnly swylke power has.
	And, ser, then sall I say certayn
16760	what myght me comforth in this case."
	The kyng grauntes ylk dele	*each part*
	to fulfyll hyr entent.
	Sho wenes all sall be wele,
	and so ther ways thei went.

[HAMAN PLANS MORDECAI'S DEATH (5:9–14)]

1398.

16765	Syr Aman wele wytt may we
	went home with mekyll pompe and pryd.
	He cald his wyfe and his meneye	*company*
	and told unto them in that tyde
	How that ther was none bed bot he	*asked*
16770	at the qweynes burd with the kyng to byde,	*table*
	And on the morn how he suld be
	in that same place sett them besyd.
	"And sen that thei do thus,
	me thynke no fawte I fele
16775	Bot fals Merdochyus	*Except*
	that to me noyght wyll knele."

1399.

	His wyfe says, "Sertes, yt is grett scorn
	that he wyll not ryse of his sette.
	Bot, ser, lett ordan fast therforn:
16780	sett up a tre both long and grette,	*gallows*
	And aske leve of the kyng at morn
	that he be hanged or ever he ete.	*before he eats anything*
	So sall his lyf by lyghtly lorn;
	then may thou be mery at thi mete."
16785	Than gart he grath men gang
	and sone sett up a sperre	*timber (gallows)*
	Of fyfty cubbettes lang	*cubits high*
	Merdochius on to marre.	*kill*

[THE KING DECIDES TO HONOR MORDECAI'S SERVICE (6:1–14; 2:19–23)]

1400.

	Bot God, that hym His helpe hath heyght,	*promised*
16790	ordand that qwayntyse forto qwell.	*scheme*
	The kyng lay wakand all the nyght,	*awake*

	and of sere maters so con he mell.	*many; so did he think*
	He bad servantes to sett up lyght	
	and cald a clerke that couth hym tell	
16795	And forto rede in romans ryght	*tales*
	what ferlys in his tym befell.	*marvels*
	That clerke then sat redand	*reading*
	full mony poyntes of price,	
	And in a sted he fand	
16800	whore wryttyn was on this wyse:	

1401.

	"Two men that wold not byde for bale	*remain [loyal] due to evil*
	thor be the way onys als thei wentt,	*there by the road (i.e., the gate) once*
	Thei counsayld same and sayd, 'We sall	*together*
	gare slay the kyng be our assent.'	*cause*
16805	And on Merdocheus herd this tale,	
	all how thei of swylke maters ment.	
	Unto the kyng he told yt hale,	*entirely*
	and els he had bene shamly shent."	*otherwise; killed*
	The kyng asked what reward	
16810	Mardocheus had here fore.	*for this*
	The clerke saw noyght declared	
	be word ne wryttyng thore.	

1402.

	By this was done, then was lyght day.	
	Ser Aman hoped to have his bone,	*reward*
16815	And in he come the kyng to pray	
	that Mardocheus were hanged soyne.	*at once*
	The kyng hym cald and bad hym say	
	what dede suld to that man be doyne	*done*
	That the kyng wold have wrschept all way:	
16820	"This wold I wytt with wordes foyne."	*few*
	Aman thynkes, "That am I	
	that the kyng wyll wrscheped be.	
	None is so wele worthy."	
	Therfor thus ordand he.	

1403.

16825	He says, "Lord, this sall be his mede	*reward*
	that the kyng wyll reverence with renown:	*who*
	He sall be cled in kynges wede	*clothes*
	and crowned with a kynges crowne.	
	He sall sytt on the kynges awn sted,	*place*
16830	and the best bachelar sall be bown	*young knights; bound*
	His brydyll bowsomly to lede	*humbly*
	and crye with trumpeyttes thrugh all the towne:	

'Thus is the kynges wyll!
  Whom he wyll wrschepe wele,
16835 That thus be done hym tyll
  and all men unto hym knele!'"

1404.

The kyng was of this purpase payd   *pleased*
  and sayd, "Loke that thou tarry not lang,
Bot sone thou loke all this geyre be grayd,   *this material be gathered*
16840 and take on of our stedes strang,   *horses*
And make Merdocheus be arayd   *arrayed*
  aftur thi wordes that noyght be wrang.
And als thou hath assygned and sayd,
  thiself sall be his brydyll gang.   *by his bridle go*
16845 And when thou has done so,
  to mete we sall go soyne."   *banquet*
Then was Aman full wo,
  bot wyghtly was yt done.

1405.

Mardocheus had grett mervell then
16850 what all thier maters myght be meyne.   *these*
Bot wele he toyght the ground began   *foundation [of them]*
  of his cosyn, the kynges qweyne.
Full sorely lett Ser Aman   *passed*
  be all ther dedes were doyne be deyne.   *until all these deeds*
16855 Unto his howse wyghtly he wan,
  and thor was sorowyng sadly seyne.
Als thei so mornyng made,   *mourning*
  on come hym to rehete   *one [man]; comfort*
And sayd the kyng abade   *was waiting*
16860 to he come to his mete.

[ESTHER'S SECOND BANQUET; HANAN EXPOSED AND KILLED (7:1–10)]

1406.

Then went he furth with syghyng sore,
  bot he behoved chaunge his sembland soyne.   *appearance quickly*
So when he come the kyng before,
  he sayd his wyll was dewly doyne.   *dutifully*
16865 Thei went to mete withoutyn more,
  and mery mad the kyng that noyne.   *noon*
The qweyn, for hyr frendes wepand wore,
  thynkes eftur mete to aske hyr boyne.   *food; reward*
Syr Aman thynkes hym shent,   *himself destroyed*
16870 no mete myght make hym glade,

For he dowtes hym to hent   *worries he might suffer*
   more harme then he yett hade.

1407.

The qweyne was fayn them forto fyll   *pleased*
   with alkyn bestes and fowls fyne,
16875 With spycery to spare or spyll;
   and when the kyng was glade with wyne,
The kyng sayd then the qweyn untyll,
   "Wyf, aske of me oght that is myne,
For half my kyngdom yf thou wyll!
16880   Aske yt and yt sal be thine."
Then down to knese sho kneled
   sum dele with drery mode,
And sayd, "Lord, God yow yeld!
   Me nedes none erthly gude.

1408.

16885 "Bot of this boyn beseke I thee:
   his strengh to stroy and to gayn stand
That wyll confownd my kyn and me
   and stroy our lynag in this land."
The kyng askes, "What herlott is he
16890   that swylke heghtnes dere take on hand?"   *pride dares*
Sho says, "Lord, yf thi lykyng be,
   Ser Aman has this care cummand."
When the kyng herd this word,
   yt merveld all his mode.
16895 He rayse up fro the burd   *table*
   and into a garthyn he yode.   *garden he went*

1409.

Thore went he hym forto avyse   *consider*
   what ware to carpe in slyke a kynd.   *say in such a situation*
The qweyn seke on hyr bed sho lys,   *fainting; she lies*
16900   for scho was moved all out of mynd.
Ser Aman then full spedely spyse   *wonders*
   how he myght any favour fynd.
Before the qweyn he knelys and cryes
   to pray hyr that he be not pynd.   *executed*
16905 The kyng com in with that,
   for greved both gull and grene,   *yellow and green [with rage]*
And sees whor Aman satt
   at the bed besyd the qweyne.

1410.

That moved hym more to tene that tyd,   *anger at that time*
16910   bot Aman withdrew hym for drede.
That unto the kyng another cryde,
        "This day is doyne a dolefull dede:
Aman has sett his howse besyd
        a gebett, large of lengh and brede,   *a gallows*
16915   Mardocheus ther with rewth to ryde.   *with grief to hang*
        Thus has he heyght, who wyll take hede."   *sworn*
The kyng asked other mo
        yf he swylk maystrys meyve.   *intended*
Thei sayd all he dyd so
16920   Mardocheus to myschefe.

1411.

The kyng then cummand his meneye,
        "Ser Aman tyte I byd yow take   *quickly*
And hang hymself on that same tre
        that he mad for Mardocheus sake."
16925   Thei were full blyth yt suld so be,   *glad*
        and sone that maystry con thei make.
And Jews that soyght to that cyté,   *journeyed*
        then mott thei wende to wynly wake.   *may they go to merry festivities*
And qweyne was glad and blyth
16930   with Merdocheus and mo.
Thei thanked God oft sythe   *often times*
        that them had socurd soo.   *succored*

[THE JEWS SAVED (8:1–10:3)]

1412.

Thus was his blyse all broyght in bale   *to sorrow*
        that to Merdocheus mened full yll.   *intended*
16935   His wyf and barnes, both grett and smale,   *children*
        were flemed ferre for that same skyll.   *driven far away*
Hys howse and all his howshald hale   *completely*
        was gyfyn to the qweyne to weyld at wyll,   *were given; wield*
And his tressour to tell be tale
16940   to Jews that were spoled forto spyll.   *plundered*
The wryttes that were enseled   *letters; officially made*
        at putt the Jews to payn,   *death*
By wrytte thei were repelyd.   *repealed*
        Then were tho folke ful fayn.   *those people very glad*

1413.

16945   So was fals Aman hanged at hame,
        als he tyll other had yll ordand.

Mardocheus was made in hys name
    stewerd in his sted to stand.   *steward in his place*
Thus whoso wyll the sakles shame   *innocent*
16950   for any lordschep in this land,
Apon themself sall fall the same
    or wers. This may we wele understand.   *worse*
God graunt us grace to end
    in luf and charité
16955   And all our myse to mend!   *misdeeds to amend*
    Amen. So mott yt be!   *may*

BOOK OF JUDITH

JUDYTH.

[NEBUCHADNEZZAR'S PRIDE AND POWER (1:1–16)]

1414.

	Dame Judyth was a gentyll Jew	*noble*
	and woman wyse whore sho suld wende.	*wise wherever she went*
	Now wyll we nevyn hyr story new,	*invoke her*
16960	for to sum men yt myght amend	*some*
	To see how sho in trewth was trew	*truth was true*
	als lang als sho in lyf con lend	*so long as she in life remained*
	And lufed the Law als lele Ebrew	*loved; as a loyal Hebrew*
	that Moyses tyll hyr kynred kend.	*to her people taught*
16965	That law forto mayntene	
	sho ordand in all thyng,	
	Als insampyll was seyn	*As example*
	and wyttenest in werkyng.	*witnessed in [her] behavior*

1415.

	Bot to mell with this mater more	*speak*
16970	this lady now wyll we leve of hand,	*leave aside (for a time)*
	And tell of fare that fell before,	*events; happened*
	als our faders before us fand.	*found*
	A kyng, Nabogodhonosour,	
	in Bablion he was dwelland.	*Babylon; dwelling*
16975	All other kynges and lordes wore	
	full stably at his stevyn to stand.	*steadfastly; command*
	All that lufed paynyms law	*loved pagan*
	and lyfed by mawmentry	*lived in idolatry*
	Aftur his dedes con draw	
16980	and lowted hym fast forthi.	*bowed to him fast therefore*

1416.

	He had this werld sett at his wyll;	
	hym toyght no noye suld neght hym nere,	*annoyance; approach*
	For all his forwardes to fulfyll	*agreements*
	all hethyn folke were full fayn in fere.	*glad together*

16985	With Ebrews oft hym angerd yll,	desired not; teaching to learn
	for them lyst not his lare to lere.	times he desired; destroy
	Oft sythys he spyed them to spyll	siege engines; many assaults
	with engynys and with sawtes sere.	crafty devices
	By sere cautels he kest	
16990	how he myght bryng them down,	
	Bot whyls thei lufed God best,	
	to beld them ay was He bown.	comfort; ever; committed

1417.

	This kyng was strang in ylke stoure,	powerful; every battle
	and in all were he wan degré;	warfare; victory
16995	And so he gat to grett honowre	
	and conquered kynges in sere cuntré,	
	Wherfor he fell in fowle errowre,	
	als men may be exempyll see.	
	He couth not knaw his creatore	
17000	bot hoped ther was no god bot he.	but himself
	On payn of lyf and lyme	limb
	he warnd his men ylkon	each one
	And bad thei suld hald hym	
	ther god and other none.	

1418.

17005	So in this errour con he dwell	
	als maystur most of more and lese,	
	Wherfore fowle vengance on hym fell	
	to lyfe als best with grouand grese.	live as a beast upon growing grass
	Bot here we have no tym to tell	
17010	the poyntes that proves all the procese.	
	Furth with our maters wyll we mell	speak
	how Jewys ware doyne to grett dystrese.	
	For then the kyng ordand	
	his ost with playn powere	army; naked power
17015	To dystroy ylka land	each land
	that his law wyll not lere.	obey

[NEBUCHADNEZZAR SENDS HOLOFERNES AGAINST THE JEWS (2:1–7:18)]

1419.

	And to fulfyll all this in dede	
	to semble folke he wold not sese.	assemble; tarry
	He ordand on his ost to lede,	one [man] his army
17020	a dughty duke heyght Olyfernes,	named Holofernes
	And bad all men to hym take hede	
	and with hym wend in were and pese.	go in war and peace
	The folke were fayn and with hym yede,	glad; went

	and for ther cheftan thei hym chese.	*declare*
17025	The kyng bad them not spare	
	bot dyng down all be deyne	*strike; everyone at once*
	That wold noyght luf ther lare,	*love their teaching*
	tyll all be conquered cleyne.	*utterly*

1420.

	This dughty duke that I of ment	*brave leader; mentioned*
17030	fro his werke wold no langer abyde.	*desist*
	With full grett ost furth is he went	*army*
	with mynstralsy and mekyll pride.	
	Cytes and burghes both thei brent,	*towns; burned*
	the Jewys to harme full fast thei hyed.	*hastened*
17035	Cornes and wynes shamly thei shent.	*Cornfields and vineyards; destroyed*
	Thor was no trews to take that tyde.	*truce; at that time*
	The Jewys that were dwelland	*dwelling*
	in Jerusalem cyté	
	Myght loke over all that land	
17040	and full grett soroyng see.	*sorrowing*

1421.

	When thei had so dystroyd and strayd	*scattered*
	and fuld the folke be fyrth and fell,	*despoiled; woods and hills*
	A sege to that cyté thei layd	*siege*
	whore Jews was dyght most forto dwell.	*were most prepared*
17045	"We sall not sese, for soth," thei sayd,	*stop; they [Holofernes' army]*
	"or all the chylder of Israel	*until*
	With all ther godes to ground be grayd.	*destroyed*
	So sall thei never of maystry mell."	*victory tell*
	Thei loged them thore to lend	*remain*
17050	and lyfyd at ther lykyng	
	Full fawrty days tyll end	
	that burgh in bale to bryng.	*city in grief*

1422.

	Bot folke within full wysly wake	*wisely are vigilant*
	ther cyté fast forto dyffend	*their; defend*
17055	With allablasters and with bows of brake	*crossbows; winches and racks*
	ay redy bown forto be bend.	*always prepared to be cocked*
	With gunys grett styfly thei strake,	*great cannons powerfully*
	within ther dynt durst no man lend.	*range; remain*
	And ever to God ther mayn thei make	*their complaint*
17060	ther mornyng with his myght to mend.	*their mourning*
	Within that cyté ere	*are*
	prestes to pray plenté,	
	And knyghtes full wyse of were	*learned in warfare*
	to govern ther degré.	*maintain their position*

1423.

17065 Bot ther degré was not to deme   *judge*
   all yf thei were dughty of dede.   *whether they were all doughty warriors*
  Ther enmyse were so bold and breme,   *fierce*
   to them thei durst not batell bede.   *engage*
  Ther byschope heyght Elyachym,   *Joakim*
17070 and unto hym holy thei yede   *as a group they went*
  And prayd hym say how yt suld seme
   them forto deme in swylka drede.   *judge under such terror*
  He commawnd then that thei
   suld both with hert and hend *heart and hand (i.e., word and deed)*
17075 Mekly unto God pray   *Meekly*
   ther myschefe to amend.

1424.

  "For so," he says, "ye sall encrese
   and nothyng of your rebels reke."   *enemies reckon*
  He sett ensampyll of Moyses
17080 and of the grett Abymalech:
  "He putt his pepyll fast in prese,   *conscription*
   to fell Goddes folke thei were full freke.   *destroy; bold*
  Bot ay whyls Moyses prayd for pese,
   God sett ther noys in ther enmys neke.   *prayers*
17085 Yf we werke on swylke wyse   *work in similar manner*
   and faynd our God to plese,   *endeavor*
  Then sall non yll enmyse   *no wicked enemies*
   unto us do dysesse."   *harm*

1425.

  Thei were full redy, os he them red,   *as he advised them*
17090 forto aray aftur his resown. *to array [themselves]; reason*
  Full bowsomly, os he them bed,   *obediently; commanded*
   on the bare erth thei sett them down.
  In hayrys and sekkes sone were thei cled *hairshirts; sackcloths; clad*
   and kest powder apon ther crown.   *cast ashes; heads*
17095 All yf ther enmyse wele were fed,   *Even*
   to fyght then had thei no fusyown.   *provisions*
  Ser Olyfernes toyght
   thei lay ther full lang whyle.
  Sere soteltes he soyght   *Many subtleties*
17100 to wyn them be sum wyle.   *stratagem*

[Holofernes cuts off water to the city; despair sets in (7:19–28)]

1426.

  He wyst wele thei wold have no dawt   *knew well; doubt*
   whyls thei had welth of waters clere.   *while*

	Therfor he gart spare ylk spowte	*made rare each drop*
	whore any wels of watur were.	*wells*
17105	He mad ther bekkes to ryn abowt	*brooks to be diverted*
	that non suld negh that cyté nere.	*come near*
	So menes he forto make them lowt	*submit*
	and be full blyth his lay to lere.	*eager his law to learn*
	Then were the Jews in wo,	
17110	when thei saw stopped ylke streme	
	Fro the cyté of Jerico	
	and fro Jerusalem.	

1427.

	Thei saw ther wellys wex all dry,	*grow*
	thei fand no tast in town ne feld.	
17115	No wounder yf thei were sory,	
	for wyn was wasted all that thei weld.	*spoiled; possessed*
	Ther price prophett then heyght Ozi,	*best; Uzziah*
	that in batell them best wold beld.	*protect*
	To hym thei come with carfull crye	
17120	and bad he suld ther bodes yeld.	*homes surrender*
	"Our lyfes so forto save,	
	for, sothly, ser," thei say,	*truly*
	"Bettur is our hele to have	*health*
	then dye all on a day."	

[UZZIAH'S PRAYER AND PROMISE IN THE TEMPLE (7:29–32)]

1428.

17125	When Ozi herd them sorowyng so	
	and lyke to lose all that land,	*likely*
	He weped and wrang his hend for wo,	*hands*
	and unto them thus he cummand	
	Unto the Tempyll all forto go	
17130	and pray ther God all-weldand	*almighty*
	"Us forto wyn out of this wo,	
	sen all our hele henges in His hand."	*since; welfare holds*
	Full prestly thore thei pray,	*earnestly*
	nevenand grett God be name,	*naming*
17135	And thus hymself con say,	*[Uzziah] himself did*
	for thei suld say that same:	

1429.

	"Lord God that mad kyrnell and corne	*seed and grain*
	and all may save be land and see,	*by; sea*
	That fed our faders fare beforn	*fathers in former times*
17140	and fro Kyng Pharo mad them free!	
	Sene Thee lykes noyght that thei be lorn	*Since; be lost*

that trewly trows and treystes in Thee,   *believes and trusts*
Have mercy on us evyn and morn.   *night and day*
Save Thi servandes and this cyté!
17145   We wott full wele us aw   *know; we ought*
for syn swylke lyf to lede,   *such*
Bot Thi mercy we knaw
is more then our mysdede.   *greater than*

1430.
"We wott wele Thou is all-weldand
17150   and all may govern gud and yll.
Agayn Thi stevyn may nothyng stand,   *voice*
all states may Thou steme and styll.   *contain and silence*
Chasty us, Lord, with Thi hand   *Chasten*
that our enmyse say not this skyll: *these words*
17155   'Ther god was wunt them to warrand,   *did formerly protect them*
now wyll he not tent them untyll.'"   *care for them so long*
Then all that pepyll prayd
full lowly, lese and more.   *meekly*
And forto make them payd   *satisfied*
17160   to them thus sayd he thore:

1431.
"I rede we fast fyve days to end   *advise*
with all wrschep we may weld,   *devotion; wield*
And see yf God wyll socour send
us forto save under His sheld.
17165   And yf no comforth then be kend,   *shown*
this cyté sone then sall I yeld   *surrender*
Our enmyse to have in ther hend,   *their power*
so that thei hete to be our beld."   *promise; protection*
Thei sayd, "We all assent
17170   this forward to fulfyll."   *agreement*
And so ther ways thei went
ylkon at ther awn wyll.

[Judith's angry response to Uzziah's promise (8:1–36)]

1432.
Bot then this wyse woman Judyth,
when scho herd of ther tythyng tell,   *heard word of these happenings*
17175   How Ser Ozi had ordand yt   *proclaimed*
ther cyté and therselfe to sell,   *their*
And how he made that mesure fytt
to dome of God fyve days to dwell,   *demand of God results in five days*
Sho wold yt wast with womans wytt,   *would undo it [their plans]; wit*
17180   and furth scho went that fare to fell.   *plan to squelch*

To the Tempyll rayked scho ryght   *she strode at once*
   and cald tho folke in fere,   *called those people together*
And up sho stud on heyght
   so that thei suld hyr here.   *should hear her*

1433.

17185   To Ozi fyrst hyr mone sho mase   *complaint she makes*
   als to most maystur tho men amang.   *most important figure those*
Sho says, "O myse thou takes thi trace,   *Amiss; your course*
   and to my wytt thi werke is wrang.
How dere thou sett in certayn space   *dare; specific time*
17190   the wyll of God to come or gang,   *go*
Sene He is gyfer of all grace   *Since; giver*
   sone forto leve or to last lang!
This is more lyke to greve   *liable to anger*
   our God, that most may gayn,   *who may help most*
17195   Then us oght to releve   *find relief*
   at put us fro this payn.

1434.

"Therfor is gud that we begyne
   of this grevance to geyte relese,   *to earn release*
And say: this sorow is sent for syn   *sin*
17200   that we have wroyght and wold not sese,   *cease*
Als was with elders of our kyn,
   Abraham, Ysaac, and Moyses.
Thei had wo, for God wold them wyn   *win them*
   aftur ther payn to endlese pese   *their; peace*
17205   And also forto prove
   with teyne and with trayveyle   *suffering and travails*
Whedder thei wold last in love   *abide*
   or fro Hym fayntly fayle.

1435.

"And for thei wold not groche agayn   *because; complain*
17210   bot schewed ay meknes more and more,   *ever showed meekness*
Als Job and Thoby dyde sertayn
   that were assayd with seknes sore,   *tried; sickness*
To Goddes bydyng ay were thei bayn;   *obedient*
   therfor ther guddes He con restore   *did restore*
17215   And put them into power playn   *manifest power*
   more fast then ever thei wore before.   *secure*
The same then sall us fall
   and we this fare fulfyll."   *if; mission*
Then Ozi and thei all
17220   graunted to werke hyr wyll.

1436.

Thei prayd hyr forto tell them to
  hyr purpase both by nyght and day.
"Now, sers," sho sayd, "sen ye wyll so,   *since*
  all myn entent I sall yow say.
17225 This nyght I wyll wende furth yow fro   *journey*
  in other place my God to pray,
And pray ye that God with me go,
  and lokes none wayte eftur my way.   *be sure that no one follows*
I kepe no cumpany
17230 bot my servand sertayn.   *except my loyal servant*
Kepes this cyté seurly   *Guard; securely*
  tyll God send us agayn."   *sends us back*

[JUDITH PREPARES HERSELF TO SAVE THE CITY (9:1–10:5)]

1437.

Sho sett yyng men to yeme the gate   *young; guard*
  and bad thei suld be redy bown   *readily prepared*
17235 To kepe hyr in the evyn late,   *To attend to her; evening*
  for that tyme wold scho wend o town.   *depart from town*
Then to hyr howse scho toke the gate   *(returned home)*
  and gart hyr servand in that sesown   *made her servant; time*
With bawme and with bathes hate   *ointment; hot baths*
17240 clense all hyr cors fro fote to crown.   *body from foot to head*
And sythyn sho hyr arayd   *then; dressed herself*
  in garmentes gud and gay,
And ever to God sho prayd
  to wyse hyr in hyr way.   *guide*

1438.

17245 With sylke and sendell and satayn   *silk and fine silk and satin*
  and baulkyn bettur non myght be,   *brocade*
Hyr pellour all of pure armyne,   *furs; ermine*
  with pyrry plett full grett plenté,   *precious stones adorned*
With gyrdyll and garland of gold fyne   *girdle*
17250 to make hyr semly unto se.   *beautiful to look upon*
Hyre maydyn bare both bred and wyne
  to fynd them fode for days thre.   *provide them with food*
God wyst wele that sho went   *knew well*
  to save His pepyll exprese.
17255 Therfor to hyr He sent
  both favour and fayrnese.

1439.

When hyr aray was all redy,
  down on hyr knesse sho kneled then,   *knees she kneeled*

And sayd, "My Lord God Allmighty,
17260   that wyll and toyght may clerly kene,   *whose; understand*
Sen in Thee lygges all vyctory,   *Since; lies*
    to me, Thi servand, myght Thou lene   *incline*
Forto overcom our yll enmy   *wicked enemy*
    and save this cyté and Thi men."   *people*
17265   Scho prayd to God thus gaite   *in this way*
    tyll lyght of day con sese.   *was gone*
Then wentt scho to the gate
    full prevely to prese.   *secretly to go forward*

[JUDITH AND HER SERVANT DEPART AND ARE CAPTURED QUICKLY (10:6–22)]

1440.

When sho come ydder, redy sho fand
17270   Ozi and other to tent ther toure.   *to guard their tower*
Sho bad that thei suld stably stand   *steadfastly*
    that cyté to save and socoure,
And that prestes suld pray with hert and hand
    that God suld be hyr governoure.
17275   So went sho furth with hyr servand
    to enmys that were strang in stoure.   *powerful in battle*
Ever to God sho prays
    to be hyr helpe and beld.   *comfort*
Wach men that kepes ways   *Watchmen who patrol the ways*
17280   fand them sone in the feld.   *found; soon; field*

1441.

Thei merveld of hyr rych aray,
    for so semly had thei sene none.   *beautiful*
Sum of them ware prowd of that pray,   *prey*
    for gay geyre had sho full gud woyne.   *fancy dress; great plenty*
17285   The asked wher scho was o way   *going*
    and why sho welke so late allon;   *walked so late alone*
And to them sothly con scho say,   *truly she did say*
    "Sers, fro my frendes thus am I gone.   *from*
I com to yow in trewse,   *truce*
17290   and that sall ye here and see.   *hear*
I am on of the Ebrews   *one*
    that wuns in this cyté.   *dwells*

1442.

"To fle ther fro I am full fayn   *eager*
    and leve both catell, kyth, and kyn.   *abandon; family; kin*
17295   For wele I wott my self certayn
    that ye and yours sone sall yt wyn.   *soon shall conquer it*
To your prince is my purpase playn,

and I sall tell hym, or we twyn,   *before we depart*
     To wyne yt wele withoutyn payn   *How to win it easily*
17300   and dystroy all that ere therin.   *are*
     Sen thei wyll not them yeld   *Since; surrender themselves*
          to men that may them save,
     Yt is no boyte to beld   *profit to help*
          them that no helpe wyll have.

1443.

17305   "Unto my hele I wyll take hede   *welfare; heed*
          and to my servand that is here.
     And, sers, I pray yow me to lede   *lead*
          unto your prince that has no pere."   *peer*
     Thei herd hyr spech was for ther sped,   *good fortune*
17310   therfor thei were full fayn in fere.   *glad together*
     To Olyfernes so thei yede   *went*
          and fand hym syttand with solace sere.   *found him sitting; apart*
     That lady in thei lad   *led*
          and told thei fand hyr flayd   *terrified*
17315   And fro hyr frenschep fled,   *their*
          and how sho to them sayd.

[JUDITH AT HOLOFERNES' TENT (10:23–12:4)]

1444.

     When Olyfernes saw this syght
          and herd ther tayles how thei con tell,   *heard*
     In hyr hys hert was ravyscht ryght   *heart*
17320   and demed that sho suld with hym dwell.
     Than, forto marre hym more in myght,   *in order to deceive him*
          full flatt unto the growND sho fell.
     He commawnd men that wer full wyght   *strong*
          to take hyr tyte up them omell.   *quickly between them*
17325   Then on hyr knese sho kneled   *knees*
          and prayd his helpe to have.
     He sayd he suld hyr beld   *comfort*
          in oght that scho wold crave.   *whatever; desire*

1445.

     Sho thanked hym frendly, noyght at hyde,   *there's no hiding it*
17330   and ryght glad in his hert was he.
     He saw hyr geyre of so heygh prid,   *apparel; high*
          he trowed sho was of grett degré.   *believed*
     He made hyr sytt hymself besyd,
          that was ryght semly syght to see.
17335   Thei fell in talkyng so that tyde   *time*
          that mery sho mad als his meneye.   *company*

Yt was solace sertayn
  to se them syt togeydder,
And fyrst he con hyr frayn   *did ask her*
17340   cause of hyr comyng ydder.   *there*

1446.
Sho sayd, "Ser, and yow lyke to here,   *if you wish to hear*
  I am an Ebrew ald and yyng.   *old and young*
My menyng is to mend your chere   *intention*
  by gud bod word that I yow bryng.   *good advice*
17345   I wyll maynteyn in my manere   *adhere; behavior [to]*
  Nabogodhonosour, your kyng,
And his law wyll me lyke to lere   *learn*
  when we have endyd other thyng.
And, ser, fully I fynd
17350   how thou has in his sted   *have; place*
Power to lowse and bynd   *loose; bind*
  als lord of lyfe and ded.   *death*

1447.
"And, ser, I se the soth certayn: *see the absolute truth*
  Ebrews, whyls thei may wepyns weld,   *weapons carry*
17355   Wyll hold yond ceté thee agayn   *against*
  and never assent yt forto yeld.   *yield*
Therfor to fle I am full fayn
  to thee, that best may be my beld.   *protection*
For wele I wott thei sal be slayn,
17360   for fawt of fode fall fay in feld.   *default of food fall dead*
And sen thei wyll not crye
  to thee, that may them save,
I hald them wele worthy
  swylk hydows herm to have.   *such hideous harm*

1448.
17365   "And therfore come I to thee here
  by certayn sygnes thee to say   *signs to tell you*
How thou sall all that kynd conquere   *people*
  lyghtly withoutyn lang delay.
Thei may not last, thus I thee lere,   *advise*
17370   because ther watur is haldyn away.   *withheld*
I herd them say with sympyll chere
  that all suld fayle or the faurt day.   *before the fourth*
And I saw, or I yode,   *before I departed*
  how thei ther bestes sloght   *beasts slaughtered*
17375   For thryst to drynke the blod,
  bot non had half enogh.

1449.
"And when I saw that thei dyd so
   and that yt wold no bettur be,
I hyde me fast to fle them fro   *hastened myself*
17380   so to save my servand and me.
Sen thei wyll not beware with wo
   to save themself and ther cyté,
Yt was Goddes wyll that I suld go
   and tell ther tythynges unto thee.   *their circumstances*
17385   Lo, ser, this is," sho sayd,
   "the cause of my comyng."
Then was the prince wele payd.   *well pleased*
   The wyn he bad them bryng.   *wine*

1450.
He dranke and bed hyr furth by raw.   *invited her to do so in turn*
17390   Sho thanked hym with hert and hende:
"Ser, me behovys lyfe eftur my Law   *it behooves me to live*
   tyll this bargan be broyght tyll ende.   *until*
We have ordand, als Ebrews aw,   *ought*
   fode ther faur days forto spend.   *food these*
17395   And, ser, by that day sall we knaw
   how wele our myrth sal be amend.
For als lang als I dwell
   His Law sadly to save,
Then wyll my God me tell
17400   how we sall helpyng have.

1451.
"And, ser, so sall I tell thee tyll   *when*
   to make asawt by sotell gyne   *assault by subtle device*
To weld the cyté at thy wyll   *conquer*
   and esely forto entur therin.   *easily*
17405   And, ser, than may thou spare or spyll
   the Ebrews ylkon or thou blyn,   *each one before you cease*
And, yf thee lyke, to lend thor styll   *to stay there still*
   or home agayn with wrschep wyn."   *return home; honors*
With gawdes thus scho hym glosed   *flatteries; deceived*
17410   to have hyr purpase playn.
Hyr sawys soth he supposed,   *words true*
   and thus he glosed agayn: *flattered her in return*

1452.
"I gyfe thee leve to make thi mese   *permission; food*
   of mete and drynke at thi lykyng,
17415   For thou ow wele thi god to plese   *ought*
   that out of bale wyll thee bryng.   *sorrow*

And when we sall the ceté sese,   *capture*
   thou sall have chose of all thyng   *choice*
And lyfe ever then at thin awn ese
17420   with Nabogodhonosour, the kyng.
For and I fynd yt fyne   *if; true*
   that thou says in thi saw,   *speech*
Then sall thi god be myne
   and I wyll luf thi law.

1453.

17425   "And all that unto hym may heve   *pertain*
   byd I thou do both nyght and day.
Yt is not gud that thou hym greve,   *grieve*
   sen he all soth to thee wyll say."   *since*
Sho sayd, "Then bus thou gyfe me leve   *must*
17430   forto have rowm and redy way   *leeway; ready access*
Evermore at mydnyght forto meve   *go*
   to certayn place my God to pray."
Of hyr wyll noyght he wyst;   *intention he knew nothing*
   therfor he graunt sone
17435   To lyf at hyr awn lyst   *live according to her desire*
   tyll all thier dedes be done.   *these deeds*

1454.

And to his kepers cummand he   *guards*
   o payn to lose both lyf and land
That thei suld to hyr bowsom be   *be obedient*
17440   and holy held unto hyr hand   *wholly*
And make uschew and entré,   *exit and entry*
   so that no stekyll agayn hyr stand.   *doorbar against*
Thei graunt ylkon in ther degré   *each one*
   kyndly to do als he them cummand.
17445   Full mery was ylk man
   and full glad of ther gest.   *guest*
So depart thei than
   and rede them all to rest.   *prepare themselves*

[JUDITH'S FOUR DAYS IN HOLOFERNES' CAMP (12:5–9)]

1455.

Then to a chamber thei hyr led
17450   that was with alkyns wrschepe wroyght.   *all manner of splendor*
All bewtese both for burd and bed   *beauteous things; board*
   with mekyll blyse was ydder broyght;
And in that sted so was sho stede   *placed*
   with alkyns solace sere unsoght.   *all manner of unsought comforts*
17455   Bot to slepe was sho never unclede,   *for sleep; undressed*

	of other thyng was mare hyr toyght.	*more*
	Ylke nyght scho toke hyr way	*Each night*
	ferre down into a dale.	*far*
	Thor menys sho, and sho may,	*There she intends, if*
17460	to hald the Ebrews hale.	*keep; healthy*

1456.

	In that ylke dale was dyght a well	*same; a well had been dug*
	with Ebrews that before had bene.	*by; in years past*
	Thorof thei dranke whore thei con dwell,	*Thereof; where; went*
	and thorin ware thei weschyn clene.	*therein were*
17465	And thore scho and hyr damsell	
	trayveld so them two betwene.	*labored*
	Thei mad a spryng that fro yt fell	
	at the cyté syde forto be sene,	
	So that thei that wund within	*dwelled*
17470	ware warescht wele of thryst.	*were relieved*
	Thus myght sho wende with win	*return with joy*
	and lend at hyr awn lyst.	*remain; own pleasure*

[JUDITH INVITED BACK TO HOLOFERNES' TENT (12:10–13:5)]

1457.

	So trayveld sho be tyms thre	*journeyed*
	into that place hyr God to pray.	
17475	Scho had fre eschew and entré,	*exit*
	and so befell on the faurt day:	
	Olyfernes bad his men suld be	
	ay redy in ther best aray.	
	For on the fyft day hoped he	
17480	the Ebrews folke to fell for ay;	*to destroy forever*
	For so had Judyth sayd.	
	he gart ordan forthi	*gave orders therefore*
	A soper gudly grayd	*banquet superbly prepared*
	for hyr sake soveranly.	

1458.

17485	When all was poynted with pomp and pryd,	*appointed*
	a knyght then unto hyr sent he	
	Forto com and sytt hym besyde	
	thar maner of solace forto se.	
	The knyght hyr told so in that tyd.	*at that time*
17490	sho thanked hym with wordes free	
	And sayd, "I sall not lang abyde,	
	for at his bydyng wyll I be."	
	Rychly sho hyr arayd	*dressed herself*
	to seme fayr in ther syght.	

17495	The pepyll were full wele payd,	*well pleased*
	and the lord was most lyght.	*wantonly cheerful*

1459.

	Befor hymself hyr sett was wroyght	*seat was made*
	full presciosly forto apere.	
	Hyr ryalnes rayvyschyd his toyght;	*queenliness*
17500	he bede hyr mete with meré chere.	*ordered her to eat; merry gladness*
	Sho ete mete that hyr maydyn broyght,	*ate food*
	and toke that coupe with wyn full clere	
	And made semland and dranke ryght noyght.	*semblance but drank nothing*
	bot Olyfernes for that fere	*companion*
17505	Of myghty wyne dranke more,	*strong wine*
	for myrth that thei were mett,	*joy; together*
	Then ever he dranke before.	
	So hymself he over sett.	*overwhelmed*

1460.

	When Judyth saw that yt was so,	
17510	of that werke was sho wele payd.	*well pleased*
	Sho made talkyng betwyx them two	
	tyll he wyst noyght wele what he sayd.	*knew not*
	He bad all men to bed suld go	
	and radly to ther rest arayd,	*promptly*
17515	And that none suld take tent hym to,	*take heed to him*
	for at his lyst he wold be layd.	*desire*
	He thynkes that he sall have	
	that lady hym forto plese.	
	Bot God wyll ever more save	
17520	His servand fro dysese.	*distress*

1461.

	Unto his bed fast con he hye	*hasten*
	hys foly fare forto fulfyll.	*foolish fancy*
	He bad that lady com lyg hym by,	*lie*
	for all the doreys ar stokyn styll.	*doors were firmly barred*
17525	Sho sayd, "Ser, I sall be redy	
	with word and werke to wyrke thi wyll.	
	Bot to my chamber wend wyll I,	*go*
	and full sone sall I come thee tyll."	*very quickly*
	To hyr chambre scho wentt	
17530	and prayd God specially,	
	Als he knew hyr entent,	
	to kepe hyr fro velany.	*villainy*

1462.

Unto God thor sho prayd and wepe	*there; wept*
forto vouchsave hyr sorow to slake.	*allay*
17535 Sone Olyfernes fell on slepe,	
for dronkyn man may not wele wake.	
Sho warnd hyr servand to take kepe	*pay attention*
that no kyns noyse suld sho make,	*no kind of noise*
And prevely als sho couth crepe	*quietly as she could creep*
17540 hyr way to his bed con sho take.	
Thor kneled sho on the ground	*There she kneeled*
and prayd God with Hys wyll	
To strengh hyr in that stownd	*strengthen; moment*
hyr forward to fullfyll.	*promise*

[JUDITH BEHEADS THE SLEEPING HOLOFERNES (13:6–10)]

1463.

17545 Sho drogh his sword full sone sertayn,	*drew*
qwylke sho fand standand in that sted,	*which; place*
And with that brand sho brest his brayn;	*sword; burst*
so with that dynt sone was he ded.	*blow*
Then cutted sho sunder synow and vayn,	*asunder sinew; vein*
17550 and fro hys halse hewed of hys hed	*neck hacked off*
And putt yt in a poket playn,	*simple bag*
whore thei befor had born ther bred.	*their bread*
Sho bad hyr maydyn yt bere	
whore als thei were wunt to pray.	*wont*
17555 Thei geydderd sayme ther geyre	*gathered together their gear*
and wyghtly went ther way.	*boldly*

[JUDITH AND HER SERVANT ESCAPE TO THE CITY (13:10–20)]

1464.

To have ther hele thei hastyd fast	*To secure their welfare*
and made no tareyng in that tyde.	*time*
Tyll tyme thei were all perels past,	*perils*
17560 thei wyst yt was no boyte to byde.	*use to tarry*
Yf yt were late, so at the last	
thei neghted nere to the cyté syde.	*approached near*
To the kepers a crye scho cast	
and bad them opyn the wekett wyde.	*wicket*
17565 Hyr voyce full wele thei knew,	
for fayn full fast thei wepe.	*joy; wept*
Full mony a bold Ebrew	
com thore hyr forto kepe.	

1465.

Thei lete hyr in with torches lyght

17570   and lowtyng low, is not to layn.   *bowing low, it is no lie*

Thei were full glad to se that syght,

    for wele thei wend sho had bene slayn.   *thought*

Sho stud up in a sted of hyght   *high place*

    that all men myght se hyr certayn.   *see her for sure*

17575 And thore scho schewed hyr releke ryght,   *revealed her relic*

    the hede out of hyr poket playn.   *head*

"Loves God," sho sayd sadly,   *Love*

    "that for you hath ordand

To sett your vyctory

17580   in a wake womans hand."   *weak*

[JUDITH'S ORDERS FOR THE CITY (14:1–10)]

1466.

Then all the pepyll in that place

    down on ther knese low thei knele.   *knees*

Thei thanked grett God of His grace

    that kyndly so thar care wold kele.   *their sorrows would relieve*

17585 When thei saw Olyfernes face,

    no wonder yf thei lyked yt wele.

Then Judyth spake furth in that space

    how thei suld do ever ylke dele.   *every part*

Sho sayd, "In this same day

17590   be lyve loke ye be bowne   *quickly; ready*

All in your best aray

    to dyng your enmys downe.   *strike your enemies down*

1467.

"Set up this hed over the gate,

    so that your enmyse may yt se.

17595 For fro thei wyt, full wele I wayte,   *For when they know, full well I know*

    that ther prince so perysched be,

His men wyll make no more debate

    bot fayn to cayre to ther cuntré.   *be eager to return to their*

                                          hotfoot (quickly)

Then sall ye folow on them fote-hate

17600   and fell them or thei ferre flee.   *destroy; before they flee far*

Thei sall lefe welth gud woyne,   *leave much desirable wealth*

    bot lokes non tent thertyll.   *but pay no attention to that*

When thei ere fled and sloyn,   *slain*

    then may ye fang your fyll."   *seize your fill*

[THE ASSYRIANS DISCOVER HOLOFERNES' DEATH AND FLEE (14:11–15:7)]

1468.

17605	Evyn als sho demed was done in hye:	*Just as she ordered; haste*
	the hede was sone sett up on the heyght.	
	Then mad thei myrth and melody	
	with bemys, als thei were bown to fyght.	*trumpets; prepared*
	And when the hethyn hard them crye	*heard*
17610	and saw a sygne sett in ther syght,	
	Thei ware full yll abayst therby.	*abashed thereby*
	To warne ther prince thei went full wyght.	*quickly*
	To his chambre thei hyed	*hastened*
	and bad his servandes say	
17615	How the Ebrews them ascryde	*cried out*
	forto have dede that day.	*to have battle*

1469.

	The chamberer durst make no dyne	*dared; noise*
	for ferd yt suld turn hym to teyne.	*fear it should get him in trouble*
	He wend the woman were within,	*presumed*
17620	and that thei both on slepe had beyne.	*been*
	Bot with hys handes he con begyn	
	to wakyn them be cowntenance cleyne.	
	And sythyn he come to the curtyn,	
	thore was no segne of solace seyne.	*pleasures seen*
17625	Then nere the bed he yode	*went*
	and fand rewfull aray:	*found rueful*
	A body laped in blod,	*lapped*
	bot the hed was away.	

1470.

	Full lowd he cryd, "Alas! Alas!	
17630	Our lyves ere lorn, my lord is ded."	*are lost*
	"How is yt so?" ylkon thei asse.	*ask*
	He sayd, "Se here, he has no hede."	
	To Judyth chamber con thei pase	*did they go*
	and saw hyr stollyn out of that sted.	
17635	Then wyst thei wele that werkyng was	
	by hyr wyles and hyr wekyd red.	*wiles and her wicked counsel*
	Thore was no boyte to byde	*no use to take time*
	there welthes o way to wyn,	*their loot to take away*
	Bot ylkon to ryn and ryd	*each one did run and ride*
17640	and forsake kyth and kyn.	

1471.

	Thus of ther rest thei were remeved,	*comforts*
	ther ryche robes thei rafe and rent.	*tattered and tore*

Ther restyng thore full sore them rewed, *rued*
 withoutyn welth away thei went.
17645 The Ebrews prestly them persewed: *quickly pursued them*
 all lost ther hedes that thei myght hent. *all they seized lost their heads*
Thor tho all that this bargan brewed, *There all those; siege dreamed up*
 full shortly were thei shamed and shent. *destroyed*
Then come Ebrews agayn
17650 whore ther enmyse had beyne. *where their; been*
Thei fand all safe certayn;
 ther was no solpyng seyne *defiling seen*

1472.

Bot only of Olyfernes blod
 that out of his body was bled.
17655 Thor ware garmentes of gold full gud
 and gold in bages abowt that bed.
The body thei kest to bestes fud *cast out as food for beasts*
 and fowles therwith forto be fede. *fowls; to be fed*
Thresour thei toke and hame thei yode, *Treasure; home they went*
17660 non other welth with them thei led.
Non other thyng thei broght
 bot of gold full gud woyn. *except; in abundance*
To Judyth sone thei soyght
 and thanked hyr ever ylkon. *each and everyone*

[JUDITH'S TRIUMPH (15:8–16:25)]

1473.

17665 Thei broyght hyr gold in bages bun, *bound*
 and bed themself at hyr wyll to be. *offered themselves*
Thei say, "We wott we have yt wun *won*
 with wyll of God and wyt of thee." *your intelligence*
Scho says, "Sen God thus has begun *Since*
17670 to save yourselfe and your cyté,
His Tempyll sall therwyth be fun *supplied*
 and goveren ever in gud degré." *governed*
Thei say, "We have leved thore *left there [in Holofernes' camp]*
 of erthly welth to wyn *material wealth*
17675 To make us mery evermore
 and comforth all our kyn."

1474.

Sho bad them wyghtly wend ther ways *bade; quickly go*
 to steyr tho folke that thei not stryfe. *guide those folk; bicker [among themselves]*
"And partyes the mobyls, sers," sho says, *divide the movable goods*
17680 "be mesure both to man and wyfe." *by just proportion*
And so thei dyd by thryty days *for thirty days*

or thei that ryches myght up ryfe.   *gather up*
Tho that before were pore to prayse   *Those who; poor to account*
   wer then relyfed for all ther lyfe.   *relieved*
17685 Grett myrth was them amang;
   thei loved God of His grace
With solace and with sange   *song*
   full specially that space.

1475.

And when that space was sped and spend   *over and past*
17690 that thryty days were fully gone,
Then Judyth bad them with hyr wend   *go*
   unto ther Tempyll ever ylkon
And love God thor with hert and hend,
   that swylke thressour had to them toyne.   *treasure; given*
17695 And thei dyd evyn als sho them kend,   *advised*
   thei offerd gold ther full grett wone.   *great amount*
Sho bad them love only
   God, that is all-weldand,   *all-powerful*
That sett Hys vyctory
17700 and ther helpe in hyr hand.

1476.

Als sho wold deme, thei dyd in dede,   *deed*
   als worthy was withoutyn were.   *doubt*
Then home to hyr hows scho yede,   *went*
   and pepyll past to ther places sere.   *their various places*
17705 A lades lyfe then con sho led,   *lady's*
   and Goddes Law lyked hyr ever to lere.   *learn (follow)*
And furth sho weryd hyr wedow wede   *wore her widow's weeds*
   bot in soverane sesons of the yere.   *except during festival seasons of the year*
Then wold sho be more gay
17710 to syght and more honest
In purpas God to pay   *please*
   for wrschepe of that fest.   *feast*

1477.

Sho had enogh of rent and land
   in ylke sted whore sho was sted
17715 Aftur Manasses, hyr husband,
   that lordly lyf before had led.
And of all that sho had in hand
   over honest spence that suld be sped,   *expense; paid*
Ther with pore folke sho fed and fand   *supplied*
17720 and beldyd both to bake and bede.   *provided; clothes and lodging*
Sho ocupyed so hyr sted
   in pennance and in prayer

Fro hyr husband was dede
    a hunderth and fyve yere. *From [the time]*

1478.

17725   Hyr servandes, man, maydyn, and knave,
    mad sho to goveren gud degré.
Then dyed scho as God vochedsave,
    for fro that fytt may no man flee. *fate*
By hyr husband thei can hyr grave *buried her*
17730   full solemply in that cyté,
And by sevyn days sorowyng thei have,
    als costome was in that cuntré.
The Jews makes hyr in mynd
    evermore to be on ment, *remembered*
17735   For scho comforth ther kynd
    when thei in bale were bent. *misery were afflicted*

1479.

Now be this werke wele may we wytt *by; know*
    how God wyll pupplysch His power *publish (make known)*
In wemen forto fall als fytt *women; fitting*
17740   als in men on the same manere.
Thus endes the Boke of Judyth,
    als clerkes may knaw by clergy clere. *as clerks may know by good scholarship*
God graunt hym hele that hath turned yt *health who has translated it*
    in Ynglysch lawd men forto lere! *English [for] unlearned; to learn*
17745   Insampyll may men here se *Examples*
    to be trew in trowyng. *loyal in belief*
God graunt us so to be
    and to His blyse us bryng!

SECOND BOOK OF MACCABEES 7

[CONCERNING JEWISH MARTYRS]

1480.

Of farly fare, whoso wyll fynd, — *wondrous things*

17750   in forme Faders is fayre to rede. — *Patristic writings; read*

Bot Crystyn folke suld carpe be kynd — *Christian; speak naturally*

    of Crystes laws, os kens our Crede, — *Christ's; as proclaimed by our Creed*

And gud marters to have in mynd — — *martyrs*

    for swylk marters may make uus mede — — *give us reward*

17755 How that thei were persewed and pynd — *pained*

    and done to ded be dyverse dede. — *tortured to death in diverse ways*

Because thei Crist wold knaw,

    wore mony sakles slayn; — *innocents*

And sum for Moyses Law

17760   were ded with dyverse payn.

[SEVEN JEWISH BRETHREN AND THEIR MOTHER ARE BROUGHT BEFORE ANTIOCHUS (7:1)]

1481.

And sone we sall sum marters nevyn — *invoke*

    that wroyght with Moyses wyll all way. — *forever*

Of aght then is yt ordand evyn

    in Holy Chyrch to syng and say,

17765 How that the mother and hyr suns sevyn

    were done to ded all on a day, — *tortured to death; in a single day*

All for thei stod with stabyll stevyn — *because they stood with unyielding faith*

    in mayntenance of Moyses Lay. — *Moses' Law*

He bad, for herd or nesch, — *for hard or soft [treatment] (i.e., come what may)*

17770   that his folke grett and small

Suld forbere swynyse flesch — *swine flesh (pork)*

    for oght that myght befall.

1482.

This woman with hyr chylder yyng — *young*

    wayted full warly, whore thei went, — *were warily watchful, wherever*

17775	To kepe and breke noyght his bydyng,	*break not*
	therfor to be in bales bent.	*in sorrow bound*
	Anthiocus, a cursed kyng,	*Antiochus IV Epiphanes*
	when he herd tell of ther entent,	
	To bare he bad men suld them bryng	*To the court of justice*
17780	and sayd thei suld with sham be shent.	*be destroyed*
	For he was paynym prowd,	*pagan*
	with mawmentes sere umsett,	*various idols surrounded*
	Goddes Law both styll and lowd	
	was his lykyng to lett,	*stop*

1483.

17785	And all Ebrews that eftur yt wroyght.	
	Therfor he charged men of myght	
	That the wyfe with hyr sevyn suns were soyght	*sons*
	and sembled sone before his syght.	*assembled quickly*
	So unto barre sone were thei broyght	*court*
17790	with bedels and with brandes bryght;	*beadles; swords*
	Bot of that noyte nothyng thei roght,	*trouble*
	ther hertes ware hale to Heven on hyght.	*their hearts were ever focused; high*
	The mother be manfull stevyn	*by powerful voice*
	both with hert and hand	
17795	Comforthys hyr suns all sevyn	
	and bad them stably stand:	*bravely stand*

1484.

	"For the luf of God to lyf and dy,	
	suns, in my blyssyng loke bown ye be.	*you should be prepared*
	I sall yow say encheson why:	*tell you the reason*
17800	none may yow help bot only He.	
	How ye were bred in my body,	*grown*
	that was nothyng be myght of me.	
	God fosterd yow thore, and not I,	
	and broyght yow furth in forme fre.	*noble shape*
17805	And, suns, He sall yow save	
	yf ye ryght spend your space,	*rightly; time [on this earth]*
	And all that ye here have	
	is gyfyn of His grace.	

1485.

	"I gaf yow nother lyfe ne lym,	*life nor limb*
17810	ne bones ne flesch to fest yow fast.	*to bind you to*
	God gaf yow lyght when ye were dym,	
	and your sawles in your corsus He cast.	*souls; bodies*
	Yf erthly payns bene grett and grym,	*pains are*
	loves now God and bees not agast,	
17815	Bot thynkes that ye sall have with Hym	

the joy and lyf that ever sall last.
Suns, yf ye suffer sore,
   that space sall sone be spend,   *time will soon be past*
And ye sall have therfore
17820   the hele that sall have non ende."   *wholeness*

1486.
Thus comforth sho that cumpany,
   both ald and yyng, ever als thei yede.   *from the eldest to the youngest; went*
The kyng spake full dyspytfully
   to make them have more dowt and dred.
17825 He sayd, "Of your hestes herd have I   *vows I have heard*
   who made yow bold forto forbede   *which*
The flesch that lele men suld lyf by,   *noble*
   that ordand is the folke to fede.   *feed*
Ye say the flesch of swyne   *pigs*
17830 suld men forsake sertayn.   *certainly*
Ye sall be putt to pyne   *pain*
   tyll ye ete yt full fayn."   *until you eat it utterly*

1487.
Thei answerd ylkon als a man   *each one*
   and sayd, "That syght sall never be seyne.   *seen*
17835 The lawes our formfaders began   *forefathers*
   ever to maynteyne sall we meyne."   *intend*
The terrand toke the eldyst than   *tyrant*
   and trayteyd hym them two betweyne,   *entreated*
And thynkes, yf he overcom hym can,
17840 then ere the other overcomyn cleyne.   *quickly*
With fayrnes fyrst he ferd   *dealt with him*
   and sythyn with noye new.   *then with troubles*
That eldyst ever answerd
   with stedfast trewth and trew.

[THE ELDEST SON REFUSES TO LEAVE MOSES' LAW (7:2)]

1488.
17845 His hert ay unto Hevyn had he,
   and thus he carped unto the kyng,   *said*
"What sekes yow, ser, of us to se?
   What wyll ye lere of our lyfyng?   *learn*
All Gods folke ow to be fre   *ought*
17850 and honor Hym over all thyng.
His Law we wyll not leve for thee,
   ne for no bale that thou may bryng.   *sorrow*
To dy is us wele lever   *we would much prefer*
   then in that Lay forfeyt

17855   That our faders used ever
           and sythyn tyll us yt seytt."

[THE ELDEST SON TORTURED AND KILLED (7:3–6)]

1489.

Then was the fend full fell of ire   *fiend*
    and manast hym with all his mayn.   *menaced; power*
He sayd, "Thou sall have thi desyre;
17860   with sorow sere thou sall be slayn."
Be lyve he gart go make a fyre   *Quickly he caused [men to]*
    in myddes the place thor on the playn   *amidst; there*
And bryn hym up both bone and lyre.   *burn; flesh*
    bot fyrst he sall fele feller payn,   *feel crueler pain*
17865   That other so may be warre   *be wary*
    and make hym ther merrowr,   *their mirror*
When thei se hym so fare
    to forsake ther errowr.

1490.

The fyr was bett at hys bydyng   *kindled*
17870   of bowes and of best byrnand geyre.   *branches; burning materials*
A led of brase then dyd he bryng,   *cauldron of brass*
    with pyke fulfylled, hym forto fere.   *pitch filled; fear*
And when yt was wele at wellyng,   *thoroughly boiling*
    his tong he bad thei suld out schere   *tongue; cut out*
17875   And als a foyle for hethyng   *contempt*
    schave of his hede both hyde and heyre.   *shave off his head; skin and hair*
All this was done in dede,   *at once*
    and wounder was to lythe: *observe*
Hys brether saw hym blede   *brothers*
17880   and bad he suld be blythe.   *cheerful*

1491.

And for he suld not chaunge his chere   *mood*
    bot with trew hert the turmentes take —   *receive the torments*
For God is of so grett power,
    of all myse may He mendes make —   *misdeeds; amends*
17885   The mother sayd, "Sun, we ere here   *are*
    redy to suffer for Goddes sake;
For He wyll foche us all in fere   *fetch us all together*
    with Hym to wun and wynly wake."   *dwell and pleasantly awake*
When the terrand herd tell   *tyrant heard*
17890   nothyng myght make them tame,
He was more fers and fell   *fierce and cruel*
    and toyght to shape them shame.

1492.

Ther myght no myrth to hym be mete

  when that he saw ther sad semlandes.   *their steadfast faces*

17895   He sayd, "We sall sone gayr them grett.   *soon make them weep*

  Tyte take this herlott thor he standes,   *Quickly; villain where*

And cutt his tase of both his fete   *toes off; feet*

  and his fyngurs of both his handes,

And haves hym then into yond hete,   *heave*

17900   and bettes hym with your byrnand brandes. *strike; burning swords*

And yf he langer last,   *lasts longer*

  lays hym ther in the led,   *lay; [molten] lead*

And make fyr under fast

  to boyle tyll he be ded."

1493.

17905   When all this dole was done and dyght,   *tragedy*

  his mother, that was most hym nere,

And his sex brether saw this syght,   *six brothers*

  how he sufferd thos sorows sere.   *various*

Thei heyved ther handes to Hevyn on hyght   *heaved*

17910   and loved God with full gud chere

And sayd that He suld se to ryght   *justice*

  and reward all that worthy were.

He wyll abate all bandes   *relieve all bondages*

  and bete ylka byttur brayd

17915   And solace His servandes,

  als Moyses sum tyme sayd.

[THE SECOND SON TORTURED AND KILLED (7:7–9)]

1494.

Thus when the fyrst had done his dett   *duty*

  and sufferd ded be dyverse payn,   *death*

The secund sone was sesed and sett   *seized*

17920   to se what he suld say certayn.

The kyng asked hym yf he wold ete

  swylk flesch os his folke were of fayn,   *his (i.e., Antiochus') people enjoyed*

Or to be mesurd with that same mett   *weighed to that same effect*

  lyke to his brother and so be slayn.

17925   He answerd sone and sayd,

  "I am not ferd therfor."   *afraid*

Then was the kyng yll payd,

  and sone he marred hym more.

1495.

Of his hed gart he scrape the skyn,   *He caused the skin to be scraped off his head*

17930   and then to hym thus con he say,

"Wyll thou yett of thin errour blyn   *cease*
    and mend thi myscheve whyls thou may,
And lere the law that we lyf in,   *accept*
    or lose thi lyms and lyf for ay?"   *forever*
17935   That other bad, "Be lyve begyn,   *Quickly*
    for, sertes, I dred nothyng that dray.   *certainly; violence*
The lawes our faders fand   *founded*
    to hald hertly I hete."   *I heartily swear to hold*
And then the kyng cummand
17940   to cutt hym hand and fete.

1496.

"And sett the fyre on ylka syde,   *each*
    sen he wyll byd no bettur bede;   *since; have no better reward*
And yf he may this bale abyde,   *sorrow survive*
    boyle hym then tyll he be ded."
17945   Then was he turment in that tyd,   *tormented at that time*
    and als thei stund hym in that stede,   *tortured; place*
Unto the kyng full lowd he cryd
    and sayd, "Thou wrech with wekyd red,   *wicked counsel*
Be thi strenght thou dystroys
17950   oure erthly lyf in land.
Bot nedleys thou the noyys;   *needlessly you commit this harm*
    our lyf sal be lastand.   *everlasting*

1497.

"God that is Kyng of creatours
    and demer both of dedes and sawys,   *judge; deeds and words*
17955   Hys servandes sadly He socours   *faithfully*
    that to His dome ther dedes drawys.   *judgment present their deeds*
Yf we now stand thus strang in stours   *hardships*
    and lefe this lyf here for His lawys,   *leave*
He sall us rayse with grett honours   *resurrect*
17960   to endlese lyf that thou noyght knawys."   *you [will] know not*
And so he gaf the gast   *gave [up] the ghost*
    to God by cours of kynd.   *by course of nature*
The kyng was made allmast   *almost crazy*
    and moved all out of mynd.

[THE THIRD SON TORTURED AND KILLED (7:10–12)]

1498.

17965   The thryd full throly then thei thrett   *violently; threaten*
    that he suld be more stratly sted   *painfully placed*
Bot he bylyve wold drynke and ete   *Unless he at once*
    swylke fode as the folke ware with fed.
The chyldes hert to Hevyn was sett,

17970	for that dray was he noyght adred.	
	Or he was auder bun or bett,	*before; either bound or beaten*
	his tong full boldly furth he bedd.	*tongue; offered [to be cut out]*
	His handes so con he schew	
	to byd that byttur brayd,	*await; torment*
17975	And his fete for to hewe;	*feet to be cut off*
	and on this wyse he sayd:	*in this way*

1499.

	"Of God fro Hevyn I had all thies	*these*
	purtrayd thrugh His power playn.	*shaped; naked power*
	Now for His Law I them dyspyse	
17980	and profers them to putt in payn.	*offer*
	For wele I wott that I sall ryse	*well I know*
	and that God sall gyfe me agayn	
	All new members and more of price.	*body parts; worth*
	Therfor to lose thies I am fayn	*these; glad*
17985	For His sake that them sentt	
	and mad them mete to me.	*suitable*
	Yf thei now take turment,	
	make them full hale may He."	*completely whole*

1500.

	The kyng then carped wordes kene,	*spoke harsh words*
17990	and to his counsayle fast he cryd.	
	Both he and thei were comberd clene	*confounded*
	of tayles ther were told that tyd.	*speeches; time*
	Thei say swylke syght was never seyne,	*such sights were; seen*
	that a yong man in his most pride	
17995	Wyll no more of his manhed mene,	*consider*
	bot be bown byttur bale to byde.	*prepared; suffering to await*
	He royght noyght of ther red,	*reckoned nothing; counsel*
	ne of all the blyse in erthe.	
	So was he done to ded,	*tortured to death*
18000	and furth thei feytt the faurth.	*fetched*

[THE FOURTH SON TORTURED AND KILLED (7:13–14)]

1501.

	The faurth was fett furth them before,	*fetched*
	and full fowly with hym thei ferd	*foully; treated*
	And sayd, bot yf he wyser wore,	*unless he were wiser*
	his spech wold sone for hym be sperd.	*shut off*
18005	Thei manast hym both lese and more,	*menaced; less*
	and when he all ther hethyng herd,	*their scorn heard*
	He had no lyst to lere ther lore,	*desire to learn their ways*
	bot herdly thus he answerd	*heartily*

And to the kyng he sayd,
   "Thiself the soth sall se: *truth*
18010

The payns thou hath purvayd
   sall make myrth unto me.

1502.

   "For God, my Mayster most of mayn,   *of most strength*
      wyll meng His mercy ever omell   *mix; among*
18015 With His servandes that ere here slayn   *are*
      by terrandes that ere fers and fell,   *tyrants that are fierce and cruel*
That thei sall ryse and lyf agayn   *rise [from the dead]*
      and at his lyst in lykyng dwell.   *desire; pleasure*
Bot of that fare be thou not fayn: *glad*
18020   thou sall never ryse, bot rest in Hell.

Thier harmes we have by thee   *These*
      with myrth sall be amend;   *rejoined*
Thi body and sawle sall be
      in wo withoutyn end."

1503.

18025 Then toyght the kyng he lyfed to lang;   *he (the boy) lived too long*
      his lyms he lythyd of fast in fere   *limbs he removed quickly together*
And put hym sythyn to payns strang   *then to terrible pains*
      tyll he was ded with doles sere.   *until; various sorrows*
The mother melled hyr ever amang;   *spoke*
18030   with murnyng mad sho mery chere   *though mourning she made*
And sayd that God suld gare them gang   *cause them to go*
      fro sorows sore to solace sere: *many solaces*
"Whoso wyll byd His bone,   *Whoever; await; reward*
      there bale full wele bese bett."   *their sorrows [will] be completely removed*
18035 Thus was the faurth fordone,   *destroyed*
      and the fyft furth was fett.   *fetched*

[The fifth son tortured and killed (7:15–17)]

1504.

The fyft full felly con thei fere,   *very cruelly did they [try to] frighten*
      and ylkon thrett hym in ther thraw.   *each one threatened; their turn*
The kyng by all his goddes con swere,
18040   "Ther lurdans sall be layd full law!"   *These villains shall be laid low*
His fyngers fast he dyd of shere;   *shear off*
      both tong and tothe he bade owt draw   *tongue; tooth; draw out*
And then to boylyng fast hym bere.   *carry*
      The chyld answerd withoutyn aw.   *awe (fear)*
18045 Unto the kyng he beheld
      in thies stoures as he stud,   *these sufferings*

	And thus his tayle he teld	*words he spoke*
	with sembland sad and gud:	*an expression firm*

1505.

	"That thou is kyng in erth to kend,	*command*
18050	that shewes thou by thi werke allway.	*you show*
	Thou proves thi myght in erthly men	*against*
	with all the malyce that thou may.	
	Whatso thee lyst, and whore and when,	*Whatever you desire*
	that bus be done ever ylk day.	*must; each single day*
18055	Bot thou suld wele avyse thee than	*better govern yourself*
	to rewle thi dede in ryght aray.	*rule your deeds*
	All yf we thus be takyn	*Even*
	and in thi pawsté pynyd,	*power pained*
	God hath us noyght forsakyn,	
18060	ne non ellys of our kynd.	*nor others*

1506.

	"Bot suffer and thiself sall se	*Wait patiently*
	in lytyll space full mekyll spede	*quickly*
	How God sall be His grett pawsté	*by; power*
	merke unto ylk man His mede,	*provide; reward*
18065	And how sere vengance sent sall be	*various*
	both on thiself and on thi sede.	*seed (family)*
	Do furth thi maystry now with me,	*mastery*
	for of thi dome have I no dred."	*judgment*
	And so he leved his lyfe	*left*
18070	or he His Law wold lett.	*before; leave*
	Thus are thei fayryn all fyfe,	*treated*
	and furth the sext was sett.	

[THE SIXTH SON TORTURED AND KILLED (7:18–19)]

1507.

	The sext was fett and sesyd sone	*sixth; fetched; seized quickly*
	to suffer ded with sorows sore.	*death*
18075	He wold abyd no bettur bone	*await; reward*
	bot als his felows ferd before.	*fared*
	When thei had dyght and to hym done	*taken*
	swylk marterdome and mekyll more,	
	He lyft his hede withoutyn hone	*lifted his head; hesitation*
18080	and to the kyng thus sayd he thore,	
	"Thou cursed commawndour,	
	that us all has sakles slayn,	*innocent*
	Sese yytt of thin errour!	*Cease yet*
	Thou trayvels all in vayn.	*travails*

1508.

18085	"Thier payns that thou hath put us in
	aftur thi wyll and wekyd toyght,
	We suffer them all for our syn
	that we agayn our Lord hath wroyght.
	To geyte His grace forto begyn
18090	with sorowyng thus our syns bene soyght,
	And so we sall to welthes wyn
	when all thi werke sall worth to noyght.
	For be ye never so lathe
	to lose this erthly lyfe,
18095	Thou sall not scape fro scath
	that agayns God wyll stryfe."

These

wicked thought

against

are
wealth be rewarded
come to nothing
loath

escape from harm

[THE MOTHER'S WORTHINESS (7:20–23)]

1509.

	And so he dyed be dyverse ded;
	he had no lenger wordes at weld.
	Ther mother was worth mekyll mede;
18100	sho sayd ever God suld be ther beld.
	When that sho saw hyr sex suns blede,
	the same ever in hyrselfe sho felyd.
	Bot of the yongest had sho dred
	that he suld turn for tender eld.
18105	Sho sayd ever thei suld ryse
	with ryghtwys men by raw
	That here themself dyspyce
	for Goddes luf and Hys Law.

died; deeds
to wield (speak)
Their; much reward
comfort

she felt

convert because of his youth

in due time
despise

[THE YOUNGEST SON TORTURED (7:24–38)]

1510.

	That cursyd Kyng Antyocus
18110	for wo in wytt he was nere wode.
	His knyghtes sayd, "Ser, tent to us,
	we con thee ken consayle full gode.
	Sen ther trayturs have tened thee thus
	and no turment may turn ther mode,
18115	Now with yond yongest boye thee bus
	with fayrnes fand to foyl that fode.
	For men uses chylder yyng
	with wordes forto tyll,
	And foyles with fayre hethyng
18120	forto werke what men wyll."

wits; nearly mad
listen
give you counsel
these; injured
change their minds
must you deal
specious words try to foul that child
young children
seduce
fouls with fair contempt

1511.

The kyng was of this purpose payd — *glad*
  and curtasly then carped he: — *courteously; said*
"Save now thiself, my sun," he sayd,
  "for, sertes, ther sall non wytt bot we. — *certainly; know*
18125   And for I wold not thou were flayd, — *would not [see that] you were flayed*
  ther sall none mell of my meneye. — *speak [of it]; company*
Full rychly sall thou be arayd
  and have my helpe, that hete I thee. — *promise*
Thou sall have toure and town — *tower*
18130   with forestes fayr and fre,
And all bowand and bown — *bowing and ready*
  at thi bedyng to be. — *bidding*

1512.

"And thresour all withoutyn tale — *treasure without reckoning*
  sall thou have in thi hurd to hyde; — *treasury*
18135   And next myself, sun, sytt thou sall — *beside*
  with solace sere on ylka syde. — *many solaces on each*
Then in thi hele thou sall be hale — *health; whole*
  and have maystry and mekyll pryd. — *power and much*
So is bettur then to be in bale, — *suffering*
18140   als thi brether have bene this tyd. — *brothers; time*
Sun, yf thou wyll acord
  with our fodes to be fede, — *food*
Thou sall lyf als a lord
  and by our lawys be led." — *laws*

1513.

18145   When the chyld herd all how he ment, — *heard; intended*
  he answerd evyn withoutyn aw — *without fear*
And sayd that he suld never assent
  to forfett in his Fader Law. — *forfeit*
Then toyght the kyng hym shamly shent — *thought; he should be shamefully destroyed*
18150   when the chyld sett nothyng by his saw; — *advice*
Bot to the woman yyt he went — *yet*
  with whyls hyr to his wyll at draw. — *wiles*
Sen other sex were slayn — *Since the other six*
  that wold no mercy crave,
18155   He wend sho wold be fayn — *thought; glad*
  hyr yyngest sun to save. — *youngest*

1514.

He carped to hyr full curtasly, — *spoke; courteously*
  and under trayn all thus he told. — *deceitfully*
"Woman," he sayd, "wonder have I
18160   how that thi hert may be so bold — *your heart*

To suffer thus thi suns to dy
  and has no mo apon this mold.   *more upon this earth*
To take the yyngest to mercy,
  that were my wyll yytt and thou wold.   *desire yet if you would [allow it]*
18165 He is a proper page
  and may grove tyll a man.   *grow into a noble man*
Now in his tender age
  were tym that he began

1515.
"To lere the law that ever sall last   *learn*
18170 and in myster most mend hym may.   *need*
Bestes of gold I sall do cast   *Beasts*
  to be his goddes full gud and gay."
The woman mad hyr forward fast   *covenant*
  that sho suld so hyr sun assay,   *test*
18175 And thynkes, when scho is from hym past,
  another poynt forto purvay.
To hyde hyr hert entent   *true intent*
  sho lowted unto hym law.   *bowed to him low*
So to hyr sun sho went
18180 and sayd to hym this saw: *these words*

1516.
"A, sun, see to thi mother here!
  Bot thou be wyse, me is full wo.   *Unless you are wise*
Thynke, sun, thou lay my hert full nere   *you lay very close to my heart*
  neyn monethes and nyghtes mo;   *months*
18185 And, sun, I sufferd sorow sere   *many sorrows*
  or tym that we were twynd in two.   *before the time; parted in two*
I fed thee of my flesch thre yere
  or thou couth speke or graydly go.   *before; walk properly*
Fro barnhed I thee broyght   *infancy; raised*
18190 to tyme that we com hydder.   *until the time; here*
Dere sun, forsake me noyght!
  Lett us go all togeydder!

1517.
"Behald, sun, to the Hevyn on hyght
  and to this werld that is full wyde,
18195 To bestes and fysch and fowles in flyght,   *beasts*
  how erth and ayre ere ocupyed,   *air are*
And how God mad all with His myght
  without substance o many syde.
And men He made of reson ryght
18200 ay in His blyse to beld and byd.   *dwell and live*
He aschys noyght ellys therfor,   *asks nothing else*

nawder in dede ne in saw,   *neither in deed nor in words*
Bot that men sall ever more   *Except*
    luf Hym and luf His Law.

1518.

18205   "Thi brether in lytyll space ere sped,   *brothers; are dead*
    and for God sake wele sufferd thei.
With hevynly fode now ere thei fed   *food*
    and lendes in lyf that last ay.   *dwell; lasts forever*
Therfor, dere sun, be not adred
18210   of yond fals domysman with his dray,   *false judge; violence*
Bot led thi lyf als thers is led,   *lead; as theirs were*
    that we may wend all away.
Of Blys bede I no more   *Bliss (Heaven) request*
    bot the barns that I boyght so dere,   *children*
18215   Sun, when I sall com thore,
    to fynd them fayr in fere."   *beautiful together*

1519.

He assent to his mother saw   *assented; mother's words*
    full wysly all yf he were yyng.   *even though he was young*
Then carped he to them all on raw   *spoke; in turn*
18220   that sat in consayle with the kyng:
"Of yowr highnes have I non aw.   *no awe*
    Why tarry ye thus of this thyng?
I oblysche me here to my law   *pledge myself*
    bot noyght unto the kynges bedyng."   *bidding*
18225   Thei toyght them then begyled;   *thought*
    the kyng was wel nere wode   *mad*
To be chawfyd with a chyld   *chafed*
    and myght not turn his mode.

[THE DEATH OF THE YOUNGEST SON AND HIS MOTHER (7:39–42)]

1520.

Unto his turmenturs he bad   *ordered*
18230   all thar payns forto purvay:
"Lyth of the lyms of that lytyll lad   *Rip off the limbs*
    and lere hym so to lake our lay.   *teach him thus to defy our law*
And the mother, that has mad them mad,   *made; mad*
    marre hyr more all that ye may!"   *mar*
18235   To go therto was sho full glad.
    So were thei ded all on a day   *in a single day*
And under a domysman,   *judge*
    the mother and hyr suns sevyn.
For thei so wyse were than,
18240   thei have ther hame in Hevyn.   *their home*

1521.

All myrthes on this mold thei myst	*earth they forsook*
the Laws of Moyses to maynteyn.	
For luf of God yt was ther lyst	*desire*
to leve all erthly comforth clene;	*comforts*
18245 And in ther blud thei were baptyst,	*their [own] blood; baptized*
als Innocentes were sythyn seyn;	*as was later seen with the [Holy] Innocents*
And Holy Chyrch hath them cananyst	*canonized*
als marters evermore forto be meyn.	*as martyrs; remembered*
God graunt us grace to trow	*believe*
18250 in Hym and in all Hys,	
And to His bydynges bow	*bidding submit*
that we may byd in Blyse!	*dwell*

SECOND BOOK OF MACCABEES 6 AND 9

DE ANTHIOCO.   *On Antiochus*

[ANTIOCHUS ABOLISHES THE LAW (6:1–9)]

1522.

	Anthiocus, that hethyn kyng,	*heathen*
	unto the Jews had ever envy,	
18255	And in hys bowndom them to bryng	*jurisdiction*
	in all his cuntré gart he cry:	
	Yf any Ebrew, old or yyng,	
	that wold not menske his mawmentry,	*honor his idolatry*
	In preson sone men suld them thryng	*prison; thrust*
18260	with dyverse doles to gare them dy,	*sorrows to cause them to die*
	Bot yf thei wold forgeyt	*Unless*
	the lyf that Moyses led,	
	And als bot thei wold ete	*also unless; eat*
	swylke flesch as he forbed.	*such flesh (i.e., pork)*

[ELEAZAR MARTYRED (6:18–31)]

1523.

18265	And als thei went, so were thei ware	*they became aware of*
	a prince that was of power grett,	
	An old Ebrew, Elyazar,	*Eleazar*
	that no forbodyn flesch wold ete.	*forbidden*
	Sone was he bun and broyght to barre,	*bound; to court*
18270	and full throly thei con hym threytt:	*fiercely; threaten*
	That he suld with Phylysteyns fare	*Philistines*
	and os on of them mete to ete.	*as one; to eat food*
	He sayd that suld he never,	
	nauder for evyn ne ode;	*neither by even nor odd (i.e., in no way)*
18275	To dy were hym wele lever	*he much preferred*
	then breke the Law of God.	

530

[Two women martyred (6:10)]

1524.

So was he ded with dole and wo,
   and furth thei soyght on ylka syde;   *each side [of the land]*
And sone thei wyst of wemen two   *knew*
18280   that ther two suns had circumscised   *their; sons*
Or thei couth other speke or go;   *Before they (the children); walk*
   and so thei hoped them forto hyd.
Bott full tyte were thei tone them fro,   *very quickly; taken*
   and over the wals thei gard them glyd.   *caused them to fall*
18285   And so this cursyd kyng,
   that of God had non aw,   *fear*
Gart stroy both ald and yyng   *Caused to be destroyed; old and young*
   that lyfed by Moyses Law.

[Antiochus' pride (9:8)]

1525.

Hym thynkes he is swylke lord in land   *such a lord on earth*
18290   that he myght conquere ylk cuntré,
All creaturs forto cummand.   *creatures*
   So that yf he wold say to the see   *sea*
Styll in a state ay forto stand,   *To stand still forever in one way*
   als he wold byd, so suld yt be.   *as he commanded*
18295   And remeve hyls ryght with his hand —   *removed hills*
   swylke hegh prid in his hert had he.   *such high pride*
Hym thynkes all erthly thyng
   suld be bowsom and bayn   *humble and obedient*
At bow to his bydyng
18300   and nothyng thor agayn.

[Antiochus attacks Jerusalem and is killed (9:1–7)]

1526.

With all swylke maystrys con he mell;   *such tyranny; busy himself*
   mete unto hym he nevyns none.   *he thinks no one equal to him*
Jerusalem, whore the Jewys con dwell,
   wyll he dystroy ever ylke stone,   *each*
18305   For in the Tempyll herd he tell
   was gold and sylver full gud wone.   *in abundance*
To foche yt and the folke to fell   *fetch; destroy*
   his purpase playnly hath he toyne.   *taken*
Bot God, ther governowre,
18310   wold not yt lynag lose.   *lose that lineage*
He sent them sone socoure
   and pared hys yll purpose.   *thwarted his wicked*

1527.

Thei geydder sone grett cumpany	*gathered*
of allablasters and of other geyre,	*arbalests; engines of war*
18315 Of charyottes and chyvalry	*chariots and knights*
that wysest were to wend in were.	*go in battle*
Hymself was sett full sekerly	*securely*
up in a chare Goddes folke to fere,	*chariot; frighten*
Bot thrugh grace of God Allmighty	
18320 his sped was spylt withoutyn spere.	*fortune; without weapon*
For all his men omell	*among*
and most in his hegh pryde,	
Out of his chare he fell	
and bressed both bake and syde.	*bruised; back*

[Sickness, false repentance, and death of Antiochus (9:8–28)]

1528.

18325 Slyke seknes sone on hym was sent	*Such sickness*
that in a lytter was he led.	*litter*
He was so bressed on that bent;	*bruised; field*
wyld bestes in his bowels bred,	*wild worms*
And qwyke out of his wome thei went.	*belly*
18330 and in swylke stynke then was he sted	*such stench; placed*
That none wold take to hym entent;	
his next frendes fast fro hym fled.	*closest friends*
When grett party were gon	*his great army*
and he allon was layd,	*alone*
18335 Falsly he mad his mone	*lament*
and sorowand thus he sayd:	*sorrowing*

1529.

"Now in myselfe the sothe se I,	*truth*
and kare me kaches kyndly to knaw:	*distress urges me naturally to confess*
All erthly men that ere dedly,	*mortal*
18340 of dew dett evermore thei aw	*proper duty; ought*
To honour a God Allmighty	
and serve Hym ever in dede and saw.	*in deed and word*
Paynyms lyf wyll I lefe forthi	*A pagan; abandon therefore*
and lere to lyf by Ebrews Law."	*learn*
18345 Thus with gabbyng he glosys;	*deceit he lies*
noyt for his syn he sore rewys,	*sorely rues*
Bot for he so supposys	
to geyt frenschep of the Jewys.	

1530.

For allways was he in dyspayre	*despair*
18350 of any helpe fro Hevyn on hyght.	

He felyd his fors full fast con pare,   *felt his life; did weaken*
  and letters gart he graydly dyght   *caused he quickly to be prepared*
Unto the Jewys and pray them fare
  forto be frendly day and nyght,
18355 Anthiocus, his sun and ayre,   *heir*
  forto releve hym in his ryght.   *to succeed*
He hetes, and he may lyf,   *promises, if*
  all that he had of thayrs   *theirs*
The dubyll agayn to gyf   *double*
18360 fro hym and fro his ayrs,   *heirs*

1531.

And to be rewled aftur ther red.   *governed; their counsel*
  Hys werke was wast withoutyn were.   *doubt*
He myght not then be styrd of sted,   *moved from that place*
  ne for stynke no man com hym nere.   *for the stench; came near him*
18365 So lay he bolnand, blo als led,   *swelling, blue as lead*
  withoutyn beld of bed or bere.   *comfort; bier*
With dyverse dole so was he dede;
  we trow his demyng to be dere.   *believe his judgment [by God] to be severe*
Pray we to God forthi,   *therefore*
18370 with the moyder and hyr suns sevyn,
That we may be worthy
  to wun with them in Hevyn!   *dwell*

Amen.

 **EXPLANATORY NOTES**

ABBREVIATIONS: *CA*: Gower, *Confessio Amantis*; *CM*: *Cursor mundi*; *CT*: Chaucer, *Canterbury Tales*; *DBTEL*: *A Dictionary of Biblical Tradition in English Literature*, ed. Jeffrey; *HS*: Peter Comestor, *Historia Scholastica*, cited by book and chapter, followed by *Patrologia Latina* column in parentheses; **K**: Kalén-Ohlander edition; *MED*: *Middle English Dictionary*; *NOAB*: *New Oxford Annotated Bible*; *OED*: *Oxford English Dictionary*; *OFP*: *Old French Paraphrase*, London, British Library, MS Egerton 2710, cited by folio and column; **Whiting**: Whiting, *Proverbs, Sentences, and Proverbial Phrases*; **York**: *York Plays*, ed. Beadle. For other abbreviations, see Textual Notes.

PROLOGUE

7   *Thrugh mediacy of Mary chast.* While there are aspects of the poem that have the ring of reform (and thus of Wycliffe and Lollardy, see the introduction), the *Paraphrase*-poet begins his story on solidly dogmatic grounds with an allusion to Mary in her role as mediatrix.

10–11   *boke ryght to aray, / Begynnyng, myddes, and end.* At the outset of his work, the *Paraphrase*-poet reveals a preoccupation with issues of literary design: he hopes to compose a book rightly from beginning to end. This concern relates to his desire to tell tales that are both entertaining and edifying, his project to "romance the Bible." Though the poet presumably could not access Aristotle's discussions of narrative structure directly, Aristotle's tripartite organization could nevertheless be known in principle from many sources: e.g., Cicero, John of Garland, and even some of the French cycles. As a formal structure it is particularly fitting for the task of translating Scripture, of course, which is defined as proceeding from the literal beginning to the presumed end of all things.

18   *the maystur of storyse.* Peter Comestor, author of the *Historia Scholastica* (c. 1170). Like many other late medieval authors of biblical commentary, the poet relies heavily on *HS* for extrabiblical embellishments and legendary materials. See, for example, the use of *HS* among such varied works as *CM*, *York*, *Northern Homily Cycle*, and *Genesis and Exodus* (Cambridge, Corpus Christi College, MS 444). The "storyse" that the poet refers to is the text of *HS*.

BOOK OF GENESIS

41–48   *God . . . with Hys Word hath wroght. . . . On the heght the Holi Gast / abown the
            waters movyd.* Much depends on the editorial act of capitalization. What the
            poet means by *hys word* (line 42), for instance, is quite uncertain due to the
            lack of standardized capitalization practices within the vast majority of
            medieval manuscripts, including those associated with the *Paraphrase.* If
            uncapitalized, the poet's phrase states only that God spoke Creation into
            existence — in accordance with the opening verses of Genesis 1. If capitalized,
            the poet's phrase states that Christ (as Word) was the acting agent of
            Creation, a theological revision of Genesis through the lens of John 1:1–3:
            "In the beginning was the Word, and the Word was with God, and the Word
            was God. The same was in the beginning with God. All things were made by
            him: and without him was made nothing that was made." As editor I have
            opted for the latter, capitalized reading, influenced by the poet's observation,
            in lines 47–48, that the Holy Spirit was likewise in presence: since the
            Council of Constantinople in 381, the co-eternal and consubstantial nature
            of the Trinity has been the mainstream doctrine of the Christian Church
            (see Bell, *Cloud of Witnesses*, pp. 65–74). It is thus both doctrinally sound and
            rhetorically expected to find both *Word* and *Holi Gast* in united substance
            and action with God from the very beginning of this mammoth biblical
            paraphrase.

49–56   *Hell He mad . . . the lyghtnes to be Day.* According to Genesis 1:1–2, Creation
            began with Heaven and earth, followed by light and darkness. The poet
            begins with a heaven, too, as well as an earth (lines 41–46); but the separ-
            ation of light and darkness is made to correspond to the creation of Hell
            (where utter darkness lies) and a more properly outfitted Heaven (where
            now light resides). The creation of Hell has no place in the Bible, and its
            place here is one we might associate with drama: the setting of the stage.
            When Lucifer falls, he must have a place to fall to, a Hell (or, as one often
            gets in the plays and in iconography, a hell-mouth). It stands to reason,
            then, that the construction of the lower, tertiary stage must occur before the
            creation of the angels. While its connection to the separation of light and
            darkness thereby seems a matter of logic, not theology, such a mythology
            makes Hell an absolute and *necessary* place — thus speaking to God's omni-
            potence and fate.

53–54   The creation of the angels is in neither the Bible nor *OFP*, but it was well
            known from numerous sources during the Middle Ages. While ultimately
            derived from Augustine and Gregorius, the poet's immediate source here is
            likely *HS.* Parallel retellings of the story can be found in *CM* and *York.*

110   *dyverse fysches to flett with fyn.* The first of those lines that clearly illustrate
            York's usage of the *Paraphrase*; compare *York* 2.65: "And othir fysch to flet
            with fyne."

115–16   *ther lyfes to lede / and same won withoutyn fynd.* This statement is, perhaps, a
            reference to the belief that most birds are monogamous. Chaucer's turtle-

dove, for example, is presented as a paragon of marital fidelity in *Parliament of Fowls*, lines 582–88 — though the mallard is quick to voice its opinion that promiscuity is fair enough. The opinion that turtledoves in particular are symbols of fidelity is supported by the *Middle English Physiologus* and its Latin tradition; indeed, it goes back at least as far as Aristotle's *Historia animalium* viii.600a 20. On avian love practices, see Bartholomaeus Anglicus' *De proprietatibus rerum* 12.1: "Among alle bestis that ben in ordre of generacioun, briddes and foules [folwen] most honest[ee] of kynde. For by ordre of kynde males seche femalis with bisynesse and loueth hem whanne they beth ifounden . . . And briddes and foules gendrynge kepith covenable tyme" (trans. Trevisa 1.597–98).

124   *and wormes on the wome to wende.* Compare *York* 2.78: "And wormis vp-on þaire wombis sall wende."

138   *a crokyd rybe, os clerkes can rede.* The idea that Eve was made from one of Adam's ribs was taken so literally in the West that it was a popular belief that all men had one less rib than women. The first clear refutation of this belief came in 1543, when Andreas Vesalius wrote otherwise in *De humani corporis fabrica libri septem* 1.19; he was roundly condemned by the Church for taking such a position. That the rib from which Eve was formed was particularly "crooked" and that this thus remarks upon her character is a long tradition that seems to have Islamic origins (see, e.g., the Tafsir Ibn Kathir on Qur'an, Surah 4:1 [An-Nisa]), but one of its clearest formations comes at the end of the Middle Ages in Kramer and Sprenger's *Malleus Maleficarum*: "There was a defect in the formation of the first woman, since she was formed from a bent rib, that is, a rib of the breast, which is bent as it were in a contrary direction to a man. And since through this defect she is an imperfect animal, she always deceives" (p. 44). For a broad look at this tradition, see Utley's *Crooked Rib*.

141   *He gafe them power playn.* The multiple possible meanings of *playn* in Middle English produce a range of theologically loaded readings of the line. The power given to Adam and Eve is at once unlimited (*playn* meaning "full"), finite ("simple"), and restricted ("honest"). How this semantically open loop will close itself off will depend, it turns out, on their own actions: "tyll thei breke Hys bydyng" (line 144).

157–60   *In myddes of Paradyse yt stud . . . suld clerly knaw both gud and yll.* There are two trees in the Garden according to Genesis 2:9: the Tree of Life and the Tree of the Knowledge of Good and Evil. The former conveyed eternal life (see Genesis 3:2, Proverbs 3:18, and Apocalypse 22:2, 14, 19), while the latter conveyed wisdom (2 Kings [2 Samuel] 14:17 and Isaias 7:15).

170   *fallyn was not fer before.* That Satan had fallen from Heaven with a host of rebellious angels is a tradition with roots in the post-exilic period of Jewish history, its primary sources being 1 and 2 Enoch, and the book of Jubilees. And while many medieval theologians endeavored to place Satan into the background — perhaps fearful that such a being might lead to Gnostic and Manichean heresics — the popularity of Satan as a figure of evil is clear enough in literature. In the fourteenth century, the devil plays a key role in

Langland's *Piers Plowman* (see, for instance, his attack on the Tree of Charity in C.16), in Chaucer's *Canterbury Tales* (e.g., in the Monk's and Friar's Tales), and, especially, in the plays. *York*, *N-Town*, *Towneley*, and *Chester* all devote plays to his fall. For an overview of the English tradition, see "Devil," *DBTEL*, pp. 199–202.

180   *them both forto gyle*. Note that *both* Adam and Eve are made subject to Satan's temptations. While this is not a direct reading of the biblical text it is, strangely, in accordance with the Qur'an, Surah 2:36 (Al-Baqarah).

184   *with woman face*. On the iconography of a woman's face on the serpent in the garden, see Flores, "'Effigies amicitiae . . . veritas inimicitiae.'" The tradition, which appears in *HS* and is prevalent in medieval art, might be traceable to the notion that Eve and the serpent work together to bring about Adam's fall. This is the case, for example, in *CM*, lines 723–30.

190   *skyll*. In his treachery, the Fiend thus turns God's ordinance into a deceit — a stratagem or ruse — that God plays on fools. The Fiend's reading is compelling since he, in earnest, mirrors such a *skyll* in himself. See *MED skil* n.6b.

224   *wyn thou thy foyd with swynke and swett*. Compare *York* 5.161: "In erthe þan shalle ye swete and swynke."

227   *manys kynd com this thyng*. The poet has carefully conveyed a complex theological concept within this phrase. On the one hand, the *thyng* is the hardships of life, which have been placed upon "mankind." In addition, however, the story of the Fall is the story of another *thyng*, original sin, which has entered into "man's kind" — i.e., human nature.

236   *cheke of an ase*. Theories about the murder weapon abound in biblical commentaries, but it is only in the English tradition that it is said to be the jawbone of an ass, a detail that perhaps owes its origin to Judges 15:15–17, where Samson utilizes such a bone to kill one thousand men. Cain is pictured with a jawbone in the eleventh-century illustrations to Ælfric's Anglo-Saxon Hexateuch in Cotton MS Claudius B.iv. Such is also made clear in Queen Mary's Psalter (fol. 8r), the Holkham Manuscript (fol. 5v), and *CM*, line 1073, a version of which our poet could well have had at hand. Neither *HS* nor *OFP* contain the detail. In the plays, see *Towneley* 1.324 and *N-Town* 2.149. Unfortunately, *York* is defective in this portion. That the "jawbone of an ass" detail has remained in currency is probably the result of its appearance, much later, in *Hamlet* 5.1.76.

239–40   *Caymys went down to Hell / and to God gaf noe lyght*. This is quite against Genesis 4:11–16, which depicts Cain as made to dwell "as a fugitive on the earth, at the east side of Eden" (4:16). The land in which he makes his dwelling place is Nod, meaning "Wandering." *CM*, lines 1223–36, agrees with the Bible here, while adding the detail that Cain and his kin were killed in the Flood. I follow K in viewing *noe lyght* as a primary reference to the lack of light from Cain's burnt offering (compare Genesis 4:4–5), a detail that fits well with the choking smoke of dramatic tradition (see, e.g., *Towneley*

2.277–92, where Cain's offering refuses to burn and only coughs up thick smoke). Stern has suggested that the line be emended to read *no delyght* (Review of *A Middle English Metrical Pharaphrase*, p. 281), but it is not necessary to emend in order to achieve the multiple levels of meaning in the term: Cain gives God no light, no figurative delight (see *MED light* n.8), and no spiritual enlightenment (n.9). The final meaning is particularly interesting, as Cain fails to gloss his relationship with God properly — in which case we might gloss the line as "demonstrated no spiritual understanding."

245–48   *Bot aftur that full mony a yer . . . the story says sexty and moe*. As Ohlander notes, *OFP* 3b follows the Bible in giving no exact number of children ("Old French Parallels," p. 204). The source for this mention of Adam and Eve's sixty-plus additional children, then, is probably *HS* Gen. 29 (1080): "Legitur Adam triginta habuisse filios, et totidem filias praeter Cain et Abel." A parallel can again be found in *CM*, lines 1215–22.

250   *lyfyd be law of kynd*. That the initial generations of mankind were apparently incestuous is here acknowledged but also excused as necessary action in keeping with the first rule of nature: to reproduce. *CM* says simply that Seth, for example, married his sister Delbora because God told him to do so (lines 1449–50).

253–54   *Of Caymys kynd come Tubulcan, / of metall mellyd he amang*. That Tubal-cain was the first metalworker reflects a long-standing tradition, rooted in Genesis 4:22. See, e.g., *CA* 4.2425–26, where he "Fond ferst the forge and wroghte it wel"; or *CM*, line 1518, where he is "þe formast smyth." See also the explanatory note to lines 257–58, below.

257–58   *Hys brothyr Juball he began / musyke, ose mynstralsy and sang*. Jubal as the inventor of music and the harp (line 559) is a detail from Genesis 4:21 (see the parallel in *CA* 4.2416–18). The listing of the occupations of Lamech's sons is, as *NOAB* observes, evidence of humanity's "[c]ultural advance" (p. 7). It is interesting, in this regard, to note the inversion of Tubal-cain and Jubal in the *Paraphrase* (Jabal, ancestor of shepherds, is not listed here). To medieval thinking, music is a far more advanced form of culture than blacksmithing.

263–64   *He wrott what dedes thei dyd / that last aftur the flode*. Perhaps a reference to the tradition in which Seth returns to Eden and receives from the archangel Michael seeds from one of the holy trees that he places in Adam's mouth after he died. In Midrash tradition there are two of these seeds, and wood from the two trees is used in building Noah's ark and Solomon's Temple. Christian exegetes added a third seed and thus a third tree (see, e.g., *CM*, lines 1363–1430), its wood being used to produce the Cross upon which Christ died. Still other Christian writers gave the number of seeds as four.

     Or has the poet confused Seth with Enoch, the son of Jareth? According to Genesis 5:24, Enoch "walked with God, and was seen no more: because God took him," a tantalizing detail that is greatly expanded in later traditions. *CM*, lines 1467–80, for example, claims that Enoch was the first man to write, and that the first books are attributable to his hand. He then was taken into Eden, where he yet lives. He will supposedly come forth from Paradise on Doomsday, when he will fight for the Christian cause only to be slain, alongside Elijah (the other Old Testament persona reportedly taken into God's presence without dying), by the Antichrist — but not before they are able to act as the two witnesses referred to in Apocalypse 11:3. This joining of Enoch, Elijah, and Doomsday was immensely popular (see, for example, the *Glossa Ordinaria* Apoc. 11 [*PL* 114.730]), taking a prominent role in some of the medieval plays, like the *Chester* Antichrist (23.253–624), where Enoch and Elijah, having not tasted death, ask to be made flesh once more in order to die and thus participate fully in Christ's gifts.

272   *thre thowssand yere for neven by nere.* Different versions of the Bible provide different timespans for the Antediluvian Age. A precise reading of the Hebrew (Masoretic) text of the chronogenealogy (I borrow the term from Hasel, "Genesis 5 and 11") of Genesis 5:1–32, for example, indicates that 1,056 years passed between the creation of Adam and the birth of Noah. Since Noah was said to have been six hundred years old when the Deluge came (Genesis 7:6), the total time span should be something like sixteen hundred years. This is the accounting that we are given in the Vulgate. The Septuagint's numbering, however, adds 586 years into the lives of the ten pre-Flood patriarchs, giving a Creation-to-Flood dating of roughly twenty-two hundred years. And some Christian commentators have chosen to disregard the numbers here in order to place the length of time as six thousand years; this allows a connection between this time span and the six days mentioned in Mark 9:2, which are also read in terms of the six days of Creation. The *Paraphrase*'s three thousand years is perhaps indebted to *CM*, lines 2005–06, which appears to be following a tradition that goes back at least to Josephus who, in *Jewish Antiquities* 1.3.3–4, gives the time span between Adam and the Flood as 2,656 years, which was then rounded up to three thousand. Josephus claims a dating based on the authority of accurate "sacred books," and we cannot discount the possibility that he was privy to sources that now elude us. It is also possible that his dating is indebted to both the Masoretic and Septuagint traditions. While the Septuagint adds one hundred years to the Masoretic accounting of six of the ten generations between Adam and Noah, Josephus has simply added a century to all ten.

273   *No rayn on erth then fell.* Compare *CM*, line 1991: "no reyn on erþe felle" (Trinity Manuscript). That no rain fell on earth prior to the Flood is a tradition that seems to arise from Genesis 9:12–14, in which God places a rainbow in the sky as a sign of his covenant with Noah. Since there had not been, up to this point in time, rainbows, some exegetes concluded that there could not have been rain. Support for this understanding was found in 2:5, where as prelude to the description of the creation of Eden it is said that there was not yet any plant life because "the Lord God had not rained upon the earth."

275–76 *faur fludes of a well / that went from Paradyce.* See Genesis 2:10–14. The four waters of Paradise — Pishon, Gihon, Tigris, and Euphrates — were well known to medieval geographers and are given some amount of explication in *HS* Gen. 14 (1068); see, too, *OFP* 2c.

301   *To make an erke.* While many Christian exegetes interpret the ark as a figure of Christ (compare 1 Peter 3:20–21), no such opportunity is taken to do so here. As discussed in the introduction, the poet only rarely makes such Christian interpretations.

318   *fyfty cubbeyttes.* Genesis 7:20 has the water being fifteen cubits over the highest mountains (so, too, *HS* and *OFP* 3c). Somewhere along the line a scribe has either misread (or misheard) his copy-text or has eyeskipped the "fyfty cubbeyttes" from line 304.

321   *monethes yt encressyd.* Genesis 7:24: "the waters prevailed upon the earth a hundred and fifty days."

322–24   That Noah's ark came to rest in Armenia (*Armynie*, line 322) is a detail repeated both in *HS* Gen. 34 (1085) and *OFP* 3c (Ohlander, "Old French Parallels," p. 205). The same location is given in both *CM*, line 1869, and *York* 9.263–64; some translations of Genesis 8:4 give Armenia, while some locate the landing, more specifically, in the mountains of Ararat (which is a region of Armenia).

329   *a dowfe he hath commawnd.* In the biblical account (Genesis 8:8–12), the dove is actually sent forth twice: the first time it returns with nothing, but a week later it retrieves the olive branch.

342   *broyght furth frutt.* Though the phrase is referring to the positive results of their newly sown crops, it might also carry a dual reference to God's command to Noah and his sons upon their leaving the ark: "Increase and multiply, and fill the earth" (Genesis 9:1, repeated at 9:7). They are thus doubly fruitful in producing both sustenance and children, the latter explicitly noted in line 344: "thei multiplyd with mony an heyre."

356   *in god degree.* Probably a reference to the detail in Genesis 9:23 that Shem and Japheth, in covering their father with a garment, walked backward and kept their faces turned away so that they would not see Noah's nakedness, thus acting more properly.

358   *he werryd hym forthi.* This is the so-called Curse of Canaan, given in Genesis 9:25–27. Canaan was a son of Ham (see Genesis 9:22 and 10:6), and it was his people who settled the land that subsequently carried his name. The curse explicitly points out that Canaan would become slave to his brothers; Canaan is, indeed, subjugated by the Israelites during the conquest.

     The cursing of Canaan for what appears in the Bible to be his father's misdeeds has often been a point of bewilderment for exegetes. It is explained in Judaic lore with the story that it was Canaan who first saw his grandfather's nakedness. He told his father, and the two of them made great mirth at Noah's expense. Therefore Canaan (and not Ham's other children) earned the curse. Another interpretation is that the text originally read "Ham," but was later changed in order to excuse Israel's treatment of the Canaanites. Yet another possibility is that Ham could not be cursed since he had already been blessed (Genesis 9:1), therefore the curse passed to his eldest son and his descendants. See Ross, "Curse of Canaan."

372   *Bablion.* That is, Babel. The odd spelling here, as Ohlander has observed, is due to both *HS* Gen. 38 (1089), which reads "De turre Babylon," and the need to meet rhyme. Comestor's confusion is also picked up by *OFP* 4a, which reads "Babiloine" ("Old French Parallels," p. 205). Though the spelling has changed, the etymology given here still follows Genesis 11:9 in relating the name to Heb. *balal*, meaning "to confuse," though *Babel* actually means "Gate of God." For his part, the poet probably has in mind an etymological connection to *babble*, which, ironically, derives from Babel as a result of this famous story.

377–79   *Yf we suld say hys suns all sere . . . Thatt lesson wer full long to leere.* A convenient way of excusing this abbreviated version of one of the more lengthy "begat" sequences in the Bible: Genesis 10 and 11:10–32.

384   *to lere our law.* As discussed in the introduction, one of the many intriguing aspects of this work is the way that it shuns anti-Semitism and accepts both Jews and Judaism as legitimate forerunners of faith. Phrases such as *our law* make clear a unity between the Jews and what is, presumably, the poet's Christian audience.

406   *twa hunderth yer.* Genesis 11:32 sets Terah's age at 205 when he died, as does *HS* Gen. 41 (1091).

433–35   *Sodome . . . / Gommer . . . / And next them was ther other thre.* The so-called Pentapolis (Wisdom 10:6) was a region dominated by five cities: Sodom, Gomorrah, Segor (Zoar), Adama, and Seboim. These cities united to resist the invasion of Chodorlahomor, referred to in stanzas 37–39 (for the fuller account, see Genesis 14:1–16).

465–68   *He wold not byd ne blyne . . . and broyght hym home agayn.* The *Paraphrase* here greatly reduces the biblical account of Abram's military prowess against the alliance of four eastern kings. Part of the reason for this might be the desire to portray Israel's ancestors as a more peaceful people than the Bible reveals them to have been.

471–74   *Melchesedeke . . . with bred and wyne.* The mysterious Melchizedek, both king of Salem (Jerusalem) and a priest of the Canaanite religion, was later interpreted to be a harbinger of the messiah. See, for instance, Vulgate Psalm 109:4 (NRSV 110:4), which says that the messiah will be a priest-king "according to the order of Melchisedech." See also Hebrews 7:1–17, where the writer "deduces that the mysterious priest-king Melchizedek, was greater than either Abraham or his descendant, Levi" and thus greater than the levitical priesthood (*NOAB*, p. 322). The *Paraphrase*-poet takes no opportunity to intrude these later messianic interpretations onto the text, even when Genesis 14:18 provides the detail that Melchizedek brought bread and wine to Abram.

499–500   A nearly identical blessing is given by God in *York* 10.15–16: "He saide my seede shulde multyplye / Lyke to þe gravell of þe see."

505–16   K (1:clxxxix–cxc), imagining the priority of the plays to the *Paraphrase*, notes that this stanza is copied "nearly word by word" from *York* 10.3, though the reverse is surely the case.

511–12   *Hyr servant prevely scho wan / tyl Abraham at hys wyll to weld.* That Sarai worked secretly (*prevely*) to provide Abram with a child is a detail in no way found in the biblical account (Genesis 16:2), which relates the decision for Abram to have sex with her slavegirl as a mutual one between husband and wife. Although *NOAB* notes that, "[a]ccording to ancient custom, a wife could give her maid to her husband and claim the child as her own" (p. 19) — a custom that is also related in Genesis 30:3 and 30:9 — the poet is apparently anxious about the perceived adultery on Abram's part. Thus, Sarai is given full responsibility for precipitating the act, and Abram is kept in the dark, as it were.

514   *beldyd.* Here, as elsewhere, the poet appears to take a decided interest in cleansing his narrative of some of the "naughty" parts. Hagar "comforts" Abram through the night, a neat euphemism for what no doubt led to Ishmael's conception. Abram's marriage to Hagar (Genesis 16:3) is also glossed over.

515   *Ysmaell.* Meaning "God hears."

522   *ever scho wrogh os woman wyse.* The fact that Sarai drives Hagar away, and that Hagar only returns after an angel orders her to do so, is omitted here (Genesis 16:6–14) and instead told at lines 649–60. See explanatory note to those lines.

530   *C wynters.* Genesis 17:1 gives Abram's age as 99, as does *HS* Gen. 50 (1097).

531–35   K notes (1:cxc) the similarity of *York* 10.44–48.

534   *Ysac.* Meaning "He laughs."

543–44   *For Abraham it is sayd schortly / that Abraham then he suld be cald.* Though the Middle English does not make the distinction quite clear, the Vulgate and Hebrew sources are specific in delineating Abraham's two names. His given name was Abram, meaning "exalted ancestor," while his post-Covenant name was Abraham, meaning "ancestor of a multitude" and referring to the peoples whose ancestry was traced to Abraham (notably the Israelites, Edomites, and Ishmaelites).

550   *ose clerkes declare it can.* It is unclear if the poet has in mind any specific authorities here or is simply thinking about the general knowledge that the Jewish faith — and thus, by extension, that of Christianity — began with the Abrahamic Covenant. See the note to lines 551–52, below, on how this notion is passed on to popular materials.

551–52   *The trowth and the begynnyng / of our fayth ther begane.* K notes (1:cxc–cxci) a similarity to *York* 10.51–53: "The grounde and þe begynnyng / Of trowthe þat tyme be-ganne."

554   *Abraham was tyllyd under a tre.* Genesis 18:1 has Abraham in a tent near the trees (usually read as oaks) of Mamre, which *NOAB* notes to be "an ancient

sacred place, slightly north of Hebron, with which Abraham was associated" (p. 17). *Cleanness* similarly omits the tent, as Abraham was "schunt to þe schadow vnder schyre leues" (line 605). There may also be some distant connection here to the notion, common in folklore, that unusual events tend to happen when one sits beneath a tree (see, e.g., *Sir Orfeo*, *Sir Degaré*, and *Sir Gowther*).

The verb *tyllyd* is interesting here. *MED* cites this instance under *tillen* v.2a, meaning, as I have glossed it here, "to stretch out." So Abraham is relaxing (see also line 55, "hym to play"). But there may be an underlying play on words here, too, as *tyllyd* could also derive from *tillen* v.1, with its various agricultural meanings of plowing, production, and toil. Thus Abraham was toiling under a tree, preparing the land for a new crop. Little does he know that his seed has already been planted: his work, as the visitors will announce, has not been for nought.

557–61   *Thre chylder . . . wer fayr to syght.* One of the three visitors proclaims them all to be messengers of God (line 566), and that his two companions are sent by God to destroy the cities of Sodom and Gomorrah. However, this third figure would seem, in accordance with the indications of Genesis 18:22 and 19:1, to be God; when the other two are gone, Abraham is no longer talking with the third visitor but with God (line 579). Then again, in lines 573–76 the poet associates the three visitors with the Trinity (Compare *HS* Gen. 51 [1098–99]), a claim that is difficult to interpret literally. On their physical appearances, see note to line 560, below.

560   *all semand on eld to be.* One might be tempted to gloss the line as all "seeming to be mature in age," following *MED elde*, but this does not fit well with their youthful appearance reported in line 557. I have followed Ohlander's glossary (K 5.30) in glossing this line as all "seeming to be in flames" (see *MED eld*). This description would certainly fit with a deity accustomed to guiding and talking to man through burning bushes, pillars of fire, and tongues of flame, and it would also make some sense in light of Genesis 18:2, where, on seeing the visitors, Abraham "ran to meet them from the door of his tent, and adored down to the ground." And while Abraham's reaction here appears to be muted from what we might expect of a man suddenly faced with three men on fire (he describes them next as only "fayr to syght" — line 561), his hailing of them ("helsyd them os hende" — line 562) carries many meanings of subservience and reverence (see *MED halsen* v.1).

581–82   *God sayd ther was non gud therin / bot Loth and tho that with hym ware.* This abbreviated version of the conversation between God and Abraham (compare Genesis 18:23–33) cuts to the chase. In the biblical account Abraham "talks down" the deity, from fifty good people as sufficient to keep God from destroying Sodom to ten good people within, to which God agrees. But ten such people are not found. The *Paraphrase* simply jumps to the conclusion: only Lot and his family are deemed salvageable, and not all of them even make it to safety.

592   *bad furth tho chylder two.* The Sodomites' reasons for wanting the two men to come forth is not given here, but at Genesis 19:5 it is said that the townsfolk desire to "know" them. It is a long-standing tradition that this euphemism implies sex; and, more specifically, homosexual relations since the speakers are presumably male (thus "sodomy"). The destruction of Sodom is thereby taken to be God's "hands-on" denouncement of homosexuality (as opposed to the mere statement of law in Leviticus 18:22 and 20:13). But the *Paraphrase*-poet makes no such claims, instead regarding the destruction as simply due to their "syns sere" (line 572).

597–600   *God mad them blynd to be / so that thei toke no tent, / Tyll Loth with hys meneye / and tho chylder wer went.* The poet makes a significant change to the biblical narrative, presumably to heighten the romance characteristics of his narrative. In the biblical account, the depraved people of the town are struck blind so that they cannot find and open the door to the house. The angels urge Lot to leave, but he cannot manage to convince his family to do so. The night passes. The angels repeatedly request evacuation in the morning, but they must eventually forcibly remove Lot and his family to the safety of the plain where, apparently, the mortals finally get the message. Here in the *Paraphrase*, however, no repeated cajoling is necessary. Indeed, we get a sequence of uninterrupted action: the wicked are struck blind, buying Lot and his family enough time to slip past them and out of the city.

608   *with sympyll chere.* The poet seems to have a measure of pity on Lot's wife that God does not; she looks back because of her sad realization that all of her friends have just been destroyed. Her pity is not unlike that of Uxor in the *York* Noah play: "wher are nowe all oure kynne / And companye we knwe before?" (9.269–70). In Genesis 19:26 no reason is given for her decision to look back.

611–12   *Scho wurthyd to an ymag / of salt and sall be evere.* Lot's wife, in effect, is turned into an image of remorse, a monument to salt tears over a lost cause.

615   *Sogor.* Zoar (meaning "little") was a small town on the southern end of the Dead Sea.

621–22   *or ever the fyne / the werld to fulfyll.* Once again, the poet seems to have a measure of pity on his characters (see note to line 608, above): Lot's daughters truly think that no one else remains in the world but the two of them and their father (an understandable conclusion after the destruction of Sodom and Gomorrah). They take the drastic measure of sleeping with their father in order to propagate the species (an act that would be in accordance with God's command to Noah in 9:1). First the eldest ("the world to maynten at hyr myght," line 626) gets him drunk enough to have sex with her, then the youngest manages to "fob" him, too (line 630); neither action is explicitly condemned. Indeed, the child of the youngest (Ben-ammi, ancestor of the Ammonites) is pointedly given the descriptor "semly" (line 632), a detail not in the Bible.

634   *in wastes that wer wyld*. Like characters in a medieval romance, Lot and his fam-
             ily are cast out beyond the margins of civilization into the wilderness where
             they must learn to survive before being brought once more into society.

635–36   *tell of Abraham and Sara and / of Ysaac that was hys chyld*. Stanza 53, in a remark-
             able transition from one brother to the other, juxtaposes the children of Lot,
             inseminated through the anxieties of his daughters to repopulate the earth,
             with Abraham and Sarah's child, Isaac, who came about through God's
             covenant with Abraham, which will populate the earth by the millions in
             times to come with God's chosen people.

649–60   The poet conflates the two banishments of Hagar and Ishmael (Genesis
             16:6–14 and 21:8–21) into a single account. While this helps Sarah to come
             off better (see explanatory note to line 522) and helps to smooth and simpli-
             fy the narrative, it does leave Hagar and Ishmael with Abraham and Sarah
             rather than in the wilderness of Paran, as the Bible would have it (Genesis
             21:21). One additional interesting aspect of this change is that Ishmael is no
             longer free to become the ancestor of the Bedouin tribes of the south; it is
             from these "Ishmaelites" that Muslims trace their ancestry to Abraham and
             to the monotheistic God of Judaism. By leaving Ishmael with Abraham
             rather than in the southern wilderness, the poet has effectively undercut
             Islam's claims of authority. If this is intended, it shows a remarkably acute
             knowledge of Islam on the poet's part. Isaac is unequivocally God and Abra-
             ham's chosen heir (line 360), as God's subsequent tests will demonstrate.

664   *sadnes*. There is perhaps dual meaning in the term. First and foremost, God
             says that he will see (investigate) Abraham's "steadfastness." That is, He will
             test Abraham's willingness to obey, even at terrible cost. The reader, how-
             ever, will no doubt sense a second meaning, "sadness," given the pathos of
             the story.

673–708   Three straight stanzas are missing a long line. I have followed K in number-
             ing these lines on the assumption that the original poem had 12-line stanzas
             throughout and to allow ease of cross-referencing with that earlier edition.
             It is tempting, however, to view these sequential omissions as intentionally
             short, helping to press speed into this exciting narrative.

673–80   *Abraham unto hys son beheld . . . And chargeyd hym with wud and fyre*. The poet
             omits the accompanying two men of the biblical account. Even more inter-
             esting, however, is the decision to heighten the emotional pull of the scene
             by allowing Abraham the chance to reflect on what *should* have been — a far
             more human reaction than his silent assent to God's will in the biblical
             account. One is reminded of the sensibilities of the Brome Abraham and
             Isaac play.

709–20   That Abraham actually notifies Isaac of his intent, and that Isaac willingly
             agrees, is not a feature of the biblical account. It is, however, a scene from
             popular interpretations of the tale. See, e.g., the Brome Abraham and Isaac
             play, or the *N-Town Cycle*, where Isaac, bearing the wood on his back (as in
             line 700 here), accepts his Christological role in the sacrifice.

723   *A wedder he saw hym besyd*. Often figured as a representation of Christ as the sacrificial lamb that takes the place of man, the ram is treated as nothing more than an unfortunate wandering beast here. The location of the sacrifice was afterward known as Jehovah Jireh (Heb. "the Lord will provide").

733–34   *Scho was woman wynsom to weld, / non heynder haldyn under Hevyn*. Keturah is little more than a name in the Bible (Genesis 25:1), but she is here given high praise for her beauty and goodness in proper romantic fashion.

740–41   *a gud wyfe to hym can he nevyn: / Rebecca, a damisell*. Here, Abraham sends his servant with the specific task of finding Rebecca. This is quite different from Genesis 24:2–4, where he asks only that the servant look for a legitimate match for Isaac.

741–44   As K notes (1:cxci), these lines, a description of Rebecca, can be found in *York* 10.365–68.

745–56   The discovery of Rebecca at the well, a rather lengthy tale in the Bible (Genesis 24:10–61), is much abbreviated here. Likely the slow pacing of the story was not in keeping with the kind of romance narrative the poet chose to produce.

762   *sexty*. The poem ought to record seventy, in agreement with the Bible, where Abraham lives 175 years rather than 165 (Genesis 25:7).

777–80   God's pronouncement to Rebecca (Genesis 25:23) is altered somewhat here. In the biblical account, the Lord says to her: "Two nations are in thy womb, and two peoples shall be divided out of thy womb, and one people shall overcome the other, and the elder shall serve the younger"; the point being that Rebecca will give birth to twins, who will in turn give rise to two nations, and that the nation of the elder child will serve the nation of the younger child. To this basic pronouncement, our poet has followed a long-standing tradition of understanding a difference in strength between the two children, in which the elder is also the stronger, so that *the more in all thyng / sall serve unto the lesse* (lines 779–80). As lines 785–86 show, this difference in strength was largely tied to the fact that Esau was the firstborn, the idea being that he literally fought his way out of her womb first (see the explanatory note to lines 781–84, below). Further evidence was seen in Esau's hairiness — a sign of testosterone long before the chemistry of the matter was known — and in Esau's reported success as a hunter, which stands in marked contrast to Jacob's willingness to stay at home in the tents with his mother (see Genesis 25:27–28). The two nations that Rebecca's twins will give rise to are those of the Edomites (from Esau, who was later called Edom — see note to lines 803–04, below) and the Israelites (from Jacob, who will later be given the name Israel — see note to lines 997–1008, below).

781–84   That Jacob and Esau fought in the womb is a long-told legend, though the poet's source is surely *HS* Gen. 66 (1109). A close parallel can also be found in *CM*, lines 3481–82. As Ohlander notes, there is no parallel in *OFP* ("Old French Parallels," p. 206).

787   *Jacob.* Genesis 25:26 relates that Jacob came out holding onto his brother
           Esau's heel. The name Jacob can mean either "He takes by the heel" or,
           more metaphorically, "He supplants." The latter meaning is clearly indicat-
           ed in lines 885–86, when Esau laments how Jacob is rightfully named since
           he has twice supplanted his older brother.

788   *ther moyder was all marryd thore.* That Rebecca suffered bodily injury as a
           result of giving birth to such fighting twins is a detail not found in the Bible.
           For more on the poet's attempts to create a more "realistic" account of the
           Old Testament, see the introduction.

803–04   Though not related here, Genesis 25:29–30 explains that it is this moment
           that gives rise to Esau's being called Edom, meaning "red": "And Jacob
           boiled pottage: to whom Esau, coming faint out of the field, said: Give me
           of this red pottage, for I am exceeding faint. For which reason his name was
           called Edom." Though the connection is here made to the red pottage (or
           perhaps to his being flushed from hunger), the attribution also connects
           back to Genesis 25:25, which relates that Esau came out of his mother's
           womb all red.

813   The abrupt introduction of the story of Esau's lost blessing is largely the
           result of the decision to excise Genesis 26 from the *Paraphrase.* In this
           chapter, Isaac goes to Gerara, at which time God twice renews with him the
           Covenant He made with Abraham, promising: "I will multiply thy seed like
           the stars of heaven: and I will give to thy prosperity all these countries: and
           in thy seed shall all the nations of the earth be blessed" (Genesis 26:4).
           Other key events in this chapter: Isaac tries to trick the Palestines into
           thinking that Rebecca is his sister (fearing that they will kill him for her if
           they know she is his wife), digs a somewhat miraculous well at a place he
           names Shibah (from which the city of Bersabee — meaning "Well of the
           Oath" — gets its name), and ultimately makes a pact with King Abimelech
           of the Palestines. In addition, Esau (now forty years old) marries two Hittite
           wives, both of whom offend the minds of his parents.

           A primary motivation for the exclusion of Genesis 26 — aside from the
           need to construct a more streamlined and exciting biblical account — might
           be that it places the story of Esau selling his birthright to Jacob and the story
           of Esau's lost blessing by his father next to one another. The resulting jux-
           taposition presumably helps to alleviate the reader's concern that Jacob is
           lying to his father, tricking him into giving him Esau's blessing. That is,
           since Esau had just sold his birthright to his younger brother Jacob, the
           blessing rightfully belongs to him. Rebecca and Jacob, then, are at worst
           guilty of a venial sin in tricking Isaac; they are preventing what would have
           been the greater wrong (Esau acquiring what he had so flippantly sold). It
           is also useful to note here that Augustine (in *Contra mendacium* 10) began a
           tradition of reading this sequence as a prefiguring of the movement of God's
           blessing from the Jews to the Gentiles (or, even more broadly, from the Jews
           to the Christians, though that might underscore the "familial" relationship
           between the two religions more than many Christians would like to admit).

821   *veneson.* That Isaac specifically requests venison is not related in the Bible, where he only asks for "some thing by hunting" (Genesis 27:3). The detail is picked up from Genesis 27:19, where Jacob asks his father to "arise, sit, and eat of my venison, that thy soul may bless me."

885   *well was he namyd.* See note to line 787.

899–900   *Thus all this werld was wroght, / evyn os God wold yt wer.* That God would will the deceiving of Isaac and the taking of the birthright from Esau has long been troubling to readers of Scripture. Some exegetes answer both objections by regarding Esau as a mere hunter, not one who could properly lead the people. His indifference toward this responsibility, according to this interpretation, is clearly shown in his willingness to sell the eternal for the temporal satisfaction of food. Their mother, recognizing this in a way that the literally and figuratively blinded father cannot, helps to rectify the situation for the greater good of the people to come, aiding Jacob in acquiring his father's blessing. While such an interpretation makes Jacob the more capable man for the job and perhaps gives a reason for the deception, it does not answer the question about whether the means to the end is morally right. On this point, however, one can point to Jacob's experience in Haran, where he will have a similar deception foisted upon him (involving a similar issue of older and younger siblings). In particular, note that in Genesis 29:25, when Jacob complains to Laban that he has been deceived, he uses the same Hebrew word that Isaac had used in 27:35. In other words, Jacob eventually gets what is coming to him and learns from it, making the original deception, if not right, at least atoned for.

913   *crown.* That the ladder reaches up from the top of Jacob's head is a detail not found in the biblical account (Genesis 28:10–22), and it may be obliquely connected to Bonaventure's *Itinerarium mentis in Deum*, which relates the mind's journey to God as an ascension of Jacob's ladder. Thus the ladder, quite logically, *should* rise from Jacob's head.

930   *Goddes awn howse.* It is from this pronouncement that the location of Jacob's dream derives its name: Bethel, meaning "House of God." The town was formerly called Luz.

935   *tokynyng.* The word serves a dual function here, especially when read against Genesis 28:22. First, Jacob raises up the stone as a marker of some kind. The Douay translation calls the raised stone a "title," whereas the NRSV calls it a "pillar." Second, the Bible records that Jacob promises at this moment that he will give a tithe, one tenth of his wealth, to God. The word *tokynyng* subsumes both meanings — a mark of remembrance and a vow to tithe — under a single term.

942   *when Rachell suld have neghyd nere.* After serving Laban for the agreed seven years in exchange for Rachel, Jacob asked for her. But Laban tricked Jacob by sending Rachel's older sister Leah into the tent instead. Only in the morning, after sleeping with her, does Jacob recognize the deceit. See Genesis 29:21–25.

957–72   Laban agrees to give Jacob any of his flocks that were odd colored; that is, those that were not a uniform white. Such colorations are the exception rather than the rule, so Laban would seem to have little to lose in the agreement. Jacob's trickery to reverse this trend, as *NOAB* points out (p. 39), fits in well with ancient understandings about the origins of the colorations: "Ancient cattle-breeders believed that the female, at the time of conception, was influenced by visual impressions which affect the color of the offspring. Jacob produced striped animals by putting striped sticks before the females' eyes while they were breeding."

985–96   Though nothing is told here of the rivalry for Jacob's attention between the two sisters, Leah and Rebecca, that story is significant for explicating the rationale behind both the naming of the children and the fact that two of Jacob's servants bear him children. First, Leah bears Reuben (1), meaning "look, a son," and then Simeon (2), whose name refers to God having "heard" her pleas. Next, Leah bears a third son, named Levi (3), meaning "joined" and pointing out (to her sister, apparently) that Leah and Jacob were clearly sharing a special bond. The fourth child is Judah (4), whose name is one meaning "praise." Rachel, still having been unable to bear Jacob any children, is put in the position of Sarah. And, like Sarah, she chooses to bear him children through the proxy of one of her maids. Thus, she gives Bilhah to Jacob, and this handmaid bears Jacob a son named Dan (5), meaning "He [God] judged," indicating the change in God's favor that she hoped she was witnessing. Bilhah then conceived a second time and gave birth to Naphtali (6), whose name refers to the "wrestling" between the two sisters. Not to be outdone, Leah then gives to Jacob *her* maid, Zilpah, who gives birth to Gad (7), meaning "fortune," and Asher (8), meaning "happy." Leah herself then gives birth to Issachar (9), whose name "my hire" refers to an exchange by which Rachel bought some of Leah's son Reuben's mandrakes — thought to be an aphrodisiac and fertility drug — in exchange for Leah "hiring" her husband's services for a night. Leah next gives birth to Zebulun (10), meaning "honor" and marking herself as honored in Jacob's eyes for having born him six sons. She then gives birth to the first daughter in the family, Dinah (11). At last Rachel herself gives a child, perhaps through the use of Reuben's mandrakes, though this point is not made explicit in the Bible. This first child she names Joseph (12), whose name means "He [God] adds." Finally, Genesis 35:16–21 relates that Rachel dies giving birth to Jacob's twelfth son (13), whose name she pronounces with her dying words: Ben-oni, meaning "son of my sorrow." Jacob, however, calls the child Benjamin, meaning "son of the right hand," which was a symbol of power and of good fortune. An alternate meaning for Benjamin might be "son of the south," which would refer to Israel's position south of Ephraim.

997–1008   Jacob's wrestling with the angel of God at a place he named Peniel ("the face of God") is an apparently very ancient tradition, marked as it is with signs of particular antiquity, such as the angel needing to disappear before sunrise (Genesis 32:26) and a concern for the power of names (32:27, 29). But these details are omitted here, where concentration is instead placed upon the angel giving Jacob the new name Israel, meaning "he who strives with God." This name, which then passed to his descendants as "children of Israel" (line 1007), is one that has particular meaning for Jews, who see in it a root of their human impulse to forever wrestle with the divine. A separate account of the renaming of Jacob is given at Genesis 35:9–15.

1012 *on hym jones the genology.* To remark that a genealogy hinges (*jones*) on Judah might have many interpretations. The poet is probably, first and foremost, referring to the genealogy of Jesus, who descends from Jacob through Judah and Tamar (see Matthew 1:1–3 and the explanatory note to lines 1169–74, below). Other meanings available here, however, are an etymology relating to the Jews and (far less likely) a reading of the story of Joseph that will follow. In the former case, the word "Jew" derives from "Judah." It was originally a term applied to only those Israelites from that land, but, in the time of David, for example, Judah dominated the other tribes to such an extent that Jew came to be applied to all Israelites. This is especially true after Judah was the only independent Israelite kingdom remaining in the Holy Land. Judah was thus given, in the Scriptures, a preeminence among the tribes; see, for example, Jacob's blessing to his sons, especially that given to Judah in Genesis 49:8–12. It is also possible that the poet is taking a particular reading of the story of Joseph, in which it is Judah who persuades his brothers not to kill Joseph (37:26–27) and, later, gives the pleading speech that convinces Joseph to reveal himself to his brothers and thus restore the house of Jacob (44:14–34). There are even some scholars who consider "Reuben" in 37:21–22 to be a scribal error for Judah, making Judah alone the sole advocate for his brother Joseph (*NOAB*, p. 49). This is certainly not the case here, however, as the opposite change occurs: Judah's role in helping to save Joseph is given over completely to Reuben (lines 1221–24).

1037–38 *For wekydly then wastyd hee / the sed that suld be multiplyd.* In Genesis 38:9 the sin of refusing to inseminate a woman is attributed to the brother Onan and given as the reason for God killing him. The circumstances Er's wickedness entailed are not given in the Bible, which only notes his being "wicked in the sight of the Lord" (Genesis 38:7; see note to line 1043).

1043 *The Fend on the fyrst nyght.* Genesis 38:7 is quite clear in attributing Er's death to God: "And Her, the firstborn of Juda, was wicked in the sight of the Lord: and was slain by him." The NRSV translates even more forcefully: "the Lord put him to death." It was apparently difficult for the poet to accept the seemingly over-sudden and severe punishment of Er, however; here God's hand has been replaced by the workings of Satan. Both this change of attribution and the added detail of the death occurring on the first night very likely have their origins in the independent story of the demon who kills the new husbands of the daughter of Raguel on their wedding night (Tobias 6:14–8:3).

1048 *ose men then in this world was wun.* Compare Deuteronomy 25:5–10, which explains that if a man dies without a son, his brother, the widow's brother-in-law, must marry her and "raise up seed for his brother," thus perpetuating the dead man's name and inheritance.

1142   *The suth sall non man spare*. Proverbial. Not cited by Whiting or Tilley.

1151–52   *By this werke now wott I well / that scho is wyser then I*. Though adultery was
             punishable by stoning (Deuteronomy 22:23–24) or burning (Leviticus 21:9),
             Tamar is excused because she did what she did to fulfill the more important
             levirate marriage requirements of continuing her husband's line.

1159–73   Tamar's twins are the ancestors to two rival clans of Judah: Perez and Zerah.
             The elder Perez, whose name means "a breach" (relating to the circum-
             stances of his birth) is noted in Ruth 4:18–22 and 1 Chronicles 2:4 as an an-
             cestor of David. She is also noted in Matthew 1:3 as being in the genealogy
             of Jesus (see explanatory note to lines 1169–74). The second son's name
             means "brightness," and he is said in Genesis 38:30 to have been born with
             a "scarlet thread" upon his hand. Here the thread is given a more realistic
             origin than one of birth: the midwife ties the thread to his hand to tell the
             brothers apart (lines 1161–64).

1169–74   The Holy Writ quoted is Matthew 1:3, part of the genealogy of Jesus: "And
             Judas begot Phares and Zara of Thamar. And Phares begot Esron."

1178–80   *hys moyder dede herd he tell. / Ysac, his fader, myght no see; / for febylnes son seke he
             fell*. Both of these details — Rebecca's death and Isaac's ill health — are un-
             recorded in the Bible, though they are referred to tangentially: in Genesis
             49:31 Jacob relates that Rebecca is buried alongside her husband, Leah,
             Abraham, and Sarah in a cave in the field at Machpelah (near Mamre in Ca-
             naan), and Isaac's death is reported in Genesis 35:27–29. The omission of
             Isaac's death is apparently the root of some confusion on the part of a scribe
             somewhere in the *Paraphrase* tradition since S, line 1209, gives Isaac as the
             one who keeps Joseph's dreams in his mind, though Genesis 37:11 clearly
             relates that it is Joseph's father, Jacob, who does this (I have altered the text
             accordingly). As Ohlander observes, the additional material here may ori-
             ginate in *HS* Gen. 85 (1123), "Venit etiam ad Isaac patrem suum in civitate
             Hebron, et jam mortuam invenit matrem," or something like *OFP* 7a: "Jacob
             trova Rebecca morte, sa mere; / Mes il trova Ysaac vif, sun pere" ("Old
             French Parallels," p. 206).

1185–88   This reference to Jacob and his sons building an altar to God is either added
             material or simply out of place. It is possible that it comes from either Gen-
             esis 35:14–15, where Jacob sets up a pillar at Bethel, the place where God
             spoke to him and (in a separate account from the wrestling with the angel
             at Peniel) renamed him Israel, or 35:20, where Jacob sets up a pillar on
             Rachel's grave on the way to Ephrath.

1211–12   *And what so suld betyde, / he prayd God to wyrke His wyll*. Genesis 37:11 says
             simply that Jacob kept "the thing with himself," that is, "kept the matter [of
             the dream] in mind" (NRSV). Here, however, Jacob seems to give a prescient
             version of part of the Lord's Prayer, from Matthew 6:9–13, particularly
             6:10b: "Thy will be done on earth as it is in heaven."

1263   *Hym toght*. Dative of agency, where the oblique case serves as subject which is acted upon or participates in an action: i.e., "a dream came to him."

1302   As K notes, this same line, a description of Joseph's brothers, is found in *CM*, line 6715.

1364   *he toght thei twa suld not twyn*. In the Bible Joseph is given no rationale for his guile against Benjamin other than, perhaps, a need to continue his testing of them. The poet, however, seems unwilling to leave such a (non)explanation standing. Instead, he posits that Joseph simply could not bear to be parted from the brother with whom he shared full blood relations — Benjamin being the only other child born of Rachel.

1380   *hyng hegh by the neke*. That Benjamin will be executed is a bit of dramatic license on the part of the *Paraphrase*-poet. Genesis 44:17 says only that he will be made a slave.

1387–88   *Lett hym go home, and dwell wyll we / in hold, wherso ye wyll us have*. Judah's offer of them all as ransom for the youngest is a subtle but significant change to Genesis 44:33, where he only offers up himself in a one-for-one exchange.

1409   *yle that hyght Jessen*. The term *yle* here means a region, especially one near the coast (*MED ile* n.2) rather than an island (*ile* n.1). Goshen is an area of land on the east side of the Nile delta, present-day Wadi Tumilat. This region is good grazing land, thus ideal for the Israelite settlers. It is presumed that because Joseph wanted to keep his family close to him, Pharaoh's capital must have been located in the delta area, probably at Rameses, as it was during the Hyksos period (1720–1550 BCE). This period of Egyptian history is also known to have been somewhat pro-Semitic.

1427–28   *Bott folke war full gud one / that com of ther kynred*. Possibly a reference to Jacob's blessing upon his sons (Genesis 49:2–28), a poem that relates the later character of the twelve tribes of Israel as blessings (and curses) upon their namesakes.

1433–34   *Thei mad grett mornyng them amell, / for Joseph was so fer them fro*. Probably a reference to Joseph's returning to Egypt after helping to bury his father in Canaan.

1435–36   *For afturwerd, os men may tell, / ther welth was turn to wer and wo*. Presumably a reference to the slavery of the Israelites, freedom from which will be dramatically presented in the book of Exodus.

BOOK OF EXODUS

1455   *And so thei fayr faur hunderth yere*. That four hundred years passed between the Israelites arrival in Egypt and Moses' birth is not recorded at this point in the Bible, but has been transferred from Exodus 12:40. If we are to associate Joseph's Pharaoh with the Hyksos period (1720–1550 BCE, see note to line 1409, above), then the oppression under the new king (line 1442) should be associated with the rise of the Nineteenth Dynasty under Seti I (1308–1290 BCE) and Rameses II (1290–1224 BCE); see *NOAB*, p. 70.

1461–64   *The kyng was kend by clerkes / a chyld of them suld spryng . . . unto bale hym bryng*. The Bible gives no rationalization for the Pharaoh's decision to curb the population. That the order to kill any male Israelite children was the result of a prophecy that one of their number would rise up to defeat him links the Pharaoh with Herod in the Gospels, who is threatened by the idea of a child to come who might displace his authority. Compare the *York* Hosier's play, where Pharaoh's first counselor warns: "Lorde, we have herde oure fadres telle / Howe clerkis, that ful wele couthe rede, / Saide a man shulde wax tham emell / That suld fordo vs and owre dede" (11.63–66). This conjoining of Moses and Jesus is rather different from the usual Old Law/New Law juxtaposition so commonplace in medieval typology.

1470   *Amryn and his wyfe, Jacabell*. The names of Moses' parents are not given in the Bible until Exodus 6:20. According to the genealogy of the Levites (Numbers 26:57–62), Amram ("friend of Jehovah") is the son of Kohath ("assembly"), son of Levi. Amram married Jochebed ("Jehovah is her glory"), who is also said to be a daughter of Levi ("adhesion") and thus Amram's aunt on his father's side. Three children are known from the union: Aaron ("mountain of strength"), Moses ("drawn from the water"), and Miriam ("their rebellion"). The *Paraphrase*, Ohlander notes, is similar to *OFP* in introducing the names so early ("Old French Parallels," p. 206).

1478   *Tremouth*. Pharaoh's daughter is unnamed in the Bible. Her name goes back at least to Flavius Josephus — who calls her Thermuthis (*Jewish Antiquities* 2.9.5) — though the *Paraphrase*-poet presumably gets the name from *HS* Exod. 5 (1143).

1487   *Moyses*. The poet alludes to the name deriving, as it does in Exodus 2:10, from the fact that he is drawn out of the water (thus corresponding to the Hebrew verb that might be behind his name, *Mosheh*). It has also been posited that *Moses* derives from an Egyptian term "meaning 'to beget a child' and perhaps once joined with the name of an Egpytian deity (compare the name Thut-mose)" (*NOAB*, p. 71).

1495–96   *Bot the barn wold not with them abyd, / ne towch ther papes for nokyns nede*. That Moses fed on the milk of his Hebrew mother, rather than that of an Egyptian, is derived from Exodus 2:8–9; yet the Bible does not add the detail that this was so because the infant Moses refused to feed at the breasts of the Egyptian women. K (1:clxxxv) notes that this additional detail derives from *HS* Exod. 5 (1143). Ohlander, however, has observed that the detail is also found in *OFP* 11d ("Old French Parallels," p. 207).

1501–02   *systur . . . then with that lady was dwelland*. Though unnamed in this account, the sister's name is Miriam; see note to line 1470, above. Her entrance into the story here differs somewhat from the biblical account (Exodus 2:4), where she has been hiding nearby and watching Pharaoh's daughter as she finds and opens the ark containing Moses. Instead, we here get a Miriam who has managed to find a place in the household of the Pharaoh and is thus in a position to offer up her mother's services as a wet nurse for the child.

1529–36   This description of Moses, not found in the Bible, may owe much to both *HS* Exod. 5 (1143–44) and *OFP* 11c–12a (printed in Ohlander, "Old French Parallels," p. 207), either of which could be the *boke* mentioned in line 1532.

1537–96   Like the childhood of Jesus, the childhood of Moses is skipped over in the Bible, picking up his post-infancy life at the point at which his career begins: in this case, the murder of an Egyptian slavemaster when Moses was probably in his fortieth year. This silence, the "white space" between Exodus 2:10 and 2:11, was subsequently filled in by Midrash writings, some of which were ultimately picked up by Christian commentators, as in the present case. The story of the infant Moses in Pharaoh's court, here deriving probably from *HS* Exod. 5 (1143–44), ultimately comes from Exodus Rabbah 1.31, which tells how Moses would play on Pharaoh's lap and take the crown from his head in order to place it on his own. The Egyptian wisemen warned Pharaoh that this act was a sign that Moses would fulfill their prophecies that a Hebrew child would grow to defeat Pharaoh. They advised Pharaoh to kill the child. But Jethro — who was a priest and would later become Moses' father-in-law (see Exodus 2:16 and 3:1) — was in court and suggested that Moses was only acting as a foolish child will. To test Moses' intent, they brought him two containers, one filled with hot coals and the other with gold. Moses actually did start to reach for the gold, we are told, but the angel Gabriel turned his hand so that he picked up a hot coal instead. This he even placed in his mouth, burning his tongue and forever giving him a speech impediment. This latter fact thus explained Moses' claim to have "impediment and slowness of tongue" (Exodus 4:10). The story as it appears here in the *Paraphrase* diverges from the tradition on several accounts: Pharaoh places the crown on Moses' head, but the child puts it onto his feet instead; Moses is given no choice of gold or coals, just shown a container of coals; and neither Gabriel nor Jethro make an appearance.

1603–04   *And sythyn when he myght wepyns weld, / he mustyrd manhed mony a tyde*. The *Paraphrase*-poet makes of Moses a late medieval military man, perhaps destined to become a great knight.

1616   *Madian*. Midian ("strife"), named for the fourth son of Abraham by Keturah.

1618   *Oreb hyll*. Horeb ("mountain of the dried-up ground") is a general name of the entire mountain range of which Sinai is a part. It is now known as Jebel Musa.

1619   *Getro*. Jethro ("his excellence"). Alternatively said to be a prince or priest of Midian, he is here said to be the local bishop. Numbers 10:29 names him Hobab ("beloved"), the son of Reuel, indicating that Jethro was likely a titular name while Hobab was an informal one.

1630   *Cephoram*. Zipporah ("female bird").

1632   *Eliazar and Gersam.* Gershom, whose name means "sojourner" and alludes to Moses being, as he says, a "stranger in a foreign land," was Moses' firstborn. While the Vulgate does relate at this time the birth of Eliezer, whose name means "my God is help," this is not the case in all stemma of the text; it is related at this point in the Masoretic text and thus in many other translations of Exodus.

1723   *Bot swylke fawt fell not in Jessen.* The *Paraphrase*-poet, always sensitive to what we might call "historical" readings of the text, transplants the exception of Goshen — the place where Joseph had settled his family and thus a substitute for the Israelites themselves — from 8:22–23, the fourth plague, to his first plague, thus illustrating that the Israelites were not affected by any of the plagues. It would not be right, after all, if the Israelites were punished by God for the Pharaoh's refusal to release them.

1733–34   K notes (1:cxci) a relationship to *York* 11.273–74: "Lorde, grete myses bothe morn and none / Bytis vs full bittirlye." The precise nature of this particular plague depends largely on the translation of Exodus 8:16, which in the Vulgate reads *sciniphes.* The AV translation is "lice," while NEB reads "maggots." *Genesis and Exodus* (line 2988) has "gnattes," and *Towneley Plays* 73.286 has "mystis." *OFP* 14c reads "pui(l)z" (K 5.61).

1743   *Grett fleand loppes over all the land.* This line has a parallel in *Towneley* 74.306: "grete loppys ouer all this land thay fly."

1772   *thei brast ther brayn.* That the hail did not just "strike down" the Egyptians but actually burst their brains from their skulls is very much a romance conceit.

1801–04   This increase in the number of Israelites — from seventy to three hundred thousand — is not found in the Bible or *HS* Exod. 27 (1155–56). As Ohlander observes, the source could be *OFP* 15b ("Old French Parallels," p. 208). The detail is subsequently picked up by *York* 11.51–56.

1811–12   *On nyghtys with flawme of fyre / in lyghtnes ware thei lede.* It is interesting that one of the most remarkable miracles of the Exodus — the presence of God that led the Israelites into the desert, during the day as a pillar of cloud and during the night as a pillar of fire — is given very little notice in the *Paraphrase.* Indeed, the pillar of fire is here so quickly glossed that it seems the poet might be uncomfortable with the notion. His reduction of what is traditionally a very large pillar to a simple *flawme* could relegate the miracle to the realm of historical probability: the flame of torches or firepits rather than the actual presence of God. The pillar of cloud, which is ever-present in Exodus from this point forward, comes off even more poorly as it merits no mention anywhere in the *Paraphrase.*

1817   *chares and mules and mekyll store.* The *Paraphrase*-poet has apparently taken the fact of an army summoned by Pharaoh, an army said to include chariots and horses (Exodus 14:6), and has perceived that far more would be required of such a substantial force — namely, mules to pull carts filled with all manner of supplies to feed, house, and clothe the army.

1818   *the Greke Se*. This would be, as I have glossed it, the Mediterranean, though
            such a route would make little sense in light of the path of the Exodus
            through known Egyptian geography. K (5:108) notes that *OFP* speaks only
            of "l'eve la mer," "la sause," and "l'element," giving no indication of a Medi-
            terranean location. *HS* Exod. 30 (1157) is similarly silent, following both the
            Vulgate and the Septuagint in giving the location as the Red Sea (*mare Rub-
            rum*). Technically speaking, the text perhaps ought to read "Sea of Reeds,"
            being not the Red Sea but a shallow body of water such as Lake Timsah, fur-
            ther north (*NOAB*, pp. 86–87). The *Pearl*-poet seems to utilize "Grece" as a
            token for any distant land (see, e.g., *Pearl*, line 231, or *Sir Gawain and the
            Green Knight*, line 2023), and this fact, along with the historical associations
            between Egypt and the Mediterranean (and the Greeks themselves), might
            be behind the discrepancy here. It is also possible that the text originally
            read "the grete se" and any number of factors contributed to a misreading.

1855–56   *Cantemus Domino Gloriose, / love we God and His power playne*. Ohlander notes
            that this Latin phrase does not occur in either the Bible or *OFP*. It does, how-
            ever, appear in *HS* Exod. 31 (1158): "Moysesque Domino canticum exposuit
            hexametro carmine, Cantemus Domino, etc. Quod quia prius legitur cæteris
            Canticum dicitur canticorum" ("Old French Parallels," p. 208).

1864–65   *A forest that was fayr to gese. / Thore fand thei wellys fayr and clere*. The *Paraphrase*
            conflates the bitter waters at Marah (Exodus 15:23–25) and the springs and
            trees of Elim (Exodus 15:17).

1871   *Moyses with hys wand*. In the Bible, Moses throws a tree (or, in some versions,
            a piece of wood) into the bitter waters to make them sweet. That it is only his
            staff (*wand*) that is used might come from either *HS* Exod. 32 (1158–59) or
            OFP 16b (Ohlander, "Old French Parallels, p. 208).

1889   *Ther cloghyng was ever in lyke clere*. The Bible notes the miraculous nature of
            the quail and manna, but it says nothing of the Israelites' clothing being
            similarly renewed by God's power. It is characteristic of the *Paraphrase*-poet
            to see past the "basic" workings of miracle stories to a more "realistic" need
            or effect: wandering in the desert for forty years would doubtless be rough
            on their garb, and the Israelites would have neither time nor material to fash-
            ion new cloth. Presumably, then, God would have provided regular replace-
            ments for their worn-out clothes.

1897–1916   There are two biblical incidents involving the drawing of water from rock
            during the sojourn in the wilderness: one here in Exodus and one in Num-
            bers. On both occasions the people cry out for water and on both occasions
            Moses strikes the rock to draw it forth. Each place is then named Meribah,
            meaning "quarrel." Unlike other seemingly twice-told tales that are accounted
            only once in the *Paraphrase*, however, Meribah is actually told twice by the
            poet (here and at lines 2335–40). Ironically, this seems accurate to history in-
            asmuch as we can treat these matters on historical principles: most critics and
            exegetes agree that the two biblical stories, while parallel, represent two dif-
            ferent events: one in Horeb (Exodus) and one in Kadesh (Numbers). The fact
            that a water-producing rock was with the Israelites in both locations gave rise

to the legend that the rock actually *followed* the Israelites through the desert, providing sustenance. It is this tradition that Paul refers to in 1 Corinthians 10:4, in which he says of the wandering Israelites: "they drank of the spiritual rock that followed them, and the rock was Christ." But while the poet has rightly recorded both of the separate events, he still seems to treat them as one (or at least as interchangeable): he only presents the story in detail here, and this in a version in which he has taken the most interesting or integral portions of the various accounts and grafted them into a more or less seamless narrative. So, for instance, Moses' success at Meribah as told in Exodus — by which he manages to bring water to his parched people — is united with his failure at Meribah as told in Numbers — in which there is an implication that Moses has failed to interpret the water as being a sign from God. It is this implied failure that is made explicit in Deuteronomy 32:50–52, where God denies Moses entrance to the Promised Land because of the incident at Meribah in Kadesh. As elsewhere, the poet does not engage in typical Christological readings of the Old Testament passage at hand: most Christian exegetes, from the *Glossa Ordinaria* (*PL* 113:242) to the *Biblia Pauperum* (plate .f.), have followed Paul's smitten-rock-as-Christ reading. The latter is especially interesting in depicting the rock "not only with the Crucifixion but also with the creation of Eve from Adam's left (*sinistra*) ribs, and with Christ's being wounded by the spear of Longinus in the right (*dextra*) side, drawing thus on the First Adam/Second Adam typology as well as contrasting the old and new command of Moses and Christ" ("Smitten Rock," *DBTEL*, pp. 718–20).

1922   *Amalec and other thre*. In the Bible, Amalek ("dweller in a valley") alone is mentioned as attacking Israel at Rephidim. It is possible that the additional kings are the result of Judges 3:12–13, where the Amelekites join with the Ammonites under the direction of King Eglon of Moab to defeat the Israelites.

1926   *Josue*. Joshua ("Jehovah is his help") is the son of Nun, son of Ephraim.

1941–44   *Getro of Madian . . . with wyf and chylder also*. Jethro's biblical role in correcting Moses and helping to organize the administration of the people (18:1–27) is here completely subsumed to the single detail (18:5) that he brought Moses' wife, Zipporah, and his two children, Gershom and Eliezer, to join with Moses and the Israelites in the wilderness. Presumably matters of legal administration, while a concern to Jethro, were of little interest to the romance narrative the poet is attempting to coalesce.

1951   *Then Commawndmentes, os clerkes says*. The *Paraphrase*-poet does not list the Ten Commandments, though they are listed in all of his assumed source texts: the Bible, *HS* Exod. 40 (1163–66), and *OFP* 16b (Ohlander, "Old French Parallels," p. 208).

1979–80   *The berdes of them wer gylt / like unto the gold wyre*. This detail is not found in either the Bible or *OFP* 16d, but probably it has its source in *HS* Exod. 73 (1189–90) (Ohlander, "Old French Parallels," p. 209). K 1:clxxxvi notes that another parallel can be found in *CM*, lines 6615–26.

1981   *Aron*. In the Bible it is Aaron who actually constructs the golden calf. Here, however, Aaron is only given the subsequent role of helping to mete justice upon the idolaters. Aaron's role as idol-builder was the subject of great discussion in exegetical traditions — higher criticism points to the passage as evidence of an attempt on the part of the Levite priests to put a band of Aaronic priests "in their place," as it were — and it is no surprise to find it missing in a paraphrase interested in a straightforward and stirring narrative.

1987   *twenty-thre milia sloyne*. The number of other Israelites slain by the Levites (Exodus 32:38) differs according to the manuscript tradition. The *Paraphrase* here follows both the Greek Septuagint and the Latin Vulgate in reporting the number as twenty-three thousand. The Masoretic text and those translations based upon it (e.g., NRSV) report only three thousand. It is somewhat interesting to note that this seemingly insignificant detail is among the bits of evidence that the "Bible" of many early Christian communities was the Septuagint: in 1 Corinthians 10:8 Paul refers to the "three and twenty thousand" who were killed as idolaters at Sinai.

2005–10   *byschop . . . prestes and dekyns . . . duke . . . prince*. In describing the formation of the priesthood and the aristocratic structure of the Israelites, the poet resorts to late medieval language, attempting to paste the familiar language of the feudal and ecclesiastical systems onto the unfamiliar notions of the text.

2015–16   *So endes the secund boke, / that of Moyses wyll mene*. One expects, based on the poem's presentation thus far, that following the account of the second book of Moses, Exodus, we will receive an account of the third book, Leviticus. And, indeed, the headings of the manuscript would indicate that this is precisely what we get, as the scribe records headings for Leviticus over the next few folios. On the contrary, the book of Leviticus is silently skipped over by the *Paraphrase*-poet, who has little use for the long sequences of priestly instructions concerning both the sacrifices at a Temple that was destroyed in 70 CE and the specific ethical obligations of what he would have considered the Old Law — replaced by the New Law of Christ a few decades before the Temple was destroyed. For more on the destruction of the Temple and the literary and theological history that developed in its wake, see *Siege of Jerusalem*, ed. Livingston, pp. 2–7 and 30–36.

BOOK OF NUMBERS

2017–20   *When Moyses thus had ordand all . . . what to werres that wyrschyp wan*. The beginning of Numbers is somewhat of a recapitulation of the laws given in Leviticus, as theory is put into practice among the people of Israel; for the poet, this material (and perhaps the whole of the book of Leviticus, too) can be reduced to these four lines stating that Moses gave instructions to the people about how to perform a proper worship service and how to conduct just wars. See explanatory note to lines 2015–16, above, for more on the "missing" book of Leviticus.

2031   *Sex hunderth and thre milia.* The exact total number in this first census, reported in Numbers 1:46, is 603,550 men over the age of twenty. By contrast, the total number in the second census, reported in Numbers 26:51, is 601,730. Twenty was the age required for military service according to Exodus 30:14.

2033–34   *And fyghand folke on fote he fand / sex hunderth and fyve milia in fere.* The poet, already having anachronistically characterized the fighting men of the Israelites as "knyghtes" (line 2032), adds in thousands of footmen unnoted in the biblical account but paralleled at this point by teh 605,000 "chavaliers" mentioned in *OFP* 17b. The result is far more the likeness of a late medieval army.

2035–36   *Withoutyn clerkes that were ordand / to serve God on sydes sere.* Moses was ordered by God not to number the tribe of Levi, for the Levites had been consecrated as a priestly class whose sole duty was the maintenance of the Tabernacle and the worship services honoring God (Numbers 1:48–53).

2044   *had to hym full grett envy.* The *Paraphrase* presents a far different rationale for the story that is about to unfold than does the Bible: Exodus 12:1 states that Miriam and Aaron speak against Moses because he has married a Cushite woman, i.e., Zipporah (Midianites being counted among the Cushites). It is possible that the poet simply found the motive of tribal tensions too difficult to convey. Perhaps even more likely, however, is the possibility that the poet has read between the lines of the tale and seen the vestiges of what scholars have called "a power struggle in the community" between these three great figures (*NOAB*, p. 182).

2049–52   *Thei sayd he was to bold . . . all ther myrth to mysse.* The specific complaint that Moses had been too hasty to get the Israelites out of Egypt belongs not to Miriam and Aaron and this story (see note to line 2044, above), but derives from the earlier complaints of the people at Numbers 11:1–35. The poet has simply conflated the two stories into one.

2077–92   Most of Moses' speech is indebted to various of his speeches that occur in Exodus, along with a reference to the Great Commandment ("Hear, O Israel, the Lord our God is one Lord. Thou shalt love the Lord thy God with thy whole heart, and with thy whole soul, and with thy whole strength" — Deuteronomy 6:4–5), which is perhaps echoed in lines 2089–92.

2099–2100   *The folke toke other ten / and send furth all togeydder.* Only Joshua and Caleb figure into the remainder of the paraphrased Old Testament, so the other ten spies listed in Numbers 13:4–15 — Shammua, Shaphat, Igal, Palti, Gaddiel, Gaddi, Ammiel, Sethur, Nahbi, and Geuel — are not notable enough for inclusion here.

2125–26   *Thei ar so grett on grone to gang: / we seme bot barns to ther bodes.* The biblical comparison is even more remarkable in differentiating the sizes of the people: "There we saw certain monsters of the sons of Enac, of the giant kind: in comparison of whom, we seemed like locusts" (Numbers 13:34). These giants are identified as the Nephilim, the giants who resulted from the union of the sons of God and the daughters of men in Genesis 6:4. The poet ignored their presence in Genesis (perhaps recognizing that such beings, if they existed, would have been destroyed in the Flood) and here both omits their name and reduces the size comparison to something more reasonable.

2176   *all that ar past over thryty yere.* Numbers 14:29 places the "cut off" age as twenty — i.e., that it is those over twenty years of age who "murmured" against God who will not be allowed to enter into Canaan (twenty being the age required for military service in Exodus 30:14 and the age of those counted in the census). That the *Paraphrase* gives the age as thirty might be attributable to a basic textual error: a copy text reading "xx" might have acquired a third "x" at some point. It is also possible that the poet (or an exemplar) has taken the age for priestly service given in Numbers 4:23 (thirty to fifty) and applied it to the unworthy Israelites who have here failed not only in their military duties but also (perhaps more importantly) in their duties of faith. From this standpoint, the application of priestly age to those who will be barred from entering the Promised Land is wholly appropriate.

2185–96   This stanza, in which God refuses to forgive the rebellious Israelites but does allow them to have light, water, food, and clothing, contains material not mentioned in the Bible or in *HS*. K states quite plainly that it has no known source (1:cxciv). Ohlander points out that lines 2195–96 (*And keped ay ther cloghyng / withowtyn wem or wast*) might be associated with *OFP* 18c, a passage connected with Exodus 16:12 and the miracle of manna falling from Heaven but nonetheless "striking" for "having no support in *Exodus* either" ("Autre miracle fist Deu pur ses genz: / Il garda si trestoz lur vestemenz / Qu'il ne purrirent ne de ren ne peirouent / El quarante anz qu'il el desert errouent"). See "Old French Parallels," p. 209.

2213–14   *Thei senssed thor and dyd servyce, / as byschoppes had before ordand.* The rebellion led by Korah, taking as its central issue whether or not the priests alone can enact religious rites, would have been of particular interest to the poet and his audience in light of Wycliffe and other reformers. In this regard, we can see that the poet's handling of his sources reveals a subtle defense against the idea that the people can take the place of the priests. The biblical account, for instance, mentions the censers only insofar as they are to be used to determine whether God's favor rests with Korah or Aaron: they will each burn incense before the Lord, and God will choose between them. The poet's alteration is subtle but of vital significance: Korah's foolish presumption is revealed in his having used a censer and having done service as if he had a right to do so. The shift of narrative marks a shift in emphasis: like so many reformers (Wycliffe included), Korah has presumed to take on duties and responsibilities that are not of his estate, and God's punishment is a clear lesson to all those who would unrightfully question the directives (and directors) of the Church. It is worth noting that this reading of the text is by no means rare. Challoner's note in his revision of the Douay-Rheims translation of the Vulgate, for instance, reads: "The crime of these men, which was punished in so remarkable a manner, was that of schism, and of rebellion against the authority established by God in the church; and their pretending to the priesthood without being lawfully called and sent: the same is the case of all modern sectaries" (p. 159).

2229   *hyght*. The sense might possibly be "hastened," though "promised" makes better sense. Often the scribe spells the word for "promised" *heyght*, as in line 2684.

2241–62   The Bible does not specify under what circumstances Korah died. In most sources, however, Korah's fate has been tied with those of the two hundred and fifty men destroyed by God's fire in Numbers 16:35 rather than with his co-conspirators Dathan and Abiram, who are swallowed by the ground in Numbers 16:31–33. The *Paraphrase*, as K notes (1:clxxxvi), is probably following *HS* Num. 20 (1230) in this regard, though Ohlander observes that *OFP* 19a is also parallel here ("Old French Parallels," p. 210). Other writers placing Korah among those burned are the early writers Josephus (*Jewish Antiquities* 4.3.4), Clement (*First Epistle to the Corinthians*), and Ignatius (*Epistle to the Magnesians*).

2270   *thonour and lefnyng down dyscend*. This stands against Numbers 16:46–50, which records that the people (14,700 of them) were felled by an unspecified "plague." That this deadly stroke might involve thunder and lightning, however, is an easy stretch of the imagination given that 16:42 notes that the Lord's cloud had covered over the Tabernacle as a sign of His anger.

2277–80   The *Paraphrase*-poet would seem to leave off the final thirty-six chapters of Numbers, ending his text after Numbers 16. As Ohlander has pointed out, *OFP* includes all of the remaining text, indicating that the decision to break off here may have been an authorial one; certainly there was also plenty of remaining material to be had from *HS*. Of course, the poet *does* include further accounts of Numbers, telling them under the rubric of Deuteronomy, lines 2281–2616. It is curious that the break between 4.3 and 4.4 of Josephus' "paraphrase," *Jewish Antiquities*, corresponds to this present authorial division between Numbers and Deuteronomy.

BOOK OF DEUTERONOMY

2281–2616   Though most of these stories occur variously in Deuteronomy, which is a book that repeats (and reinterprets) the events of the Mosaic time, they are given here in accordance with the ordering and accounting of Numbers, not Deuteronomy. Deuteronomy proper, therefore, is given relatively small attention: lines 2617–77. While the treatment of Numeric material as Deuteronomistic seems authorial (see note to lines 2277–80, above), the omission of all but the end of Deuteronomy is in keeping with *OFP*, which relates only the death of Moses ("Old French Parallels," p. 209). It would seem, then, that the *Paraphrase*-poet has taken *OFP* (or its like) as a model for the sequence and extent of his paraphrase, but has opted to alter the location of the division between books in order to produce a more uniform length between books.

2333   *To Cades then thei toke the gatte.* The *Paraphrase*-poet has confused the geography of the wanderings in the wilderness, mistaking Paran (lines 2021–22) as a separate location from the oasis of Kadesh. But these seem to be one and the same place, Kadesh being the specific location within the region of Paran. Rather than a sequence of stops as the *Paraphrase* presents it, the Bible seems clear in presenting a direct migration from Sinai to Kadesh in Paran within roughly nine months of the theophany. It was at this oasis that the Israelites spent the majority of their forty years in the wilderness. Thus most of Numbers, from 10:11 to 21:3, deals with the various events that occurred at the Kadesh oasis. Numbers 13:26 explicitly records that the spies were sent into Canaan from the encampment at Kadesh, and it was there that both the rebellion of Korah, Dathan, and Abiram and the blooming of Aaron's rod occurred.

2335–40   This second mention of an incident at Meribah is greatly abbreviated. The first paraphrased Exodus 17:1–7; see explanatory note to lines 1897–1916.

2339–40   *qwylke was cald / allway the Watur of Stryfe.* See Numbers 20:13, which makes the etymology clear: the place was called Meribah, which means "quarrel."

2341   *Becawse of stryvyng in that stede.* There is no biblical connection made between Miriam's death and the various incidents at Kadesh, though one can imagine how such a tradition began, given the proximity of the events in the Bible.

2353   *Herrott, the kyng of Cananews.* There is confusion about whether Arad (*Herrott*) is a location or the name of the otherwise unidentified Canaanite king. While the poet follows the Vulgate in assuming the latter, other texts (e.g., the Masoretic) take Arad as the name of a town roughly twenty miles southeast of Hebron near Masada.

2407   *Seon was strekyn with his awn stave.* The detail that Sihon is killed with his own sword is not found in the Bible, nor in *HS*, nor older sources such as Josephus, whose *Jewish Antiquities* 4.5.2 reports only that Sihon was killed. The idea of a tyrant or enemy struck down with his own blade is a common biblical trope, however. David beheads Goliath with the giant's own blade, for instance, and Judith does the same to Holofernes.

2503–08   *And Balam ther mad prophecyse / that Crist suld come amang ther kynd . . . of Israel owt suld spryng.* Numbers 24 obviously makes no attempt to read Christ into the interpretation of Balaam's prophecy. On the sudden intrusion of a Christological reading at this point in the narrative, see the introduction.

2523–32   Numbers 25:1 does not mention Balaam's role in advising Balak to tempt the Israelites with beautiful young Moabite women, saying only that the men began to have sex with them. The blame of Balaam comes later, in Numbers 31:16, the discrepancy probably being the result of the separate strands of traditional material being redacted together here. The connection of Balaam to the apostasy at Peor was a strong one, however, being also reported in 2 Peter 2:15, Jude 11, and Apocalypse 2:14. As K notes (1:clxxxvi), the *Paraphrase*-poet is probably deriving his account at this point from *HS* Num. 34 (1239). The poet might also be looking at *OFP* 21a (Ohlander, "Old

French Parallels," p. 210). Both sources move up the attribution of Balaam's guilt from 31 in order to meet the initial discussion of the apostasy.

2551   *twenty milia went.* Numbers 25:9 gives the number dead in this latest plague as 24,000.

2573   *He fand thre hunderth thowssand men.* This number stands quite against Numbers 26:51, where the total number of Israelites counted is 601,730.

2587   *Fyve hethyn kynges.* Unnamed here, the five kings of Midian are Evi, Rekem, Zur, Hur, and Reba (Numbers 31:8).

2627–28   *And ye sall hald Josue / your duke when I am dede.* One of many anachronistic applications of medieval conventions onto the biblical narrative. Note also that Joshua must be *duke* of the Israelites because God is implicitly king.

2655   *A whyt clowde down fro Hevyn dyscend.* Neither the Bible nor *HS* Deut. 20 (1259–60) say anything about Moses ascending into Heaven within a white cloud, a detail, as Ohlander notes, that is akin to *OFP* 22a ("Old French Parallels," p. 210). The association of a cloud with Moses' death goes back to rabbinical literature, but it can also be found in Josephus, *Jewish Antiquities* 4.8.48, where it is said that "as he was going to embrace Eleazar and Joshua, and was still discoursing with them, a cloud stood over him on the sudden, and he disappeared in a certain valley, although he wrote in the holy books that he died, which was done out of fear lest they should venture to say, that because of his extraordinary virtue he went to God." Although Josephus seems hesitant to affirm the ascension of Moses, other Jewish sources are clear in making the connection. One tradition even provides a rationale for the cloud: God wrapped Moses in the cloud in order to protect him from the angels who were jealous of the man and might well have attacked him upon his arrival in Heaven. Other Jewish traditions, however, follow the Bible in clearly stating that Moses' body remains in an unmarked grave yet on the earth, where he was perhaps buried by God Himself (following one reading of Deuteronomy 34:6).

2671–72   *Wherfor we wott withowtyn were / his sawle unto Hevyn is hent.* The move to the present tense in this unequivocal statement hints at an unspoken theological conclusion: from a Christian perspective, Moses can only be in Heaven if he participated in Christ's Grace at the Harrowing of Hell. The poet's opinion, shared by most exegetes, is that there is "no doubt" that he did so.

BOOK OF JOSHUA

2711–12   *scho was commyn kend / as hostler evyn and morn.* Rahab is called a prostitute in both Joshua 2:1 and *HS* Jos. 2 (1261). The *Paraphrase*-poet is somewhat oblique in referencing her trade here, however, describing her status in terms that are what the reader makes of them. She is *commyn kend as hostler*, which could mean either that she is "commonly known as one who runs a hostel," or that she is "commonly known," and that she welcomes men into her hostel (with its various allusions) both morning and evening, as an inn-keeper should do. Note that the modern slang term *hustler* to refer to a prostitute is unrelated to these terms, as it derives from the verb *hustle*, itself a late-seventeenth-century derivation from various possible High and Low German dialects. The *OED* thus lists an initial instance of *hustler* meaning "prostitute" as dating from 1924.

2765   *Elyazar has ordand then.* The order, according to Joshua 4:1, comes not from Eleazar but from God Himself. It is possible that the poet is here trying to make a theological point about the place of the priest as conduit to God in a post-Mosaic world, though elsewhere he seems unshy about allowing God the ability to still speak directly to the people (e.g., lines 3023–24, where God reassures Joshua).

2789–90   *thei suld syng solemp song / and make all maner of mynstralsy.* The seven trumpets and the shouts of the people and the circling of the city seven times are here omitted in favor of solemnity. And the association between the shout of the people and the breaching of the wall (Joshua 6:20) is similarly left out in lines 2819–20, where the active hand is that of God alone, acting on His own accord. The omission is, perhaps, part of a "historization" of the text, where the poet regards the trumpets and shouts as more "mythic" or "fantastic" than the active intercession of God.

2825   *Achor.* In Hebrew, "trouble"; his activities befit his name, or the reverse.

2836   *Adan.* As Ohlander notes, the *Paraphrase*-poet has taken the name of the town not from the Vulgate but from *OFP* 24a or an Old French source very similar to it, where the name "Ai" has been altered to "Adan" in order to meet rhyme: "Pur aseger la vile d'Adan / Qui est assise sur le flum Jordan" ("Old French Parallels," p. 205).

2839   *thryty thowssand on a thrum.* Joshua 7:4 reports three thousand men, rather than thirty thousand. It is possible that the number of men sent against Ai in the second assault (Joshua 8:3) may have simply been transfered to the first. Also of note, however, is *HS* Jos. 6 (1265), where Comestor records three thousand before noting that Josephus gives the number as thirty thousand.

2860   *he parted hys pepell evyn in two.* Joshua 8:12 gives the number in the ambushing party as five thousand. The *Paraphrase*-poet has apparently here opted for the exigencies of rhyme over text.

2894   *thei had no bodes them to beld.* The contrast is clearly with Rahab and her family, who had gained assurances of safety that were granted when Jericho was taken. The people of Ai made no such deals.

2939–40   *To bere wode and fuell / ther sacurfyce to begyne.* That is, the Gibeonites were tasked with producing wood and water for the sacrifices that took place in the Israelite services. The story thus serves to explain both "the presence of non-Israelites in the service of Israelite sanctuaries" and "the survival of some Canaanites despite the command to exterminate them" (*NOAB*, p. 281).

2968   *lenghed that day two days space.* That the lengthened day was of two days in duration is an extrabiblical detail (compare Joshua 10:12–14) derived from *HS* Jos. 9 (1267), where the additional day gained here is contrasted with the ten hours gained by Isaias as proof for Hezekiah (see 4 Kings [2 Kings] 20:7–11 and Isaias 38:7–8).

2977–3000   The sense of what is happening here may be in need of explanation. Joshua has ordered the five kings brought out from the cave in which they were hiding and has bound them (lines 2977–84). He makes them lie down upon the ground, and then the Hebrews walk among them (lines 2985–88). Joshua tells his men that they are to have no more fear of other kings than they have of these five bound ones, for God will give them such power over them all, just as He has promised (lines 2989–96). The five kings are then hanged as an example before they move on (lines 2997–3000). Making the sense particularly difficult to construe is line 2990, *that fulse them heyr under your fette.* The word *fulse* means to "oppress," "subdue," or "trample down" (*MED fullen* v.2[c]), making this line a further explication of the *ye* referred to in both the preceding and succeeding lines. Thus Joshua says to his men that they, who are trampling upon these five kings with their feet, will be thus always victorious against the enemy. What can only be inferred here, but is plain from Joshua 10:24–25, is that this trampling of the kings is no metaphor: "he called all them men of Israel, and said to the chiefs of the army that were with him: Go, and set your feet on the necks of these kings. And when they had gone, and put their feet upon the necks of them lying under them, He said again to them: Fear not, neither be ye dismayed, take courage, and be strong: for so will the Lord do to all your enemies, against whom you fight."

3011   *Kyng Jabyn of Dasore.* The *Paraphrase*-poet has once again (see note to line 2836) taken the name of a town not from the Vulgate but from a French source. *OFP* 25c reads "Li reis Jabin dasor" (= "d'Asor").

3015–17   The description of Jabyn's army, which the *Paraphrase* gives as three hundred chariots and four hundred thousand armed men, is not based on any clear source. Joshua 11:1–5 gives no specific number of men, while Judges 4:3 gives only nine hundred chariots. *HS* Jos. 10 (1267) reads: "Egressique sunt viginti quatuor reges, cum turmis suis, habentes secum trecenta millia armatorum, et duo millia curruum" (i.e., two thousand chariots and three hundred thousand men). And *OFP* 25c reduces *HS*'s chariots by tenfold: "Dous cent curres, treis cent millers de gent" (Ohlander, "Old French Parallels," p. 211).

3035   *faur hunderth thowssand.* See note to lines 3015–17.

3040   *schamly schent.* The poet's comment here, which is unparalleled in his primary sources (Bible, *HS*, *OFP*), is striking in its candor. It certainly seems to invert one reading of the preceding lines, which have reported the slaughter so factually as to imply approval of the devastation. The comment goes far toward painting a picture of the *Paraphrase*-poet as a man of peace who, though he recognizes and cannot deny the historicity and efficacy of such destruction, cannot wholly approve of it. He would take a place, then, along with other late-fourteenth-century poets who are espousing irenic goals in works as varied as *Siege of Jerusalem*, Gower's *Confessio Amantis*, and Langland's *Piers Plowman*.

3051–52   *Thyrty kynges to ded was done / withowtyn dukes and knyghtes kene.* Joshua 12 provides a comprehensive listing of the many kings killed by the Israelites.

BOOK OF JUDGES

3165–67   *The cyté of Salem . . . Sythen cald Jerusalem.* Judges 1:21 does not give the earlier name of the town. Nor does Joshua 15:63 or 2 Kings (2 Samuel) 5:6. The *Paraphrase* is parallel to *OFP* 26d here ("Tant unt conquis qu'il venent a Salem / Que chrestiens apelent Jerusalem"), which has probably either picked up the old name from Vulgate Psalm 76:2 or *HS* 2 Reg. 7 (1329), which corresponds to the 2 Kings passage cited above and in which Comestor discusses the etymology and history of the name Jerusalem (Ohlander, "Old French Parallels," p. 211).

3187–88   *Bot in Ebron fast have soyght / unto mowntans wher gyantes dweld.* These two lines, K notes (1:clxxxvi), do not correspond precisely with Judges 1:20. The spies sent by Moses to reconnoiter the Promised Land report back, in Numbers 13:33, that giants — the Nephilim of Genesis 6:4 — live in the area, and among those locations that they have specifically visited is, indeed, Hebron. This exchange is perhaps behind *HS* Jud. 2 (1273): "Ascendit et Caleb in Hebron terram, scilicet gigantum, et percussis hostibus, plenius possedit eam," which in turn has given the detail to *OFP* 26d (Ohlander, "Old French Parallels," p. 212).

3239   *Next Salen nere besyde.* "Gibeah is identified with Tell el Ful, four miles north of Jerusalem" (*NOAB*, p. 327).

3241–88   The vengeance upon Benjamin for the rape and murder of the Levite's concubine is out of place here, as it should follow Samson and Delilah rather than precede it. This alteration of events has no parallel in either *HS* or *OFP*, though Ohlander points out that the latter does, at least, correspond with the *Paraphrase* in ending Judges with Samson's death ("Old French Parallels," p. 212).

3245–46   *An Ebrew com ther in the way / with his wyfe, full fayre and fre.* Judges 19:1 specifies that the man is a Levite from near Ephraim, and the woman is his concubine from Bethlehem, rather than his wife.

3247–48   *Amang themself then can thei say, / "Yond woman this nyght weld wyll we."* The *Paraphrase*-poet has omitted some of the less-savory details of this gruesome event. The man and his concubine, foreigners in the area, found shelter in the home of an old man, and the townspeople (all reported to be Benjaminites) surrounded the house and demanded that the foreigner be brought out so that they could "abuse him" (i.e., have intercourse with him, Judges 19:22). In order to prevent his own rape, the man took his concubine — most commentators, like the *Paraphrase*, have read this as his own wife — and "abandoned her to their wickedness" (Judges 19:25), allowing her to be raped all night. The woman manages to crawl back to the house at dawn but dies with her hand upon the threshold, where her master/husband finds her in the morning.

3257   *He sent to cetys lesse and more*. Again, the poet has cleaned up his text (see note to lines 3247–48, above), as Judges 19:29–30 reports that he does not just send word to all the parts of Israel that she needs to be avenged: using his sword he hacks her body into twelve pieces to be sent to the twelve parts of Israel.

3263   *Ten thowsand sone*. Presumably this is the first wave of fighting, led by Judah, in which Judges 20:21 reports Israelite losses as twenty-two thousand.

3267–68   *For Fynyes then was not fayn / of the feyghyng, for all ware Jews*. Phinehas' reluctance short-circuits the biblical story, as it should not occur until a second day of the fighting, after several defeats. It is then that he asks God whether or not they should thus fight and kill their kin (Judges 20:28). The Lord answers yes, and He promises to deliver the Benjaminites into their hands on the third day.

3271   *Twenty milia sone ware slayn*. Judges 20:35 indicates that 25,100 Benjaminites were killed in Phinehas' decisive attack.

3277–88   The twin stories of the women of Shiloh are here omitted entirely, probably as the picture they paint of Israelite behavior is far too dark for the positive account that the poet wished to create. According to Judges 21:1, the Israelites had sworn an oath not to give any of their daughters to the six hundred surviving men of the Benjaminites. Yet having wiped out all of the remainder of that lineage, they came to realize that they were facing the extinction of one of the twelve tribes of Israel. Unable to provide wives from their own peoples due to the oath, the Israelites opted for two different methods of procuring wives for the six hundred. The first (Judges 21:1–14) involved a technical loophole: the town of Jabesh-gilead had sent no one to make the oath, so their daughters were fair game. The rest of the Israelites promptly killed all of the town's inhabitants aside from four hundred young virgins who were brought to Shiloh where they were given to the surviving Benjaminites. Unfortunately, two hundred men were still without wives. So the Israelites then allowed the Benjaminites to abduct girls from the town of Shiloh when they were dancing in the fields (21:15–24). In other words, to repopulate the nearly extinct tribe the "other tribes resorted to murder, kidnap, and rape," which "paints a pathetic picture of Israelite society" to close out the book of Judges (*NOAB*, p. 330). Here, of course, the book does not end, as the story has been moved to set the stage for the coming of Samson, marking him even more as an early "savior" of his people.

3279   *Bot sex hunderth that fled on lyve*. Judges 20:47 explains that the six hundred survivors fled to the rock of Rimmon, where they remained for four months while the victors pillaged their lands and set their homes to the torch. These survivors were all fighting men. See the note to lines 3277–88.

3313   *Cenys.* The *Paraphrase*-poet has misunderstood the name of this early judge. Properly speaking, this hero is not Kenaz, but the son of Kenaz, named Othniel (compare Judges 3:9). This is probably the result of misreading *HS* Jud. 5 (1274): "Othoniel, fratrem Caleb, quem Josephus Cenem vocat, quasi equivocum patri. Et dicitur Cenem, quasi Cenezaeus a loco."

3355   *aghtene yeres.* Judges 3:30 has eighty years, as does *HS* Jud. 6 (1275).

3368   *in batell to hym them betwene.* Compare *CM* Cotton, line 16454.

3376–78 *for hungar . . . no fode thei fand.* That the Israelites were first stricken with a seven-year famine and then by the power of the Midianite and Amelekite invasions stands somewhat against Judges 6:1–6. In the biblical account, it is the invaders who for seven years cause the famine by destroying Israel's crops. Perhaps the *Paraphrase*-poet desires to provide a stronger Israel that could not have been susceptible to attack.

3389   *He in His trowth was trew.* That is, God is true to His promise to protect Israel against its enemies.

3398   *in a prevé stede.* Judges 6:11 explains that Gideon did this work in private in order to keep it from the prying eyes of the oppressors, who would have destroyed or looted such things.

3405–08 *he suld asay . . . that God His servant had hym sent.* The poet skips over Gideon's specific doubts and the first signs of divine presence, which are accounted in Judges 6:13–35. Instead, the *Paraphrase* moves quickly to the sign of the fleece.

3434   *and fenys not for scheld ne spere.* The detail about the men's treatment of their weaponry is apparently an attempt on the part of the poet to produce a rational explanation for this puzzling biblical story. The Bible says nothing about weapons, explaining only that those who draw the water to their mouths will be better fighters than those who draw their mouths to the water. The former are associated with dogs in the Bible, just as the latter are associated with mules in the *Paraphrase*. The poet, clearly dissatisfied with such "explanations," tries to explain that those who draw water to their mouths do so because they do not want to set down their weaponry and thus make better fighters.

3464   *sexty fayr suns.* Both Judges 8:30 and *HS* Jud. 9 (1281) agree on the number of sons as seventy.

3478   *for gold and grett maystry.* Again and again the *Paraphrase*-poet marks the falling away of the Israelites into idolatry as a result of avarice (compare line 3230), whereas the Bible tends more to view their wanderings from God as simple issues of religion: they are habitual idolaters, not habitual misers. That the *Paraphrase* alters this perception could be due to any number of factors, but two possibilities stand out most strongly. First, the poet may be altering in accordance with the stereotypical presentation of Jews as rich, greedy, and miserly. While this accords well with many late medieval perceptions of the Jews, it stands somewhat at odds with the otherwise positive portrayal of the Jews in his account. Another possibility, then, is that the poet is altering for the purpose of example, projecting a primary vice of his time back onto the biblical story in order to make a moral point for his audience.

3493   *Gepte was a knyght in armys clere*. Jephthah's position as an outcast is unmentioned here. Judges 11:1–3 relates that he was the son of a prostitute who was driven away from his father's home due to his unsavory mother. Perhaps such details are unworthy of the noble light that the poet seems so keen on casting upon his biblical subjects.

3517–88   In his edition of the story of Jephthah and his daughter, Peck observes that the *Paraphrase*-poet "alters several details of the Vulgate text by developing Jephthah's concern for his daughter, his falling from his horse in grief, his daughter's self-sacrificing responses to his vow; by deleting the daughter's lament for her virginity; and by adding details of Jephthah's execution of the vow with beheading and cremation" (*Heroic Women from the Old Testament*, p. 148). It is interesting to note that the poet does not follow *HS* Jud. 13 (1284) in his expansion and alteration of the tale. Clearly the drama of the story itself moved him to make such shifts.

3557   *graunteys me grace two wekes to wake*. Judges 11:37 records that she was given two months in order to mourn her virginity. Here, however, such mourning is done away with and replaced by what Peck calls "a premium on virginity" (*Heroic Women from the Old Testament*, p. 149). Thus, like the condemned Virginia in Chaucer's Physician's Tale, Jephthah's daughter celebrates rather than mourns her chaste death; indeed, Virginia cites Jephthah's daughter as an example for her willingness to suffer death at the hand of her father (*CT* VI[C]235–50).

3573–76   *Therfor hyr fader noyght leved . . . and bad scho suld be brent*. The detail of the beheading, like so many of the details in this expansion of the biblical story, is from the hand of the poet (see note to lines 3517–88). Both the Bible and *HS* record the offering as a burnt offering, saying nothing of her execution prior to being put to the flames. The added detail here — in addition to heightening simultaneously the horror and the mercy of the scene — emphasizes Jephthah's blind obedience and nobility. He is noble in smiting off his daughter's head with one clean stroke, thus diminishing her suffering, but he is also foolish in admirably not breaking his vow, as the poet protests: he should never have given the vow to begin with, and, having given the vow, he probably should not have kept it (lines 3581–84). The story, no doubt like Jephthah's blade, is double-edged.

3592   *Achyron*. As Ohlander has observed, the *Paraphrase*-poet is in accordance with *OFP* 30b ("Apres cestui regna Abialon; / Dis anz apres e puis regna abdon") in mistaking the burial place of the judge Elon for his name. Thus we have here not Elon, but Aijalon, the place where Elon is buried ("Old French Parallels," p. 212); compare Judges 12:11–12.

3601–4440   It is interesting to compare the story here with other Samson stories in Middle English, such as *CM*, lines 7083–7262, Chaucer's Monk's Tale (*CT* VII [B²]2015–94), and Lydgate's *Fall of Princes* 2.6336–6510. Generally, these fictional retellings emphasize the heroic quality of Samson's story and his fall at the hands of a woman, rather than any theological characteristics (compare, too, Gower's *CA* 8.2703–04, where Samson is with the company of the ill-fated lovers Paris, Troilus, and Hercules [*CA* 8.2529–60]). The *Paraphrase*, not surprisingly, follows precisely this line of purpose, treating the story as a romantic narrative. The poetic license that the *Paraphrase*-poet takes in working to this end is notable and, as Ohlander has observed, often parallels *OFP* ("Old French Parallels," pp. 212–13). To record all variances of the *Paraphrase* from the biblical account would be superfluous, as this story has the feel of a set piece dropped into the otherwise straightforward paraphrasing of the Bible. For an overview of literary treatments of Samson, see *DBTEL*, pp. 677–79.

3605   *Was haldyn chefe of chewalry*. The Bible gives little detail about Manoah, but the poet seems to have no difficulty filling in the blanks with an anachronistic reference to his chivalric qualities. It would make sense, of course, for the great warrior Samson to come from such stock.

3609–12   The mourning of Manoah's wife over their inability to conceive a child stands in juxtaposition with the mourning over Jephthah's daughter about her virgin fate.

3670   *bare withowtyn blame*. The language here, giving details original to the poet, borders on that reserved for Mary and the Immaculate Conception and birth of Christ. The basic features of that story have certainly been put into place here: a couple with no children, an annunciation by God's angel, the doubts of the husband, a miraculous birth that leaves no blemish on the woman. Such relationships were familiar in the allegorical tradition of Christian biblical exegesis, where Samson was often viewed as a prefiguration of Jesus (see, e.g., Augustine's *Sermo de Samsone* [*PL* 39:1639–45] or Isidore of Seville's *Mysticorum expositiones sacramentorum* [*PL* 83:389–90]). But while the poet has heightened such connections with his various alterations to the story, he stops short of producing definite parallels. That is, though the poet pushes against the envelope of a literal reading of the text here, he does not go so far as to cross the border into allegorical exegesis: in the end the elusive parallels remain only allusive hints of deeper significance. On the essentially Victorine quality of such behavior, see the introduction.

3701   *Hym toyght her*. The poet's use of dative of agency here is interesting. It is as if her beauty possesses him, making him passive in the face of it — which is, indeed, how most of Samson's troubles begin.

3713   *His moyder morned*. The detail is not in the Bible, but the personal touch fits well with the poet's work to heighten verisimilitude throughout this poem.

3845   *Of turnamentes ther*. The poet continues to paint his story in contemporary chivalric strokes, here presenting the tournaments that would accompany a fourteenth-century aristocratic wedding. In addition to presenting Samson as a man of knightly excellence, such details would no doubt put the poet's audience into the romantic mindset, associating Samson more with Guy of Warwick, Bevis of Hampton, and other romance figures than with Gideon, Saul, and other biblical figures. For more on the blurring of the line between romance and Scripture in the *Paraphrase*, see the introduction.

3849–56   *Becawse he was so strang . . . for ferd of fare that myght befall.* The *Paraphrase* neatly explains the cause of the thirty people who follow Samson about the town, an offhand and unexplained detail given in Judges 14:11, by claiming that Samson's prowess was so great that the people feared to leave him alone in town.

3873–74   *Avyse yow . . . the question this es.* The poet emphasizes Samson's skills in rhetoric here and elsewhere. This brand of oratory in dialogue, a mannered rhetoric, heightens the ties to romance in this section of the poem.

3875–76   *Owt of the herd come fode, / and of the swalowand swettenes.* The need to meet rhyme has apparently taken precedence over the need to present an accurate rendition of the riddle: the terms have here been reversed. Judges 14:14 presents the riddle thus: "Out of the eater came forth meat, and out of the strong came forth sweetness." Strangely, the "revised" version of the riddle is almost more intelligible: "Out of the strong came forth food, and out of the eater came forth sweetness."

3881   *Of sevyn days respeyt thei hym prayd.* In Judges 14:12 Samson presents a seven-day window as a part of the initial riddle agreement. The poet alters this, perhaps, to heighten Samson's magnanimity, as he graciously allows them a full week at their request. Even his reply picks up the language of authority and grace: "I grawntt your askyng, sers" (line 3883).

3889   *When thei had soyght faur days or fyve.* The detail here, though seemingly insignificant, might tell us a great deal about the biblical text that the poet has at hand, as the Vulgate reads seven days, following the Hebrew (as does *HS* Jud. 17 [1287]). But the Greek (LXX) and Syriac versions of the text read four (a reading followed in most modern translations, such as NRSV). It is possible, then, that such a small difference provides further evidence of the poet's reliance on Cassiodorus' translation (see the introduction).

3985–4020   Samson's response to the people of Timnah and his subsequent attack on Ashkelon are presented quite differently than they are in the Bible. Here, Samson's response is to determine that he is at a disadvantage among the Philistines in Timnah, as they have a thirty-brute squad watching his every move. Samson is thus a calculating hero, willing to bide his time for revenge. Ashkelon becomes a way of passing the time, apparently, as he goes to rescue the beleaguered city and hand it over to its rightful owner, the Jews, who not incidentally point out that all of their grief is due to the Philistines (Ashkelon was actually historically a Philistine city, on the southern coast of the Mediterranean). The Bible, on the other hand, presents Samson as a man of immediate action in response to the deceptive Philistines in Timnah: he sets off at once for Ashkelon, and he plunders it for the reward that he gives to the men who "solved" the riddle. Such action, of course, does not well fit the romance hero that the *Paraphrase*-poet is working to present.

4043–44   *Of swylke maner he noyed / Phylysteyns for his wyfe*. The fate of Samson's wife is not here given. Judges 15:6–8 relates that the Philistines, when they learned that Samson had destroyed their crops because of Samson's wife, took the young woman and her father (who had given her to the second man) and burned them both. Samson, angered at this action, too, makes great slaughter among them to avenge the deaths of those whose actions had set in motion his initial need for vengeance. The tempestuousness of this Samson is here reduced, as the two sides, Philistine and Jew, good and evil, believer and pagan, hero and enemy, Samson and all comers, are much more clearly defined.

4097   *He fand a cheke bone of an asse*. The detail of the killing weapon (given in Judges 15:15–17) might be the ultimate source for the tradition that such an object was also utilized by Cain in killing Abel (see the note to line 236). A jawbone weapon, whether in the hands of Cain or Samson, is not as far-fetched as it might seem at first glance: *NOAB* notes that jawbones can easily be "worked into a sickle" (p. 322). Samson's early story thus has vestiges of crops and harvesting throughout (note, for instance, the need for water in Samson's "seson" in line 4127).

4184   *Tabor, that was a heygh hyll*. The *Paraphrase* ought to read Hebron, as does *HS* Jud. 18 (1289), following Judges 16:3. Tabor is, indeed, a high hill, but it is in the wrong part of the Holy Land, being in the north, near the Sea of Galilee, rather than in the south near the Dead Sea. To be sure, the geography is exaggerated in either case — Gaza to Hebron is almost a fifty mile trek with a vertical ascent of over three thousand feet — but we can hardly suspect that the poet knew enough of the geography (or intended his audience to be familiar enough with it) to make the exaggeration that much more exaggerated by tripling the distance that Samson carries the gates of Gaza. Perhaps, then, the poet has mistakenly transplanted Tabor from elsewhere in Judges: it is the staging ground for Deborah and Barak in 4:6, and it is where Gideon's brothers are killed in 8:18.

4201   *With wemen wold he wun and wend*. The *moralia* of the story are clear, as the indomitable Samson proves Herculean to the core. Such readings of the story were common, especially in the all-too-often misogynist Middle Ages. See, for example, Abelard's *Planctus Israel super Samson*, where connections, too, are made to Adam's fall at the hand of a woman's wiles.

4225   *Dalida, doyghtur dere*. The Bible does not actually say that Delilah was a Philistine, the Sorek valley being of mixed population. Nevertheless, her willingness to aid the Philistines has long been taken as indicative of her own ancestry — though this is only assumption. That Delilah is a harlot is not made clear in the Bible, but that tradition, too, has a long history, reaching back at least as far as Josephus (*Jewish Antiquities* 5.8.11). Pseudo-Philo not only regards her as a harlot but also as Samson's wife (43.5).

4229   *Wold thou qwayntly of hym enquere*. It is difficult not to see a pun on *qwayntly*, which I have here glossed as "cunningly." Delilah will no doubt use her cunning to achieve her ends, but she will also use her cunt to effect her desires. The same pun is famously utilized in Chaucer's Miller's Tale, when Nicholas, who is "ful subtile and ful queynte," catches Alisoun by her "queynte" and has sex with her (*CT* I[A]3275–76).

4233–36   *So may thou stynt all stryve, / and gyftes we sall thee gyfe / To lede a ladys lyve, / os lang os thou may lyfe*. Though the poet follows so much of the tradition in associating Delilah with dangerous lust and wanton sexual behavior, thus making the story one that follows antifeminist traditions, he is apparently reluctant to allow such generalizations to stand without comment. Thus he problematizes such readings by introducing the possibility that Delilah is acting, if not entirely honorably, at least with ultimately good intentions: she is told that learning Samson's secrets might lead to peace in the land. Even more, she is given the chance to lead the life of a "lady," a term that would resonate in the late Middle Ages as the marker of a good woman, far from the life of harlotry that Delilah had previously led. These possible excuses are not paralleled in the Bible, but we must also observe that the poet is ultimately quite condemning of her despite these additional details; see line 4311.

4311   *I deme hyr a dewle os I dare*. A rare seemingly personal comment from the poet — whose occasional first-person intrusions are generally of simple narrative relation (e.g., "as I told you earlier") — but an intrusion that fits in perfect consort with the long tradition of antifeminist readings of the Samson and Delilah story. E.g., Abelard, toward the end of his short poem *Planctus Israel super Samson*, writes:

> O semper fortium
> Ruinam maximam,
> Et in exitium
> Creatam feminam! (lines 54–57)

> [O woman, always the greatest ruin of the strong,
> and created to destroy!]

Even more pertinent for the *Paraphrase*-poet, of course, is Comestor, *HS* Jud. 19 (1289–90), who also regards Delilah as a type of the inconstant woman and makes a succinct and devastating attack on women in concluding his tale: "Omnis enim mulier fere naturaliter avara, et levis, unde addam: Quid levius flumine? flamen. Quid flamine? fama. Quid fama? mulier. Quid muliere? nihil" [Everyone knows woman to be naturally greedy and fickle, to which I will add: What is more fickle than the river? Fire. What more than fire? Fame. What more than fame? Woman. What more than woman? Nothing].

4313–14   *Now nedes Sampson forto beware, / les he be wrethed with his awn wand*. The poet seems to be pushing a pun upon *wand*: if Samson might be chastised with a metaphorical rod of his own making it will be because of his inability to control the urging of his physical rod.

4339   *Scho dyd hym drynke of dyverse wyn.* In Judges 16:19 Samson simply falls asleep
            in Delilah's lap. Here she gets him to drink himself into a stupor. This change
            clearly compounds her duplicity, while it also makes his lack of awareness
            more plausible. In addition, it allows the poet to make a moral point about the
            dangers of alcohol as well as the foolish rituals of sexual infatuation.

4341   *So yll wemen wyll glose.* Glossing, the act of interpreting a text (by com-
            menting that can either clarify or obscure its meaning), has various rever-
            berations in Middle English, ranging from the Summoner's famous state-
            ment that "Glosynge is a glorious thyng, certeyn, / For lettre sleeth, so as we
            clerkes seyn" (*CT* III[D]1793–94) to the Wife of Bath's happy proclamation
            that her fifth husband could wel "glose" her in bed when he handled her
            "bele chose" (*CT* III[D]509–10). The *Paraphrase*-poet, being a man of the
            letter, would surely attack the Summoner, but he might well confirm the
            Wife of Bath's pride as the mark of a wicked woman's glossing and its effects.
            It is interesting to note, in this regard, that the Wife of Bath reports that her
            husband Jankyn read her a sequence of stories about wicked women in order
            to convince her to behave more properly, beginning with the biblical exam-
            ples of Eve and Delilah (*CT* III[D]721–23). His plan famously failed as she
            turned the tables (and the book) on him and got more of the marriage bri-
            dle in her hand than ever before. Chaucer's repeated use of Delilah, an exe-
            getical type of the inconstant woman, in the Wife's Prologue is no mistake.

4343–44   *For men sall not suppose / in them none yll entent.* The sententious statement
            here functions like a full stop, tying up what has gone before. This literary
            device is used with frequency through Samson's story.

4351   *Hys hare scho cutt of ylka dele.* In Judges 16:19 she calls a man into the room
            to shave off his hair, but in most popular imaginings of the tale, as here, she
            does the deed herself. Compare, for example, Milton's *Samson Agonistes* or
            Albrecht Dürer's 1493 woodcut.

4368   *lady of landes.* The legality of this title is noteworthy, as it makes Delilah into
            a woman of property, of estate and entitlement. See note to lines 4421–22.

4411–12   *And on a pyller war thei brayd / that bare up all on ylka syde.* Judges 16:29 re-
            cords the structure as supported by two pillars, but the *Paraphrase* here par-
            allels *OFP* in providing only one. Likely such a "centerpole" structure was
            more easily understood by poet and audience alike.

4419   *ther by his bake myght rest.* This additional detail (Judges 16:26 says only that
            he wants to "rest a little") is a part of Samson's lie, his use of rhetoric to
            destroy his enemies.

4421–22   *Dame Dalyda on deese was drest / with mony a wyght in worthy wede.* The *Para-
            phrase*-poet follows both popular tradition and *OFP* in specifically men-
            tioning Delilah as present in the destruction and thereby killed (Ohlander,
            "Old French Parallels," p. 213). The Bible says nothing of her fate.

4427–28   *Bot the boy, that he can warne / to wend owt of the wons.* That Samson warns the
            boy who has brought him to the pillar, and thus gives him time to escape the

destruction, is a detail not found in the Bible. The *Paraphrase* is here parallel to *OFP* (Ohlander, "Old French Parallels," p. 213).

4431   *All for he wold that woman slo.* Judges 16:28 gives Samson's rationale as vengeance for the taking of his eyes, but the majority of medieval accounts, as here, center the vengeance on Delilah's treachery. In *CM*, for instance, we find the remarkable detail (apparently original) that Samson pulls down the pagan temple not at a feast in honor of Dagon but at Delilah's marriage feast (she having become engaged to a fellow Philistine behind Samson's back); see *CM*, lines 7247–62. Later Renaissance retellings shifted the purpose of Samson's final action once more, regarding Samson (in exegetical incarnation as a prefiguration of Christ) as a martyr whose sole desire in destroying the temple is to fulfill God's bidding against the Philistines and their pagan god, Dagon (thus Milton's *Samson Agonistes* or Francis Quarles' *Historie of Sampson*). To some degree, this Renaissance view moves the commentary of the tale full circle, as Josephus, one of the first writers to treat Samson in any large way, casts Samson in a very sanctified light (see *Jewish Antiquities* 5.8.12).

4435–36   *So wakynd weyre and mekyll wo / all throw a wekyd woman wyle.* Ohlander notes ("Old French Parallels," p. 213) that the *Paraphrase*-poet diverges from *OFP* considerably at this point:

> The OFr. poet denounces woman's cunning most energetically, one might say with great personal engagement. He addresses to Samson an earnest entreaty not to let himself be deceived, he holds up Adam and Joseph as warning examples. Then he exclaims: "Pur nent, seignurs, pur nent les chastiun, / L'engin de femme l'ad pris en mal laçun" (fol.33d). Against the background of this personal approach the ME. poet seems rather tame in his matter-of-fact statement.

4440   *more yett men may lere.* The *more* immediately to follow is Ruth, since the poet has altered the order of Judges (see note to lines 3241–88). The result juxtaposes Samson and Delilah with Ruth: Samson was unable to control his sexual impulses and could at times be disloyal to the Jewish cause; Ruth is profoundly loyal to the Jews (even if she is not one herself) and is in complete control of her impulses. Delilah is made the epitome of the worst of women; Ruth is made the best. Delilah is "wyld" while Ruth is "tame" (see line 4441). Though we cannot know whether this juxtaposition was intentional, it is effective. If one of the lessons of the Samson story as told by the poet is that people get what they deserve, it is a lesson that is continued in the story of Ruth. There is, indeed, more that *men may lere*.

BOOK OF RUTH

4441   *both wyld and tame.* See note to line 4440.

4442   *our spekyng.* The use of first-person commentary on the text, which the poet had slipped into increasingly in the story of Samson, continues here.

4451–52   *Of hyr kynred com Cryst / and of the Jewes gentyll blud.* That Jesus descends from Ruth is not mentioned in *HS*, though *OFP* 34c does have the detail (Ohlander, "Old French Parallels," p. 213). The connection appears in the genealogy of Jesus, Matthew 1:3–6. The *gentyll blud* of the Jews refers to the Davidic line of kings, as Ruth's son Obed was the grandfather of King David (see Ruth 4:17).

4453   *Aftur Sampson dede.* The link to what the poet presents as the last story in Judges is not biblical and helps to underscore the deliberate juxtaposition of these stories. See note to line 4440.

4458   *Emalec.* In Hebrew, his name means "my God is king." This is among the many facts that the narrative played out after his death by his wife and daughter-in-law will show.

4459   *Neomy.* In Hebrew, her name means "pleasant," and it stands in sharp contrast to the name that she tells the people of Bethlehem to call her as a result of her misfortunes: Mara, meaning "bitter" (Ruth 1:19).

4462–64   *Chelon . . . Maalon.* That Naomi's two sons will die is hardly surprising given that in Hebrew their names mean "consumption" and "sickness," respectively.

4474   *Orafayn.* Orpah's name in Hebrew seems to mean "neck." According to Midrash this figuratively relates to the fact that she, unlike Ruth, turns her head away from Naomi.

4475   *Ruth.* In Hebrew her name means "compassion." According to some traditions, she and Orpah are sisters, the daughters of the king of Moab, Eglon, but there is no sense of this here.

4479   *Phylysteyns ware tho fayre wemen.* Ruth and Orpah are not, technically speaking, Philistines, who are a people from a stretch of land along the Mediterranean coast in and around Gaza. Rather, they are Moabites, a separate people who lived in Moab, a land east of the Dead Sea. *Philistine*, long before the late Middle Ages, had become a sort of catchall general term for a pagan, a sense that continues today. The Moabites are related to the Israelites through Lot (Genesis 19:37), the nephew of Abraham, but the two peoples had a long history of conflict between them due to claims upon the same territories (see, e.g., Deuteronomy 23:4).

4495–98   *Scho tuke Ruth furth to be hyr by, / and in that land scho leved Orfayn. / Of on enogh hyr toyght / to led the landes throgh.* That Naomi chose to bring Ruth and to leave Orpah stands much in contrast to the biblical narrative on these points, where Naomi asks them both to stay behind. Ruth refuses and Naomi does not bother to argue about the matter (see Ruth 1:11–18). While the alteration slightly weakens the portrayal of Ruth as a woman of undying loyalty, it also makes her seem less stubborn. At the same time, it strengthens the image of her as a worthy woman since Naomi chooses to bring her (and not Orpah) back to Bethlehem.

4538   *Neomy, thy nevow grett.* The Bible says only that Naomi is a kinswoman to Boaz through her husband. The change here helps to account for Boaz's familial duties to Naomi and her daughter-in-law, as Ruth 3:9 presents Ruth claiming connection to Boaz as next-of-kin. And, according to Jewish law, the next-of-kin must protect the honor and rights of such a family (see, e.g., Leviticus 25:25 on the passing of property, or Joshua 20:3 on blood vengeance). While the necessity of Boaz's actions are less clear in the biblical account due to their only being kinsfolk, the alteration in the family structure here makes the law more binding.

4576   *a yong man with ryve elders rent.* Ruth 3:12–13 explains the events a bit more clearly: Boaz is willing to act as next-of-kin (see note to line 4538), but he knows that there is someone with a closer family claim that must be respected. If the other man refuses the duty, Boaz will do it. The language here in the *Paraphrase*, while less clear, does add in minor points not present in the Bible: the other man's youth and, depending on how one reads *ryve elders rent*, his wealth. Ruth's loyalty to Boaz thus becomes a more worthy thing, done not for money or youthful passions.

First Book of Kings

4669   *bred and wyne.* The Bible and *HS* relate only that the family brought sacrifices to the Temple at Shiloh (not the Temple at Jerusalem, which had yet to be built). That such a sacrifice would consist of bread and wine, the food and drink of the Mass, would certainly seem fitting in a Christian exegetical tradition, though no expansion on the point is made here.

4673–74   *He parted then Anna to pyne, / for unto hyr he gaf bot one.* The single portion agrees with the Vulgate, but stands against some translations of 1 Kings (1 Samuel) 3:4–5, where Hannah is given a double portion — twice as much as Peninnah — because of Elkanah's strong love and pity for her (thus, e.g., NRSV). The Septuagint can be translated as "prime portion."

4681–92   Hannah appears to have set herself within a kind of psychological prison built of her anxiety about her failure to have children, a kind of interior devastation that is akin to the dread of purposelessness that Chaucer's Parson describes as leaving its victims in a self-inflicted darkness, a "lond of misese" (*CT* X[I]185). Hannah's place in this perpetual darkness is here exemplified in her lamenting sleeplessness (*withoutyn rest*, line 4681), which grows so profound that the high priest, Eli, thinks her mad (*wode*, line 4688). His advice to her accords well both with the Parson's dictum that remembrance of the good that one has left to do can provide a way out of overwhelming despair and with Boethius' therapeutic ideas of self-governance: having lost her sense of self-purpose she acts improperly, forgetful of self-watchfulness as if she were drunk. Worse, the projection of her anguish on the world reflects poorly on her, as it threatens to *greve* God (line 4692) in a kind of transference of psychological condition to external surrounds that would be familiar from many religious writings. See, for instance, the fourteenth-century lyric "In a Valley of This Restless Mind," where the soul's disunity from God affects a kind of psychological topography of despair (in

Fein, *Moral Love Songs and Laments*, pp. 68–71), or Boethius' *Consolation of Philosophy* 1, where the narrator displaces his condition of imprisonment on Lady Philosophy (trans. Chaucer, *Boece* 1.pr.3.11–12).

4690–91   *thou takes no kepe / All yf thou dronkyn be.* 1 Kings (1 Samuel) 1:13–14 relates that due to the silent fervency of her prayer, Eli accuses Hannah of being drunk. But the accusation here is not just one of excess drinking: it is the lack of self-governance that such a condition would imply that is of concern to Eli (see note to lines 4681–92, above).

4692   *Go slepe.* Eli's advice reverberates not only with his thinking that she might be literally drunk and thus need to "sleep it off" (see note to lines 4690–91), but also with the possibility that her anxiety has divorced her from having any rest, leaving her sleepless in her despondency (see note to lines 4681–92, above). As Hannah will note, however, Eli misunderstands her ministrations before God (see note to line 4695).

4695   *To God is that I cry and pray.* In response to the priest's concern over her mental state and the way that it threatens to directly aggrieve God (see note to lines 4681–92), Hannah concedes that she intends to do just that, the implication being that a just and loving God should indeed grieve for the griefs of His Creation. When Eli learns that Hannah intends to make what offering she can as part of her prayer for an audience — that her child, should she conceive one, will be God's servant — he agrees to join her plea (lines 4699–4700).

4707–08   *a sun heyght Samuell, / as scho full oft cane aftur crave.* The point being that the child was named Samuel because of her prayers that God provide her with just such a child: in Hebrew Samuel means "God has appointed."

4719–24   K notes (1:clxxxvi–clxxxvii) that Samuel's early start on prophecy, here given as well established by age twelve, derives from *HS* 1 Reg. 4 (1298): "Rediit Elcana in domum suam, et Samuel ministrabat anti Heli, et dicit eum Josephus anno duodecimo pleno prophetasse." The passage in Josephus which Comestor refers to is *Jewish Antiquities* 5.10.4. Ohlander observes that the detail is also given in *OFP* 36a ("Old French Parallels," p. 214). The age might have been considered particularly appropriate to Christian exegetes since Luke 2:42 gives it as the age at which Jesus first began to teach at the Temple.

4733   *lechery.* In the biblical account, Eli's sons are primarily noted for their stealing of sacrifices at the Temple (1 Kings [1 Samuel] 2:12–17); only later is it recorded "how they lay with the women that waited at the door of the tabernacle" (2:22). Here, however, the poet has reversed the order of their sins and thereby the emphasis upon them, choosing to highlight their sexual immorality and to background their sacrificial improprieties — presumably due to the fact that the specifics of the latter acts would be too far foreign for the intended audience. That the two sons are priests is not directly stated here, but it is implied in the sermonlike aside that follows (see note to lines 4741–52).

4741–52	The poet uses the improper behavior of Eli's sons to make a comment about the proper behavior of all priests at all times — though we might surmise that his attack on those who soil hallowed things and do not dress in a matter fitting of their station is aimed specifically at circumstances in his own personal surrounds since these were among the accusations made by the Lollards against the contemporary priesthood.
4748	*for dowt of Hym that all sall deme.* That is, for fear of Jesus, who was traditionally figured to be the arbiter of final judgment on the Day of Doom. As noted in the introduction, direct reference to Christ is rare in this "literal" text. Even oblique references, such as this here, are remarkably infrequent.
4753	*rede and reherse.* It is possible that the direction could be taken literally to indicate the oral means by which the *Paraphrase* was intended to be delivered: the text would be read out loud and subsequently rehearsed by its listeners, effectively allowing them to memorize parts of the text.
4761–62	*wyll ye oght, / I com yow forto kepe.* While the Bible has Samuel say only "Here am I: for thou didst call me" (1 Kings [1 Samuel] 3:5), the poet expands his words to point out Eli's inability to comprehend fully the words that he hears. One understanding of young Samuel's statement is, as I have glossed it, that if Eli wants something Samuel will go fetch it for him. But Samuel, as we have been told, is also a prophet. At that level of understanding, he tells the old priest that what Eli ought to be doing — the proper rites and directives of God — he (Samuel) will do. This does, indeed, prove true.
4764	*go slepe.* Eli instructs the boy, just as he had his mother Hannah, to go to sleep. But, as before, Eli misunderstands the situation. Hannah did intend to grieve God with her pleas, and Samuel has, indeed, been called by his master.
4777	*He sleped in his howse at hame.* The *Paraphrase* seems to suggest here that Samuel leaves the Temple and goes to rest in another location; this would appear to stand against the Bible, which says only that he goes to sleep "in his place" ("in loco suo," 1 Kings [1 Samuel] 3:9) — his previous place of rest being given in 3:3 as "in the temple of the Lord, where the ark of God was." So, too, *HS.* If this change in location is intentional, it could either be a subtle means of undercutting the authority either of the Temple (and thus of any Jewish privilege that might be associated with it) or of the Church's claims about the necessity of a mediating priesthood in general.
4783–84	*All Jacob suns sall suffer schame / for wekyd dedes that thei have wroght.* That is, the whole of Israel (all of its twelve tribes) will suffer for its wicked deeds. While God does pronounce direct action against Eli and his family in 1 Kings (1 Samuel) 3:11–14, He says nothing there of action against Israel at large, only that what He will do to Eli will be heard throughout that land. This change may go some way toward emphasizing the possible undercutting of the Jews noted for line 4777, above.
4822	*ten thowssand, says the Boke.* The Bible reports a death count of four thousand (1 Kings [1 Samuel] 4:2), a detail number followed in *HS* 1 Reg. 7 (1300).

4859–62 K (1:clxxxvii) terms this account of a plague of mice that eat the Philistines as extrabiblical, not appearing at this point in the narrative and only subsequently being alluded to at 1 Kings (1 Samuel) 6:4–5. The lines are parallel to *HS* 1 Reg. 8 (1301) and, as Ohlander observes, *OFP* 36d ("Old French Parallels," p. 214). But while the account does not appear in the now-standard copies of the Vulgate, it is indeed found in a great many copies of that text as an extension of 1 Kings (1 Samuel) 5:6. Thus it appears, for instance, in both the Douay-Rheims and NRSV translations.

4897–4920 That two oxen pull the Ark to Beth-shemesh stands against the Bible (1 Kings [1 Samuel] 6:7) and *HS* (1 Reg. 8 [1301]) which describe them as two milch cows. The *Paraphrase* here agrees with *OFP* 37a (Ohlander, "Old French Parallels," p. 214).

4929–30 *Vengiance com sone unsoyght / apon sexty thowssand.* The *Paraphrase*-poet has rounded off the number of curious onlookers slaughtered by God; *HS* 1 Reg. 8 (1302) follows 1 Kings (1 Samuel) 6:19, which reads: "seventy men, and fifty thousand of the common people." Despite the fact that the fifty thousand are in the Hebrew, many translations disregard it and only report the death of seventy men (e.g., NRSV), which accords with Josephus, *Jewish Antiquities* 6.1.4.

5017 *In Masphat sojournd Samuel.* That Samuel goes to Mizpah to mourn for Israel before he seeks out its king is found neither in the biblical narrative nor in *HS*. The detail apparently derives from the earlier incidents at Mizpah (not narrated here) in which Samuel leads Israel in confessing their sins against God, an act that leads directly to a defeat of the Philistines and in honor of which Samuel dedicates a shrine at Eben-ezer, between Mizpah and Jeshanah (1 Kings [1 Samuel] 7:2–14). The *Paraphrase*-poet seems to consider this shrine to be that to which Samuel is making his way when he meets Saul (1 Kings [1 Samuel] 9:14). Since Mizpah is also the location where Samuel will proclaim Saul king before the people (1 Kings [1 Samuel] 10:17–27), the poet is thus able to condense the geography of his story considerably.

5111 *Thre loyvys sall thei gyf thee.* According to 1 Kings (1 Samuel) 10:4, Josephus (*Jewish Antiquities* 6.4.2), and *HS* 1 Reg. 11 (1304), Saul will be offered two loaves.

5213 *Ther settes he gybcrokes and engyns.* The siege of Jabesh-gilead is presented as a medieval siege, complete with all the implements thereof, sights that perhaps would have been familiar to the poet's audience from wars in France or elsewhere. Aside from creating a more familiar and thus more historically plausible atmosphere for his contemporaries, the poet's "medievalizing" of the narrative through these details further underscores the romance nature of his work: the resulting text is thus a generic hybrid in much the same way as another popular text of the period: *Siege of Jerusalem*.

5272–74 *sex hunderth thowssand men myghty, / And of Juda als fell ther fell, / the nowmers ar not forto dyscrye.* **HS** 1 Reg. 12 (1305), following 1 Kings (1 Samuel) 11:8, puts the number of Israelite warriors at 300,000, with the men of Judah being 30,000 more; Josephus' numbers are 700,000 and 70,000 (*Jewish Antiquities* 6.5.3).

5301–06   *Kyng Saul slogh that day / a hunderth with his handes, / And wan wrschepe. . . . This was fyrst chaunce of chevalry / that Kyng Saul fell in this case.* After expanding his account of the siege of Jabesh-gilead in terms of a medieval battle (both in its fictional and historical qualities, see note to line 5213), the poet concludes the sequence by making Saul into a type of the medieval knight familiar to medieval romance, his deeds turning him into a chivalric leader whose doughty deeds win him glory and honor *to hym and all his landes* (line 5304).

5331–32   *He wyll that we forgyf gladly / all tho that to us have trespast.* The poet here has Samuel echo Matthew 6:12, part of the Lord's Prayer.

5353–64   The mention that Saul came to rule over "kynredes twelve / that Jacob suns was cald" (lines 5351–52) leads the poet into a short, seemingly personal (n.b. the first-person pronoun in line 5354) digression on the different terms used to refer to the Jews. Regardless of the word used to collect them, he says, they are the same people, one loved by God as long as they followed His rule. It may well be that the poet intends a subtle comment on the contemporary place of Jews in his world: while they once were His people, they have been replaced in God's sight by virtue of their denial of Him in Christ.

5443–48   *That sexty thowsand sone had thei / of knyghtes . . . thrytty thowsand els . . . And mo that no man tels / on futte full wyght in were.* The numbers here are not quite in agreement with 1 Kings (1 Samuel) 13:5 (or *HS* 1 Reg. 13 [1306]), which records 30,000 chariots, 6,000 horsemen, and an uncountable number of men: "like the sand on the seashore." Josephus concurs, though he specifies the number of footmen as 300,000 (*Jewish Antiquities* 6.6.1). Here the horsemen have become knights and have increased tenfold, while the charioteers have become the additional category of fighters.

5505–08   *For he had messege sent . . . Or he com in present / to make no sacrafyce.* In the biblical account Samuel had made no such earlier pronouncement to Saul. Rather, it is simply implied that Saul has done ill in overstepping the implicit bounds of his kingship (his duty — see line 5496) by taking on priestly duties. This issue of proper and improper areas of influence would have been a familiar one to the poet and his audience, as the imposition of the State on the Church was an active source of both condemnation and glorification in the late Middle Ages, seen in texts as diverse as the popular *Siege of Jerusalem* and Gower's formal *In Praise of Peace*.

5513–14   *Bycawse thou hath done this owtrage, / that suld not passe bot be presthed.* In this extrabiblical statement, Samuel here emphasizes that Saul's misdeed was in taking on duties reserved for the priesthood. Not only does this have political ramifications to the *Paraphrase*-poet's contemporary surrounds (see note to lines 5505–08, above) but it also reflects the very serious issue of Lollardy, and the question of whether or not the laity can effectively replace the ordained officials of the Church. The poet's answer, if we can presume to allow the prophet to speak for him, is that they cannot: the priesthood must be maintained if for no other reason than that they alone can properly conduct the rites sacred to God and man.

5515   *God hath ordand a lytyll page.* I.e., David, who is here defined as a *page* in accordance with late medieval structures of knighthood. In 1 Kings (1 Samuel) 13:14 (and *HS* 1 Reg. 13 [1307]) Samuel is far less specific, saying God will appoint "a man."

5559–64   *On of them wyst well who yt wase . . . soyne ware thei feld that myght not flee.* In the biblical account of this incident (1 Kings [1 Samuel] 14:1–15), the sign of God's favor that Jonathan looks for is whether or not he and his armorbearer are invited up to engage against the Philistines. Once invited up, the two of them make a direct assault on the enemy that, when it proves successful, causes the ensuing chaos. Here, however, the sign is whether or not they recognize Jonathan; and their awareness of his presence alone puts them into flight. The alteration seems intended mainly to add dimension to Jonathan's character, presenting him as such a well-known, stalwart knight that his name itself strikes fear into the hearts of his enemies.

5610   *Achyas heyght he, os we rede.* The priest is unnamed here in 1 Kings (1 Samuel), though the name Ahijah for Saul's primary priest is found earlier at 14:3 and 9. Josephus, *Jewish Antiquities* 6.6.5, does name the priest at this point, as does *HS* 1 Reg. 14 (1308).

5663   *Sexty thowsand ware slayn.* This summary of the total number of Philistines killed in the war, which here acts to close off the account of it, is not biblical in origin, nor can it be found in *HS*. It does, however, appear in Josephus, *Jewish Antiquities* 6.6.6.

5718   *sexty thowsand at a syght.* 1 Kings (1 Samuel) 15:4 and *HS* 1 Reg. 15 (1309) place the total number of men at 200,000 Israelites and 10,000 men of Judah. Josephus, *Jewish Antiquities* 6.7.2, gives the numbers as 400,000 and 30,000. The source for the number given here is unknown.

5731–48   *Of knyghtes kene and princes of price . . . in ways withowtyn heuyd.* The detail of the pageantry of the armies has a clear "medieval" feel to it, as knights sally forth with pennons and banners above their gleaming arms. The poet deftly turns away from the glory of this earthly finery, however, in presenting the simple image of the bloody aftermath of the battles being undertaken: riderless horses walking aimlessly amid the headless corpses on the field.

5817–18   *Sone fro that pepyll he past / ryght way to Ramatha.* That is, Samuel started to make his way toward Ramah, not that he actually went there. According to 1 Kings (1 Samuel) 15:34 and *HS* 1 Reg. 15 (1310), and as is shown here in lines 5853–54, Samuel actually makes his way to Ramah after the tearing of his cloak and the slaughter of Agag (15:27–33). The biblical encounter between the two men described here, rather, takes place at Gilgal (see 15:12).

5889   *Sex suns ware sett on raw.* There were, according to 1 Kings (1 Samuel) 16:10 (which is followed by *HS* 1 Reg. 16 [1310] and *CM*, line 7350), a total of seven sons of Jesse that God rejects before settling on the youngest, David, who is at first away, tending to the sheep. Thus Jesse, as stated clearly in 17:12, had a total of eight sons. The alteration on the part of the *Paraphrase*-poet surely originates in his awareness that in 1 Chronicles 2:13–15 David is named as the seventh and last son of Jesse. This discrepancy has led to much speculation aimed at resolution, including the possibilities that one of the sons who passed before Samuel was adopted and thus not counted in the later enumeration, or that one of them died shortly afterwards, so that it could be said with equal accuracy that Jesse had seven or eight sons. The *Paraphrase*-poet takes instead the apparently unique position of simply altering the Kings text so that no discrepancy occurs, though one wonders why he would do so given the fact that Chronicles is not incorporated in his poem. It is possible, then, that an added benefit in the alteration is in making David a seventh son (as opposed to an eighth), seven being a number of totality.

5894   *the eldyst two*. Unnamed here, the two sons singled out in 1 Kings (1 Samuel) 16:8–9 are Abinadab and Shammah, though the names of the eldest sons in 1 Chronicles 2:13–15 are Eliab and Abinadab. See note to line 5889, above.

5909–24   *The prophett hym in armys hentt . . . grett lordschep sal be thee lentt.* This long sequence regarding Samuel's recognition of David and bestowal of honors upon him prior to the anointing is extrabiblical and, with details such as the *deyse* ("dais," line 5917) upon which David is set, somewhat anachronistic. It does, however, derive much of its power from that very anachronism, showing an acknowledgment of power relationships in very feudal terms, with further ritualized presentations like Samuel's public embrace of the boy and the dinner at which individuals are arranged according to *ther degree* (line 5915).

5923–24   *To warn thee of His wyll allway: / grett lordschep sal be thee lentt.* Samuel's reminder that lordship over men is only a temporary state of affairs, and that this lordship is dependent on God's grace, finds echo in the writings of Gower, especially in his *In Praise of Peace*, itself an extended elaboration of these themes written in warning to a new king (Henry IV). Gower's advice in that poem opens by underscoring the observation, noting time and again "that Henry is not himself responsible for having attained the crown. He is not a conqueror by right of martial arms but a passive tool in the active hand of God" (*In Praise of Peace*, ed. Livingston, p. 119).

5931   *The gud gast, that in Saul was.* I have glossed this "good spirit," though it is tempting to read here something more like "Holy Spirit," thus paralleling the line with the imagery of the later Acts of the Apostles, where the Holy Spirit comes down to rest in believers. *HS* 1 Reg 16 (1310) makes just such a parallel, though it is only partially picked up in *CM*, lines 7405–06.

5941–52   This extrabiblical stanza, in which Samuel gives the young David advice on how to rule himself and thus his kingdom, again has parallels with Gower's work. See the explanatory note to lines 5923–24.

5965–76   K notes (1:clxxxvii) that the advice of Saul's physicians and clerks, that only music can drive away the evil spirit plaguing him (1 Kings [1 Samuel] 16:16 puts the matter less directly and in the mouth of servants), comes from *HS* 1 Reg. 16 (1310). Ohlander points out that similar advice is given in *OFP* 44b, though Comestor specifically mentions "servi," "physici," and "mathematici" as those giving advice ("Old French Parallels," p. 214).

6027–30   *Under a banke, wher thei abyde . . . Kyng Saul on the other syde, / the hyll betwen, was on a grett heght.* The geography is difficult to construe here, as it seems to indicate that the two forces are arrayed on opposite sides of a single mountain. 1 Kings (1 Samuel) 17:3 is more clear: "the Philistines stood on a mountain on the one side, and Israel stood on a mountain on the other side: and there was a valley between them."

6049–60   Goliath's armor as described here does not conform to the description given in the Bible (1 Kings [1 Samuel] 17:5–7), but it does correspond to that found in *OFP* 44d (Ohlander, "Old French Parallels," p. 215). Ohlander also notes that the *Paraphrase*-poet, though willing to spend time with the details of this extrabiblical description, omits the famous physical description of Goliath's height: "six cubits and a span" (1 Kings [1 Samuel] 17:4). Goliath's remarkable height is picked up, however, in *CM*, line 7451.

6068   *yond warlaw.* The epithet appears to have been borrowed from *CM*, line 7478, which in several versions has Saul attaching the term to Goliath when he decries his inability to find a man to match the Philistine's challenge (e.g., "yon warlau" in the Cotton). Note that *warlaw* here means simply a "monstrous or hideous creature" (*MED warlou* n.3) or, as I have glossed it here, an "infidel" (n.1b). The term does not indicate, as it does in most modern parlance, someone who "practices occult arts" (n.1c) — though the latter meaning *is* that which is used in line 11130 of the present poem, where it is applied to the unknown power sought by Ahab, whom the king believes to have caused a great drought; Ahab finds, instead, Elijah (3 Kings [1 Kings] 18:2–6).

6101–08   David and Goliath's exchange of words across the field before they engage in battle is more brief here than it is in the Bible or in *CM*, for instance. The brevity, however, presents us with a chance for increased characterization on the part of David who, rather than presenting a drawn-out speech about God's influence in battle, is a straightforward man of action, whose return of Goliath's mockery is a true one-liner (line 6104) that cuts directly to the heart of their coming fight. David, it seems, does not have time for more speech. Thus it is not surprising to find that his response to Goliath's subsequent insult — that David is infantlike (line 6106) — is to ignore it: in determined silence David simply whirls his sling into action and strikes him down with one shot to the brain.

6129   *Thryty milia war slayn.* Ohlander notes that neither 1 Kings (1 Samuel) 17:52 nor *HS* give a specific number to the slain Philistines. *OFP* 45c reads "Treis mile," while another copy of that poem, Oxford, Corpus Christi College, MS

36, fol. 92a, meets the *Paraphrase* precisely: "Trente mil" ("Old French Parallels," p. 215).

6141–43   *Tho wyfes sang . . . The madyns sang.* 1 Kings (1 Samuel) 18:7 simply says that women sang of Saul's slaying his thousands and David his ten thousands. The *Paraphrase*-poet adds a romance twist as the maidens answer the wives, who praise Saul, with laughter and adoration of the young hero, the idea being repeated in lines 6146–48. The girls have a soft spot for David from the get-go, which anticipates Michal's attraction to him, which is so strong that she withers at a mere frown (see lines 6197–6200).

6184   *he bare the flour.* That is, he achieved victory. The phrase is a chivalric one, once more marking David as part of a late medieval culture of knighthood.

6197–6214 *Mycoll . . . hyr fayrnes fast can fale.* The poet takes nearly two stanzas expanding on a few words from 1 Kings (1 Samuel) 18:20 ("Michol, the other daughter of Saul, loved David"), further blending the elements of romance into his narrative.

6225–26   *Heydes of Phylesteyns / two hunderth suld he bryng.* 1 Kings (Samuel) 18:25–27 puts Saul's demand as one hundred *foreskins*, and says that David produces two hundred. *HS* agrees with the Bible, while *OFP* 46d gives the command to bring "mil chefs," a charge that David fulfills to the letter as opposed to doubling (Ohlander, "Old French Parallels," p. 215). Here he is charged to produce two hundred hides of Philistines, but he brings in five hundred hides instead, which he presumably flays (line 6240).

6285–88   That Michal saves her husband from Saul's spear, as K notes (1:cxciv), has no known source. It is not in the biblical account, nor in *HS* or *CM*. Ohlander does not find it in *OFP*, either ("Old French Parallels, p. 215). Josephus, *Jewish Antiquities* 6.11.3–4 may be of note here, as it adds a detail that David was able to avoid Saul's spear because he "was aware of it before it came," alluding to the possibility that he had been warned. Since the immediately following event is Michal's warning David about her father's intention of killing him in the morning (and her aiding his escape), one might see that the Josephan tradition is the first step in a conflation of the events, by which Michal becomes the one to warn him. It makes sense that Michal would be attending her father, but also that she likes to hear David play.

6317   *Scho layd a dry stoke in his bed.* According to 1 Kings (1 Samuel) 19:13 it is the image (Vulgate *statuam*; so, too, *HS*) of one of the household gods that Michal places in the bed. The alteration to a log is in keeping with the folkloristic conventions and avoids the affiliation of images with idols.

6325   K notes a close parallel line in *Sir Gawain and the Green Knight*, line 226: "Gladly I wolde se þat segg in syght."

6335–36   Again we find a ten-line stanza. The "missing" lines may never have been written, but I have maintained the line count of earlier editors and scholarship on the poem.

6349–60   The poet greatly condenses the narrative here, omitting the account of Samuel's supernatural ability to put David's pursuers, ultimately including Saul, into a "prophetic frenzy" that rendered them naked at his feet (1 Kings [1 Samuel] 19:19–24).

6380   *or ever I ette*. The *Paraphrase* reduces the elaborate arrangement for notifying David of the results of Jonathan's questioning (1 Kings [1 Samuel] 20:12–23), noting instead that the sign will be Jonathan's refusal to eat, which in the Bible is a result of his recognition of his father's anger, but one independent of his communications with David (20:34).

6388   *sothly*. A line-filler here, but perhaps a subtle point, too, in that Jonathan questions his father in honest need to understand the truth of what is happening in the court, and that he does so without lying himself, something he is guilty of in the biblical account of this exchange (see note to lines 6388–6402).

6389–6402   Jonathan's speech about David's worth, and his question about why, therefore, he is not at the feast, is extrabiblical; 1 Kings (1 Samuel) 20:24–29 has instead Saul asking the question regarding David's absence and Jonathan telling a lie about it in an effort to sound out his father (on Jonathan's truthfulness here, see the note to line 6388). The alteration allows the poet to once more emphasize David's excellence, which culminates in speaking of his comeliness as a *knyght* (line 6401).

6457   *Myn armour gart thei me forgete*. David initially asks only for food in 1 Kings (1 Samuel) 21:3, but his request for armor here is certainly in fitting with the chivalric presentation of him as a knight, now temporarily divested of his position at court.

6496   *Sephyn*. Ziph, though it is not so named until much later in the biblical narrative: 1 Kings (1 Samuel) 23:15.

6497–6504   *Thore come men to hym . . . of cosyns and of other kyn. . . . owtlayd or exyld . . . fawre hunderth folke in fere*. 1 Kings (1Samuel) 22:2 describes David's band of brothers thus: "And all that were in distress, and oppressed with debt, and under affliction of mind, gathered themselves unto him: and he became their prince, and there were with him about four hundred men." To the notion that David's army is made up of the dispossessed and downtrodden the *Paraphrase*-poet has introduced the further characteristic of outlawry, a designation enwrapped in specifically medieval notions of both justice and romance. David thereby stands in the place of Robin Hood for the poet. Or, perhaps more accurately, Robin Hood can stand in the place of David.

6501–02   *bede hym forto be / his men*. In addition to presenting David as captain of a band of outlaws (see note to lines 6497–6504), the poet also reveals his relationship with his subjects to be one of proper feudal oaths, as the men swear to be *his* men in all things. This formal reciprocative structure stands in marked contrast to Saul's court, where the king's jealousy of the success of one of his sworn and loyal lieutenants (David) is cause for anxiety and strife.

6505–6708   These two stories, David's rescue of the city of Keilah (lines 6506–6624) and the betrayal of Doeg the Edomite (lines 6625–6708), appear in reverse order from the Bible, where they are in 1 Kings (1 Samuel) 23 and 22, respectively. Ohlander notes that both *HS* and *OFP* follow biblical order ("Old French Parallels," p. 216). The reversal here in *Paraphrase* emphasizes David's romantic role as an outlaw captain, righting the wrongs of the establishment and protecting the common people.

6650   *popelard*. The word, meaning "hypocrite" or "traitor," derives from OF *papelart*, with K querying whether the spelling of the term here shows influence by *pope* (5:69). If this possibility were true, it would certainly be a strong piece of evidence in debates about whether this text reveals Wycliffite tendencies (or at least reformist ones) — though one wonders how much weight such a minor point of orthography can stand in a text of this length. More likely to be the case here, however, is that the spelling is a result of regional variation, especially since it occurs, too, in the *Chester Plays* (15.362, 17.157, and in the H-variant of 5.233), which can hardly bear the blanket accusation of Lollardy. In addition, the word here is from Saul, describing Ahimelech, a character that is utterly blameless from any other perspective — including that of Saul's own men, most of whom will refuse to kill "Goddes byschop blyst" (line 6678).

6769–92   *He saw David was well arayd . . . he wyst no bettur wone*. The *Paraphrase*-poet presents an ulterior motive to Saul's actions in En-gedi. In the biblical account Saul's decision to exchange oaths with David is depicted as one of genuine remorse, as he weeps (1 Kings [1 Samuel] 24:16) and declares himself in the wrong. Here, however, Saul's decision is an act not of contrition but of self-preservation: he sees that David has the advantage of superior numbers and thus cuts a deal to escape (even though David has not threatened him with harm). The poet illustrates the separation between Saul's words and his intent by pointing out that on leaving David once more had to go to his outlaw encampment, nothing better being offered to him.

6803–04   *he lyfed not by the law / of Moyses and Josue*. Nabal's status as a nonobservant Jew appears to be original to the *Paraphrase*.

6879–80   *In gud garmentes scho made hyr gay / with pelure and with pyrre fyne*. While the story of Abigail is omitted in *CM* and Peter Riga's *Aurora*, and only briefly told in *HS*, the *Paraphrase*-poet utilizes the story further to incorporate romantic conceits with the Scriptures, something clearly seen in his unique description of Abigail's singular beauty and finery — especially her expensive clothes, furred and inwoven with precious stones — that signify her nobility rather than her vanity.

6928   *weded hyr unto his wyfe*. David's marriage to Abigail was seen as a tribute to her worship and wisdom. She is regularly cited in the Christian marriage service, along with Rebecca, Judith, and Esther, as wise women and counselors. E.g., see Chaucer's Tale of Melibee (*CT* VII[B²]1096–1102) and Merchant's Tale (*CT* IV[E]1362–74).

6933–34   *Another he wan also / thrugh dughty dedes he dyde.* The third wife, unnamed here (and omitted, too, in *HS*), is Ahinoam of Jezreel. That he won her hand through his brave deeds is nowhere directly described in the Bible, with most translations reading 1 Kings (1 Samuel) 25:43 simply as a statement of marriage: "Moreover David took also Achinoam of Jezrahel" (Douay), or "David also married Ahinoam of Jezreel" (NRSV). The Latin of the Vulgate, however, is more flexible than this: "Ahinoem accepit David de Iezrahel," which could be translated "David took Ahinoam out of Jezreel." It is the implication of action in this latter reading that seems the origin of the *Paraphrase* here; interestingly, the same reading appears strongly in the Greek Septuagint. A fourth wife, Bathsheba (2 Kings [2 Samuel] 11), appears later in the David story.

6964   *Abyathar.* According to 1 Kings (1 Samuel) 26:6, this must be Ahimelech the Hittite, though the spelling here would appear to have confused him with Abiathar the priest, a confusion I have found nowhere else.

6965   *Thoo three ther gatte.* That all three men enter Saul's encampment stands against the Bible, where David asks Ahimelech and Abishai which of them will accompany him, and it is only Abishai who is chosen. Similarly, in *HS* 1 Reg. 25 (1319) and *CM*, line 7717, only the presence of Abishai is remarked.

6977–78   *a grett coupe of gold full gud / and als the kynges chefe chasyng spere.* These proofs are not those retrieved by David in 1 Kings (1 Samuel) 26:11–16 and *HS* 1 Reg. 25 (1319–20), where David takes the spear and a jug of water. Ohlander notes that the *Paraphrase* is in accordance with *OFP* 53c ("Old French Parallels," p. 216).

7065–66   *Achys noyght understud / what Phylesteyns can fele.* Assuming a lack of knowledge about the geography of the ancient Holy Land, one wonders how much the audience of the *Paraphrase* might sympathize with Achish. The rather subtle point here is that the Amalekites and the Geshurites (along with David's other victims during this period) are subjects of Achish. On each raid, "David wasted all the land, and left neither man nor woman alive" (1 Kings [1 Samuel] 27:9) to tell the truth of his deeds; he would then lie to Achish, claiming that his booty was had from among the lands of the Jews.

7110   *wyche.* 1 Kings (1 Samuel) 28:7 has Saul request "a woman that hath a divining spirit" ("mulierem habentem pythonem" — compare *HS* 1 Reg. 26 [1320–21]). In his Friar's Tale Chaucer calls this same female conjuror a "phitonesse" (*CT* III[D]1510), a term derived from the Latin of the Vulgate here, and one that Chaucer earlier associated plainly with witches in *House of Fame*, lines 1261–63: "phitonesses, charmeresses, / Olde wicches, sorceresses, / That use exorsisaciouns." Gower and Lydgate, too, call the medium of Endor a "phitonesse" in *CA* 6.2387 and *Fall of Princes* 2.434, respectively. Though many scholars have claimed that the identification of the medium with the term *witch* derives from the King James translation of the Bible, which uses the designation "Witch of Endor" as a heading for this chapter (see, e.g., *DBTEL*, pp. 840–41), we see here in *Paraphrase* evidence going back much further than that. Since the story is untold in *CM*, one wonders where the poet derived his terminology. One intriguing possibility in this regard is a short passage in Anglo-Saxon affiliated with a few manuscripts of Ælfric's *De Auguriis*, which utilizes the story of Saul and the medium as an exemplum against the trickeries of the Devil. In this passage, which may or may not be by Ælfric himself, she is consistently termed a "wicce" (Ælfric, *Homilies of Ælfric: Supplementary*, 2:786–98).

7115   *with your lefe*. I have glossed and punctuated this phrase on the assumption that it is Saul's advisor asking leave to speak, rather than a reference to the witch living in En-dor through Saul's permission. 1 Kings (1 Samuel) 28:9 makes clear that Saul had, in fact, rid Israel of such mediums and that the witch thus operates in fear of his reprisals.

7155–56   *This is the same / that maydyns made of in ther sang*. A reference back to lines 6147–48, where the women praised Saul for killing thousands but David for killing tens of thousands.

7250   *and chefe of all his chevalry*. The same phrase occurs in *The Alliterative Morte Arthure*, where the description is of Arthur's knights of the Round Table "That chef were of chivalry" (line 18).

7254   *lawles*. Perhaps one ought to produce the word as *Law-less*, since the "law" in question is not about secular legal systems but about the Law of Moses, the Torah. This point is made again a few lines later when it is repeated that Saul would rather die than live with "folke of fals lyvyng" (line 7258), meaning "people of false belief systems."

7261–68   The death of Saul is here given in accordance with 2 Kings (2 Samuel) 1:6–10 rather than 1 Kings (1 Samuel) 31:4, where Saul kills himself without the aid of the young man. The later story of Saul's death, in addition to being fitted into this earlier account, is also told in full in lines 7327–56. The *Paraphrase* parallels *OFP* 55d–56a and 56d in both accounts, whereas *HS* matches the biblical account (Ohlander, "Old French Parallels," p. 216).

SECOND BOOK OF KINGS

7365–80   The deeply romantic nature of David's lament, complete with swooning and weeping and wringing of hands, is set in place of David's elegy given in 2 Kings (2 Samuel) 1:19–27. As Ohlander notes, David's lament does not fit "with the ideal of the gallant knight," forcing an anonymous duke to tell him to cease weeping like an old woman (line 7377–78) and to take his anger against their enemies instead: "The whole passage gives a good idea of how the writer has adapted the biblical narrative to his own time and its literary tastes and traditions. Carried away by the felicity of his colourful tale he starts the next stanza in the same popular vein. . . . Needless to say there is nothing of this in the Bible" nor in *HS*, though *OFP* 57a–57b contains the same account (with a baron in place of the duke); see "Old French Parallels," p. 217.

7394   *kyng by comyn crye*. That is, king by the assent of the common people, or popular acclaim. David is thus doubly anointed: of God, and of the people he will rule. Notably absent from this ideal combination is force of arms, with David's strength said to be the result of his kingship rather than the other way around. These conditions compare favorably to those presented by Gower in his work (see, especially, his *In Praise of Peace*).

7398   *chefe of his chevalry*. See note to line 7250.

7400   *Aghaell and Abaghai*. Asahel and Abishai are not named in the biblical narrative until 2 Kings (2 Samuel) 2:18.

7444   *so wyght a stede*. 2 Kings (2 Samuel) 2:18 attributes Asahel's speed not to his steed but to the man himself, calling him "a most swift runner, like one of the roes that abide in the woods." Either the simile was too unrealistic for the poet's taste or he simply took the opportunity to introduce yet another element of romantic knighthood to his story.

7445–48 *When Abnare saw he sewed so sore / and to his hele wold take no hede . . . he suld gyf hym gold to mede*. The *Paraphrase*-poet makes clear Abner's concern for the younger warrior, who is taking no care for his own safety in rushing after the more veteran fighter. The details here are more personal than Abner's reasoning in the Bible: "Go off, and do not follow me, lest I be obliged to stab thee to the ground, and I shall not be able to hold up my face to Joab thy brother" (2 Kings [2 Samuel] 2:22). Certainly here in the *Paraphrase* the sense one gets of Abner is of his chivalrous quality in trying to put off the unfair fight, even offering money to the younger man if he should stop (line 7448).

7559–60 *Bot Abnare ay before / was honerd next hymselfe*. This detail of the seating arrangements at the feast is not to be found in either the biblical source (2 Kings [2 Samuel] 3:20–21) or in *HS* (2 Reg. 5 [1327]), but it sets up the coming extrabiblical account of Joab's envy.

7569   *he suld be nare*. Joab's reason for anger is here given as envy: he thought that he was the closest man to David, only to learn that Abner had been given pride of place in his absence. In the Bible (2 Kings [2 Samuel] 3:27 and 30) his cause is specifically given as one of vengeance for his brother Asahel's death at Abner's hand. One might speculate that the poet is uncomfortable with David's subsequent condemnation of Joab for Abner's death — a condemnation that could be perceived as harsh given the somewhat just cause of fraternal piety.

7613   *togh*. K (5:89) glosses as "tough, 'elaborate' (tale)," noting derivation from OE *toh*. The *MED* reveals more nuance, however, listing the specific construction *maken hit tough*, meaning "to be arrogant or obstinate," under *tough* adj.3b. Given the poet's highlighting of Joab's envy in this passage (see the explanatory note to line 7569, above), it is this more negative connotation that seems intended here.

7617–20 *Bot als men may suppose . . . that he had forto lede*. As one might expect, this aside regarding the real reason for Joab's act — envy — is absent from the

	Bible, which twice gives his cause as one of simple vengeance for his brother. See the explanatory note to line 7569, above.
7681–7716	No such census is recorded in this location in the Bible or *HS* (2 Reg. 6 [1327–28]). It has been moved, apparently, from 2 Kings (2 Samuel) 24. Ohlander observes that "[t]he result of the census described here is with two exceptions the same as that in [*OFP*]. A slight difference is noticeable as regards Naphtali. In the [*Paraphrase* (lines 7705–06)] . . . that tribe is simply said to be innumerable, whereas [*OFP* 60c] reads 'De Nephtalim mil princes a guerreier. / La gent qu'il meinent nuls nes pot acunter.' In the [*Paraphrase* (lines 7709–11)] Reuben, Gad, and Manasseh number six hundred thousand altogether. The OF text says 'cent vint mil'" ("Old French Parallels," p. 218). The origin of the numbers provided is, in any case, unknown. The results of the census in both the Vulgate and Septuagint are an Israel numbering 800,000 able-bodied men, and a Judah of 500,000, while a retelling of the census in 1 Chronicles 21:1–6 gives the numbers as 1,100,000 and 470,000, respectively. No further numbers are provided in the Bible, and other potential sources provide no clues for the detailed accounting given here: on the census *CM* is silent, and Peter Riga's *Aurora* and Comestor's *HS* give no more than the biblical enumerations.
7693	*lygh als levyn.* K rightly notes this to be an *epitheton ornans* (5:55), a line-filling rhetorical epithet that perhaps owes something to the role of the Levites in the priesthood (though the precise connection is unclear). Alternatively, the phrase could be a description of the speed by which the Levites were counted, a usage that may be paralleled in the counting of the people of Zebulon in line 7703.
7741–54	*The folke within . . . this sotelty . . . done in dyspytt.* The story reported here is an expansion and explanation of the Jebusites' boast to David in 2 Kings (2 Samuel) 5:6: "Thou shalt not come in hither unless thou take away the blind and the lame that say: David shall not come in hither." This obscure reference has been subject to much interpretation, the one apparently known to the *Paraphrase*-poet relating ultimately to the explanation from Josephus (via *HS*), who explained that even the blind and lame could defend Jerusalem's walls due to their excellent design. The Jebusites' ruse, then, is that David's army will see the blind and lame guarding the walls and despair at the confidence of the inhabitants.
7763–64	*Tho that wore maysturs most / had takyn a towr for strengh.* That the capture of Jerusalem occurred in two stages — first, the taking of the city itself and, second, the taking of a tower within the city where stalwart defenders had holed up — comes not from the Bible. 2 Kings (2 Samuel) 5:6–8 presents the taking of Jerusalem in short fashion, with few details beyond the Jebusites' boast involving blind men (see note to lines 7741–54, above), and the parallel account of the event in 1 Chronicles 11:4–6 is similarly sparse on details, though it adds in the fact of David's challenge to his men (see note to lines 7769–88, below). The two-stage scenario may rather owe something to the commonplace of the tower of Sion within Jerusalem. See, for instance, *Hali*

Meithhad, where this tower represents virginity; Millett notes that the description in that text of Sion as "a tower" (*tur*), follows "the traditional (though inadmissable) etymology of *Sion* as *specula* 'watch-tower'" (*Hali Meiþhad*, ed. Millett, p. 26n2/5). The image of Sion as Jerusalem's tower, however, is no doubt older in origin. Vulgate Psalm 75:3 records that God's "place" is in Salem, an early name for Jerusalem, while his "home" is Sion, and 1 Chronicles 11:5 comes close to a distinction between the city and the citadel within when it says that "David took the castle of Sion, which is the city of David," i.e., Jerusalem. The longest of Jerusalem's hills, and the city's highest point, is thus known as the Mount of Sion, itself able to function metaphorically as the "high tower" from which so much can be seen. Aside from such biblical exegesis, however, one wonders if these depictions of a tower within the city — especially as in the present case, where the tower represents the final stage of defense for the besieged city — owe much to the strands of history and legend surrounding the siege and destruction of Jerusalem in 70 CE. In that famous event, the city was indeed taken in stages, one of the hardest of which was the towerlike Fortress Antonia (see *Siege of Jerusalem*, ed. Livingston, pp. 4–5). Perhaps the 1099 siege of Jerusalem in the First Crusade might well be of note, too, since while the Romans took the city proper in one massive assault after the walls were breached, the Muslim governor was able to maintain control over the Tower of David, a medieval citadel, until he was granted free leave out of the city by the victorious crusaders.

7769–88   David's challenge to his men comes not from 2 Kings (2 Samuel), but from the retelling of the event in 1 Chronicles 11:4–6, though the biblical challenge is for the first man to kill a Jebusite whereas here it is for the first man to enter the besieged tower.

7791   *The folke then namyd yt David Towre.* See note to lines 7763–64, above.

7835–36   *A wyfe bare Absolon / and his suster Thamar.* Absalom and Tamar are not mentioned in the list of children born to David in Jerusalem that appears at this point in the Bible (2 Kings [2 Samuel] 5:13–16; so, too, *HS* 2 Reg. 7 [1329]). Rather, Absalom is mentioned in the earlier list of children born to him in Hebron (3:2–5), briefly told here in lines 7499–7500, and Tamar is named first at 2 Kings (2 Samuel) 13:1, at the beginning of the lengthy sequence involving her and her brother Absalom and half-brother Amnon. Their appearance here in the course of the narrative is surely due to their prominent roles to come.

7917–20   *This lesson wyll us lere: / non suld neght howled thyng / Bot thei that have power / grauntyd of Goddes gyfyng.* The lesson is vaguely like that which Comestor attributes to Josephus: "Dicit Josephus eum percussum, quia tetigit arcam cum sacerdos non esset" (*HS* 2 Reg. 9 [1330]). The additional weight given to the *exemplum*, however, might well be appropriate to the late medieval struggles over the priesthood in the poet's contemporary surrounds.

8030–36   The treatment of David's messengers is one that is picked up in a number of contemporary poems, including *Siege of Jerusalem* (lines 357–74) and *The Alliterative Morte Arthure* (lines 2330–70).

8105   *I wott full well.* David does, indeed, know her loneliness full well, his statement a self-incrimination before the very man he has made a cuckold.

8114   *his wyfe to glose.* The use of the verb *glosen* here is interesting. The term typically means to gloss something (commonly a text) or to flatter a person, but the implication here is undoubtedly sexual, as if to beget a new meaning. David hopes that Uriah can *glose* Bathsheba, thus creating the illusion that David's child is actually Uriah's. This sexual allusion will remind readers of the several uses of the word in Chaucer, particularly the Wife of Bath's statement about her fifth husband, that "So wel koude he me glose / Whan that he wolde han my *bele chose*" (*CT* III[D]509–10), where the implication is more of performance than mere flattery or coaxing.

8225–32   That David's response to God's announcement of punishment is to compose psalms is a detail recorded in neither the Bible at this point nor in *HS*. It does, as K notes (1:clxxxvii), match *OFP* 125c. Though there are three psalms that begin *Miserere mei Deus* (line 8225) — Vulgate Psalms 50, 55, and 56 — the specific psalm referred to here is no doubt the first of these, which is so often used in Church liturgy and music as to be referred to often as simply "the Miserere." This psalm, the fourth of the so-called penitential psalms, has traditionally been tied to David's confession of his sin with Bathsheba (see Vulgate Psalm 50:1), an association that appears in even the earliest Greek and Hebrew records and surely functions as the source for its incorporation into the narrative here.

8245–48   *He dyde away his garmentes gud, / and in a seke he sett hym down. / He weped . . . and kest powder apon his crown.* The specifics of David's behavior are given in 2 Kings (2 Samuel) 12:16–20 as a refusal to change clothes and the undertaking of a solitary fast. The further details here — a casting away of garments in order to sit in sackcloth and ashes — are traditionally attributed to the scene as a result of the proverbial nature of such a penitential act (see, e.g., Daniel 9:3, Judith 4:15, and Esther 4:1).

8271   *fawt of fode.* As 2 Kings (2 Samuel) 12:26 relates, the vital lack is not that of food but of water.

8281–83   *Anon, the kyng of Amonys . . . His crown.* The crown, according to 2 Kings (2 Samuel) 12:30, is not from the head of Ammon but from the (presumably statuary) head of Milcom, the god of the Ammonites (see also 4 Kings [2 Kings] 11:5).

8333–34   *Then wysed he all his men away / and bad them spere all as thei yede.* That Amnon orders his men to bar the doors behind them as they leave, effectively locking him and his sister into his bedroom, is not biblical. The locking of the doors does, however, add a chilling precognition to Amnon's plan: he *expects* that he will resort to rape — a fact confirmed by his awareness, in line 8361, that "all was sperd" for him to take her by force.

8343–60   The biblical account of Tamar's reaction to Amnon's desires (2 Kings [2 Samuel] 13:12–13) is substantially different. There, Tamar complains that it would be shameful for Amnon to rape her, especially when they can, as only half-siblings, rightfully marry (a practice only later forbidden it seems; see Leviticus 18:9). Tamar therefore suggests that Amnon present his suit to David. We get none of this in the *Paraphrase*, however, where the poet omits any chance whatsoever of a proper union between the half-siblings and instead presents a deeply frightened but nevertheless remarkably calm Tamar chastising Amnon in the manner of a preacher or confessor, advising him to throw the intent of his heart to Heaven, to ask God's forgiveness for such evil thoughts. She says, too, that she would rather lose her inheritance and be exiled from her homeland than to have sex with him. Tamar's simultaneous roles as victim and counselor, and her resolute determination to remain a virgin no matter the cost, no doubt owe much to hagiographical traditions, where such behavior is often the norm with many female saints and martyrs.

8393   *So all this stryfe was haldyn styll.* Following *HS* 2 Reg. 14 (1335), the *Paraphrase*-poet omits a substantial subtext to the biblical account of this story: David's knowledge. 2 Kings (2 Samuel) 13:21 makes clear that David learns about the rape almost immediately, yet he does nothing to punish Amnon. The poet, we might assume, is not satisfied with the rather soiled image of David thus painted, and so he falls silent on the question of David's knowledge (indeed, he does not even indicate that David learns about the tragedy after Amnon's murder).

8439   *Jessor with the kyng of Cirre.* That Talmai, king of Geshur, is also thereby king of Syria is an association not made at this point in the Bible or in *HS*. We later learn that Geshur is an Aramean kingdom (see 2 Kings [2 Samuel] 15:8]), but not the identification of Aram with Syria.

8440   *his syb man on his moyder syde.* Absalom's kinship with Talmai, the king of Geshur — Talmai is his grandfather through Absalom's mother Maacah — is not mentioned at this point of the Bible but earlier, at 2 Kings (2 Samuel) 3:3.

8493–94   *Then ware thei frendes fast, / the kyng and Absolon.* According to 2 Kings (2 Samuel) 14:24 David ordered Joab to retrieve Absalom to Jerusalem and to "let him return into his house" but "let him not see my face." While these biblical facts are followed in *HS* (2 Reg. 14 [1336]), the *Paraphrase*-poet again seems at pains to clear away any stain on David's reputation in this sordid family affair.

8497–8504   *DBTEL* observes that of all the potential responses to Absalom and his life, medieval writers seem most preoccupied with his beauty; thus "Absalom's name appears frequently in the interminable lists of *Ubi sunt?* poems, a popular poetic form emphasizing the transitoriness of life and the fragility of beauty" (p. 12). This concentration on Absalom's physical appearance,

	especially his luxurious hair, led to Absalom becoming "a type of feminine beauty." Nowhere is this perhaps more evident than in Chaucer's Prologue to *The Legend of Good Women* (F.249, G.203), where Absalom is the first name listed in his balade cataloguing beautiful women (see also his characterization of Absolon in The Miller's Tale).
8501	*Of twenty libri wegh was his hare.* This weight corresponds to *OFP* 67d ("vint livres"), whereas both 2 Kings (2 Samuel) 14:26 and *HS* 2 Reg. 14 (1336) give the weight as two hundred shekels (Ohlander, "Old French Parallels," p. 218). Two hundred shekels, according to Josephus (*Jewish Antiquities* 7.8.5), would equate to five pounds.
8507–08	*and he ware oght greved, / then was he fell os fyre.* In these two lines the poet alludes to the whole of 2 Kings (2 Samuel) 14:28–33, which describes how Absalom, after living two years in Jerusalem under a sort of house arrest (see note to lines 8493–94), summons Joab to argue his case before the king. When Joab twice fails to come to Absalom, Absalom orders his servants to set fire to Joab's fields. The conflagration stirs Joab's attention, and he at last manages to reconcile Absalom and David.
8517	*be faur yeres ware past.* 2 Kings (2 Samuel) 15:7 reads forty years in the Hebrew and the Vulgate, whereas the *Paraphrase* follows the Septuagint and Josephus, *Jewish Antiquities* 7.9.1, in reading four years. *HS* 2 Reg. 15 (1337) notes the discrepancy, and Ohlander observes that *OFP* parallels the *Paraphrase* here, too ("Old French Parallels," p. 218).
8546	*knyght, swyer, knave, and page.* There is, of course, no biblical parallel for such a list, which is clearly medieval.
8657–60	*Bot aftur sone, os men may rede, / this grome . . . Be David dome . . . lost his lyf, yf yt ware late.* Though David refuses to react to Shimei's insults at this time, and he will later swear not to kill Shimei (see 2 Kings [2 Samuel] 19:18–23), his dying words, it seems, are to instruct his son and heir Solomon to at last be avenged upon him (see 3 Kings [1 Kings] 2:8–9, 36–46).
8687–88	*That Natan told before / bud unto end be broght.* Though *HS* 2 Reg. 16 (1338) does not make this association, the poet follows the tradition that identifies the "neighbor" of Nathan's pronouncement in 2 Kings (2 Samuel) 12:11 as Absalom, whose family comes from a neighboring land (see Josephus, *Jewish Antiquities* 7.9.5).
8717	*Take me ten thowsand men of myght.* This does not match the number as given in the Bible or in *HS*, both of which record 12,000. A parallel can be found, as K notes (1:clxxxvii), in *OFP*; and Josephus, *Jewish Antiquities* 7.9.6 also puts the number at 10,000.
8783–84	*Ne thei dowt no dele / for gune ne grett ingyne.* The poet's depiction of siege warfare is once again anachronistically medieval.

8787   *Faur barons wuned ther besyde.* 2 Kings (2 Samuel) 17:27 gives three aides, naming all three. That there were four men, barons all, corresponds to *OFP* 70a (Ohlander, "Old French Parallels," pp. 218–19).

8792   *faur thowsand.* The size of David's army is not given in the Bible. The *Paraphrase* here fits with Josephus' description of the size (*Jewish Antiquities* 7.10.1), but it conflicts with *HS* 2 Reg. 18 (1339), which reports that it is seven thousand strong. It is difficult to know whether this is firm evidence of the poet's direct use of Josephus or simply a scribal error in which the numeral for four has been introduced by scribal eye-skip from line 8787.

8828   *I hope thei held all that thei hette.* A rare interjection on the part of the poet, who seems swept up in the narrative himself.

8849–50   *The wynd heyved up his hare on hyght / so that yt cached into a tre.* 2 Kings (2 Samuel) 18:9 says only that Absalom's head was caught in the branches of an oak, but the *Paraphrase* follows a very old tradition (see, e.g., Josephus, *Jewish Antiquities* 7.10.2), building on the description of Absalom in 14:26, that he was caught by his hair.

8851   *His sted.* 2 Kings (2 Samuel) 18:9 places Absalom upon a mule, a detail supported by *HS* 2 Reg. 17 (1339). Both the *Paraphrase* and *OFP* (70c) place him upon the far more knightly horse (Ohlander, "Old French Parallels," p. 219).

8859–60   *He bede a boy fyfty schylyng / to sla hym.* The payment is in accordance with *OFP* 70d (Ohlander, "Old French Parallels," p. 219) and Josephus, *Jewish Antiquities* 7.10.2. 2 Kings (2 Samuel) 18:11 places the price at "ten sicles [shekels] of silver and a belt."

8879–80   *And hedyd was Amon / for Thamar.* The recollection of Absalom's beheading of his half-brother for Tamar's rape effectively sums up Absalom's life.

8943   *A bryg full wysly have thei wroyt.* 2 Kings (2 Samuel) 19:18 gives no impression of a bridge. Indeed, the Vulgate explicitly refers to David crossing a ford in the Jordan. The Septuagint refers to a ferry built by the Benjaminites that carries the king across the river. The *Paraphrase* here follows *HS* 2 Reg. 18 (1340), which is itself probably derived from Josephus, *Jewish Antiquities* 7.2, who describes a crossing made on a bridge of boats.

8971   *Joab wold full fayn have hym aflayd.* In 2 Kings (2 Samuel) 19:21 and *HS* 2 Reg. 18 it is Joab's brother Abishai who desires to wreak vengeance upon Shimei; the alteration here might be the result of the poet's efforts to simplify the biblical narrative by streamlining characters whenever possible.

9025–26   *Syr Cyba, that I of ayre sayd, / was lord of Myfbosett land.* Ohlander was the first to realize that the *Paraphrase*-poet is here guilty of "a remarkable confusion of persons" ("Old French Parallels," p. 221). The present man, who rebels against David's rule, is Sheba, the son of Bochri, a Benjaminite (2 Kings [2 Samuel] 20:1). The earlier man with whom the poet has mingled Sheba's identity (first noted at line 2621) is Ziba, a man who was first a servant of Saul and later became the steward of Mephibosheth (2 Kings [2 Samuel] 9:2–13).

The Bible is clear in delineating the identities of the two men, as are *HS* and *OFP*. The poet's confusion is no doubt the result of their names being both very similar in Latin (Siba and Seba) and identical in Old French (Siba).

9137   *A lady*. 2 Kings (2 Samuel) 20:16 identifies her as a "wise woman."

9187   *Natan the prophett*. In both the Bible (2 Kings [2 Samuel] 21:1) and *HS* (2 Reg. 20 [1342]) David receives his answer directly from God. Whether the poet derives this unique detail from another unknown source, or makes the alteration for other reasons — perhaps to reinforce the necessity of the priesthood, for instance — is unknown.

9189   *Duke Josue*. Joshua first made contact with the people of Gibeon in Joshua 9:3–27.

9222   *gud wone*. 2 Kings [2 Samuel] 21:6–9 specifies that only seven of Saul's male heirs were handed over to the Gibeonites, a detail repeated in *HS*.

9233–34   *Diligam te, Domine, / this salme he sett and sayd yt fast*. This is Vulgate Psalm 17. Both *HS* 2 Reg. 21 (1343) and *OFP* 74b provide the Latin title.

9258   *fyfty milia rekynd ryght*. This number is tenfold shy of both the Bible (2 Kings [2 Samuel] 24:9) and *HS* (2 Reg. 23 [1345]), both of which record 500,000. A parallel, as K notes once again (1:clxxxviii), is *OFP*.

9273–76   *HS* 2 Reg. 23 (1346) and *OFP* 75a both follow 2 Kings (2 Samuel) 24:13 in giving the choice between seven years of famine, three months of war, or three days of pestilence. The *Paraphrase*-poet has the choice between seven years of war, three years of famine, and three days of pestilence. I know of no source for this change.

9319–24   2 Kings (2 Samuel) 24:18 labels the site of David's altar only as the threshing-floor of Araunah the Jebusite. *HS* 2 Reg. 23 (1346) follows Josephus (*Jewish Antiquities* 7.13.4) in making the further association of the site with the hill whereupon Abraham offered up his son Isaac. The final connection of the location with Mount Calvary is found in the French tradition; e.g., *OFP* 75b (Ohlander, "Old French Parallels," pp. 221–22).

9337–9625   The poet subsumes the final events of David's reign, which are told in the first chapters of 3 Kings (1 Kings) into his paraphrase of 2 Kings (2 Samuel). This makes a clear and logical sense, and actually follows the division of books in Josephus' *Jewish Antiquities* 7–8, though whether the poet would have access to this fact is subject to question. See also the explanatory note to lines 9469–9618, below.

9386   *Naomy*. According to all known sources, this should be Benaiah the son of Joiada, as it is in *OFP* 76c.

9422   *well that is named Wyon*. That Gihon was a principal source of water for Jerusalem is a detail found in 2 Chronicles 32:30.

9469–9618   The death of David, in which he names his son Solomon as his sole heir and entrusts his care to the lords of the land, is greatly expanded from its biblical source, 3 Kings (1 Kings) 1–2. Both its displacement to the end of 2 Kings and its expansion to this very medieval, feudal setting, is in accordance with *OFP* (Ohlander, "Old French Parallels," p. 222).

9611   *Begynnyng, myddes, and ende.* The poet clearly thinks of his presentation of the life of David as a narrative unit, a tale of the triumphs and woes of kingship.

THIRD BOOK OF KINGS

9680   K notes comparison with *Genesis and Exodus*, lines 1425–26: "Siðen men auen holden skil, / first to freinen ðe wimmanes will" (*Story of Genesis and Exodus*, ed. Morris).

9714   *heldyd.* See the note to line 9986.

9734   *Ebron.* As K notes, 3 Kings (1 Kings) 3:4 and *HS* 3 Reg. 5 (1351) call the place Gibeon, whereas Hebron appears in *OFP* 79c. This alternative location is mentioned in *HS* as being that given by Josephus, which is true (*Jewish Antiquities* 8.2.1).

9783, 86   *delyver . . . delyver.* In both cases, the word is being used as an adjective. K notes a parallel in *Purity*, line 1084.

9821–22   *Thei say, "Yt wele is sene this tyd / of a new kyng a new comyn case."* K calls attention to *OFP* 80b, which reads: "sa gent se gabent, se jurent lur lei: "ceste semble agard ("decision") de jovene rei." Compare lines 9829–40.

9849–52   K notes to compare *HS* 3 Reg. 7 (1352): "admirati sunt assessores ejus, qui prius sententiam, quasi ab adolescente prolatam deridebant."

9883   *Fawr thowssand yeres fyfty and fyve.* 3 Kings (1 Kings) 6:1 dates the start of the building to 480 years after the Exodus (440 years in the Septuagint), though *HS* 3 Reg. 9 (1354) notes that Josephus gives a different date, including the fact that from the creation of Adam 3,102 years had passed (compare *Jewish Antiquities* 8.3.1). The number of years here, 4,455, might, as K observes, be compared to *OFP* (see Baker, *Die versifizierte Übersetzung*, p. 37).

9893   *The suteltes of science sevyn.* K notes the similarity to *Seven Sages*, line 48 (in Weber, *Metrical Romances*, 3:5): "The suteltè of science seuyn." The seven sciences are the seven liberal arts that were the mainstay of a medieval education. These seven areas of learning were divided into the trivium — grammar, rhetoric, and dialectic (also sometimes called logic) — and the quadrivium — music, mathematics, geometry, astronomy.

9951   *Synophogy.* "The Feast of Tabernacles." Compare Leviticus 23:33, Numbers 29:12, 1 Kings 8:65, and 2 Chronicles 7:8, as well as *HS* 3 Reg. 21 (1366–67).

9961–63   *Another hows then ordand he . . . mad in yeres thre.* The sequence here is not biblical, which presents the details of Solomon's house between those about the Temple and its dedication, but it corresponds to that in many sources, such as Josephus and *HS*.

9963   *yeres thre*. According to 3 Kings (1 Kings) 7:1, Solomon's palace was thirteen years in the making, not three. I have found no source for the lower number and can only speculate either scribal contamination or, as a distant possibility, the poet's interest in having Solomon spend fewer years on his palace than were spent on the Temple (seven). In the latter case, the numerology of the figures used could come into play.

9974   K notes a parallel usage of this use of "reason" in *Purity*, line 194.

9986   *held*. From OE *heldan*, meaning "to incline or bow." K notes (3:17) that the "associative influence from *hold* is suggested by *with* for normal *(un)to*," and compares lines 1194 (which K, 1:lxviii, had wrongly defined as "hold"), 1412, 9714, and 10121.

9988   *fyrth*. K notes (3:17) comparison with lines 7866 and 8854.

10037–40   *God was greved . . . And sent the prophet Achyas / to warn hym*. In 1 Kings (3 Kings) 11:11–13 God directly rebukes Solomon; here, in accordance with *HS* 3 Reg. 27 (1371), it is God's prophet who delivers God's condemnation, a scene brought forward from Ahijah's encounter with Jeroboam on the road (1 Kings [3 Kings] 11:29–39).

10161–63   *Faur score . . . nyne score yere and faur*. 3 Kings 11:42 and 2 Chronicles 9:30 record Solomon's reign as lasting forty years, as does *HS* 3 Reg. 27 (1371), which also states that the length of Solomon's life is ninety-four years. Josephus, in *Jewish Antiquities* 8.7.8, gives the numbers as eighty and ninety-four, respectively, as does *OFP* 85d. It would seem, therefore, that either *score*, in this poet's hands, unique in Middle English, means "ten" rather than "twenty"; or, more likely, the *score* of line 10163 is a scribal error.

10317–452   Beginning here the poet moves far from the 3 Kings (1 Kings) narrative to tell the story of Rehoboam, about whom little is said in that book or in *HS*; the details here derive from 2 Chronicles 11–12. The sequence of the narrative is likewise distant from the Bible and *HS*. In both these characteristics he follows Josephus, *Jewish Antiquities* 8.10, though presumably the poet's immediate source is *OFP*.

10317   *Aght milia knyghtes kene*. 2 Chronicles 11:1 reports 180,000 rather than 8,000; Josephus says "many ten thousand men" (*Jewish Antiquities* 8.10.1).

10330   *other thryty and one*. 2 Chronicles 11:21 gives the number of other concubines as sixty; Josephus, *Jewish Antiquities* 8.10.1, claims thirty, as does *HS* 3 Reg. 30 (1375) and *OFP* 87b.

10331–32   *Thamar, / the doyghtur of Absolon*. The syntax here is difficult, since the meaning must be "the daughter of Tamar by Absolom," a woman named Maacah (compare 2 Chronicles 11:20–21 and *HS* 3 Reg. 31 [1375]). 3 Kings (1 Kings) 15:2 also gives the wife's name as Maacah but says nothing of this ancestry, instead calling her simply the daughter of Abishalom. We find the same apparent error in *OFP* 87b. If someone has mistaken the name of Maacah for Tamar, it may well be due to *HS*, which reads "nomen matris ejus

Maacha, filia Thamar, filiae Abessalon," and thus could easily have been corrupted by eye-skip.

10371–76   *A mille charyottes had he . . . And knyghtes . . . sexty milia . . . And folke on fote . . . faurty milia.* 2 Chronicles 12:3 cites 1,200 chariots, 60,000 cavalry ("knights"), and countless infantry. Josephus, *Jewish Antiquities* 8.10.2, numbers the footmen as 400,000. *OFP* 87c follows the Bible up to the numbering of the footmen, which are, as in *Paraphrase*, accounted to be 40,000. The origin of the *Paraphrase*-poet's specific sequence of numbers is thus unknown.

10443–45   *In aghtene yeres his lordschep last . . . fyfty yeres.* According to 3 Kings (1 Kings) 14:21, 2 Chronicles 12:13, and Josephus, *Jewish Antiquties* 8.10.4, Rehoboam's reign lasted seventeen, not eighteen, years. *HS* 3 Reg. 30 (1374) gives the number of years as twenty-six. In addition, these sources agree that Rehoboam took the throne at the age of forty-one, leaving his age at his death as either fifty-eight or, in *HS*, sixty-seven. We find the same numbers as the *Paraphrase* in *OFP* 88c.

10633–56   That the false prophet knows his fault and the truth of God's prophet yet nevertheless works to convince Jeroboam that he should rebuild the altar and thus continue to provoke God's wrath is contrary to 3 Kings (1 Kings) 13:33 and *HS* 3 Reg. 29 (1374), which places guilt upon Jeroboam alone, not on the further machinations of the false prophet. For the tradition followed here, see Josephus, *Jewish Antiquities* 9.1.

10669–728 As with the story of Rehoboam (see note to lines 10317–452, above), the poet makes heavy use of 2 Chronicles to tell the story of Jeroboam's war against Abijah, which is only given passing reference in 1 Kings (3 Kings) and *HS*.

10679–80   *He had at his ledyng / fayr folke fawrty thowssand.* According to 2 Chronicles 13:3, Abijah's army numbered 400,000. So, too, Josephus, *Jewish Antiquities* 8.11.2. The number here also appears in *OFP* 89d, however.

10726   *fyve thowssand sloyn.* 2 Chronicles 13:17 numbers the fallen as 500,000. So, too, Josephus, *Jewish Antiquities* 8.11.3.

10747   *Thre yere.* So *OFP* 90a. 3 Kings (1 Kings) 15:25 states that Nadab ruled two years, as does Josephus, *Jewish Antiquities* 8.11.4, and *HS* 3 Reg. 32 (1376).

10761–64   *Thas that in towns war dede / howndes laped ther blode. / That dyed in other sted / ware leved to foyles fode.* The gruesome specificity of the murder of Jeroboam's family comes not from the Bible or *HS* but from Josephus, *Jewish Antiquities* 8.11.4.

10823–24   *kyng of Matenours, / Benedab by name.* S gives his name, here and elsewhere, as *Amynadab.* Compare 3 Kings (1 Kings) 15:18 and 2 Chronicles 16:2, where Ben-hadad is the king of Syria. *HS* 3 Reg. 32 (1376) reads "Benadad regem Syriæ," and *OFP* 91a has the similar "Benadab"; so the origin of S's *Amynadab* is unclear. The *Paraphrase*-poet does seem indebted to something like *OFP* in replacing "Syria" or "Damascus" with *Matenours* (the reading in both S and L): *OFP* introduces him as king of "Mascedonurs," a reference I can find nowhere else.

10847–48   *He byged yt wele and fayre / with store that he thore fand.* This stands contrary to
           3 Kings (1 Kings) 15:22 (and Josephus and *HS*), which clearly states that,
           rather than finishing Baasha's fortification of Ramah, Asa razed the con-
           structions and used the materials to build Geba and Mizpah.

10859   *Agary.* 3 Kings (1 Kings) 16:9 calls him Zimri, as does Josephus, *Jewish Antiqui-
           ties* 8.12.4, and *HS* 3 Reg. 32 (1377). The source for the *Paraphrase* here ap-
           pears to be *OFP* 91a: "Edementers le trahi azarie, un son ebreu, si li toli la vie"
           — though where *OFP* derived this unique form of his name remains unknown.

10966   *Tyre.* Compare 3 Kings (1 Kings) 16:31, or *HS* 3 Reg. 34 (1378), where he
           is simply king of the Zidonians. Our poet is here following the *OFP* 91d: "la
           fille al rei de tir e de sydun" — though this connection between Tyre and
           Sidon is made clear earlier in 3 Kings (1 Kings) 5:1–6.

11365–11460 In the Bible (3 Kings [1 Kings] 20–21), the Naboth episode follows the siege
           of Samaria, whereas here it precedes it. *HS* 3 Reg. 37–39 (1381–86) follows
           the Bible. The change is in accordance with *OFP* (see Bonnard, *Les Tradu-
           ctions de la Bible*, p. 102) and in line with Josephus, *Jewish Antiquities* 8.13.7–8.

11502   *Chylder.* While the primary meaning of the word, "children," cannot be wholly
           discounted here — it would almost certainly call up images of the so-called
           Children's Crusade of 1212 — it is more likely that a secondary use of the
           term, meaning "youth in service" is meant here (*MED child*, n.5b). This latter
           option would be consistent with 3 Kings (1 Kings) 20:14, which calls them
           "servants of the princes of the provinces" (so, too, *HS* 3 Reg. 37 [1382]).

11506   *faur hunderth.* 3 Kings (1 Kings) 20:15 gives the number of servants as 232,
           as do Josephus, *Jewish Antiquities* 8.14.2, *HS* 3 Reg. 37 (1382), and *OFP* 94c.

11513   *Fyve thowsand.* That 5,000 were slain is not recorded in either the biblical
           source (3 Kings [1 Kings] 20:20–21) or *HS* 3 Reg. 37 (1382). K notes (3:59)
           that the number derives from *OFP* 94c: "Si unt Ebreu plus de cinc mile ocis."

11545   *A hunderth thowssand and wele mo.* The *wele mo* includes, as related in 3 Kings
           (1 Kings) 20:29, 27,000 men killed when the wall falls upon them. *HS* 3 Reg.
           38 (1383) omits this detail, as does *OFP* 94d.

11589   *A prophett, Machias.* 3 Kings (1 Kings) 20:35 does not name the prophet,
           though Micaiah's subsequent antagonistic appearance at 22:8 might well
           explain his association with this earlier prophet. This identification appears
           in *HS* 3 Reg. 38 (1383), but it goes back to Josephus, *Jewish Antiquities* 8.14.5.

11650   *In preson he dyd hym cast.* Ahab takes no such action to the unnamed prophet
           in 3 Kings (1 Kings) 20:43. The response to imprison him appears in Jose-
           phus, *Jewish Antiquities* 8.14.5, and thereafter in *HS* 3 Reg. 38 (1383), pro-
           bably coinciding with the king's response to Micaiah's predictions of failure
           at 22:26–28.

11670   *Godely.* See 4 Kings (2 Kings) 8:18, 26 and 2 Chronicles 21:6, 22:2, where
           she is called "Athaliah," as she is in *HS* 3 Reg. 39 (1384). Nevertheless, the
           Paraphrase-poet follows *OFP* in consistently terming her "Godolie."

11733–44   *I sall hym stryke in the face . . . and he stroke hym with all his mayn.* This test by
            striking is far different than 3 Kings (1 Kings) 22:24–25 and *HS* 3 Reg. 39
            (1385), though it is that presented by Josephus, *Jewish Antiquities* 8.15.5.

11745–52   This digression on the paradoxical failure and success of testing a prophet
            appears to be unique to the *Paraphrase*. Not even Josephus, who appears to
            be the ultimate source for this particular test (see note to lines 11733–44,
            above), bothers to address the issue.

FOURTH BOOK OF KINGS

11913–16   The poet is probably thinking of Romans 15:4, though similar statements
            by Paul can be found in 1 Corinthians 9:9 and 2 Timothy 3:16.

12001–02   *Thore in that cyté wonned a man / that Moyses Law wold never lett.* In 4 Kings (2
            Kings) 1:13, the third individual sent to fetch Elijah is not, as here, a loyal
            Jew sent alone. Rather, he is another captain, leading a third company of
            fifty men. The poet's source for this change is unknown.

12006   *within his sell whore he was sett.* The Bible specifically describes Elijah as sitting
            atop a hill (4 Kings [2 Kings] 1:9), a location followed by *HS* 4 Reg. 1 (1387).
            The poet's alteration from hilltop to a cell — a small, secluded dwelling —
            brings Elijah into the hagiographic tradition of hermit saints living in soli-
            tude in the wilderness.

12053–55   Enoch and Elijah, both taken up by God without dying (for the account of
            the former, see Genesis 5:22–24), were the source of much postbiblical com-
            mentary, especially among Christian writers who could not rationalize ad-
            mittance to Heaven without acceptance of Christ as God — an impossibility
            for two men who lived long before the birth of Jesus of Nazareth. These wri-
            ters eventually came to agreement that the two men had been transported
            to the Earthly Paradise where they awaited Christ's Second Coming. As early
            as the time of Justin Martyr in the second century, Enoch and Elijah were
            thus identified as the Two Witnesses of Apocalypse, two mysterious figures
            who will appear at the end-times to witness for Christ in the final battle
            against the Antichrist. This identification grew more secure in the Middle
            Ages; it is accepted essentially as dogma, for instance, in the twelfth-century
            Glossa Ordinaria. Building out of Apocalypse 11:3–13, it was said in these tra-
            ditions that during the Apocalypse Enoch and Elijah would preach against
            the Antichrist and convert the Jews; the Antichrist would then kill the two wit-
            nesses, who would willingly offer up their lives so that they could participate
            fully in the love of Christ by being resurrected into their "purified" forms. It
            was thought that they would, indeed, be resurrected three and a half days
            later, and thereafter taken into Heaven just prior to the Second Coming.
            Though reference to this legend is not made in *HS*, the stories of Enoch and
            Elijah were very much a part of the Middle English literary landscape, ap-
            pearing in works as widespread as *CM* and *The Pricke of Conscience* to perfor-

mative works like the mystery plays (see especially *Chester*'s "Harrowing of Hell," "Prophecies of Antichrist," and "Antichrist" plays).

12072　　　*two hunderth shepe be yere*. 4 Kings (2 Kings) 3:4 and *HS* 4 Reg. 4 (1388) both number the tribute as 200,000 sheep in total. This much smaller (and, frankly, more realistic) number also appears in *OFP* 98a.

12129–32　　Similar comments about the identical names but separate identities of the kings of Israel and Judah at this point in the narrative occur in *HS* 4 Reg. 1 (1387) and *OFP* 98d.

12134　　　*Godolé*. See note to line 11670.

12158　　　*my husband . . . Obedias*. The husband is not named in the Bible (4 Kings [2 Kings] 4), but compare 3 Kings (1 Kings) 18:3 and stanza 927. *HS* 4 Reg. 5 (1389), gives the name here: "uxor scilicet Abdiæ," an identification also found in *OFP* 99a: "Femme ert Obedias et sa muiller." These identifications appear to derive ultimately from Josephus, *Jewish Antiquities* 9.4.2.

12174–75　　*my sun that is full fayr and free, / Thei say thei sall have hym forfett*. In 4 Kings (2 Kings) 4:1, the widow is threatened with the taking of two children into slavery, not one. So, too, *HS* 4 Reg. 5 (1389).

12355　　　*flesch*. K suggests that in order to maintain the rhyme *flesch* should be pronounced "fless," as if *sch* = *s* (1:cxxviii). The end-rhyme would thus be only orthographically broken, perhaps evidence that the text of this Yorkshire poem (where –*sh* appears as –*s*; see, e.g., *Joas* for *Joash* in line 13619) has passed through more southern scribal hands. Note, however, that the current text is consistent in its presentation of *flesch(e)* in all positions, even appearing to demand an –*sh* pronunciation for rhyme at lines 12046, 48 (*flesch* : *fresch*). Another explanation, therefore, might be that the palatization of *s* to *sh* is underway in the poet's own dialect, in which case the present line may simply be an off-rhyme.

12479–80　　*Thus may men lyghtly lere / forto trow wemens tales*. Naaman's conclusion that his experience can serve as a pedagogical exercise for all men who might think to believe the words of women is neither biblical nor from Comestor (*HS* 4 Reg. 8 [1391]). It appears the *Paraphrase*-poet has instead added this embellishment to further underscore the positive actions of Naaman's loyal Israelite serving-girl, whose central role in revealing God's power to the Aramean otherwise goes largely unnoted.

12679–80　　In 4 Kings (2 Kings) 6:6, the axhead is retrieved when Elisha throws a stick into the water, which miraculously causes the iron to float. So, too, *HS* 4 Reg. 9 (1392). Compare *OFP* 102a.

12761–64　　*Then forto loke he led his knave . . . for baners and for basnettes bryght*. These lines are difficult to construe, even more difficult to get to match the biblical source. In 4 Kings (2 Kings) 6:16–17, the theme of vision in this story is underscored in the fact that the servant is pointedly unable to see Elisha's army until the prophet prays that his eyes be opened. Only then is the army revealed: made up of horses and chariots of fire (an image hearkening back to the taking of Elijah into Heaven).

12802   *thei wend all had bene feld*. The appearance of *feld* here, echoing back to line 12734 and the plan to assassinate Elisha, serves as a further marker of divine justice: the Arameans have, both narratively and orthographically, had the tables turned on them.

12821   *Sauns fayle*. While it is true that this particular French expression, and a few others like it, had by the time of the composition of the *Paraphrase* become common in English, it is hard not to wonder if there might not be subtle political points being made in its usage. The only other appearance of the phrase in the poem is at line 8721, where it is spoken by Absolom.

12929–32   *The prophett that wyll noyght for us pray . . . sall be done to dede this day / for all the tales that he has told*. 4 Kings (2 Kings) 6:31 gives no explanation why the king's wrath turns against Elisha, but Josephus comments that this is because Elisha failed to "pray to God to provide them some exit and way of escape out of the miseries with which they were surrounded" (*Jewish Antiquities* 9.4.3), a detail picked up by Comestor. The blameworthy *tales* Elisha *has told* (line 12932) would thus seem to be either his statements of being both in God's favor and in favor of Israel, or, sarcastically, his lack of words before God.

13002   *Arabys*. The poet thus replaces the Hittites of 4 Kings (2 Kings) 7:6, who would be unfamiliar to his audience.

13035   *spyre and spye*. K (3:102) notes the same phrase in *Gawain*, line 2093.

13075   *Evyn in the entryng was he slayn*. Implied here, but specified in 4 Kings (2 Kings) 7:20 and *HS* 4 Reg. 11 (1394), is the detail that the unbeliever is trampled to death by the people as they seek out the food.

13085–86   *For als He made both erth and ayre / and with His Word all wardly wyght*. I have capitalized *Word* in accordance with the extended Christological readings of John 1:1, which would regard the "active" half of God's speeches in Genesis as the second person of the Trinity. This would seem very much in keeping with the theological position of the *Paraphrase*-poet, who makes clear his own Trinitarian leanings.

13109–10   *Of holy men then here wyll He / that for us profers ther prayer*. While one could read this as referring to either the intercession of saints (to which we might compare the poet's earlier praise of Mary and her "mediacy" in our salvation — lines 7–8) or the efficacy of confession (to which we might compare Samuel's earlier comments on the necessity of maintaining a priesthood — lines 5513–14), the poet seems to intend both. In the following lines he deems it "gud wysdome" (line 13111) to send prayers to God via the saints, and that we should, here on earth, listen to those we know are wise (which has all the ring of a plug for the priesthood). These positions, it must be noted, would stand very much against those of Wycliffe and the Lollards.

13131–40   In both the Bible and *HS*, the story of the siege of Samaria is followed by the story of the Shunammite woman whose lands are restored to her by Elisha's actions (which is a continuation of 4 Kings [2 Kings] 4:8–37). This story includes Gehazi and ignores his curse of leprosy (and his implied exile), which earlier occur in 5:27. It may be the case, then, that the *Paraphrase*-poet recognized the story as potentially out of chronology and omitted it. For certain, his omission of the story allows him to dwell on the aftermath of the siege by tying Ben-hadad's illness to his defeat, a connection not made in the Bible but appearing in Josephus, *Jewish Antiquities* 9.4.6, whence it appears in *HS* 4 Reg. 12 (1394).

13163–64   *Els may thou mater gyf / to do hym more dysese*. This original line is a clever one: on the surface it reads simple enough, stating that to tell the king the truth — that he will soon die — would cause him more discomfort than a lie. In light of Hazael's subsequent regicidal actions, however, it also carries the weight of foreshadowing on the part of the prophet: to do other than talking to the king would be causing him more discomfort. See explanatory note to lines 13193–94.

13193–94   *yll lechyng for hym he layd / so that his lyf last not lang*. Ill-doctoring, indeed: 4 Kings (2 Kings) 8:15 tells how Hazael, having relieved the king's anxieties by assuring him of a full recovery, spread a wet cloth over the king's face and smothered him. Thus, as reported in line 13202, Hazael makes himself king of Syria.

13209   *Godolé*. See note to line 11670.

13227–29   *Sant Elysew . . . Ely*. Both the Bible (2 Chronicles 21:12) and Josephus (*Jewish Antiquities* 9.5.2) agree in identifying the prophet-writer of the rebuke as Elijah, and are silent regarding Elisha's possible involvement. This would be difficult to correlate with biblical timelines, which record Elijah's ascension as occurring about four years earlier. Comestor, apparently aware of this chronological issue, alters his text to term Elisha the writer and is silent about Elijah's possible involvement (*HS* 4 Reg. 13 [1395]). The *Paraphrase* takes an intriguing middle ground that remains true to the Bible while maintaining the chronology: the letter is a prophecy of Elijah, written before his ascension and delivered, years later, by Elisha (see *OFP* 105c).

13263   *With Ethyopes and Arabyse*. *HS* 4 Reg. 13 (1395) says nothing of Ethiopians, while 2 Chronicles 21:16 identifies the advancing Arabs as being those who live near the Ethiopians. The *Paraphrase*-poet follows *OFP* 105c, however, in identifying them equally as attackers.

13266   *the eldest, Occozias*. 2 Chronicles 21:17 and 22:1 call Ahaziah his youngest son. *HS* 4 Reg. 13 (1395) and *OFP* 105d do not mention his age. The poet, it seems, has let an expectation of primogeniture dictate his reading of the text.

13278   *Kyng Benedab*. Both copies of the *Paraphrase* (and its other editors) agree on the reading here, which follows *OFP* 105d in identifying the besieged king as Ben-hadad. This is surely a mistake, however. The poet told the story of

Ben-hadad's death less than a hundred lines earlier, along with the information that Hazael succeeded him (lines 13129–13200). Likewise, the primary authoritative sources (see, e.g., 4 Kings [2 Kings] 9:14 and 2 Chronicles 22:5), identify the besieged king as Hazael.

13380   *Godolé*. See note to line 11670.

13427   *Sant Elysew*. Both copies of the *Paraphrase* (and its other editors) read thus, which appears to be a mistake original to the poet. The prophecy was made by Elijah, as rightly referenced in 4 Kings (2 Kings) 9:36 and in both *HS* 4 Reg. 14 (1396) and *OFP* 106c.

13442   *sexty chylder*. 4 Kings (2 Kings) 10:1 gives the number of sons as seventy, as does *HS* 4 Reg. 15 (1396). The *Paraphrase*-poet here follows something like *OFP* 107a.

13532   *Byschop Joiada*. Jehoiada cannot, of course, be a bishop (a Christian title) in the context of his Jewish milieu. The decision to term him thus, rather than the more historical "priest," is a means for the poet to help his readers relate to the Old Testament.

13533   *his wyf*. That the woman who helps Jehoiada to hide the child is the priest's wife is a detail not from 4 Kings (2 Kings) but from 2 Chronicles 22:11, where she is also named Jehoshabeath.

13677–78   *yeres aght and fawrty / regned he*. According to 2 Chronicles 24:1, Joash reigned for forty years, coming to the throne at age seven (so, too, Josephus, *Jewish Antiquities* 9.8.4, and *HS* 4 Reg. 16 [1398]).

13681   *Long aftur this so yt befell*. The poet skips the reign of Jehoahaz of Israel, son of Jehu, to go to his son named Joash.

13758   *thryty thowssand*. 4 Kings (2 Kings) gives no number to the size of Amaziah's army, while 2 Chronicles 25:5 gives the count as 300,000 (so, too, Josephus, *Jewish Antiquities* 9.9.1). The number here appears to come from *OFP* 109d.

13767   *A thowsand men*. Judah's hiring of a mercenary army from Israel is noted in 2 Chronicles 25:26, where the number of men given is 100,000, which is followed by *HS* 4 Reg. 19 (1399) and Josephus, *Jewish Antiquities* 9.9.1. The source for the *Paraphrase*-poet's number is not known.

13782   *Moabyse*. 4 Kings (2 Kings) 14:7 and 2 Chronicles 25:14 refer to his target as Edom and the Edomites. So, too, *HS* 4 Reg. 19 (1400) and *OFP* 109d. The poet's source is unknown.

13824   *Ozi*. 4 Kings (2 Kings) 15 names him Azarias, but 2 Chronicles 26 calls him Ozias (Uzziah). I have followed the latter not only for its closeness to the Middle English, but also for its clearer differentiation from other characters of the same name.

13825–14004   This digression into the story of Jonas (based on the book of Jonas) is interpolated into the account at 4 Kings (2 Kings) 14:25. Comestor did not include Jonas in *HS*, so the poet is perhaps following something like *OFP* (see

Bonnard, *Les Traductions de la Bible*, p. 102, and Baker, *Die versifizierte Übersetzung*, p. 38) as both a source of the story and its interpolation here. Jonas' story is also famously told in Middle English in the poem *Patience*.

13862   *Cecile*. Jonas 1:3 gives their destination as Tarshish. The *Paraphrase*-poet has apparently copied over the error from *OFP* 110c, which reads "cesile." K (3:125) explains the discrepancy: "Tarshish, traditionally located in Spain, here probably identified with Tarsus, Lat. *T(h)arsus* or *T(h)arsi*, capital of Cilicia. This name was easily confused with Sicily." Compare, too, Baker, *Die versifizierte Übersetzung*, p. 38.

13921   *Your Savyour thus has me send*. This slip into a Trinitarian reading of God is, as far as I can tell, original to the *Paraphrase*. It is striking not only for the paucity of Christ references in the poem but also for the clever way it sets up the parallel between Jonas' experience and Christ's (see note to lines 13965–68).

13927–28   *To Hell your cyté sall dyscend, / als other fyfe hath done before*. The parallel being made, apparently original to the poet, is to the destruction by God of Sodom and Gomorrah and the other cities of the Pentapolis (see note to lines 433–35, above).

13965–68   *As the prophet Jonas / was thre days in the se, / So Cryst in erthe here was / bered be days thre*. This parallel between Jonas' three days in the whale and Christ's three-day burial has its basis in Matthew 12:40 and does not appear in *OFP*. It does, however, have a long tradition in exegesis; see, for example, its appearance in the *Biblia Pauperum* (plate .g.). Interestingly, L does not include the parallel, reading instead: "Thus this prophet Ionas / was come vnto Ninive. / And thurgh it gun he pas / prechand be days thre."

14012   *Ozi*. See note to line 13824.

14077–88   The *Paraphrase*-poet completes the books of Kings with a stanza informing his audience that Uzziah's pride and punishment ought to be a warning against those who would question the Church and try to take on those tasks meant for its ordained churchmen. One would be hard-pressed not to see in this a rebuke of reformative movements like those associated with Lollardy.

14088b   *EXPLICIT LIBRI REGUM*. Not hardly. The poet has paraphrased up to 4 Kings (2 Kings) 15:7, leaving him some ten chapters shy of completing the fourth and final book. Surprisingly, there is no indication that this material, which includes such important and fascinating stories as the Assyrian conquest of Israel, the story of Sennacherib and Hezekiah, the reformations of Josiah, and the conquest of Judah by the Babylonian king Nebuchadnezzar, is missing. The majority of this material is found in *HS*, so one wonders at its absence here. Of perhaps no coincidence, *OFP* similarly breaks off from its own narrative near to this point, ending incomplete (in midcouplet) in the midst of the story of Ahaz, king of Judah (4 Kings 16). It may be that the *Paraphrase*-poet, knowing that *OFP* was soon to end and seeing nothing of concern in the few French lines remaining (which summarily relate a sequence of inconsequential kings in Israel and Judah), decided to wrap up his own narrative in a seemingly more "complete" fashion by turning to a final exemplum.

BOOK OF JOB

The book of Job is omitted by Comestor, who turns from the fourth book of Kings to Tobit (Tobias), which here in the *Paraphrase* follows Job. Neither is this particular order of books indebted to the traditional sequence of the major biblical traditions. The Vulgate passes from the books of Kings and the Chronicles (the latter largely subsumed into the paraphrase of the former here and thus not expected to appear), to Ezra, Nehemias, Tobit, Judith, and Esther, before turning at last to Job. The Septuagint more or less agrees with the Vulgate up to Nehemias, but then turns to the Psalms, the Prayer of Manasseh, Proverbs, Ecclesiastes, Song of Songs, before Job occurs — we are then given Wisdom of Solomon, Wisdom of Sirach (Ecclesiasticus), Esther, and Judith before Tobit. Only in the nine-volume bible of Cassiodorus do we find some semblance of the order given here: after his section of the "Kings" (which includes the Chronicles) Cassiodorus' next division is the "Prophets" (Isaiah, Jeremiah, Lamentations, Ezekiel, and the twelve minor prophets), followed by Psalms and the five books of "Wisdom." None of these texts lend themselves to the kind of reconstructive, "historical" narrative that concerns the *Paraphrase*-poet. The next division, however, is "Hagiography": Job, Tobit, Esther, Judith, Maccabees, and Esdras — precisely the same order of texts (aside from the missing Esdras) that appears in the *Paraphrase*. One of the poet's presumed sources for much of his work up to this point has been *OFP*, but that ends abruptly in the middle of the fourth book of Kings (see explanatory note to line 14088b, above). His sources for the remainder of his work are far less certain. Perhaps as a result of these circumstances, or perhaps because Job can be so inspiring to poets and artists alike, the *Paraphrase*-poet is at his most distant from the biblical text when he moves through this book. Though one might say, from a strictly scriptural standpoint, that the *Paraphrase*'s text is thus "garbled," it is an inspired refashioning, a subtle, theologically profound permutation of what Bloom calls "one of the world's great poems" (*Where Shall Wisdom*, p. 13).

14118	*fyfty yoke of oxyn.* Job 1:3 gives the number of Job's oxen as five hundred. Since neither *HS* nor *OFP* include Job within their paraphrase, and the Middle English poem *Pety Job* does not include these opening details as it concentrates on Job's Dirige, the derivation of this number is unknown.
14138	*putt hym furth in prese.* The image, as in Job 1:6, is of a council of heavenly beings, among whom is Satan: one of many beings greater than man but lesser than (and subservient to) God. This depiction is far different from the "Devil" figure familiar to most of the West; for discussion of the development of Satan over time, see Elaine Pagels' informative and fascinating *Origin of Satan*.
14142	*to gette hym leve, this is no lese.* The *Paraphrase*-poet here admits the unfamiliarity of a Satan obedient to God; see note to line 14138.
14213–14	*A sodan fyre . . . so brym.* The poet's choice of the term *brym* is no elaboration: Job 1:16 describes the fire that consumes Job's stock as a fire from God in Heaven, i.e., brimstone.

14289–92   K (4:14) regards these lines as "anacoluthon" — that is, lacking sequence — since it would make more sense for them to occur before Job's preceding lament.

14315–16   *Bot luke that thou not greve / his sawle bot kepe yt clene.* God's command to Satan in Job 2:6 is not that Job's soul be saved, but his life. The poet's alteration from life to soul might well result from the significant interest in the late Middle Ages on the soul and salvation as revealed in the many medieval works incorporating debates between the soul and body.

14347   *yll are.* The concern of Job's contemporaries with his "ill air" reflects an understanding of disease as being related to invisible but poisonous pockets of air. This concept lasted well into the nineteenth century in the West; the term *malaria*, for instance, which according to the *OED* first appeared in 1740, literally means "bad air."

14357   *Blyse.* So Job 2:9 in the Hebrew and in the Vulgate ("Benedic Deo"), though many modern translations have replaced the term with "Curse." The original is wholly accurate, however, to what we might call a sarcastic stance on the part of Job's wife.

14363–64   *Thou spekes evyn als a foyle / that hath no womans wytt.* In Job 2:10 he says his wife speaks "like one of the foolish women." The change here is intriguing: her foolish speech is emblematic not of being a woman but of being less than a woman. This is yet one more revelation of the relatively high regard in which the poet seems to hold women, a regard that, at times, quietly pushes even Scripture aside.

14408   *sex days.* According to Job 2:13, the three men sit with him for seven days and nights.

14447   *Man, knaw thiselfe.* The advice is proverbial, deriving from (at least) the Ancient Greeks (the originating source varies, but it was famously inscribed on the walls of the forecourt of the Delphic Oracle). For some of its many appearances in Middle English, see Whiting K100.

14494–95   *penauns ordand wore / Eftur mens dedes wore done.* Job recommends that the pains of penance (more properly speaking, the acts of satisfaction that reflect the penitent's contrition) ought to equate to the pains of the sins to which they correspond; this advice is in perfect theoretic keeping with the dicta of the Church.

14501   *when the Day of Dome is dyght.* Job's reference to Judgment Day here is perhaps surprising given Western associations between this subject and Christian theology, especially as it is derived from the misunderstood book of the Apocalypse (Revelation). Yet, as Daniel 12:1–3 shows, the doctrine of resurrection and judgment does have some roots in late Jewish thought (for discussion of the history, see Segal's *Life after Death*). Beginning with Clement of Rome, Christian exegetes have also pointed to Job 19:25–27 as a reference to Christian understandings of life after death (thus, e.g., Augustine, *City of God* 22.29), seeing in these "difficult, probably textually corrupt, verses" (*NOAB*, p. 645) a "*locus classicus* of the doctrine of resurrection" (Zink, "Impatient Job," p. 147). By the later Middle Ages, this connection was generally considered factual, no doubt largely due to Jerome's Christologically-influenced translation of the lines in the Vulgate. Thus "Domesday" also appears in *Pety Job*; see especially line 255.

14523   This line, an echo of Proverbs 24:16 ("Septies enim cadet iustus et resurget"), does not appear in Job or in *Pety Job*.

14539   *For dome is His forto dystrye.* Ohlander's glossary ("Old French Parallels," p. 28) lists *dystrye* under the verb *dystroy(e)*, meaning "to destroy." Though unnoted by the *MED*, a far more likely meaning would be related to the verb *distreinen*, meaning "to compel."

14557–616   The poet (or his source) is paraphrasing Job very loosely throughout, which makes it difficult to correspond between *Paraphrase* and Bible at any given point. This section, for instance, seemingly ought to be Job's first response to Bildad (chapters 9–10), but it is, instead, his second (chapter 19).

14595   *My Sayvyour lyfes.* Job's reference to Christ is a technically ahistorical appearance of Christianity in the poet's paraphrase of this Jewish text, but it is one with origins in the Church Fathers.

14633   *Of gud werke God dose ylk dele.* Zophar's point, one that does not explicitly appear in Job, is one of deep theological import: whether or not humans can "effect" grace — whether they are capable of doing good without God actually doing the good for them. The question came to a forefront in the early fifth century, as a result of the teachings of the British monk Pelagius, who "could not accept that human beings were so corrupted at birth that they could not help sinning" (Bell, *Cloud*, p. 144). This position brought Pelagius into conflict with Augustine, who believed that the Fall left mankind inherently "fallen, damned, doomed, condemned. At birth we are simply 'one lump of sin' and because we are so totally, so helplessly corrupted, we can no more do good of our own power than a blind man can see" (Bell, *Cloud*, p. 147). Pelagianism was condemned in the West, partly due to Augustine's reputation, but the issue continued to resurface for centuries, requiring repeated condemnations. Thomas Bradwardine, for example, felt it was necessary to write a full treatise denouncing the belief in fourteenth-century England (*De causa Dei contra Pelagium et de virtute causarum*). As we see here, the *Paraphrase*-poet is in keeping with the orthodox position.

14682   *to make me turment on a tre.* The point seems to be that even if God were to crucify him, Job would still maintain his integrity. He will not betray his righteousness so long as he believes in a righteous (if incomprehensible) God (see the following lines). At the same time, it is difficult not to see in this nonbiblical insertion to Job's reply a reference to Christ. Though Job suffers terribly, the *Paraphrase*-poet also seems to say, Christ suffered more: the torment of the Crucifixion lies far beyond even Job's experience.

14713–24   The parable of the rich man and the leper, often entitled "Dives and Laza-
            rus," was a popular one in the Middle Ages. It appears, for instance, in Chau-
            cer's Summoner's Tale, where the friar notes that "Lazar and Dives lyveden
            diversly, / And divers gerdon hadden they therby" (*CT* III[D]1877–78). The
            poet's use of the parable is interesting here for its ambiguity. Spoken by Eli-
            phaz, it nevertheless appears to support Job's Lazarus-like position against
            the self-assured self-righteousness of his friends. Eliphaz thus incriminates
            his own actions by being unable to recognize the leper before him.

14748   *no malyse mene*. Job insists that his intentions are benevolent toward the
            friends who rebuke him — and toward the God that may or may not have
            kind intentions. Job's insistence on his integrity allows the line to be read in
            several ways given the variant meanings of the verb *mene* in Middle English:
            to intend, speak, comprehend, or explain (*MED menen*, v.1–2).

14845–64   Job's assessment of what is going on is remarkably accurate. He neither
            judges nor blames God, but rather attempts to acknowledge what he is ex-
            periencing. Job sees that the Fiend cannot touch his soul and, in articulating
            so clearly the leeway God has given the Fiend, indirectly praises God for
            granting him control over his own soulful decisions.

14896   *Mary His moyder*. There is, of course, no precedent in the biblical book of Job
            for a reference to Mary as Mater Dei, but the insertion reveals the universal
            appeal of the Job story, which remains as profound for its medieval Chris-
            tian readers as it did for its antique Hebrew writers. At the same time, its
            inclusion here is highly ambiguous. Zophar appears to acknowledge God as
            a redemptive principle, yet his words are more judgmental than merciful.
            Like Bildad, he is more committed to his understanding of righteous retri-
            bution than truth.

14917–20   K notes (1:cxcii) an echo of *Pety Job*, lines 289–90. The Latin is from Job
            14:1, the fifth lesson of the Dirge (see explanatory note to line 14941).

14941   Job begins his "playnt" (line 14939) with a proclamation of his complete trust
            in God's power as he prays for mercy. This Latin phrase, from Job 7:16, is
            the first of the Nine Lessons of the Dirge, a sequence of verses drawn from
            Job (Job 7:16–21 [lesson 1], 10:1–7 [2], 10:8–12 [3], 13:22–28 [4], 14:1–6 [5],
            14:13–16 [6], 17:1–3 and 11-25 [7], 19:20–27 [8], and 10:18–22 [9]) recited
            during the Matins of the Office of the Dead (*Moral Love Songs*, ed. Fein, p.
            289). Fein characterizes the late Middle Ages as "a culture that fully em-
            braced the Office of the Dead as a ritualized way to enclose and confront
            death, or at least to accept its mystery through time-honored words of ear-
            nest entreaty, rebellion, questioning, and submission. . . . Repetition of the
            Latin — whether fully understood or not by auditors — would most likely
            have been a somber but comforting experience" (p. 289). The first of these
            devotions became representative of the whole sequence in symbolizing the
            condition of man; it serves, for instance, as the end-stanza refrain in *Pety Job*,
            just as it has a prominent place in several other similarly penitential works.

14946   *teche me forto take Thi trace*. The line may well owe something to the antiphon that begins the first nocturn of Matins, "*Dirige, Domine Deus meus*" ("Direct my path, O Lord my God"), from which the Dirge takes its name (see explanatory note to line 14941). The term *trace*, as Job uses it here, appears to be influenced by the kind of Platonic theological philosophies associated with Bonaventure; this same mode of thinking also deepens our understanding of Job's further request to "have mynd of Thee" in the following linc: Job understands that it is his mind that interposes obstacles between him and his goal, so he asks God for guidance in using his mind.

14965–68   K notes (1:cxcii) an echo of *Pety Job*, lines 157–59. The Latin is from Job 10:9, the third lesson of the Dirge (see explanatory note to line 14941).

14966   *umthynke*. The verb is most often reflexive in Middle English, especially when directed toward God, and it reflects the unbiased circumspection Job desires from his prosecutors, the kind of perspective only God can provide.

14977–94   Job's discourse on God's merciful power leads the poet to incorporate two New Testament stories into his text: the raising of Lazarus and the Gospel story of the thief upon the cross. One implication of this seems to be that the book of Job, with its troubling questions of evil, power, and justice, is an asynchronous text: not constrained to any one time or timeline but for all times, existing outside of timelines. The overlay is thus not unlike the climax of *Piers Plowman*, in which the mind, functioning outside time and space, can join Abraham and Moses in racing to witness the Crucifixion, deliverance, and resurrection of Christ, "that redeeming aspect of Trinity whereby eternity is realized in time and space" (Peck, "Number," p. 38).

15008   *be my frend als Thou was before*. The *Paraphrase*-poet emphasizes the value of friendship as Job, whose public, conventional friends have proved to be inadequate, nevertheless desires friendship. As Laelius notes in Cicero's *De amicitia* 19, the need for companionship is part of human nature. Job's concern, then, is that he seems to have lost his one truly adequate friend, God.

15038   *Thi man ay whyls I moght*. Job places himself in the subservient position of a feudal relationship with God, a bond built on personal loyalty and the exchange of a vassal's support for the lord's protection. Homage, the act of thus becoming another's "man" (Latin *homo*), involved the vassal kneeling before the lord and placing his joined hands (as in prayer) between those of his lord. The relationship was technically indissoluble, like marriage, yet what Job seeks is the reassurance that these bonds still function. It is worth noting that, although as a vassal he might doubt his lord's protection in his case (given the attacks to which he has been made subject), Job does not waver in his support for his Lord.

15049–15104   God's reply to Job is substantially different from that which appears at the end of the biblical text. Most noticeable in its absence is God's long sequence of rhetorical questions in Job 38–41 that famously puts Job and all mortals "in their place": "Canst thou draw out the Leviathan with a hook? . . . Will he make a covenant with thee, and wilt thou take him to be a servant for ever?" (Job 40:20–23). Instead of this "bombardment of exuberances" that "is unanswerable, and substitutes power for justification" (Bloom, *Where Shall Wisdom*, p. 17), the *Paraphrase*-poet has God simply insist on Job's need to be submissive before Him, and to admit to his own inherent sinfulness before the perfection of the Divine. In this regard, God's speech seems most indebted to the words of the missing fourth friend, Elihu (Job 33–37), a fact that may lie behind God's strange shift to speaking in the third person starting in line 15079.

15058   *als thee thynke in thi toyght*. God makes clear that He knows even Job's unspoken thoughts, a fact that Job states in the biblical text (Job 42:2).

15093–94   God's statement that all who are born after the Fall are *unclene / and evyll in all degré* acknowledges the basic need for baptism, which Job has not participated in. At the same time, Job's movement beyond complaint toward the expression of his complete love of God in stanza 1260 opens the way for him to participate in God's will that "is ever of mercy free" (line 15050). Note that Job's "wo is went away" (line 15114) once God addresses him, and he prays that he might "clensed be" (line 15139).

15133–36   K notes (1:cxcii) an echo of *Pety Job*, lines 660–61. The Latin is from Job 10:20, the ninth lesson of the Dirge (see explanatory note to line 14941).

15139–44   Compare Chaucer's Parson's Tale, which cites this passage in Job as a step in the contritional process that leads to satisfaction (*CT* X[I]175–87).

15170   *then was his grefe all gon, I geyse*. The *Paraphrase*-poet's tag, *I geyse*, introduces some interesting ambiguities. On the one hand, it might indicate an experiential truth ("I perceive") that testifies to the efficacy of devout prayer; on the other hand, it might indicate an experiential doubt ("I guess") about Job truly being relieved of the grief of losing so many of his loved ones as a result of God allowing the Fiend to do so much physical harm to the loyal man.

15197–15204 The poet infuses his conclusion with romance elements as Job's good ending is shown by the worshipful heritage of his children. Thus Job's "myrth wold multyplye" (line 15208), along with his wealth (line 15212).

15211   *fresch*. See explanatory note to line 12355, above.

15213–16   *God graunt us grace to lyfe / in luf and charité, / That we our gast may gyfe / to myrth*. The poet's prayer restates the theme of love and charity expressed most clearly in his New Testament insertions to the narrative (Dives and Lazarus, the thief on the cross), and his specificity about the reception of *grace* — that it gives mirth to the soul, rather than the body — underscores the fundamental lesson of Job.

BOOK OF TOBIAS

Unlike the preceding book of Job, the book of Tobias (or Tobit) can be found paraphrased by Comestor in *HS*, though it is uncertain if the poet truly used Comestor as a source for this section of his text. For instance, whereas *HS* dutifully follows the Bible (Tobias 3:7–17) in introducing Raguel's daughter Sarah and her torments at the hands of the demon Asmodeus between Tobit's prayer and Tobit's instruction to Tobias concerning the monies left in Media, the *Paraphrase* omits Sarah until after Tobias has left home. The result is a more streamlined and focused text, unwaveringly following the actions of father and son. Also of note: there are significant differences between the Vulgate text of Tobias and that found in many other versions of the Bible, like the NRSV. The latter version, for instance, has the book partially told from the first-person point of view of Tobit, whereas the *Paraphrase* joins *HS* and the Vulgate in keeping to third-person. Other points of difference can be found within the explanatory notes below. Regarding the non-Vulgate order of presenting Tobias immediately following Job, Morey characterizes both main characters as men "tried by God" (*Book and Verse*, p. 152).

15227–28	*To love God lowd and styll, / what soynd so He wyll send.* The presumed moral — to love God regardless of God's actions toward you — is especially poignant given the ordering of the books in the *Paraphrase*: surely no better example of such humility under discussion can be had than Job (lines 14531–32), which the poet echoes here.
15331	*Sevyn hunderth and twenty libras weyd thei.* The weight of the ten talents left with Gabael is not given in the Bible or *HS*; it apparently derives from the *Catholicon* mentioned in line 15336.
15336	*Catholicon.* K notes (1:cxciii) that these facts cannot be found in the 1483 *Catholicum Anglicum*. Compare Liljegren, Review of *A Middle English Metrical Paraphrase*, p. 228.
15404	*to werke his wyll.* Compare line 15495. One central topic of the story is the seeking of a way to work one's will (effect one's desire). Gower hits on the same idea, noting that, once Tobias and Sarah complete their prayers, "Thobie his wille hadde" (*CA* 7.5361).
15440	*swolws nest.* In certain translations of Tobias 2:10 (e.g., NRSV), the birds are sparrows. *HS* Tob. 1 (1433) agrees with the Vulgate, however, in having a swallow's nest ("ex nido hirundinum").
15469–70	*This wo I wott I am worthy / for weked werkes that I have wroyght.* The humility of Tobit's response demands comparison with the preceding book of Job, a connection made explicitly in *HS* Tob. 1 (1433). See explanatory note to lines 15227–28.
15661–68	*A lytyll hund . . . wold stably with hym stand.* K notes (4:53) that "the dog has caught the poet's fancy in a way that has no correspondence in the Bible." Indeed, Tobias 6:1 notes only that when Tobias goes to the river Tigris "the dog followed him." *HS* Tob. 1 (1434) adds little more. The poet seems to be building on the intimate portrayal of the dog at 11:9 of the Vulgate (this latter verse lacks the dog in some traditions; see, e.g., NRSV), here paralleled in lines 16209–12 and 16219–20, which corresponds to *HS* Tob. 1 (1436): "Tunc praecurrit canis, qui simul fuerat in via, et quasi nuntius adveniens blandimento suae caudae gaudebat."

15767	*or thei neghed hyr nere.* The phrase, appearing similarly at line 15944, is rather blunt and to the point. *MED* (*neighen*, v.1, 7a) gives such definitions as "have sexual intercourse with" and "impregnate." But a glance at the other examples listed points out the "dirtiness" with which the word is often used, a crudity that certainly fits well with the context here. A better gloss, then, might be "before they fucked her" since it drives home both the moral and physical implications of the act.
15791–92	*Thus dyd scho days thre / withoutyn drynke or mette.* These details, which appear in the Vulgate (3:10), are missing from some versions of the Bible (e.g., NRSV).
15833	*maw.* Rather than the fish's stomach, Tobias 6:5 gives the third portion as the liver.
15913–36	Raphael's instructions to Tobias are far more detailed from those found in the Bible. His somewhat amusing explanation that the smoke and stench is the active agent driving away the demon, for instance, has no parallel in 6:19, which makes no effort to provide a realistic mechanism for such a supernatural event.
16063	That the couple decides together (following Raphael's advice to Tobias) to spend their first three nights together in prayer before they consummate the marriage is found in the Vulgate (Tobias 8:4), which is followed by *HS* Tob. 1 (1435). It is absent, however, in some other versions (e.g., NRSV).
16209–20	See the explanatory note to lines 15661–68.
16303–04	K notes "the humorously popular style sometimes affected by the poet" in these lines (4:70).
16381–88	Something has clearly gone wrong somewhere in the textual tradition. Line 16388 tells us that Tobit lived to be 102, a fact confirmed by Tobias 14:2. We are also told in lines 16381–86, however, that he went blind at the age of seventy and remained blind for fifty-three years, after which he could see for another forty-two, making him an entirely contradictory 165 years old when he died. The numbers in Tobias 14:1–3, on the other hand, add up correctly: Tobit lost his sight at fifty-six, gained it back at sixty, and had forty-two years of restored sight before his death at 102. L is no help here, as it agrees with the numbers in S with the exception of Tobit's age when he lost his sight: rather than sixty, L reads an even more unlikely seventeen. So the error lies somewhere behind both existing texts of the *Paraphrase*, an unsurprising fact given the discrepancies even in biblical texts concerning his age — NRSV gives the age at which he lost his eyesight as sixty-two, while still others read fifty-eight. *HS* Tob. 1 (1437–38) gives 56.
16434	That Tobias died at the age of ninety-nine is consistent with both Tobias 14:14 and *HS* Tob. 1 (1438). Other authorities give different numbers however: e.g., the AV gives 127, and the NRSV gives 117.

BOOK OF ESTHER

By moving directly from Tobias to Esther, the *Paraphrase*-poet omits two books of Comestor's *HS* entirely (Ezechiel and Daniel) and inverts the Vulgate (and *HS*) order of Judith and Esther. As noted in the introduction, however, this odd ordering of books replicates that found in the canon of Cassiodorus.

16482	*faurty days.* Esther 1:4 reads "a hundred and fourscore days" (180 days), while *HS* Esther 1 (1489) reads "centum et septuaginta diebus" (170 days). I can find no source for the far shorter number found here.
16505	*aghtyn day.* Esther 1:10 reads "seventh day," as does *HS* Esther 1 (1490).
16539	*to princes he con hym pleyne.* Esther 1:13 terms those consulted "wise men," or "sages" — men who knew the laws and could properly judge the course of action to take. The *Paraphrase*-poet, ever attentive to differences between the world of his text and the world of his audience, shifts this to the more contemporary idea of a king among his aristocratic peerage.
16600	*his brother doyghtur.* Compare Esther 2:7, "his uncle's daughter."
16629	*festes thre.* Neither the Bible nor *HS* Esther 1 (1491) provide a specific number.
16794–96	*cald a clerke . . . forto rede in romans ryght / what ferlys in his tym befell.* The story that the king will hear is told earlier, at Esther 2:19–23. That the poet associates this tale with a romance narrative is itself interesting: the Vulgate describes the reading material as "historias et annales," casting Mordecai's previous service to the crown in a historical light rather than in an adventurous one.
16869–72	Haman's lack of appetite and general sense of foreboding are details added by the *Paraphrase*-poet; the biblical source has nothing of the kind.
16949–52	*Thus whoso wyll the sakles shame / for any lordschep in this land . . . or wers.* As the poet quickly sums up the remaining chapters of the biblical text, which focus primarily on the aftereffects of Haman's execution, he sets aside the liturgical importance of the story for Jews: the fact that these events are annually recounted during the festival of Purim. Instead, he turns to a lesson more fitting for his own contemporary audience.

BOOK OF JUDITH

As with several books of the Bible (see, e.g., Tobias), there are significant differences between the Vulgate text of Judith and that found in many other versions of the Bible, like the NRSV. In the case of Judith, there are four extant Greek versions, two Latin ones, one in Syriac, and at least three later versions in Hebrew. Though I have found no direct correlations between it and the present work, it is also of note that the story of Judith survives as one of the most famous surviving works of Old English, an incomplete verse epic in the *Beowulf*-manuscript.

The *Paraphrase*-poet's manipulation of the figure of Judith has been studied at length by Squires, who argues that the *Paraphrase*, "by its linguistic choices and by its emphases, transmutes the biblical figure, reducing the sense of her beauty and sexuality, and moulding her to fit acceptable contemporary stereotypes . . . to de-fuse the threat that her powerful femininity poses" ("Treatment," pp. 189, 196). I make references to Squires' work throughout the notes that follow.

17007–08   *Wherfore fowle vengance on hym fell / to lyfe als best with grouand grese.* As Squires points out ("Treatment," p. 197n13), the poet here "conflates the Nebuchadnezzar of the Book of Judith with that of Daniel" as the latter's end, recorded in Daniel 4:33, is transferred to the former: "This indicates the non-scholarly nature of the text," Squires writes, because "Comestor certainly distinguishes" them.

17037–40   *The Jewys that were dwelland / in Jerusalem cyté / Myght loke over all that land / and full grett soroyng see.* Peck notes the oddness of the implication in these lines — and subsequent references to the Temple — that the city around which the main action of the story takes place is Jerusalem: the Vulgate clearly gives the name of the besieged city as Bethulia, an otherwise unknown location. The poet's confusion between locations might well be due to Comestor's lack of clarity on the matter, however, and it is certainly not specific to the *Paraphrase*: Chaucer's Monk places the story in Bethulia (*CT* VII[B²]2551–74), while Gower's *Mirour de l'Omme* places it in Jerusalem (lines 17461–72). Further clouding our ability to be certain what location was on the *Paraphrase*-poet's mind is his reference, in line 17112, to Holofernes shutting off a watercourse coming "fro Jerusalem," which hardly makes sense if Jerusalem is besieged but would, perhaps, be fitting of a nearby town.

17038   *cyté.* Peck maintains the general capitalization of the noun throughout Judith, wondering whether this is meant to "focus attention on the Jews' special dwelling place," thus relating it to Jerusalem (see note to lines 17037–40, above). I have chosen not to follow suit, given that the word is capitalized elsewhere in the base manuscript of the *Paraphrase*, where such implication cannot be inferred.

17080   *Abymalech.* Peck notes that the poet seems to have confused Amalech, from the Judith 4:12 in the Vulgate, with Abimelech, from Genesis 20–26.

17112   *fro Jerusalem.* See note to lines 17037–40.

17179   *Sho wold yt wast with womans wytt.* Squires observes that "the phrase 'woman's wytt' is curiously ambiguous since it would appear to refer to her use of feminine wiles to defeat Holofernes but in the context of her 'wise woman' designation and her immediate behaviour towards Ozias and the Bethulians this is far from obvious" ("Treatment," p. 191).

17181–82   *To the Tempyll rayked scho ryght / and cald tho folke in fere.* Squires points out that "[f]rom the moment that she enters the action her voice is one of authority" ("Treatment," p. 191). "Indeed once Judith has entered the action, with the

exception of one speech of sixteen lines of Holofernes, four lines of excla-
mation when Holofernes' body is discovered and one stanza (1473) of dia-
logue between Judith and the victorious warriors, all direct speech belongs
to Judith" (p. 198n21).

17183–84   *up sho stud on heyght / so that thei suld hyr here.* Judith "does not discuss the
matter of the city's proposed surrender with the leaders in private (as in the
Bible) but, standing in a prominent position, rebukes their leader . . . in
public . . . for the policy he has proposed. Her tone has the uncompromising
ring of the female saint or female authority figure like the Pearl maiden"
(Squires, "Treatment," p. 191).

17211   *Job and Thoby.* Judith's connection of present circumstance to those of the
books of Job and Tobias is not biblical, nor can I find any other telling of the
story in which she does so. It is fitting here, however, given the proximity of
those tales to hers in the *Paraphrase*; the poet's characters thus aid him in
making his work more unified. The fact that, despite these efforts and
traditional orders to the contrary, the poet nevertheless places Esther be-
tween Job and Tobias and the present book is yet more evidence that he is
faithful to a source with this order already in place, which could be, though
is not necessarily, Cassiodorus. See the introduction.

17223   *Now, sers.* Squires notes Judith's shift in tone after the capitulation of the
male authorities to her will, as "she responds more politely" to them in this
subsequent speech ("Treatment," p. 192).

17241–50   *sho hyr arayd / in garmentes gud and gay . . . to make hyr semly unto se.* Squires
makes much of the *Paraphrase*-poet's keen interest in the material aspect of
Judith's appearance: "the chief emphasis of this text is not on Judith's
beauty but rather is transferred onto the richness of her clothing" ("Treat-
ment," p. 190). See note to line 17250.

17250   *semly unto se.* Though I have glossed *semly* as "beautiful," Squires notes that
the vocabulary "not only reduces markedly such explicit reference to her
beauty but uses language for it which converts it from the sexually dan-
gerous to the socially acceptable. . . . It is not a vocabulary choice which sug-
gests the beauty of the seductress but the outer beauty which matches and
mirrors the inner beauty of spirit" ("Treatment," p. 189). Such observations
aside, we might note, too, that it is not Judith herself who is "semly" in this
text: it is her clothing, a transference that further reduces the threat of her
sexuality. See note to lines 17241–50.

17321–22   *forto marre hym more in myght, / full flatt unto the grownd sho fell.* Squires points
out that Judith's "behaviour towards Holofernes at their first meeting seems
to play more on Holofernes' sense of power than on his lust, and to relate
to Judith's social status rather than her physical desirability" ("Treatment,"
p. 191). Again and again she presents herself as submissive to his authority,
while at the same time appearing, both in her speech and garments, to be
a woman "of grett degré" (line 17332), which pleases Holofernes greatly.

17455–60	*Bot to slepe was sho never unclede.* Squires observes that the poet "contrasts [Judith's] labour with the luxury that Holofernes is offering her. . . . Far from revelling in the physical luxury as would a Delilah, she does not even undress but deprives herself of sleep and engages in hard labour for the good of her people" ("Treatment," p. 193). In addition, one might note that the observation that Judith never undresses further underscores her devotion to God's Law and the celibacy that it requires of her. See, too, the note to lines 17525–40.
17461–70	While in the Bible Judith goes to the well to purify herself and pray to God for support, here in the *Paraphrase* she goes to the well to bring water to the water-starved city. Peck notes: "in romance tradition the woman normally needs a guardian for her well (e.g., Chrétien de Troyes' *Yvain*). Here Judith tends the well herself for the benefit of the whole city" (*Heroic Women from the Old Testament*, p. 152n1456.1–10).
17525–40	The Bible makes no mention of Judith ever leaving Holofernes' side between the banquet and his beheading. The poet's addition of having her temporarily leave the bedchamber, however, ensures his audience that Judith never comes close to compromising the celibacy of her widowhood.
17556	*wyghtly went ther way.* Peck glosses *wyghtly* as "manfully," presumably echoing the Douay-Rheims translation of Joachim's praise of Judith's actions at Judith 15:11. While I have not followed the gloss — the Middle English is not necessarily as gendered — it is an interesting consideration, especially in light of the tale's deep interests in issues of gender. See, too, notes to lines 17577–604 and 17675.
17575	*scho schewed hyr releke ryght.* "Although the word 'releke' can be used without religious connotations . . . there does seem [to be] deliberate irony in the choice of this term. The beheading of Holofernes and removal of his head forms an interesting parallel to martyrdoms which require decapitation to kill a saint. For example in the legend of St Margaret of Antioch . . . her head [is] taken to Paradise in the embrace of angels while her body remains behind as a relic working healing miracles. Holofernes' fate is almost a parody of this: his head is borne into Bethulia/Jerusalem in Judith's food bag and his body remains behind to perform the 'miracle' of sending his invincible army in headlong flight" (Squires, "Treatment," p. 198n24).
17577–604	Judith's speech, which begins, as Squires notes, "with a series of imperatives," marks her as "the sole authority figure" in the city. "Judith as God's representative and instrument has become both the civil and religious leader of her people," a "figure of the powerful female" that the poet will subsequently work to mediate ("Treatment," p. 192).
17651–78	*Thei fand all safe certayn . . . that thei not stryfe.* This sequence, in which the Assyrian camp remains untouched by the victorious Jews until they have brought Holofernes' personal goods to Judith and received her wise direction regarding the orderly division of the spoils, stands against the known texts of the biblical tale. In the Bible, the camp is plundered even as the

Assyrians are fleeing, and details about specific treasures being set aside for Judith are not given until the triumphant return of all to the city. One obvious result of the *Paraphrase*'s different account, for which I can find no source, is that the Jewish forces are presented as remarkably controlled and orderly from beginning to end. They are loyal to the social authoritative structures of their world — especially those associated with religion, whether rooted in the traditional location of the Temple or the quite nontraditional location of the figure of the uncompromising Judith.

17675   *To make us mery evermore.* Both extant manuscripts read *To make us men evermore* (see textual note). While I have followed previous editors in emending the line, it is not without some hesitation; the manuscript reading presents a very interesting admission on the part of those speaking (presumably the town elders): Judith's gender-infused victory, and its subsequent triumphant spoils, have restored a traditional gender balance to the community: the men have now resumed their masculine roles, and Judith will return once more to her widow's weeds. See note to lines 17703–35.

17703–36   Unlike the Bible, which presents the fact of Judith's widowhood at the moment of her first appearance, the *Paraphrase* only mentions it here, at the end of the narrative. The alteration provides the poet with an opportunity to focus the whole of his conclusion on a portrayal of Judith as "not the wise and commanding leader, nor, exactly, the wealthy and noble 'lady,' but an even more acceptable development of that image, the pious, chaste, charitable and retiring widow who remains content with devotion to the memory of a single husband." Thus the *Paraphrase*-poet "makes it appear that the dramatic events of the narrative had no permanent effect on Judith. As soon as her role as God's agent is complete, she immediately retires to her 'proper' female role of managing her house and her servants, and caring for the poor" (Squires, "Treatment," p. 195).

17707–08   *sho weryd hyr wedow wede / bot in soverane sesons of the yere.* The detail that she did not wear her widow's weeds during holidays, derived from Judith 16:27 in the Vulgate, does not appear in all versions of the Bible due to the multiple recensions of the book of Judith. It is lacking, for instance, in the NRSV. See headnote.

17715–16   *Manasses . . . that lordly lyf before had led.* Squires wonders at the fact that the *Paraphrase* makes no mention of the manner of Manasses' passing: "Is this because his death while working in the fields at harvest does not match the image of a wealthy landowner for the poet?" ("Treatment," p. 198n19).

SECOND BOOK OF MACCABEES 7

It is an open question whether the poet paraphrases so little of the books of Maccabees because he lacks the sources to do otherwise (that is, he had only fragments of the books to work with), or because he deliberately chooses to highlight these particular passages. The cohesive specificity of the stories he provides — the best-known martyrdoms of the Old

Testament and the death of the pagan emperor to blame for them — argues for the latter position, though it does not necessitate it. It is also worth observing the length he devotes to these subjects despite their brevity in the Bible. On some of the many implications of these Jewish stories for the poet's presumably Christian audience, see the explanatory notes (especially that to lines 17761–62), below.

17750   *in forme Faders is fayre to rede.* The stories of the "Maccabean martyrs" — the martyrdom of the Jewish mother and her seven sons, told here, and that of the priest Eleazar, told subsequently — are "so powerful . . . that they served the church fathers as a paradigm for Christian martyrdom" (Patterson, "'Living Witnesses,'" p. 522, who cites Frend, *Martyrdom*, pp. 22–57); they thus appear, for example, in the writings of John Chrysostom, Ambrose of Milan, and Augustine. For a thorough discussion of the medieval reception and propagation of these stories, see Joslyn-Siemiatkoski, "Maccabean Martyrs."

17754   *swylk marters may make uus mede.* It is unclear whether the *Paraphrase*-poet here reinforces the principles of devotional reading or the doctrine of the intercession of saints — whether it is reading about the martyrs that will do his audience good or whether it is the martyrs themselves, called upon to intercede on the reader's behalf.

17761–62   *we sall sum marters nevyn / that wroyght with Moyses wyll all way.* The poet's statement that the Maccabean martyrs were Jews *all way*, though easily passed over, is nonetheless loaded with implications. Their story had captivated Christians from an early date (see note to line 17750), causing the martyrs to shift, as Joslyn-Siemiatkoski puts it, "from being liminal figures in late antiquity, whose Christian authenticity had to be proven, to being standard elements of the medieval Christian narrative of biblical and salvation history" ("Maccabean Martyrs," p. 10). Indeed, they became central enough to the life of the Church that they were eventually included in the calendar of the saints, with a feast day alongside the Christian martyrs. The fact of their Jewish faith, however, was a lingering concern. Bernard of Clairvaux, for instance, dwells at some length on why, "alone of all the righteous men of the old Law," these particular Jewish martyrs are so honored, especially given that, as Jews, Christian doctrine dictated that they were denied heavenly reward upon the instant of their martyrdom (Evans, *Bernard*, p. 73). Bernard, among others, ultimately argues that they were "Christian in spirit from a carnal Israel," a typological, supersessionist understanding of their tale that ultimately led Christian exegetes, Comestor among them, to argue "that the fullest meaning of their martyrdom is found by the light of the incarnation of Jesus Christ. Thus the value of dying for the Law of Moses is superseded by the value of dying for the Gospel. In this way, Christian historical exegesis of 2 Maccabees 7 presents the Church as the true Israel in contrast to contemporary Judaism" (Joslyn-Siemiatkoski, "Maccabean Martyrs," pp. 10–11). For more on the Christian cult of the Maccabean martyrs, see also Rouwhorst, "Cult."

17763–64   *Of aght then is yt ordand evyn / in Holy Chyrch to syng and say.* Until the twentieth-century suppression of the feast, the Maccabean martyrs were celebrated on the Roman Catholic calendar of the saints (1 August). The poet's reference to their number as eight is technically accurate, insofar as he refers now specifically to the martyrdom of the seven brothers and their mother in 2 Maccabees 7, though many Christian writings omit the mother in their reckoning, referring to them collectively as the "Seven Maccabees." For many exegetes, this was particularly fitting given the fact that, as Caxton writes in his translation of Jacobus de Voragine's *Golden Legend*, "the church maketh solemnities of the Maccabees, howbeit that they descended into hell" (4.153). Among the other reasons Caxton provides to explain this discrepancy, he observes their association with "the representation of the mystery," because "the number of seven is universal and general." Thus, "in these seven is done reverence to them all. For as it is said by the number of seven is assigned an university."

17801–03   *How ye were bred in my body . . . God fosterd yow thore.* The mother's speech, which, like much in this discursive opening, has no biblical counterpart, here touches on a late medieval outgrowth of the Christian fascination with the Maccabean martyrs: "a typological connection between the mother who witnesses the death of her sons and the Virgin Mary, who keeps watch at the foot of the cross at the crucifixion of her son Jesus Christ" (Joslyn-Siemiatkoski, "Maccabean Martyrs," p. 11).

17804   *in forme fre.* The mother perhaps references the tradition that mankind is formed in God's "noble" image (Genesis 1:26).

17888   *with Hym to wun and wynly wake.* While bodily resurrection is an evolving concept in the history of Judaism (see, too, the note to line 14501), it is firmly stated in the biblical passage here paraphrased (2 Maccabees 7:9), a fact that did not go unnoticed by Christian exegetes.

18240   *thei have ther hame in Hevyn.* The *Paraphrase* here stands against traditional exegetical understandings of the martyrs, which often place them, despite their sacrifices, in (at best) limbo. See the notes to lines 17761–62 and 17763–64, above.

18245–46   *in ther blud thei were baptyst, / als Innocentes were sythyn seyn.* The *Paraphrase*-poet, as is the case with many Christian exegetes, associates the dead children with the Holy Innocents of Bethlehem said in Matthew 2:16–18 to have been massacred by Herod the Great in his effort to kill the infant Jesus. Aside from the more ready and graphic meaning of baptism by blood, the poet's focus on their blood in connection to the Innocents might have additional meaning: Christian martyrs were often characterized by the manner of their deaths. Regarding the Christmas feasts of the martyrs — St. Stephen, St. John of Patmos, and the Holy Innocents, whose feast days immediately follow the Nativity — Jacobus de Voragine summed up the exegetical position by observing that Stephen was a martyr by will and by blood (that is, he willingly shed his blood for Christ), John by will alone (he devoted his life to Christ, but died a natural death), and the Innocents by blood alone (though they did not know it, they shed their blood for Christ).

SECOND BOOK OF MACCABEES 6 AND 9

The *Paraphrase*-poet's presentation of the story of Eleazar after the story of the more famed Maccabean martyrs stands against that of Comestor, who passes on his information in biblical order. The alteration is put to good use here, however; it allows the poet to provide a brief recapitulation of Antiochus' wickedness, in the form of additional martyrological exempla, before he concludes the whole of his work with an illustration of God's ultimate, if perhaps belated, justice.

18303–04   *Jerusalem, whore the Jewys con dwell, / wyll he dystroy ever ylke stone.* The Bible mentions Antiochus' intention to desconstruct the city itself only in passing during discussion of his deathbed sorrows (2 Maccabees 9:14). An oath to unmake Jerusalem would perhaps be familiar to the poet's audience, however, in the form of the destruction of Jerusalem by the Roman armies under the command of future emperors Titus and Vespasian in the year 70. In the Middle English *Siege of Jerusalem*, for instance, Vespasian swears not to leave the Holy Land until "no ston in the stede [is] stondande alofte, / Bot alle overtourned and tilt, Temple and other" (ed. Livingston, lines 1019–20).

18305–08   Antiochus' interest in the wealth of Jerusalem's treasury has no source in the Bible or *HS* (though 2 Maccabees 9:16 reports that on his deathbed he regrets having previously plundered the Temple). It may be transposed from an identical interest in the riches of Persepolis' temples: according to 2 Maccabees 9:1–4, it was his rage at being defeated in that pursuit that put him in mind to take his anger out on the Jews and to make Jerusalem their burial ground. It is also worth observation, however, that the pillaging of the Temple's treasures stands as one of the acts of Jerusalem's Roman conquerors in the final stanza of *Siege of Jerusalem* (ed. Livingston, lines 1337–40); perhaps imperial (or ecclesiastical?) Rome, too, has been guilty of overweaning pride.

18313–16   *Thei geydder sone grett cumpany . . . to wend in were.* 2 Maccabees 9 says nothing of an army on either side: in his rage Antiochus spurs his charioteer to take him to Jerusalem as quickly as possible, the lack of an accompanying force to help him destroy the Jews yet one more outward sign of his inner arrogance in thinking himself of equal power to God. The siege of Jerusalem quickly sketched here, however, would be a familiar one from the many legends surrounding the historical siege in 70. Antiochus' "chare" (line 18318) might thus remind readers of the "chayre" in which Caiaphas sits during one of the first battles in the Middle English *Siege of Jerusalem* (ed. Livingston, line 471).

18325–32   On the worm-infected body of the diseased Antiochus, whose stench of rotting flesh was so great that none, even his fast friends, dared approach him, compare Chaucer's Monk's Tale (*CT* VII[B²]2615–20).

18369–72   *Pray we to God forthi, / with the moyder and hyr suns sevyn, / That we may be worthy / to wun with them in Hevyn.* The *Paraphrase*-poet completes his Old Testament paraphrase by using prayer to fuse his account of 2 Maccabees 9 to 2 Maccabees 7. The poet, underscoring his conclusion that the martyred mother and her seven sons are saved (see explanatory note to lines 17761–62, above), thus leaves the reader with an understanding that the whole of the Old Testament serves as a proto-Christian text.

🌿 Textual Notes

As noted in the introduction, the orthography of L differs significantly from that of S. As a result, Kalén and Ohlander often altered spellings from L when emending from that manuscript, making an effort to "match" orthography as well as possible to that of their base text, S. I have followed this same principle. As a result, I have chosen to ignore minor spelling variations when compiling these notes. The actual readings of line 1737 in the two manuscripts, for example, are: "Nothyng myght byde theire byt" (L) and "No thyng myg3t byte þerof" (S). Following K, I have emended this to read "Nothyng myght byd ther byte" and attributed the reading to L. The minor orthographic variations in such instances (here being *byd* for *byde*, *ther* for *theire*, *byte* for *byt*) seem largely inconsequential and have thus been ignored. For the reader wishing such precision, however, K provides all relevant details, and I have found its readings to be generally accurate.

For the most part (see, e.g., lines 49–52 for an exception), the base text (S) of the poem preserves the lines in pairs, two to a line; thus lines 1–2 appear as a single line, lines 3–4 appear as the next, etc. Like previous editors, I have regularized this across the whole of the poem in both the numbering and the indented presentation of the text.

ABBREVIATIONS: L: MS Longleat 257; **H**: Heuser edition (partial); **K**: Kalén-Ohlander edition; **O**: Ohlander's corrigenda to K; **P**: Peck edition (partial); **S**: MS Selden Supra 52 (base text for this edition).

PROLOGUE

above 1	Marginalia in S (at right of fol. 2r): *Samuel Purchas*.
	Marginalia in S (at top of fol. 2r): *Genesis*.
1–1472	**Missing in L.**
1, 3	Lines indented to leave space for an initial capital; first letter of line 1 written in the middle of the space.
7	*Mary*. S: *r* inserted above the line.
20	*schort*. So K. S: *schortes*.
30	*ever*. So K. S: *ouer*. H reads *on*.
31	*wer*. So S, K. H reads *wur*.
32	*kawn*. So S. H emends to *knawn*, but K suggests that *kawn* is the past participle of Old English *ceowan*. Thus *kawn* has the Middle English sense of "mediated on" or, more literally, "chewed over."

Book of Genesis

39	*cald is.* So H. S: *cald.* K:*[is] cald.*
40	*see.* S: second *e* inserted above the line.
	unsoght. S, K: *vnsogh.*
42	*wroght.* S, K: *wrogh.*
49–52	Written as separate lines in S.
52	*forever and.* S: *for.* K: *for [euer and].*
57	Marginalia (top of fol. 2v): *de casu lucifer. Genesis.*
	Of. So K. S: *On.*
62	*sone can.* So K. S omits.
67	*to.* So O. S, K omit.
70	*kend.* S: ~~clerkes~~ *kendes.* K's emendation.
72	*the.* S: *ther.* K's emendation.
74	*were.* Second *e* is inserted above the line.
95	*forto.* K omits.
98	*to moyv.* So K. S: *the moyn.*
99	*and.* K omits.
113	Marginalia in S (at top of fol. 3a): *Genesis.*
116	*won.* So K. S: *wons.*
118	*no.* K marks this as an emendation, though S is clear.
148	*in.* So K. S omits.
153	*tresses.* K emends to *tress.*
158	*frut fayr.* K emends to *frut [so] fayr.*
159–60	Written as separate lines in S.
159	*fang.* S: ~~fand~~ *fang.*
164	*to.* K emends to *thou.*
167	*That.* S: ~~S~~ *That.*
	bad. S: inserted above the line.
169	Marginalia in S (at top of fol. 3v): *Genesis.*
177	*yt.* So S. K omits.
183	*sen.* So K. S: *sent.*
184	*free.* So K. S: *clere.*
187	*wold.* So K. S: *wole.*
200	*kyne.* So S. K: *kynd.*
214	*forbeyd.* S: ~~forso~~ *forbeyd.*
220	*erth.* S: inserted above the line.
229	Marginalia in S (at top of fol. 4r): *Genesis.*
240	*lyght.* So S, K. Stern (Review, p. 281) suggests *delyght.*
251	*loke.* S: *k loke.*
259	*harpe.* So K. S: *happe.*
264	*last.* So K. S: *lastur.*
266	Marginalia in S (at left of fol. 4r): four illegible words.
	Marginalia in S (at right of fol. 4r): *Mattussile lameth Noe.*
272	*yere.* So K. S omits.
	by. S: ~~in~~ *by.*
281	*non aw.* S: *non* ~~na~~; *aw* inserted above the line.

284	*be*. So K. S omits.
290	*hath*. So S. K emends to *have*.
294	Marginalia in S (at top of fol. 4v): *Noye*.
298	Marginalia in S (at right of fol. 4v): *Arca Noe*.
303	*Thre*. So K. S: *thro*.
312	*of ylka kynd a*. So K. S: *mony of ylka*, with *kynd a* inserted above the line.
314	*wyll*. S: inserted above the line.
321	*monethes*. S: *ne* inserted above the line.
342	*thei*. S, K: *the*.
348	*werld*. So K. S: *welrd*.
350	*wych*. S, K: *wyhc*.
354	*Cham*. So O. S: *k Caym*, followed by K.
357	Marginalia in S (at top of fol. 5r): *Genesis. Turris babilonis*.
	When. S: *ff When*.
370	*foyn*. S: *foynd*, with *d* canceled.
374	*bod dy*. S: inserted above the line.
379	*Thatt*. So K. S: *latt*.
396	*worthay*. S: *worthy*, with *a* inserted above the line.
398	*In*. S: *I*, with *n* inserted above the line.
410	*fune*. S: ~~sure~~ *fune*.
419	Marginalia in S (at top of fol. 5v): *Genesis*.
426	*thei*. S, K: *the*.
430	*hym*. S: inserted above the line.
434	*nere*. S: *t nere*.
452	*full*. S: ~~fer~~ *full*.
460	*thei*. So K. S: *the*.
464	*of*. So K. S omits.
465	*wold*. So K. S: *wole*.
470	*pyn*. S: corrected from *payn*.
478	*lay*. S: ~~law~~ *lay*.
481	Marginalia in S (at top of fol. 6r): *Genesis. Abram*.
489	*emong*. K calls this a later addition to S, though I can find no evidence of this being the case.
490	*I have*. K inverts to *have I* in order to indicate an interrogative statement.
499	*gravell*. S: *ra* inserted above the line.
502	*hevyn*. So K. S: *heuenyn*.
514	*beldyd*. So K. S: *beldyld*.
539	*circumscisyd*. So S. K: *circumcisyd*.
543	*it*. S: inserted above canceled *yrtt*.
544	*he*. S: inserted above the line.
545	Marginalia in S (at top of fol. 6v): *Genesis*.
548	*circumsysed*. S: inserted above canceled *cursyd*.
555	*hy*. So K. S: *hym*.
559	*And*. So K. S: *In*.
565	Marginalia in S (at right of fol. 6v): *signum trinnitatis*.
567	*unto*. So K. S: *forto*.
572	*down*. S: *n* inserted above the line.

576	*one*. S: *b one*.
580	*fro*. So O. S, K: *for*.
596	*byttur*. S: inserted above canceled *bett*.
603	Marginalia in S (at top of fol. 7r): *Genesis*.
607	*wyf*. S: inserted above the line.
612	*be*. S: inserted above the line.
621	*fyne*. So O. S: *syne*, followed by K.
633	Marginalia in S (at right of fol. 7r): *Abraham Sara Ysac*.
	wonnand. So S. K omits.
635	*and Sara*. So S. K omits.
638	*thei*. S: *the*, followed by K.
	lend. S: inserted above the line.
642	*myrth*. S: corrected from *myʒth*. Both meanings would, in fact, work. Sara has shown strength in her dealings but also her being comforted in line 640 would give ample cause for her happiness.
654	*suld*. S: inserted above the line.
656	*acord*. S: *a* inserted above the line.
661	Marginalia in S (at top of fol. 7v): *Genesis*.
662	*yf*. S: *he yf*.
668	Marginalia in S (at right of fol. 7v): *imolacio de Ysac*.
669	*theron*. S: *or þer*.
670	*Me*. S: *tyll me*.
681–82	Incomplete stanza indicates that perhaps lines are missing here. Though I am reluctant to do so, I have opted to number these missing lines in order to maintain number count with the existing edition of K.
692	*for to Hys*. So K. S: *fforto do hys*.
694–95	Missing lines. See textual note to lines 681–82, above.
702–03	Missing lines. See textual note to lines 681–82, above.
719	*God*. S: *h God*.
721	*have*. So K. S: *hath*.
722	*noght*. So S. K: *not*.
723	Marginalia in S (at top of fol. 8r): *Genesis*.
725	*tyd*. S: inserted above the line.
730	Marginalia in S (at right of fol. 8r): *de secunda uxore Abree*.
740	*gud*. So K. S: *guf*.
741	Marginalia in S (at right of fol. 8r): *de uxore Ysac*.
742	*fayrer*. So K. S: *fader*.
763	*Then*. S: *W Þen*.
768	*be*. So K. S omits.
780	*the*. So K. S omits.
784	Marginalia in S (at top of fol. 8v): no heading.
801	*hir*. S: inserted above canceled *hys*.
817	*He*. So K. S: *The*.
819	*wun*. So K. S: *wunt*.
833	*feld*. So K. S: *fold*.
	fon. So K. S: *fynd*.
841	Marginalia in S (at top of fol. 9r): *Genesis. Jacob et Rebecca*.

845	*hym.* S: inserted above the line.
858	*be felyn.* So S, K. O suggests *not be felyn*, assuming *felyn* to mean "feeling." If the term is parallel with our modern "felon," however, no emendation is necessary.
872	*Then.* So K. S: *the.*
877	*then.* S: inserted above the line.
882	*myn.* S: *n* inserted above the line.
889	*yow now.* So S. K inverts.
894	*howshald.* So K. S: *howshad.*
904	Marginalia in S (at top of fol. 9v): *Genesis. de dormicione iacob et scala domini.* *and grett.* So K. S: *and with grett.*
910	*sclepand.* So S. K: *slepand.*
912	*hyght.* S: inserted above canceled *ryght.*
915	*angels.* S: ~~at~~ *angels.*
927	*in.* S: inserted above the line.
944	*schawyd no chere.* So K. S: *schawnyd chere.*
949	*elder.* S: ~~ell~~ *elder.*
955	*hym.* S: ~~y~~ *hym.*
959	*mad Jacob mony.* So K. S: *mad full soyn Iacob þerof mony.*
961	Marginalia in S (at top of fol. 10r): *Genesis.*
966	*or.* So O. S, K: *of.*
979	*Jacob.* S: ~~Go~~ *Jacob.* *fro.* So O. S, K: *for.*
980	*made.* So K. S omits.
985	*Lya.* So K. S: *Lyi.*
987	*tha.* So K. S: *thei.*
988	*war.* So S. K inserts *trewly* before.
994	*scho.* So S. K omits. *that.* S: inserted above the line.
999	*bryght.* S, K: *brygh.*
1000	*schent.* S: inserted above the line.
1003	*Israell.* So K. S: *Iraell.*
1010	*the.* So K. S: *ther.*
1011	*brothyr.* So K. S: *broythyr.*
1013	*has.* So S. K omits.
1014	*Chanaan.* So S. K emends to *Chanany.*
1015	*in.* So K. S omits.
1021	Marginalia in S (at top of fol. 10v): *Genesis.*
1026	*afore.* So S. K emends to *a fother.*
1031	Marginalia in S (at left of fol. 10v): *Judas.*
1032	*name.* So K. S: *naman.*
1035	Marginalia in S (at left of fol. 10v): *Thamar.*
1059	*yt is.* So K. S: *is yt.*
1064	*then.* So K. S: *the.*
1071	*lever.* S: *r* inserted above the line.
1082	*hir.* S: *his.* K emends to *gart hir.*
1083	*And cled.* So K. S: bottom corner of the page is missing.

1084	*jape*. So S. K: *rape*.
1085	Marginalia in S (at top of fol. 11r): no heading.
1093	*hyr*. S: inserted above the line.
1104	*hir*. So K. S: *his*.
1106	*scho*. S: inserted above canceled *k*.
1112	*and*. So S. K omits.
	prevely. S: ~~pro~~ *prevely*.
1119–20	Missing lines. See textual note to lines 681–82, above.
1121	*monethyse*. So K. S: *mothneyse*.
1128	*hange*. S: *e* inserted above the line. K: *hang*.
1133–34	Missing lines. See textual note to lines 681–82, above.
1137	*was*. S: ~~r~~ *was*.
1139	*wroght*. S, K: *wrogh*.
1145	*gold*. S: ~~god~~ *gold*.
1146	*ther*. S: inserted above the line.
1147–48	Missing lines. See textual note to lines 681–82, above.
1151	Marginalia in S (at top of fol. 11v): no heading.
	By. So K. S: *Now by* inserted above the line, but *now* is repetitive within the line.
	I well. S: inserted above the line.
1152	*that*. S: ~~and~~ *that*.
1174	Marginalia in S (at right of fol. 11v): *Reversus est Jacob*.
1188	Marginalia in S (at top of fol. 11v): *de sompnio josephi*.
1189	*dremyd with*. So K. S: *dremyd then with*, but the second *then* is unnecessary.
1193	*schefe*. S: *f schefe*.
1194	*can*. S: inserted above the line.
1200	*me*. So K. S omits.
1203	*deme*. So O. S, K: *dreme*.
1205	*sall*. S: altered from *fall*.
1209	*Jacob*. So O. S, K: *Isac*. The error is certainly scribal, as Isaac is dead; Joseph's father is Jacob. Compare Genesis 37:11.
1213	Marginalia in S (at top of fol. 12r): *Genesis*.
1214	*more*. S: inserted above the line.
1228	*wyld*. So K. S: *wyldes*.
1230	*thei*. S: inserted above the line.
1236	*Egype*. S: inserted above canceled *ferr*.
1250	*namys call*. S: *mamys call*, corrected to *namys call*. K emends to *namys thei call*.
1253	*And*. S: *d* inserted above the line.
1255	*all scathe*. So K. S omits.
1264	*com fatt*. So S. K emends to *fatt com*.
	folde. So S. K emends to *flode*.
1268	*stud*. S: inserted above the line.
1269	*the clerkes*. So K. S omits.
1273	Marginalia in S (at top of fol. 12v): *Genesis*.
1274	*bend*. So K. S: *lend*.
1284	*hungur*. So K. S: *hugur*.
1290	*gret*. So S. K: *grett*.

1297	*ther then.* So K. S omits *ther.*
1298	*corn yf.* So K. S: *corn þer þen yf.*
1302	*ware.* So S. K omits.
1310	*down.* So O. S, K: *drownd.*
1333	Marginalia in S (at top of fol. 13r): *Genesis.*
1338	*have.* S: inserted below the line.
1345	*thei.* S: ~~he~~ *þei.*
1368	*Benjamyn.* S: *i* inserted above the line.
1393	Marginalia in S (at top of fol. 13v): no heading.
1399	*sayd.* So K. S: *say.*
1414	*sevyn.* So K. S: *xiiii.*
1417	*weld.* So K. S: *werld.*
1421	*when.* So K. S: *whe.*
1422	*ten and.* So S. K emends to *and X.*
1430	*multyplyd.* So S, O. K: *myltyplyd.*
1432	*schonged.* So K. S: *schonegd.*

BOOK OF EXODUS

1441	Marginalia in S (at top of fol. 14r): *Exodus.*
1441, 43	Lines indented to leave space for an initial capital; first letter of line 1441 written in the middle of the space.
1448	*gret.* So K. S: *gre.*
1451	*them.* So S, O. K: *the.*
1454	*forne.* S: ~~fore~~ *forne.*
1455	*yere.* S: *f ʒere.*
1468	*bot.* So K. S omits.
1470	*Amryn.* So K. S: *Maryn.*
1473	**The text of L begins here.**
1474	*thei.* S: *ł þei.*
	durst. S: ~~a~~ *durst.*
1475	*hym.* So L, K. S: *hyd.*
1476	Marginalia in S (at right of fol. 14r): *Inuencio Moysen.*
1477	*then.* So L, K. S omits.
1487	*name.* So L, K. S: *namyd.*
1496	*papes.* So L, K. S: *pape.*
1501	Marginalia in S (at top of fol. 14v): no heading.
1504	*socur.* So L, K. S: *socurd.*
1507	*dyd.* So L, K. S: *dyr.*
1520	*ben.* So S, L. K: *been.*
	ylk dele. S: inserted below the line.
1524	*cummand.* So O. S, K: *cunnand.* L: *connand.*
1534	*oft sythe.* So L, K. S: *of syght.*
1538	*with.* So L, K. S omits.
1543	*of.* So K. S omits.
1561	*thies.* S: *e* inserted above the line.
1562	*said.* So L, K. S: *fand.*

1563	Marginalia in S (at top of fol. 15r): *Exodus.*
1566	*Therfor.* S: ~~*that*~~ *þerfor.*
	with wordes fone. S: inserted above canceled *that same is hee.*
1568	*ne bettur.* So S. L, K emends to *no bettur.*
1576	*ys.* So L, K. S omits.
1577	*seyn.* S: inserted above the line.
1578	*bryn.* So S, O. L, K: *bryng.*
1579	*with.* So L, K. S omits.
1580	*soyn them hentt.* So K. S: *them hee hent.* L: *soone theym hent.*
1609	*meud.* So K. L: *meved.* S: *moud.*
1621	*keped.* So L, K. S omits.
1622	*than cumonly.* So L, K. S: *þam cumly.*
1623	Marginalia in S (at top of fol. 15v): no heading.
1628	*he.* So L, K. S omits.
1636	*yt.* So L, K. S omits.
1644	*bot.* So L, K. S: *bo.*
1646	*swylk.* So L, K. S: *swyll.*
1649	*I am.* S: inserted above the line.
1678	*their.* So L, K. S: *þoir.*
1681	Marginalia in S (at top of fol. 16r): *Pharo. Leviticus.*
1702	*say.* So L, K. S omits.
1708	*ase.* S: ~~*at*~~ *ase.*
1710	*sone.* So L, K. S omits.
1715	*bondom.* So O. S, K: *bondon.* L: *bondage.*
1717, 19	Lines indented to leave space for an initial capital; first letter of line 1717 written in the middle of the space.
1718	*so forto make theym turne theire moode.* So L, K. S: *wele wers then euer þei were* ~~*blode*~~.
1720	*blude.* S: inserted above the line.
1721	*noght.* So L, K. S omits.
1723	*fawt.* So K. L: *faute.* S: *faw.*
1726	*them.* So L, K. S omits.
1733	*syne.* So L, K. S: *soyne.*
1737	*byd ther byte.* So L, K. S: *byte þerof.*
1741	Marginalia in S (at top of fol. 16v): no heading.
1753	*come.* So L, K. S: *con*, inserted above the line.
	fast. So L, K. S: *fall.*
1754	*well wers.* So K. L: *mych wars.* S: *was well wers.*
1765	*over.* S: inserted above canceled *or.*
1766	*sone.* So L, K. S omits.
	blayne. So L, K. S: *blake rayn.*
1770	*and rayn.* So L, K. S omits.
1771	*With.* So L, K. S: *And with.*
	stryve. So L, K. S: *stroye.*
1775–76	So L, K. S omits lines.
1780	*tre.* S: inserted above the line.
1781	*then.* So L, K. S omits.

1790	*wold.* So L, K. S: *wer told.*
1792	*thei herd ther talys bee told.* So L, K. S: *þer talys bee.*
1794	*old.* S: inserted above the line.
1795	*tyme.* So S, L. K: *tyms.*
1801	Marginalia in S (at top of fol. 17r): *leviticus.*
1806	*na.* So L, K. S: *a.*
1818	*gart.* S: ~~gt~~ *gart.*
1830	*lyse.* So L., K. S: *lastes.*
1832	*have.* So L, K. S omits.
1842	*God.* S: ~~to~~ *god.*
	thor. S: inserted above the line.
1855	Marginalia in S (at right of fol. 17r): *Cantemus.*
1857	Marginalia in S (at top of fol. 17v): no heading.
1874	*that for them.* So L, K. S: *þerfor þei.*
1875	*sojourned.* So L, K. S: *suffern.*
1879	*theim.* So L, K. S: *þei.*
1891	*the.* So L, K. S: *þei.*
1892	*lyved.* So L, K. S: *lyve.*
1897	*fand thei non.* So L, K. S: *non þei fand*, with *non* inserted above the line.
1915	Marginalia in S (at top of fol. 18r): *leuiticus and Amalett.*
	sall. So L, K. S: *satt.*
1916	*I.* So L, K. S omits.
1922	*Amalec.* So L, K. S: *Amalet.*
1938	*gyfyn.* So L, O. S, K: *ȝfyn.*
1939	*wyse.* So L, K. S: *wyses.*
1956	S: lines 1951–52 after this line repeated, then canceled.
1970	*to.* So L, K. S: *at.*
1975	*On.* So L, K. S: *And.*
1977	Marginalia in S (at top of fol. 18v): no heading.
1984	*was.* S: ~~wax~~ *was.*
1985	*with.* So L, K. S omits.
1989	*them fald.* So L, K. S: *þen fall.*
1990	*them.* So L, K. S omits.
1992	*in.* So L, K. S: *on.*
1993	*An.* So L, K. S: *And.*
2002	*of*: S: ~~and~~ *of.*

BOOK OF NUMBERS

2017, 19	Lines indented to leave space for an initial capital; first letter of line 2017 written in the middle of the space.
2020	*wyrschyp.* So L, O. S, K: *wrschyp.*
2022	*heght.* S: *g* inserted above line.
2025	*Hys Jew.* So L, K. S: *that hys jews.*
2033	Marginalia in S (at top of fol. 19r): *Numeri.*
2037	*thei.* So L, K. S omits.
2039	*To.* S: two letters canceled before.

2054	*Hymself.* So L, K. S: *hymsef.*
2056	S: line transposed with line 2058.
2058	S: line transposed with line 2056.
	hys. So L, K. S: *hyr.*
	he. So L, K. S: *scho.*
2059	*down.* So L, K. S: *dow.*
2081	*soundly.* So K. S: *soudanly.* L: *savely.*
2087	Marginalia in S (at top of fol. 19v): no heading.
2105	*that.* So L, K. S: *and.*
2120	*nevyn.* S: inserted under the line.
2126	*bot.* So L, K. S: *bo.*
2127	*cetes.* S: ~~se~~ *cetes.*
2130	*lyse.* S: ~~is~~ *lyse.*
2131	*thor.* S: inserted over canceled *m.*
	them. So L, K. S: *þan.*
2133	*sayd.* So S, L. K: *say.*
2135	*betrayde.* So S, L. K: *betray.*
2139	Marginalia in S (at top of fol. 20r): no heading.
2143	*them.* So L, K. S: *hym.*
2148	*yow.* So S. L, K: *you.*
2150	*fell.* S: inserted above three canceled letters.
2153	*we.* So L, K. S omits.
	do. So K. S: *de,* which could have been intended to read *deschend.* L omits.
2176	*thryty.* So L, K. S: *thryrty.*
2188	*done.* So L, K. S omits.
2190	*moyne.* S: inserted below the line.
2191	Marginalia in S (at top of fol. 20r): no heading.
2197	*For.* S: *ffro* corrected to *ffor.*
2204	*them.* So L, K. S: *þen.*
2208	*fondly.* So K. S: *fendly.* L: *fowly.*
2220	*ther.* So L, K. S: *te.*
2242	*fele.* So L, K. S: *few.*
2243	Marginalia in S (at top of fol. 21r): no heading.
2254	*way.* S: ~~wax~~ *way.*
2258	*sense.* So K. L: *encence.* S omits.
2270	*thonour.* S: inserted above ~~tharne~~.
2272	*to.* So L, K. S omits.
2279	*new.* S: *w* inserted above line.

BOOK OF DEUTERONOMY

2281, 83	Lines indented to leave space for an initial capital; first letter of line 2281 written in the middle of the space.
2291	Marginalia in S (at top of fol. 21v): no heading.
2300	*twelft.* S: ~~th~~ *twelft.*
2312	*awn.* So L, K. S: *all.*
2342	*Moyses.* S: *y* inserted above the line.

2345	Marginalia in S (at top of fol. 22r): no heading.
2348	*welth.* So L, K. S: *mony welth.*
2358	*bot.* So L, K. S: *be.*
2366	*fyne.* S: inserted above the line.
2368	*rowed.* So L, K. S: *sowed.*
	syne. So L, K. S: *synd.*
2373	*releved.* So L, K. S: *rewled.*
2397	*Seon.* So L, K. S: *was kyng Seon.*
2401	Marginalia in S (at top of fol. 22v): no heading.
2404	*to.* S: inserted above canceled *and.*
2408	*that.* S: *at* inserted above the line.
2410	*of.* S: inserted above the line.
2432	*hym.* So L, K. S: *þem.*
2433	*consell.* So L, K. S: *conse.*
2438	*mo than.* So L, K. S omits.
2439	*To fyght.* So L, K. S omits.
2441	*Balam.* S: inserted above canceled *Abram* in another ink.
2451	*Balam.* S: inserted above canceled *Abram.*
2452	*cummand.* So L, K. S: *cunnand.*
2453	Marginalia in S (at top of fol. 23r): no heading.
2454	*Balame.* S: inserted above canceled *Abram.*
2462	*Amoryse.* So L, O. S, K: *Amonyse.*
2466	*beste wyse.* So L, K. S: *best awyce.*
2467	*He.* S: inserted above the line.
2474	*suld.* S: inserted above the line.
2475	*Ser.* So L, K. S: *sers.*
2477	*that.* So K. S, L omit.
2481	*Ye.* So L, K. S: *The.*
2492	*he.* S: inserted above the line.
2503	Marginalia in S (at top of fol. 23v): no heading.
	prophecyse. So L, K. S: *prophecy.*
2534	*for.* So L, K. S omits.
	fand. So L, K. S: *cowd fand.*
2535–36	So L, K. S omits lines.
2537	*way.* S: inserted above the line, *waye* or *wayd.*
2555	Marginalia in S (at top of fol. 24r): no heading.
2556	*flee.* S: *flere flee.*
2568	*Calaphe.* S: *Car Calaphe.*
2570	*foes.* So L, K. S: *fors.*
2578	*host.* So L, K. S: *hest.*
2580	*had.* So L, K. S: *þen had.*
2605	Marginalia in S (at top of fol. 24v): no heading.
	throly. S: inserted above the line.
2611	*cuntré.* S: *g cuntre.*
2622	*I.* So L, K. S omits.
2629	*you avayle.* So K. S: *abayle.* L: *avale.*
2635	*ne.* So L, K. S: *þen.*

2637	*how.* So S, L. K: *hou.*
2658	*well.* S: inserted below the line.
2659	Marginalia in S (at top of fol. 25r): no heading.

BOOK OF JOSHUA

2677, 79	Lines indented to leave space for an initial capital; first letter of line 2677 written in the middle of the space.
2683	*cuntré.* So L, K. S omits.
2704	*ways.* So L, K. S: *be ways.*
2709	Marginalia in S (at top of fol. 25v): no heading.
2715	*wardyns.* So L, K. S: *wardyn.*
2728	*govern.* So L, K. S: *gouerd.*
2741	*had to.* So L, K. S omits.
2744	*slayn.* S: inserted above the line.
2751	*ordan.* So K. S: *ordans,* with *s* canceled. L: *ordand.*
2762	*full strang.* S: inserted below the line.
2763	Marginalia in S (at top of fol. 26r): no heading.
2773	*when.* So L, K. S omits.
2787	*Arke.* S: inserted above the line in different ink.
2789	*song.* So K. S, L: *sang.*
2809	*commawnment.* So L, K. S: *commawment.*
2814	*and.* So L, K. S omits.
2815	Marginalia in S (at top of fol. 26v): no heading.
2816	*ewyn.* So L, K. S: *wyn.*
2817	*can.* So L, K. S omits.
2823	*Bot.* So L, K. S: *Bo.*
2835	*afferrom.* So L, K. S: *afforrom.*
2852	*myscheved.* S: *ved* inserted below the line.
2856	*this.* So L, K. S: *þs.*
2857	*he.* So L, K. S omits.
2867	Marginalia in S (at top of fol. 27r): no heading.
2873	*dowt.* S: *đ dowt.*
2875	*to.* S: inserted above the line.
2881	*can.* So K. L: *gun.* S omits.
2884	*one.* So S, O. L, K: *wone.*
2918	*knew.* S: inserted below the line.
2919	Marginalia in S (at top of fol. 27v): no heading.
2923	*By.* So L, K. S: *Bot.*
2924	*When.* S: *ff when.*
	new. S: inserted above the line.
2935	*Bot.* S: *t* inserted above the line in different ink.
2954	*wold.* So L, K. S: *was.*
	last. So L, K. S: *fast.*
2961	*them.* So L, K. S: *hym.*
2973	Marginalia in S (at top of fol. 28r): no heading.
2978	*byd$_2$.* So L, O. S, K: *abyd.*

2980	*in.* So L, K. S: *made.*
2981	*them.* So L, K. S: *þen.*
2990	*fulse.* So S, O. L, K: *sulse.*
2996	*your God with gud wyll.* So L, K. S: *wyll your god with gud.*
3000	*maystry.* So O. S, K: *maystur.* L: *maistres.*
3007	*myrth.* So L, K. S: *mrth.*
3008	*werke.* S: *r* inserted above the line.
3010	*noyd.* S: inserted above canceled *new.*
3023	Marginalia in S (at top of fol. 28v): no heading.
3032	*paynyms.* So L, K. S: *pynyms.*
3054	*betwene.* S: *twene* inserted below the line.
3061	*arayse.* So L, K. S: *he rayse.*
3064	*hyght.* So O. S, L, K: *myght.*
3066	*heyght.* S: inserted below the line.
3072	*fulfylled.* S: l_1 inserted above the line.
	and. S: *d* inserted above the line.
3075	Marginalia in S (at top of fol. 29r): no heading.
3085	*fayre.* So L, K. S: *þei fayre.*
3086	*mett.* So L, K. S: *wett.*
3114	*is₂.* So L, K. S omits.
3120	*kyde.* S: ~~dede~~ *kyde.*
3123	Marginalia in S (at top of fol. 29v): no heading.
3125	*gud wone.* So L, K. S: *when þei can wun.*
3126	*of.* So L, K. S omits.
3130	*bot.* So L, K. S: *be.*
3135	*Cananews.* So L, K. S: *Canews.*
3136	*nacion.* So L, O. S: *nacon*, with *n* inserted above the line, followed by K.
	your awn. So L, K. S: *yf ȝe be ouer drawn.*
3137	*schrews.* So L, K. S: *schews.*
3138	*drawn.* So L, K. S omits.
3140	*sall.* So L, K. S: *sad.*
3142	*thyng.* S: *thynges.*
3155	*other.* So L, K. S: *other ther.*
3156	*Judicum.* S: *Iudicium*, with last *i* canceled.

BOOK OF JUDGES

3157, 59	Lines indented to leave space for an initial capital; first letter of line 3157 written in the middle of the space.
3171	Marginalia in S (at top of fol. 30r): no heading.
3175	*layd.* S: inserted above the line.
3176	*fell.* So S, O, Stern (p. 281). L, K: *few.*
3184	*bot.* So L, K. S: *bo.*
	unteld. So L, K. S: *vntyll.*
3191	*land.* So L, K. S: *landes.*
3197	*thore.* S: ~~þer~~ *þore.*
3207	*God.* So L, K. S omits.

3210	*whyls*. So L, K. S: *whys*.
3219	Marginalia in S (at top of fol. 30v): no heading.
3228	*kepe to*. So L, K. S: *to kepe*.
3235	*Bynjamyns*. S: ~~*beniam*~~ *byniamyns*.
3239	*nere*. S: *þ nere*.
3248	*we*. S: inserted above the line.
3250	*qwat₂*. So S. L: *what*. K: *qwatt*.
3263	*thei*. S, L, K: *the*.
3266	*rews*. S: *s* inserted below canceled *ed*.
3273	Marginalia in S (at top of fol. 31r): no heading.
3276	*syn*. So L, K. S: *sym*.
3278	*pyn*. So L, K. S: *payn*.
3281	*thryve*. So L, K. S: *thyrn*.
3282	*acordyd*. So L, K. S: *acordyng*.
3297–98	So L, K. S omits lines.
3302	*maynten*. So L, K. S: *mayntem*.
	hym. So L, K. S: *he*.
3308	*them*. So L, O. S, K: *thei*.
3323	*come the*. So L, O. S, K: *come to the*.
3327	Marginalia in S (at top of fol. 31v): no heading.
3353	*then ordand*. So L, K. S: *ordand þen*.
3356	*surely*. So L, K. S: *serely*.
3357	*regned*. So L, K. S: *remeued*.
3381	Marginalia in S (at top of fol. 32r): no heading.
3386	*thei*. So L, K. S: *þat*.
	Hys. So L, K. S: *hy*.
3417	*the*. S: ~~*vnto þe cuntre*~~.
3431	Marginalia in S (at top of fol. 32v): no heading.
3445	*Gedion*. So K. S: *Gedian*. L: *Gedeon*.
	yt. So L, K. S: *ys*.
3447	*panyms*. So L, K. S: *payms*.
3453	*and*. S: *and þ*.
3458	*folke*. So L, K. S omits.
3466	*pyn*. So L, K. S: *payn*, with *a* canceled.
3473	*harnys*. So L, O. S, K: *armys*.
	owt. So L, O. S, K: *of*.
3481	Marginalia in S (at top of fol. 33r): no heading.
3491	*Gepte*. So K. L: *Iepta*. S: *Septe*.
3493	*Gepte*. So K. L: *Iepta*. S: *Septe*.
3499	*os*. So L, K. S: *of*.
3502	*to*. So L, K. S omits.
	myght. So L, K. S omits.
3505	*hertly*. So L, K. S: *herthy*.
3520	*home*. So L, K. S omits.
3521	*byd*. So L, K. S: *hyd*.
3523	*saw*. So L, K. S omits.
3526	*not*. So L, K. S omits.

3529	Marginalia in S (at top of fol. 33v): no heading.
3538	*comforth.* So L, K. S: *comferth.*
3546	*schent.* S: inserted below the line.
3554	*gud.* S: ~~gy~~ *gud.*
3555	*Leues.* S: ~~leys~~ *leues.*
	fader. So L, K. S omits.
3570	*fader.* So L, K. S omits.
3575	*swopped.* So K. S, L: *swapped.*
3577	Marginalia in S (at top of fol. 16v): no heading.
3580	*heddyd.* S: ~~he~~ *heddyd.*
3581	*be.* So L, K. S omits.
3582	*avysed.* So L, O. S, K, P: *abayst.*
3583	*Foyle vow.* So L, K. S: *ffeyle bow.*
3584	*sakles.* So L, K. S: *sakes.*
3587	*Both of.* So S, L. K: *of.*
3592	*Achyron.* So S, K. L: *Ailaon.* The judge's name is Elon (or Ahialon), as the L reading correctly reads. S's *Achyron* appears to be tainted by Aijalon, which is the name of the place where Elon is buried.
3593	*aght.* Stern: *VIII* (Review, p. 281). S, K: *XX.* L: ?????? Compare Judges 12:14.
	yere. So S, Stern (Review, p. 281). L, K omit.
3600	*ware.* S: inserted above canceled *whar.*
3603	*in.* So L, K. S: *and.*
3605	*chewalry.* S: ~~chyl~~ *chewalry.*
3606	*worthy.* So L, K. S: *worth.*
3612	Marginalia in S (at right of fol. 34v): *Sampson.*
3625	Marginalia in S (at top of fol. 34v): no heading.
3627	*of.* So L, K. S omits.
3641	*ferse.* So L, K. S: *forse.*
3652	*bycause.* S: *u* inserted above the line.
3660	*process.* So L, K. S: *processer.*
3679	Marginalia in S (at top of fol. 35r): no heading.
3694	*Tanna.* S: *tannar.*
3706	*ther lay.* So L, K. S: *þat lady.*
3720	*he hys hert hade.* So L, K. S: *hys hert to hyre hade.*
3724	*kyng.* So L, K. S: *ȝyng.*
3729	Marginalia in S (at top of fol. 35v): no heading.
3745	*not.* So L, K. S omits.
3763	*forto.* So L, K. S: *fort.*
3781	Marginalia in S (at top of fol. 36r): no heading.
3816	*to.* S: inserted above canceled *owt of.*
3831	Marginalia in S (at top of fol. 36v): no heading.
	wore. So L, K. S: *was borne.*
3835	*to.* So L, K. S omits.
3841	*of.* S: ~~oser~~ *of.*
3852	*tresty.* So S. L: *thryfty.* K: *trefty.*
3864	*abays.* So O. S: *abayst.* L, K: *abavst.*
3868	*it.* So L, K. S omits.

3872   *mony*. S: inserted above canceled *many*.

                 to. S: inserted above the line.

3874   *this*. So L, K. S: þis þis.

3884   *in hy*. So L, K. S: *a way*.

3885   Marginalia in S (at top of fol. 37r): no heading.

3890   *clene*. So L, K. S: *clere*.

3902   *thiselfe*. So S, L. K: *thi folke*.

3924   *thryty*. So L, K. S: *thryrty*.

3925   *fayre*. S: ~~fader~~ *fayre*.

3939   Marginalia in S (at top of fol. 37v): no heading.

3941   *How*. So K. S, L: *And how*.

3944   *lyon*. S: inserted above the line.

3948   *dyscrye*. S: ~~dr~~ *dsycrye*.

3951   *I not*. So L, K. S: *not I*.

3956   *fro*. So L, K. S: *to*.

3957   *is*. So L, K. S omits.

3958   *say*. S: ~~see~~ *say*.

3962   *sett*. S: inserted above the line.

3968   *mett*. S: inserted below the line.

3987   *if*. So L, K. S: *of*.

3988   *tyme*. So L, K. S omits.

3990   *well to deme*. S: inserted below the line.

3991   Marginalia in S (at top of fol. 38r): no heading.

3992   *fayn*. So L, K. S omits.

3997   *has*. S: corrected from *hath*.

4000   *told*. S: inserted above the line.

4010   *fayn*. S: inserted above the line.

4036   *fers foxys*. So Stern (Review, p. 281). S: *fers wulfes*. K: *wulfes*. L: *wolves*, corrected to *foxes* by a later hand.

4043   Marginalia in S (at top of fol. 38v): no heading.

4046   *was born*. S: inserted above the line.

4058   *mone*. S: inserted above the line.

4062   S: scribe mistakenly copied line 4064 before canceling it and copying the correct line in the interlinear space.

4065   *bynd*. S: ~~bryng~~ *bynd*.

4071   *lordes*. So L, K. S: *lord*.

4075   *he*. So L, K. S omits.

4076   *that ryot*. So L, K. S: *yt*.

4083   *bede*. So L, K. S: *bode*.

4089   *thei*. So L, K. S: þer.

4090   *thei*. So L, K. S, Stern (Review, p. 281): þat.

4093   Marginalia in S (at top of fol. 39r): no heading.

4094   *well he*. So L, K. S omits.

4099   *panyms*. So L, K. S: *payms*.

4106   *them*. So L, K. S omits.

4108   *in*. S: ~~son~~ *in*.

4117   *God*. S: ~~w~~ *god*.

4122	*a.* So L, K. S omits.
4134	*moyght.* S: inserted above canceled *myȝt.*
4141	Marginalia in S (at top of fol. 39v): no heading.
4165	*whatso.* S: *t* inserted above the line.
4179	*fro.* S: corrected from *for.*
4180	*His.* So L, K. S omits.
4182	*postes.* So L, O. S, K: *postrons*
	tyll. S: inserted below the line.
4185	*that.* So L, K. S: *þen,* altered from *þem.*
4189	Marginalia in S (at top of fol. 40r): no heading.
4198	*he.* So L, K. S omits.
4203	*yf.* So L, K. S: *of.*
4205	*Soreth.* So L, K. S: *secrett.*
4207	*hert all hale to.* So L, K. S: *hale.*
4218	*thei.* So L, K. S omits.
4222	*dyssayve.* So S, L. K: *dyssauyue.*
4230	*wyghtnes.* S: *t* inserted above the line.
4238	Marginalia in S (at bottom of fol. 40r): *quintus.*
4239	Marginalia in S (at top of fol. 40v): no heading.
4243	*myghtis.* So L, O. S, K: *myghis.*
4251	*me.* So L, K. S omits.
4288	*scho.* S: *scho ~~sch~~.*
4290	*and.* So L, K. S: *A.*
4291	Marginalia in S (at top of fol. 41r): no heading.
4300	*wast.* S: inserted above the line.
4310	*hed.* So L, K. S: *hend.*
4314	*be.* So L, K. S omits.
4330	*by.* So L, K. S omits.
4333	*pyn.* So L, K. S: *payn.*
4337	*fyn.* So L, K. S: *feyn.*
4345	Marginalia in S (at top of fol. 41v): no heading.
4353	*delfull.* So L, K. S: *defull.*
4358	*hyd.* S: inserted above the line.
4362	*byd.* S: inserted below the line.
4365	*Gaza.* So L, K. S: *ga all.*
	ga. So L, K. S omits.
4380	*gret.* So L, K. S: *gre.*
4386	*hyd.* S: inserted below the line.
4388	*dyd.* So L, K. S: *dyȝt.*
4389	*hir.* So L, K. S: *his.*
4399	Marginalia in S (at top of fol. 42r): no heading.
4424	*that.* S: *and that.*
4438	*he.* So L, K. S omits.

BOOK OF RUTH

4441, 43	Lines indented to leave space for an initial capital; first letter of line 4441 written in the middle of the space.
4447	Marginalia in S (at top of fol. 42v): no heading.
4449	*pupplyst.* S: *þ pupplyst.*
4454	*we.* S: *e* inserted above the line.
4460	*and in ther tyme.* So L, K. S omits.
4462	*Chelon.* S: *chelyon,* with *y* canceled.
4464	*Maalon.* S: ~~*Thal*~~ *Maalon.*
4486	*left.* So L, K. S: *led.*
4499	Marginalia in S (at top of fol. 43r): no heading.
4509–10	So L, K. S omits lines.
4511	*The God.* S: *The law of god.*
4513	*of hew and hyd.* So L, K. S: *hyd and hew.*
4520	*as for hyr dew.* So L, K. S: *for þei non sew.*
4537	*sojourns.* S: *u* inserted above the line.
4542	*sal.* So L, K. S: *sab.*
4544	*so.* So L, K. S: *hyr.*
4549	Marginalia in S (at top of fol. 43v): no heading.
4562	*felles.* So L, K. S: *feldes.*
4574	*unto.* S: *vn* inserted above the line.
4575	*wuns.* S: ~~*vn*~~ *wuns.*
4581	*forthi.* S: *for* inserted above canceled *to dwell.*
4589	*cyteseyn.* So L, K. S: *certayn.*
4602	*yt is ryght.* So L, K. S: *I haue heyȝt.*
4603	Marginalia in S (at top of fol. 44r): no heading.
4615	*withowtyn.* So L, K. S, Stern (Review, p. 281): *was withowtyn.*
4616	*was rutt; of hym.* So L, K. S: *of hym was rutt.* Stern (Review, p. 281) emends this line to *Jesse the Jew. Of hym we rede,* taking *the Jew* from L, deleting a dittograph *was,* and assuming the existing *rutt* to be a marginal notation (for "Ruth") that has slipped into the text. I have treated the matter more simply, repunctuating K but assuming *rutt* to mean "begot" (from *rutte*).

FIRST BOOK OF KINGS

4633, 35	Lines indented to leave space for an initial capital; first letter of line 4633 written in the middle of the space.
4641	*prophetes.* So L, K. S: *prophet.*
4642	*banere.* So L, O. S, K: *private.*
4649	Marginalia in S (at top of fol. 44v): no heading.
4666	*wyfes.* So L, K. S: *wyfe.*
	chylder. So L, K. S: *chyld.*
4669	*Thei.* So L, K. S: *he.*
4681	*withoutyn.* So S, L. K: *withowtyn.*
4688	*wode.* S: inserted below the line.
4691	*yf.* So L, K. S: *of.*

4698	*he.* So L, K. S: *I.*
4699	Marginalia in S (at top of fol. 45r): no heading.
4711	*to.* S: blotted.
4721	*The.* So L, K. S: *he.*
4724	*well.* S: inserted above the line.
4730	*both.* So L, K. S: *bot.*
4741	*ys.* So L, K. S: *hys.*
4743	*Be.* So L, K. S: *Bot.*
4744	*beyryng.* S: inserted above 6 canceled letters (*byrnyg*?).
4748	*dowt.* So L, K. S: *dow.*
4749	Marginalia in S (at top of fol. 45v): no heading.
4753	*ryght.* So L, K. S omits.
4758	*sithes Ser.* So L, K. S: *s.*
4759	*wyght.* So L, O. S, K: *wygh.*
4767	*certayn.* So L, K. S omits.
4780	*he.* So L, K. S omits.
	servaunt. So S. L, K: *seruant.*
4798	*sew.* S: ~~be~~ *sew.*
4801	Marginalia in S (at top of fol. 46r): no heading.
4815	*Trowghowt.* S: *t* inserted above the line.
4839	*Felesteyns.* S: e_3 inserted above the line.
4844	*for.* So L, K. S: *or.*
4855	Marginalia in S (at top of fol. 46v): no heading.
4877	*fyve.* L, K: *V.* S: *VII.*
4884	*Arke.* S: ~~t~~ *arke.*
4891	*clenely.* So L, K. S: *clene.*
4909	Marginalia in S (at top of fol. 47r): no heading.
4919	*jewells.* So L, K. S: *jews.*
4922	*were.* S: *were* ~~so nere~~.
4944	*nothyng.* S: *no* ~~no~~.
4952	*mare.* S: *þ mare.*
4953	*Fro.* So L, O. S, K: *ffor.*
4954	*fold.* So L, K. S: *sold.*
4961	Marginalia in S (at top of fol. 47v): *liber primus Samuel.*
4996–97	So L, K. S omits lines.
5008	*space.* So L, K. S: *place.*
5012	*our.* So L, K. S omits.
5013	Marginalia in S (at top of fol. 48r): *Samuel, Saule.*
5016	*then.* So L, K. S: *þem.*
5021	*Saul.* S: *Saule,* with canceled *e.*
5024	*rachyd.* So L, K. S: *rachayd.*
5067	Marginalia in S (at top of fol. 48v): no heading.
5087	*be.* So L, K. S: *he.*
5117	*profecyes.* So L, K. S: *profecye.*
5120	*Saul.* S: *saule,* with canceled *e.*
5121	Marginalia in S (at top of fol. 49r): no heading.
5140	*myghty.* So L, K. S: *myȝt.*

5146	*begyne.* So L, K. S: *be gane.*
5150–51	So L, K. S omits lines.
5163	*call.* So L, K. S: *cald.*
5165	*Then.* So L, K. S: *þem.*
5174	*spyll.* S: inserted above canceled *pyn.*
5177	Marginalia in S (at top of fol. 49v): no heading.
5190	*that.* So L, K. S: *yt.*
5197	*towns.* So L, K. S: *towas.*
5200	*also.* So K. L: *theym.* S: *so.*
5202	*tho.* So L, K. S: *þor.*
5204	*dewlfull.* So L, K. S: *dewfull.*
5210	*encrese.* So L. S: *encreses.* K: *encresse.*
5212	*Jabese.* So L, K. S: *Jabase.*
5218	*have.* So L, K. S: *saue.*
5219	*weld.* So L, K. S: *well.*
5220	*save.* So L, K. S: *haue.*
5228	*tho.* So L, K. S: *two.*
5230	*to.* So L, K. S: *so.*
5233	Marginalia in S (at top of fol. 50r): no heading.
	The. So L, K. S omits.
5234	*same.* So L, K. S omits.
5239	*of.* So L, K. S omits.
	new. S: *o new.*
5242	*us.* S: *t vs.*
5258	*sone.* S: inserted above the line.
5259	*bryng.* So L, K. S: *kyng.*
5261	*sere.* So L, O. S, K: *thre.*
5271	*of₁.* So L, K. S omits.
5276	*have.* So L, K. S omits.
5278	*that.* S: *it þat.*
	outrayd. So L, K. S: *ouerrayd.*
5286	*on.* So L, K. S omits.
	he. So L, K. S: *forto.*
5287	Marginalia in S (at top of fol. 50v): no heading.
	down. So S, L. K: *doun.*
5294	*bot.* So L, K. S: *be.*
5313	*gat.* S: *gra gart.*
5315	S: *at* at end of line.
5316	*than.* So L, K. S: *þat.*
5329	*gyfyn.* So L, O. S, K: *yfyn.*
5331	*we.* So L, K. S: *he.*
5334	*frendschep.* S: *d* inserted above the line.
5337	*frend.* So L, K. S: *frendes.*
5340	*to.* S: *h to.*
	bod. S: *bode,* with canceled *e.*
5341	Marginalia in S (at top of fol. 51r): no heading.
5342	*God.* So L, K. S: *to god.*

5346	*Saul.* S: inserted above canceled *samuel.*
5389	*harvest.* So L, K. S: *hardnes.*
5391	Marginalia in S (at top of fol. 51v): no heading.
5396	*bot.* So L, K. S: *both.*
5405	*hym.* So L, K. S: *all.*
5406	*he.* So L, K. S, Stern (Review, p. 281): *ȝe.*
	wend. So L, K. S omits.
5412	*gentyll.* So L, K. S omits.
5414	*new tythandes.* So L, K. S: *noe.*
5418	*them.* So L, K. S omits.
5420	*to.* So L, K. S omits.
5428	*never.* So L, K. S omits.
5430	*say.* So K. S: *þei say.*
	the. So L, K. S omits.
5436	*to.* So L, K. S omits.
5441	*them.* So L, K. S: *þei.*
5443	Marginalia in S (at top of fol. 52r): *liber primus Regum.*
5444	*kene.* So L, K. S omits.
5445	*els.* So L, K. S: *als.*
5450	*chyvalry.* S: ~~chyl~~ *chyvalry.*
5464	*ware.* S: inserted above the line.
5467	*abyd.* So L, K. S: *to abyd.*
5470	*his.* So L, K. S: *he.*
5475	*he.* So L, K. S omits.
5488	*he.* So L, K. S omits.
	bestes. So L, K. S: *best.*
5491	*on.* So L, K. S omits.
5494	Marginalia in S (at bottom of fol. 52r): *sextus.*
5495	Marginalia in S (at top of fol. 52v): no heading.
5508	*no.* So L, K. S omits.
5509	*Therfor.* So L, K. S: *þer.*
5510	*and.* S: letter canceled before.
5518	*kyng.* So L, K. S omits.
5520	So L, K. S omits line.
5536	*yf.* So L, K. S: *of.*
5549	*thei.* So L, K. S omits.
5551	Marginalia in S (at top of fol. 53r): no heading.
5557	*payn so.* So L, K. S: *so payn.*
5571	*when.* So L, K. S: *whe.*
5573	*relyed.* So L, K. S: *releved.*
5580	*prestely.* So L, K. S: *presthely.*
5581	*velany.* S: *f velany.*
5586	*swere.* S: letter canceled before.
5589	*sun.* So L, K. S omits.
5591	*thore.* S: inserted above canceled *whore.*
5596	*honycamys.* S: letter canceled before.
	camys. S: ~~comy~~ *camys.*

5603	Marginalia in S (at top of fol. 53v): no heading.
5605	*thei*. So L, K. S: *thet*.
5645	*have*. S: corrected from *nave*.
5654	*mekyll*. So L, K. S omits.
5655	Marginalia in S (at top of fol. 54r): no heading.
5656	*hole*. So S. L, K: *hold*.
5669	*hym meld*. So L, K. S: *to mell*.
5670	*bot*. So L, K. S: *bo*.
5676	*hym*. S: *a hym*.
5680	*wan*. So L, K. S: *wang*.
	grett. S: *þ grett*.
5687	*was*. So L, K. S omits.
5688	*Mycoll*. So L, K. S: *was mycoll*.
5702	*pyn*. So L, K. S: *payn*.
5708	*fayntnes*. S: *s* inserted above the line.
5709	Marginalia in S (at top of fol. 54v): *liber primus Regum*.
5712	*els*. So L, K. S: *þat*.
	thou. So L, K. S: *þe*.
5715	*commawndment*. So L, K. S: *commawndmentes*.
5727	*wyse*. S: inserted above canceled *was*.
5758	*ne*. So L, K. S: *þei ne*.
5759	*Both*. So L, K. S: *Bot*.
5763	Marginalia in S (at top of fol. 55r): no heading.
5766	*help*. So L, K. S omits.
5768	*them*. So L, K. S: *hym*.
5788	*bryng*. S: inserted above the line.
5792	*thyng*. S: letter canceled before.
5795	*gyfes*. So L, K. S: *gyfe*.
5797	*gre*. S: *gre we*.
5798	*sayd*. So L, K. S omits.
5800	*thou*. So L, K. S: *þei*.
5810	*space*. So L, K. S: *place*.
5817	Marginalia in S (at top of fol. 55v): no heading.
5821	*well*. So L, K. S omits.
5822	*hym*. So L, K. S omits.
5824	*yt*. So L, K. S omits.
5869	Marginalia in S (at top of fol. 56r): no heading.
5899	*Ya*. S: *y ȝa*.
5900	*is*. So L, K. S: *yt is*.
5923	Marginalia in S (at top of fol. 56v): no heading.
5954	*wher*. So S, K. L: *where*.
5958	*mynstralcy*. So L, K. S: *maystry*.
5960	*ever*. So L, K. S omits.
5964	*Saul*. S: *saule*, with *e* canceled.
5965	*spake of*. So L. S, K: *of spake*.
5967	*sare*. So L, K. S: *sere*.
5969	*wyd*. So L, K. S: *wyld*.

5970	*was.* So L, K. S omits.
5972	*mend.* S: inserted above the line.
5973	S: the scribe mistakenly copies line 5981 before canceling it.
5975	Marginalia in S (at top of fol. 57r): no heading.
6002	*belufed.* L, K: *be lufed.* S: *he lufed.*
6013	*them.* So L, K. S omits.
6022	*in.* So L, K. S omits.
6025	*wold.* S: inserted above canceled *was.*
6029	Marginalia in S (at top of fol. 57v): no heading.
6055	*of:* S: ~~ost~~ *of.*
6073	*tythand.* S: ~~th~~ *tythand.*
6079	*holy.* So L, K. S: *hely.*
6081	Marginalia in S (at top of fol. 58r): no heading.
6090	*bere.* S: inserted above the line.
6107	*thou fro come.* So L, K. S: *fro con fall.*
6109	*his.* So L, K. S omits.
6117	*lerd.* So L, K. S: *lernyd.*
6119	*his.* So L, K. S omits.
6121	*note new.* So K. S: *note of new.* L: *tythandes new.*
6133	Marginalia in S (at top of fol. 58v): no heading.
6134	*doyghtynes.* So L, K. S: *doyghty dede.*
6136	*price.* So S. L, K: *þrice.*
	that prowesse. So L, K. S: *þer prownesse.*
6142	*hand.* So L, K. S: *handes.*
6150	*not.* So L, K. S: *no.*
6151	*hert he.* So L, K. S: *hert hele hent he.*
	holy. So L, K. S omits.
6152	*certayn.* So L, K. S omits.
6153	*He.* So L, K. S: *Hys.*
6157	*yf.* So L, K. S: *of.*
6167	*For.* S, L, K: *Fro.*
6169	*fayged.* So L, K. S: *fayg.*
6175	*for.* So L, K. S: *forus.*
6180	*in.* So L, K. S: *on.*
6185	Marginalia in S (at top of fol. 59r): *liber primus Regum. Saul and David.*
6200	*glad.* S: inserted above the line.
6203	*dysplessyd.* So L, K. S: *dysessyd.*
6206	*no.* So L, K. S omits.
	hire. So L, K. S: *his.*
6208	*was.* So L, K. S: *wad.*
6210	*scho myght ever.* So K. S: *noyȝt to.* L: *if she myght.*
6217	*If.* So L, K. S: *Of.*
6218	*to gyf.* S: ~~to h~~ *to gyf.*
6223–24	So L, K. S omits lines.
6233	*that.* So L, K. S: *þar.*
6239	*when.* S: ~~wh~~ *when.*
6241	Marginalia in S (at top of fol. 59v): no heading.

6245–6968	**Missing in L (fols. 145–148 lost).**
6245	*sterd*. S: *ferd sterd*.
6246	*hedes*. So K. S: *hendes hom*.
6247	*then*. S: altered from *þem*.
6248	*was*. So K. S omits.
6250–95	The overall numbering of these lines in K is incorrect due to miscounting.
6260	*heyght*. So K. S: *dyd*.
6270	*lede*. S: *lerde*.
6272	*hym spede*. So K. S: *to hym speke*.
6297	Marginalia in S (at top of fol. 60r): no heading.
6303	*not*. So K. S: *no*.
6308	*that*. So K. S omits.
6315	*ded*. S: *dr ded*.
	was. S: *r was*.
6319	*dede*. So K. S: *lede*.
6324	*went*. So K. S: *well*.
6331	*thei*. S, K: *the*.
6335–36	Lines missing in S (and L, see textual note to lines 6245–6968).
6342	*that*. So K. S omits.
6350	*the*. S: *he þe*.
	kyng. So K. S omits.
	kindes. So K. S: *knds*, with an *e* marked for insertion between *k* and *n*.
6353	Marginalia in S (at top of fol. 60v): no heading.
6355	*that con hym quell*. So K. S: *he wold*.
6356	*he wold bot wytt*. So K. S: *bot wytt he wold*.
6360	*abate*. S: *a*₁ inserted above the line.
6370	*all*. So K. S: *a*.
6373	*To*. So K. S omits.
6375	*spare*. S: *fare spare*.
6390	*dedes*. S: *h dedes*.
6407	Marginalia in S (at top of fol. 61r): no heading.
6419	*he*. S: *hy he*.
6426	*sped*. S: *stede sped*.
6433	*sen*. So S. K omits.
6452	*meneye*. S: *ne* inserted above the line.
6463	Marginalia in S (at top of fol. 61v): no heading.
6465	*Bot*. S: *Bor*, with *t* inserted above the line.
6471	*then*. So K. S: *þem*.
6474	*store*. So K. S: *stere*.
6477	*thore*. So S. K: *fore*.
6484	*aspy*. S: *a* inserted above the line.
6490	*he*. So K. S omits.
6502	*in all*. So K. S: *all in*.
6509	*maystrays*. S: *rays* above canceled *ters*.
6517	Marginalia in S (at top of fol. 62r): no heading.
6518	*he*. So K. S: *þei*.
6522	*Go*. So K. S: *do*.

6524	*unto.* So K. S: *vnt.*
6532	*to.* S: ~~town~~ *to.*
6535	*So.* S: *Soí.*
6538	*wedys.* S: *weddys.*
6545	*tythyng.* S: ~~th~~ *tythyng.*
6554	*to.* So K. S omits.
6563	*to be.* S: *to ~~be~~ be.*
6571	Marginalia in S (at top of fol. 62v): no heading.
6572	*lett.* So K. S: *sett.*
6575	*ferther.* So K. S: *fererther.*
6577	*to.* So K. S omits.
	Gedyn. So S. K: *Geden.*
6579	*Then.* So K. S: *Bot.*
6583	*glad.* So K. S omits.
	wyn. So K. S: *wysch.*
6585	*when thei.* So K. S: *when þat þei.*
6590	*threpe again.* So K. S: *þre ennen in.*
6592	*governd.* K notes this and an instance in line 9343 as cases of inverted spelling.
	in. So K. S omits.
6593	*thin.* So K. S: *in.*
6619	*uncertayn.* S: *un* inserted above an uncanceled *in.*
6625	Marginalia in S (at top of fol. 63r): no heading.
6629	*to.* So K. S: *forto.*
6632	*to.* S: *to ~~by~~.*
6640	*con.* S: corrected from *com.*
6642	*bede.* So K. S: *be.*
6651	*made.* So K. S omits.
6660	*bot.* S: *t* inserted above the line.
6662	*two.* So K. S: *o* and part of *w* lost due to trimming.
6668	*wo.* So K. S: *fo.*
6675	*cummand.* So K. S: *cumnand* or *cunnand* (minim missing from written nasal).
6679	Marginalia in S (at top of fol. 63v): no heading.
6680	*werke.* So K. S: *werke hym.*
	hys. So K. S omits.
6683	*thor.* So S. K: *þer.*
6686	*all.* S: inserted above *that₁.*
6692	*otterest.* So K. S: *ottest.*
6694	*non away.* So K. S: *non of þem away.*
6718	*time.* So K. S: *tome.*
6721	*raythely.* So K. S: *rayly.*
6729	*Bot.* So K. S: *Bor.*
6732	*the soth.* S: *þe ~~sone wo~~ soth.*
6735	Marginalia in S (at top of fol. 64r): no heading.
6740	*thee.* So K. S omits.
6752	*yt.* S: inserted above canceled *he.*
	slytt. S: inserted above canceled *kytt.*

6777	Marginalia in S (at right of fol. 64r): *Saul and David unitas*.
6786	*thou*. S: inserted above canceled *I*.
6789	*then hyne*. So K. S: *with hym*.
6791	Marginalia in S (at top of fol. 64v): no heading.
	To. S: ~~And~~ *To*.
6808	*do*. So K. S: *to*.
6818	*als*. So K. S: *& als*.
6825	*the*. S: inserted above the line.
6831	*In*. So K. S omits.
6833–34	Lines missing in S (and L, see textual note to lines 6245–6968).
6837	*wyght*. So K. S: *wyghty*.
6845	*Who*. So K. S: *When*.
6849	Marginalia in S (at top of fol. 65r): no heading.
6851	*All*. S: ~~als~~ *all*.
6867	*aftur*. So K. S omits.
6872	*had*. So K. S omits.
6880	*pelure*. So K. S: *penure*.
6881	*presentes scho*. So K. S: *present sch*.
6889	*kynd*. S: ~~kyng~~ *kynd*.
6900	*fud*. So K. S: *gud*.
6901	*knight*. So S. K: *knyȝt*.
6905	Marginalia in S (at top of fol. 65v): *liber primus Regum. De nupciis david and Abygay*.
6909	*mett*. S: ~~þer~~ *mett*.
6937	*Then folke*. So K. S: *þen grett folke*.
6952	*buske*. S: ~~but I~~ *buske*.
6963	Marginalia in S (at top of fol. 66r): no heading.
6965	*ther*. So K. S: *þei*, above canceled *þor*.
6969	**The text of L continues here (fol. 149r).**
6972	*sure*. So L, K. S: *sone*.
6981	*on*. So L, K. S omits.
6982	*thei*. So L, K. S: *þat*.
6984	*wake₂*. So L, K. S: *make*.
6988	*heryng*. So L, K. S: *hethyng*.
6992	*Saul*. S: *u* inserted above the line.
6997	*begun*. So L, K. S omits.
7001	*thou me*. So L, K. S: *I þe*.
	fun. So L, K. S: *slayn*.
7010	*of*. S: *of* ~~w~~.
7012	*unto*. So L, K. S: *to*.
7013	*lefes*. So L, K. S: *lofes*.
	lessons. So L, K. S: *lessens*.
7016	*that*. So L, K. S omits.
7021	Marginalia in S (at top of fol. 66v): no heading.
7028	*went*. So L, K. S: *ware*.
7032	*the*. So L, K. S omits.
7035	*a*. So L, K. S omits.

7039	*wene.* So L, K. S: *were.*
7042	*thei.* So K. S: *þat.* L alters line.
7045	*landes.* S: three letters canceled before.
7048	*to₂.* S: inserted above the line.
	of his. S: inserted above the line.
7051	*wo.* So K. S: *mo.* L: *fayle.*
7056	*Cananews.* So K. S: *phylysteyns.* L: *Philistiens.*
7072	S: line 7075 canceled after.
7073	*men.* So L, K. S omits.
7077	Marginalia in S (at top of fol. 67r): no heading.
7083	*fare.* So L, K. S omits.
7087	*soundly.* So L, K. S: *sodanly.*
7088	*grett.* S: *gt grett.*
7089	*And.* So L, K. S: *All.*
7092	*byd.* So K. S: *abyd.* L: *abyde.*
7103	*howsoever.* L, K: *how s[o] euer.* S, O: *how sum ever.*
7105	*prophettes.* So L, K. S: *prophett.*
	prays. So L, K. S: *prayd.*
7106	*helpe.* So L, K. S: *hym.*
7107	*God not pays.* So L, K. S: *god was not payd.*
7108	*sum.* So L, K. S: *of sum.*
7110	*wyche.* S: inserted above canceled *wythe.*
	hym. So L, K. S: *Them.*
7115	*One.* S: in left margin, before canceled *And.*
7123	*asked.* So L, K. S: *aske.*
7129	*beforne.* S: *n* inserted above the line.
7137	Marginalia in S (at top of fol. 67v): no heading.
7145	*borows.* So K. S: *brorows.* L: *Burghes.*
7147	*wyghtly.* So L, K. S: *wyttely.*
7148	*non.* So K. S: *no.* L: *noone.*
7161	*us.* So L, K. S: *was.*
7167	*to.* So L, K. S: *to he to.*
7183	*spoyle.* So L, K. S: *speke.*
7186	*them.* So L, K. S: *þem þem.*
7193	Marginalia in S (at top of fol. 68r): no heading.
7195	*Thei.* S: *Đ þei.*
	hamwerd. So L, K. S: *hanwerd.*
7204	*for mete.* So K. S: *forthermer.* L: *farthere.*
7227	*telle.* S: second *e* inserted above the line.
7251	Marginalia in S (at top of fol. 68v): no heading.
7257	*past.* So L, K. S: *pist.*
7266	*be rownde.* S: *ro* inserted above the line.
7273	*tyll.* S: *to tyll.*
7278	*that.* S: *at* inserted above the line.
7289	*thei.* S: *of þei.*
7294	*lade.* So L, K. S: *lede.*
7303	*hedes.* So K. S: *hed.* L: *hevedes.*

7306	*worthy.* So L, K. S: *vnworthy.*
7307	Marginalia in S (at top of fol. 69r): no heading.
7309	*When.* S: *h When.*
	was. So L, K. S omits.
7310	*had.* So L, K. S omits.
7312	*he.* S: *hed.*
7316	*kynges.* So L, K. S: *kyng.*
	in. So L, K. S: inserted above *to.*
7317	*Forther.* So L, K. S: *For heyr.*

SECOND BOOK OF KINGS

7321–7504	**Missing in L (fol. 151 lost).**
7321, 23	Lines indented to leave space for an initial capital; first letter of line 7321 written in the middle of the space.
7328	*wyst.* So K. S: *þen wyst.*
7336	*I.* S: *& I.*
7337	*Then.* So K. S: *Þe.*
7339	*From.* So K. S omits.
	Jews. So K. S: *Iewas,* with *a* inserted above the line.
7340	*seygne.* So S. K: *seygns.*
7345	*hyt.* So S. K: *yt.*
7349	*syre.* S: *ser syre.*
7350	*towre and town.* So K. S: *town & towre.*
7357	Marginalia in S (at top of fol. 69v): no heading.
7361	*ne.* So K. S: *no.*
7366	*hend.* So K. S: *hand.*
7370	*guyse.* So K. S: *gryse.*
7380	*ther.* So K. S: *þei.*
7385	*Whore.* So S. K: *where.*
7388	*Israel.* So O. S, K: *Israhel.*
7390	*chose.* So K. S: *he chose.*
7405	*We told.* S: inserted above two canceled words.
7406	*in.* So K. S: *&.*
7408	S: written below canceled line 7410.
7409	Marginalia in S (at top of fol. 70r): no heading.
7410	*Ysboset.* S: *yseb ysboset.*
	unweld. S: *weld* inserted above the line.
7422	*Kyng.* So K. S omits.
	Israel. So O. S, K: *Israhel.*
7424	*Kyng.* S: corrected from *kynd.*
7430	*feyght on.* So S. K: *feyȝht in.*
7438	*tell.* So K. S: *fell.*
7463	Marginalia in S (at top of fol. 70v): no heading.
	werke. S: *he werke.*
7464	*clerly.* So S. K: *derly.*
7465	*well.* S: inserted above the line.

7483	*yt.* S: *ꝫ yt.*
7484	*kepe.* S: *ħ kepe.*
7488	*rested.* S: word (*reste?*) canceled before.
7490	*feld.* S: inserted above the line.
7496	*all way.* So K. S: *ouer.*
7504	*fare.* So K. S: *dwell.*
7505	**The text of L continues here (fol. 152r).**
7507	*con.* So K. S: *con he.* L: *gun.*
7508	*fore.* So S. L, K: *for.*
7517	Marginalia in S (at top of fol. 71r): no heading.
7518	*bundom.* So K. S: *bomdom.* L: *gouernaunce.*
7528	*of.* S: letter canceled before.
7539	*of.* So L, K. S: *of all.*
7540	*small.* S: inserted above the line.
7549	*we.* So L, K. S: *þei.*
7556	*he.* So L, K. S: *be.*
7568	*suld so.* So L, K. S: *suld go so.*
7569	Marginalia in S (at top of fol. 71v): no heading.
7574	*is all.* So L, K. S: *all his.*
7588	*best.* So L, K. S: *bestes.*
7589	*he.* So L, K. S: *be.*
7590	*blyn.* So L, K. S: *wyn.*
7593	*sone.* So L, K. S: *sone he.*
7605	*an evyll.* So L, K. S: *a gentyll.*
7623	Marginalia in S (at top of fol. 72r): *liber Regum ijus.*
7628	*Israel.* So O. S, K: *Israhel.*
	cuntré. So L, K. S: *te cuntre.*
7636	*therfore.* So L, K. S: *þore.*
7646	*is trist.* So L, K. S: *has.*
7647	*prevey.* S: corrected from *preuely.*
7648	*to.* So L, K. S: *two to.*
	in. So L, K. S omits.
7654	*qwen.* S: letter canceled before.
	thei. So L, K. S omits.
7659	*Kyng.* So L, K. S: *þe kyng.*
7661	*there.* So L, K. S: *þe.*
	thee. So L, K. S omits.
7670	*lordes.* So K. S: *lo lordes.* L: *the lordes.*
7671	*knaw.* So L, K. S: *knew.*
7675	Marginalia in S (at top of fol. 72v): no heading.
7684	*thei.* S, K: *þe.*
7705	*Neptalim.* So L, K. S: *neptalinm.*
7706	*com.* So K. S: *con,* inserted above canceled *neuyn.* L: *cum.*
7717	*was.* So L, K. S omits.
7729	Marginalia in S (at top of fol. 73r): no heading.
7730	*thei.* S, K: *þe.*
7735	*schrews.* So L, K. S: *scherws.*

7768	S: written above canceled line 7770.
	to. S: *to he.*
7769	S: written after canceled line 7771.
7774	*decré.* S: *degre decre.*
7779	Marginalia in S (at top of fol. 73v): no heading.
7783	*as.* So L, K. S: *all.*
7806	*Aram.* S: corrected from *Iram.*
7807	*syder wod.* So K. S: *syper wod,* with *syder wyn* canceled above the line. L: *Cedre wod.*
7817	*gart.* S: *gart gart.*
7819	*them.* So L, K. S: *þen.*
7827	*bune.* So K. S: *bene.* L: *bonne.*
	and. So L, K. S omits.
7829	*howses.* So L, K. S: *halles.*
7833	Marginalia in S (at top of fol. 74r): no heading.
7835–36	So L, K. S omits.
7840	*goverand.* So K. S: *gouerard.* L: *governe.*
7841	*Thei.* S: corrected from *þem.*
7864	*wend thou then.* So K. S, L: *wend þen.*
7873–8240	**Lines missing in L (fols. 154–155 lost).**
7887	Marginalia in S (at top of fol. 74v): no heading.
7897	*purpase.* S: *vp purpase.*
7941	Marginalia in S (at top of fol. 75r): no heading.
7945	*os.* So K. S: *o.*
	understode. So K. S: *vnderstand.*
7952	*and.* S: *r and.*
7965	*ald.* So K. S: *all.*
7968	*in.* S: inserted above canceled *&.*
7984	*os.* So K. S omits.
7990	*soveran.* So S. K: *soverin.*
7994	*a.* So K. S: *I.*
7997	Marginalia in S (at top of fol. 75v): no heading.
8007	*frendchep.* S: *d* inserted above the line.
8032	*wer served.* So K. S: *wer sertes serue.*
8051	Marginalia in S (at top of fol. 76r): no heading.
8060	*to.* So K. S omits.
8068	*Kyng.* So K. S: *kynd.*
8070	*was.* So K. S omits.
8076	*forto.* So K. S: *fort.*
	in. S: *vn in.*
8077	*on.* S: inserted above canceled *at.*
8084	*ordan.* S: *ordand.*
8098	*com.* So K. S: *com to.*
8099	*done.* So K. S omits.
8105	Marginalia in S (at top of fol. 76v): no heading.
8120	*lyfes lose.* So K. S: *lyfes to lose.*
8126	*rest.* So K. S: *treyst.*

8130	*knew*. S: inserted above the line.
8145	*saklese*. So K. S: *slaklese*.
8151	*forto*. So K. S: *fort*.
8154	S: inserted above canceled line 8156.
8161	Marginalia in S (at top of fol. 77r): no heading.
8183	*pure*. So K. S: *purys*.
	mans. S: *s* inserted above the line.
8185	*of thee*. So K. S omits.
8210	*helpe*. S: *& helpe*.
8215	Marginalia in S (at top of fol. 77v): *ijus liber Regum*.
8234	*delyvered*. So K. S, O: *delyuer*.
8241	**The text of L continues here (fol. 156r).**
8250	*ne*. So L, K. S: *ne of*.
8251	*myrth*. So L, K. S: *thyng*.
8253	*sevynt*. S: ~~XH~~ *VII*.
	day. So L, K. S omits.
8257–68	So L, K. S omits.
8274	*thei*. So L, K. S omits.
	thare. S: word canceled before.
8275	*to*. So L, K. S omits.
8276	*that himself*. So L, K. S omits.
8284	*hent*. So L, K. S: *hend*.
8285	Marginalia in S (at top of fol. 78r): no heading.
8293	*had*. So L, K. S: *bad*.
8294	*os*. So K. S: *o*. L: *as*.
	beforne. So L, K. S: *to be fore*.
8297	*Amon*. So L, K. S: *Donon*.
8300	*to be lorn*. So S. L, K: *be lorn*.
8302	*not*. S: ~~not say~~ *not*.
8304	*peryst*. So L, K. S: *prayd*.
8306	*his*. So L, K. S omits.
8331	*So*. So L, K. S: *Tyll*.
	on. So L, K. S: *or*.
8332	*forto*. So L, K. S omits.
8341	Marginalia in S (at top of fol. 78v): no heading.
8353	*Amone*. So L, K. S: *a none*.
8358	*the*. So K. S omits. L: *othre*.
8364	*hyr*. So K. S: *hys*. L: *hire*.
8375	*Evyll hurled hed and hare*. So L. S: *Euyll hyr yryhed hyde & hare*. K: *hyr hed [scho] hyde and hare*.
8379	*go*. So L, K. S: *so*.
8399	Marginalia in S (at top of fol. 79r): *liber ijus Regum*.
8402	*mangery*. S: corrected from *mangere*.
8414	*perfyt*. S: *perfyt~~ly~~*.
8418	*hed*. S: inserted above the line.
8424	*payn*. S: ~~pyn~~ *payn*.
8429	*dole*. So K. S: *Duke*. L: *doell*.

8430	*Alas*. So L, K. S: *als*.
8434	S: transposed with line 8436.
8436	S: transposed with line 8434.
	wrake. So L, K. S: *wreke*.
8453	*heyr*. S: *ɫ heyr*.
8457	Marginalia in S (at top of fol. 79v): no heading.
8461	*con*. So L, K. S: *he con*.
8462	*wyll*. So L, K. S omits.
8484	*thou*. So L, K. S: *þat þou*.
8498	*syght*. So L, K. S: *fyȝt*.
8508	*os*. So K. S: *of*. L: *as*.
8513	Marginalia in S (at top of fol. 80r): no heading.
8516	*wylly*. S: inserted above the line, after *ware*.
8522	*at*. So L, K. S: *all*.
8527	*in*. S: corrected from *im*.
8528	*of*. S: *ơ of*.
8546	*knave*. So L, K. S omits.
8554	*sewrty*. So S. K: *seurty*.
8565	*cummand*. So K. S: *cumnand* or *cunnand*. L: *commant*.
8566	*forto*. So L. S: *so forto*. K: *so to*.
8567	Marginalia in S (at top of fol. 80v): no heading.
8572	*with*. So L, K. S omits.
8577	*toke*. So K. S: *take*. L: *tuke*.
8578	*seged*. So L, K. S: *sege*.
8611	*with*. So L, K. S omits.
8614	*more*. So L, K. S: *& more*.
8619	*Mifbosett*. So K. S: *Misbosett*.
8620	*Jonatha*. S: ~~Ioratha~~ *Ionatha*.
8621	Marginalia in S (at top of fol. 81r): *liber ijus*.
8622	*and*. So L, K. S: *at*, above canceled *þat*.
8624	*frend*. So L, K. S: *frendes*.
8625	*Ser*. So L, K. S: *sers*.
8640	*Myfbosett*. So K. S: *Misbosett*.
8644	*Semey*. So L, K. S: *Seney*.
8647	*fowles fene*. So L, K. S: *fowled kene*.
8673	*thei*. So L, K. S: *þou*.
8675	Marginalia in S (at top of fol. 81v): no heading.
8677	*glose*. S: letter canceled before.
8701	*Godes*. So L, K. S: ~~lykes~~ *god*.
	is. S: inserted above the line.
	wyll. S: inserted below the line.
8703	*thee*. So L, K. S: *to þe*.
	untyll. So L, K. S omits.
8715	*ryght*. So L, K. S: *myȝt*.
8719	*be*. So L, K. S omits.
8721	*fayle*. S: corrected from *fayll*.
8731	Marginalia in S (at top of fol. 82r): no heading.

8735	*more*. So L, K. S: *of*.
8736	*of*. So L, K. S omits.
8737	*all*. So L, K. S omits.
8741	*mene*. So L, K. S: *menyd*.
8757	*he was*. So L, K. S: *lest*.
8758	*at*. So L, K. S: *of*.
8759	*This tale*. So K. S: *þs tale*. L: *The mater*.
8787	Marginalia in S (at top of fol. 82v): no heading.
8791	*tell*. So L, K. S: *tell in*.
8799	*thei*. So L. S, K: *þe*.
8812	*thei*. So L, K. S: *þi*.
8817	*sith*. So L. S, K: *sythis*.
8819	*lith*. So L. S, K: *lythes*.
8828	*all*. S: inserted above the line.
8829	*with*. So L, K. S: *with his*.
8830	*past*. So L, K. S: *he past*.
8837	*byd abyde*. So L, K. S: *byde*.
8843	Marginalia in S (at top of fol. 83r): no heading.
8848	*beldyd*. So L, K. S: *belyd*.
8853	*fere*. So L, K. S: *fare*.
8854	*fryd*. S, L, K: *fyrth*. The rhyme (: *David*) in both manuscripts is broken. My solution is to posit an original form *fryd* that has undergone metathesis in the copy shared by both existant manuscripts.
8857	*tythyng*. S: ~~th~~ *tythyng*.
8859	*boy*. So L, K. S: *body*.
8860	*sla*. So K. L: *sloo*. S: *sha*.
8883	*well*. So L, K. S: *wall*.
8885	*hym*. So L, K. S omits.
8886	*hale*. So K. S: *half*. L: *hoal*.
8897	Marginalia in S (at top of fol. 83v): no heading.
8900	*that doylefull dede*. So L, K. S: *with byttur bede*.
8903	*hym*. So L, K. S: *his*.
8920	*shamely*. So L, K. S: *shamesly*.
8931	*with*. So L, K. S omits.
8935	*kynred*. So L, K. S: *kyng*.
8937	*For*. So L, K. S: *Fro*.
8939	*fyrst*. So L, K. S omits.
	furth. S: inserted above canceled *fyr*.
8940	*cité*. So L, K. S: *cuntre*.
8941–64	S: these two stanzas, 746 (lines 8941–52) and 747 (lines 8953–64), are transposed in S. Like K, I have followed the order in L.
8942	*thousandes*. So L, K. S: *þer sandes*.
8956	*welthis*. So K. S: *wethis*. L: *welth*.
8963	Marginalia in S (at top of fol. 84r): no heading.
8970	*ther*. So L, K. S: *on þer*.
8973	*tyll*. S: ~~vntyll~~.
8978	*Mifbosett*. So L, K. S: *Misbosett*.

8983	*The.* So L, K. S: *þeі.*
8990	*as man.* So L, K. S: *man as.*
8994	*lyyse.* So L, K. S: *lyyfe.* L: *wyse.*
8998	*he.* So L, K. S: *be.*
9004	*with.* S: inserted above the line.
9005	Marginalia in S (at top of fol. 84v): no heading.
9015	*then.* S: altered from *thei.*
9028	*furth.* So L, K. S: *futh.*
9042	*woo.* So L, K. S omits.
9046	*forto.* So L, K. S: *fort.*
9047	*We.* So L, K. S: *with.*
9051	*he began.* So L, K. S: *he he gan.*
9056	*to.* So S. L, K: *þe.*
9059	Marginalia in S (at top of fol. 85r): no heading.
9065	*lend.* So L, K. S: *wend.*
9067	*Folke.* So L, K. S: *And folke.*
9068	*fayn.* S: inserted above the line.
9094	*cosyn.* So L, K. S: *counsell.*
9100	*yt.* So L, K. S omits.
9106	*murtherd.* S: ~~musche~~ *murtherd.*
9108	*Amasan.* So L, K. S: *masan.*
9113	Marginalia in S (at top of fol. 85v): no heading.
9114	*and.* So L, K. S omits.
9115	*his.* So L, K. S omits.
9135	*folk.* So L, K. S: *fok.*
9141	*Ser.* So L, K. S: *Som.*
9145	*here thou.* So K. S: *þat here.* L alters line.
9146	*theym morne and none.* So L, K. S: *more & myne.*
9152	*Delyver.* So S. L, K: *Deliver.*
9156	*to lose oon.* So L, K. S: *losso on.*
9158	*them.* S: inserted above canceled *scho.*
9160	*thei.* So L, K. S: *þat þei.*
	hent. So L, K. S omits.
9162	*unto.* So L, K. S: *to.*
9166	*frendes.* So L, K. S: *frend.*
9167	Marginalia in S (at top of fol. 86r): no heading.
9170	*rewlys.* So L, K. S: *rowlys.*
9175	*for.* So L, K. S: *furth.*
9179	*fell sodan.* So L, K. S: *sodanly.*
9183	*pure.* S: ~~pr~~ *pure.*
9205	*he.* So L, K. S omits.
9210	*seson.* S: ~~reson~~ *seson.*
9223	Marginalia in S (at top of fol. 86v): *liber iіus Regum.*
	Tho. So L. S: *þei.* K: *þe.*
9224	*sessyd.* So L, K. S: *sessyn.*
9229	*in.* S: inserted above the line.
9233	*Diligam.* So L, K. S: *Deligam.*

9243	*no.* So L, K. S omits.
9253	*hym.* So L, K. S: *to hym.*
9262	*tent.* S: *a tent.*
9264	*no.* S: inserted above the line.
9266	*greved.* So L, K. S omits.
9267	*rekynyng.* S: corrected from *rekyngng.*
9268	*oft.* S: letter canceled before.
9269	*was.* S: inserted above canceled *wog.*
9271	*new.* So L, K. S: *ew.*
9277	Marginalia in S (at top of fol. 87r): no heading.
9280	*fro.* So L, K. S: *for.*
9281	*he wyst wele.* So L, K. S: *wyst wele he.*
9292	*fyght.* So L, K. S: *flyȝt.*
9295	*on.* S: inserted above canceled *in.*
9305	*on.* S: corrected from *om.*
9309	S: after canceled line 9311.
9327	Marginalia in S (at top of fol. 87v): no heading.
9336	*thei.* S: *ȝ þei.*
9341	*thyng.* So L, K. S: *thynges.*
9349	*David.* So L, K. S omits.
9357	*tell.* So L, K. S: *tyll.*
9366	*for.* S: ~~fare~~ *ffor.*
9381	Marginalia in S (at top of fol. 88r): *liber ijus Regum.*
	then war. So L, K. S: *was,* inserted above the line.
9383–84	S: inserted in right margin.
9386	*Naomy.* So S. L, K: *Neomi.*
9390	*made.* So L, K. S omits.
	fest. So L, K. S: *frest.*
	fare. S: ~~per~~ *fare.*
9392	*that.* S: corrected from *þaf.*
9409	*Ser.* So L, K. S: *sers.*
	is this. So L, K. S: *This is.*
9410	*Adonay.* So L, K. S: *I Adonay.*
9430	*that$_1$.* So K. S: *of þat.* L: *all.*
9433	*Thurghoute.* So L, K. S: *Thurgh.*
9437	Marginalia in S (at top of fol. 88v): no heading.
9447	*Abyathar.* So S, L. K: *Abhyathar.*
9448	*set.* So L, K. S: *sent.*
9464	*in.* So L, K. S: *on.*
9467	*mett.* So L, K. S: *made.*
9474	*bad.* So L, K. S: *bad þat.*
9487	*I.* So L, K. S omits.
9488	*os.* S: *r os.*
9493	Marginalia in S (at top of fol. 89r): no heading.
9495–9500	The overall numbering of these lines in K is incorrect due to miscounting.
9498	*beseke.* So L, K. S: *leseke.*
9506	*of.* S: ~~or~~ *of,* with *over* canceled above the line.

	ever. S: inserted above the line.
9525	*fyne*. So L, K. S omits.
9547	Marginalia in S (at top of fol. 89v): no heading.
9554	*at*. S: *& at*.
	med. S: inserted above the line.
9556	*and*. So L, K. S: *a*.
9564	*all*. So L, K. S: *all þi*.
9571	*dare*. So L, K. S: *dere*.
9578	*oon*. So L, K. S: *þem*.
9581	*maynteyned*. So L, K. S: *maynteyn*.
9595	*God*. So L, K. S: *go*.
9601	Marginalia in S (at top of fol. 90r): no heading.
9608	*grauntyng*. So L, K. S: *graunted*.
	sum. So L, K. S omits.
9614	*sone*. S: ~~sun~~ *sone*.
9615	*so*. So L, K. S: *for*.
9619	*werkes*. So L, K. S omits.
9621	*story*. S: ~~storr~~ *story*.

Third Book of Kings

9625, 27	Lines indented to leave space for an initial capital; first letter of line 9625 written in the middle of the space.
9640	*forto*. So L, K. S: *so to*.
9647	Marginalia in S (at top of fol. 90v): no heading.
9657	*bargan*. So L, K. S: *barga*.
9682	*that*. S: altered from *þou*.
9699	Marginalia in S (at top of fol. 91r): no heading.
9703	*so*. S: inserted above canceled *l*.
	so had ther. So L, K. S: *so þer had þer*.
9706	*as*. So L, K. S: *a*.
9710	*als*. So L, K. S: *and als*.
9718	*all folke*. So L, K. S: *all þo folke*.
9732	*on*. So L, K. S: inserted above canceled *of*.
9737	*then*. So L, K. S: *þe*.
9738	*calves*. So L, K. S: *camels*.
9741	*what thou*. So L, K. S: *what at þou*.
9742	*thou*. So L, K. S: *þat*.
9748	*on*. So K. S, L omit.
9749	Marginalia in S (at top of fol. 91v): *liber iijus Regum*.
9750	*boyth*. S: *y* inserted above the line.
9755	*mas*. So L, K. S: *mad*.
9762	*thei*. So L, K. S: *þou*.
9770	*a torfer*. So L, K. S: *aftur*.
9774	*myght*. S: inserted above the line.
9776	*dome*. So L, K. S: *domes*.
9803	Marginalia in S (at top of fol. 92r): *iudicium Salamonis*.

9805	*fyrst unto the kyng then cryse*. So L, K. S: *fyrst þen vnto þe kyng cryse*.
9809	*full lowde*. So L, K. S: *and foly sayd*.
9810	*bot*. So L, K. S: *bo*.
9821	*is*. So L, K. S omits.
9824	*graunt me*. So L, K. S: *graunt to me*.
9832	*is*. So L, K. S omits.
9856	Marginalia in S (at top of fol. 92v): no heading.
9858	*named*. So L, K. S: *name*.
9863	*his bokes*. So L. S, K: *þis boke*.
	here. So L, K. S: *lere*.
9866	*drese*. So L, K. S: *dryse*.
9879	*strykes*. So L, K. S: *mesurs*.
9885	Marginalia in S (at left of fol. 92v): *Templum*.
9888	*ymages*. So L, K. S: *ymage*.
9890	*flygh*. S: inserted above the line.
9901	*sett*. So L, K. S: *sell*.
9913	Marginalia in S (at top of fol. 93r): no heading.
9941	*space*. So L, K. S: *place*.
9950	*dene*. S: inserted above canceled *twen*.
9951	*named*. So L, K. S: *made*.
9958	*city*. So L, K. S: *sett*.
9961	*Another*. So L, K. S: *And other*.
9963	*was*. So L, K. S: *wad*.
9965	*the thryd*. So L, K. S: *þer*.
9966	*when*. So L, K. S: *whe*.
9969	Marginalia in S (at top of fol. 93v): no heading.
9975	*full fayre*. So L, K. S: *fayre full*.
9986	*wyll*. S: altered from *with*.
9998	*on mys*. So L, K. S: *onnys*.
10010	*wold*. S: inserted above the line.
10025	Marginalia in S (at top of fol. 94r): no heading.
10026	*ever had*. So L, K. S: *euer he had*.
10035	*he*. So K, S, L omit.
10051	*saw*. So L, K. S: *sal be*.
10062	*that*. S: corrected from *ther*.
10063	*have*. So L, K. S omits.
10064	*be*. So L, K. S omits.
10076	*thi*. So L, K. S: *þou*.
10081	Marginalia in S (at top of fol. 94v): no heading.
10097	*bed*. So L, K. S: *boyd*.
10102	*kyn*. So L, K. S: *kyn told*.
10104	So L, K. S: *to stroy both ȝyng and old*.
10111	*A new*. So L, K. S: *Anab*.
10118	*seys*. So L, K. S: *sesys*.
	twyn. S: corrected from *twon*.
10136	Marginalia in S (at top of fol. 95r): no heading.
10139	*mo commynté*. So K. S: *mo of þe commynte*. L: *more commonalte*.

10146	*bot fro his welth.* So L, K. S omits.
10153	*prowyse.* So L, K. S: *promyse.*
10157	*So.* S: *Sor.*
10161	*Faur.* So L, K. S: *ffor IIII.*
10166	*gyfyn.* So L, K. S: *yfyn.*
10172	*man.* So L, K. S omits.
10173	*Sychem.* So L, K. S: *sych.*
10185	*fayne.* So L, K. S omits.
	plese. S: followed by three canceled letters.
10191	Marginalia in S (at top of fol. 95v): no heading.
10201	*When.* So L, K. S: *whem.*
10209	*then.* So L, K. S: *end.*
10219	*yf.* So L, K. S omits.
10224	*a.* So L, K. S omits.
10225	*hers.* So L, K. S: *herd.*
10226	*this.* So L, K. S: *and þis.*
10229	*Omys this men.* So L, K. S: *onys þis mon.*
10232	*schortly.* So L, K. S: *chortly.*
10235	*The.* S: *þe sall.*
10243	*scorpions.* So L, K. S: *scoppions.*
10247	Marginalia in S (at top of fol. 96r): no heading.
10252	*lent.* So L, K. S: *went.*
10256	*the.* S: *thei.*
10257	*sen.* So L, K. S: *so.*
10299	*Jeroboam.* So L, K. S: *Ioroboam.*
10301	*Israel.* So O. S, K: *Israhel.*
10305	Marginalia in S (at top of fol. 96v): *liber iijus Regum.*
10306	*barn.* S: one letter canceled after.
10309	*two.* So L, K. S omits.
10319	*clene.* So L, K. S: *kene.*
10322	*stif.* So L, K. S: *fyrst.*
10332	*doyghtur.* So L, K. S: *systur.*
10341	*No.* S: *No na.*
10344	*fulli.* S: *i* inserted above the line.
10351	*nevyn.* So L, K. S: *euyn.*
10361	Marginalia in S (at top of fol. 97r): no heading.
10362	*noyght.* So L, K. S: *noyt.*
10370	*Egyp.* S: *egyp,* with a letter canceled after.
10376	*wyll noyght.* So L, K. S: *well myȝt.*
10385	*forto.* S: *to* inserted above line.
	grete. So L, K. S: *wepe.*
10392	*gretand.* So L, K. S: *wepand.*
	sore. S: corrected from *sory.*
10404	*or.* S: *of or.*
10408	*bot this connand.* So L, K. S: *be þis commaundment.*
10415	Marginalia in S (at top of fol. 97v): no heading.
	is. So L, K. S: *was.*

10417	S: stanza marker missing.
	Thor. S: *þor* ~~thr~~.
10422	*well.* S: a word canceled after.
10423	*Potes.* So L, K. S: *Petes.*
10425	*kynges.* S: three letters canceled after (*pab?*).
10435–42	S is deficient here, as line 10435 leads into 10442. The scribe has copied some of the missing lines into the left margin and (wrongly) marked them for insertion before 10435. Lines 10437–38 are clearly visible, as are the letter tops of what seems to be line 10439. Unfortunately, the trimming of the outer edge has removed the rest of the correction. I have followed K in liberally emending from L here.
10436	So L, K. S omits line.
10437–38	S: written along left margin.
10439–41	So L, K. S omits lines.
10447	*so.* So L, K. S omits.
10450	*wher his.* So L, K. S: *wher oþer of his.*
10455	*Jeroboam.* So L, K. S: *Ioroboam.*
10460	*governyng.* So L, K. S: *gouerdyng.*
10477	Marginalia in S (at top of fol. 98r): *liber iijus Regum.*
10481	*there.* So L, K. S: *so.*
10495	*we are as.* So L, K. S: *we aftur are.*
10504	*you.* So L, K. S: *your.*
10506	*space.* S: ~~place~~ *space.*
10511	*have.* So L, K. S omits.
10512	Marginalia in S: *De vitulo aureo.*
10531	*The.* So L, K. S: *þei.*
10534	*ther.* So L, K. S: *þei.*
10537	Marginalia in S (at top of fol. 98v): *De distruccione altaris et De vindicatione Ieroboam.*
	can begyn. So L, K. S: *hath be gun.*
10539	*Thou.* So L, K. S: *The.*
	is. So L, K. S omits.
10543	*myn.* S: ~~ny~~ *myn.*
10587	*pas.* So L, K. S: *past.*
10591	*as.* So L, K. S: *has.*
10595	Marginalia in S (at top of fol. 99r): *liber iijus Regum.*
10599	*agayn.* So L, K. S: *agay.*
10620	*to.* S: inserted above the line.
10621	*By.* S: inserted above canceled *bott.*
10627	*he suld.* So L, K. S: *he beryd suld.*
10628	*beryd.* So L, K. S omits.
10653	Marginalia in S (at top of fol. 99v): *liber iijus Regum.*
	kyng ay. So L, K. S: *kyng þen ay.*
10669	*mynd.* So L, K. S: *tyme.*
10672	*noyght.* So L, K. S: *noyt.*
10685	*are.* So L, K. S omits.
	one. So L, K. S: *ones.*

10690	*cause thou.* So L, K. S: *cause þat þou.*
10694	*forfett.* So L, K. S: *for sett.*
10701	*thi.* So L, K. S: *þou.*
10706	*his.* So L, K. S: *þis.*
10711	Marginalia in S (at top of fol. 100r): *liber iijus Regum.*
10715	*As.* So L, K. S: *Hase.*
10718	*strake.* So K. S: *stared.* L: *faght.*
10726	*feld.* So L, K. S: *fele.*
10728	*noyght.* S: *o noyȝt.*
10730	*turned agayn.* So L, K. S: *turned sone agayn.*
10735	*yll.* So K. S: *styll.* L: *evyll.*
10740	*cald.* So L, K. S: *cale.*
10756	*Nabad.* So L, K. S: *Naab.*
10766	*was for.* S: *was ~~sen~~ for.* L: *was sent for.* K retains *sen.*
10769	Marginalia in S (at top of fol. 100v): *liber iijus Regum.*
10771	*sayd.* S: *d* inserted above the line.
10774	*in hand.* So L, K. S: *in his hand.*
10787	*him.* So L, K. S: *he.*
10789	*ay.* S: *~~all~~ ay.*
10790	*be.* So K. L, S: *he.*
10798	*mystrewth hym betrayd.* So L, K. S: *myse mad hym to be trayd.*
10808	*gyle.* S: inserted above canceled *whylle.*
10813	*make.* So L, K. S: *be in.*
10814	*for₂.* So L, K. S omits.
10821	*socours.* So L, K. S: *socour.*
10824	*Benedab.* So L, K. S: *Amynadab.* See the explanatory note to lines 10823–24.
10827	Marginalia in S (at top of fol. 101r): *liber iijus Regum.*
10829	*Benedab.* So L, K. S: *Amynadab.*
10840	*rescow.* So L, K. S: *rescows.*
10842	*burgh.* So L, K. S: *burght.*
10845	*Rama.* So L, K. S: *Ramatha.*
10849	*Benedab.* So L, K. S: *Amynadab.*
10859	*An.* So L, K. S: *And.*
10860	*slogh.* So L, K. S omits.
10863	*progeny.* S: *pgeny* (missing mark of abbreviation).
10867	*kyng.* S: inserted above canceled *knyȝt.*
10868	*Israels.* So S, L. K: *israel.*
10881	*furth.* So S. L, K omits.
10887	Marginalia in S (at top of fol. 101v): no heading.
10905	*send.* S: inserted above canceled *sented.*
10906	*unto.* So L, K. S: *to.*
10909	Marginalia in S (at left of fol. 101v, partially cut off): *. . . Rex . . . [Aas]a dis-cipli . . . deo.*
10911	*told.* S: *~~hym~~ told.*
10915–16	So L, K. S omits lines.
10927	*bounté.* So L, K. S: *bewte.*
10940	*mys.* So L, K. S: *myrth.*

10949	Marginalia in S (at top of fol. 102r): *liber iijus Regum.*
10955	Marginalia in S (at left of fol. 102r): *Acab.*
10965	*Jesabell.* So L, K. S: *Iosabell.*
10973	*Beall.* S: inserted above canceled *B be all.*
10974	*god of Tyre.* So L, K. S: *gud of tre.*
10995	*has His.* So L, K. S: *hyr.*
	slayn. So L, K. S: *slyn.*
10997	*Within.* S: *with with in.*
10998	*apeyre.* So L, K. S: *ayre.*
11002	*begyld.* S: altered from *be gyled.*
11005	Marginalia in S (at top of fol. 102v): no heading.
	in. S: inserted above the line.
11011	*rayvyns.* So L, K. S: *raymyns.*
11015	*monthes.* So L, K. S: *mothnes.*
11019	*hym.* So L, K. S omits.
11025	*ther.* So L, K. S: *thor.*
11035	*to.* So L, K. S omits.
11041	*affrayd.* So L, K. S: *amate.*
11057	*ete.* S: *eteþ.*
	and. So L, K. S omits.
11059	*both.* So L, K. S: *bot.*
11062	Marginalia in S (at top of fol. 103r): no heading.
11071	*wold.* So L, K. S omits.
	fyne. So L, K. S omits.
11081	*gretand.* So L, K. S: *wepand.*
11082	*be.* So L, K. S: *be þe.*
11083	*Schew.* S: *Schew ~~thou~~.*
11089	*hyr.* So L, K. S: *his.*
11101	*then.* So L, K. S: *þer.*
11104	*forto.* S: *forto ~~er~~.*
11105–06	So L, K. S omits lines.
11111	*or.* S: inserted above the line.
11113	*then.* So L, K. S omits.
11115	*Obedyas.* So K. S: *þen Elydeas.* L: *Abdias.*
11117	Marginalia in S (at top of fol. 103v): no heading.
11120	*day.* S: *day s.*
11121	*hid.* So L, K. S: *his.*
11125	*Acab.* S: *Acab m.*
11151	*gyfyn.* So L, O. S, K: *yfyn.*
11155	*I.* S: corrected from *&.*
11173	Marginalia in S (at top of fol. 104r): *De rege Acab et seruo eius. liber iijus Regum.*
11188	*dekyns.* So L, K. S: *dekyng.*
11189	*he thus.* So L, K. S: *is.*
11222	*hunderth.* L, K: *C.* S: *s.*
11229	Marginalia in S (at top of fol. 104v): *liber iijus Regum.*
11243	*kepe.* So L, K. S: *hede.*

11254	*was agrayd.* So L, K. S: *was it agrayd.*
11272	*on hym.* So L, K. S: *þen cowd.*
11273–76	Lines 11273–74 and 11275–76 are transposed in S.
11273	*mad thei.* So L, K. S: *had mad þer.*
11276	*send.* S: *y* has been inserted and then canceled above *d*.
11283	Marginalia in S (at top of fol. 105r): *liber iijus Regum.*
11306	*ferre.* S: *fr ferre.*
11307	*alone.* S: inserted above canceled *anone.*
11315	Marginalia in S (at right of fol. 105r): *De dormicione Ely sub iunipero.*
11319	*come and.* So L, K. S: *con.*
	spake. So L, K. S: *speke.*
11329	*tyme.* So L, K. S: *þat.*
11333	*grayd.* S: *y* inserted above the line.
11335	Marginalia in S (at right of fol. 105r, partially cut off): *Et ambula[t] in forti-tudi[ne] cibi illius vsque ad m[ontem] dei.*
11336	*thynke.* S: *h* inserted above the line.
11339	Marginalia in S (at top of fol. 105v): no heading.
11342	*into.* S: *to* inserted above the line.
11344	*and.* S: inserted above the line.
	ete. So L, K. S: *hete.*
11372	*os.* So L, K. S: *of.*
11374	*God.* So L, K. S: *go.*
11376	*Nabod.* S: *naꜩbod.*
11377	*Jezerael.* So L, K. S: *israel.*
11389	*And.* S: ~~Ante~~ *And.*
11391–99	The overall numbering of these lines in K is incorrect due to miscounting.
11394	Marginalia in S (at top of fol. 106r): no heading.
11397	*thynke.* So L, K. S: *thynkes.*
11400	*bot.* So L, K. S: *bo.*
11413	*hand.* S: *hand,* with a canceled nasal abbreviation over the *n*.
11424	*sayd.* S: *sayd ɓ.*
	sore be. So K. S: *be sore.* L: *dere be.*
11444	*Ely.* So K. S: *in hy.* L: *hely.*
11453	Marginalia in S (at top of fol. 106v): no heading.
11458	*thryty.* So L, K. S: *thryrty.*
11481	*that.* So L, K. S omits.
11485	Marginalia in S (at left of fol. 106v): *Rex Acab.*
11491	*erthe.* So L, K. S: *hyll.*
11502	*no chyvalry.* So L, K. S: *chylualry.*
11503	*the.* So L, K. S omits.
11508	*with.* S: *with ꝥ.*
11511	Marginalia in S (at top of fol. 107r): no heading.
	paynyms. S: corrected from *paymyms.*
11512	*thei.* So S. L, K: *þai.*
11534	*in.* So K. S: *i.* L omits.
11535	*noyght.* So L, K. S omits.
11540	*as.* S: ~~als~~ *as.*

11541	*assayld*. So L, K. S: *assayd*.
11544	*done*. So L, K. S: *donyng*.
11555	*soght and*. S: *sogh and*, with *t* inserted above line.
11569	Marginalia in S (at top of fol. 107v): *liber iijus Regum*.
	S: line 11581 mistakenly copied here before being canceled and replaced.
11572	*with*. S: inserted above the line.
11574	*when*. So L, K. S *whe*.
	fun. So L, K. S: *wun*.
11584	*tyme*. So L, K. S omits.
	were. So L, K. S: *we*.
11590	*lendyd*. S: *yd* inserted above the line.
11597	*breke*. S: ~~*gayr*~~ *breke*.
11600	*me*. So L, K. S omits.
	never. S: corrected from *mever*.
11608	*Have*. S: ~~*and*~~ *haue*.
11609–12	Lines 11609–10 and 11611–12 are transposed in S and marked for correction in the margin.
11611	*hed*. So L, K. S omits.
11621	Marginalia in S (at top of fol. 108r): no heading.
11622	*away*. So L, K. S: *sway*.
11623	*tane*. So K. S: *tone*.
11625	*Sine*. So L, K. S: *sone*.
11630	*this*. So S. L omits. K: *þat*.
	the. S: *þi*, with *e* inserted below line.
11634	*dowm to have thou aw*. S: *dowm þou aw* ~~*to have*~~, with *to have* then added above the line.
11642	*pawsté*. S: inserted above canceled *power*.
11668	S: lines 11669 and an incorrect 11672 (*by Iesabell his moyder ryȝt*) copied as one line here and then canceled.
11675	Marginalia in S (at top of fol. 108v): no heading.
11679	*frend*. S: *n* and *d* share a minim in an inadvertent ligature.
11680	*conferm cours*. So L, K. S: *comfern corns*.
11686	*hend*. So L, K. S: *hand*.
11692	*burghes*. So L, K. S: *burgh*.
11694	*dwels*. So L, K. S: *dewels*.
11701	*now*. So L, K. S: *we now*.
11714	S: an incorrect line 11727 (*Swylke cause he may not before knaw*) copied and canceled here.
11722	*beforn*. S: *be* ~~*fore*~~ *forn*.
11728	*privaté*. So S. L, K: *prevate*.
11729	Marginalia in S (at top of fol. 109r): no heading.
11730	*heyght*. S: *t* inserted above the line.
11733	*hym stryke*. So L, K. S: *stryke hym*.
11735	*I*. S: inserted above canceled *he*.
11743	*kynges*. So L, K. S: *kyng*.
11747	*mirakle*. So L, K. S: *murake*.
11748	*the*. So L, K. S: *to*.

11751	*And.* So L, K. S: *þen.*
11756	*hym.* So L, K. S omits.
11761	*whore.* S: ~~þei~~ *whore.*
11773	*rewled.* So K. S: *dewled.* L: *ordand.*
11774	*fro.* So K. S: *fore.* L: *for.*
11785	Marginalia in S (at top of fol. 109v): *liber iijus Regum.*
11787	*with.* So L, K. S omits.
11795	*he dyed.* So L, K. S: *ded.*
11802	*sayd.* So L, K. S: *profecyd.*
11804	*awn.* So L, K. S: *aw.*
11819	*His.* So L, K. S: *hym.*
11822	*Ser.* So L, K. S omits.
11823	*Acab.* So L, K. S omits.
11824	*Goddes.* S: ~~of~~ *goddes.*
11826	*suld.* So L, K. S: *sal.*
11827	*Bot that.* So L, K. S: *waryn.*
11832	*or.* S: ~~and~~ *or.*
11834	*kyn.* So L, K. S: *his.*
11837	*thei.* So S. L, K: *ther.*
11841	Marginalia in S (at top of fol. 110r): *liber iijus Regum.*
11845	*sone.* S: ~~sone~~ *sone.*
11853	*the.* S: inserted above the line.
	prayd. So L, K. S omits.
11861	*Out.* So L, K. S: *gate.*
11865	*swylk.* S: ~~sent~~ *swylk.*
11867	*paynym.* So L, K. S: *paymyn.*
11882	*kin.* So L, K. S: *in.*
11883	*gold.* So L, K. S: *wold.*
11886	*come.* So L, K. S: *como.*
11892	*Commawndmentes.* So L, K. S: *commawndment.*
11898	*then.* So L, K. S omits.
11899	Marginalia in S (at top of fol. 110v): *liber iijus Regum.*
11904	*Amen.* So L, K. S: *Ame.*

FOURTH BOOK OF KINGS

11905, 96	Lines indented to leave space for an initial capital; first letter of line 11905 written in the middle of the space.
11921	*godes.* So L, K. S: *god.*
11922	*used.* So L, K. S: *useid.*
11923	*bun.* S: corrected from *bin.*
11924	*beld.* S: ~~frend~~ *beld.*
11934	*hymself.* S: *hym* ~~self~~ *self.*
11951	*leves.* So L, K. S: *leue.*
11955	Marginalia in S (at top of fol. 111r): *liber iiijus Regum.*
11960	*his.* So L, K. S omits.
11962	*this.* So L, K. S: *and this.*

11967	*has.* S: ~~has~~ *has.*
11971	*angred.* So L, K. S: *angard.*
11973	*Bot wyghtly.* So L, K. S: *wyttely.*
11994	*prophet.* So S, L. K: *prophett.*
12005–08	Lines 12005–06 and 12007–08 are transposed in S and marked for correction in the margin.
12013	Marginalia in S (at top of fol. 111v): *liber iiijus Regum.*
12017	*se.* So L, K. S: *sent.*
12020	*we.* So L, K. S: *þou.*
12021	*We.* So L, K. S: *he.*
12022	*to.* So L, K. S: *forto.*
12041	*Joram.* So L, K (*ioran*). S: *Iotan.*
12076	Marginalia in S (at top of fol. 112r): no heading.
12086	*and.* So L, K. S omits.
12091–92	So L, K. S omits lines.
12097	*mekyll.* So L, K. S: *myld.*
12100	*thei.* So L. S, K: *the.*
12127	*hys.* So L, K. S: *hym.*
12131	Marginalia in S (at top of fol. 112v): *liber iiijus Regum.*
12144	*of.* So L, K. S: *þat fell of.*
12145	*then.* So L, K. S omits.
12150	*helpe.* S: ~~hes~~ *helpe.*
12157	*knew.* So L, K. S: *knaw.*
12160	*allas.* So L, K. S: *he was.*
12164	*whyls.* S: *wyhyls.*
12168	*fro.* So L, K. S: *for.*
12169	*seler.* So L, K. S: *soler.*
	sytt. So L, K. S: *fytt.*
12180	*sytt.* So L, K. S: *flytt.*
12187	Marginalia in S (at top of fol. 113r): *liber iiijus Regum.*
12199	*thou.* So L, K. S: *so.*
12202	*cover.* So L, K. S: *couerd.*
12209–12	Lines 12209–10 and 12211–12 are transposed in S and marked for correction in the margin.
12225	*hyr.* So L, K. S omits.
12231	*Chyld.* So L, K. S: *schyld.*
12236	*I.* So L, K. S: *þat.*
12238	*dyseve.* So L, K. S: *dysese.*
12244	Marginalia in S (at top of fol. 113v): no heading.
12246	*wun.* So L, K. S: *went* (inserted above the line).
12258	*myschef.* So K. L: *myschieve.* S: *mysche.*
12271	Marginalia in S (at left of fol. 113v): *gofy* or *gosy* (this may be the end of a phrase cut off in trimming).
12275	*To.* S: corrected from *Th.*
12278	*fete.* So L, K. S: *fote.*
12298	*to.* S: *l to.*
12301	Marginalia in S (at top of fol. 114r): *liber iiijus Regum.*

12312	*prophett*. So L, K. S: *prophe*.
12319	Marginalia in S (at left of fol. 114r): *Elysew*.
12326	*sytt*. So L, K. S: *titt*.
	S: line 12333 copied and then canceled after this line.
12337	*Go*. So L, K. S: *so*.
12341	*dyd*. S: *dyd ʒ*.
12349	*of*. S: ~~*o ser*~~ *of*.
	Sarsynes. So K. S: *sarsyns*. L: *Saresins*.
12350	*Benadab*. So S. L, K: *Benedab*.
12351	*prowes*. So L, K. S: *prows*.
12357	Marginalia in S (at top of fol. 114v): *liber iiijus Regum*.
	grett. So L, K. S: *a grett*.
12364	*was*. S: *a* inserted above the line.
12370	*that*. So L, K. S: *þer*.
12377	*unto*. So L, K. S: *to*.
12378	*lykyng*. S: ~~*k*~~ *lykyng*.
12380	*me*. So L, K. S: *þe*.
12381	*The*. So L, K. S: *he*.
12391	*lech ylk*. So L, K. S: *lech of ylk*.
12395	*sall*. So L, K. S: *self*.
12396	*thi*. S: ~~*þat*~~ *þi*.
12398	S: line 12404 copied and then canceled, correct line inserted above.
12412	*pyrry*. S: ~~*y*~~ *pyrry*.
12413	Marginalia in S (at top of fol. 115r): no heading.
12416	*He*. So L, K. S: *whore he*.
12421	*So*. So L, K. S: *gone*.
12436	*to₂*. S: ~~*r*~~ *to*.
12441	*er*. So L, K. S: *þe*.
12443	*hele*. So L, K. S: *he*.
12451	*bad*. S: ~~*sayd*~~ *bad*.
12454	*I*. So L, K. S: *þat I*.
12462	*space*. So L, K. S: *place*.
12469	Marginalia in S (at top of fol. 115v): *liber iiijus Regum*.
12474	*helyd*. So L, K. S: *lelyd*.
12476	*wole*. So L, K. S: *wele*.
12478	*bete*. So L, K. S: *bote*.
12489	*gyfyn*. So L, K. S: *yfyn*.
12496	*cowrse*. So S. L, K: *course*.
12500	*fest*. S: inserted above the line.
12513	*may*. So L, K. S: *make*.
12527	Marginalia in S (at top of fol. 116r): no heading.
12547	*heled*. S: ~~*leh*~~ *heled*.
12569	*his*. S: inserted above canceled *ser*.
12574	*bene*. So L, K. S: *haue bene*.
12576	*thy*. So L, K. S: *his*.
12585	Marginalia in S (at top of fol. 116v): no heading.
12587	*do*. S: inserted above the line.

12589	*charge*. So L, K. S: *charged*.
	bad. So L, K. S: *had*.
12590	*drewres*. So L, K. S: *drewrers*.
12591	*I hym*. So L, K. S: *yf I*.
12592	*thanke*. So L, K. S: *thynke*.
	of myn. So L, K. S: *forto*.
	hele. S: *ł hele*.
12599	*have*. So L, K. S: *had*.
12601	*knave*. So L, K. S omits.
12620	*sede*. So L, K. S: *stede*.
12623	*mesellri*. So L, K. S: *mesell*.
12640	Marginalia in S (at top of fol. 117r): no heading.
12649	*banke*. So S. L, K: *bank*.
12650	*bowand*. So L, K. S: *bownd*.
12658	*felows*. So O. S, K: *felews*. L: *fellays*.
12668	*becaws*. So L, K. S: *be caw*.
12674	*about*. So L, K. S omits.
	the. S: *ʊnto þe*.
12679	*boyld*. S: *byt boyld*.
12680	*yrn*. S: corrected from *yrne*. K: *yrne*.
12691	*Joram*. So L, K. S: *þem*.
12692	*quayntyse*. So L, K. S: *quaynty*.
12694	*Joram*. So L, K. S: *Iordan*.
12695	Marginalia in S (at top of fol. 117v): no heading.
12698	*kenest*. So L, K. S omits.
12702	*forto*. So L, K. S: *fort*.
12706	*fro*. So K. L: *for*. S: *frod*.
12710	*was₁*. So L, K. S omits.
12726, 28	These lines are transposed in L, with *that* in line 12726 altered to *he*. I have maintained the reading of S, despite my feeling that the original might well have followed L.
12729	*Dotaym*. So L, K. S: *Dotan*.
12733	*go*. So L, K. S omits.
12734	*and*. So L, K. S: *and bad*.
12741	*Dataym*. So L, K. S: *Datan*.
12744	*sonderman*. So L, K. S: *sondran*.
12746	*in*. So L, K. S omits.
12748	*heuyd*. So L, K. S: *fete*.
12750	*Alas, alas*. So L, K. S: *als*.
	full. So L, K. S: *fowle*.
12753	Marginalia in S (at top of fol. 118r): *liber iiijus Regum*.
	sertes. So S. L, K: *certes*.
	we be. So L, K. S: *be we*.
12760	*ryght*. S: *r* corrected from *ʒ*.
12763	*stave*. So L, K. S omits.
12769	*of*. So L, K. S omits.
12776	*sone*. So L, K. S: *sum*.

12787	*we.* So L, K. S: *be.*
12801	*ware.* So L, K. S: *þei.*
12806	*prayd God to.* So L, K. S: *prayd to god.*
12807	Marginalia in S (at top of fol. 118v): *liber iiijus Regum. De actes Elysew.*
12819	*kyng.* So L, K. S omits.
12821	*con.* So K. S: *þus he.*
	Sauns fayle. So L, K. S omits. Compare 727:9.
12836	*lete.* So S, L. K: *lette.*
12845	*knyght.* So L, K. S: *kyng.*
12864	Marginalia in S (at top of fol. 119r): no heading.
12866	*wo may.* So L, K. S: *wo men may.*
12882	*and.* S: inserted above canceled *of.*
12894	*shetyng and.* So L, K. S: *sewtyng.*
12897	*ware.* S: *g̶ ware.*
12902	*ther.* So L, K. S: *oþer.*
12916	*for.* So L, K. S: *forto.*
12917	*Another.* So L, K. S: *And other.*
12919	Marginalia in S (at top of fol. 119v): no heading.
12930	*us.* So L, K. S omits.
12939	*sent men.* So L, K. S: omits.
	to. So L, K. S: *forto.*
12940	*come.* So L, K. S omits.
12964	*befor.* So L, K. S: *for.*
12968	*slyke.* So L, K. S: *skyke.*
12969	*prophet.* So L, K. S: *prophe.*
12971	*for.* So L, K. S: *for þat.*
12975	Marginalia in S (at top of fol. 120r): no heading.
12991	*comys.* So L, K. S: *comyn.*
12998	*beld.* S: altered from *byld.*
13002	*Arabys.* So L, K. S: *armys.*
13020	*that.* So L, K. S omits.
13022	*trussed.* So L, K. S: *trassed.*
13032	*and.* So L, K. S: *bot.*
13033	Marginalia in S (at top of fol. 120v): no heading.
	of. So L, K. S omits.
13035	*this spech.* So L, K. S omits.
13037	*may.* So L, K. S: *make.*
	by. So L, K. S omits.
13042	*als.* S: inserted above canceled *all.*
	the. S: ~~when~~ *þe.*
13053	*vitaylyng.* So L, K. S: *waytyng.*
13054	*all.* So L, K. S: *of.*
13057	*sawes.* So L, K. S: *sanges.*
13063	*in fere.* So L, K. S omits.
13078	*he.* S: *þ he.*
13083	*That.* S: ~~Nat~~ *þat.*
13085	Marginalia in S (at top of fol. 121r): no heading.

13087	*amend.* So L, K. S omits.
13089	*Who.* So L, K. S: *whoso.*
13094	*sayve.* So S. L, K: *save.*
13114	*are.* So L, K. S: *ware.*
13117	*forto.* So L, K. S: *fort.*
13126	*to forsake.* So K. S: *forto sake.* L: *forto forsake.*
13129	*forthir.* So L, K. S: *forþi.*
13130	*processe.* So S, L. K: *process.*
13136	*hym cover.* So L, K. S: *couer hym.*
13140	Marginalia in S (at top of fol. 121v): no heading.
13142	*he angred.* So L, K. S: *þe Angor.*
13144	*take tressour.* So L, K. S: *take of his tressour.*
13149	*knew.* So L, K. S: *hew.*
13152	*his.* So L, K. S omits.
13163	*thou.* So L, K. S: *þe.*
13170	*con.* So L, K. S: *con hym.*
13172	*sorows.* So L, K. S: *sorow.*
13178	*this.* So L, K. S: *is.*
13193	*yll.* S: inserted above canceled *ylke.*
13197	Marginalia in S (at top of fol. 122r): *liber iiijus Regum.*
	rewled. So L, K. S: *saued.*
13200	*had.* So L, K. S omits.
13202	*ma.* S: *make.*
13204	*tyme.* So L, K. S omits.
13205	*Of.* So L, K. S: *And of.*
13214	*hym.* So L, K. S omits.
13217	*brethyr.* So L. S, K: *broþer.*
13226	*myght.* So L, K. S: *þat myȝt.*
13237	*has.* S: *a* inserted above the line.
13239	*doos.* So L, K. S omits.
13242	*brethyr.* So L. S, K: *broþer.*
13244	*how.* So L, K. S: *hole.*
13257	Marginalia in S (at top of fol. 122v): no heading.
13272	*lest.* So L, K. S: *left.*
13289	*that.* So L, K. S: *yt.*
13291	*had.* So L, K. S: *bad.*
13293	*Jezeraell.* So L. S: *ierusalem.* K: *Ieȝerael.*
13303	*Jezeraell.* So L, K. S: *ierusalem.*
13304	*as.* S: *has as.*
13305	*So.* So L, K. S: *To.*
13308	*turn.* So L, K. S: *turm.*
13313	*ser.* So L, K. S: *of.*
13314	*con.* So S. L, K: *can.*
13317	Marginalia in S (at top of fol. 123r): no heading.
13321	*kyn.* So L, K. S: *kyng.*
13322	*eld.* S: *n eld.*
13326	*scheld.* So L, K. S: *cheld.*

13339	*pepyll.* S: *ff pepyll.*
13352	*was.* S: inserted above canceled *I.*
13358	*wound.* So L, K. S: *wenyng.*
13373	Marginalia in S (at top of fol. 123v): no heading.
13374	*men.* So L, K. S: *me.*
13375	*thrast.* So L, K. S: *trayst.*
13382	*Jezeraell.* So L, K. S: *Ieraraell.*
13385	*contrarye.* So L, K. S: *conrarye.*
13391	*Thou.* So L, K. S: *þat.*
13392	*sakles.* So L, K. S: *slakles.*
13396	*ye.* S: letter canceled before (*ȝ*?).
13398	*two.* So L, K. S: *þo.*
	wyghtly. S: *t* inserted above the line.
13408	*of.* So L, K. S: *on.*
13415	*To.* So L, K. S: *So.*
13416	*bot.* So L, K. S: *bo.*
13422	*wyt.* S: inserted above the line.
13427	*sayd.* S: inserted above the line.
13431	Marginalia in S (at top of fol. 124r): no heading.
	sen. So L, K. S: *son.*
	God. S: inserted above canceled *þof.*
13433	*both.* So L, K. S: *before.*
13435	*kynred.* S: letter (*c*?) canceled before.
13445	*forthy.* So L, K. S: *in hy.*
13450	*sone.* So L, K. S: *saue.*
13451	*them.* So L, K. S: *he þem.*
13458	*down.* S: *downn̄.*
13478	*hym.* So L, K. S omits.
13479	*thei hym.* So S, O. L, K: *thei to hym.*
13480	*thor.* S: ~~þer~~ *þor.*
13481	*ther owt.* So L, K. S: *þe rowt.*
13491	Marginalia in S (at top of fol. 124v): no heading.
13498	*tone.* S: altered from *tene.*
13502	*unto.* So L, K. S: *to.*
13514	*held.* So K. S: *hald.* L: *had.*
13518	*hyr.* So L, K. S: *his.*
13532	*Joiada.* So L, K. S: *Iorada.*
13540	*Joiada.* So L, K. S: *Iorada.*
13547	Marginalia in S (at top of fol. 125r): no heading.
13561	*in.* So L, K. S omits.
13564	*hyr.* So L, K. S: *þer.*
13585	*than.* S: inserted above the line.
	Joiada. So L, K. S: *Iorada.*
13587	*mony.* S: *ny* inserted above the line.
	ma. S: ~~and~~ *ma.*
13591	*thei ta.* S: ~~þei ta~~ *þei ta.*

13596	*Joiada.* So L, K. S: *Iorada.*
	last in. So K. S: *lysted.* L: *lasted.*
13600	*wyll.* S: ~~wll~~ *wyll.*
13609	Marginalia in S (at top of fol. 125v): no heading.
13613	*Joacas.* So O. S, L, K: *Ioatas.*
13623	*Joiada.* So L, K. S: *Iorada.*
13634	*and.* So L, K. S omits.
13636	*Joiada.* So L, K. S: *Iorada.*
13648	*Joiada.* So L, K. S: *Iorada.*
	he has. So L, K. S: *yt was.*
13649–50	So L, K. S omits lines.
13653	*Azaell.* S: *a* inserted above the line.
13657	*townes.* So L, K. S omits.
13669	*Phylysteyns.* S: *ff Phylysteyns.*
13671	Marginalia in S (at top of fol. 126r): *liber iiijus Regum.*
	hom. So L, K. S: *whom.*
13681	*this.* So L, K. S omits.
13687	*so.* So L, K. S omits.
13693	*comforth.* S: *þan* inserted before, then canceled.
13694	*The soth we sone sall knaw.* So K. S: *þat sath sall sone be knaw* ꝛ. L: *the soth sone shal we knaw.*
13695	*lang lyf.* So L. S: *lyf lang lyf.* K: *lyf lang.*
13699	*desiring.* So L, K. S: *lykyng.*
13700	*both.* So L, K. S: *beth.*
13701	*Thre.* So L, K. S: *þe.*
13702	S: line 13700 mistakenly copied and then canceled; line 13702 inserted above.
	he layd. So L, K. S: *can he lay.*
13705	*sayd.* So L, K. S: *say.*
13711	*When he.* So L, K. S: *whe.*
13717	*his.* S: ~~þer~~ *his.*
13719	*murdred.* So L, K. S: *menturd.*
13722	*of.* So L, K. S omits.
	werkyng. S: ~~his~~ *werkyng.*
13723	*hid.* So L, K. S omits.
13725	*neghted.* So L, K. S: *neght.*
13729	Marginalia in S (at top of fol. 126v): *liber iiijus Regum.*
13735	*schew.* So S. L, K: *shew.*
13756	*them.* So L, K. S: *þei.*
13769	*full redy.* So L, K. S: *full wele redy.*
13782	*Moabyse.* S: ~~Mob~~ *Moabyse.*
13785	Marginalia in S (at top of fol. 127r): no heading.
13814	*long.* So L, K. S: *to long.*
13822	*wrscheply.* So L, K. S: *wrschepfully.*
13824	Marginalia in S (at right of fol. 127r): *Jeroboam.*
13843	Marginalia in S (at top of fol. 127v): *liber iiijus Regum.*
13852	*hym.* So L, K. S: *þem.*

13854	*therfore*. So L, K. S: *þore*.
13860	*Hym*. So L, K. S: *he*.
13887	Marginalia in S (at left of fol. 127v, partially cut off): *[J]onas [sca]pham*.
13901	Marginalia in S (at top of fol. 128r): *liber iiijus Regum. Jonas*.
13902	*unwysly*. S: altered from *wnwysly*.
13910	*to*. S: ~~do~~ *to*.
13911	*Then*. So L, K. S: *þei*.
	way. So L, K. S: *ways*.
13912	*delese*. So L, K. S: *dolese*.
13914	*and*. S: *yt and*. K reads *þe and*.
13915	*that any man may*. So L. S: *þat anyman þat may*. K: *any man þat may*.
13916	*in*. So L, K. S: *of*.
13924	*graunt*. So L, K. S: *graunt yow*.
13941	*thei*. So L, K. S: *þou þei*.
13943	*over*. S: *of ouer*.
13947	*suld in sekkes*. So L, K. S: *in sekkes suld*.
13949	*barns*. So L, K. S: *barons*.
13950	*ware*. So L, K. S: *þat*.
13956	Marginalia in S (at top of fol. 128v): *liber iiijus Regum*.
13974	*he*. S: inserted above canceled *yt*.
13976	*pennance*. So S. L, K: *penance*.
13982	*sone may*. So L, K. S: *may sone*.
13983	*an*. S: *an* ~~hyll euer~~.
13992	*yvyn*. So L, K. S: *euyn*.
14002	*we*. So L, K. S omits.
	thynges. So L, K. S: *kynges*.
14004	*to end*. So L, K. S: *to þe end*.
14005	*Jeroboam we told of*. So K. S: *Ioroboam*. L: *Ieroboam that we told of* (omits *Kyng*).
14011	Marginalia in S (at top of fol. 129r): *liber iiijus Regum*.
14012	*carpe*. So L, K. S: *cappe*.
14025	*Goddes*. So S, L. K: *Godes*.
14033	*surquidry*. So L, K. S: *syche degre*.
14051	*ware*. So L, K. S: *warer*.
14063	*meselry*. S: ~~melle~~ *meselry*.
14065	Marginalia in S (at top of fol. 129v): no heading.
14067	*felows*. So L, K. S: *felews*.
14070	*cyté*. S: inserted above canceled *reme*.
14079	*ylke*. S: ~~yll~~ *ylke*.
14084	*drese*. So L, K. S: *drefe*.
14087	*trowth*. So L, K. S: *trowt*.

Book of Job

14090	*helfull*. So L, K. S: *lefull*.
	here. So L, K. S: *lere*.
14091	*whoso*. S: *so* inserted above the line.
14098	*erthly*. S: *ly* inserted above the line.

14113   Marginalia in S (at top of fol. 130r): *Job*.
14114   S: line 14116 written and canceled, line 14114 inserted above.
14148   *He*. So K. S: *hym*.
14169   Marginalia in S (at top of fol. 130v): no heading.
14175   *may*. S: *mayn*.
14185   *fayren*. So K. S: *fayrer*. L: *part*.
14203   *enogh*. S: *o* inserted above the line.
14209   *to me*. So L, K. S omits.
14225   Marginalia in S (at top of fol. 131r): no heading.
14231   *Hyder*. So L, K. S: *hylder*.
14233   *then*. So L, K. S: *þem*.
14236   *syghtys se*. So L, K. S: *fyghtyns fle*.
14239   *on*. S: inserted above canceled letters.
14264   *of₂*. S: inserted above the line.
14277   Marginalia in S (at top of fol. 131v): no heading.
             S: lines 14277–95 are repeated with minor variations after line 14331 (at the top of fol. 132r).
14281   *Thou*. S: corrected from *þi*.
14282   *werldly*. So L, K. S: *worthy*.
             weld. So L, K. S: *wend*. The correct reading, *weld*, is properly copied in the canceled rewrite of this line following line 14331. See textual note to line 14277.
14286, 88   So L, K. S: lines transposed both here and in the canceled rewrite of these lines following line 14331. See textual note to line 14277.
14286   *no*. So L, K. S omits here, but includes in the canceled rewrite of this lines following line 14331 (though the rewrite mistakenly copies *ferrer* for *ferther* at that point). See textual note to line 14277.
14288   *Thi*. So L, K. S: *þe*. The correct reading, *þi*, is properly copied in the canceled rewrite of this line following line 14331. See textual note to line 14277.
14296   *greve*. So L, K. S: *geue*.
14306   *not*. So L, K. S omits.
14317   *forthy*. So L, K. S omits.
14331   Marginalia in S (at top of fol. 132r): *Job*.
             See textual note to line 14277.
14335   *Bot*. So L, K. S: *bo*.
14336   *allone*. So L, K. S: *at þe last*.
14342   *cors*. So L, K. S omits.
14347   *and*. So L, K. S omits.
14351   *releve*. So L, K. S: *relesch*.
14352   *owt*. So L, K. S: *ow*.
14367   Marginalia in S (at top of fol. 132v): no heading.
14373   *gyfes*. So L, K. S: *gyf*.
14378   *yt*. S: *and yt*. Compare L, however: *naked and nedy is noght to layne*.
14388   *his*. S: *y his*.
14393   *space*. S: *place space*.
14401   *Bot*. So L, K. S: *Bon*.

14402	*and bett.* S: inserted above the line.
14405–08	Lines 14405–06 and 14407–08 are transposed in S, but marked for correction in the margin.
14408	S: line 14409 copied and then canceled before being recopied in its proper place.
14422	*to.* So L, K. S: *into.*
14423	*non me.* So L, K. S: *non then me.*
14425	Marginalia in S (at top of fol. 133r): *Job.*
	Elyphath. So L, K. S, O: *Elypagh.*
14427	*it had lent.* So L, K. S: *he had hent.*
14440	*that thee is sent thies.* So L, K. S: *for þi is sent þe.*
14442	*all.* So L, K. S: *als.*
14446	*slyke.* So L, K. S: *syke.*
14454	*be.* So L, K. S omits.
14458	*sythes.* So K. S *swylke.* L: *such.*
14465	*faurth.* So L, K. S: *faruth.*
14469	*wogh.* So L, K. S: *wagh.*
14474	*and.* So L, K. S omits.
14479	Marginalia in S (at top of fol. 133v): *Job.*
14483	*laythes.* So L, K. S: ~~lath~~ *laythers.*
14487	*That.* S: *þat Ɫ.*
14489	*as.* So L, K. S omits.
14492	*mo.* So L, K. S omits.
14495	*mens.* So L, K. S: *men.*
14509	*Then Baldath.* So L, K. S: *þe Balath.*
14510	*to.* So L, K. S: *so.*
14516	*men.* S: inserted above canceled *man.*
14537	Marginalia in S (at top of fol. 134r): *Job.*
	Allmighty. S: *ty* inserted above the line.
14551	*fare.* So L, K. S omits.
14567	*gabbyng.* So L, K. S: *galbyng.*
14577	The line as it stands is defective in both S and L, breaking the rhyme. Line 14579 in S is also defective, though I have followed K in emending that line from L. On this line, K notes (4.22) that adding "*wele* after *wryttyn* would save the rime but make the line too long." Another possibility would be to alter the ending to *ware wryt wele,* or *ware wryt full,* but neither is plausible enough to convince me to alter the text.
14579	*a poyntyll of steylle.* So L, K. S: *with steylle satyt þerfor.* The line in S is clearly defective as it fails to hold the rhyme. See textual note to line 14577.
14581	*myght ever more.* So L, K. S: *euer more myȝt.*
14593	Marginalia in S (at top of fol. 134v): *Job.*
14595	*Sayvyour.* S: *y* inserted above the line.
14605–06	So L, K. S: missing lines.
14609	*come.* So L, K. S: *come not.*
	men. S: *mene.*
14610	*sore.* S: inserted above the line.
14621	*thou.* So L, K. S: *þen.*

14644	*dyd.* So L, K. S: *dyll.*
14646	*he.* So L, K. S omits.
14653	Marginalia in S (at top of fol. 135r): *Job.*
14682	S: inserted above canceled line 14684.
14683	*ryghtwysnes.* So L, K. S: *ryghtwyse.*
14691	*lyfes.* So L, K. S: *lyf.*
14707	Marginalia in S (at top of fol. 135v: *Job.*
14725	*Forthi.* S: *ffor ꝥ þi.*
14733	*it.* So L, K. S omits.
14738	*kavtels.* S: *v* inserted above the line.
14739	*That.* So L, K. S omits.
14748	*malyse.* So S. L, K: *malyce.*
14754	*then.* So L, K. S: *þem.*
14761	Marginalia in S (at top of fol. 136r): *Job.*
14766	S: inserted above canceled line 14768.
14774	*thi.* So L, K. S omits.
14780	*bot.* So L, K. S: *bo.*
14788	*hame.* S: inserted above canceled *name.*
14802	*solace.* So L, K. S: *salace.*
14810	*other.* S: corrected from *uther.*
14819	Marginalia in S (at top of fol. 136v): *Job.*
14826	*fro.* So L, K. S: *for.*
14828	*levere.* So L, K. S: *levare.*
14841	*Ne.* So L, K. S: *he.*
14843	*mysgovernaunse.* So L, K. S: *mysgouernse.*
14845	*Bot.* So L, K. S: *Bo.*
14875	*yow₁.* S: *ħ yow.*
	yow₂. S: inserted above the line.
14879	Marginalia in S (at top of fol. 137r): *Job.*
14931	*Fayrewele.* So L, K. S: *Fayre.*
14935	Marginalia in S (at top of fol. 137v): *Job.*
14955	*men.* So L, K. S: *me.*
14968	*me.* So L, K. S omits.
14974	*lyges.* So S. L, K: *lygges.*
14979	*faur.* L, K: *IV.* S: *XL.* L is confirmed by John 11:17, 39: "four days."
14993	Marginalia in S (at top of fol. 138r): *Job.*
	Thou. So L, K. S: *þat.*
14995	*wrang.* S: letter (y?) canceled before.
14997	*stale.* So L, K. S: *stae*, with a faint curl above the *e.*
15002	*Thi wyll.* So L, K. S: *in whyls.*
15013	*governd.* So L, K. S: *gouernernd.*
15014	*dere.* So L, K. S: *drere.*
15015	*wrschept.* So S. L: *worship.* K: *wurschept.*
15022	*wyll.* So L, K. S: *lyf.*
15026	S: much of line written above an incorrect and canceled line 15028.
15027	*Myn.* S: *n* inserted above the line.
	wayn. So L, K. S: *hay.*

15049	Marginalia in S (at top of fol. 138v): *Job.*
15055	*herd.* S: corrected from *hard.*
15070	*to be.* So L, K. S omits.
15075	*how.* So L, K. S omits.
15084	*can serve.* So L, K. S: *cawse.*
15095	*what.* So L, K. S: *how.*
15105	Marginalia in S (at top of fol. 139r): *Job.*
15125	*no.* S: ~~not~~ *no.*
15126	*to.* So L. S, K: *te.*
15131	*By.* So L, K. S: *bot.*
15142	*wott.* S: inserted above the line.
15145	*governs.* So L, K. S: *gouerans.*
15146	*sand.* So L, K. S: *loue.*
15161	Marginalia in S (at top of fol. 139v): *Job.*
15193	*When.* S: ~~To god~~ *when.*
15207	*God.* S: *god* ~~lese~~.
15208	*multyplye.* So L, K. S: *multyplyed.*

BOOK OF TOBIAS

15217	Marginalia in S (at top of fol. 140r): *Thobie.*
15217, 19	Lines indented to leave space for an initial capital; first letter of line 15217 written in the middle of the space.
15217	*trew.* So L, K. S omits.
	we. S: *e* inserted above the line.
15223	*kynred.* S: *r* inserted above the line.
15224	*connyng.* S: n_2 inserted above the line.
15250	*foylies.* S: *i* inserted above the line.
15254	*or.* So L, K. S: *r of.*
15255	*cum furth.* S: written above canceled *comforth.*
15269	Marginalia in S (at top of fol. 140v): *Toby.*
	went withoutyn. S: written twice, neither canceled.
15277	*Ana, as.* So L, K. S: *Analas.*
15278	*hyre.* S: corrected from *here.*
15302	*gold.* So L, K. S: *gald.*
	gyfyn. So L, K. S: *yfyn.*
15313	*the.* So L, K. S omits.
15317	*not sese.* So L, K. S: *no se.*
15325	Marginalia in S (at top of fol. 141r): *Toby.*
15326	*wherfor.* So L, K. S: *whefor.*
15339	*therto.* S: *ther* inserted above the line.
15385	Marginalia in S (at top of fol. 141v): *Thoby.*
15395	*of.* So L, K. S: *on.*
15436	*of swylke werke.* So L, K. S: *swylke were.*
15441	*eyelyddes.* S: ~~hee~~ *eye liddes.*
15443	Marginalia in S (at top of fol. 142r): *Thoby.*
	brydes. So K. S: *byrdes*, but compare line 14422, *bryth.* L: *birds.*

15452	*ded.* So L, K. S: *dyd.*
15462	*he.* So L, K. S omits.
15477	*dysesse.* So L, K. S: *hym dysessed.*
15479	*That.* So L, K. S: *þei.*
	them. S: inserted above ~~hym~~.
15480	*then.* So L, K. S: *þou.*
15484	*in.* So L, K. S: *an.*
15488	*feche.* So L, K. S: *seche.*
15499	Marginalia in S (at top of fol. 142v): *Thoby.*
	myn. S: ~~nyn~~ *myn.*
15504	*lorn.* S: ~~for~~ *lorn.*
15508	*to.* S: inserted above the line.
	the lordes that. So L, K. S: *þat lordes.*
15513	*I.* So L, K. S: *he.*
15517	*sone.* So L. S: ~~sone~~ *sun.* K: *sun.*
15518	*a.* So L, K. S: *I.*
15550	*tyll.* So L, K. S: *tyll þat.*
15556	*to take.* So L, K. S: *tyll takent.*
15557	Marginalia in S (at top of fol. 143r): *Thobie.*
15568	*leyn.* S: inserted above canceled *leuyt.*
15573	*saw unsoght.* So L, K. S: *sone hym soght.*
15574	*the.* So L, K. S: *to.*
15595	*then.* S: corrected from *þem.*
	me to. So L, K. S: *vn to me to,* with *vn* inserted above the line.
15604	*prove.* S: ~~pr~~ *proue.*
15605	*it.* So L, K. S: *he.*
15613	Marginalia in S (at top of fol. 143v): *Thoby.*
15619	*I.* So L, K. S: *he.*
15626	*me.* So L, K. S omits.
15637	*The.* S: ~~An~~ *þe.*
15653	*them.* So L, K. S: *þen.*
15658	*moyder.* So L, K. S: *his moyder.*
15665	*hym.* So L, K. S: *þem.*
15666	*he.* So L, K. S omits.
15671	Marginalia in S (at top of fol. 144r): *Thoby.*
15689	*mowrne.* S: *w* inserted above the line.
15716	*falys.* S: *y* inserted above the line.
15727	Marginalia in S (at top of fol. 144v): *Thoby.*
15750	*on.* So L, K. S: *of.*
15766	*worthy.* So L, K. S, O: *worthly.*
15769	*the.* So L, K. S omits.
15770	*swylke.* S: ~~swylke~~ *swylke.*
15772	*in.* So L, K. S omits.
	them. So L, K. S: *þan.*
15774	*she.* So K. S: *he.* L omits.
	not fare. So L, K. S: *no ferre.*
15775	*sevyn husbandes dy.* L, K: *VII husbandes dy.* S: *þi husbandes VII be.*

15778	*foles*. So L, K. S: *felos*.
15781	Marginalia in S (at top of fol. 145r): *Thoby*.
15782	*hyr*. S: inserted above canceled *yt*.
15814	*whyls thei*. So L, K. S: *whyls þat þei*.
15831	*Undoo*. So L, K. S: *vnder*.
15833	Marginalia in S (at top of fol. 145v): *Thoby*.
15835	*Salt*. So L, K. S: *Salt of*.
15846	*thei*. So L, K. S: *þi*.
	medsyn. So S. L: *medicyn*. K: *medcyn*.
15872	*outt*. So S, L. K: *out*.
15875	*for*. So L, K. S: *furth*.
15876	*that*. S: *y that*.
15884	*wold*. So L, K. S: *wold þat*.
15887	Marginalia in S (at top of fol. 146r): *Thoby*.
	than. S: ~~ewyn~~ *þan*.
15894	*thi*. So L, K. S: *þe*.
15904	*scherwes*. So K. S: *scherwrs*. L: *shrews*.
15906	*weddyng*. So L, K. S omits.
15908	*that*. So L, K. S omits.
15914	*graydly*. So S. L: *grathly*. K: *gradly*.
	go. So L, K. S: *lyge*.
15916	*non*. So L, K. S: *no*.
15941	Marginalia in S (at top of fol. 146v): *Thoby*.
15949	*dede*. So L, K. S: *dele*.
15950	*course*. So L, K. S: *coure*.
15955	*enogh*. S: *enoght*.
15985	*Sen*. So L, K. S omits.
15989	*ys*. S: inserted above canceled *is*.
15991	*Then*. S: inserted above canceled *Our cosyn*.
	ferleys. So L, K. S: *felows*.
15997	Marginalia in S (at top of fol. 147r): *Thoby*.
	ever. S: inserted above canceled *neuer*.
16012	*maryed*. S: *y* inserted above the line.
16014	*he wold not*. So L, K. S omits.
16023	*of*. So L, K. S: *on*.
16033–36	Lines 16033–34 and 16035–36 are transposed in S, but marked for correction in the margin.
16049	Marginalia in S (at top of fol. 147v): *Thoby*.
16060	*hyr*. So L, K. S omits.
	his. So L, K. S: *þis*.
16069	*hend*. So L, K. S: *hand*, corrected from *hond*.
16070	*maw*. S: inserted above canceled *mawys*.
16080	*noyght*. So L, K. S: *and noyȝt*.
16082	*angel*. So L, K. S: *Ange*.
16085	*Asmodeus*. So L, K. S: *Asmodus*.
	at. So L, K. S: *a*.
16101	Marginalia in S (at top of fol. 148r): *Thoby*.

16102	*thei knaw.* S: ~~was þei knew~~ *knaw.*
16105	*then.* S: *thens.*
16107	*forto.* So L, K. S: *for.*
16115	*Go.* So L, K. S: *To.*
16119	*Thoby.* So L, K. S omits.
16123	*wele.* S: inserted above canceled *weld.*
16126	*all ther.* So L, K. S: *all þat þer.*
16141	*made.* So L, K. S omits.
16154	*lete.* S: inserted above canceled *lett.*
16156	*fader.* So L, K. S omits.
	moyder. So L, K. S: *hyr moyder.*
16157	Marginalia in S (at top of fol. 148v): *Thoby.*
16165	*nete.* So L. S, K: *nawte.*
16166	*and.* So L, K. S omits.
16172	*when.* S: letter (*m?*) canceled before.
16174	*in werld.* So L, K. S: *inwardly.*
16182	*in.* So L, K. S omits.
16184	*parfytt.* S: ~~rr~~ *parfytt.*
16205	*eyne.* S: ~~weyne.~~
16213	Marginalia in S (at top of fol. 149r): *Thoby.*
16215	*wrast.* So L, K. S: *wratht.*
16218	*moght.* S: *t* inserted above the line.
16247	*wentt.* S: ~~went~~ *wentt.*
16269	Marginalia in S (at top of fol. 149v): *Thoby.*
16270	*ryches.* So L, K. S: *ryche.*
16276	*had spede.* S: inserted above canceled *was wede.*
16286	*untyll.* S: *vn-* written above canceled *þer.*
16289	*syne.* So L, K. S: *sone.*
16298	*his.* So L, K. S: *hyr.*
16303	*weyne.* S: ~~may~~ *weyne.*
16304	*qwer.* S: inserted above canceled *qwyl.*
	stewerd. So L, K. S: *stewer.*
16312	*to.* So L, K. S: *two.*
16315	*we.* S: *we* ~~t~~.
16324	*has.* S: *has* ~~P~~.
16325	Marginalia in S (at top of fol. 150r): *Thoby.*
16326	*ar grayd.* So L, K. S: *agrayd.*
16336	*ye.* S: letter (*I?*) canceled before.
16365	*beforne.* So L, K. S: *before.*
16367	*that.* S: inserted above the line.
16375	*kepe.* So L, K. S omits.
16379	*then.* So L, K. S: *þe.*
16381	*sevynty.* So L, K. S: *seynty.* See explanatory note to lines 16381–88.
16383	Marginalia in S (at top of fol. 150v): *Thoby.*
16388	*in.* So L, K. S: *and.*
16398	*that.* S: ~~fro~~ *þat.*
16409	*agayn.* So L, K. S: *agayn agayn.*

16410	*send.* S: inserted above the line.
16412	*that.* So L, K. S: *of.*
	be. So L, K. S: *to be.*
16422	*were then.* So L, K. S: *vnto.*
	so were. So L, K. S: *þen ere.*
16441	Marginalia in S (at top of fol. 151r): *Hester.*

BOOK OF ESTHER

16453, 55	Lines indented to leave space for an initial capital; first letter of line 16453 written in the middle of the space.
16470	*erles.* So L, K. S: *erthyls.*
16480	*his.* So L, K. S: *in his.*
16491	*Ther.* So L, K. S: *þei.*
16493	Marginalia in S (at top of fol. 151v): *Hester.*
16504	*abowt.* So L, K. S: *a bow.*
16509	*meyne.* S: *y* inserted above the line.
16511	*aftur.* So L, K. S: perhaps corrected from *eftur.*
16514	*tent.* S: *tentes.*
16523	*say.* S: *sayd.*
16535	*price.* So L, K. S: *prince.*
16537	*yt.* So L, K. S omits.
16538	S: lines 16551–52 copied and then canceled after the line.
16549	Marginalia in S (at top of fol. 152r): *Hester.*
16561	*this.* S: *is þis.*
16563	*noyght. noyȝt b.*
16564	*are.* S: *h are.*
16568	*sene.* So L, K. S: *meynd.*
16585	*fra.* So S. L, K: *fro.*
16588	*to.* S: *s to.*
16590	S: lines 16587–88 copied and then canceled after the line.
16591	*manly.* So L, K. S: *namly.*
16603	Marginalia in S (at top of fol. 152v): *Hester.*
	meneys. So K. S: *moneys.* L: *meues.*
16610	*with.* So L, K. S: *we.*
16619	*Hester.* S: *Aftur,* with *Hester* added in the left margin.
16621	*mery.* S: letter canceled before.
16625	*kyned.* S: corrected from *kyn.*
16646	*evyn als.* So L, K. S: *als euyn.*
16647	*yt.* So L, K. S omits.
16648	*his.* S: *his mete.*
16652	*bot.* So L, K. S: *bo.*
16663	Marginalia in S (at top of fol. 153r): *Hester.*
16678	*suld.* So L, K. S omits.
16682	*man.* So L, K. S: *mony.*
16701	*thyng.* So L, K. S: *tythyng.*
16719	Marginalia in S (at top of fol. 153v): *Hester.*

16722	*when.* So L, K. S: *whe.*
16729	*and.* S: inserted above the line.
16732	*I.* S: ~~in~~ *I.*
16748	*hyr.* So L, K. S omits.
16754	*space.* S: inserted above canceled *god.*
16770	*qweynes.* So L, K. S: *kynges.*
16775	Marginalia in S (at top of fol. 154r): *Hester.*
	Merdochyus. So S. L, K: *Mardochyus.*
16779	*therforn.* So L, K. S: *therfor.*
16780	*a.* So L, K. S: *þe.*
16787	*cubbettes.* So L, K. S: *cublettes.*
16791	*all the.* So L, K. S: *on a.*
16798	*full.* S: ~~ful~~ *full.*
16804	*be.* S: inserted above canceled ~~of~~.
16817	*kyng.* S: ~~k~~ *kyng.*
16822	*kyng.* So L, K. S omits.
16829	Marginalia in S (at top of fol. 154v): *Hester.*
	on. So L, K. S: *in.*
16838	*not.* So L, K. S: *no.*
16858	*hym.* So L, K. S: *in.*
16861	*with syghyng.* So L, K. S: *syghand.*
16880	*thine.* S: corrected from *thnne.*
16883	Marginalia in S (at top of fol. 155r): *Hester.*
16892	*Ser.* So L, K. S: *for.*
	cummand. So L, K. S: ~~commawnd~~ *cumnand.*
16893	*this word.* So L, K. S: *thies wordes.*
16894	*yt.* So L, K. S: *he.*
16906	*grene.* So L, K. S: *gryme.*
16908	*bed.* S: *be ꝛ*, with *d* inserted above the line.
16918	*yf.* S: ~~of~~ *yf.*
16921	*cummand.* So L, K. S: *cumnand.*
	his. S: ~~he~~ *his.*
16927	*to.* So L, K. S omits.
16937	Marginalia in S (at top of fol. 155v): no heading.
16938	*weyld.* So L, K. S: *veyld.*
16947	*name.* S: ~~nane~~ *name.*
16954	*in.* So L, K. S: *and.*

BOOK OF JUDITH

16957, 59	Lines indented to leave space for an initial capital; first letter of line 16957 written in the middle of the space.
16969	*with.* So L, K. S, P omit.
16970	*of.* So L, K, P. S: *on.*
16972	*our.* So L, K, P. S: *fell.*
16987	Marginalia in S (at top of fol. 156r): *Judyth.*
	them. So L, K, P. S omits.

16999	*not.* S: *t* inserted above the line.
17001	*On.* So L, K, P. S: *Of.*
17013	*then.* So L, K, P. S: *þem.*
17023	*folke.* So L, K, P. S: *foke.*
17041	Marginalia in S (at top of fol. 156v): *Judythe.*
17044	*dyght most.* So L, K, P. S: *most dyȝt.*
17047	*ther.* So L, K, P. S omits.
17054	*forto.* So L, K, P. S: *to.*
17072	*deme in.* So K. S, P: *deme.* L: *do in.*
17079	*of Moyses.* So L, K, P. S omits.
17089	*he.* S: inserted above the line.
	them. So L, K. S: *þan.* P omits.
17097	Marginalia in S (at top of fol. 157r): *Judyth.*
17101	*thei.* So S, P. L: *they.*
17105	*ryn.* S: ~~rynd~~ *ryn.*
17107	*lowt.* So L, K, P. S: *bowt.*
17118	*them.* S: ~~þen~~ *þem.*
17128	*cummand.* So L, K, P. S: *cumnand.*
17129	*Tempyll.* S: inserted above ~~pepyll~~.
17130	*God all.* So L, K, P. S: *all god.*
17134	*nevenand.* So L, K, P. S: *nevan and.*
17138	*land.* So L, K, P. S: *sand.*
17144	*this.* S: *s* inserted above the line.
17151	Marginalia in S (at top of fol. 157v): *Judyth.*
17168	*to.* S: ~~t~~ *to.*
17170	Marginalia in S (at right of fol. 157v): *Judyth.*
17195	*us.* So L, K, P. S: *was.*
17207	Marginalia in S (at top of fol. 158r): *Judyth.*
17208	*fayle.* S: ~~fall~~ *fayle.*
17220	*graunted.* S: ~~at~~ *graunted.*
17221	*them.* S: ~~to~~ *þem.*
17222	*both.* So L, K, P. S omits.
17247	*pellour.* So L, K, P. S: *plessour.*
17249	*of.* So L, K, P. S omits.
17258	*then.* S: inserted above ~~down~~.
17259	*God.* So L, K, P. S omits.
17263	Marginalia in S (at top of fol. 158v): *Judyth.*
	yll. S: corrected from *ell.*
17266	*lyght.* S: ~~scho~~ *lyȝt.*
17280	*fand them sone.* S: *sho fand þem sone.* L, P: *toke theym sone.* K: *[sone] fand þem.*
17281	*Thei.* So S, L, P: *They.*
17282	*semly.* S: *sembly.*
17284	*geyre.* S: *y* inserted above the line.
17286	*so late.* So L, K. S: *solace.*
17300	*ere therin.* So L, K, P. S: *þer ere in.*
17315	Marginalia in S (at top of fol. 159r): *Judyth.*
17331	*geyre.* So L, K, P. S: *gyrde.*

17336	*sho.* So L, K, P. S omits.
17338	*them.* So L, K, P. S: *þen.*
17341	*here.* S: ~~tere~~ *here.*
17350	*how thou.* So L, K, P. S: *how þat þou.*
	his. So L, K, P. S omits.
17360	*of fode fall.* So L, K, P. S: *fell.*
17367	Marginalia in S (at top of fol. 159v): *Judyth.*
17388	*bryng.* S: ~~by~~ *bryng.*
17396	*amend.* So L, K, P. S: *mend.*
17403	*thy.* So L, K, P. S omits.
17417	*when.* So L, K, P. S omits.
17423	Marginalia in S (at top of fol. 160r): *Judyth.*
17425	*unto hym may heve.* So L, P. S: *vnto þe may heue.* K: *to hym may be leue.*
17437	*cummand.* So L, K, P. S: *cumnand.*
17442	*hyr stand.* So L, K, P. S: *hyr suld stand.*
17444	*cummand.* So L, K, P. S: *cumnand.*
17449	*a.* So L, K, P. S omits.
17453	*that.* S: inserted above *þar.*
17460	*Ebrews.* So L, K, P. S: *Ebrew.*
17462	*Ebrews.* So L, K, P. S: *Ebrew.*
17469	*within.* So L, K, P. S omits.
17471	*win.* So L, K, P. S: *in.*
17481	Marginalia in S (at top of fol. 160v): *Judyth.*
17498	*presciosly.* So L, K, P. S: *presciosusly.*
17508	*over.* So L, K, P. S: *our.*
17512	*wele.* So L, K, P. S omits.
17533	*and wepe.* S: inserted above line.
	wepe. So L, K, P. S: *vepe.*
17537	*warnd.* S: *warrnd.*
17538	*sho.* So L, K, P. S: *no man.*
17543	Marginalia in S (at top of fol. 161r): *Judyth.*
17548	*so.* So L, K, P. S: *& so.*
17549	*synow.* So L, K, P. S: *syn.*
17554	*whore.* So L, K, P. S omits.
17579	*To.* So L, K, P. S: canceled.
17584	*thar.* So L, K, P. S: *þan.*
17588	*do.* So L, K, P. S omits.
17595	*For.* S: ~~ffr~~ *ffor.*
17598	*bot.* So L, K, P. S: *bo.*
17603	Marginalia in S (at top of fol. 161v): *Judyth.*
17642	*ryche.* So L, K, P. S: *ryches.*
	thei rafe. So L, K. S, P: *all rafed.*
17646	*ther.* S: ~~t~~ *þer.*
17661	Marginalia in S (at top of fol. 162r): *Judyth.*
	broght. So L, P. S: ~~borogh.~~ K: *brogh.*
17666	*hyr.* S: ~~h~~ *hyr.*
17667	*wun.* S: ~~wone~~ *wun.*

17671	*therwyth*. So L, K, P. S: *wyt*.
17672	*goveren*. So L, K, P. S: *goveren yt*.
17675	*mery*. So K, P. S, L: *men*.
17682	*thei*. So L, K, P. S omits.
17700	*ther*. S: letter canceled before.
17702	*were*. So L, K, P. S: *wene*.
17707	*wede*. S: ~~hede~~ *wede*.
17719	Marginalia in S (at top of fol. 162v): *Judyth*.
17733	*hyr*. S: inserted above the line.
17738	*power*. S: inserted above the line.
17748	*us*. So L. S, K, P: *to*.

Second Book of Maccabees 7

17749, 51	Lines indented to leave space for an initial capital; first letter of line 17749 written in the middle of the space.
17753	*marters*. So K. S, L: *maters*.
17754	*marters*. So K. S, L: *maters*.
17761	*sone*. So L, K. S: *sene*.
	marters. So K. S, L: *maters*.
17770	*his*. So L, K. S: *þies*.
17771	Marginalia in S (at top of fol. 163r): *De matre cum vij pueris*.
17772	*that myght befall*. So L, K. S: *þat þei myȝt fall*.
17785	*Ebrews*. So L, K. S: *Hebrew*.
17792	*Heven*. So L, K. S: *heue*.
17798	*be*. So L, K. S: *ȝe*.
17800	*He*. S: ~~I~~ *he*.
17804	*and*. So L, K. S omits.
	in forme fre. S: inserted above ~~yow iiij j in fere~~.
17808	*gyfyn*. So L, K. S: *yfyn*.
17812	*corsus*. S: inserted above ~~cour sus~~.
17813	*Yf*. So K. S: *þe*. L: *Thogh*.
17814	*now*. So L, K. S omits.
17825	Marginalia in S (at top of fol. 163v): *vij filii cum matre*.
	hestes. So L, K. S: *hertes*.
17829	*the*. So L, K. S: *ȝe*.
17836	*meyne*. So L, K. S: *weyne*.
17841	*ferd*. So L, K. S: *herd*.
17853	*dy*. So L, K. S: *day*.
17866	*make*. S: ~~ma t~~ *make*.
17867	*fare*. S: ~~ferre~~ *fare*.
17881	Marginalia in S (at top of fol. 164r): *De matre et vij filiis*.
17893	*hym be*. So L, K. S: *be hym*.
17899	*then*. S: corrected from *them*.
17900	*bettes*. So L, K. S: *lettes*.
17911	*that*. So L, K. S omits.
17914	*bete*. So L, K. S: *bate*.

17918	*and.* So L, K. S: *he.*
17938	Marginalia in S (at top of fol. 164v): *De matre et vij filiis.*
17943	*this.* So L, K. S omits.
17961–64	S: these two pairs of lines (17961–62 and 17963–64) are transposed in S. Like K, I have followed the order in L.
17975	*for.* S: inserted above the line.
17989	*then.* S: corrected from *them.*
17993	Marginalia in S (at top of fol. 165r): *De vij pueris cum matre.*
18001	*before.* So L, K. S: *be forn.*
18004	*spech.* So L, K. S omits.
	sperd. So L, K. S: *spred.*
18017	*thei.* So L. S, L: *the.*
18032	*sore.* So L, K. S omits.
18042	S: inserted above canceled line 18044.
18043	*boylyng.* S: ~~by~~ *boylyng.*
18044	*The.* S: ~~þus~~ *þe.*
18046	*as.* So L, K. S: *all as.*
18047	Marginalia in S (at top of fol. 165v): *De vij pueris cum matre.*
18059	*us noyght.* So L, K. S: *noyȝt vs.*
18074	*sore.* S: ~~sere~~ *sore.*
18082	*sakles.* So L, K. S: *slakly.*
18085	*in.* So L, K. S omits.
18095	*fro.* So L, K. S: *for.*
18103	Marginalia in S (at top of fol. 166r): *De matre cum vij filiis.*
18109	*cursyd.* So L, K. S: *cursyd cursyd.*
18113	*ther.* So L, K. S: *þeþer.*
18116	*foyl.* So K. S: *foyb.* L alters line.
18159	Marginalia in S (at top of fol. 166v): no heading.
18160	*that.* So L, K. S omits.
18166	*grove.* So K. S, L: *prove.*
18174	*assay:* two canceled letters before.
18215	Marginalia in S (at top of fol. 167r): no heading.
18218	*all yf.* So K. S: *al of.* L: *althogh.*
18219	*he.* S: *he* ~~þan.~~
18221	*yowr highnes.* So L, K. S: *yow.*
18232	*lay.* S: ~~law~~ *lay.*
18241	*myrthes.* So L, K. S: *marters.*
18250	*in₁.* So L, K. S: *& in.*

SECOND BOOK OF MACCABEES 6 AND 9

18253, 55	Lines indented to leave space for an initial capital; first letter of line 18253 written in the middle of the space.
18258	*not.* So L, K. S omits.
18267	Marginalia in S (at top of fol. 167v): *Anthiocus.*
18279	*thei.* So L. S, K: *þe.*
18286	*had.* So L, K. S omits.

18291	*cummand*. So L, K. S: *cumnand*.
18297	*thyng*. S: *ꝫ thyng*.
18312	*hys*. S: ~~yl his~~ *hys*.
18320	*spylt*. So L, K. S: *spyll*.
18323	Marginalia in S (at top of fol. 168r): no heading.
18326	*led*. So L, K. S: *layd*.
18328	*bred*. So L, K. S: *breyd*.
18337	*in*. So L, K. S omits.
18347	*so*. So L, K. S omits.
18349	*allways*. So L, K. S: *all*.
18352	*graydly*. So L, K. S: *gayly*.
18361	*be*. S: inserted above the line.
18368	*to*. So K. S omits. L alters line.

❦ BIBLIOGRAPHY

Ælfric of Eynsham. *The Homilies of the Anglo-Saxon Church*. Ed. and trans. Benjamin Thorpe. 2 vols. London: Ælfric Society, 1844–46. Rpt. New York: Johnson Reprint, 1971.

———. *Homilies of Ælfric: A Supplementary Collection*. Ed. John C. Pope. 2 vols. EETS o.s. 259–60. London: Oxford University Press, 1967–68.

———. *Preface to Genesis*. See *The Old English Version of the Heptateuch*.

Annals of Ulster, otherwise, Annals of Senat: A Chronicle of Irish Affairs from A.D. 431, to A.D. 1540. Ed. and trans. William M. Hennessy. 4 vols. Dublin: Alexander Thom & Co., 1887–1901.

Aristotle. *History of Animals*. Trans. Richard Cresswell. London: Henry G. Bohn, 1862.

Arngart, O. "St Avitus and the *Genesis and Exodus* Poet." *English Studies* 50 (1969), 487–95.

Aston, Margaret. *Lollards and Reformers: Images and Literacy in Late Medieval Religion*. London: Hambledon Press, 1984.

Augustine. *The Confessions and Letters of St. Augustin*. In Schaff, *Select Library*, vol. 1.

———. *St. Augustin's City of God and Christian Doctrine*. In Schaff, *Select Library*, vol. 2.

Baker, Alfred Thomas. *Die versifizierte Übersetzung ver französischen Bibel in Handschrift Egerton 2710 des British Museum: Eine Untersuchung des Inhalts und der Sprache*. Cambridge: Universitäts-druckerei, 1897.

Barber, Charles. *Figure and Likeness: On the Limits of Representation in Byzantine Iconoclasm*. Princeton, NJ: Princeton University Press, 2002.

Beadle, Richard. "The Origins of Abraham's Preamble in the York Play of Abraham and Isaac." *Yearbook of English Studies* 11 (1981), 178–87. [Argues, contra Kalén, that *Paraphrase* pre-dates *York*.]

Bede. *Ecclesiastical History of the English People*. Ed. and trans. Bertram Colgrave and R. A. B. Mynors. Oxford: Clarendon Press, 1969. Rpt. 1992.

Bell, David N. *A Cloud of Witnesses: An Introductory History of the Development of Christian Doctrine*. Kalamazoo, MI: Cistercian Publications, 1989.

———. *Many Mansions: An Introduction to the Development and Diversity of Medieval Theology, West and East*. Kalamazoo, MI: Cistercian Publications, 1996.

Besserman, Lawrence. *Chaucer's Biblical Poetics*. Norman: University of Oklahoma Press, 1998.

The Bible of the Poor [Biblia Pauperum]: A Facsimile and Edition of the British Library Blockbook C.9 d.2. Ed. and trans. Albert C. Labriola and John W. Smeltz. Pittsburgh: Duquesne University Press, 1990.

Biblia Pauperum. See *The Bible of the Poor*.

Bird, Ruth. *The Turbulent London of Richard II*. London: Longmans, Green, and Co., 1949.

Blamires, Alcuin. "The Limits of Bible Study for Medieval Women." In Smith and Taylor. Pp. 1–12.

Bloom, Harold. *A Map of Misreading*. New York: Oxford University Press, 1975.

———. *Where Shall Wisdom Be Found?* New York: Riverhead, 2004.

Bloom, Harold, and David Rosenberg. *The Book of J*. New York: Grove Weidenfeld, 1990.

Boethius. *The Consolation of Philosophy*. In *Boethius*. Ed. and trans. H. F. Stewart, E. K. Rand, and S. J. Tester. Cambridge, MA: Harvard University Press, 1973.

Boffey, Julia, and A. S. G. Edwards. *A New Index of Middle English Verse*. London: British Library, 2005.

Bonnard, Jean. *Les Traductions de la Bible en vers français au moyen âge*. Paris: Imprimerie Nationale, 1884. Rpt. Geneva: Slatkine, 1967.

Brown, Michelle P. "Preaching with the Pen: The Contribution of Insular Scribes to the Transmission of Sacred Text, from the 6th to 9th Centuries." University of London Annual Palaeography Lecture, 22 January 2004. School of Advanced Study, Institute of English Studies, University of London, Centre for Manuscript and Print Studies.

Bruce-Mitford, Rupert. "The Art of the Codex Amiatinus." *Journal of the Archaeological Association* 32 (1969), 1–25. [First given as a Jarrow Lecture, 1967.]

Brunner, Ingrid. Review of *A Middle English Metrical Paraphrase of the Old Testament II*, ed. Urban Ohlander. *Word* 12 (1956), 476–79.

Buehler, Philip G. *The Middle English Genesis and Exodus: A Running Commentary on the Text of the Poem.* The Hague: Mouton, 1974. [Designed as an alternative commentary to Arngart's edition.]

Bühler, Curt F. "A Lollard Tract: On Translating the Bible into English." *Medium Ævum* 7 (1938), 167–83.

Butler, William. "Determination against Biblical Translation, 1401 1401; also the burning of English Bibles previous to 1401." Ed. Margaret Deansley. In Deanesly, *The Lollard Bible and Other Medieval Bible Versions*. Appendix II.1. Pp. 399–418. [Based on Oxford, Merton College, MS K.2.2, fols. 202r–204v.]

Cassiodorus. *Cassiodori Senatoris Institutiones.* Ed. R. A. B. Mynors. Oxford: Clarendon Press, 1937.

Catholicon Anglicum, an English-Latin Wordbook, Dated 1483. Ed. Sidney J. H. Herrtage. EETS o.s. 75. London: N. Trübner, 1881. Rpt. Milwood, NY: Krause Reprint, 1973.

Caviness, Madeline H. "Biblical Stories in Windows: Were They Bibles for the Poor?" In *The Bible in the Middle Ages: Its Infuence on Literature and Art*. Ed. Bernard S. Levy. Medieval and Renaissance Texts and Studies 89. Binghamton, NY: Medieval and Renaissance Texts and Studies, 1992. Pp. 103–47.

Cawley, A. C. Review of *A Middle English Metrical Paraphrase of the Old Testament*, Part II, ed. Urban Ohlander. *Modern Language Review* 52 (1957), 454.

Caxton, William. *The Golden Legend.* 7 vols. London: J. M. Dent & Sons, 1900. Rpt. New York: AMS Press, 1973. [See also Jacobus de Voragine.]

Challoner. See *Holy Bible.*

Chaucer, Geoffrey. *The Riverside Chaucer.* Third ed. Gen. ed. Larry D. Benson. Boston: Houghton Mifflin, 1987.

Chaytor, H. J. *From Script to Print: An Introduction to Medieval Literature.* Cambridge: Cambridge University Press, 1945.

The Chester Mystery Cycle. Ed. R. M. Lumiansky and David Mills. 2 vols. EETS s.s. 3, 9. London: Oxford University Press, 1974–86.

Cleanness. In *The Poems of the Pearl Manuscript: Pearl, Cleanness, Patience, Sir Gawain and the Green Knight.* Ed. Malcolm Andrew and Ronald Waldron. Rev. ed. Exeter: University of Exeter Press, 1996. Pp. 111–84.

Comestor, Peter. *Historia Scholastica.* Ed. J.-P. Migne. Patrologiae cursus completus: Series Latina 198. Paris: Migne, 1855. Cols. 1050–1722.

Copeland, Rita. "The Fortunes of 'non verbum pro verbo': or, Why Jerome Is Not a Ciceronian." In *The Medieval Translator: The Theory and Practice of Translation in the Middle Ages.* Ed. Roger Ellis. Cambridge: D. S. Brewer, 1989. Pp. 15–35.

Cottle, Basil. Review of *The Middle English Genesis and Exodus*, ed. Olaf Arngart. *Journal of English and Germanic Philology* 69 (1970), 163–65.

Cross, Claire. "'Great Reasoners in Scripture': The Activities of Women Lollards 1380–1530." In *Medieval Women.* Ed. Derek Baker. Oxford: Basil Blackwell, 1978. Pp. 359–80.

Crossan, John Dominic. *The Historical Jesus: The Life of a Mediterranean Jewish Peasant.* San Fransisco, CA: HarperSanFrancisco, 1991.

Cursor Mundi: A Northumbrian Poem of the XIVth Century in Four Versions. Ed. Richard Morris et al. 7 vols. EETS o.s. 57, 59, 62, 66, 68, 99, 101. London: K. Paul, Trench, Trübner, & Co., 1876. Rpt. London: Oxford University Press, 1966.

Dahmus, Joseph H. *The Prosecution of John Wyclyf.* New Haven, CT: Yale University Press, 1952.

Daly, Saralyn R. "Peter Comestor: Master of Histories." *Speculum* 32 (1957), 62–73.

Davis-Weyer, Caecilia. *Early Medieval Art 300–1150: Sources and Documents*. Toronto: University of Toronto Press, 1986.

Dean, James M., ed. *Medieval English Political Writings*. Kalamazoo, MI: Medieval Institute Publications, 1996.

Deanesly, Margaret. *The Lollard Bible and Other Medieval Biblical Versions*. Cambridge Studies in Medieval Life and Thought. Cambridge: Cambridge University Press, 1920.

Decrees of the Ecumenical Councils. Ed. and trans. Norman P. Tanner. 2 vols. Washington: Georgetown University Press, 1990.

de Lubac, Henri. *Medieval Exegesis*. Trans. E. M. Macierowski. 2 vols. Grand Rapids, MI: William B. Eerdmans, 2000.

De Rossi, G. B. *La Bibbia offerta da Ceolfrido Abbate al Sepolchro di S. Pietro. Al Sommo Pontefice Leone XIII omaggio giubilare della Biblioteca Vaticana*. Vatican: Vatican Publications, 1888.

A Dictionary of Biblical Tradition in English Literature. Gen. ed. David Lyle Jeffrey. Grand Rapids, MI: William B. Eerdmans, 1992.

Doherty, Earl. "The Jesus Puzzle: Pieces in a Puzzle of Christian Origin." *Journal of Higher Criticism* 4 (1997), 68–102.

Dove, Mary. *The First English Bible: The Text and Context of the Wycliffite Versions*. Cambridge: Cambridge University Press, 2007.

Duffy, Eamon. *The Stripping of the Altars: Traditional Religion in England, c.1400–c.1580*. New Haven, CT: Yale University Press, 1992.

Eusebius. *The Ecclesiastical History*. Ed. and trans. Kirsopp Lake. Vol. 1. Loeb Classical Library 153. Cambridge, MA: Harvard University Press, 1926.

Evans, G. R. *Bernard of Clairvaux*. Oxford: Oxford University Press, 2000.

Fein, Susanna Greer, ed. *Moral Love Songs and Laments*. Kalamazoo, MI: Medieval Institute Publications, 1998.

Ferrante, Joan M. *Woman as Image in Medieval Literature: From the Twelfth Century to Dante*. New York: Columbia University Press, 1975.

Flores, Nona C. "'Effigies amicitiae . . . veritas inimicitiae': Antifeminism in the Iconography of the Woman-Headed Serpent in Medieval and Renaissance Art and Literature." In *Animals in the Middle Ages: A Book of Essays*. Ed. Flores. New York: Garland Publishing, 1996. Pp. 167–95.

Fowler, David C. *The Bible in Early English Literature*. Seattle: University of Washington Press, 1976.

———. *The Bible in Middle English Literature*. Seattle: University of Washington Press, 1984.

Frend, W. H. C. *Martyrdom and Persecution in the Early Church: A Study of a Conflict from the Maccabees to Donatus*. Oxford: Blackwell, 1965.

Friedman, John B., and Jessica M. Wegmann. *Medieval Iconography: A Research Guide*. New York: Garland Publishing, 1998.

Gameson, Richard. "The Cost of the Codex Amiatinus." *Notes and Queries* 237 (1992), 2–9.

Garrucci, Raffaele. *Storia della arte cristiana nei primi otto secoli della chiesa*. 6 vols. Prato: G. Guasti, 1872–81.

Geisler, Norman, and William Nix. *A General Introduction to the Bible*. Chicago: Moody Press, 1968.

Ghosh, Kantik. *The Wycliffite Heresy: Authority and the Interpretation of Texts*. Cambridge: Cambridge University Press, 2002.

Glossa ordinaria. Ed. J.-P. Migne. Patrologiae cursus completus: Series Latina 113. Paris: Migne, 1852.

Goodman, Anthony. *John of Gaunt: The Exercise of Princely Power in Fourteenth-Century Europe*. New York: St. Martin's Press, 1992.

Gospel of Nicodemus. In *The Middle-English Harrowing of Hell and Gospel of Nicodemus*. Ed. William Henry Hulme. EETS e.s. 100. London: Oxford University Press, 1907.

Gower, John. *Confessio Amantis*. Ed. Russell A. Peck, with Latin translations by Andrew Galloway. 3 vols. Kalamazoo, MI: Medieval Institute Publications, 2000–04.

———. *In Praise of Peace*. Ed. Michael Livingston. In *Minor Latin Works with In Praise of Peace*. Ed. and trans. R. F. Yeager. Kalamazoo, MI: Medieval Institute Publications, 2005. Pp. 89–133.

Hali Meiþhad. Ed. Bella Millett. EETS o.s. 284. London: Oxford University Press, 1982.

Hahn, Thomas. "Early Middle English." In *The Cambridge History of Medieval English Literature*. Ed. David Wallace. Cambridge: Cambridge University Press, 1999. Pp. 61–91.

Hanna, Ralph. "English Biblical Texts Before Lollardy and Their Fate." In *Lollards and Their Influence in Late Medieval England*. Ed. Fiona Somerset, Jill C. Havens, and Derrick G. Pitard. Woodbridge: Boydell Press, 2003. Pp. 141–53.

Hasel, Gerhard F. "Genesis 5 and 11: Chronogenealogies in the Biblical History." *Origins* 7 (1980), 23–37.

Heffernan, Thomas J., ed. *The Popular Literature of Medieval England*. Knoxville: University of Tennessee Press, 1985.

Henderson, George. *From Durrow to Kells: The Insular Gospel-Books, 650–800*. London: Thames and Hudson, 1987.

Heuser, W. "Die alttestamentlichen dichtungen des ms. Seld. Supra 52 der Bodleiana: Ein vergessenes werk und ein überschenes manuskript." *Anglia* 31 (1908), 1–24. [Provides a few excerpts of the *Paraphrase*.]

Higden, Ranulf. *Polychronicon Ranulphi Higden Monachi Cestrensis; Together with the English Translations of John Trevisa and of an Unknown Writer of the Fifteenth Century*. Ed. Churchill Babington and Joseph Rawson Lumby. Rerum Britannicarum medii aevi scriptores (Rolls Series) 41. 9 vols. London: Longman & Co., 1865–86. [See also Trevisa, John.]

Hinckley, Henry Barrett. "The Riddle of *The Ormulum*." *Philological Quarterly* 14 (1935), 193–216.

Hindman, Sandra. "Fifteenth-Century Dutch Bible Illustration and the *Historia Scholastica*." *Journal of the Warburg and Courtauld Institutes* 37 (1974), 131–44.

"The Historye of the Patriarks." Ed. Saralyn Ruth Daly. Ph.D. dissertation, Ohio State University. 1950.

The Holkham Bible Picture Book. Ed. W. O. Hassall. London: Dropmore Press, 1954.

The Holy Bible, Translated from the Latin Vulgate; Diligently Compared with the Hebrew, Greek and Other Editions in Divers Languages. The Old Testament First Published by the English College at Douay, A. D. 1609, and the New Testament First Published by the English College at Rheims, A. D. 1582; with Annotations, References and an Historical and Chronological Table. Baltimore, MD: John Murphy Company, 1914.

Horrall, Sarah M. "'Man Yhernes Rimes for to Here': A Biblical History from the Middle Ages." In *Art into Life: Collected Papers from the Kresge Art Museum Medieval Symposia*. Ed. Carol Garrett Fisher and Kathleen L. Scott. East Lansing: Michigan State University Press, 1995. Pp. 73–93.

Horstmann, C., ed. "Nachträge zu den Legenden." *Archiv* 79 (1887), 411–70. [Item 8 (of 10) is "De matre et VII pueris" (pp. 447–54).]

Hudson, Anne. "The Debate on Bible Translation, Oxford 1401." *English Historical Review* 90 (1975), 1–18. Rpt. in *Lollards and Their Books*. London: Hambledon Press, 1985. Pp. 67–84.

———. *The Premature Reformation: Wycliffite Texts and Lollard History*. Oxford: Clarendon Press, 1988.

Hugh of St. Victor. *The Didascalion of Hugh of St. Victor: A Medieval Guide to the Arts*. Trans. Jerome Taylor. New York: Columbia University Press, 1991.

Institoris, Heinrich, and Jakob Sprenger. *Malleus Maleficarum*. Trans. Montague Summers. London: John Rodker, 1928.

Isidore of Seville. *Quæstiones in Vetus Testamentum*. Ed. J.-P. Migne. Patrologiae cursus completus: Series Latina 83. Paris: Migne, 1850. Cols. 201–434.

Jacob and Josep: A Middle English Poem of the Thirteenth Century. Ed. Arthur S. Napier. Oxford: Clarendon Press, 1916.

Jacobus de Voragine. *Legenda aurea*. Ed. Johan Georg Theodor Grässe. Dresden: Impensis Librariae Arnoldianae, 1846.

———. *The Golden Legend*. Trans. Granger Ryan and Helmut Ripperger. New York: Arno Press, 1969.

———. *Legenda aurea: Edizione critica*. Ed. Giovanni Paolo Maggioni. 2 vols. Rev. ed. Florence: SISMEL, Edizioni del Galluzzo, 1998.

Jeffrey, David Lyle. "Chaucer and Wyclif: Biblical Hermeneutic and Literary Theory in the XIVth Century." In *Chaucer and Scriptural Tradition*. Ed. Jeffrey. Ottawa: University of Ottawa Press, 1984. Pp. 109–40.

Jellicoe, Sidney. *The Septuagint and Modern Study*. Oxford: Clarendon Press, 1968.

Jones, Timothy S. "'Job the Gentyl Jew' in the Middle English Metrical Paraphrase of the Old Testament." Unpublished essay.

Josephus, Flavius. *The Works of Flavius Josephus*. Trans. William Whiston. Baltimore: Armstrong and Plaskitt, 1830.

Joslyn-Siemiatkoski, Daniel E. "The Maccabean Martyrs in Medieval Christianity and Judaism." Ph.D. dissertation, Boston College, 2005.

Judah, Rabbi. *Tosephta*. Ed. M. S. Zuckermandel. Jerusalem: Bamberger & Wahrmann, 1937.

Käsmann, Hans. Review of *A Middle English Metrical Paraphrase of the Old Testament*, vol. 2, ed. Urban Ohlander. *Anglia* 75 (1957), 245.

———. Review of *A Middle English Metrical Paraphrase of the Old Testament*, vol. 3, ed. Urban Ohlander. *Anglia* 80 (1962), 326.

Kelly, T. D., and John T. Irwin. "The Meaning of Cleanness: Parable as Effective Sign." *Mediaeval Studies* 35 (1973), 232–60.

King Henry's Bible: MS Bodley 277, the Revised Version of the Wyclif Bible. Ed. Conrad Lindberg. 2 vols. Stockholm: Almqvist and Wiksell, 1999.

Kinneavy, Gerald Byron. *A Concordance to The York Plays*. New York: Garland Publishing, 1986.

Knighton, Henry. *Knighton's Chronicle: 1337–1396*. Ed. and trans. G. H. Martin. Oxford: Clarendon Press, 1995.

Kölbing, E. "MS. 25 der Bibliothek des Marquis of Bath." *Englische Studien* 10 (1887), 203–06. [Description of the manuscript and a few brief excerpts.]

Kramer, Heinrich, and James Sprenger. *Malleus Maleficarum*. New York, 1971.

Krouse, F. Michael. *Milton's Samson and the Christian Tradition*. Princeton, NJ: Princeton University Press, 1949; rpt. 1962.

Krummel, Miriamne Ara. "The Semitisms of Middle English Literature." *Compass*. <http://www.literature-compass.com/>. February 2005.

Lamb, J. A. "The Place of the Bible in the Liturgy." In *The Cambridge History of the Bible*. Vol 1: *From the Beginnings to Jerome*. Ed. P. R. Ackroyd and C. F. Evans. Cambridge: Cambridge University Press, 1970. Pp. 563–86.

Langland, William. *Piers Plowman: The A Version, Will's Visions of Piers Plowman and Do-Well*. Ed. George Kane. London: Athlone Press, 1960.

Levy, Bernard S. *The Bible in the Middle Ages: Its Influence on Literature and Art*. Binghamton, NY: Medieval and Renaissance Texts and Studies, 1992.

Lewis, Jack P. "Jamnia Revisited." In *The Canon Debate*. Ed. Lee Martin McDonald and James A. Sanders. Peabody, MA: Hendrickson, 2002.

Light, Laura. "French Bibles c. 1200–30: A New Look at the Origin of the Paris Bible." In *The Early Medieval Bible: Its Production, Decoration, and Use*. Ed. Richard Gameson. Cambridge Studies in Palaeography and Codicology. Cambridge: Cambridge University Press, 1994. Pp. 155–76.

Liljegren, S. B. Review of *A Middle English Metrical Paraphrase of the Old Testament*, ed. Herbert Kalén. *Anglia Beiblatt* 34 (1923), 227–28.

Little, A. G., and F. Pelster. *Oxford Theology and Theologians, c. A.D. 1282–1302*. Oxford: Clarendon Press, 1934.

Long, Lynne. *Translating the Bible: From the 7th to the 17th Century*. Aldershot: Ashgate, 2001.

Luscombe, David. "Peter Comestor." In *The Bible in the Medieval World: Essays in Memory of Beryl Smalley*. Ed. Katherine Walsh and Diana Wood. Oxford: Basil Blackwell, 1985. Pp. 109–29.

Manly, John M., and Edith Rickert. *The Text of The Canterbury Tales: Studied on the Basis of All Known Manuscripts*. Vol. 1: *Descriptions of the Manuscripts*. Chicago: University of Chicago Press, 1940. [Pp. 339–42 discuss the Longleat Manuscript.]

Marsden, Richard. "Job in His Place: The Ezra Miniature in the Codex Amiatinus." *Scriptorium* 49 (1995), 3–15.

———. *The Text of the Old Testament in Anglo-Saxon England*. Cambridge: Cambridge University Press, 1995.

McGerr, Rosemarie Potz. "Guyart Desmoulins, the Vernacular Master of Histories, and His Bible Historiale." *Viator* 14 (1983), 211–44.

McIntosh, Angus, M. L. Samuels, and Michael Benskin, eds., with the assistance of Margaret Laing and Keith Williamson. *A Linguistic Atlas of Late Mediaeval English*. 4 vols. Aberdeen: Aberdeen University Press, 1986.

McKisack, May. *The Fourteenth Century: 1307–1399*. Oxford: Clarendon Press, 1959.

McSheffrey, Shannon. "Literacy and the Gender Gap in the Late Middle Ages: Women and Reading in Lollard Communities." In Smith and Taylor. Pp. 157–70.

———. *Gender and Heresy: Women and Men in Lollard Communities, 1420–1530*. Philadelphia: University of Pennsylvania Press, 1995.

Mercer Dictionary of the Bible. Gen. ed. Watson E. Mills. Macon, GA: Mercer University Press, 1990.

Metzger, Bruce M. *The Bible in Translation: Ancient and English Versions*. Grand Rapids, MI: Baker Academic, 2001.

Meyvaert, Paul. "Bede, Cassiodorus, and the Codex Amiatinus." *Speculum* 71 (1996), 827–83.

———. "The Date of Bede's *In Ezram* and His Image of Ezra in the Codex Amiatinus." *Speculum* 80 (2005), 1087–1133.

Michelli, Perette. "What's in the Cupboard? Ezra and Matthew Reconsidered." In *Northumbria's Golden Age*. Ed. Jane Hawkes and Susan Mills. Stroud: Sutton, 1999. Pp. 345–58.

Middle English Dictionary. Gen. ed. Hans Kurath and Sherman M. Kuhn. Ann Arbor: University of Michigan Press, 1952–2003.

A Middle English Metrical Paraphrase of the Old Testament. Ed. Herbert Kalén. Gothenburg: Elanders Boktryckeri, 1923. [Includes the first 6,000 lines and a detailed philological discussion of the poem; continued and completed by Ohlander.]

———. Ed. Urban Ohlander. 4 vols. Gothenburg: Elanders Boktryckeri, 1955–72. [Continues and completes the work begun by Kalén; the final volume contains a glossary and index.]

———. In *Heroic Women from the Old Testament in Middle English Verse: The Storie of Asneth, The Pistel of Swete Susan, The Story of Jephthah's Daughter, The Story of Judith*. Ed. Russell A. Peck. Kalamazoo, MI: Medieval Institute Publications, 1991. [Includes the Prologue (stanzas 1–3), The Story of Jephthah and His Daughter (stanzas 292–99), and The Story of Judith (stanzas 1414–79), pp. 109–53.]

The Middle English Physiologus. Ed. Hanneke Wirtjes. Oxford: Oxford University Press, 1991.

Minnis, A. J. *Chaucer and Pagan Antiquity*. Woodbridge: D. S. Brewer, 1982.

———. *Medieval Theory of Authorship: Scholastic Literary Attitudes in the Later Middle Ages*. London: Scolar Press, 1984.

———. "Medium and Message: Henry of Ghent on Scriptural Style." In *Literature and Religion in the Later Middle Ages: Philological Studies in Honor of Siegfried Wenzel*. Ed. Richard G. Newhauser and John A. Alford. Binghamton, NY: Medieval and Renaissance Texts and Studies, 1995. Pp. 209–35.

Mitchell, Bruce, and Fred C. Robinson. *A Guide to Old English*. Fifth ed. Oxford: Blackwell, 1992.

Morey, James Henry. "'Coram Laycis': Spreading the Word in Early Middle English." Ph.D. dissertation, Cornell University, 1990. *DAI* 51.04A (1990): 1224.

———. "Peter Comestor, Biblical Paraphrase, and the Medieval Popular Bible." *Speculum* 68 (1993), 6–35.

———. *Book and Verse: A Guide to Middle English Biblical Literature*. Urbana: University of Illinois Press, 2000.

Morin, Germain, ed. *Anecdota maredsolana*. 5 vols. Maredsous, 1893–1903.

Muir, Laurence. "Translations and Paraphrases of the Bible, and Commentaries." In Severs 2:381–409, 534–52.

Muir, Lynette R. *The Biblical Drama of Medieval Europe*. Cambridge: Cambridge University Press, 1995.

Mum and the Sothsegger. In *Richard the Redeless and Mum and the Sothsegger*. Ed. James M. Dean. Kalamazoo, MI: Medieval Institute Publications, 2000. Pp. 75–169.

Murdoch, Brian. *The Medieval Popular Bible: Expansions of Genesis in the Middle Ages*. Cambridge: D. S. Brewer, 2003.

Mustanoja, Tauno F. Review of *A Middle English Metrical Paraphrase of the Old Testament*, vols. 2 and 3, ed. Urban Ohlander. *Neuphilologische Mitteilungen* 62 (1961), 234–36.

Newman, Robert C. *The Council of Jamnia and the Old Testament Canon*. Hatfield, PA: Interdisciplinary Biblical Research Institute, 1983.

The New Oxford Annotated Bible, with the Apocryphal/Deuterocanonical Books. Ed. Bruce M. Metzger and Roland E. Murphy. New York: Oxford University Press, 1991. [Based on the New Revised Standard Version.]

The Northern Homily Cycle: The Expanded Version in MSS Harley 4196 and Cotton Tiberius E.vii. Ed. Saara Nevanlinna. Mémoires de la Société Néophilologique de Helsinki 38 (1972), 41 (1973), 43 (1984).

Northern Passion: Four Parallel Texts and the French Original, with Specimens of Additional Manuscripts. Ed. Frances A. Foster. 2 vols. EETS o.s. 145, 147. London: Kegan Paul, Trench, Trübner, & Co., 1913–16. Rpt. New York: Kraus Reprint, 1971.

Oakden, J. P., with Elizabeth R. Innes. *Alliterative Poetry in Middle English: A Survey of the Traditions*. Manchester: Manchester University Press, 1935.

Ohlander, Urban. "Old French Parallels to a Middle English Metrical Paraphrase of the Old Testament." In *Contributions to English Syntax and Philology*. Ed. Frank Behre. Gothenburg: Almqvist & Wiksell, 1962. Pp. 203–24.

The Old English Version of the Heptateuch, Ælfric's Treatise on the Old and New Testament and His Preface to Genesis. Ed. S. J. Crawford. EETS o.s. 160. London: Oxford University Press, 1922. Rpt., with additional material by N. R. Ker, 1969.

Orrm. *The Ormulum*. Ed. Robert Holt, with notes and glossary by R. M. White. 2 vols. Oxford: Clarendon Press, 1878.

Oxford English Dictionary. Second edition. Ed. J. A. Simpson and E. S. C. Weiner. Oxford: Clarendon Press, 1989.

Owst, G. R. *Literature and Pulpit in Medieval England: A Neglected Chapter in the History of English Letters and of the English People*. Second ed. Oxford: Oxford University Press, 1961. Rpt. 1966.

Pagels, Elaine. *The Origin of Satan*. New York: Vintage Books, 1996.

Panofsky, Erwin. *Renaissance and Renascences in Western Art*. New York: Harper and Row, 1960. Rpt. 1972.

Patience. In *The Poems of the Pearl Manuscript: Pearl, Cleanness, Patience, Sir Gawain and the Green Knight*. Ed. Malcolm Andrew and Ronald Waldron. Rev. ed. Exeter: University of Exeter Press, 1996. Pp. 185–206.

Patterson, Lee. "'The Living Witnesses of Our Redemption': Martyrdom and Imitation in Chaucer's Prioress's Tale." *Journal of Medieval and Early Modern Studies* 31 (2001), 507–60.

Paues, A. C. "An Earlier Discovery of MS. Selden Supra 52." *Anglia* 31 (1908), 256. [Claims priority over Heuser.]

Peck, Russell A. "Number as Cosmic Language." In *Essays in the Numerical Criticism of Medieval Literature*. Ed. Caroline D. Eckhardt. Lewisburg, PA: Bucknell University Press, 1980. Pp. 15–64.

———, ed. *Heroic Women from the Old Testament in Middle English Verse*. See *Middle English Metrical Paraphrase of the Old Testament*.

Pety Job. In Fein, *Moral Love Songs and Laments*. Pp. 289–359. [*PJ*.]

Remley, Paul G. *Old English Biblical Verse: Studies in Genesis, Exodus and Daniel*. Cambridge: Cambridge University Press, 1996.

Riga, Peter. *Aurora: Petri Rigae biblia versificata: A Verse Commentary on the Bible*. Ed. Paul E. Beichner. 2 vols. Notre Dame, IN: University of Notre Dame Press, 1965.

Robertson, D. W., Jr. *A Preface to Chaucer: Studies in Medieval Perspectives*. Princeton, NJ: Princeton University Press, 1962.

Robertson, Elizabeth. *Early English Devotional Prose and the Female Audience*. Knoxville: University of Tennessee Press, 1990.

Ross, Allen P. "The Curse of Canaan." *Bibliotheca Sacra* 137 (1980), 223–40.

Rouwhorst, Gerard. "The Cult of the Seven Maccabean Brothers and Their Mother in Christian Tradition." In *Saints and Role Models in Judaism and Christianity*. Ed. Marcel Poorthuis and Joshua Schwartz. Leiden: Brill, 2004. Pp. 183–204.

Saintsbury, George. *A History of English Prosody from the Twelfth Century to the Present Day*. 3 vols. Second ed. New York: Russell and Russell, 1923; rpt. 1961.

Schaff, Philip, et al., eds. *A Select Library of the Nicene and Post-Nicene Fathers of the Christian Church*. 14 vols. New York: Christian Literature, 1886–90. Rpt. Edinburgh: T&T Clark, 1991–97.

Segal, Alan F. *Life after Death: A History of the Afterlife in the Religions of the West*. New York: Doubleday, 2004.

Severs, J. Burke, and Albert E. Hartung, gen. eds. *Manual of the Writings in Middle English: 1050–1500*. 10 vols. to date. New Haven: Connecticut Academy of Arts and Sciences, 1967–98.

Seybolt, Robert Francis. "The *Legenda Aurea*, Bible, and *Historia Scholastica*." *Speculum* 21 (1946), 339–42.

Siege of Jerusalem. Ed. Michael Livingston. Kalamazoo, MI: Medieval Institute Publications, 2004.

Smalley, Beryl. "Stephen Langton and the Four Senses of Scripture." *Speculum* 6 (1931), 60–76.

———. *The Study of the Bible in the Middle Ages*. Third ed., rev. Oxford: Basil Blackwell, 1983.

Smeets, Jean Robert. "Les traductions, adaptations, et paraphrases de la Bible en vers." In *La Littérature Didactique, Allégorique et Satirique*. Vol. 6 of *Grundriss der romanischen Literaturen des Mittelalters*. Gen. ed. Hans Robert Jauss. Heidelberg: Carl Winter, 1968–70. Pp. 48–57 [text] and 81–96 [notes].

Smith, Lesley, and Jane H. M. Taylor, eds. *Women, the Book and the Godly: Selected Proceedings of the St Hilda's Conference, 1993*. Vol. 1. Cambridge: D. S. Brewer, 1995.

Squires, Ann. "The Treatment of the Figure of Judith in the Middle English Metrical Paraphrase of the Old Testament." *Neuphilologische Mitteilungen* 97 (1996), 187–200.

A Stanzaic Life of Christ: Compiled from Higden's Polychronicon and the Legenda Aurea, Edited from MS. Harley 3909. Ed. Frances A. Foster. EETS o.s. 166. London: Oxford University Press, 1926. Rpt. New York: Kraus Reprint, 1971.

Stern, Gustaf. Review of *A Middle English Metrical Paraphrase of the Old Testament*, ed. Herbert Kalén. *Englische Studien* 59 (1925), 280–86.

Stevens, Martin. *Four Middle English Mystery Cycles: Textual, Contextual, and Critical Interpretations*. Princeton, NJ: Princeton University Press, 1987.

The Story of Genesis and Exodus: An Early English Song, about 1250. Second ed., rev. Ed. Richard Morris. EETS o.s. 7. London: N. Trübner & Co., 1873. Rpt. New York: Greenwood Press, 1969.

———. Ed. Olaf Arngart. *The Middle English Genesis and Exodus*. Lund: Gleerup, 1968.

Taylor, John. *The "Universal Chronicle" of Ranulf Higden*. Oxford: Clarendon Press, 1966.

Ten Brink, Bernhard. *History of English Literature*. Trans. Horace M. Kennedy. New York: Holt, 1883.

Thompson, John J. "Popular Reading Tastes in Middle English Religious and Didactic Literature." In *From Medieval to Medievalism*. Ed. John Simons. New York: St. Martin's Press, 1992. Pp. 82–100.

———. "The *Cursor Mundi*, the 'Inglis tong', and 'Romance.'" In *Readings in Medieval English Romance*. Ed. Carol M. Meale. Cambridge: D. S. Brewer, 1994. Pp. 99–120.

———. *The Cursor Mundi: Poem, Texts and Contexts*. Medium Ævum Monographs n.s. 19. Oxford: Society for the Study of Medieval Languages and Literature, 1998.

Thoresby, John. *The Lay-folks' Catechism, or, The English and Latin Versions of Archbishop Thoresby's Instruction for the People*. Ed. Thomas Frederick Simmons and Henry Edward Nolloth. EETS o.s. 118. London: Kegan Paul, Trench, Trübner, and Co., 1901. Rpt. Millwood, NY: Kraus Reprint, 1972.

Tilley, Morris Palmer. *A Dictionary of the Proverbs in England in the Sixteenth and Seventeenth Centuries*. Ann Arbor: University of Michigan Press, 1950.

Trevisa, John. *On the Properties of Things: John Trevisa's Translation of Bartholomæus Anglicus De proprietatibus rerum: A Critical Text*. Gen. ed. M. C. Seymour. 3 vols. Oxford: Oxford University Press, 1975.

————. *A Dialogue on Translation*. In "The English *Polychronicon*: A Text of John Trevisa's Translation of Higden's *Polychronicon*, Based on Huntington MS. 28561." Ed. Richard Arthur Seeger. Ph.D. dissertation, University of Washington, 1974.

Twomey, Michael W. "*Cleanness*, Peter Comestor, and the *Revelationes Sancti Methodii*." *Mediaevalia* 11 (1989 for 1985), 203–17.

————. "Falling Giants and Floating Lead: Scholastic History in the Middle English *Cleanness*." In *Marvels, Monsters, and Miracles: Studies in the Medieval and Early Modern Imaginations*. Ed. Timothy S. Jones and David A. Sprunger. Kalamazoo, MI: Medieval Institute Publications, 2002. Pp. 141–65.

Usk, Adam. *The Chronicle of Adam Usk: 1377–1421*. Ed. and trans. C. Given-Wilson. Oxford: Clarendon Press, 1997.

Utley, Francis Lee. *The Crooked Rib: An Analytical Index to the Argument about Women in English and Scots Literature to the End of the Year 1568*. Columbus: Ohio State University, 1944. Rpt. New York: Octagon Books, 1970.

Vauchez, André. *The Laity in the Middle Ages: Religious Beliefs and Devotional Practices*. Ed. Daniel E. Bornstein, trans. Margery J. Schneider. Notre Dame, IN: University of Notre Dame Press, 1993.

Walsh, Katherine, and Diana Wood, eds. *The Bible in the Medieval World: Essays in Memory of Beryl Smalley*. Oxford: Published for the Ecclesiastical History Society by Blackwell, 1985.

Walsingham, Thomas. *The St Albans Chronicle: The Chronica maiora of Thomas Walsingham*. Vol. 1: *1376–94*. Ed. and trans. John Taylor, Wendy R. Childs, and Leslie Watkiss. Oxford: Clarendon Press, 2003.

Weber, Henry, ed. *Metrical Romances of the Thirteenth, Fourteenth, and Fifteenth Centuries: Published from Ancient Manuscripts*. 3 vols. Edinburgh: A. Constable and Co., 1810.

Weitzmann, Kurt. *Late Antique and Early Christian Book Illumination*. New York: George Braziller, 1977.

Wells, John Edwin. *A Manual of the Writings in Middle English: 1050–1400 and Supplements 1–9*. New Haven: Connecticut Academy of Arts and Sciences, 1916–51. [Superseded by Severs.]

Whiting, Bartlett Jere, with the collaboration of Helen Wescott Whiting. *Proverbs, Sentences, and Proverbial Phrases from English Writings Mainly before 1500*. Cambridge, MA: The Belknap Press of Harvard University Press, 1968.

Wilson, David M. *Anglo-Saxon Art: From the Seventh Century to the Norman Conquest*. Woodstock, NY: Overlook Press, 1984.

Wilson, Derek. *The People and the Book: The Revolutionary Impact of the English Bible 1380–1611*. London: Barrie and Jenkins, 1976.

Woolf, Rosemary. *The English Mystery Plays*. Berkeley: University of California Press, 1972.

Workman, Herbert B. *John Wyclif: A Study of the English Medieval Church*. 2 vols. Oxford: The Clarendon Press, 1926. Rpt. as 1 vol., Hamden, CT: Archon, 1966.

Wyclif(fe), John. *Select English Works of John Wyclif*. Ed. Thomas Arnold. 3 vols. Oxford: Clarendon Press, 1869–71.

————. *The English Works of Wyclif Hitherto Unprinted*. Ed. F. D. Matthew. Second ed. EETS o.s. 74. London: Kegan Paul, Trench, Trübner & Co., 1880.

————. *Johannis Wyclif Opera Minora*. Ed. Johann Loserth. Wyclif's Latin Works 21. London: Wyclif Society, 1913. Rpt. New York: Johnson, 1966.

————. *On the Truth of Holy Scripture*. Trans. with an introduction and notes by Ian Christopher Levy. Kalamazoo, MI: Medieval Institute Publications, 2001.

The York Plays. In *The York Plays: The Plays Performed by the Crafts or Mysteries of York on the Day of Corpus Christi in the 14th, 15th, and 16th Centuries*. Ed. Lucy Toulmin Smith. New York: Russell & Russell, 1963.

————. Ed. Richard Beadle. London: Edward Arnold, 1982.

Zink, James K. "Impatient Job: An Interpretation of Job 19:25–27." *Journal of Biblical Literature* 84 (1965), 147–52.

MIDDLE ENGLISH TEXTS SERIES

The Floure and the Leafe, The Assembly of Ladies, The Isle of Ladies, edited by Derek Pearsall (1990)

Three Middle English Charlemagne Romances, edited by Alan Lupack (1990)

Six Ecclesiastical Satires, edited by James M. Dean (1991)

Heroic Women from the Old Testament in Middle English Verse, edited by Russell A. Peck (1991)

The Canterbury Tales: Fifteenth-Century Continuations and Additions, edited by John M. Bowers (1992)

Gavin Douglas, *The Palis of Honoure,* edited by David Parkinson (1992)

Wynnere and Wastoure and The Parlement of the Thre Ages, edited by Warren Ginsberg (1992)

The Shewings of Julian of Norwich, edited by Georgia Ronan Crampton (1994)

King Arthur's Death: The Middle English Stanzaic Morte Arthur and Alliterative Morte Arthure, edited by Larry D. Benson, revised by Edward E. Foster (1994)

Lancelot of the Laik and Sir Tristrem, edited by Alan Lupack (1994)

Sir Gawain: Eleven Romances and Tales, edited by Thomas Hahn (1995)

The Middle English Breton Lays, edited by Anne Laskaya and Eve Salisbury (1995)

Sir Perceval of Galles and Ywain and Gawain, edited by Mary Flowers Braswell (1995)

Four Middle English Romances: Sir Isumbras, Octavian, Sir Eglamour of Artois, Sir Tryamour, edited by Harriet Hudson (1996; second edition 2006)

The Poems of Laurence Minot, 1333–1352, edited by Richard H. Osberg (1996)

Medieval English Political Writings, edited by James M. Dean (1996)

The Book of Margery Kempe, edited by Lynn Staley (1996)

Amis and Amiloun, Robert of Cisyle, and Sir Amadace, edited by Edward E. Foster (1997; second edition 2007)

The Cloud of Unknowing, edited by Patrick J. Gallacher (1997)

Robin Hood and Other Outlaw Tales, edited by Stephen Knight and Thomas Ohlgren (1997; second edition 2000)

The Poems of Robert Henryson, edited by Robert L. Kindrick with the assistance of Kristie A. Bixby (1997)

Moral Love Songs and Laments, edited by Susanna Greer Fein (1998)

John Lydgate, *Troy Book Selections,* edited by Robert R. Edwards (1998)

Thomas Usk, *The Testament of Love,* edited by R. Allen Shoaf (1998)

Prose Merlin, edited by John Conlee (1998)

Middle English Marian Lyrics, edited by Karen Saupe (1998)

John Metham, *Amoryus and Cleopes,* edited by Stephen F. Page (1999)

Four Romances of England: King Horn, Havelok the Dane, Bevis of Hampton, Athelston, edited by Ronald B. Herzman, Graham Drake, and Eve Salisbury (1999)

The Assembly of Gods: Le Assemble de Dyeus, or Banquet of Gods and Goddesses, with the Discourse of Reason and Sensuality, edited by Jane Chance (1999)

Thomas Hoccleve, *The Regiment of Princes,* edited by Charles R. Blyth (1999)

John Capgrave, *The Life of Saint Katherine,* edited by Karen A. Winstead (1999)

John Gower, *Confessio Amantis,* Vol. 1, edited by Russell A. Peck; with Latin translations by Andrew Galloway (2000; second edition 2006); Vol. 2 (2003); Vol. 3 (2004)

Richard the Redeless and Mum and the Sothsegger, edited by James M. Dean (2000)

Ancrene Wisse, edited by Robert Hasenfratz (2000)

Walter Hilton, *The Scale of Perfection,* edited by Thomas H. Bestul (2000)

John Lydgate, *The Siege of Thebes,* edited by Robert R. Edwards (2001)

Pearl, edited by Sarah Stanbury (2001)

The Trials and Joys of Marriage, edited by Eve Salisbury (2002)

Middle English Legends of Women Saints, edited by Sherry L. Reames, with the assistance of Martha G. Blalock and Wendy R. Larson (2003)

The Wallace: Selections, edited by Anne McKim (2003)

Richard Maidstone, *Concordia (The Reconciliation of Richard II with London),* edited by David R. Carlson, with a verse translation by A. G. Rigg (2003)

Three Purgatory Poems: The Gast of Gy, Sir Owain, The Vision of Tundale, edited by Edward E. Foster (2004)

William Dunbar, *The Complete Works,* edited by John Conlee (2004)

Chaucerian Dream Visions and Complaints, edited by Dana M. Symons (2004)

Stanzaic Guy of Warwick, edited by Alison Wiggins (2004)

Saints' Lives in Middle English Collections, edited by E. Gordon Whatley, with Anne B. Thompson and Robert K. Upchurch (2004)

Siege of Jerusalem, edited by Michael Livingston (2004)

The Kingis Quair and Other Prison Poems, edited by Linne R. Mooney and Mary-Jo Arn (2005)

The Chaucerian Apocrypha: A Selection, edited by Kathleen Forni (2005)

John Gower, *The Minor Latin Works*, edited and translated by R. F. Yeager, with *In Praise of Peace*, edited by Michael Livingston (2005)

Sentimental and Humorous Romances: Floris and Blancheflour, Sir Degrevant, The Squire of Low Degree, The Tournament of Tottenham, and The Feast of Tottenham, edited by Erik Kooper (2006)

The Dicts and Sayings of the Philosophers, edited by John William Sutton (2006)

Everyman and Its Dutch Original, Elckerlijc, edited by Clifford Davidson, Martin W. Walsh, and Ton J. Broos (2007)

The N-Town Plays, edited by Douglas Sugano, with assistance by Victor I. Scherb (2007)

The Book of John Mandeville, edited by Tamarah Kohanski and C. David Benson (2007)

John Lydgate, *The Temple of Glas*, edited by J. Allan Mitchell (2007)

The Northern Homily Cycle, edited by Anne B. Thompson (2008)

Codex Ashmole 61: A Compilation of Popular Middle English Verse, edited by George Shuffelton (2008)

Chaucer and the Poems of "Ch," edited by James I. Wimsatt (revised edition 2009)

William Caxton, *The Game and Playe of the Chesse*, edited by Jenny Adams (2009)

John the Blind Audelay, *Poems and Carols*, edited by Susanna Fein (2009)

Two Moral Interludes: The Pride of Life and Wisdom, edited by David Klausner (2009)

John Lydgate, *Mummings and Entertainments*, edited by Claire Sponsler (2010)

Mankind, edited by Kathleen M. Ashley and Gerard NeCastro (2010)

The Castle of Perseverance, edited by David N. Klausner (2010)

Robert Henryson, *The Complete Works*, edited by David J. Parkinson (2010)

John Gower, *The French Balades*, edited and translated by R. F. Yeager (2011)

🙢 COMMENTARY SERIES

Haimo of Auxerre, *Commentary on the Book of Jonah*, translated with an introduction and notes by Deborah Everhart (1993)

Medieval Exegesis in Translation: Commentaries on the Book of Ruth, translated with an introduction and notes by Lesley Smith (1996)

Nicholas of Lyra's Apocalypse Commentary, translated with an introduction and notes by Philip D. W. Krey (1997)

Rabbi Ezra Ben Solomon of Gerona, *Commentary on the Song of Songs and Other Kabbalistic Commentaries*, selected, translated, and annotated by Seth Brody (1999)

John Wyclif, *On the Truth of Holy Scripture*, translated with an introduction and notes by Ian Christopher Levy (2001)

Second Thessalonians: Two Early Medieval Apocalyptic Commentaries, introduced and translated by Steven R. Cartwright and Kevin L. Hughes (2001)

The "Glossa Ordinaria" on the Song of Songs, translated with an introduction and notes by Mary Dove (2004)

The Seven Seals of the Apocalypse: Medieval Texts in Translation, translated with an introduction and notes by Francis X. Gumerlock (2009)

The "Glossa Ordinaria" on Romans, translated with an introduction and notes by Michael Scott Woodward (2011)

🙢 DOCUMENTS OF PRACTICE SERIES

Love and Marriage in Late Medieval London, selected, translated, and introduced by Shannon McSheffrey (1995)

Sources for the History of Medicine in Late Medieval England, selected, introduced, and translated by Carole Rawcliffe (1995)

A Slice of Life: Selected Documents of Medieval English Peasant Experience, edited, translated, and with an introduction by Edwin Brezette DeWindt (1996)

Regular Life: Monastic, Canonical, and Mendicant "Rules," selected and introduced by Douglas J. McMillan and Kathryn Smith Fladenmuller (1997); second edition, selected and introduced by Daniel Marcel La Corte and Douglas J. McMillan (2004)

Women and Monasticism in Medieval Europe: Sisters and Patrons of the Cistercian Reform, selected, translated, and with an introduction by Constance H. Berman (2002)

Medieval Notaries and Their Acts: The 1327–1328 Register of Jean Holanie, introduced, edited, and translated by Kathryn L. Reyerson and Debra A. Salata (2004)

John Stone's Chronicle: Christ Church Priory, Canterbury, 1417–1472, selected, translated, and introduced by Meriel Connor (2010)

MEDIEVAL GERMAN TEXTS IN BILINGUAL EDITIONS SERIES

Sovereignty and Salvation in the Vernacular, 1050–1150, introduction, translations, and notes by James A. Schultz (2000)

Ava's New Testament Narratives: "When the Old Law Passed Away," introduction, translation, and notes by James A. Rushing, Jr. (2003)

History as Literature: German World Chronicles of the Thirteenth Century in Verse, introduction, translation, and notes by R. Graeme Dunphy (2003)

Thomasin von Zirclaria, *Der Welsche Gast (The Italian Guest),* translated by Marion Gibbs and Winder McConnell (2009)

Ladies, Whores, and Holy Women: A Sourcebook in Courtly, Religious, and Urban Cultures of Late Medieval Germany, introductions, translations, and notes by Ann Marie Rasmussen and Sarah Westphal-Wihl (2010)

VARIA

The Study of Chivalry: Resources and Approaches, edited by Howell Chickering and Thomas H. Seiler (1988)

Studies in the Harley Manuscript: The Scribes, Contents, and Social Contexts of British Library MS Harley 2253, edited by Susanna Fein (2000)

The Liturgy of the Medieval Church, edited by Thomas J. Heffernan and E. Ann Matter (2001; second edition 2005)

TO ORDER PLEASE CONTACT:

Medieval Institute Publications
Western Michigan University
Kalamazoo, MI 49008-5432
Phone (269) 387-8755
FAX (269) 387-8750
http://www.wmich.edu/medieval/mip/index.html

Typeset in 10/13 New Baskerville
and Golden Cockerel Ornaments display
Designed by Linda K. Judy
Manufactured by Cushing-Malloy, Inc.

Medieval Institute Publications
College of Arts and Sciences
Western Michigan University
1903 W. Michigan Avenue
Kalamazoo, MI 49008-5432
http:/ /www.wmich.edu/medieval/mip

 WESTERN MICHIGAN UNIVERSITY